The Legal Writing Handbook

The Legal Writing Handbook

Analysis, Research, and Writing

Fourth Edition

Laurel Currie Oates
Director, Legal Writing Program
Seattle University School of Law

Anne Enquist
Associate Director,
Legal Writing Program
Seattle University School of Law

ΛSPEN

PUBLISHERS

76 Ninth Avenue, New York, NY 10011
http://lawschool.aspenpublishers.com

Aspen Publishers
Attn: Permissions Department
76 Ninth Avenue, 7th Floor
New York, NY 10011-5201

Printed in the United States of America.

1 2 3 4 5 6 7 8 9 0

ISBN 0-7355-5568-0

Library of Congress Cataloging-in-Publication Data

Oates, Laurel Currie, 1951-
    The legal writing handbook : analysis, research, and writing / Laurel Currie Oates, Anne Enquist. — 4th ed.
        p. cm.
    Includes index.
    ISBN 0-7355-5568-0
    1. Legal composition.   2. Legal research — United States.
I. Enquist, Anne, 1950-   II. Title.
KF250.O18 2006
808'.06634 — dc22   2005037192

About Aspen Publishers

Aspen Publishers, headquartered in New York City, is a leading information provider for attorneys, business professionals, and law students. Written by preeminent authorities, our products consist of analytical and practical information covering both U.S. and international topics. We publish in the full range of formats, including updated manuals, books, periodicals, CDs, and online products.

Our proprietary content is complemented by 2,500 legal databases, containing over 11 million documents, available through our Loislaw division. Aspen Publishers also offers a wide range of topical legal and business databases linked to Loislaw's primary material. Our mission is to provide accurate, timely, and authoritative content in easily accessible formats, supported by unmatched customer care.

To order any Aspen Publishers title, go to *http://lawschool.aspen publishers.com* or call -800-638-8437.

To reinstate your manual update service, call 1-800-638-8437.

For more information on Loislaw products, go to *www.loislaw.com* or call 1-800-364-2512.

For Customer Care issues, e-mail *CustomerCare@aspenpublishers.com*; call 1-800-234-1660; or fax 1-800-901-9075.

Aspen Publishers
a Wolters Kluwer business

To my parents, Bill and Lucille Currie,
my husband, Terry, and my children, Julia and Michael.
Thank you.

To my family, Steve, Matt, and Jeff Enquist,
for their love, support, and patience.

Summary of Contents

Contents

Preface

One of the first things that you learn as a first-year law student is that law school textbooks are big. The casebooks for your doctrinal courses are big, and this book, your legal writing textbook, is also big.

While we will let your other professors explain why their casebooks are so big, we want to take a moment to explain the size of this book. First, it is big because it is really five books in one. We hope you will think of that as a bargain and not a burden. Book 1 is designed to be read during orientation and provides you with an introduction to the United States legal system, legal research, and legal reading. Books 2 and 3 walk you step-by-step through the process of writing objective memoranda, opinion letters, trial-level briefs, and appellate briefs. If your school has a one-year legal writing course, you may not have enough time to cover some of these chapters in these books. You will, however, find the chapters useful once you get your first job. If your school has a three- or four-semester legal writing program, you will probably use the material in Book 2 in your first year of law school and the material in Book 3 in your second year. Books 4 and 5 contain information on writing effectively and correctly. Think of these two books as reference books that you will use both in law school and in practice.

Second, this book is big because it contains numerous examples. Our experience as legal writing professors has taught us that the majority of students find models and examples an important key to their learning. So, instead of just telling you what to do, this book shows you what to do. Think of this approach as a kind of apprenticeship. Imagine that you are sitting next to an expert legal writer and researcher and learning by observing how he or she does things. For example, in Book 2 we walk you through the process of researching, analyzing, and writing three different types of memos and an opinion letter, and in Book 3, we walk you through the process of writing a trial-level brief and an appellate brief and we explain how to do an oral argument. Similarly, in Books 4 and 5, we provide you with numerous examples, often showing you how to revise a draft to make the writing more effective or to correct errors in grammar or punctuation.

Finally, this book is big because learning to become a good legal writer is a complex process that takes most individuals years to master. Although many of the individuals who come to law school are good writers, few are good legal writers. Thus, even though you may be able to write a good term paper, a good business letter, or a good report, if you are going to write a good objective memo or a good appellate brief, you will need help: you will need help in learning how to do legal research; you will need help in learning to read and analyze the information that you find in doing that research; you will need help in learning the conventional formats for memos, letters, and briefs; and you will need help in learning how to present complex ideas and arguments clearly and concisely and without any mistakes in grammar or punctuation.

Thus, our hope is that this book will provide you with more than a weightlifting program. Yes, it is big and a bit heavy, so you may actually develop a few muscles carrying it around. The muscles we care about, though, are the mental ones that will make you a successful attorney. It is in that vein that we hope you will see this book as just what you need — the perfect exercise for the well-built legal mind.

Acknowledgments

One of the special pleasures of writing a fourth edition of a book is that it allows the authors to think about all the people who have helped them along the way. Some colleagues and friends were particularly instrumental in the early years when we were first writing. Others have been steady supporters through all four editions, and some are relatively new friends, colleagues, and students who have shared their insights and given us encouragement.

Mary Beth Harney was critical to the book's development in the early stages. She helped conceptualize the book and allowed us to use many examples of her own writing. Our friend and colleague Marilyn Berger introduced us to the people at Little, Brown (now Aspen Publishers) and encouraged us to persevere. At Little, Brown and later at Aspen, we have been fortunate to have wonderful editors, Betsy Kenny and Peter Skagestad.

Three law school deans have been significant supporters of this project. Former Dean Fred Tausend gave us the "green light" in the early years; former Dean Jim Bond provided institutional support and personal encouragement; and our current dean, Kellye Testy, has continued that support and encouragement.

We have been fortunate throughout this process to have had the critiques and counsel of numerous colleagues who have taught legal writing. A heartfelt thank you to our longtime colleagues Lori Bannai, Janet Dickson, Connie Krontz, Susan McClellan, Chris Rideout, and Mimi Samuel and to our newer colleagues, Mary Bowman, Pat Brown, Janet Chung, Lucas Cupps, Julie Heintz-Cho, and Margaret Lent. We would also like to give a special thanks to our friend and colleague from Maine, Jessie Grearson.

In addition, we have benefited from the knowledge and advice of many other faculty members at the Seattle University School of Law: Janet Ainsworth, Melinda Branscomb, Annette Clark, Sid DeLong, Paula Lustbader, John Mitchell, Mark Reutlinger, John Strait, John Weaver, Carmen Gonzalez, and Maggie Chon. In addition, we would like to give a special thanks to our former co-author, Kelly Kunsch, for his continued research assistance.

Perhaps the most important collaborators in this project have been our students. Their writing appears throughout the book, and they were our first readers. So many made recommendations and allowed us to use their writing that we cannot mention them all, but we want them to know how much we appreciate their part in what we think of as "their book."

Some students made substantial contributions and deserve special recognition. Thanks to Ashley Tam for helping capture many of the screen shots that appear on the CD that comes with this edition; to Elaine Conway for allowing us to use a copy of her memo and the chart that she developed; to Fletcher Barkdull, Chad Kirby, and Kelly Wood for allowing us to reprint their memos; to Erin Shea and Mary Shea for their assistance with the bias-free language section; to Kelly Dalcin for her work updating many examples; and to Carmen Butler for her research on procrastination. We would also like to thank former students Susan McClellan, Annette Clark, Luanne Coachman, Mary Lobdell, Eileen Peterson, Lance Palmer, Edwina Martin-Arnold, Vonda Sargent, Melissa May, Kevin Dougherty, Cindy Burdue, Amy Blume, Chris Fredrikson, Daryl Wareham, and Monique Redford.

The chapter on "Legal Writing for English-as-a-Second-Language Law Students" would not have been possible without the help of several colleagues and students. Thanks to Donn R. Callaway for his guidance as we first began to explore this topic, to Dana Yaffee and Linda Chu for their excellent research, and to Jessie Grearson and Jeffrey Gore for their comments and suggestions on early drafts. Thanks, too, to our many ESL law students who inspired us with their dedication and hard work. We are particularly grateful to Stephanie Ko, Neli Espe, Nikolay Kvasnyuk, Masha Fartoutchnaia, Linda Chu, Meihuei Hu, and Julian Lin for allowing us to use their writing as examples and for reading early drafts of the chapter and suggesting changes.

The diagnostic test that is available with this edition has also been a collaborative effort. Special thanks to Connie Krontz and Judi Maier for their help with early versions of the test, to all the Seattle University School of Law legal writing faculty in 2001-02 for helping us iron out the kinks, and to Professor Nancy Wanderer and her students at the University of Maine School of Law for "testing the test" in the fall of 2001.

We also want to thank our secretary, Lori Lamb, who was an instrumental part of the earlier editions of the book and in assembling this edition and Steve Burnett, who helped us think about and develop a website for this book.

The Legal Writing Handbook

An Introduction to Law

Introduction

It is an experience we have all had. We show up a bit late, and our family or friends are a half hour into a movie that we have been dying to see. Confident that we can figure out the characters and plot, we settle in. Sometimes all goes well. There are just a few characters, and the plot is one that we have seen a thousand times before: boy meets girl, girl is engaged to someone else, at the last minute girl sees the light and falls in love with the boy. At other times, though, there are numerous characters and the plot is complicated. While at first we think we have figured out who is who, we eventually realize that we have misunderstood not only the characters' roles but the point that the director was trying to make.

Unfortunately, the same thing happens to some law students. During the first week, month, or even semester of law school, they feel as if they have walked into a movie part way through and that everyone else in the room knows what is going on. They feel, at least figuratively, as though they are in the dark. While their classmates seem to have a sophisticated understanding of the roles that the executive, legislative, and judicial branches play, the less confident students feel like they are relying on what they learned in eighth grade. Everyone else seems to understand things like the difference between mandatory and persuasive authority, but to the baffled students all cases look the same. Speaking of cases, each one seems to have a secret code: What do all of those numbers and letters after the case names mean and how can the student use them to find a case in the library or on a computer? Even the reading assignments are intimidating. These students do the reading but wonder all the time whether they are doing it right. Like filmgoers who stop at the level of plot and character, they are amazed by the insight of others who seem to see so much more in the legal stories they are assigned.

The material in this book, Book 1, was written to give you just the right kind of head start on law school and to put what is going on into a meaningful context. Chapter 1 introduces the characters in the United States legal system and the relationship between the federal and state courts. Chapters 2 and 3 build on Chapter 1, and provide you with an introduction to legal research. Chapter 2 introduces the four categories of sources — primary authorities, secondary authorities, finding tools, and citators; explains the difference between mandatory and persuasive authority; and teaches you to read and use citations to find cases and statutes. Chapter 3 explains how to use citators to determine whether a particular case or statute is still good law or to find cases and other authorities that have cited to a case, statute, or other authority. We then end Book 1 with a discussion of what is possibly *the* skill that may determine how well you do as a law student and as a lawyer: legal reading. Chapter 4 distinguishes between the types of reading laypeople do and the reading lawyers do and gives you some practical advice about how to read as a lawyer.

So sit back, grab a bowl of popcorn, and know that Book 1 will set the scene for all that follows.

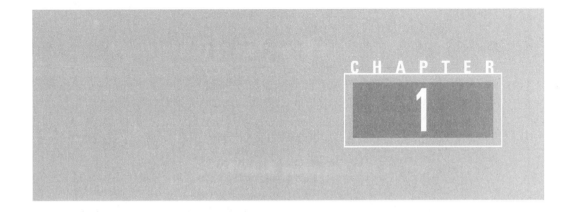

The United States Legal System

The United States system of government. For some, it is the secret to democracy, the power to elect one's leaders and the right to speak freely. For others, it is a horrendous bureaucracy, a maze through which one must struggle to obtain a benefit, to change a law, or to get a day in court. For still others, it is more abstract — a chart in an eighth-grade civics book describing the three branches of government and explaining the system of checks and balances.

For lawyers, the United States system of government is all of these things and more. It is the foundation for their knowledge of the law, the stage on which they play out their professional roles, the arena for the very serious game of law.

No matter which metaphor you prefer — foundation, stage, arena — the point is the same. To be an effective researcher, you must understand the system. You must know the framework before you can work well within it.

Like most complex systems, the United States system of government can be analyzed in a number of different ways. You can focus on its three branches — the executive branch, the legislative branch, and the judicial branch — or you can focus on the system's two parts, the federal government and the state governments.

In this chapter we do both. We look first at the three branches, examining both their individual functions and their interrelationships. We then examine the relationship between state and federal government, again with an eye toward their individual functions and powers.

§ 1.1 The Three Branches of Government

Just as the medical student must understand both the various organs that make up the human body and their relationship to each other, the law student must understand both the three branches of government and the relationships among them.

§ 1.1.1 The Executive Branch

The first of the three branches is the executive branch. In the federal system, the executive power is vested in the President; in the states, it is vested in the governor. (See Article II, Section 1 of the United States Constitution and the constitutions of the various states.) In general, the executive branch has the power to implement and enforce laws. It oversees public projects, administers public benefit programs, and controls law enforcement agencies.

The executive branch also has powers that directly affect our system of law. For example, the President (or a governor) can control the lawmaking function of the legislative branch by exercising his or her power to convene and adjourn the Congress (or state legislature) or by vetoing legislation. Similarly, the President (or a governor) can shape the decisions of the courts through his or her judicial nominations or by directing the attorney general to enforce or not to enforce certain laws.

§ 1.1.2 The Legislative Branch

The second branch is the legislative branch. Congress's powers are enumerated in Article I, Section 8, of the United States Constitution, which gives Congress, among other things, the power to lay and collect taxes, borrow money, regulate commerce with foreign nations and among the states, establish uniform naturalization and bankruptcy laws, promote the progress of science and the useful arts by creating copyright laws, and punish counterfeiting. Powers not granted Congress are given to the states or left to the people. (See the Tenth Amendment to the United States Constitution.) The state constitutions enumerate the powers given to the state legislatures.

Like the executive branch, the legislative branch exercises power over the other two branches. It can check the actions of the executive branch by enacting or refusing to enact legislation requested by the executive, by controlling the budget and, at least at the federal level, by consenting or refusing to consent to nominations made by the executive.

The legislative branch's power over the judicial branch is less obvious. At one level, it can control the judiciary through its power to establish courts (Article I, Section 8, grants Congress the power to establish inferior federal courts) and its power to consent to or reject the executive branch's judicial nominations. However, the most obvious control it has over the judiciary is its power to enact legislation that supersedes a common law or court-made doctrine or rule.

The legislative branch also shares its law-making power with the executive branch. In enacting legislation, it sometimes gives the executive branch the power to promulgate the regulations needed to implement or enforce the legislation. For example, although Congress (the legislative branch) enacted the Internal Revenue Code, the Internal Revenue Service (part of the executive branch) promulgates the regulations needed to implement that code.

§1.1.3 The Judicial Branch

The third branch is the judicial branch. Article III, Section 1, of the United States Constitution vests the judicial power of the United States in one supreme court and in such inferior courts as Congress may establish. The state constitutions establish and grant power to the state courts.

a. The Hierarchical Nature of the Court System

Both the federal and the state court systems are hierarchical. At the lowest level are the trial courts, whose primary function is fact-finding. The judge or jury hears the evidence and enters a judgment.

At the next level are the intermediate courts of appeals. These courts hear the majority of appeals, deciding (1) whether the trial court applied the right law and (2) whether there is sufficient evidence to support the jury's verdict or the trial judge's findings of fact and conclusions of law. Unlike the trial courts, these courts do not conduct trials. There are no witnesses, and the only exhibits are the exhibits that were admitted during trial. The decisions of the appellate courts are based solely on the written record and the attorneys' arguments.

At the top level are the states' highest courts and the Supreme Court of the United States. The primary function of these courts is to make law. They hear only those cases that involve issues of great public import or cases in which different divisions or circuits have adopted or applied conflicting rules of law. Like the intermediate courts of appeals, these courts do not hear evidence; they only review the trial court record. See Chart 1.1.

An example illustrates the role each court plays. In *State v. Strong*, a criminal case, the defendant was charged with possession of a controlled substance. At the trial court level, both the State and the defendant presented witnesses and physical evidence. On the basis of this evidence, the trial court decided the case on its merits, with the trial judge deciding the questions of law (whether the evidence should be suppressed) and the jury deciding the questions of fact (whether the State had proved all of the elements of the crime beyond a reasonable doubt).

Both issues were decided against the defendant: the trial court judge ruled that the evidence was admissible, and the jury found that the State had met its burden of proof. Disagreeing with both determinations, the defendant filed an appeal with the intermediate court of appeals.

In deciding this appeal, the appellate court could consider only two issues: whether the trial court judge erred when he denied the defendant's motion to suppress and whether there was sufficient evidence to support the jury's verdict.

Because the first issue raised a question of law, the appellate court could review the issue *de novo*. The court did not need to defer to the judgment of the trial court judge. Instead, the appellate court could exercise its own independent judgment to decide the issue on its merits.

The appellate court had much less latitude with respect to the second issue. Because the second issue raised a question of fact rather than law, the

---

Chart 1.1 **The Roles of the Trial, Intermediate, and Supreme Courts**

Trial Court

- The trial court hears witnesses and views evidence.
- The trial court judge decides issues of law; the jury decides questions of fact. (When there is no jury, the trial court judge decides both the questions of law and the questions of fact.)

Intermediate Court of Appeals

- The intermediate court of appeals reviews the written record and exhibits from the trial court.
- When an issue raises a question of law, the intermediate court of appeals may substitute its judgment for the judgment of the trial court judge; when an issue raises a question of fact, the appellate court must defer to the decision of the finder of fact (the jury or, if there was no jury, the trial judge).

Supreme, or Highest, Court

- Like the intermediate court of appeals, it reviews the written record and exhibits from the trial court.
- Like the intermediate court of appeals, it has broad powers to review questions of law: it determines whether the trial court and intermediate court of appeals applied the right law correctly. Its power to review factual issues is, however, very limited. Like the intermediate court of appeals, it can determine only whether there is sufficient evidence to support the decision of the jury or, if there was no jury, the decision of the trial court judge.

appellate court could not substitute its judgment for that of the jury. It could only review the jury's findings to make sure that they were supported by the evidence. When the question is one of fact, the appellate court may decide only (1) whether there is sufficient evidence to support the jury's verdict or (2) whether the jury's verdict is clearly erroneous. It may not substitute its judgment for the judgment of the jury.

Regardless of the type of issue (fact or law), the appellate court must base its decision on the written trial court record and exhibits and the attorneys' arguments. Consequently, in *Strong*, the intermediate court of appeals did not see or hear any of the witnesses. The only people present when the appeal was argued were the appellate court judges assigned to hear the case and Strong's and the State's attorneys. Not even the defendant, Strong, was present.

If Strong lost his first appeal, he could petition the state supreme court (through a petition for discretionary review) and ask that court to review the intermediate court of appeals' decision. If the state supreme court granted the petition, its review, like that of the intermediate court of appeals, would be limited. Although the supreme court would review the issue of law *de novo*, it would have to defer to the jury's decision on the questions of fact.

Chart 1.2   The Thirteen Federal Judicial Circuits

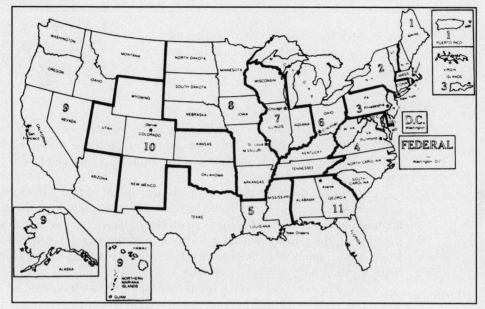

Reprinted from *Federal Reporter* (West's National Reporter System) with permission of West, a Thomson business.

Most of the cases that appear in law school casebooks are appellate court decisions, decisions of the state or federal intermediate courts of appeals or Supreme Court. These cases, however, represent only a small, and perhaps not representative, percentage of the disputes that lawyers see during the course of their practice.

Thus, as you read the cases in the casebooks, remember that you are seeing only the proverbial tip of the iceberg. For a case to reach the United States Supreme Court, the parties must have had the financial means to pursue it, and the Court must have found that the issue raised was significant enough to grant review.

b. The Federal Courts

In the federal system, most cases are heard initially in the federal district courts, the primary trial courts in that system. These courts have original jurisdiction over most federal questions and have the power to review the decisions of some administrative agencies. Each state has at least one district court, and many have several. For example, Indiana has the District Court for Northern Indiana and the District Court for Southern Indiana. Cases that are not heard in the district court are usually heard in one of several specialized courts: the United States Tax Court, the United States Court of Federal Claims, or the United States Court of International Trade.

In the federal system, the intermediate court of appeals is the United States Court of Appeals. There are currently thirteen circuits: eleven numbered circuits, the District of Columbia Circuit, and the Federal Circuit. See Chart 1.2. The Federal Circuit, which was created in 1982, reviews the decisions of the United States Court of Federal Claims and the United States Court of International Trade, as well as some administrative decisions.

For an electronic copy of a map showing the federal circuits, see http://www.uscourts.gov/images/CircuitMap.pdf

P R A C T I C E
POINTER

The highest federal court is the United States Supreme Court. Although many people believe that the Supreme Court is all-powerful, in fact it is not. As with other courts, there are limits on the Supreme Court's powers. It can play only one of two roles.

In one role, the Supreme Court is similar to that of the state supreme courts. In the federal system it is the highest court, the court of last resort. In contrast, in its other role, it is the final arbiter of federal constitutional law, interpreting the United States Constitution and determining whether the federal government or a state has violated rights granted under the United States Constitution.

Thus, although people often assert that they will take their case all the way to the Supreme Court, they may not be able to. The Supreme Court may hear a case only if it involves a question of federal constitutional law or a federal statute. The Supreme Court does not have the power to hear cases involving only questions of state law. For example, although the United States Supreme Court has the power to determine whether a state's marriage dissolution statutes are constitutional, the Court does not have the power to hear purely factual questions, such as whether it would be in the best interests of a child for custody to be granted to the father or whether child support should be set at $300.00 rather than $400.00 per month.

Each year the United States Supreme Court receives more than 7,000 requests for review (writs of certiorari). Of the approximately 100 cases that the Court actually hears, the overwhelming majority are appeals from the federal courts.

Chart 1.3 illustrates the relationships among the various federal courts.

Because the United States District Court and Court of Appeals hear so many cases, not all of their decisions are published. When they are published, district court opinions are published in either the *Federal Supplement* or *Federal Rules Decisions*, and current Court of Appeals decisions are published in *Federal Reporter, Third Series*. (Decisions from the specialized courts are published in specialized reporters.)

All United States Supreme Court decisions are published. The official reporter is *United States Reports*, and the two unofficial reporters are West's *Supreme Court Reporter* and *United States Supreme Court Reports, Lawyer's Edition*.

c. State Courts

A number of courts operate within the states. At the lowest level are courts of limited jurisdiction. These courts hear only certain types of cases or cases

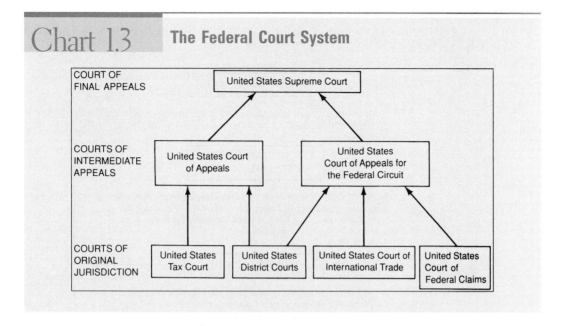

Chart 1.3   **The Federal Court System**

involving only limited amounts of money. Municipal or city courts are courts of limited jurisdiction, as are county or district courts and small claims courts.

At the next level are courts of general jurisdiction. These courts have the power to review the decisions of courts of limited jurisdiction and original jurisdiction over claims arising under state law, whether it be under the state constitution, state statutes, or state common law.

About three-quarters of the states now have an intermediate court of appeals. These courts hear appeals as of right from the state courts of general jurisdiction, and the bulk of their caseload is criminal appeals. Because of the size of their workload, many of these courts have several divisions or districts.

Every state has a state "supreme" court. These courts review the decisions of the state trial courts and courts of appeals and are the final arbiters of questions of state constitutional, statutory, and common law. Chart 1.4 illustrates the typical relationship among the various state courts.

Not all states call their highest court the supreme court. For example, in New York, the highest court is called the Court of Appeals, and the trial courts are called the supreme courts.

P R A C T I C E

Decisions of state trial courts are not usually published. In addition, because of the volume, not all decisions of intermediate state courts of appeals are published. Those that are, and all decisions of the state supreme court, appear in one of West Publishing Company's regional reporters and the state's official reporter, if one exists.

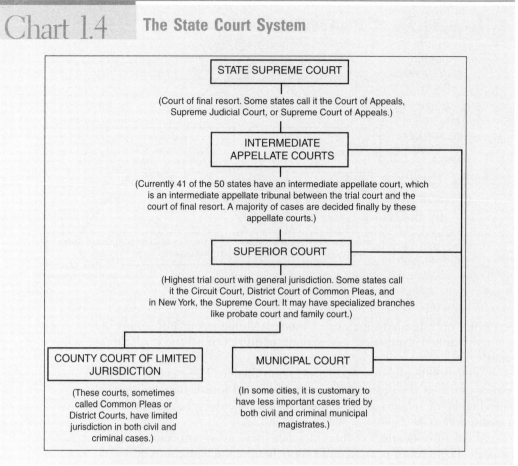

Chart 1.4   The State Court System

STATE SUPREME COURT

(Court of final resort. Some states call it the Court of Appeals,
Supreme Judicial Court, or Supreme Court of Appeals.)

INTERMEDIATE
APPELLATE COURTS

(Currently 41 of the 50 states have an intermediate appellate court, which
is an intermediate appellate tribunal between the trial court and the
court of final resort. A majority of cases are decided finally by these
appellate courts.)

SUPERIOR COURT

(Highest trial court with general jurisdiction. Some states call
it the Circuit Court, District Court of Common Pleas, and
in New York, the Supreme Court. It may have specialized branches
like probate court and family court.)

COUNTY COURT OF LIMITED
JURISDICTION

(These courts, sometimes
called Common Pleas or
District Courts, have limited
jurisdiction in both civil and
criminal cases.)

MUNICIPAL COURT

(In some cities, it is customary to
have less important cases tried by
both civil and criminal municipal
magistrates.)

d. Other Courts

There are also several other court systems. As sovereign entities, many
Native American tribes have their own judicial systems, as does the United
States military.

§ 1.2 The Relationship Between the Federal and State Governments

It is not enough, however, to look at our system of government only from the
perspective of its three branches. To understand the system, you must also
understand the relationship between the federal and state governments.

§ 1.2.1 A Short History

Like most things, our system of government is the product of our history.
From the early 1600s until 1781, the "united states" were not united. Instead,
the "country" was composed of independent colonies, all operating under
different charters and each having its own laws and legal system. Although the
colonies traded with each other, the relationship among the colonies was no

closer than the relationship among the European countries prior to 1992. It was not until the Articles of Confederation were adopted in 1781 that the "states" ceded any of their rights to a federal government.

Even though the states ceded more rights when the Constitution became effective in 1789, they preserved most of their own law. Each state retained its own executive, its own legislature and laws, and its own court system.

Thus, our system of government is really two systems, a federal system and the fifty state systems, with the United States Constitution brokering the relationship between the two.

§ 1.2.2 The Relationship Between Laws Enacted by Congress and Those Enacted by the State Legislatures

As citizens of the United States, we are subject to two sets of laws: federal law and the law of the state in which we are citizens (or in which we act). Most of the time, there is no conflict between these two sets of laws: federal law governs some conduct; state law, other conduct. For example, federal law governs bankruptcy proceedings, and state law governs divorce.

Occasionally, however, both Congress and a state legislature enact laws governing the same conduct. Sometimes these laws coexist. For example, both Congress and the states have enacted drug laws. Acting under the powers granted to it under the Commerce Clause, Congress has made it illegal to import controlled substances or to transport them across state lines. The states, acting consistently with the powers reserved to them, have made illegal the possession or sale of controlled substances within the state. In such instances, citizens are subject to both laws. A defendant may be charged under federal law with transporting a drug across state lines and under state law with possession.

There are times, however, when federal and state law do not complement each other and cannot coexist. An act can be legal under federal law but illegal under state law. In such instances, federal law supersedes state law, provided that the federal law is constitutional. As provided in the Supremacy Clause, laws enacted by Congress under the powers granted to it under the Constitution are the "supreme Law of the Land; and the Judges in every State shall be bound thereby. . . ."

The issue is different when the conflicting laws are from different states. Although there are more and more uniform laws (the Uniform Child Custody Act, the Uniform Commercial Code), an activity that is legal in one state may be illegal in another state. For instance, although prostitution is legal in Nevada as a local option, it is illegal in other states.

§ 1.2.3 The Relationship Between Federal and State Courts

The relationship between the federal and state court systems is complex. Although each system is autonomous, in certain circumstances the state courts may hear cases brought under federal law, and the federal courts may hear cases brought under state law.

For example, although the majority of cases heard in state courts are brought under state law, state courts also have jurisdiction when a case is brought under a provision of the United States Constitution, a treaty, and certain federal statutes. Similarly, although the majority of cases heard in the federal courts involve questions of federal law, the federal courts have jurisdiction over cases involving questions of state law when the parties are from different states (diversity jurisdiction).

The appellate jurisdiction of the courts is somewhat simpler. In the state system, a state's supreme, or highest, court is usually the court of last resort. The United States Supreme Court may review a state court decision only when the case involves a federal question and there has been a final decision by the state's highest court. If a state has an intermediate court of appeals, that court has the power to review the decisions of the lower courts within its geographic jurisdiction.

In the federal system, the United States Supreme Court is the court of last resort, having the power to review the decisions of the lower federal courts. The United States Court of Appeals has appellate jurisdiction to review the decisions of the United States District Courts and certain administrative agencies.

§1.2.4 The Relationship Among Federal, State, and Local Prosecutors

The power to prosecute cases arising under the United States Constitution and federal statutes is vested in the Department of Justice, which is headed by the Attorney General of the United States, a presidential appointee. Assisting the United States Attorney General are the United States Attorneys for each federal judicial district. The individual United States Attorneys' offices have two divisions: a civil division and a criminal division. The civil division handles civil cases arising under federal law, and the criminal division handles cases involving alleged violations of federal criminal statutes.

At the state level, the system is slightly different. In most states, the attorney for the state is the state attorney general, usually an elected official. Working for the state attorney general are a number of assistant attorney generals. However, unlike the United States attorneys, most state attorney generals do not handle criminal cases. Their clients are the various state agencies. For example, an assistant attorney general may be assigned to a state's department of social and health services, the department of licensing, the consumer protection bureau, or the department of worker's compensation, providing advice to the agency and representing the agency in civil litigation.

Criminal prosecutions are handled by county and city prosecutors. Each county has its own prosecutor's office, which has both a civil and a criminal division. Attorneys working for the civil division play much the same role as state assistant attorney generals. They represent the county and its agencies, providing both advice and representation. In contrast, the attorneys assigned to the criminal division are responsible for prosecutions under the state's criminal code. The county prosecutor's office decides whom to charge and then tries the cases.

Like the counties, cities have their own city attorney's office, which, at least in large cities, has civil and criminal divisions. Attorneys working in the civil division advise city departments and agencies and represent the city in civil litigation; attorneys in the criminal division prosecute criminal cases brought under city ordinances. State, county, and city prosecutors do not represent federal departments or agencies, nor do they handle cases brought under federal law.

§ 1.3 A Final Comment

Although there are numerous other ways of analyzing the United States system of government, these two perspectives — the three-branches perspective and the federal-state perspective — are the foundation on which the rest of your study of law will be built. Without such a foundation, without a thorough understanding of the interrelationships among the parts of the system, many of the concepts that you will encounter in law school would be difficult to learn.

This is particularly true of legal writing. If you do not have a good understanding of the the United States system of government, you will find it difficult to do legal research and legal analysis. Thus, if you have questions about the United States system of government, this is the time to ask those questions. A question asked now will make the next three years much easier.

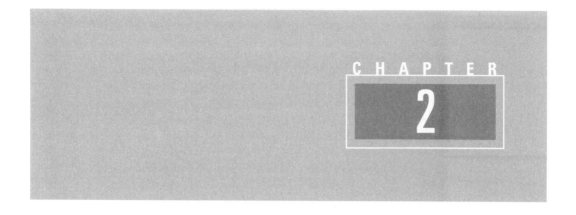

Introduction to Legal Research

While Chapter 1 provided you with an introduction to the United States system of government, this chapter provides you with an introduction to legal research. In particular, this chapter describes some of the sources that you will use in doing your research, it explains how to use citations to find those sources both in books and in electronic sources, and it describes the process of determining how much weight to give to a particular source.

§ 2.1 The Sources

Most law librarians talk about four types of sources: (1) sources that contain primary authority, (2) sources that contain secondary authority; (3) finding tools; and (4) citators. Although some sources have just one type of information, other sources have several types. Thus, you may be able to use a single source as a finding tool and as a source for primary and secondary authority.

§ 2.1.1 Sources Containing Primary Authority

Primary authority is the law itself. For example, federal and state constitutions, federal and state statutes, federal and state regulations, federal and state cases, and federal and state court rules are all primary authority. In addition, at the local level, county and city charters and county and city ordinances are primary authority. Chart 2.1 lists the types of primary authorities. The sources for finding these authorities are then described in more detail in Chapters 6, 9, and 12. You can also find brief descriptions of each of these sources in the Glossary, which begins on page . . . .

Most primary authorities are available in both book and electronic formats. For instance, you can find federal statutes in four different sets of books (*Statutes at Large, United States Code, United States Code Annotated,* and *United States Code Service*) and on a number of different free and fee-based websites.

See **Exercise 2A**, which is in the *Practice Book.*

§ 2.1.2 Sources Containing Secondary Authority

Secondary authorities summarize, analyze, or comment on the law. As a researcher, you will use secondary authorities in two different ways: at the beginning of a research project, you will use secondary authorities to familiarize yourself with the issue that you have been asked to research, and near the end of the project you will use them to gain a more sophisticated understanding of the issue. For example, if you are asked to research a federal

Chart 2.1   List of Primary Authorities

	Federal Law	State Law	Local Law
Constitutions	United States Constitution	State constitutions	County or city charter
Statutes	Federal session laws *United States Code*	State session laws state codes	County or city ordinances
Regulations	Federal regulations	State regulations	Department or agency rules and procedures
Cases	United States Supreme Court decisions	Decisions from the state's highest appellate court	Decisions by local departments, agencies, and courts
	United States Court of Appeals decisions	Decisions from the state's intermediate level appellate court or courts	
	United States District Court decisions	Decisions from state trial courts (as a general rule, these decisions are not published)	
	Decisions from special federal courts, for example, Bankruptcy Court decisions		
Court Rules	Federal rules	State rules	Local rules

statute, you might begin your research by reading about the statute on a government website that summarizes and explains that particular statute. Then, after you have located and analyzed the applicable primary authorities, you might look for a law review article or treatise that critiques those authorities.

Chart 2.2 lists some of the secondary authorities that are available. (Chapters 6, 9, and 12 discuss these sources in more detail.) You can also find brief descriptions of these sources in the Glossary.

Like primary authorities, most secondary authorities are available in both book and electronic formats. The exception, of course, is websites.

See Exercise 2B, which is in the *Practice Book*.

Chart 2.2　　　**List of Secondary Authorities**

	Federal Issues	State Issues	Local Issues
Secondary Sources that can be used for background reading	▪ Federal websites ▪ Federal practice books ▪ Hornbooks ▪ *Nutshells* ▪ Legal encyclopedias	▪ State practice books ▪ Hornbooks ▪ State websites ▪ *Nutshells* ▪ Legal encyclopedias	▪ State practice books ▪ Hornbooks ▪ Local websites ▪ *Nutshells* ▪ Legal encyclopedias
Secondary Sources that can be used to gain a more sophisticated understanding of a particular issue	▪ Law reviews ▪ Treatises ▪ Loose-leaf services ▪ A.L.R. Fed.	▪ Law reviews ▪ Treatises ▪ A.L.R. 4th, A.L.R. 5th	▪ Law reviews ▪ Treatises ▪ A.L.R. 4th, A.L.R. 5th

§ 2.1.3 Finding Tools

Finding tools are what the name suggests: they are tools that help you locate primary and secondary authorities. Some examples of finding tools are annotated codes, digests, and search engines. The following chart, Chart 2.3, shows you some of the finding tools that you can use to find primary and secondary authorities. (These finding tools are discussed in more detail in Chapters 6, 9, and 12.)

See Exercise 2C, which is in the *Practice Book*.

§ 2.1.4 Citators

Citators are used in two ways: (1) you use them to determine whether a particular source — for example, a case — is still good law; and (2) you use them to locate additional authorities that might be on point.

Historically, there was only one citator, the book version of *Shepard's®*. Today, few attorneys use the print version of *Shepard's*. Instead, most attorneys use the electronic version of *Shepard's*, which is on LexisNexis; GlobalCite, which is on Loislaw; or KeyCite®, which is on Westlaw. For a more complete description of citators, see Chapter 3.

Chart 2.3	List of Finding Tools

	Finding Tools
Statutes	▪ Subject indexes in codes.
	▪ References to statutes in cases, practice manuals, hornbooks, law review articles, and other secondary sources.
	▪ Terms and connectors, natural language, or table of contents searches on fee-based services like LexisNexis,® Loislaw, VersusLaw, and Westlaw.
Cases	▪ References to cases in other cases, practice manuals, hornbooks, law review articles, and other secondary sources.
	▪ Digests.
	▪ *American Law Reports* (A.L.R).
	▪ Terms and connectors or table of contents searches on fee-based services like LexisNexis, LoisLaw, VersusLaw, and Westlaw.
	▪ Citators—for example, *Shepard's* and KeyCite.
Secondary Authorities	▪ Cross-references in annotated codes.
	▪ References in cases, practice manuals, law review articles, and other secondary sources.
	▪ Directories and database lists on fee-based services like LexisNexis, Loislaw, VersusLaw, and Westlaw.
	▪ Citators—for example, *Shepard's* and KeyCite.
	▪ Internet search engines.

§ 2.2 Using Citations to Locate Information in Book and Fee-Based Services

In addition to knowing the sources, you also need to know how to locate information in those sources. The key to this step in the process is learning how to read and use legal citations.

Although there are a number of different citation systems,[1] each of these systems requires similar types of information in a similar order. Thus, once you learn one citation system, transferring that knowledge to a different system is relatively easy.

---

1. The two most commonly used citation systems are set out in the *ALWD Citation Manual* and *The Bluebook*. Some states also have their own citation systems.

In addition to giving you the information that
you need to find a particular source, citations also
give you information that you can use in determining
how much weight to give to a particular source.

For example, case citations tell you which court decided the case and when the
case was decided.

§2.2.1 Citations to Constitutional Provisions, Statutes, Regulations, and Court Rules

a. Constitutional Provisions

Citations to constitutional provisions contain two types of information: an abbreviation that identifies the constitution and a number or set of numbers that identify a particular article, section, or amendment. In the following example, the abbreviation tells you that the citation is to the United States Constitution, and the number tells you that it is a reference to a particular article and section within that article.

Example:

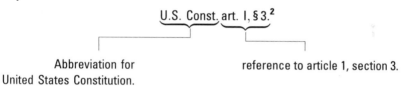

b. Statutes and Regulations

Like the citations to constitutional provisions, most citations to statutes and regulations contain two types of information: an abbreviation that identifies the "code" in which the statute or regulation can be found and a number that identifies the specific section. This number often includes a reference to the title under which the section is codified and a number that identifies either the specific section or the specific chapter and section.

Examples:

---

2. The citations set out in this chapter comply with the rules for memoranda and briefs set out in both the *ALWD Citation Manual* and *The Bluebook*.

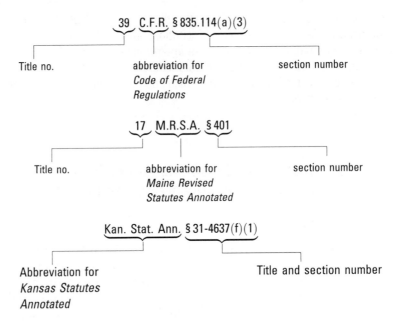

By now you have probably figured out that the "§" stands for "section." If you are referring to more than one section, use §§. For example, 17 M.R.S.A. §§ 401-410.

c. Court Rules

Most citations to court rules include an abbreviation that identifies the set of rules and a number that identifies the specific rule. In addition, under some citations systems, you need to include the year of the code.

Example :

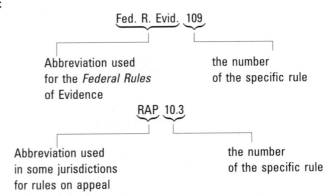

§ 2.2.2 Citations to Cases

Citations to cases contain more information. In addition to giving you the name of the case, the citation gives you information about where you can find a copy of the case and information you can use to determine if the case is mandatory or persuasive authority. These pieces of information are usually set out in the following order: case name, volume number of the reporter, page number, court, and year of decision.

Examples :

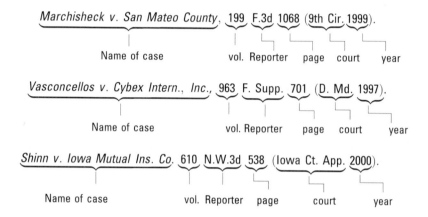

If the case appears in more than one reporter,[3] the citation may also contain a parallel citation — that is, a reference to the other reporters in which you can find a copy of the case. For example, the United States Supreme Court's decision in *Terry v. Ohio* appears in three reporters, *United States Reporters*, *Supreme Court Reporter*, and *Supreme Court Reporter, Lawyer's Edition Second*. The first reference is to the official reporter, and the second and third references are parallel cites to unofficial reporters.

Example:

> *Terry v. Ohio,* 393 U.S. 1, 100 S.Ct. 1870, 64 L. Ed. 3d 497 (1968)
>
>   Official cite   parallel cite   parallel cite

In addition to setting out the page on which the opinion begins, there may be a pinpoint cite (also known as a jump cite) that refers the reader to a specific page in the opinion. For instance, in the following example, the citation tells readers that the Ninth Circuit's decision in *Humanitarian Law Project* begins on page 383 in volume 353 of the *Federal Reporter, Third Series*. In addition, the citation pinpoints the page on which the language that the author is relying on can be found. Thus, instead of reading the entire opinion, the reader can simply turn to page 390.

---

3. A reporter is a set of books in which cases are published. For a more detailed explanation of reporters, see pages 80-82.

Example:
Humanitarian Law Project v. United States Dept. of Justice, 353 F.3d 383, 390 (9th Cir. 2003).

Finally, if there was another subsequent opinion in the same case, the citation may include that subsequent history. In the following example,[4] the *"review denied"* and following reference to volume 146 of *Washington Reports, Second Series,* is the subsequent history.

Example:
State v. Larry, 108 Wn. App. 894, 908, 34 P.3d 341 (2004), *review denied,* 146 Wn. 2d 1033 (2005).

§ 2.2.3 Citations to Secondary Authorities

There are different citations forms for different types of secondary authorities. However, most of these citations include the following information: (1) the name of the source, (2) a reference to a volume number, page number, or section number in the source; and (3) a parenthetical that gives the date that the source was published. In addition, citations to books and law review articles set out the author's or authors' names. For instance, in the following example, a citation to a law review article, the authors' names are set out first, the name of the article is set out second, the reference to the law review in which the article is published is set out third, and the year in which the article was published is at the end.

Example:
David Cole & James X. Dempsey, *Terrorism and the Constitution: Sacrificing Civil Liberties in the Name of National Security,* 101 Mich. L. Rev. 1408, 1433 (2003).

In doing your research, always record all of the information that you will need for your citation. You do not want to have to go back to the source at a later date to find the author's name, the pinpoint cite, or the year. An easy way to obtain this material is to use the "copy with reference" function that is on most of the fee-based services.

P R A C T I C E

See Exercise 2D, which is in the *Practice Book.*

---

4. In this example, we have used the Washington Citation Rules, which are set out at www.courts.wa.gov/appellate_trial_courts/supreme/?fa=atc_supreme.style

§ 2.2.4 Using the Citations to Find Material in a Book

To find material in a book, use your library's electronic card catalog to find where the particular set of books or book is shelved in your library. Once you find the set, use the citation to find the particular statute, case, or section. For example, if you are looking for a statute, find the volume that contains the title set out in your citation, and then look through that volume to find the appropriate section or chapter and section. Similarly, if you are looking for a case, locate the correct reporter, and then use the citation's volume number to find the right volume. Once you have found that volume, use the page number to find the case.

See Exercise 2E, which is in the *Practice Book.*

§ 2.2.5 Using Citations to Find Material on a Free Website or Fee-Based Service Like LexisNexis, Loislaw, VersusLaw, or Westlaw

If the material that you are looking for is in book form in your firm's library or on a free website, look up the statute, case, or authority there. If, however, you cannot find the material in a "free" source, you can find it by clicking on "Get a Document" on LexisNexis or by clicking on "Find by Citation" on Westlaw. To find the material on Westlaw,[5] follow the following steps.

Step 1: Sign on to Westlaw.

Locate the Westlaw website for students by typing in *www.lawschool. westlaw.com.* When the Westlaw screen appears, type in your password. If you do not have a password, get one from your legal writing professor, law librarian, or Westlaw representative. See Exhibit 2.1, which is on the CD that came with this book.

Keep in mind that all of the services change the "look" of their pages on a regular basis. Thus, your screens may not look exactly like the ones set out in the exhibits. When you click on "Go," a "welcome" screen will appear. See Exhibit 2.2, which is on the CD that came with this book.

Because you will be using LexisNexis, Loislaw, VersusLaw, or Westlaw on a regular basis, think about creating a link to one or more of these sites on your toolbar or desktop. In addition, think about saving your password so that you do not need to sign on each time.

P R A C T I C E
POINTER

---

5. Although we show you how to use Westlaw, the process is similar for LexisNexis, Loislaw, and VersusLaw. Although the surface features may be different, the underlying structures are the same.

Step 2: Type Your Citation in the "Find by Citation" Box.

When the welcome screen appears, find the "Find by citation" box and type in your citation. If the citation form that you use is not correct, a box will appear that will help you determine the correct form. For example, if you want to find *Humanitarian Law Project v. United States Dept. of Justice*, 353 F.3d 383, 390 (9th Cir. 2003), type "353 F.3d 383" into the "Find by citation" box. Do not type in the name of the case or the material in the parenthetical. See Exhibit 2.3, which is on the CD that came with this book. When you click on "GO," a screen like the one in Exhibit 2.4 should appear. You can use the same process to find regulations, law review articles, restatement sections, and numerous other types of authority.

Step 3: Save or Print a Copy of the Document.

If you think that you will need to look at a document again, email a copy of the document to yourself, save a copy of that document to your computer, or print out a copy. Because in practice you may be charged each time you use the "Get a document" or "Find by citation" feature, emailing, saving, or printing the document may save your client money.

As a law student using your law school password, your use of LexisNexis, Loislaw, VersusLaw, and Westlaw is "free."[6] However, in practice, these services are not free. Some firms pay a transactional
rate, which means that they pay for each search they do or for each case they cite check or print out. In contrast, other firms pay a flat fee. That fee may, however, be determined by how much the firm uses the service.

To print, email, or save a document, click on the icon that is at top of your document screen. See Exhibit 2.5, which is on the CD. When you do, a pull-down menu like the one in Exhibit 2.6 should appear.

See Exercise 2F, which is in the *Practice Book*.

§ 2.3 Deciding How Much Weight to Give to a Particular Authority

Not all enacted and common law is given equal weight. In deciding which law to apply, courts distinguish between mandatory and persuasive authority.

Mandatory authority is law that is binding on the court deciding the case. The court *must* apply that law. In contrast, persuasive authority is law that is

---

6. Most schools have contracts with the various services for which the school pays a flat fee to the service and the school's faculty and students have unlimited access to all or some of the service's databases. The services hope that students will like their service and, after graduation, subscribe.

not binding. Although the court may look to that law for guidance, it need not apply it.

Determining whether a particular statute or case is mandatory or persuasive authority is a two-step process. You must first determine which jurisdiction's law applies (that is, whether federal or state law applies and, if state law applies, which state's law). You must then determine which of that jurisdiction's statutes and cases are binding on the court that will be deciding the case.

§ 2.3.1 Which Jurisdiction's Law Applies?

Sometimes determining which jurisdiction's law applies is easy. For example, common knowledge (and common sense) tells you that federal law probably governs whether a federal PLUS loan constitutes income for federal income tax purposes. Similarly, you can probably guess that a will executed in California by a California resident would be governed by California state law. At other times, though, the determination is much more difficult. You probably would not know which jurisdiction's law governs a real estate contract between a resident of New York and a resident of Pennsylvania for a piece of property located in Florida.

Although the rules governing the determination of which jurisdiction's law applies are beyond the scope of this book (they are studied in courses on Civil Procedure, Federal Courts, and Conflicts), keep two things in mind.

First, remember that in our legal system, federal law almost always preempts state law. Consequently, if there are both a federal and a state statute on the same topic, the federal statute will preempt the state statute to the extent that the two are inconsistent. For example, if a federal statute makes it illegal to discriminate in the renting of an apartment on the basis of familial status but under a state statute such discrimination is lawful, the federal statute governs — it is illegal to discriminate on the basis of familial status. There are a few instances, however, when a state constitutional provision or a state statute will govern: if the state constitution gives a criminal defendant more rights than the United States Constitution, the state constitution applies. States may grant an individual more protection. They may not, however, take away or restrict rights granted by the United States Constitution or a federal statute.

Second, although legal scholars still debate whether there is a federal common law, in the federal system there is not the same body of common law as there is in the states. Unlike in the state systems, in the federal system there are no common law rules governing adverse possession or intentional torts such as assault and battery, false imprisonment, or the intentional infliction of emotional distress. Thus, if the cause of action is based on a common law doctrine, the case is probably governed by state law, not federal law.

§ 2.3.2 What "Law" Will Be Binding on the Court?

Within each jurisdiction, the authorities are ranked. The United States Constitution is always the highest authority, binding on both state and federal courts. Under the United States Constitution is other federal and state law. In the federal system, the highest authority is the Constitution, and under the Constitution are federal statutes and regulations, and under the federal statutes and regulations are the cases interpreting and applying them.

In the state system, the ranking is similar. The highest authority is the state constitution, followed by (1) state statutes and regulations and the cases interpreting and applying those statutes and regulations and (2) the state's common law.

In addition, the cases themselves are ranked. In both the federal and state systems, decisions of the United States Supreme Court carry the most weight: when deciding a case involving the same law and similar facts, both the courts of appeals and the trial courts are bound by the decisions of the supreme, or highest, state courts. Decisions of intermediate courts of appeals come next; the trial courts under the jurisdiction of the intermediate court of appeals are bound by the court of appeals' decisions. At the bottom are the trial courts. Trial court decisions are binding only on the parties involved in the particular case.

Statutes and cases are also ranked by date. More recent statutes supersede earlier versions, and more recent common law rules supersede earlier rules by the same level court. Courts are bound by the highest court's most recent decision. For example, if there is a 1967 state intermediate court of appeals decision that makes an activity legal and a 1986 state supreme court decision that makes it illegal, in the absence of a statute, the 1986 supreme court decision governs. The 1986 decision is mandatory authority, and all of the courts within that jurisdiction are bound by that decision.

See Exercise 2G, which is in the *Practice Book*.

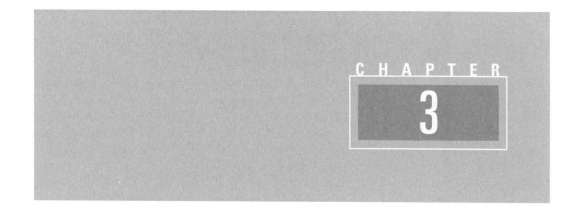

Citators

One of the most embarrassing things that can happen to you as an attorney is to discover that the statute you are relying on has been amended or repealed or that a case you have cited was either reversed on appeal or overruled in a subsequent case. The conversation usually goes something like this:

Attorney: Your Honor, our case is almost identical to *State v. Smith*, a 2002 court of appeals decision. In that case, . . .

Judge: [interrupting the attorney] Counsel, are you aware that the Court of Appeals overruled *State v. Smith* earlier this month?

Attorney: [long pause] No, Your Honor, I was not.

To make sure that you do not find yourself in this position, cite check every statute and case that you cite in your memos and briefs. In addition, cite check every statute and case that your opponent relies on in his or her brief. One of the easiest ways to win a case is to show that the authority that the other side has relied on is no longer good law.

§ 3.1 Introduction to Citators

Citators serve two purposes. First, they are used to determine whether a particular authority — for example, a statute or case — is still good law. Second, they are used to find other authorities that have cited to a particular statute, case, or other authority.

Case citators work as follows. Each time a court publishes a decision, an attorney who works for the company that produces the citator reads the case and determines whether the case reverses or overrules an earlier decision. A decision is *reversed* when, in the same case, a higher court reverses the decision of a lower court. In contrast, a case is *overruled* when, in a different case, a court determines that in an earlier decision the court applied the wrong rule of law.

After determining whether the case reverses or overrules an earlier decision, the attorney who works for the company that publishes the citator examines each of the cases that are cited in each new case determining how, in that new case, the court treated the cases that it cites as authority. Does the court distinguish the cases that it cites as authority? Does the court criticize the courts' reasoning in the cases it cites? Does it follow or apply the rules set out in the cases it cites or do something else — for example, simply cite the cases? This information is then collected and placed in the citator. For example, if in Case D the court distinguishes Case A, this information will be listed in the citator under Case A. Similarly, if Case D follows Case B, this information will be listed in the citator under Case B.

Thus, when you enter the citation for a case, you will find (1) its prior and subsequent history, (2) citations to other cases that have cited to the case, and (3) citations to selected secondary sources that have cited to the case.

Although the publishing companies will list all of the cases that cite a particular case, they do not list all of the secondary sources. For example, typically KeyCite® lists only those secondary sources that are on Westlaw.

P R A C T I C E

POINTER

In addition to cite checking cases, you can also cite check a variety of other sources. For example, if you want to find cases that have cited a particular statute, you can cite check that statute. Similarly, if you want to find cases that have cited to a particular restatement section or a particular law review article, you can cite check those sources.

§ 3.2 The Book Versions of *Shepard's*® *Citators*

Until a few years ago, most attorneys checked their citations using the book version of one of *Shepard's Citators*. Recently, however, most attorneys have abandoned the book versions of *Shepard's* in favor of either KeyCite, which is on Westlaw, or the online version of *Shepard's*, which is on LexisNexis. The online versions of KeyCite and *Shepard's* provide the attorney with more up-to-date information than the book version of *Shepard's* and are easier to use.

Because so few attorneys use the book versions of *Shepard's*, we do not discuss their use in this book. If you need to use them, read the introductory material found at the beginning of each hardbound volume of *Shepard's* or ask a librarian or a more experienced attorney to show you how to *shepardize*™ using books.

Just as individuals who ask you to Xerox a case are not asking you to copy a case using a machine sold by Xerox, attorneys who ask you to *shepardize* a

case are not asking you to cite check the case using *Shepard's.* They are simply asking you to check the case to make sure that it is still good law, and you can do that using KeyCite, *Shepard's,* or another cite-checking product.

---

§ 3.3 KeyCite

If you like West's Key Number system, you will probably want to do your cite checking using KeyCite, which is on Westlaw.

§ 3.3.1 Using KeyCite to Determine If a Case Is Good Law

To determine whether a case is still good law, sign on to Westlaw and, when the welcome screen appears, type the citation that you want to cite check in the KeyCite text box. For example, if you want to determine if *Rendon v. Valleycrest Productions, Ltd.*, 294 F.3d 1279 (11th Cir. 2002),[1] is still good law, type "294 F.3d 1279" into the KeyCite text box. See Exhibit 3.1 which is on the CD that came with this book.[2]

When you click on "GO," the screen set out in Exhibit 3.2 appears. The flag to the left of the case name tells you the case's status. The window on the left allows you to select "Full History," "Direct History — Graphical View," or "Citing References."

Look first at the status flag that is in the upper left-hand corner in the main text box. These flags, assigned by the KeyCite editors, tell you that the case has a negative history that you should investigate. To see what the flags mean, click on KeyCite on the menu bar that is near the top of the page. See Exhibits 3.3 and 3.4.

---

1. In *Rendon*, a group of individuals with hearing and upper-body mobility impairments sued the producers of the television game show, "Who Wants to be a Millionaire," alleging that the use of an automated fast finger telephone selection process violated the Americans with Disabilities Act because it excluded disabled individuals from participating. *Id.* at 1320.

2. Because Westlaw is always updating its product, your screens may not look the same as the screens that are set out on the CD that came with this book.

You may be able to use a case that has a red flag.
For example, if the court reversed or overruled a
case on one point but affirmed or agreed with the
court's reasoning on a second or third point, you can use the case for the second or
third points. You will, however, need to include the case's subsequent history and,
perhaps, a parenthetical indicating that the case was reversed or overruled on
other grounds.

In our example, *Rendon* has a yellow flag, which means that *Rendon* has
some negative indirect history. Next to the yellow flag in the left pane is a
statement that says that *Rendon* has some negative history but that it has not
been overruled. See Exhibit 3.5 on the CD.

To find that negative history, scroll down. When you do, you find a reference to *Access Now*, a 2002 decision from the United States District Court for
the Southern District of Florida that distinguished *Rendon*. Although *Access
Now* is a district court decision and therefore not mandatory authority, you
should read the case to see what the *Access Now* court says about *Rendon*. To see
a copy of *Access Now*, click on the "<u>4</u>" that is next to *Access Now*'s citation. The
link takes you to the place or places in *Access Now* in which the *Access Now*
court discusses *Rendon*. See Exhibits 3.6 and 3.7 on the CD.

When the screen containing *Access Now* appears,
select "Maximize." Then use the "Term Search"
button that is on the bottom of the page to find
all of the places in *Access Now* in which the *Access Now* court discusses *Rendon*.

At this point, read *Access Now*, looking carefully at what the *Access Now*
court says about *Rendon* and making your own decision about whether
Rendon is a case that you want to rely on in your memo or brief. In general,
in deciding whether the case that you are cite checking is still good law,
consider three factors. First, think about the relationship between the citing
court and the court that decided the case you are cite checking. It is one thing
for the United States Supreme Court to question a United States Court of
Appeals decision and another thing for a United States District Court to do so.
Second, look carefully at what the citing court says about the case that you
are cite checking. Is it responding to the losing side's argument, distinguishing the facts in the two cases, or questioning the court's reasoning? In this
last situation, consider the third factor: the persuasiveness of each court's
reasoning.

In the present situation you determine that you are comfortable relying
on *Rendon*. While *Rendon* is a Court of Appeals decision, *Access Now* is a

District Court decision. In addition, it appears that in *Access Now*, the court is distinguishing *Rendon* on its facts: while in *Rendon* the game show took place at a physical, public accommodation (a television studio), *Access Now* involves a website. Finally, after considering the reasoning in both cases, you decide that there might be a flaw in the *Access Now* court's reasoning.

In addition to providing a case's full history, Westlaw now allows you to see a graphical view of your case's prior and subsequent history. To see this view, click on the link to "Direct History — Graphical View." See Exhibit 3.8 on the CD. When you do, the "chart" set out in Exhibit 3.9 appears. Decisions from lower courts are set out at the bottom of the screen, and decisions from higher courts are set out at the top.

§ 3.3.2 Using KeyCite to Locate Additional Cases and Other Authorities

In addition to using KeyCite to determine whether a case is still good law, you can use KeyCite to find additional, more recent, cases that have discussed your case and the rules of law that it sets out. To find these citing references, click on the "Citing References" link, which is on the left-hand side of the screen. See Exhibit 3.10. When you click on the "Citing References" link, you find not only a reference to *Access Now*, but also links to cases, administrative decisions, and secondary sources that have cited *Rendon*. See Exhibit 3.11.

Note that the parenthetical under "Citing References" tells you that there are 96 documents that have cited *Rendon*. The citations to these documents are listed in the following order: (1) cases that have treated *Rendon* negatively (for example, cases that have overruled or distinguished *Rendon*); (2) cases that have treated *Rendon* positively (for example, cases that have followed or explained *Rendon*; and (3) secondary authorities. Within each category, sources are listed according to the depth of the discussion. Four-star sources — that is, sources that have an extended discussion of *Rendon*, are listed first, and one-star sources — that is, ones that only mention *Rendon*, are listed last. A description of Westlaw's star system is set out in Exhibit 3.12.[3]

Quotation marks mean that the citing reference quoted the source that you are cite checking.	

If there are only one or two cases that have cited your cases, checking those cases is easy. Simply click on the link to the cases and read through them

---

3. To find this information, click on KeyCite on the toolbar near the top of the page and then on "Depth of Treatment."

to determine whether they contain information that you can use. Can you use the cases as more recent authority for a rule, as an analogous case, or to rebut an argument that the other side might make?

If, however, a number of cases have cited your case as authority, you need a more efficient way of locating cases that are on point. The easiest way to do this is to use KeyCite's "Limit Key Cite Display" function. To use this function, click on the link, which is at the bottom of the page. See Exhibit 3.13. When you click on the link, the screen set out in Exhibit 3.14 appears.

The "KeyCite Limits" screen allows you to limit the KeyCite display to cases that have cited *Rendon* for the point of law set out in a particular headnote or set of headnotes. For instance, to limit the KeyCite display to those cases that have cited *Rendon* for the point of law set out in headnote 1 of *Rendon*, check the box next to the bracketed 1. In doing so, note the number set out in parentheses: It tells you how many documents have cited to *Rendon* for the point of law set out in headnote 1. In this instance, there are 42 sources that have cited *Rendon* for the point of law set out in headnote 1. See Exhibit 3.15.

You can limit the citing references display even further by selecting additional boxes from the list set out on the left-hand side of the screen. For example, if you click on the "Depth of Treatment" link, the screen appears in Exhibit 3.16. To retrieve only those sources that have a substantial or extended discussion of *Rendon*, check the first two boxes and then "Apply."

On the day that we ran the search, we retrieved 38 documents that have either a substantial or extended discussion of the point of law set out in headnote 1 in *Rendon*. See Exhibit 3.17.

§ 3.3.3 Using KeyCite to Make Sure That a Statute Is Still Good Law

In addition to using KeyCite to make sure that a case is still good law, you can use it to track changes in statutes and regulations and to locate sources that have cited to secondary sources — for example, to a particular law review article.

§ 3.3.4 Other Features

KeyCite also has a number of other "bells and whistles." For instance, if you are expecting "action" on a case or statute, you can monitor that case or statute using "KeyCite Alert." When you use this feature, you will be notified by email each time there is a change to the KeyCite information. If the only thing that you request is a list of citations, then KeyCite Alert is free.

§ 3.4 The Online Version of *Shepard's*

The online version of *Shepard's* is on LexisNexis. Like KeyCite, you can use the online version of *Shepard's* to determine whether an authority is still good law and to find other authorities that have cited the authority you are cite checking.[4]

§ 3.4.1 Using *Shepard's* to Determine Whether a Case Is Good Law

Begin by logging on to LexisNexis. When the opening screen appears, click on the *Shepard's* tab. See Exhibit 3.18, which is on the CD that come with this book.

When the next screen appears, type in the citation that you want to *shepardize* and click on "*Shepard's* for Validation."

Presume that you want to determine whether *Rendon v. Valleycrest Productions, LTD*, 294 F.3d 1279 (11th Cir. 2002) is still good law. To do this, you type in the citation for *Rendon* and click on "*Shepard's* for Validation." See Exhibit 3.19. When you click on "Check," and then the "Full Screen" view, the screen set out in Exhibit 3.20 appears.

The "*Shepard's* FULL Summary" box sets out the *Shepard's* status signals and the information that the *Shepard's* editors relied on in assigning that signal. To find the chart that explains the symbols, scroll to the bottom of the page. See Exhibit 3.21.

Just as you can sometimes use a case that has one of KeyCite's red flags, you may be able to use a case that has one of *Shepard's* red circles.

P R A C T I C E

POINTER

For example, if the court reversed or overruled a case on one point but affirmed or agreed with the court's reasoning on a second point, you can use the case for the second point. You will, however, usually need to include either the case's subsequent history and a parenthetical indicating that the case was reversed or overruled on other grounds.

As the chart on the screen in Exhibit 3.21 tells you, the blue circle with an A inside it means that there are citing references that have analyzed *Rendon*. The *Shepard's* editors did not, however, believe that this analysis was either positive or negative.

As this example illustrates, the KeyCite and *Shepard's* editors do not always assign the same status flags. While the KeyCite editors gave *Rendon* a yellow flag, which means that there is some negative indirect history, the *Shepard's* editors assigned *Rendon* a blue circle with an A inside, which means that there are sources that have analyzed *Rendon* but that their analysis is neutral.

Most of the time, these differences reflect the differences in meaning that each company has attached to its symbols. A red flag on KeyCite does not

---

4. Just as the KeyCite screens change, the *Shepard's* screens also change. Thus, the screens that you see on your computer may not look like the screens that are set out on the CD.

mean the same thing as a red circle on *Shepard's*. There are, however, times when the KeyCite and *Shepard's* editors read the cases differently or when one of them simply makes a mistake. Consequently, always make your own determination about whether a particular case is or is not good law.

Like KeyCite, *Shepard's* also gives a case's prior and subsequent history. Look, for example, at Exhibit 3.22. The citation following number 1 is the citation to the United States District Court's opinion in *Rendon*; the citation next to the green arrow is the citation for the case that you are *shepardizing*, the United States Court of Appeals decision in *Rendon*; and the citation next to the number 2 gives *Rendon's* subsequent history.

§ 3.4.2 Using *Shepard's* to Find Citing References

You can also use *Shepard's* to find cases and other sources that have cited your case. To find these cases and sources, click on "*Shepard's* for Research" on the opening *Shepard's* screen. See Exhibit 3.23.

Although the cases are listed in different orders, KeyCite and *Shepard's* list the same four cases: *Plante*, which is an unpublished decision; *Druskin*, *Bautista*, and *Access Now*. They do not, however, list the same secondary sources. While both KeyCite and *Shepard's* list the law review articles that have cited *Rendon*, the list of other sources is different. KeyCite lists sources published by Thomson West that cite to *Rendon*, and *Shepard's* lists sources included in the LexisNexis databases.

In addition, like KeyCite, *Shepard's* allows you to filter your results to find the sources that are most on point. To filter your results, use the following links: "All Pos," "All Neg," "Custom," or "Focus," which are near the top of the screen. See Exhibit 3.24.

When you select "All Neg," your search retrieves only those sources that have treated the case you are cite checking negatively; when you select "All Pos," your search retrieves only those sources that have treated the case you are cite checking positively. If you click on "Custom," the screen set out in Exhibit 3.25 appears.

Note that while you can filter the citing references by jurisdiction and by date, you cannot filter them by headnotes. Because the *Federal Reporters, Third Series*, is published by Thomson West, *Shepard's* does not have access to its headnotes. You can, however, filter cases by using the "Focus^{TM}" option. You can this function to identify citing references that set out a particular rule or that contain a particular set of facts. See Exhibit 3.26.

For more information about *Shepard's* see the following website: *http://support.lexis-nexis.com/*

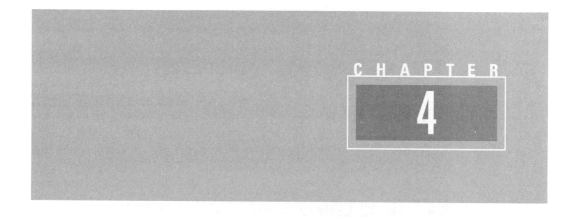

Reading and Analyzing Statutes and Cases

W hen you think about becoming a lawyer, what image comes to mind? Do you see yourself cross-examining a witness? Making an impassioned argument to a jury? Hugging your client when the jury returns the verdict in his or her favor?

Although some lawyers do these things, these are more likely the images of TV lawyering than they are of real lawyering. Real lawyers spend much of their time reading and writing. Consider the following quotation from an associate at a major law firm.

> My view of lawyering has changed dramatically since I entered law school. In my first year of law school, I saw myself as a trial lawyer. I thought that most of my time would be spent either preparing for trial or in trial. The truth of the matter is that I have been inside the courthouse only three or four times during the last year and that was to look through court files. Instead, most of my time is spent reading and preparing documents, doing legal research, and writing memos and briefs. Don't get me wrong. The work that I do is extremely

interesting. It is just that I never saw myself spending seven or eight hours a day reading and writing.

— Second-year associate at a large law firm

The way in which lawyers read is not, however, the way in which most individuals read. Therefore, part of learning how to think like a lawyer is learning how to read like a lawyer. In this chapter, we describe some of the strategies that lawyers use in reading statutes and cases.

§4.1 Good Lawyers Are Good Readers

Good lawyers are good readers. When they read a document, statute, or case, they read exactly what is on the page. They do not skip words, read in words, or misread words. In addition, they have good vocabularies. They recognize and understand most of the words that they read, and the ones they do not recognize or understand they look up in a dictionary.

There are a number of good, free dictionaries online. For example, Merriam-Webster Online dictionary is at *http://www.m-w.com/*; the Cambridge Dictionaries Online is at *http://dictionary. cambridge.org/*; JURIST's legal dictionaries are at *http://jurist.law.pitt.edu/dictionary.htm;* Findlaw's legal dictionary is at *http://dictionary.lp.findlaw.com/*, and The Concise Law Encyclopedia is at *www.thelawencyclopedia.com*

P R A C T I C E
POINTER

Poor reading skills can significantly affect your ability to understand what it is that you are reading. For instance, in the following example, which is taken from the transcript of a law student reading a case aloud, Jackie, a first year student, mispronounced and apparently did not recognize the word "palatial."

EXAMPLE

Transcript of a Student, Jackie, Reading Case Aloud

Some months prior to the alleged imprisonment, the plaintiff, while in Jaffa, announced her intention leave the sect. The defendant, with the help of the plaintiff's husband, persuaded the plaintiff to return to the United States aboard the sect's [platial] yacht, the Kingdom.

James, another student who read the same case, misread the following sentence. The first example shows how the sentence appears in the casebook. The second sentence shows how James read it when he read the sentence aloud.[1]

---

1. The examples in this section come from the following article: Laurel Currie Oates, *Beating the Odds, Reading Strategies of Law Students Admitted Through Special Admissions Programs,* 83 Iowa L. Rev. 139 (1997).

Sentence as it Appears in the Case Book

EXAMPLE

According to the uncontradicted evidence, at no time did anyone physically restrain the plaintiff except for the defendant's refusal once the plaintiff announced her decision to quit the yacht to let the plaintiff use a small boat to take herself, her children and her belongings ashore.

How James Read the Sentence.

EXAMPLE

According to the uncontradicted evidence, at no time did anyone physically restrain the plaintiff except for the defendant's [pause] defendant's refusal once [pause] defendant's refusal once [pause] the plaintiff announced her decision to the quit the yacht to let the plaintiff use a small boat to take herself, her children, and her belongings ashore.

When questioned about what the court was saying in this sentence, James stated that the defendant had, on one occasion, refused to let the plaintiff take the boat. In fact, the court says that the refusal came once the defendant announced her decision to quit the yacht.

Although at first these errors may seem insignificant, in each instance they resulted in the student misunderstanding the case and thus the rules and the court's reasoning. In addition, in both instances, the errors were a harbinger of things to come. Both students ended up doing poorly on their exams. At the end of the first year, Jackie was in the bottom 20 percent of her class, and James had flunked out.

To determine whether you may be misreading cases, make two copies of one of the cases in your casebook. Keep one copy for yourself and give the other to a trusted classmate or teaching assistant. Then read aloud from your copy while your partner follows along on his or her copy, highlighting any words or phrases that you misread and any words that you mispronounce or do not appear to understand. After you have finished your reading of the case, compare your understanding of the case with your partner's. Did you both read the case in essentially the same way? If your partner noted more than one or two problems or if your understanding of the case is substantially different from your partner's understanding of it, try the following. First, try reading more slowly. You may be trying to read the material too quickly. Second, take the time to look up any words that you do not recognize or are not sure that you understand. Third, if the problems appear to be serious, ask your school's learning center if it can provide you with a more thorough evaluation of your reading skills.

§ 4.2 Good Legal Readers Read and Reread Material Until They Are Sure That They Understand It

While in some types of reading you can skip sections that you do not completely understand, such a strategy does not work when you are doing legal reading. If the document, statute, or case is one that is relevant to your problem, you need to read and reread it until you are sure that you understand it.

The following example shows how a student, William, stayed with a case until he was sure that he understood it. The material in the regular typeface is the text of the case. The material in italics is what William said after he had read that section of the text.

EXAMPLE

Transcript of Student, William, Reading Case Aloud

WHITTAKER v. SANFORD

110 Me. 77, 88 S. 399 (1912)

Savage, J. Action for false imprisonment. The plaintiff recovered a verdict for $1100. The case comes up on defendant's exceptions and a motion for a new trial.

So the defendant is the appellant and is appealing the verdict of $1100.

The plaintiff had been a member of a religious sect which had colonies in Maine and in Jaffa, Syria, and of which the defendant was a leader. Some months prior to the alleged imprisonment, the plaintiff, while in Jaffa, announced her intention to leave the sect.

I need to reread this again. [Rereads sentence.] So just prior to the alleged imprisonment the plaintiff was in Jaffa and expressed an intention to leave the sect. At this point, I am a bit confused about who the parties are. I need to reread this to make sure that I have the facts straight. [Rereads from the beginning.] OK. This is an action for false imprisonment. The plaintiff recovered a verdict for $1100. The case came up on the defendant's exceptions. The plaintiff is a member of the sect and the defendant is the head of the sect so Whittaker is the member of the sect and Sanford is its leader.

Although it took William more time to read the case than some other students took, the payoff was substantial. Although his undergraduate GPA and LSAT placed William in the bottom 10 percent of his entering law school class, at the end of his first year, he was in the top 10 percent.

There are several things that you can do to make sure that you understand the cases that you are reading. First, see if you can diagram the action. At the trial court level, who sued whom and what was the cause of action? Who "won" at trial, who filed the appeal, and what is the issue on appeal?

In some instances, you may be able to compare your chart showing the case's prior and subsequent history with the chart that is on KeyCite® under "Direct History, Graphical View." For more information about this KeyCite feature, see page 33 in Chapter 3.

P R A C T I C E
POINTER

Second, do not underestimate the value of preparing your own case briefs. While it may be faster and easier to highlight sections of a statute or case, highlighting does not ensure that you understand the material you are reading. In fact, there is some evidence that students who highlight remember less than students who do not highlight. In highlighting a section, some students focus their attention on the process of highlighting, not on the material they are highlighting. As a result, when they are asked to recall what it is that they just highlighted, they are unable to do so.

Finally, after reading a section, test yourself to make sure that you understood what it is that you have just read. After you have finished reading a statute or case, close the book or your computer and summarize what the statute or case said. If you cannot do this, you need to go back and reread the material until you can.

§ 4.3 Good Legal Readers Engage in Both Analysis and Synthesis

In addition to reading accurately and until they understand the materials, good legal readers analyze and synthesize the material that they read.

Analysis is the process of taking a statute or case apart. In reading statutes, you analyze each section and subsection, making sure that you understand each. In reading cases, you identify the issue that was before the court, the rule or rules that the court applied in deciding that issue, the facts that the court considered in applying those rules, and the court's reasoning or rationale. When you "brief" a statute or case, you are engaging in analysis.

In contrast, synthesis is the process of putting the pieces together. You take each of the statutory sections and cases you have read and try to make sense of them. Are they consistent? What are the steps in the analysis? How do they fit into your existing conceptual frameworks? See pages 113-119.

The following example shows how a law professor engaged in both analysis and synthesis. Note both how she analyzes the case she is currently reading and how she tries to reconcile what the court says in that case with the restatement section that set out the elements of false imprisonment. The text is set out in regular type and the professor's comments are in italics.

Transcript of Professor Reading Case Aloud

EXAMPLE

There was evidence that the plaintiff had been ashore a number of times, had been on numerous outings and had been treated as a guest during her stay aboard the yacht. According to the uncontradicted evidence, at no time did anyone physically restrain the plaintiff except for the defendant's refusal, once the plaintiff announced her decision to quit the yacht, to let the plaintiff use a small boat to take herself, her children, and her belongings ashore.

I'm sort of getting a visual image of the boat that she was in and out of... uhm.... the plaintiff had been ashore. I'm thinking about the elements that I just read [a reference to the restatement section that had been set out immediately before the case] *and I'm trying to see how, I guess, frankly how I would decide the case on a certain level before I even want to know what Judge Savage thought.* [Pause.] *I need to look at the Restatement section.* [Looks back at the *Restatement* section.] *Is the defendant acting to or with the intent to confine the plaintiff? She got off the boat. That kind of bothers me. That results directly or indirectly in confinement. Maybe that's relevant here. The other is conscious of the confinement or is harmed by it. Given the facts, that bothers me too.*

Doing analysis and synthesis is both time-consuming and hard work. You are no longer reading just for information. Instead, as you are reading, you are either placing new information into existing conceptual frameworks or constructing completely new frameworks.

If you are like most law students, at some point you will argue that law school would be a lot easier if your professors put the pieces together for you, if they just gave you their conceptual frameworks. If you had come to law school just to learn the law, you would be right. It would be easier for both you and your professors if they just gave you the law. However, there is a lot more to law school than just learning the law. Although you will learn some law while you are in law school, the real reason that you came to law school was to learn to think like a lawyer. Thus, the primary skills that you will need to teach yourself while you are in law school are how to do legal analysis and synthesis. You need to be able to look at a statute and a group of cases and determine what the law is and how it might be applied in a particular situation.

§ 4.4 Good Legal Readers Place the Statutes and Cases They Read into Their Historical, Social, Economic, Political, and Legal Contexts

Good legal readers understand that statutes are usually enacted to solve a problem or to promote certain interests and that judicial decisions reflect, at least in part, the time and place in which they were written. As a consequence, in reading statutes and cases, good legal readers place them in their historical, social, economic, political, and legal contexts. They note the date that the statute was enacted and amended and the year in which the case was decided. They think about the social and economic conditions during those periods and about the political issues that were in the headlines when the statute was enacted or the case was decided. Finally, they place the case in its larger legal context. They determine how the particular issue fits into the broader area of law, they note whether the decision is from an intermediate court of appeals or the highest court in the jurisdiction, and they read the court's decision in light of the standard of review that the court applied. Was the court deciding the issue *de novo,* or was it simply looking to see whether there was sufficient evidence to support the jury's verdict?

If you do not know what the phrase *"de novo"*
means, look it up in a book or online dictionary.
When you use the link on Findlaw.com, you retrieve
the following information:

> [de̱-'no̱-vo̱, da̱-] Medieval Latin, literally, from (the) new: over again: as if for the first
> time: as **a:** allowing independent appellate determination of issues (as of fact or law)
> Example: **a** *de novo* review **b:** allowing complete retrial upon new evidence (compare
> *abuse of discretion clearly erroneous*).
> *Note: A* de novo *review is an in-depth review. Decisions of federal administrative
> agencies are generally subject to* de novo *review in the United States District
> Courts, and some lower state court decisions are subject to* de novo *review at
> the next level.*

In reading the case that was described earlier in this chapter, the professor
placed the case in its historical, social, and political context. First, she noted
that the case was an old one. It was decided by the Supreme Court of Maine
in 1912. Second, she noted that in 1912, $1,100 would have been a substan-
tial sum of money. Third, she considered the social climate in 1912: the role
of women and their rights and the public's attitudes about "religious cults."
She knew that in 1912 women had far fewer rights. For instance, it was often
the husband who determined where the couple lived and what religion they
practiced. What she did not know is how religious cults were viewed. In 1912
did people view religious cults in the same way that most people view them
today? Were cults seen as a problem? How did these factors influence the
court's decision and the way it wrote its opinion?

You need to think about the cases that you read in similar ways. When
you are reading cases, pay close attention to the dates of the decisions and the
courts that issued them. If you read the cases in chronological order, can you
discern a trend? Over the last fifty, twenty-five, or five years, have the rules or
the ways the courts apply those rules changed? If the answer is yes, what social,
economic, or political events might account for those changes? In contrast, if
you arrange the decisions by jurisdiction, does a pattern appear? For example,
do industrial states tend to take one approach and more rural states another?
Are some jurisdictions more conservative while others more liberal? As you
read between the lines, what do you think motivated the judges and persuaded them to decide the case in one way rather than another?

§ 4.5 Good Legal Readers "Judge" the
Statutes and Cases They Read

As a beginning law student, you may be tempted to accept everything you
read. Who are you to judge the soundness of a Supreme Court Justice's
analysis or Congress's choice of a particular word or phrase? Do not give
in to this temptation. If you are going to be a good legal reader, you need
to question and evaluate everything you read.

In judging the cases you read, make sure you do more than evaluate the facts. Although in the following example William engages in some evaluation, it is the evaluation of a nonlawyer. William evaluates the witness's testimony, not the court's choice of rule, application of the rules to the facts, or reasoning. Once again, the text of the case is set out in a regular typeface and William's comments are in italics.

EXAMPLE   ### Transcript of Student, William, Reading Case Aloud

There was evidence that the plaintiff had been ashore a number of times, had been on numerous outings and had been treated as a guest during her stay aboard the yacht.

So at this point I'm getting a picture of what happened.... I'm not sure though. There is evidence that the plaintiff had been ashore so at this point I'm thinking was she really held against her will? So I have doubts, doubts about the plaintiff's story at this point.

According to the uncontradicted evidence, at no time did anyone physically restrain the plaintiff except for the defendant's refusal, once the plaintiff announced her decision to quit the yacht, to let the plaintiff use a small boat to take herself, her children, and her belongings ashore.

Well, ... the defendant by this point isn't really stopping the plaintiff from leaving. Throughout the entire episode the plaintiff's husband was with her and repeatedly tried to persuade her to change her mind and remain with the sect.

At this point, mentally, I think, ... I don't think the plaintiff's story doesn't hold water, ... that's what I am thinking. Because her husband was there so maybe you, there's in my mind that her story doesn't hold water. So I am thinking at this point that the court might end up reversing her position.

In contrast, the professor evaluated the court's conclusion and reasoning. After she finished reading the case, the professor made the following comments. Note how the professor talks about the elements of the tort and how she poses a hypothetical.

EXAMPLE   ### Transcript of Professor's Comments

I'm not sure that the plaintiff proved all of the elements of false imprisonment. For example, I'm not sure that the plaintiff proved that the defendant intended to confine the plaintiff. If I remember correctly, [pause] on a number of occasions he allowed her to go ashore. He just wouldn't let her use the small boat to take her children and their things ashore. It would have been interesting to know what would have happened if a boat had come to get the plaintiff. Would the defendant have let her go? If he would have, there wouldn't have been false imprisonment. [Pause.] The facts may, however, support a finding that the defendant's actions resulted in confinement. In those days, the plaintiff may not have had a way to contact anyone on shore to ask them to come get her. Although the court may have reached the right result, I wish that Judge Savage had done more analysis. [Pause.] I get the feeling that he had made up his mind, maybe he didn't like cults, and then just tried to justify his conclusion.

§ 4.6 Good Legal Readers Read for a Specific Purpose

The reading that you do for your law school classes is very different from the reading you will do in practice. In law school, you read so that you will be prepared for class. Consider the following comment made by James.

> When I read cases, I usually read them not for briefing cases per se, but more out of fear of being called on in class. I don't want to look like a fool so I just want to know the basic principles.

In contrast, in practice you will read for a specific purpose. For example, you will read to keep up to date in an area of law, to find the answer to a question that a client has posed, to find statutes or cases to support your client's position, or to find holes in your opponent's arguments.

In reading the statutes and cases for your legal writing assignments, read not as a student, but as a lawyer. Initially, read to find out what the law is. Analyze the statutes and cases that you have found and then put the pieces together. Then read the cases as the parties and the court would read them. Begin by putting yourself in your client's position. How can your client use the statutes and cases to support its position? Put yourself in the other side's shoes. How could the opponent use the same statutes and cases to support his or her position? Finally, put yourself in the court's position. If you were the judge, how would you read the statutes and cases?

§ 4.7 Good Legal Readers Understand That Statutes and Cases Can Be Read in More Than One Way

Different people have different beliefs about text. While some people believe that there is a right way to read each statute or case, others believe that most statutes and cases can be read in more than one way. For those in the first group, the meaning of a particular text is fixed. For those in the second group, the meaning of a particular text is "constructed" by juries and judges and the attorneys who talk to them.

As a general rule, the students who seem to have the easiest time in their first year of law school are those who believe that statutes and cases can be read in more than one way, that the meaning of a particular text can be socially constructed. These students have an easier time seeing how each side might interpret a particular statute and stating a rule so that it favors their client's position. When they talk about a court's holding, they refer to it as "*a* holding," not "*the* holding."

If you are a student who believes that meaning is fixed, be aware of how your belief system is affecting the way in which you read statutes and cases and the way in which you make arguments. In reading cases, can you see how both the plaintiff and the defendant might be able to use the same case to support its argument? In making arguments, are you able to see what the other side might argue and how you might be able to respond to those arguments? Are you spending too much time looking for the correct answer and not enough time creating that answer? In contrast, if you are a student who believes that meaning is socially constructed, be careful that you do not become cynical or only a hired gun. Although there may be many ways of reading a particular statute or case, not all of those readings will lead to a "just" result.

     Reading and thinking like a lawyer are not skills that you can learn overnight. There are no crash courses, short cuts, or magic wands. Instead, you will learn to read and think like a lawyer through trial and error and by observing how real lawyers, not TV lawyers, read and think about statutes and cases.

Introduction to Legal Research and Objective and Advisory Writing

Introduction

Imagine for a moment that, instead of applying to law school you applied to film school. The first week has been a whirlwind of activity with welcomes from the dean and famous alums, form after form that had to be filled out, and a series of introductory classes that have provided you with information about the history of film and the current technologies. All is going well until one of your professors tells you that you need to write the screenplay for a one-hour drama and, please, turn in something of professional quality by Monday.

You have, of course, seen hundreds if not thousands of television dramas. You have not, however, ever seen the "paper" that is behind those dramas. Thus, although you think you know how to write the dialogue, how do you indicate the settings, the camera angles, and the music? How can you write a screenplay if you have never seen one?

The good news is that you have been accepted into law school and not film school. The bad news is that your legal writing professor wants you to research and write an office memo, you do not know how to do legal research, and the only memos you have seen are business memos. We are not, however, going to do what the film school professor did and ask you to write an office memo without showing you what one looks like or without walking you through the process. If you read, and perhaps reread the chapters in this book, Book 2, you will have a good start on researching, writing, and revising, editing, and proofreading an objective memo.

Chapter 5 introduces the objective memo. The chapter explains the memo's audience, purpose, and conventional formats and provides three sample memos. Think of Chapter 5 as the chapter in which the film school professor shows you some sample screen plays. The remaining chapters in Book 2 walk you through the process of researching and writing three objective memos.

Part 1 of Book 2 shows you how to research and write a relatively simple memo that involves a state statute that has three elements, or requirements. Chapter 6 shows you how to research an issue governed by state statutes and cases using both book and electronic sources. Chapter 7 shows you how to draft the memo, and Chapter 8 shows you how to revise, edit, and proofread the memo. In the revising and editing sections of Chapter 8 we focus on how to use roadmaps, signposts, and transitions effectively, and on how to write effective sentences.

Part 2 of Book 2 takes a similar approach, showing you how to research and write about a more difficult problem that involves a common law issue with five elements. Chapter 9 shows you how to research common law issues. Chapter 10 walks you through the process of preparing the first draft of the memo, and Chapter 11 shows you how to revise, edit, and proofread the memo with a focus on writing precisely and concisely.

The last part of Book 2, Part 3, takes a slightly different approach. First, instead of showing you how to research and write a memo involving state law, we show you how to research and write a memo involving federal law. Second, instead of writing an objective memo to an attorney in your own firm, we show you how to write a prehearing or bench memo for a judge. Finally, instead of showing you how to write a memo in which you apply well-established law to a particular set of facts, we show you how to write a memo when the issue is one of first impression — that is, an issue in which the courts in your jurisdiction have never decided what the law is.

In writing the chapters on researching and writing memos we have tried to be as explicit as possible. We provide you not only with information but also with descriptions of the process and with numerous examples. Researching and writing a memo is not, however, the same as making brownies from a box. Thus, do not treat the plans and templates that we provide for you as recipes. Instead, treat them as what they are: starting points. Although there are some wrong ways to research and write an objective memo, there is no one right way to research, one right way to do the analysis, or one right way to organize the discussion section. Do not leave your common sense at the law school door.

Finally, keep in mind that learning to research and write a memo is much more difficult than learning to make hamburgers at McDonald's. In fact, it may be more difficult to learn how to research and write a memo than it is to learn how to diagnose a heart defect or cancer. There is, in fact, a reason why you spend three years in law school.

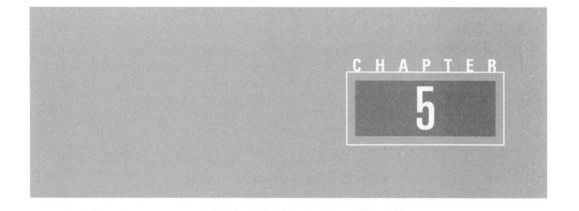

The Objective Memorandum: Its Purpose, Audience, and Format

I f you work as a legal intern after your first year of law school, you will
probably spend most of your time researching and writing objective
memoranda, which are also known as office memos. An attorney will
ask you to research a question, you will research it, and then you will
present your research and analysis to the attorney in a written memo.
The attorney who assigned the project will then read your
memo and, using the information contained in it, advise a client, draft a
document, negotiate with an opposing party, or prepare a brief or oral
argument.

Thus, office memos are in-house documents that have as their primary
audience attorneys in the office and that have as their primary purpose providing those attorneys with information. In addition, sometimes a copy of the
memo is sent directly to the client, who will read it to determine what his or
her options are.

Although the format of a memo will vary from law firm to law firm, most attorneys want the following sections: a heading, a statement of facts, a formal statement of the issue, a brief answer, a discussion section, and a formal conclusion.

Set out below are three memos written by first-year law students. As you read through them, ask yourself the following questions.

- What types of information are contained in the memos?
- In what order is that information presented?
- In presenting the information, what role did the students assume? Did they simply play the role of a "reporter," summarizing what they had found, or did they do more?
- What types of authority did the students cite? How did they use those authorities?
- Are the memos well written? Why or why not?

EXAMPLE 1 **Sample Memo**

To: Connie Krontz

From: Thomas McMurty

Date: September 18, 2006

Re: Boliver Custom Carpets, File No. 06-478

Statement of Facts

Our client, Boliver Custom Carpets (BCC), a Colorado corporation doing business in Colorado, wants to know whether it can enforce an oral contract for three rugs that were manufactured to the buyers' specifications.

The buyers, Mr. and Mrs. McKibbin, first contacted BCC in June of this year, asking whether BCC could replicate the original rugs in the Reutlinger mansion, which Mr. and Mrs. McKibbin were refurbishing and turning into a bed and breakfast. Around the perimeter of each rug was a twelve-inch maroon strip; in the center was beige carpet with the Reutlinger family flower woven into the carpet at one-foot intervals.

After examining a picture of the rugs, BCC called its manufacturer. The manufacturer told BCC's sales representative that it could produce the rugs. Although the looms would have to be specially set, standard dyes could be used. On June 19, 2006, the sales representative sent the McKibbins a proposal setting out the specifications and the price, $16,875.

On June 29, 2006, Mrs. McKibbin called the sales representative and told him that she and her husband wanted to purchase the rugs. The next day, the salesperson ordered the rugs from the manufacturer. A written contract was not sent to the McKibbins.

On August 4, 2006, Mrs. McKibbin called BCC and told the sales representative that, because her husband had fallen from the roof of the mansion, they were canceling their order. BCC called its manufacturer the same day. Unfortunately, the rugs had already been completed, and BCC was forced to accept delivery of the rugs at a cost of $13,500.

On August 15, 2006, BCC sent the McKibbins a bill for the proposal price of the rugs. Last week, BCC received a letter from the McKibbins' attorney stating that, because the contract was not in writing, it was not enforceable under the UCC Statute of Frauds.

BCC sold the rugs to a wholesaler on September 1, 2006, for $10,000. BCC has done business with this wholesaler on one prior occasion. Similar rugs are not available from other carpet stores.

BCC is a specialty carpet firm that specializes in custom work. It has been in business for only one year and is in financial trouble.

Issue

Under Colorado's UCC Statute of Frauds exception for specially manufactured goods, Colo. Rev. Stat. § 4-2-201(3)(a) (2005), is an oral contract for the sale of rugs enforceable when (1) the rugs were manufactured to the buyers' specifications, (2) the same rugs are not available at other outlets, (3) the buyers told the seller that they did not want the rugs after the rugs had been completed, and (4) the seller sold the rugs to a wholesaler with whom it had done business on one prior occasion?

Brief Answer

Probably. Although the formal requirements of the Statute of Frauds are not met, the contract is probably enforceable under the exception for specially manufactured goods: to produce the rugs, the manufacturer had to specially set its looms, and the rugs were sold not to a retail customer but to a wholesaler at a loss.

Discussion

Specially manufactured goods are exempt from the writing requirement because the very nature of the goods serves as a reliable indicator that a contract was indeed formed. *Colorado Carpet Installation, Inc. v. Palermo*, 668 P.2d 1384, 1390 (Colo. 1983). When the goods conform to the special needs of a particular buyer and are not, therefore, suitable for sale to others, not only is the likelihood of a perjured claim diminished, but denying enforcement of such a contract would impose a substantial hardship on the aggrieved party. *Id.*; *accord Webcor Packaging Corp. v. Autozone, Inc.*, 158 F.3d 354 (6th Cir. 1998). Thus, even if the formal requirements of the UCC Statute of Frauds are not met, a contract is enforceable if the goods were specially manufactured. *Id.* The applicable portion of the Colorado statute reads as follows.

> (3) A contract which does not satisfy the requirements of subsection (1) but which is valid in other respects is enforceable
>   (a) if the goods are to be specially manufactured for the buyer and are not suitable for sale to others in the ordinary course of the seller's business and the seller, before notice of repudiation is received and under circumstances which reasonably indicate that the goods are for the buyer, has made either a substantial beginning of their manufacture or commitments for their procurement. . . .

Colo. Rev. Stat. § 4-2-201(3)(a) (2005).

Thus, in this case BCC must prove the following: (1) that the rugs were specially made for the McKibbins; (2) that the rugs were not suitable for sale to others in the ordinary course of BCC's business; (3) that BCC had manufactured the rugs or had made a commitment for their procurement; and (4) that the manufacture or commitment commenced under circumstances reasonably indicating that the goods were for the McKibbins and prior to BCC's receipt of notification of contractual repudiation. *See Colorado Carpet,* 668 P.2d at 1389-91.

In this case, the first two elements will be in dispute. While BCC will argue that the rugs were specially manufactured for the McKibbins and that they could not be resold in the ordinary course of its business, the McKibbins will argue that the rugs were not specially manufactured and that BCC was able to resell the rugs. The third and fourth elements are not, however, in dispute. The third element is met because the rugs were completed before Ms. McKibbin called to cancel the order. The fourth element is met because the circumstances indicate that the rugs were in fact manufactured for the McKibbins.

1. Specially Manufactured for the Buyer

Although the term "specially manufactured" is not defined in the statute, the Colorado Supreme Court has held that it refers to the nature of the goods and not to whether the goods were made in the usual course of the seller's business. *Colorado Carpet Installation, Inc. v. Palermo,* 668 P.2d 1384, 1390 (Colo. 1983).

In the only Colorado case discussing the exception for specially manufactured goods, the Colorado Supreme Court held that carpeting that was available from other carpet outlets and that had not been cut to unusual shapes or subjected to special dyeing, weaving, or other procedures was not specially manufactured. *Id.* In contrast, in other states the courts have held that goods are specially manufactured if the goods have been produced with either the buyer's name or logo on them. For example, in a Virginia case, the Virginia Supreme Court held that wrapping material imprinted with the buyer's name and unique artwork and cut to the buyer's specifications was specially manufactured. *Flowers Baking Co. of Lynchburg, Inc. v. R-P Packaging, Inc.,* 329 S.E.2d 462, 464 (Va. 1985); *accord Smith-Scarf Paper Co. v. P.N. Hirsch & Co. Stores, Inc.,* 754 S.W.2d 928 (Mo. Ct. App. 1988) (holding that cellophane imprinted with the defendant's logo and cut to the size specified by the defendant was specially manufactured).

In the present case, BCC can argue that the rugs were specially manufactured for the buyer. Relying on the plain language of the statute, BCC can argue that the rugs were, in fact, specially manufactured: BCC had to make special arrangements with the manufacturer, and to produce the rugs, the manufacturer had to specially set its looms.

BCC can also contrast the facts in its case to the facts in *Colorado Carpet.* Unlike *Colorado Carpet,* in this case identical rugs are not available from other carpet outlets. Instead, the rugs in question are one of a kind: they were made to fit specific rooms, and special weaving was required. The case is more like *Flowers.* Like the wrapping material, the rugs were personalized. The Reutlinger family flower is as distinctive as any company name or logo and, as a consequence, rugs with such a flower woven into them are of little value to a third party.

Finally, BCC can argue policy. In this instance, the rugs themselves are evidence that a contract was formed. BCC probably would not have produced rugs matching the original rugs in the Reutlinger mansion had there not been a contract. In addition, if the court does not enforce the contract, BCC, a small business that is already in financial trouble, will suffer a substantial loss.

In response, the McKibbins will argue that the rugs were not specially manu-factured. Unlike *Flowers,* in which the buyer's name was imprinted on the packing material, in this case it is only the Reutlinger family flower that is woven into the rugs. Furthermore, the flower is not particularly unusual; BCC was able to sell the rugs to a wholesaler with little or no difficulty.

The McKibbins' best argument is, however, a policy argument. They can argue that under the UCC oral contacts should be the exception rather than the rule. Thus, a seller whose only business is custom or specially manufactured goods should not be exempt from the Statute of Frauds simply because its goods are specially manufactured. If all of such a seller's goods are custom-made, a written contract will never be necessary, and written contracts will become the exception, not the rule. In addition, the McKibbins can argue that a seller who deals only in custom goods is just as likely to fabricate a contract for custom goods as is a seller who deals in ready-made merchandise.

BCC can respond to such an argument by citing *Impossible Electronic Techniques Inc., v. Wackenhut Protection Systems, Inc.*, 669 F.2d 1026 (9th Cir. 1982), a case in which the seller sold custom closed-circuit television cameras. In holding that the cameras were specially manufactured, the court said the fact that the seller is in the business of manufacturing custom-designed and custom-made goods does not necessarily preclude a finding that the goods are specially manufactured. *Id.* at 1037.

The court will probably conclude that the rugs were specially manufactured for the McKibbins. The rugs were not available from other outlets and, to produce the rugs, the manufacturer had to specially set its looms. Although BCC is in the business of producing custom carpets, it is not likely that it would have produced rugs with the Reutlinger family flower woven into them unless it had been requested to do so.

2. Not Suitable for Sale to Others in the Ordinary Course of the Seller's Business

In determining whether goods are suitable for sale to others in the ordinary course of the seller's business, the courts look first at the nature of the seller's business and then at whether the seller could reasonably be expected to find a buyer for the goods. *See Colorado Carpet Inc.*, 668 P.2d at 1391. For example, in *Colorado Carpet*, the court first identified the nature of Colorado Carpet's business and found that its business was to purchase carpet from wholesalers and then to resell the carpet to retail purchasers at a price that included a labor charge for installation. The court then looked at whether it was reasonable to expect that Colorado Carpet could resell the carpets. In deciding that it was reasonable, the court considered three factors: (1) Colorado Carpet dealt in similar carpets on a regular basis, (2) the carpets were large enough that they could be cut to other dimensions, and (3) Colorado Carpet had in fact been able to resell the carpets. Colorado Carpet returned some of the carpets to the manufacturer and sold the rest to a local purchaser. *Id.* at 1391. Thus, the court concluded that the goods were suitable for sale to another in the ordinary course of Colorado Carpet's business and that the exception for specially manufactured goods did not apply.

BCC can argue that it was not able to sell the goods in the ordinary course of its business. Unlike Colorado Carpet, BCC does not deal in standard carpets in standard sizes and shapes. The individuals with whom BCC does business are looking for rugs designed to their specifications. In addition, the rugs cannot be altered to make them suitable for another customer. The rugs cannot be cut to another size or shape, and the colors and flower design cannot be changed. Finally, BCC can argue that it was not able to sell the goods to a retail customer. It had to resell them to a wholesaler.

The McKibbins will respond by arguing that BCC was able to resell the goods. While BCC did not resell them to a retail customer, BCC did resell them to a wholesale dealer with whom it had done business in the past. In addition, the facts do not indicate that BCC made any attempt to resell the rugs to a retail customer.

Because BCC's ordinary course of business is selling to retail customers, not to wholesale companies, a court is likely to decide that the rugs were not suitable for sale to others in the ordinary course of BCC's business. It is not reasonable to expect that BCC could find a retail customer that would want rugs in those sizes and colors and with that particular design.

Conclusion

Although the formal requirements of the UCC Statute of Frauds are not met, the contract between BCC and the McKibbins is probably enforceable under the exception for specially manufactured goods.

BCC should be able to prove the first element, that the rugs were specially manufactured for the McKibbins. The rugs were made to the McKibbins' specifications: the manufacturer specially set its looms to weave the Reutlinger family flower into the rugs.

BCC should also be able to prove the second element, that the goods are not suitable for sale to others in the ordinary course of BCC's business. BCC's ordinary course of business is selling carpets to retail customers, not wholesalers.

The third element, that the seller had manufactured or made a commitment to procure the goods before repudiation, and the fourth element, that the evidence reasonably indicates that the goods were for the McKibbins, are not likely to be in dispute. The rugs had been completed at the time Mrs. McKibbin canceled the order, and the family flower is evidence that the goods were for the McKibbins.

Because it is likely that a court would enforce the contract, we should advise BCC to pursue this action. We can either contact the McKibbins' attorney and attempt to settle the matter or file a complaint.

EXAMPLE 2   ## Sample Memo

To: Margaret Anne Graham
         Senior Prosecutor, King County

From: Samuel Jones
         Assistant Deputy Prosecutor

Date: September 8, 2006

Re: Case No. 02-08-6695
         Doug Richardson, Possession of Stolen Property

Statement of Facts

You have asked me to evaluate the State's case against Doug Richardson, who has been charged with Possession of Stolen Property in the First Degree.

On April 17, 2006, the owner of the Last Chance Tavern purchased a Rocket Blaster pinball machine, serial number A47699942, for $3,900.00. On July 6, 2006, the machine was stolen from the tavern.

On August 21, 2006, the police executed a search warrant for the house located at 2204 65th Ave in Seattle, Washington. In the living room, the police located a Rocket

Blaster pinball machine with the serial number A47699942. There was a 4" × 8" identification decal visible on the front of the pinball machine. Although some of the label had been scratched off, the letters "Prop of L st C nce Tavern" were still visible. The coin box had been disabled so that coins were not necessary to operate the machine. The police did not dust the machine for fingerprints.

At the time of the search, Richardson was the sole occupant of the residence. He told the police that he was housesitting for his friend, Stan Coming, for six weeks, beginning on July 15, 2006. Richardson told the police that although he was not paying rent, he had agreed to pay for his long distance phone calls and for the pay-for-view movies that he ordered. Richardson had a key to the residence, and the police found a number of Mr. Richardson's belongings in the house, including clothing, a radio, text-books, class notes, and a checkbook. Richardson told the police that he had his own apartment. The police have not yet verified this fact.

In response to questions about the pinball machine, Richardson told the police that Coming had told him that he had purchased the pinball machine from a "fence."

Issue Statement

Under RCW 9A.56.150,[1] can the State prove all of the elements of Possession of Stolen Property in the First Degree when (1) the pinball machine had been purchased for $3,900 approximately four months earlier; (2) the pinball machine had the same serial number as the one stolen from the tavern; (3) the defendant had been told that the pinball machine had been purchased from a fence; and (4) the defendant had been housesitting at the house for four weeks, had clothing, books, and his checkbook at the house, and had paid his share of some of the bills?

Brief Answer

Probably not. Although the State will be able to prove that the pinball machine was stolen, that it was worth more than $1,500.00, and that Richardson knew that it was stolen, the State will not be able to prove that Richardson had either actual or constructive possession of the pinball machine. The pinball machine was not in Richardson's personal custody, and Richardson did not have dominion and control over either the pinball machine or the house where it was found.

Discussion

A person is guilty of possession of stolen property in the first degree if he or she knowingly possesses stolen property valued at more than $1,500. RCW 9A.56.150. The phrase "possessing stolen property" is defined as follows:

> "Possessing stolen property" means knowingly to receive, retain, possess, conceal, or dispose of stolen property knowing that it has been stolen and to withhold or appropriate the same to the use of any person other than the true owner or person entitled thereto.

RCW 9A.56.140(1).

Therefore, to obtain a conviction, the State must prove each of the following elements: (1) that the act occurred in the State of Washington; (2) that the value of

---

1. Because this memo was written for a Washington attorney, the author has used the Washington citation rules.

the pinball machine exceeded $1,500; (3) that the pinball machine was withheld or appropriated from the true owner — that is, that the pinball machine was "stolen"; (4) that Richardson knew that the pinball machine was stolen; and (5) that Richardson had active or constructive possession of the pinball machine. *See* WPIC 77.02.

The State can easily prove the first four elements. First, the State can prove that the pinball machine was found in a residence in Seattle, Washington; therefore, the alleged act took place in the State of Washington. Second, the State can prove that the value of the pinball machine exceeds $1,500. "'Value' means the market value of the property or services at the time and in the approximate area of the criminal act." RCW 9A.56.010(18)(a). The price paid for an item of property, if not too remote in time, is proper evidence of value. *State v. Melrose*, 2 Wn. App. 824, 470 P.2d 552 (1970). Because the tavern had purchased the machine for $3,900 only four months earlier, it is unlikely that Richardson will be able to demonstrate that the current value is less than $1,500.

Third, the State can prove that the pinball machine was stolen property. The serial number on the machine found at the Coming residence matches the serial number on the machine stolen from the tavern. In addition, the fact that the pinball machine was found at the Coming residence supports the conclusion that the pinball machine was being withheld or appropriated from its true owner.

Fourth, the State will be able to prove that Richardson knew the machine was stolen. Richardson has admitted that Coming told him that he had purchased the pinball machine from a fence.

The State may, however, have difficulty proving the fifth element, that Richardson had possession. Possession may be either actual or constructive. *State v. Summers*, 45 Wn. App. 761, 763, 728 P.2d 613 (1986). A defendant has actual possession when the property is in his or her personal custody. *Id.* In this case, the State will not be able to prove that Richardson had actual possession of the pinball machine. At the time the police searched the house, Richardson was not playing or even standing near the pinball machine. In addition, the State may have trouble proving that Richardson had constructive possession.

A defendant has constructive possession of stolen property when he or she has dominion and control over the premises on which the property was located or the property. *See, e.g., State v. Summers*, 45 Wn. App. at 763. In determining whether a defendant has dominion and control, the courts look at the totality of the circumstances. Mere proximity to stolen merchandise is not enough to establish dominion and control over it. *Id.*

In the cases in which the courts have found that there was sufficient evidence to support a finding of constructive possession, the defendant had been staying on the premises for more than a few days and had no other residence; had personal property on the premises; and had done some act that indicated that he had dominion and control over the premises. *See, e.g., State v. Weiss*, 73 Wn.2d 372, 438 P.2d 610 (1968); *State v. Collins*, 76 Wn. App. 496, 886 P.2d 243 (1995). For example, in *Collins*, the defendant admitted staying on the premises fifteen to twenty times during the prior month and having no other residence; boxes filled with the defendant's personal property were found in a hallway; and, while the police were in the house, the defendant received several phone calls. *Id.* at 499. Similarly, in *Weiss* the evidence indicated that the defendant had been staying on the premises for more than a month and had helped pay the rent; a bed belonging to the defendant was found in the house; and the defendant had invited others to spend the night. *Id.* at 374. In both cases, the courts held that the facts were sufficient to support the jury's verdict that the defendant had dominion and control over both the premises and the drugs.

In contrast, in the cases in which the courts have found that there was not sufficient evidence to support a finding of constructive possession, the defendant was only a temporary visitor. *See, e.g., State v. Callahan*, 77 Wn.2d 27, 459 P.2d 400 (1969); *State v. Davis*, 16 Wn. App. 657, 558 P.2d 263 (1977). In *Callahan*, the defendant, Hutchinson, had been on the houseboat for only a few days, had only a limited number of personal possessions on the premises, and was not paying rent. In addition, another individual admitted that the drugs belonged to him. Based on these facts, the court held that the defendant did not have constructive possession of either the premises or the drugs, which were found on a table next to the defendant. *Id.* at 32. Likewise, in *Davis*, the court held that the defendant did not have dominion and control over either the premises or the drugs when the defendant was staying at the apartment for only the weekend while his mother entertained guests at home. Even though the defendant's clothing and sleeping bag were found in the apartment, the court held that the presence of these items was not enough to establish constructive possession. *Id.* at 658-659.

In this case, it is unlikely that the State can prove that Richardson had constructive possession of either the premises or the stolen pinball machine. First, the jury will probably find that Mr. Richardson was only a temporary visitor. Although Richardson had been staying on the premises for more than a few days, the facts in his case can be distinguished from the facts in *Collins* and *Weiss*. Unlike Collins and Weiss, Richardson was not paying rent, and he had another residence. The facts in this case are more like the facts in *Callahan* and *Davis*. Like the defendants in those cases, Richardson was just a temporary visitor. Just as Davis was spending the weekend at a friend's house, Richardson was staying for a relatively short period of time at a friend's house.

Second, the jury will probably find that the personal possessions that were found in the house are not sufficient to establish that Richardson had dominion and control over the premises. The State will argue that the personal possessions found on the premises indicate that Richardson was using the house as his home. When the police searched the premises, they found clothing, books, class notes, and a checkbook belonging to Richardson. In contrast, the defendant will argue that the personal possessions found on the premises are not sufficient to support a finding that he had constructive possession. Unlike Weiss, who had brought his bed into the house, and Collins, who had boxes of his personal possessions on the premises, Richardson had just a few items. There is no evidence that indicates that the police found personal items such as Richardson's toothbrush or razor on the premises. In fact, the evidence indicates that Richardson had even fewer personal possessions on the premises than did the defendant in *Davis*.

Third, it is unlikely that the jury will find that the other evidence is sufficient to establish that Richardson had dominion and control over the premises. Even though Richardson had a key to the premises, his possession of the key is consistent with his claim that he was only housesitting. In addition, even though Richardson paid some bills, he was only paying for his share of the phone and cable bills. There is no evidence that he paid rent or utilities.

Finally, as a matter of public policy, it is unlikely that the jury will find a person who was only housesitting guilty of possession of stolen property in the first degree. While we can argue that Richardson had an obligation to report the presence of the pinball machine to the police, it is unlikely that the jury will want to impose such a duty on housesitters. At this point, the law does not require that individuals contact the police each time they notice stolen property in another person's possession or on the individual's premises. For example, dinner guests are not required to contact the police to tell them that their host was serving dinner on stolen china, and repairpersons are not required to contact the police to tell them that they were asked to repair stolen property. Although the jury may hope that such individuals will report the presence of stolen property, it is unlikely that jurors will find that an individual is guilty of a felony if he or she does not do so.

Conclusion

It is unlikely that the State will be able to prove all five elements of Possession of Stolen Property in the First Degree. Although the State will be able to prove that the act occurred in the State of Washington, that the value of the pinball machine exceeded $1,500, that the pinball machine was stolen, and that Richardson knew that it was stolen, it will not be able to prove possession. Because Richardson was not playing or even standing near the pinball machine, the State will not be able to prove that he had actual possession. In addition, the State will not be able to prove that Richardson had constructive possession. Richardson was only a temporary visitor at the house, the police found only a few of his personal possessions on the premises, and there is no evidence that Richardson was paying rent or doing any other act that indicated that he had dominion and control over the premises. The fact that he had a key to the premises and that he paid his share of the phone and cable bills is consistent with his claim that he was housesitting. Finally, it is unlikely that a jury would convict an individual of Possession of Stolen Property in the First Degree when the individual was only house-sitting for a friend.

EXAMPLE 3   ## Sample Memo

To: Supervising Attorney

From: D. Elaine Conway, Legal Intern

Date: August 29, 2005

Re: Elder Care; Mary Smith; FMLA Leave

Statement of Facts

We represent Martha McLean, the owner of Elder Care, a small business that provides in-home care to elderly clients. You have asked me to determine whether Mary Smith, one of Ms. McLean's employees, has a claim under the Family and Medical Leave Act (FMLA).

Elder Care is a small business that employs approximately sixty-sixty five employees who provide daily in-home care to elderly clients. Mary Smith was a specialist at Elder Care for two years and, while generally a good worker, Ms. Smith was late to work several times and used all of her sick and vacation time. Three weeks ago, Ms. McLean received an email from Ms. Smith, in which Ms. Smith stated (1) that she had "been at the hospital all night"; (2) that she "needed to take care of some family matters"; and (3) that she was sorry, but that she would be gone for about a month.

Ms. Smith also asked Ms. McLean to respond to the email because Ms. Smith could not be reached by phone. Ms. McLean did not respond to the email. Instead, she hired a replacement to take over Ms. Smith's clients.

There was no contact between Ms. Smith and Ms. McLean until two days ago, when Ms. Smith returned to work. At that point, Ms. Smith told Ms. McLean that she had missed work because her husband had physically abused her: Ms. Smith's husband had hit Ms. Smith so hard that Ms. Smith had gone to the emergency room. Ms. Smith spent the night at the emergency room, meeting with both a doctor and a clinical social worker. Although Ms. Smith was not admitted to the hospital, the doctor told her that she should not work for a week. In addition, the social worker told Ms. Smith that she had to leave the home before her husband killed her. Ms. Smith immediately went into hiding at a women's shelter; it is not, however, clear whether the social worker specifically recommended that she check into such a shelter.

Because of Ms. Smith's lengthy absence, Ms. McLean was unable to hold Ms. Smith's position open for Ms. Smith. Thus, when Ms. Smith returned to work, Ms. McLean told Ms. Smith that she had filled her position. Ms. McLean did, however, offer to hire Ms. Smith as a part-time office coordinator. In this new position, Ms. Smith would make approximately 75% of her previous salary and receive partial benefits. Ms. Smith says that an advocate at the shelter told her that she was entitled to FMLA leave and that Elder Care has to give her job back to her.

Issues

1. Under the FMLA, is Elder Care a covered employer and is Mary Smith a covered employee when a) Elder Care has between sixty-sixty five employees; b) more likely than not, Elder Care's employees all work within seventy five miles of the main office; and c) Mary Smith has worked for Elder Care for at least twelve months and probably worked at least 1,250 hours in the last twelve months?

2. Under the FMLA, did Mary Smith give Elder Care sufficient notice when a) Ms. Smith notified Elder Care of her unforeseeable absence the day after the injury occurred; b) Ms. Smith's email stated that "she had been at the hospital all night" and "needed to take care of some family matters"; and c) Ms. McLean did not respond to Ms. Smith's email to inquire further into the details of Ms. Smith's leave request?

3. Under the FMLA, does Mary have a serious health condition when a) domestic violence is not specifically mentioned as a qualifying condition in the text of the FMLA or the governing regulations; b) Ms. Smith was not admitted to the hospital the night of her injury; c) Ms. Smith met with both a doctor and a clinical social worker while at the hospital and was told not to work for the rest of the week; and d) the social worker told Ms. Smith she had to get out of the situation at home right away?

Brief Answers

1. Probably. Elder Care and Mary Smith probably meet the requirements for coverage under the FMLA.

2. Probably not. Although Ms. Smith gave notice within the required time frame, the substance of her notice was insufficient to create a reasonable belief that she was taking FMLA leave.

3. Probably not. Domestic violence is not mentioned specifically in the FMLA, and a court will probably determine that it is not a serious health condition under the FMLA.

Discussion

In 1993, Congress enacted the Family and Medical Leave Act (FMLA) to provide job security for employees who have serious health conditions that prevent them from working for temporary periods. 29 U.S.C. § 2601(a)(4) (2000). The Act is intended to balance the "demands of the workplace with the needs of families" as well as entitle "employees to take reasonable leave for medical reasons." 29 U.S.C. § 2601(b)(1) (2000). The Act seeks to accomplish its purposes "in a manner that accommodates the legitimate interests of employers." 29 U.S.C. § 2601(b)(3) (2000).

Issue 1: Is Elder Care a Covered Employer, and Is Ms. Smith a Covered Employee?

Under the FMLA, an employer is a covered employer if it 1) is engaged in commerce and 2) employs fifty or more employees working within seventy five miles of the work-site. 29 C.F.R. § 825.104 (2005). In this instance, Elder Care is a covered employer because it is engaged in commerce and employs fifty or more employees. We should, however, verify that at least fifty of these employees work within a seventy five-mile radius.

Under the FMLA, an employee is a covered employee if he or she 1) has been employed by the employer for at least twelve months, and 2) has been employed for at least 1,250 hours of service during the twelve-month period immediately preceding the commencement of the leave. 29 C.F.R. § 835.110(a)(1) (2005). Thus, in this case, Ms. Smith is a covered employee if she worked at least 1,250 hours during the past twelve months and has not already used twelve weeks of FMLA leave.

Issue 2: Did Ms. Smith Provide Elder Care with Appropriate Notice?

The FMLA's notice requirement is met when the employee gives notice to the employer as soon as practicable, or within no more than one or two working days of learning the need for leave. 29 C.F.R. § 825.303 (2005). If there is a medical emergency, the employee need not follow the employer's usual procedures for requesting leave. *Id.* The regulations further state that the notice requirement is met if the employee provides notice to the employer either in person or by some electronic means. *Id.* When the employee gives this notice, the employee does not have to request FMLA leave or even mention the FMLA; the employee only needs to state that he or she needs leave. *Id.* Once the employee has given notice, the burden then shifts to the employer to obtain any additional required information. *Id.*

Courts have not required employees to use the specific language of the FMLA to invoke FMLA rights and benefits. Instead, the notice requirement is met if an employee's notice to his or her employer is sufficient to create a reasonable belief that the employee is requesting FMLA leave. *See, e.g., Aubuchon v. Knauf Fiberglass, GMBH,* 359 F.3d 950, 952 (7th Cir. 2004); *Collins v. NTN-Bower Corp.,* 272 F.3d 1006, 1008 (7th Cir. 2001); *Stoops v. One Call Communications, Inc.,* 141 F.3d 309, 312-313 (7th Cir. 1998).

In the cases in which the notice requirement was met, the employee told his or her employer that he or she had received medical care and that he or she needed to take medical leave. *See, e.g., Price v. City of Fort Wayne,* 117 F.3d 1022, 1025 (7th Cir. 1997); *Haschmann v. Time Warner Entertainment Co., L.P.,* 151 F.3d 591, 595 (7th Cir. 1998). For instance, in *Price,* a decision vacating a district court's grant of summary judgment for the employer, the court held that an employee's notice was sufficient when the employee's request for medical leave was accompanied by a physician's note requiring the employee to take time off. *Price*, 117 F.3d at 1025. In contrast, in the cases in which courts have held that the notice requirement was not met, the employee's statements were vague. *See, e.g., Collins*, 272 F.3d at 1008; *Hauge v. Equistar Chem. Co.*, 2002 U.S. Dist. LEXIS 15822 (D. III. 2002). For example, in *Collins*, the court held that the notice requirement was not met when the employee merely "called in sick" for two days without giving the employer additional information. *Collins*, 272 F.3d at 1008. In its opinion, the court stated that employers "are entitled to the sort of notice that will inform them not only that the FMLA may apply but also when a given employee will return to work." *Id.*

Although it is possible that a court would determine that Ms. Smith's need for leave was foreseeable, it seems unlikely that a court would make that determination. Even if Ms. Smith's husband has abused her before, more likely than not, the court would decide that this particular incident was not foreseeable. In addition, more likely than not, the court would determine that Ms. Smith provided Elder Care with notice as soon as was practicable: Ms. Smith sent an email message to Ms. McLean the day after she had gone to the hospital.

The court will, however, probably determine that Ms. Smith's email was not sufficient to put Elder Care on notice that Ms. Smith was requesting or was entitled to FMLA leave. While in her email Ms. Smith stated that she had been at the hospital and that she needed to take care of some family matters, she did not say why she had been at the hospital or what type of family matters she needed to take care of. Thus, the court will probably determine that this case is more similar to *Collins* than it is to *Price*. Although Ms. Smith gave Elder Care more information than Collins gave her employer, Ms. Smith did not go into the detail that Price did. For example, Ms. Smith did not say that she had been injured, that she had received treatment at the hospital, or that she needed to leave home. Although as a matter of public policy the courts may not want to require employees to tell their employers that they have been the victim of domestic violence, employers should not be required to investigate every employee absence to determine whether the employee is entitled to FMLA leave.

Issue 3: Did Ms. Smith Have a Serious Health Condition?

The FMLA defines the term "serious health condition" as "an illness, injury, impairment, or physical or mental condition that involves A) inpatient care in a hospital, hospice, or residential medical care facility or B) continuing treatment by a health care provider." 29 U.S.C. § 2611(11). Therefore, to establish that she had a serious health condition, Ms. Smith must prove the following: 1) that she had an illness, injury, impairment, or physical or mental condition that prevented her from working for three weeks and 2) either a) that she received inpatient care or b) that she received continuing treatment.

1. Did Ms. Smith Have an Illness, Injury, Impairment, or
  Physical or Mental Condition That Prevented Her from
  Working for Three Weeks?

Under the FMLA, the employer may require that a request for leave be supported by "a certification issued by the health care provider" that states that the employee or eligible relative has a qualifying illness, injury, impairment, or physical or mental condition. 29 U.S.C. § 2613. Although neither the statute nor the applicable regulations state what does and does not constitute an illness, injury, impairment, or physical or medical condition, the courts have held that cancer, severe depression, and a terminal illness fall within the definition. *Collins,* 272 F.3d at 1008; *Sherry v. Protection, Inc.,* 981 F. Supp. 1133, 1135 (D. Ill. 1997). *See also Ragsdale v. Wolverine World Wide, Inc.,* 535 U.S. 81, 84 (2002). Thus, Ms. Smith's head injury would constitute an injury. However, that injury lasted, at most, one week, and Ms. Smith missed three weeks of work. Thus, Ms. Smith may try to argue that that domestic violence falls within the definition of an illness, injury, impairment, or physical or medical condition or that she suffers from Post Traumatic Stress Disorder.

Although Ms. Smith will make a number of public policy arguments about the need for FMLA coverage for victims of domestic violence, at this time neither the statute nor the cases support her argument. It is, however, worth noting that the Alaska Supreme Court has decided a case involving an FMLA claim based partially on domestic abuse. *Municipality of Anchorage v. Gregg,* 101 P.3d 181 (Alaska 2004). In *Gregg,* the Alaska Supreme Court affirmed the trial court's decision for the employee, concluding that the employee suffered from the cumulative effect of several physical and mental conditions that constituted a serious health condition. *Id.* The court further stated that, while a victim of domestic violence is not automatically entitled to FMLA protection, a victim who meets the test for a serious health condition has a right to the statutory leave. *Id.*

Additionally, Congress is currently considering a proposed amendment to the FMLA. The Family and Medical Leave Expansion Act 2005 includes language that would allow employees to take FMLA qualifying leave resulting from domestic violence. The Family and Medical Leave Expansion Act, § 282, 109th Cong. (2005). This proposed amendment helps our client in that it indicates that the FMLA does not currently cover domestic violence. If the FMLA currently covered domestic violence, there would be no need for an amendment. However, if this Act passes, our case will deteriorate rapidly. Because of the proposed expansion of the FMLA and the possibly persuasive power of the *Gregg* case, we should consider the possibility of settlement with Ms. Smith.

2. Did Ms. Smith Receive Either Inpatient Care or Continuing Treatment?

In addition to proving that she had an illness, injury, impairment, or physical or mental condition that prevented her from working for three weeks, Ms. Smith must also prove that she received either a) inpatient care or b) continuing treatment. 29 C.F.R. § 825.800(1) (2005).[1]

a. Did Ms. Smith Receive Inpatient Care?

The regulations require that a qualifying condition involve inpatient care in a hospital, hospice, or residential medical care facility. 29 C.F.R. § 825.800(1)(i) (2005). In this instance, Ms. Smith will not be able to prove that she received inpatient care in a hospital. Although Ms. Smith spent the night at the emergency room, she was not admitted and, therefore, never received inpatient care. Telephone Interview with John Doe, Hospital Administrator, Providence Hospital (August 27, 2005).

It also seems unlikely that Ms. Smith will be able to prove that the shelter was a residential medical care facility. Whether this particular requirement is met depends on the composition of the staff at the women's shelter. If the shelter employs qualifying

---

1. Information found in 29 C.F.R. § 825.800 can also be found in 29 C.F.R. § 825.114.

medical professionals, Ms. Smith's claim that it should be considered a residential care facility might be successful. If, though, the shelter does not offer continuing treatment by health care providers as defined in the regulations, this requirement will not be met.

From the information we have thus far about the facility, it does not appear to employ a health care provider such as a doctor. Although Ms. Smith will likely argue that her feeling dizzy while at the shelter is evidence that she was suffering from continued symptoms, this argument will, in fact, benefit Elder Care. Ms. Smith states that she did not return to the doctor because she was afraid to leave the shelter. This statement indicates that there was no doctor present at the shelter that she could see, and thus the statement strengthens our argument that the shelter was not a residential care facility.

b. Did Ms. Smith Receive Continuing Treatment?

In the alternative, Ms. Smith can try to prove that she received continuing treatment. To do this, she will have to prove 1) that she was incapacitated for three or more days and at least one of the following: A) she received treatment two or more times by a health care provider, by a nurse or physician's assistant under direct supervision of a health care provider, or by a provider of health care services under orders of, or on referral by, a health care provider; or B) she received treatment by a health care provider on at least one occasion that results in a regimen of continuing treatment under the supervision of the health care provider; or C) she suffered from a chronic health condition. 29 C.F.R. § 825.800(1)(iii).

1. Was Ms. Smith Incapacitated for Three or More Days?

The regulations define incapacity as an inability to work, attend school, or perform other regular daily activities because of the serious health condition, treatment therefore, or recovery therefrom, or any subsequent treatment in connection with such inpatient care. 29 C.F.R. § 825.800(1)(i). Elder Care should concede that Ms. Smith suffered a period of incapacity of three or more days. The doctor who examined her at the emergency room told her not to work the rest of the week and to get as much bed rest as possible.

A. Did Ms. Smith Receive Two or More Treatments?

While conceding that Ms. Smith was incapacitated for three or more days, Elder Care can argue that the other requirements are not met. Although Ms. Smith will argue that she meets the first requirement because she met with both a doctor and a social worker while in the emergency room, the court will likely reject that argument because consulting with two health care providers during the same visit to the emergency room does not constitute two or more treatments. In reaching this conclusion, the court may rely on a Ninth Circuit case involving a boy who was treated in the emergency room and then sent home without being admitted to the hospital. *Marchisheck v. San Mateo County*, 199 F.3d 1068 (9th Cir. 1999). In that case, the court concluded that the boy had not been treated two or more times by a health care provider because he had only been to the emergency room once. *Id.* at 1075. While Ms. Smith will attempt to distinguish *Marchisheck* by arguing that during her visit to the emergency room she was treated by two different health care providers, more likely than not, the *Marchisheck* boy was also seen by at least two health care providers while he was at the emergency room. For example, he was probably seen by both a nurse and a doctor.

Because most individuals see more than one health care provider during a single visit, it is unlikely that a court will decide that Ms. Smith's single visit to the emergency room counts as two or more treatments by a health care provider. In the alternative, Ms. Smith may argue that she received two or more treatments because she went to the emergency room and she was seen by a health care provider while she was at the shelter. If it turns out that Ms. Smith consulted a qualified health care provider at the shelter on more than one occasion, a court will likely find that Ms. Smith had continuing treatment by a health care provider.

B. Did Ms. Smith Receive Treatment Once, Combined with a Regimen of Continuing Treatment Under the Supervision of the Health Care Provider?

In the alternative, Ms. Smith may argue that she received treatment once, combined with a regimen of continuing treatment under the supervision of a health care provider. In making this argument, Ms. Smith will argue that she received one treatment at the emergency room and that she then received a regimen of continuing treatment when, on the recommendation of the social worker, she went to the shelter. However, based on what we now know, it appears that the social worker only told Ms. Smith that she needed to get out of the situation at home immediately. It does not appear that she told Ms. Smith to go to a shelter. If it is true that the social worker did not tell Ms. Smith to go to the shelter, the court will reject this argument.

C. Did Ms. Smith Suffer from a Chronic Health Condition?

Finally, the regulations consider any period of incapacity or treatment for such incapacity due to a chronic serious health condition as a qualifying condition. A chronic serious health condition is one which 1) requires periodic visits for treatment by a health care provider, or by a nurse or physician's assistant under direct supervision of a health care provider; 2) continues over an extended period of time (including recurring episodes of a single underlying condition); and 3) may cause episodic rather than a continuing period of incapacity (*e.g.*, asthma, diabetes, epilepsy, etc.).

Ms. Smith will make a public policy argument that domestic violence is a chronic serious health condition. Ms. Smith may try to point to her use of her vacation and sick leave to deal with the abusive situation at home as an indicator that the condition was chronic. In addition, she will attempt to draw a correlation between herself and the employee in a case involving multiple illnesses. *See Price v. City of Fort Worth*, 117 F.3d 1022, 1025 (7th Cir. 1997). In *Price,* the employee suffered from a combination of numerous illnesses. The court decided that, although none of the employee's individual illnesses constituted a serious health condition, the combination of them could. *Id.* at 1023; *accord Municipality of Anchorage v. Gregg*, 101 P.3d 181 (Alaska 2004). Similarly, Ms. Smith may try to persuade the court that it should take into consideration her physical disabilities resulting not only from the assault but also from prior incidents, of domestic violence. There are, however, important differences between Ms. Smith and the employee in *Price.* For example, in *Price*, the employee saw her doctor on many occasions and was under his continuing supervision. *Id.* at 1025. In addition, while the doctor in *Price* ordered the employee not to work for three weeks, *id.,* in the present case the doctor told Ms. Smith not to work for the rest of the week. In addition, while the employee in *Price* suffered from reoccurring physical ailments, Ms. Smith suffered from only one physical injury.

Conclusion

It is unlikely that a court will find that the content of Ms. Smith's notice to Elder Care was sufficient to make Elder Care aware that Ms. Smith's leave was FMLA qualifying. In addition, it is unlikely that a court will find that Ms. Smith suffered from a serious health condition. If, however, Ms. Smith is able to establish the elements of her *prima facie* case, the burden will then shift to Elder Care to prove that it did not violate the FMLA in demoting Ms. Smith. Furthermore, the legislative and judicial basis for our case are subject to change. Even though the law may support Elder Care's position, we should talk to Ms. McLean about some type of settlement. For example, if turnover is high, it may be possible for Elder Care to reinstate Ms. Smith sometime in the near future.

Researching and Writing a Memo Involving State Statutes

Introduction: The Assignment

Imagine for a moment that it is the summer after your first year of law school and that you are working as a law clerk for an attorney in Miami, Florida. On your first day, the attorney hands you the following memo.

To: Legal Intern

From: Christina Galeano

Date: August 28, 2006

Re: Case No. 06-478, Default Judgment

Memo to File: Facts in the Elaine Duncan Case

Elaine Duncan has requested our help in overturning a default judgment that has been entered against her. The judgment terminated her parental rights.

- Ms. Duncan says she never received the summons and, as a result, did not respond.
- On Wednesday July 25, 2006, a process server went to Ms. Webster's house and asked for Elaine Duncan. (Ms. Webster is Ms. Duncan's sister.) When Ms. Webster told the process server that "Elaine isn't here today," the process server handed what was probably a summons and complaint to Ms. Webster and told Ms. Webster that Ms. Duncan "needed to go to court."
- On February 1, 2006, Ms. Duncan entered an inpatient drug treatment program in Miami. She remained in the program until March 27, 2006, when she moved into a "halfway" house for recovering addicts.
- During April, May, and June, Ms. Duncan was a full-time resident at the halfway house. She had a bedroom in the house, ate her meals there, and had some of her possessions there.
- When Ms. Duncan renewed her driver's license in August 2006, she listed Ms. Webster's address as her address.
- Beginning in July 2006, Ms. Duncan began spending less time at the halfway house and more time with her sister, Elizabeth Webster. During July and August 2006, Ms. Duncan usually spent weeknights at the halfway house and Friday, Saturday, and Sunday nights at her sister's house. Because she was spending time at her sister's house, she moved some of her clothing and personal effects into her sister's house.
- Ms. Webster is 32. She will testify that she never gave the summons to her sister. Because she thought that paper related to some of Ms. Duncan's unpaid bills, she simply put the summons in a shoebox in the kitchen with a stack of Ms. Duncan's other mail.
- From April and May 2006, Ms. Duncan put the halfway house address on employment applications. However, her driver's license showed her sister's address as her address. Her voter registration shows the address where she lived prior to entering the treatment program.
- On September 1, 2006, Ms. Duncan moved into her own apartment. Since August 1, 2006, she has worked part time.
- I looked at the return on the service of process and everything appears to be in order.
- There is nothing in the record that indicates whether the defendant tried to personally serve Ms. Duncan or whether it tried to serve her at the halfway house.

As the first step, I would like to determine if the service of process is valid under the applicable Florida statute or statutes. Thus, please research the service of process issue for me. Because I am meeting with Ms. Duncan on Thursday morning, I need your memo by noon on Wednesday.

The next three chapters walk you through the process of researching and writing the memo that the supervising attorney has requested. In particular, Chapter 6 walks you through the process of researching the service of process issue using both book and electronic sources; Chapter 7 walks you through the process of writing the first draft of the memo; and Chapter 8 walks you through the process of revising, editing, and proofreading that draft. The final draft of the memo is set out at the end of Chapter 8.

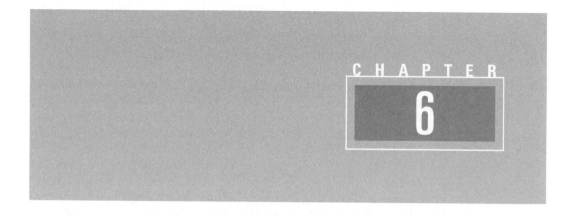

Researching an Issue Governed by State Statutes

B ecause this your first case, you want to do well. You are not, however, sure where to start. Fortunately, we have an easy answer. Start each research project by asking yourself two questions: (1) What issue have I been asked to research?, and (2) What law governs that issue?

In our first example problem, the attorney has not asked you to determine whether the court erred in terminating Ms. Duncan's parental rights. Instead, she has asked you to research a much narrower issue: whether the service of process was valid. In addition, in our first example problem, the attorney has told you what law governs: Florida statutes.

With the answers to these two questions in hand, you are ready to move to the next step, which is to research the issue. However, before you can do that, you need to develop a research plan, and you need to learn about the sources that you will use in executing that plan.

§ 6.1 Creating a Research Plan for an Issue Governed by State Statutes

When it is time to go grocery shopping, do you write out your menus for the week and then make a list, or do you go into the store, wander up and down the aisles, and pick out things that look good or things that you think you might need? Although both approaches have their pluses and minuses, those individuals who use the first approach almost always come home with the ingredients that they need.

The same is true of legal research. While there are pluses and minuses to researching with and without a plan, those individuals who develop and use a research plan almost always spend less time researching than do those individuals who research without a plan. In addition, those individuals who develop and use a research plan almost always do more thorough and more sophisticated research. Thus, while you can continue to grocery shop however you like, when it comes time to do legal research, make a research plan and use it.

The research plan for an issue governed by a state statute usually involves four steps: (1) doing background reading to familiarize yourself with the area of law; (2) locating, reading, and analyzing primary sources; (3) cite checking the primary sources to make sure that they are still good law; and (4) if appropriate, looking for cases from other jurisdictions, law review articles, or other commentaries. Thus, a generic research plan for an issue governed by a state statute would look like the one set out below.

Research Plan for an Issue Governed by State Statutes

Jurisdiction:	[Enter the name of the applicable state.]
Type of Law:	Enacted law.
Preliminary Issue Statement:	[Put your first draft of the issue statement here.]
Step 1:	Spend thirty to sixty minutes doing background reading.
Step 2:	Locate the governing statutes and regulations and the cases that have interpreted and applied those statutes and regulations.
Step 3:	Cite check the cases that you plan to use to make sure that they are still good law.
Step 4:	If appropriate, locate cases from other jurisdictions, law review articles, or other commentaries that might be on point.

§ 6.2 Sources for State Statutory Research

It is not, however, enough to have a research plan. You must also know the names of the sources and how to use them. The following chart lists some, but not all, of the sources that you can use in researching an issue governed by state statutes and regulations. Because the names of the sources vary by state, we have listed the sources using generic labels and not by specific names. For a list of the names of the sources in a particular state, see the listing for that state in Appendix 1 of the *ALWD Citation Manual* or Table 1 in

The Bluebook. Finally, note that not all states will have all of the sources listed. For example, not all states have both an unannotated and an annotated code.

Chart 6.1:	**Sources for Researching an Issue Governed by State Statutes**
	State Law
Background Reading	▪ State practice manuals and practice books ▪ Hornbooks ▪ *Nutshells* ▪ The Internet
State Session Laws (statutes in order enacted)	▪ State session laws
State Codes (statutes organized by topics)	▪ Unannotated code ▪ Annotated code
State Regulations	▪ Administrative code
Cases Interpreting and Applying Statutes	▪ State reporter setting out decisions from the state's highest appellate court ▪ State reporter setting out decisions from the state's intermediate appellate court ▪ West regional reporter that contains decisions from the state's highest appellate court and the state's intermediate appellate court ▪ Fee-based services like LexisNexis, Loislaw, VersusLaw, and Westlaw ▪ Free Internet sites like Findlaw.com, lexisone.com, or a state government website
Cite Checking	▪ KeyCite ▪ *Shepard's*®
Secondary Authorities	▪ Attorney general opinions ▪ *American Law Reports*, (for example, A.L.R.3d, A.L.R.4th, and A.L.R. 5th) ▪ Law review articles

§6.2.1 Sources for Background Reading

If you are familiar with the area of law that you have been asked to research, you can skip this step. If, however, the area is one that is new to you, begin your research by spending thirty to sixty minutes doing background reading.

a. Practice Manuals and Practice Books

For issues governed by state law, the best source for background reading is almost always a practice manual or book. In most states, these manuals and books are written by practitioners and provide the reader with an overview of the area of law and citations to key statutes, regulations, and cases. In addition, some practice books set out sample forms and practice pointers. Although most practice manuals and books are updated regularly, some are not. Therefore, before relying on the information in a practice book, check to see when the manual or book was last updated.

Historically, most practice books were only available in book form. Today, however, many of these books and manuals are available on fee-based computer services. For example, practice books published by West, a Thomson business, are available on Westlaw, and some of the practice books published by state bar associations are available on Loislaw.

To find the book version of a practice book, use your library's electronic card catalog and do key word searches using the name of the state and one or more of the following words: "practice," "procedure," and "manual." To find out what practice books are available on a particular fee-based service, check that service's list of databases or ask a colleague or your service's sales representative.

See Exercise 6A, which is in the *Practice Book*.

b. Hornbooks and *Nutshells*

If the practice books do not discuss the issue that you have been asked to research, look for a hornbook or a *Nutshell*. Hornbooks are one-volume hardbound books that provide the reader with an overview of an area of law — for example, civil procedure, contract law, property law, or tort law. *Nutshells* are shorter one-volume paperbacks designed primarily as study tools for law students. Like hornbooks, *Nutshells* deal with broad areas of law. Although hornbooks and *Nutshells* will not tell you what the law is in your state, they can provide you with general information about the area of law. To find copies of hornbooks and *Nutshells*, use your library's electronic card catalog. For example, to find a *Nutshell*, do a title or key word search using the word "Nutshell" and a word or phrase describing the area of law.

See Exercise 6B, which is in the *Practice Book*.

c. The Internet

While the Internet may not be the best source for issues governed by state statutes and regulations, it may have some information that is useful. Using the Advanced Search Option on Google or a similar search engine, type in the words relating to your issue, the name of your state, and a word or phrase like "introduction," "overview," "summary," or "research guide." If you get more than one hit, look first at the sites that tend to be most reliable. For example, look first at government-sponsored sites (.gov), educational sites (.edu), and sites sponsored by reliable organizations (.org).

To use the "Advanced Search" Option go to "Google.com." When the first screen appears, click on the link "Advanced Search."

P R A C T I C E
POINTER

See Exercise 6C, which is in the *Practice Book*.

§6.2.2 Sources for Statutes

Most state statutes come in three forms. You can find a particular statutory provision in the state's session laws, in its unannotated codes, and its annotated code or codes. Although the session laws are usually found only in books, unannotated and annotated versions of codes can usually be found in both book and electronic formats.

a. Session Laws

Session laws are the statutes published in the order in which they were enacted. At the end of a legislative session, the statutes enacted during that session are collected and arranged, not by topic, but by date. For instance, statutes enacted during the 2000 legislative session will be set out in date order in one volume; statutes enacted during the 2001 legislative session will be set out in date order in another volume; and so on. To find a session law, you need to know when the statute was enacted and its number. In most state codes, that number is set out at the very end of the statute. See, for example, Exhibit 6.1, which is on the CD. The information set out in the "CREDIT(S)" section tells you when the statute was amended and the chapter and section numbers where those amendments are set out.

The only time that you will use session laws is when you are doing a legislative history. For other types of statutory research, use an unannotated or annotated code.

b. Unannotated Codes

Statutes are "codified" when they are arranged, not in the order in which they were enacted, but by topic. Thus, in a code all of the statutes relating to a particular topic will be placed together. For instance, all of the statutes relating to criminal law will be placed under the "title" or subject heading "Criminal Law"; all of the statutes relating to marriage will be placed under another title or subject heading; and all of the statutes relating to commercial transactions will be placed under yet another title or subject heading. The decision about where to place a particular statute is made not by the legislative body itself but by attorneys who work for the state as "code revisers."

An unannotated code sets out the statutes themselves and historical notes and little else. Therefore, you should use an unannotated code when all you want is the text of the statute. In particular, use an unannotated code when your issue is governed by several different statutory sections. Because the statutory sections are close together, it will be easier to see how the various sections work together.

An unannotated code may be a state's official code or its unofficial code. Most unannotated codes are available both in book form and, if the unannotated code is the state's official code, on the state's webpage.

As a practicing attorney, you will probably use the state's official webpage frequently. It is, therefore, a good idea to spend some time exploring that site to see what is and is not there. In addition, think about adding your state's webpage to your list of favorites.

P R A C T I C E
POINTER

---

c. Annotated Codes

An annotated code is a code that has been — you guessed it — annotated. In addition to setting out the statutes by topic, an annotated code contains historical notes, cross-references to other sources published by the same publisher, and notes of decisions, which are one-paragraph descriptions of cases that have discussed the statute. Thus, an annotated code is primary authority[1] because it sets out the law itself and is also a finding tool because you can use it to find other primary authority (cases that have interpreted and applied the statute).

Historically, most states published their own unannotated code and private publishing companies published the annotated codes. Some states have, however, stopped publishing the unannotated version of their state code and have entered into a contract with a private publishing company to make the publishing company's annotated code its official state code. For example, both Maine and New Jersey use the West versions of the code as their official codes. Annotated codes are available both in book form and on one or more of the following fee-based services: LexisNexis, Loislaw, VersusLaw, and Westlaw. The annotated versions of codes are not, as a general rule, available on free Internet sites.

You should use an annotated code when you are interested not only in the text of the statute but also in how the courts have interpreted and applied the statute. Read the statute, determine which elements are likely to be in dispute, and then locate cases that have discussed those elements using the notes of decision. For more on identifying the elements and determining which are likely to be in dispute, see pages 86-87.

Most citation systems require you to cite to the official rather than the unofficial version of the code unless the material that you are citing appears in only the unofficial version. See Rule 14.1 in the *ALWD Citation Manual* and 12.2.1(a) in *The Bluebook*.

P R A C T I C E
POINTER

See **Exercise 6D** in the *Practice Book*.

§6.2.3 Sources for State Regulations

In enacting a state statute, the state legislature may grant a state administrative agency the power to promulgate regulations. When the proper procedures have been followed, those regulations have the effect of law and are, therefore, primary authority.

---

1. For a definition of the terms "primary authority," "secondary authority," and "finding tools," see pages 17-19 or the Glossary of Terms at the end of the book.

Although the process varies from state to state, in most states proposed regulations are first published in a state register and then in the state's administrative code. In most states, the register and the administrative code are published in both book form and on the state's website. In addition, many states' regulations are available on Findlaw.com.

See Exercise 6E in the *Practice Book.*

§ 6.2.4 Locating Cases That Have Interpreted or Applied a State Statute

a. Notes of Decision

When the statutory language itself answers the legal question, you do not need to look for cases that have interpreted or applied the statute. However, when the statutory language is ambiguous, you will need to find cases that have interpreted or applied the statute. One of the easiest ways to find these cases is to use an annotated code.

As soon as they release an opinion, most courts send an electronic copy of the opinion to the online services (for example, to LexisNexis, Loislaw, VersusLaw, and Westlaw). Attorneys who work for these services read the opinions and write a one-sentence summary of each point of law set out in the opinion. In addition to placing these one-paragraph summaries at the beginning of the opinion, if the summary relates to a particular statute, the publishing company will place that summary after the statute. When the summary appears at the beginning of an opinion, it is called a "headnote." When it appears after the text of a statute, it is called a "note of decision."

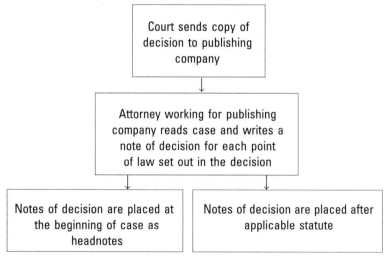

If there are relatively few cases that have discussed a particular statute, all of these notes of decision will be listed together after the statute. If, however, there are a number of cases that have discussed a particular statute, the notes of decisions will be organized by subtopics. Your job as a legal researcher is to read through the relevant notes of decision and then locate and read the cases that appear to have the types of information that you need. See Exhibit 6.2, which is on the CD.

As a general rule, decisions from higher courts will be listed before decisions from lower courts and, if there is more than one decision from a particular court, newer cases will be listed before older cases.

Although notes of decision set out points of law, the notes are only finding tools and not a source that you can rely on or cite to in a memo or a brief. Thus, use the notes of decisions as finding tools, not as authority.

See Exercise 6F in the *Practice Book*.

b. Reporters

You can find copies of the cases referred to in the notes of decision in the book version of reporters; on fee-based services like LexisNexis, Loislaw, VersusLaw, and Westlaw; and sometimes on a state's website or another free website. No matter which source you choose, you will need to use the citation to the reporter to find a particular case. Therefore, even if you do not think that you will ever use the book version of a reporter, you need to understand the reporter system.

A "reporter" is a set of books in which court decisions are reported. In many states, the decisions of a state's highest court are placed in one reporter, and the decisions of a state's intermediate court of appeals are placed in a separate reporter. For example, in Georgia, copies of the Supreme Court of Georgia's opinions are published in *Georgia Reports*, and copies of the Georgia Court of Appeals decisions are published in *Georgia Appeals Reports*. In addition, both the Georgia Supreme Court and the Georgia Court of Appeals decisions are published in a regional reporter, the *Southeastern Reporter*, which is published by West, a Thomson business, and which is part of West's National Reporter System.

When the decisions of a particular court are published in more than one reporter, one of those reporters will be designated as the official reporter and the other reporter(s) will be designated as the

unofficial reporter(s). For example, in Georgia, *Georgia Reports* and *Georgia Appeals Reports* are the official reporters and *Southeastern Reporter* is the unofficial reporter.

In other states, the decisions of both the state's highest court and intermediate court of appeals are published in the same state reporter. For instance, in New Mexico the decisions of both the New Mexico Supreme Court and the New Mexico Court of Appeals are published in *New Mexico*

Reports. In addition, the decisions of both the New Mexico Supreme Court and the New Mexico Court of Appeals are published in the *Pacific Reporter,* which is another one of West's regional reporters.

In still other states, the state has stopped publishing its own reporter. In these states, the state's decisions can be found only in the regional reporter. See, for instance, Kentucky. Since 1951, Kentucky decisions have been published only in the *South Western Reporter.*

To find the names of the reporters in which a particular court's decisions are published, see Appendix 1 in the *ALWD Citation Manual* or Table 1 of *The Bluebook.* To find a list of the  reporters published by West, go to *http://west.thomson.com/government/ officialpublications.*

See Exercise 6G in the *Practice Book.*

Like session laws (see page 77), reporters are organized chronologically. Cases decided in 1995 appear before cases that were decided in 2000, and cases that were decided in 2000 appear before cases that were decided in 2005. In addition, a case that was decided on May 20 will appear before one that was decided on May 21.

When two cases are published in the same reporter, you can use the citation to tell you which case is more recent. The case with the higher volume number is the more recent case.  Similarly, if the cases appear not only in the same reporter but in the same volume of that reporter, the case with the higher page number will be the more recent case.

To find a case in either the book version of a reporter or on a fee-based service like LexisNexis, Loislaw, VersusLaw, or Westlaw, you need three pieces of information: (1) the name of the reporter; (2) the volume in which the case appears; and (3) the page on which the case begins. This information is buried in the citation that appears at the end of each note of decision. Look, for example, at the following citation, which is taken from the notes of decisions following section 48.031 of the *Florida Statutes Annotated.*

Thompson v. State, Dept. of Revenue, App. 1 Dist., 867 So. 2d 603 (2004).

Although this citation is not in the form specified by either the *ALWD Citation Manual* or *The Bluebook,* it does give you the information you need to find the case. This citation tells you that the court's opinion in *Thompson v.*

State, Dept. of Revenue can be found in volume 867 of the *Southern Reporter, Second Series*, beginning on page 603. In addition, the citation tells you that the opinion was issued in 2004 and that the case was heard and decided by the First District Appellate Court. Because the citation appears in the annotation to the *Florida Statutes*, you can infer that the case is a Florida case. For more on reading citations, see pages 22-23.

It is not uncommon for a publishing company to use its own citation rules rather than the citation rules set out in the *ALWD Citation Manual* or *The Bluebook*. If you are citing the case in a memo or brief, you need to use the citation rules used in your jurisdiction, not the publishing company's rules. In other words, do not just cut and paste the citation in your memo or brief without first checking to make sure that the citation complies with your jurisdiction's rules.

P R A C T I C E
POINTER

To find a copy of the court's opinion using Westlaw,[2] log on and select the Westlaw tab. Then, using the "Find by citation" box, type in the volume number, abbreviation for the reporter, and the page number. See Exhibit 6.3, which is on the CD.

When you click on "GO," the case will then appear.[3] See Exhibit 6.4, which is on the CD.

See Exercise 6H in the *Practice Book*.

§6.2.5 Sources for Secondary Materials

When the statutes, regulations, and in-state cases do not answer the question that you were asked to research, you may need to look at cases from other jurisdictions or other secondary sources.

a. State Attorney General Opinions

As we explained in Chapter 1 (see pages 14-15), the state attorney general is the state's attorney. As the attorney for the governor, the legislature, and state agencies, the state attorney general will sometimes prepare written opinions in which he or she analyzes, explains, or evaluates a state statute or regulation. While these opinions are only opinions and do not have the force of law, they

---

2. The process is similar on LexisNexis, Loislaw, and VersusLaw. Although the surface features may be different (for example, the screens may look different and the boxes may have different labels), the underlying structures are the same. For a discussion of surface features and underlying structures, see Chapter 1.

3. Because the services update their products on a regular basis, the name or location of the box may change from time to time. There should, however, always be a box that allows you to find a source by citation.

do provide insight into how the state believes the statute or regulation should be interpreted and applied.

In most states, the state attorney general's opinions are available both in books and on the state's website.

b. American Law Reports

American Law Reports (A.L.R.) was first published in 1919 to compete with West's National Reporter System. Instead of publishing every state and federal opinion, A.L.R. is selective: it publishes only those cases that it deems to be "significant." For each of these significant cases, it includes an annotation that collects and discusses other cases that deal with the issue raised in the significant case.

Today, most researchers use A.L.R. not as a source for the text of an opinion but for its annotations. In particular, researchers use A.L.R. as a finding tool to locate summaries of cases from around the country that deal with a particular issue of law.

Like other reporters, A.L.R. is arranged chronologically. Annotations dealing with state issues are set out in A.L.R., A.L.R.2d, A.L.R.3d, A.L.R.4th, and A.L.R.5th. Annotations dealing with federal issues are set out in A.L.R. Fed.

A.L.R.	1919-1948
A.L.R.2d	1948-1965
A.L.R.3d	1965-1980
A.L.R.4th	1980-1991
A.L.R.5th	1992-current
A.L.R. Fed.	1969-current

A.L.R. is available both in book form and on LexisNexis and Westlaw. The books have subject indexes.

Because you want the most current information, look first for annotations published in A.L.R.4th and A.L.R.5th or A.L.R. Fed. In addition, if you are using the book version, be sure to check the pocket parts for more recent cases.

P R A C T I C E

POINTER

---

c. Law Reviews and Journals

Law reviews and journals publish articles written by law school professors, judges, practitioners, and law students. While most law reviews and journals are published by law schools, some are published by organizations.

Occasionally you will find a law review article that analyzes the state statute that governs your case or that analyzes one of the cases that has interpreted and applied that statute. In addition, occasionally you will find a law review article that analyzes an identically or similarly worded statute from another state. In these instances, the law review article can provide you with arguments that you or the other side might use.

The easiest way to find a law review article is to do a search on a fee-based service such as LexisNexis or Westlaw. After signing in, select the law reviews and journals database and then construct a search using the citation to the statute, the name of one or more of the parties in the case that discusses that statute, or key concepts as search terms. If your search retrieves more than one document, look first at the articles published in law reviews or journals from your state's law schools: most of the articles that deal with a specific state statute are published in that state's law schools' law reviews and journals.

§ 6.3 Researching the Service of Process Issue Using Book Sources

Historically, most attorneys researched issues governed by state statutes using books. They would do their background reading in the book form of a practice book; they would locate the applicable statutes in the book form of an annotated code and the cases in the book form of the state or regional reporter; and they would shepardize™ the statutes and cases using the book form of *Shepard's®*. However, as the cost of maintaining a book library has increased and the cost of doing electronic research has dropped, more and more attorneys are using electronic sources to research issues governed by state law. As a consequence, we show you how to research the service of process issue in both book sources and electronic sources. In this section we walk you through the process using book sources to do your background reading and to find the applicable statutes and cases. In section 6.4 we repeat the process, showing you how to find the same materials using electronic sources. The exception is cite checking. Because few attorneys use the book version of *Shepard's*, we do all of the cite checking electronically.

Modified Research Plan: Researching an Issue Governed by Florida Statutes and Cases Using Book Sources

Jurisdiction:	Florida
Type of Law:	Enacted law
Preliminary Issue:	Was the service of process valid?

Step 1:   Do background reading on service of process in the book version of *Trawick's Florida Practice and Procedure* or another Florida practice book.

Step 2:   Locate the applicable statutory section or sections in the book version of *Florida Statutes Annotated*. Specifically, locate the service of process statute that was in effect on July 26, 2006, and the cases that have interpreted and applied that statute.

Step 3:   Before deciding to use a case, use the online version of *Shepard's* or KeyCite to determine (1) whether the case is still good law and (2) whether there are any additional cases. Look up and, if appropriate, cite check any additional cases that you locate through cite checking.

Step 4:   If appropriate, locate the book versions of out-of-state cases, law review articles, or other materials that might be on point.

Step 1: Background Reading

You start your research in the clinic's library, looking for background information in *Trawick's Florida Practice and Procedure,* a multivolume practice set that provides attorneys with information about Florida law. You locate the volume containing the index and look up "service of process." See Exhibit 6.5, which is on the CD that came with this book.

At first, you may have trouble determining what words or phrases to look up in an index. This is normal. If you get stuck, think some more about the issue that the attorney asked you to research. Does

P R A C T I C E

POINTER

it involve a particular area of law — for example, property law? If it does, look up "Property" in the index. If you do not know the area of law, try to think of words that describe the "action." For example, in our example problem, the action was serving a summons. Thus, you could look up "service" or "summons." If you really get stuck, ask for help from the attorney who assigned the project or from a colleague.

Under "Process and Service of Process," you find the subheading "service on natural persons." Although you may not know what a "natural" person is, you do know that Ms. Duncan is a person. Therefore, you decide to look at section 8.6, which is set out in Exhibit 6.6, which is on the CD.

Under "Process," you find the subheading "Service," and under that heading you find the heading, "Abode, place of." Because you have been asked to determine whether the summons was left at Ms. Duncan's usual place of abode, you decide to look up Section 8.6 in *Trawick's.* See Exhibit 6.6.

At this point, you need to spend five to ten minutes reading section 8.6, in Exhibit 6.6. In addition to familiarizing yourself with the area of law, look for citations to the governing statute and to cases that might be on point. If you find citations, copy them into your research notes. See Exhibit 6.7 on the CD.

At this point, take a few minutes to read section 8.6 in *Trawick's.*

In this instance, the material in the practice book is relatively easy to read and understand. This will not, however, always be the case. As a consequence, as a researcher, you need to distinguish between material that is difficult because it deals with difficult concepts and material that is difficult because it is poorly written. If the material is difficult because it deals with difficult concepts, take the time to work through the text. If the material is difficult because it is poorly written, look for a different practice book.

Step 2: **Locating Primary Authority**

Having familiarized yourself with the area of law, it is time to locate the governing statute. Because the governing statute was listed in section 8.6 in footnote 1, use that citation to find the statute. Go to the book version of *Florida Statutes Annotated*, and select the volume that contains section 48.031. When you locate that section, you find five pages setting out the text of the statute; credits; historical notes; cross-references to practice books, A.L.R. Annotations, and law review articles; a table of contents for the notes of decision; and the notes of decision themselves. Exhibit 6.7 shows you excerpts from the book version of the statute.

It is not enough, however, to find the statute. You must analyze it. In this instance, the statute seems to set out four requirements, or elements.[4] Service is valid when (1) the summons is left at the person's usual place of abode; (2) the summons is left with a family member who is more than 15 years old; (3) the person with whom the summons was left was residing therein; and (4) the process server tells the person with whom the summons is left about the contents of the summons.

More often than not, there is more than one way to list the elements. You could treat each word as a separate element, or you could lump lots of things together. If the statute enumerates the elements, use that list. If the statute does not enumerate the elements, come up with a tentative list and then modify that list once you see how the courts list the elements.

In the Duncan case, the second element is not in dispute. The summons was left with Ms. Webster, Ms. Duncan's 22-year-old sister. The first and fourth elements are, however, in dispute. Ms. Duncan can argue that the summons was

---

4. In law, the word "element" is a term of art. Use the word "element" to describe a requirement set out in a statute, a common law rule, or a court rule.

not left at her usual place of abode and that the process server did not tell her sister about the contents of the summons. In contrast, the State can argue that Ms. Duncan's sister's house was Ms. Duncan's usual place of abode and that the process server's statement to Ms. Webster was sufficient.

Having found the applicable statute, identified the elements, and made a tentative determination about which elements are likely to be in dispute, create a template that you can use to guide you both through the rest of your research and through the drafting process.

Although there is no standard format for a template for research notes, in most instances your template will have a section in which you set out general rules — for example, the language of the governing statute, rules relating to the burden of proof, and policies underlying the governing statute. In addition, if the statute requires proof of a series of elements or requirements, your template will have a subsection for each element. When you are doing your research using book sources, you can create the template on a piece of paper or on your computer. If you are doing your research using electronic sources, you will usually want to create the template on your computer so that you can cut and paste relevant information from the electronic sources into your template.

Note that the template serves both as a shopping list for your research and as an outline of the discussion section. See Chart 6.2

Chart 6.2   **Sample Template for Researching and Writing the Duncan Memo**

Introduction

A. Policies underlying general rule

B. Text of applicable statute

FSA § 48.031(1)(a)

"Service of original process is made by delivering a copy of it to the person to be served with a copy of the complaint, petition, or other initial pleading or paper or by leaving the copies at his or her usual place of abode with any person residing therein who is 15 years of age or older and informing the person of their contents. Minors who are or have been married shall be served as provided in this section."

- List of elements
    (1)   the summons is left at the person's usual place of abode;
    (2)   the summons is left with a family member who is more than 15 years old;
    (3)   the person with whom the summons was left resided therein; and.
    (4)   the process server tells the person with whom the summon is left about the contents of the summons.

I. Usual Place of Abode (probably in dispute)

A. Rules ("test" that courts use in determining whether summons was left at individual's usual place of abode)

B. Analogous Cases
   1. Cases in which the court held that the summons was left at the individual's usual place of abode.
   2. Cases in which the court held that the summons was not left at the individual's usual place of abode.

C. Possible Arguments
   1. Arguments that we can make
   2. Arguments that the State can make

II. Summons Left with Family Member Who Is at Least 15 Years Old

   Rules

III. Person With Whom Summons Is Left Is Residing Therein

   Rule

IV. Process Server Tells Person Served About Contents of Summons (probably in dispute)

A. Rules ("test" that courts use in determining whether process servers provided sufficient notice)

B. Analogous Cases
   1. Cases in which the court held that the process server gave sufficient notice
   2. Cases in which the court held that the process server did not give sufficient notice

C. Possible Arguments
   1. Arguments that we can make
   2. Arguments that the State can make

Because you have found the general rule, which in this instance is the statute, you turn your attention to the elements that are likely to be in dispute To find cases that have interpreted the first and third elements, turn to the notes of decision that follow F.S.A. § 48.031. Begin by scanning the table of contents, identifying the subsections that deal with the first and third elements, "usual place of abode" and "telling the person served about the contents of the summons." You identify two sections, "Notification of contents 11" and "Usual place of abode 10," which appear to be on point. See Exhibit 6.8, which is on the CD.

When you turn to subsection 10, you find the material set out in Exhibit 6.9, which is on the CD.

At this point, take five or ten minutes to read through the notes of decision, identifying the one, two, three, or four cases that appear to be most on point.

In selecting cases, look for two types: (1) cases that set out definitions or rules and (2) cases that have facts that are similar to yours. In selecting "rules cases," select the highest authority:  select cases from higher courts over cases from lower courts and more recent cases over older cases. In selecting analogous cases, select the cases that have facts that are similar to the facts in your case.

After reading through all of the notes of decision listed in subsection 10, you select, as your first case, *Thompson v. State, Department of Revenue.* Even though the *Thompson* decision is a decision of the Florida Court of Appeals, not the Florida Supreme Court, you decide to read the case because it sets out what seems to be one of the basic rules (several of the notes set out the same rule) and because it is recent.

Using the citation "867 So. 2d 603," go to the library, locate the place where *Southern Reporter, Second Series,* is shelved and pull volume 867 off the shelf. Then locate page 603.

Make sure that you find the *Southern Reporter, Second Series,* not the *Southern Reporter.* While the *Southern Reporter* has cases decided between 1886 and 1941, the *Southern Reporter, Second Series,* has cases decided since 1941. See Appendix 1  in the *ALWD Citation Manual* for the dates of coverage for each state's reporters. The same information is available online at *http://www.alwd.org/cm/cmAppendices/SecondEditionAppendices/.*

Because *Thompson* is short, you should read the entire case. Had it been longer, you would have used the headnotes set out at the beginning of the case to locate the relevant portions of the case. For instance, if you were interested in the point of law set out in headnote 1, you would page through the text of the case until you found a "[1]." The text following the "[1]" would be the text from which headnote 1 was drawn. See Exhibit 6.10, which is on the CD.

You may not cite to the headnotes. They are written by attorneys working for the publishing company, not by the court. Instead, cite to the part of the decision  from which the headnote was drawn.

As you read *Thompson,* you copy information from it into your template. For example, copy the rule for usual place of abode. Although you think about using the case as an analogous case, a close reading of the case reveals that the case deals more with who has the burden of proof than it does with whether the summons was or was not left at Thompson's usual place of abode. Thus, you do not list the case as a possible analogous case. You do, however, copy the rules about the burden of proof into the general rule section of your template. See Chart 6.3.

In recording the information, remember to include the page numbers from which you took the information. You will need these page numbers for your pinpoint or jump cites.

P R A C T I C E

Chart 6.3   Excerpt from Sample Template for Researching and Writing the Duncan Memo

Introduction
A. Policies underlying general rule
B. Text of applicable statute

FSA § 48.031(1)(a)
"Service of original process is made by delivering a copy of it to the person to be served with a copy of the complaint, petition, or other initial pleading or paper or by leaving the copies at his or her usual place of abode with any person residing therein who is 15 years of age or older and informing the person of their contents. Minors who are or have been married shall be served as provided in this section."

C. List of elements
    (1) the summons is left at the person's usual place of abode;
    (2) the summons is left with a family member who is more than 15 years old;
    (3) the person with whom the summons was left was residing therein; and
    (4) the process server tells the person with whom the summon is left about the contents of the summons.

D. Burden of proof
From page 605 in *Thompson*
"[A] process server's return of service on a defendant which is regular on its face is presumed to be valid absent clear and convincing evidence presented to the contrary." *Telf Corp. v. Gomez,* 671 So. 2d 818 (Fla. 3d DCA 1996). Although simple denial of service is not sufficient, *id.* at 819, "Thompson's motion and affidavit are based on the fact that the service did not comply with section 48.031 and was therefore legally deficient. *National Safety Associates, Inc. v. Allstate Insurance Co.,* 799 So. 2d 316, 317 (Fla. 2d DCA 2001). Thompson's affidavit makes a *prima facie* showing that he was not served at his usual place of abode by valid substituted service."

II. Usual Place of Abode (probably in dispute)

E. Rules ("test" that courts use in determining whether summons was left at
   individual's usual place of abode)
Thompson, from page 605
"[s]ection 48.031 expressly requires that substituted service be at the person's usual place of
abode." *Shurman v. Atlantic Mortgage & Investment Corp.,* 795 So. 2d 952, 954 (Fla. 2001). The
requirement "usual place of abode" means "the place where the defendant is actually living at the
time of service." *Id., citing State ex rel. Merritt v. Heffernan, 142 Fla. 496, 195 So. 145, 147 (1940).*

In addition to reading *Thompson,* you need to read the other cases that
appear to be on point. Thus, spend the next hour or two looking up and
reading the relevant portions of the other cases set out in the notes of decision
and looking up and reading the relevant portions of the cases that are cited in
those cases. As you do so, continue filling in your template.

Do not, however, treat filling in the template as an exercise in filling in
the blanks. While the template can remind you about the types of information
that you need to find and about the types of information that you have already
found, it is not a substitute for thinking. Thus, as you read through the cases,
think about how you might use them to support your client's position and
about how the State might use them to support its position. For more on
analyzing and synthesizing cases, see pages 147-157.

As a general rule, stop looking for rules when you begin to see the same
rules in case after case. In addition, stop looking for analogous cases when you
find one or more cases that are factually analogous to your case or when, after
spending an hour or two looking, you determine that there is no case that is
factually analogous. You can stop looking for arguments when you feel comfortable that you can construct an effective argument or set of arguments for
your client and when you believe that you can anticipate, with some accuracy, the arguments that the other side is likely to make.

Sometimes students ask how many cases they
should find or how many cases they should use in
their memo or brief. At least in practice, this
question is impossible to answer. Because he or

P R A C T I C E

POINTER

she has not done the research, the supervising attorney cannot tell you how many
cases there are, let alone how many you need. Instead, stop researching when
(1) you have found mandatory authority that answers your question or (2) the
cases that you are finding are cases that you have already seen.

Note that in this case we did not look for regulations. There were three reasons for not doing so. First, based on our knowledge of the law, we knew that it was unlikely that there would be any regulations. Given the nature of the statute, it was unlikely that the legislature would have given a state agency the power to promulgate regulations. Second, in doing our background reading, we did not see any references to state regulations. Finally, in reading the cases, we did not see any references to state regulations.

There will, however, be cases in which there are regulations. In those cases you should look for these regulations and, if you find them, analyze them. The easiest way to find them is to use the citations set out in the background reading or in the cases. You can, however, also find them using the tables that are set out in many of the book versions of the state regulations, by using the tables and links that are on many of the state's websites, or by doing a terms and connectors search on a free website or on one of the fee-based websites.

Step 3: Cite Check to Make Sure That the Cases You Plan to Use Are Still Good Law

Even if you do the rest of your research using books, you should cite check online. Online cite checking is more up-to-date and more reliable. To learn how to cite check using *Shepard's* and KeyCite, see page 99 in this chapter and Chapter 3.

Step 4: If Appropriate, Locate Out-of-State Cases, Law Review Articles, or Other Materials That Might Be on Point

Do not spend your time, and your client's money, looking for out-of-state cases, law review articles, or other materials until you have taken a close look at your statute and the in-state cases. If the statute and the in-state cases answer your question, stop researching. If they do not, and you have the resources to do so, continue your research.

In our sample problem, the statutes and cases are sufficient. Thus, you can stop your research and begin to write. See Chapter 7.

§ 6.4 Researching the Issue Using Electronic Sources

If you decide to research the issue online, you have several choices: You can do the research using one of the "big two," fee-based services, LexisNexis or Westlaw, or you can use one of the newer services — for example, Loislaw or VersusLaw. In addition, sometimes you can use a free site — for example, your state's website, Findlaw, or Casemaker.

For purposes of this problem, assume that the law clinic has a contract with Westlaw that allows the clinic unlimited use of Westlaw's Florida databases for a flat fee.

Step 1: Background Reading

To speed up your research on Westlaw, create a "Florida Tab." To do this, sign on to Westlaw and, when the welcome page appears, click on the "My Westlaw" link that is shown in Exhibit 6.11, which is on the CD.

You can create as many tabs you need. As a practicing attorney, you will probably want to create a tab for the state in which you practice, one for federal law, and one for your practice area.

P R A C T I C E

POINTER

When the "My Westlaw" page appears, scroll through the options and select "Florida." See Exhibit 6.12, which is on the CD. Then scroll to the bottom of the page and click on "Next," and then, when the next screen appears, click on "Save."

See Exercise 6I, which is in the *Practice Book*.

Once you have created a Florida tab, scroll through the list of databases until you find "Treatises, CLE's and Practice Materials." Read through the list of databases and select the one that looks most helpful. In this instance, the two that are most likely to be helpful are the online version of *Trawick's Florida Practice and Procedure* and *West's Florida Practice Manual*. Although both of these sources are good, you decide to use *Trawick's Florida Practice and Procedure*. See Exhibits 6.13 and 6.14, which are on the CD.

The next step is to construct a search. As a general rule, start with a relatively broad search and then, if you get too many "hits," narrow your search. For example, begin by identifying the area of law and the element that you want to research. Then, if you need to narrow the search, add additional search terms.

In the Duncan case, the area of law is service of process, and the first element is usual place of abode. Thus, you start with the terms "service of process" and "usual place of abode." There are several ways to set out these terms. One way is to put quotation marks around each of the phrases.

"service of process"
"usual place of abode"

If you use quotation marks, your search will retrieve only those documents that contain the quoted phrases. You will not retrieve documents that contain only one of the words inside the quotation marks or the words in a different order.

Once you have selected your search terms, you need to connect those terms. To find a list of connectors, click on the link that is just below the search box. See Exhibit 6.15, which is on the CD.

When you click on this link, the screen in Exhibit 6.16 appears. Thus, you could connect your two terms using an "and," an "/s," a "/p," or one of the other connectors that Westlaw recognizes. Depending on the connector that you use, your search will retrieve more or fewer documents.

Chart 6.4 Terms-and-Connectors Search

Search	Number of documents that search retrieved on the day that we ran the search in the Florida cases database
"service of process" and "usual place of abode" (retrieves documents in which the phrases "service of process" and "usual place of abode" appear anywhere in the document)	90 documents
"service of process" /p "usual place of abode" (retrieves documents in which the phrases "service of process" and "usual place of abode" appear in the same paragraph)	48 documents
"service of process" /s "usual place of abode" (retrieves documents in which the phrases "service of process" and "usual place of abode" appear in the same sentence)	33 documents
"service of process" /20 "usual place of abode" (retrieves documents in which the phrases "service of process" and "usual place of abode" appear within 20 words of each other) (excludes conjunctions, articles, and other "noise" words)	19 documents

See Exercise 6J in the *Practice Book*.

Instead of using the phrases "service of process" and "usual place of abode" you could search for individual terms or you could search for individual terms plus one or more phrases. For example, instead of using the phrase "service of process" as one of your search terms, you could use the word "service" or "serv!" If you use the word "service," your search will retrieve documents that contain the word "service," whether or not that word is part of the phrase "service of process." If you use the root word "serv" with an exclanation mark at the end — "serv!" — you will retrieve documents that contain any word that has the root word "serv." For example, you will retrieve "service," "served," "serving," and even "servant."

Although using single words and root words can help ensure that you do not miss documents, it will also increase the number of documents that your search retrieves. Consequently, you need to use judgment: when the phrase is a well-established one, use the phrase in quotation marks. If, however, the phrase is not well established or your first search produces no results or very few results, broaden your search by using expanders, by changing your connectors, or by adding synonyms. To find a list of synonyms, click on the link to the "Thesaurus," which is just under the link to the list of expanders and connectors.

In constructing the search for our sample problem, you decide to take a middle ground. Because you are not sure whether the documents will use "summons" or "service of process," you decide to use synonyms: "service" or "summons." You are, however, quite sure that the documents that you are looking for will contain the well-established phrase "usual place of abode." In addition, you make an educated guess about where the terms are likely to occur. Although they may not appear in the same sentence or paragraph, they should appear in the same section. Thus, you decide to connect the two parts of your search using "and," which means "in the same document." Although you do not need to include the parentheses, parentheses can help you control and see how the computer will run your search. See Exhibit 6.17, which is on the CD.

When you run this search in the *Trawick's Florida Practice and Procedure* database, it retrieves three documents.[5] See Exhibit 6.18, which is on the CD.

On Westlaw, the word "document" is used to refer to a number of different things. For example, in this instance, a document is a section in *Trawick's*. In another database, it might be a case or statutory section.

PRACTICE POINTER

When you select the first document, you retrieve the information set out in Exhibit 6.19, which is on the CD. Note that your search terms are highlighted.

This section, section 8.6, is the same section that you located when you did your research in the book version of *Trawick's Florida Practice and Procedure*. Thus, if you have already read the section, you do not need to reread it.

Once you go into practice, you will need to think about how much it costs to use Westlaw or another fee-based service such as LexisNexis, Loislaw, or VersusLaw. If you are being charged

PRACTICE POINTER

by the search, you can read the section while online. If, however, you are being charged by the minute, think about emailing the section to yourself, downloading it, or printing it. Although there is a charge for emailing, downloading, and printing, that charge may be less than the cost of the time you spend reading the section online.

---

5. If *Trawick's Florida Practice and Procedure* is revised, your search may retrieve more or fewer documents.

Step 2: Locating the Governing Statute

If your search produced a section in a practice book that discusses your statute, locating the text of the governing statute is easy. You simply go to the place in the practice book that contains a reference to the statute and click on the link to the statute. For instance, in our case, footnote 1 cites to the statute. See Exhibit 6.20, which is on the CD.

When you click on the link, you are taken to the list of footnotes at the end of section 8.6. See Exhibit 6.21, which is on the CD.

When you click on the link to the statute, the text of the statute appears. See Exhibit 6.22 on the CD. Keep in mind that when you are using a fee-based service, the link may or may not take you to the official version of the state's code. For example, on Westlaw, the links will take you to the code that is published by Westlaw's parent company, Thomson. In Florida, this is the *Florida Code Annotated*, which is not Florida's official code. (Florida's official code is *Florida Statutes*, which is unannotated.) Although you can rely on the information set out in the *Florida Code Annotated*, your citation will be to *Florida Statutes*.

To find out which code is a state's official code and which codes are unofficial, see Appendix 1 in the *ALWD Citation Manual* or Table 1 in *The Bluebook*.   **P R A C T I C E**

To enlarge the window that sets out the text of the statute, click on "maximize." See Exhibit 6.23, which is on the CD.

Note that the text of the statute is the same as the text that you found when you looked up the statute in the book version of *Florida Statutes Annotated*. See page 86.

If you were familiar with the area of law and did not do background reading or if you were unable to find a section in the practice book that discussed your state's statute, you can find the governing statute in one of three ways.

Method 1: Use the "Find by Citation" Option

If you know the citation to the statute, type your citation into the "Find by citation" box and search. See Exhibit 6.24, which is on the CD, and pages 24-25.

Method 2: Use the "Table of Contents" Option

If you do not know the citation, you can find the statute by using the Table of Contents option. Click on the link to the "Table of Contents" database, select "State Statutes," select the Florida statutes, and then select the appropriate chapter, etc. Exhibits 6.25 through 6.30 on the CD walk you through the process. Note that you may have to make an educated guess about where to look.

Method 3: Use a "Terms and Connectors" Search

The last, and usually most difficult, method is to use a "terms and connectors" search. Construct a search that is likely to retrieve the governing statute and then run that search in one of the statute's databases. See Exhibit 6.31.

At this point the process is the same as it was when you did the research using the books. First, analyze the statute, tentatively identifying the requirements or elements. See page 86. In this instance, the statute seems to set out three elements: for the service on Duncan to have been valid, (1) the summons must have been left at her usual place of abode; (2) the summons must be left with a family member who is more than 15 years old who is residing therein; and (3) the person serving the summons must have told the person with whom the summons was left about the contents of the summons.

Second, determine which elements are not likely to be in dispute and which elements are likely to be in dispute. In our example, the second element is not in dispute: the summons was left with Ms. Duncan's 22-year-old sister. The first and third elements will, however, be in dispute. See pages 86-87. Third, research the elements that are likely to be in dispute, identifying the test that the courts use in determining whether those elements are met and the analogous cases. See pages 86-87. Fourth, develop and begin filling in a template. See page 87.

Although there is more than one way to find cases online, the easiest way is to use the Notes of Decision in *Florida Statutes Annotated*. Following the text of F.S.A. § 48.031 is a table of contents for the notes of decision and then the notes themselves. Because the Westlaw version of the *Florida Statutes Annotated* is the same as the book version of *Florida Statutes Annotated*, you choose the same two topic headings: "Notification of contents 11" and "Usual place of abode 10." See page 88. See Exhibits 6.32 and 6.33.

The easiest way to get to the Notes of Decision is to use the link in the window on the left-hand side of the screen. Click on "Section Outline," and then "Notes of Decision." See Exhibit 6.31, which is on the CD.

P R A C T I C E

To get to the subsection dealing with notification, click on the "11" following "Notification of contents." To get to the subsection dealing with "usual place of abode," click on the "10" following "Usual place of abode." When you click on the "10," the screen in Exhibit 6.34 appears.

When the subsection appears, read through the notes of decision, identifying the one, two, three, or four cases that appear to be most on point.

Regardless of whether you are doing your research using books or an online service, you are looking for two types of cases: cases that set out rules or definitions and cases that have facts that are similar to yours. In selecting "rules cases," select cases from higher courts over cases from lower courts and more recent cases over older cases. In selecting analogous cases, select cases in which the facts are similar to the facts in your case.

Finding the text of the cases cited in the notes of decision is easy. To read one of the cited decisions, simply click on the link to the case. For instance, to read *Thompson v. State, Department of Revenue*, simply click on the name of the case. When you do, you are taken to the screen set out in Exhibit 6.35.

Maximize the screen and then scroll through the opinion identifying those headnotes that appear to be on point. To find that portion of the case from which a particular headnote was drawn, just click on the headnote's number: the link will take you to the appropriate place in the opinion. See Exhibits 6.36 and 6.37 on the CD.

This point bears repeating: you cannot cite to the headnotes: they are written by attorneys working for the publishing company, and not the court. Instead, cite to the part of the decision from which the headnote was drawn.

Spend the next sixty to ninety minutes looking up and reading the relevant portions of the cases set out in the notes of decision and recording the information that you find in your template. To copy material from the case into your template, simply highlight the material that you want to copy, click on "Copy," open the window that holds your template, and then paste the material into your template. See Exhibits 6.38 and 6.39 on the CD. In doing so, make sure that you record the source, including the pinpoint cite.

You can also email a copy of the document to yourself, print out a copy, or save a copy to your hard drive. To email, print, or copy, go the top of your screen and click on the "Email"/"Print"/"Save" icon. See Exhibit 6.40 on the CD.

When you click on one of these icons, the screen set out in Exhibit 6.41 appears. To see the drop-down menu, click on the arrow that is just to the left of the word "Properties." This drop-down menu allows you to select from a number of options, including whether you want to include the KeyCite flags and a summary page. You can also add a note that will remind you about why you chose to email, print, or download the documents.

Last but not least, keep in mind that you do not need to read or email/print/download every case. You can stop looking for rules when you have identified the rule or rules that apply in your case. In addition, you can stop looking for analogous cases when you find cases that are factually analogous to your case or when, after a reasonable search, you determine that there is no case that is factually analogous. Similarly, you can stop looking for arguments when you feel comfortable that you can construct an effective argument or set of arguments for your client and when you believe that you can anticipate the arguments that the other side is likely to make. In other words, use common sense.

Step 3: Cite Check to Make Sure That the Cases You Plan to Use Are Still Good Law

Before you use a case, it is essential that you cite check it to make sure the case is still good law. To do this using Westlaw, use KeyCite®.

If you do not have the case on your screen, select KeyCite from the menu bar that is just under your "My Westlaw" tab and then type in the cite. If you have the case on your screen, click on the link to "Full History" in the KeyCite box. See Exhibit 6.42 on the CD. The screen that appears will show you whether the court's decision has been reversed or affirmed by a higher court or whether, in a different case, the court has overruled the court's decision in your case.

For example, when you look at the history for *Thompson v. State, Department of Revenue,* you find only one entry, a citation to the case you are KeyCiting. See Exhibit 6.43 on the CD. Because there are no other citations, you know that your decision is still good law: neither Thompson nor the Department of Revenue appealed the Court of Appeals' decision and, in other cases, the courts have not overruled the court's decision in *Thompson.* For a more detailed description of cite checking, see Chapter 4.

Step 4: If Appropriate, Locate State Attorney General's Opinions, Cases from Other Jurisdictions, Law Review Articles, or Other Materials That Might Be on Point

In some cases, you will want to look for a state attorney general's opinion. While these opinions are not primary authority, they can provide insight into how the state attorney general believes that the statute and regulations should be interpreted. In this case, because the Florida statutes and cases answer the question, you need not spend the time and money that it would take to look for one. Similarly, because the Florida statutes and cases answer the question, you need not spend the time or money to look for out-of-state cases, law review articles, A.L.R. annotations, or other materials. Know when to stop.

See Exercise 6K in the *Practice Book*.

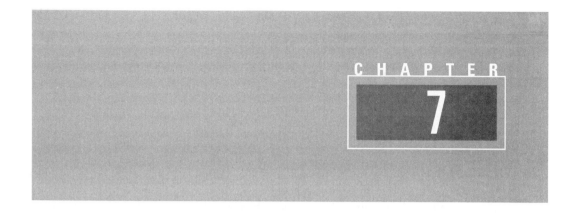

Drafting Memo 1

Having completed most of the research for Memo 1, it is now time to move to the second part of the process: preparing the first draft of the memo. In this chapter we walk you through that process. In doing so, we have two goals. First, we want to introduce the format for a "formal" in-house memo. Although in practice the attorneys you work for may have you use a less formal format, if you know how to write a formal memo, making the switch to a less formal format is easy. Second, and more important, we want to show you how the format for a formal memo reflects the way attorneys think about legal issues. Thus, this chapter is as much about learning to think like a lawyer as it is about learning how to write a memo.

At first, you may have trouble fitting information into the templates we set out. For example, you may have trouble writing an issue statement using the "under-does-when" format or, in drafting the discussion section, you may have trouble figuring out what goes in the general rule section and what goes in the discussion of a specific element. Don't[1] worry. As you learn to think like a lawyer, it will become second nature to draft your issue statement so that it sets out the reference to the rule of law first, the legal question second, and the key facts last. Similarly, it will become easier and easier to determine what is a general rule and what is a specific rule. You will know that you have begun to think like a lawyer when the format for a formal memo makes perfect sense.

---

1. Because we have written this book using an informal style, we sometimes use contractions. You should not, however, use contractions in a formal memo or in a brief to a court unless the contraction appears within a quotation.

§ 7.1 Understanding What You Have Found

If you have done the research described in Chapter 6, you have done most of the research. In addition, if you recorded your research notes on the template that was set out in that chapter, you have a good start on understanding what it is you have found. For example, you will have identified the applicable statute and its elements, and you will have located not only the general rules but also the rules that the courts use in determining whether an element is or is not met and cases that illustrate how the courts have applied those specific rules in cases that are analogous to your case. The following chart shows you what your completed template might look like.[2]

Chart 7.1   Completed Template

Research Notes

General Rule Section

A. *Policies Underlying General Rule*

Excerpt from Page 586 in *Torres v. Arnco Constr., Inc.,* 867 So. 2d 583
(Fla. 5th DCA 2004).

"The purpose of service of process is to advise the defendant that an action has been commenced and to warn the defendant that he or she must appear in a timely manner to state such defenses as are available. *See Shurman v. Atlantic Mortg. & Inv. Corp.,* 795 So. 2d 952 (Fla. 2001); *Abbate v. Provident Nat'l Bank,* 631 So. 2d 312 (Fla. 5th DCA 1994)."

Cite checked: No cases have cited *Torres.*

Excerpt from Pages 953-54 in *Shurman v. Atlantic Mortg. & Inv. Corp.,*
795 So. 2d 952 (Fla. 2001).

"It is well settled that the fundamental purpose of service is "to give proper notice to the defendant in the case that he is answerable to the claim of plaintiff and, therefore, to vest jurisdiction in the court entertaining the controversy." *State ex rel. Merritt v. Heffernan,* 142 Fla. 496, 195 So. 145, 147 (1940); *see also* *954 Klosenski v. Flaherty,* 116 So. 2d 767, 768 (Fla.1959) (quoting *Heffernan*); *Clark v. Clark,* 158 Fla. 731, 30 So. 2d 170, 171 (1947) ("The purpose of constructive or substituted service is to bring knowledge of the pending litigation to the defendant in order that he may appear and guard his interests."); *Gribbel v. Henderson,* 151 Fla. 712, 10 So. 2d 734, 739 (1942); *Arcadia Citrus Growers Ass'n v. Hollingsworth,* 135 Fla. 322, 185 So. 431, 434 (1938). In other words, the purpose of this jurisdictional scheme is to give the person affected notice of the proceedings and an opportunity to defend his rights."

Cite checked: Citing references but no negative history.

B. *Applicable Statute*

"48.031. Service of process generally; service of witness subpoenas

---

2. Note that much of the information in Chart 7.1 are quotes that have been cut and pasted from the electronic versions of the cases. Thus the citations may not conform to the rules set out in the *ALWD Citation Manual.* or *The Bluebook.*

(1)(a) Service of original process is made by delivering a copy of it to the person to be served with a copy of the complaint, petition, or other initial pleading or paper or by leaving the copies at his or her usual place of abode with any person residing therein who is 15 years of age or older and informing the person of their contents. Minors who are or have been married shall be served as provided in this section."

C. List of Elements

(1)　Usual place of abode
(2)　Any person residing therein who is 15 years of age or older
(3)　Informing the person of their contents

D. Burden of Proof

Excerpt from Page 605 in *Thompson v. State, Dept. of Revenue,* 867 So. 2d 603 (Fla. 1st DCA 2004).

"Turning to the merits, "[s]ection 48.031 expressly requires that substituted service be at the person's usual place of abode." *Shurman v. Atlantic Mortgage & Investment Corp.,* 795 So. 2d 952, 954 (Fla. 2001). The requirement "usual place of abode" means "the place where the defendant is actually living at the time of service." *Id., citing State ex rel. Merritt v. Heffernan, 142 Fla. 496, 195 So. 145, 147 (1940).* The burden of proof to sustain the validity of service of process is upon the person who seeks to invoke the jurisdiction of the court and, without proper service of process, the court lacks personal jurisdiction over the defendant. *M.J.W. v. Department of Children and Families,* 825 So. 2d 1038, 1041 (Fla. 1st DCA 2002)."

[4] [5] "[A] process server's return of service on a defendant which is regular on its face is presumed to be valid absent clear and convincing evidence presented to the contrary." *Telf Corp. v. Gomez,* 671 So. 2d 818 (Fla. 3d DCA 1996). Although simple denial of service is not sufficient, *id.* at 819, Thompson's motion and affidavit are based on the fact that the service did not comply with section 48.031 and was therefore legally deficient. *National Safety Associates, Inc. v. Allstate Insurance Co.,* 799 So. 2d 316, 317 (Fla. 2d DCA 2001). Thompson's affidavit makes a *prima facie* showing that he was not served at his usual place of abode by valid substituted service. *See, e.g., S.H. v. Department of Children and Families,* 837 So. 2d 1117, 1118 (Fla. 4th DCA 2003) (invalidating substituted service on father at mother's address, where mother's residence was not father's "usual place of abode" at the time of service); *Gonzalez v. Totalbank,* 472 So. 2d 861 (Fla. 3d DCA 1985) (invalidating substituted service when wife was separated from husband and not living at address where service was attempted). Having raised the issue of personal jurisdiction, Thompson's motion and accompanying affidavit placed the burden on the Department to establish the validity of service of process. *M.J.W.,* 825 So. 2d at 1041. Accordingly, the case is reversed and remanded for an evidentiary hearing to determine whether the attempted service of Thompson pursuant to section 48.031, *Florida Statutes* (2003), was valid. *See Venetian Salami,* 554 So. 2d at 502-03; *Mowrey Elevator of Florida, Inc. v. Automated Integration,* 745 So. 2d 1046, 1047-48 (Fla. 1st DCA 1999).

REVERSED and REMANDED."
Cite checked — Citing references but no negative history.

Excerpt from Pages 818-19 in *Telf Corp. v. Gomez,*
671 So. 2d 818 (Fla. 3d DCA 1996).

"We affirm the order of the trial court denying appellants' respective motions to quash service of process. It has well been established that a process server's return of service on a defendant which is regular on its face is presumed to be valid absent clear and convincing evidence presented to the contrary. *Florida Nat'l Bank v. Halphen,* 641 So. 2d 495 (Fla. 3d DCA 1994); *Lazo v. Bill Swad Leasing Co.,* 548 So. 2d 1194 (Fla. 4th DCA 1989); ***819** Slomowitz v. Walker,* 429 So. 2d 797 (Fla. 4th DCA 1983); *Brugh v. Savings & Profit Sharing Pension Fund of United Ins. Co. of Am.,* 211 So. 2d 613 (Fla. 1st DCA 1968). Further, a defendant may not impeach the validity of the summons with a simple denial of service, but must present 'clear and convincing evidence' to corroborate his denial. *Halphen,* 641 So. 2d at 496; *Jefferson Bank & Trust v. Levy,* 498 So. 2d 450 (Fla. 3d DCA 1986)."

Cite checked — Only negative history is *National Safety Associates, Inc. v. Allstate Ins. Co.,* 799 So. 2d 316, 317+ (Fla. 2d DCA 2001), which declined to extend rule to case in which return was not regular on its face.

Excerpt from page 1035 in *Magazine v. Bedoya,*
475 So. 2d 1035 (Fla. DCA 3d 1985).

"A presumption of valid service arises from evidence of a return of service which is regular on its face. *Klosenski v. Flaherty,* 116 So. 2d 767 (Fla. 1959). The party challenging the service must overcome that presumption by clear and convincing evidence. *Montano v. Montano,* 472 So. 2d 1377 (Fla. 3d DCA 1985); *Slomowitz v. Walker,* 429 So. 2d 797 (Fla. 4th DCA 1983)."

Cite checked: Still good law. Only negative history is a Minnesota case.

E. Other Rules

Excerpt from Page 586 in *Torres v. Arnco Constr., Inc.,* 867 So. 2d 583
(Fla. 5th DCA 2004).

"The statutes regulating service of process are to be strictly construed to assure that a defendant is notified of the proceedings. *See Abbate; see also Carter v. Lil' Joe Records, Inc.,* 829 So. 2d 953 (Fla. 4th DCA 2002). Indeed, because statutes authorizing substituted service are exceptions to the general rule requiring a defendant to be served personally, due process requires strict compliance with their statutory requirements. *See Monaco v. Nealon,* 810 So. 2d 1084 (Fla. 4th DCA 2002); *Mercy Lu Enters., Inc. v. Liberty Mut. Ins. Co.,* 681 So. 2d 758 (Fla. 4th DCA 1996)."

Cite checked: No cases have cited *Torres.*

First Element: Usual Place of Abode

A. Specific Rules

Excerpt from Page 605 in *Thompson v. State, Dept. of Revenue,* 867 So. 2d 603
(Fla. App. 1 Dist. 2004).

"Turning to the merits, "[s]ection 48.031 expressly requires that substituted service be at the person's usual place of abode." *Shurman v. Atlantic Mortgage & Investment Corp.,* 795 So. 2d 952, 954 (Fla. 2001). The requirement "usual place of abode" means "the place where the defendant is actually living at the time of service." *Id., citing State ex rel. Merritt v. Heffernan*, 142 Fla. 496, 195 So. 145, 147 (1940)."

Cited checked — Citing references but no negative history.

Excerpt from Page 586 in *Torres v. Arnco Constr., Inc.*, 867 So. 2d 583 (Fla. 5th DCA 2004).

"In *State ex. rel. Merritt v. Heffernan*, 142 Fla. 496, 195 So. 145, 147 (1940), the Florida Supreme Court defined the term "usual place of abode" as the place where the defendant "is actually living at the time of service." The word "abode" means "one's fixed place of residence for the time being when service is made." *Id.* If a person has more than one residence, he must be served at the residence in which he is actually living at the time of service. *Id.* The Florida Supreme Court noted later in *Shurman v. Atlantic Mortgage & Investment Corp.*, 795 So. 2d 952, 954 (Fla. 2001), that courts have frequently invalidated substituted service of process in cases where the defendant was not actually living at the place where service was made, even though process might have been delivered to a relative. *See, e.g., Alvarez v. State Farm Mut. Auto. Ins. Co.*, 635 So. 2d 131 (Fla. 3d DCA 1994); *Stern v. Gad*, 505 So. 2d 531 (Fla. 3d DCA 1987)."

Cite checked: No cases have cited *Torres.*

Excerpt from Page 954 in *Shurman v. Atlantic Mortg. & Inv. Corp.*, 795 So. 2d 952 (Fla. 2001).

"Going one step further, "usual place of abode" is the place where the defendant is actually living at the time of the service. The word "abode" means one's fixed place of residence for the time being when the service is made. Thus, if a person has several residences, he must be served at the residence in which he is actually living at the time service is made."

And in *Mygatt v. Coe*, 63 N.J.L. 510, 512, 44 A. 198, 199, the following pertinent statement appears:

"The statute does not direct service to be made at the "residence" of the defendant, but at his "dwelling house" or "usual place of abode," which is a much more restricted term. As was said in *Stout v. Leonard*, 37 N.J.L. 492, many persons have several residences, which they permanently maintain, occupying one at one period of the year and another at another period. Where such conditions exist, a summons must be served at the dwelling house in which the defendant is living at the time when the service is made."

Heffernan, 195 So. at 147. *See also Milanes v. Colonial Penn Ins. Co.*, 507 So. 2d 777, 778 (Fla. 3d DCA 1987); *Panter v. Werbel-Roth Securities, Inc.*, 406 So. 2d 1267, 1268 (Fla. 4th DCA 1981); *Hauser*, 341 So. 2d at 532.

Cite checked: Citing references but no negative history.

B. Description of Analogous Cases

1. Case in Which the Court Held That the Element Was Met:

State ex rel. Merritt v. Heffernan, 142 Fla. 496, 195 So. 145, 147 (1940).

Facts:

Defendant maintained a permanent residence in Minnesota, where he had an office, voted, and paid taxes.

Two months before service of process, the defendant moved his family to an apartment in Miami. The defendant visited his family twice "during the season."

One hour before the summons was served, the defendant boarded a train to go back to Minnesota.

The summons was left with the defendant's wife.

Issue:

The case involved a complicated procedure, and it is not clear what exact issue was before the court.

Holding:

The court determined that the summons had been left at the defendant's usual place of abode and that justice had been done and affirmed the decision.

Reasoning:

Quote from page 501:

"In the instant case the relator had established his family in an apartment in Miami Beach, where they had been living for about two months and where he had visited them. Although his permanent residence was in a distant state, we think that his then place of abode was where his family was living. We can attach little importance to the fact that an hour or so before the summons was delivered to his wife he had left by train for his northern residence or place of business. Certainly it could not be said that his place of abode was on a common carrier. He was not accompanied by his family, who remained in this State for a considerable length of time after his departure. There was no convincing proof that he did not intend to return to Florida, and the principal purpose, as we have stated, was to advise him of the pendency of the suit, which was accomplished by the delivery of a copy of the writ to his wife. We do not hold the view that Florida was the permanent residence of the defendant, but we do feel that in the circumstance reflected in the record, it was his ****148** usual place of abode in contemplation of that expression as used in the statute. His family resided in this State at the time and had done so for a period of approximately two months. Nor do we feel that the plaintiff is within the classification of persons who had at the time of service lost one place of residence and had not yet established another."

2. Cases in Which the Court Held That the Element Was Not Met:

Alvarez v. State Farm Mut. Auto Ins. Co., 635 So. 2d 131, 132 (Fla. 3d DCA 1994).

Facts:

Cousin was served at what the plaintiff alleged was the defendant's usual place of abode.

However, affidavits and supporting documentation—including a telephone bill and marriage license—established that Alvarez was not living at that address on the date of service or for some time before.

Issue:

Did the trial court err when it denied the defendant's motion to set aside a default judgment?

Holding:

Service of law was ineffective as a matter of law. Therefore, default and default judgment were void and had to be set aside.

Reasoning:

Court just sets out rules and facts.

"The defendant below seeks review of an order denying her rule 1.540(b) motion to set aside a default and default judgment entered against her. We reverse.

Substituted service of process in this accident case was secured on Alvarez under section 48.031, Florida Statutes (1991) by serving her cousin at what was allegedly her "usual place of abode" at a home in Hialeah. The affidavits and supporting documentation—including a telephone bill and marriage license—submitted in support of appellant's motion below, however, established uncontradictedly that Alvarez was not living at that address on the date of service or for some time before. *See Hunt Exterminating Co. v. Crum,* 598 So. 2d 113 (Fla. 2d DCA 1992); *Partrade, Inc. v. Marchiano,* 566 So. 2d 588 (Fla. 3d DCA 1990); *Marshall Davis, Inc. v. Incapco, Inc.,* 558 So. 2d 206 (Fla. 2d DCA 1990). It is therefore apparent that the purported service of process was ineffective as a matter of law, *see Kennedy v. Richmond,* 512 So. 2d 1129 (Fla. 4th DCA 1987), and that the default and default judgment were therefore void and must be set aside. *See Falkner v. AmeriFirst Fed. Sav. & Loan Ass'n,* 489 So. 2d 758 (Fla. 3d DCA 1986); *Sams Food Store, Inc. v. Alvarez,* 443 So. 2d 211 (Fla. 3d DCA 1983); *Hyman v. Canter,* 389 So. 2d 322 (Fla. 3d DCA 1980)."

Shurman v. Atlantic Mortg. & Inv. Corp., 795 So. 2d 952 (Fla. 2001).

Facts:

The defendant had been incarcerated for at least nine months. Service was made on the defendant's wife.

Issue:

Was the defendant properly served at his usual place of abode?

Holding:

The defendant was not properly served at his usual place of abode.

Reasoning:

Excerpt from pages 995-96:

"Although Atlantic argues that Shurman's "usual place of abode" was where he lived with his family before being incarcerated, Shurman was "actually living" in prison at the time of service. Thus, under our obligation to strictly construe the statutory notice provisions and our analysis in *Heffernan*, it is apparent that Shurman's "usual place of abode" was prison, not his prior residence. *See Heffernan*, 195 So. at 147.

We find additional support for our decision in *Heffernan* and our conclusion that prison was Shurman's "usual place of abode" in *Fidelity & Deposit Co. v. Abagnale,* 97 N.J. Super. 132, 234 A.2d 511 (1967), and *Saienni v. Oveide,* 355 A.2d 707 (Del. Super. Ct. 1976)."

The court then goes on to distinguish out-of-state cases that reached the opposite conclusion.

"However, we believe that the better view is that one's "usual place of abode" is where the person is actually living at the time of service, even in cases involving prisoners.

The law in this State has developed in somewhat rigid conformity to the principle that provisions for substituted service, being in derogation of the common law, must be strictly construed. Hence, the rule has been consistently applied ***956** that one's "dwelling house or usual place of abode" is limited in its meaning to the place where one is "actually living" at the time when service is made. . . . The expectation that a defendant will normally receive notice of process served through a competent member of his household living at the same place of abode as he, does not, it seems to me, prevail in the setting of familial disorganization frequently ensuing where the head of the household is committed to prison. *Abagnale,* 234 A.2d at 519 (citations omitted). While the court recognized some jurisdictions had concluded that an incarcerated party's usual place of abode continues to be where his family resides, it distinguished those cases on the basis that they were "largely influenced, if not governed, by a hybrid of residence and domicile. *Id.*"

Torres v. Arnco Constr., Inc., 867 So. 2d 583 (Fla. 5th DCA 2004).

Facts:

Mr. Torres submitted an affidavit stating that he had been a resident of New York for fifty seven years and that for twelve years his residence and usual place of abode was at the address in New York where the defendant had attempted to serve him. Mr.Torres also indicated that he never received process in this case and that no one was authorized as his agent to accept service for him. Finally, he said that he had no residence or usual place of abode in Florida.

The New York process server indicated in his affidavit that he "verified" with a neighbor that Mr. Torres lived at the New York address, but that he was often out of town and was expected to return in two weeks.

The Florida process server made a notation that Mr. Torres's mother said that Mr. Torres would be home soon.

Issue:

Was substituted service made on the defendant at his usual place of abode?

Holding: Service of process was valid.

Reasoning:

Quoting from page 586-87:

"Our standard of review of an order ruling on a motion to vacate a default judgment is whether there has been a gross abuse of discretion by the trial court. *See North Shore Hosp., Inc. v. Barber*, 143 So. 2d 849 (Fla.1962). We make a number of observations in this regard. First, there was no live testimony considered by the trial court in denying the motion to set ***587*** aside final judgment. Rather, the court relied only on documents and arguments of counsel in concluding that it had personal jurisdiction. As a result, this is not a case where the trial court evaluated the demeanor and credibility of live witnesses. Second, we note that the party seeking to invoke the court's jurisdiction has the burden to prove the validity of service of process. *See M.J.W. v. Dept. of Children & Families*, 825 So. 2d 1038 (Fla. 1st DCA 2002); *Gilliam v. Smart*, 809 So. 2d 905 (Fla. 1st DCA 2002). We conclude that the record does not reflect competent evidence that Arnco met this burden.

The affidavit of Mr. Torres specifically denies that his place of abode is in Florida, and specifically avers that his place of abode is in New York where Arnco, which was apparently aware of this, tried unsuccessfully to serve him. Moreover, the affidavit of the New York process server tends to support the position of Mr. Torres that his place of abode is in New York. In particular, the process server confirmed with neighbors that, indeed, Mr. Torres lived there. Finally, the primary item that might support the trial court's order — the Florida process server's notation that Mr. Torres's mother said that Mr. Torres would be home soon — is ambiguous at best. As Arnco did not meet its burden of proving that it served Mr. Torres in his place of abode, we conclude that it was error not to grant the motion of Mr. Torres for relief from judgment. Accordingly, we reverse and remand for proceedings not inconsistent with this opinion."

"GRIFFIN, J., dissenting.

I respectfully dissent. The trial court had two key items of information to consider. One was the affidavit of Mr. Torres in which he states in conclusory fashion that: "[I] do not have a residence or a place of abode in the State of Florida." Given the verb tense, this would mean that on the date of execution of the affidavit, February 20, 2003, he did not have a place of abode in Florida. This tells us nothing about what his circumstances were in August 2002 when service was made. The affidavit of attempted service in New York recites conversations with neighbors who related that Torres "lived [at the New York address] but was rarely home," and that on July 27th a neighbor said that he was "possibly visiting in Florida and would be back in approximately two weeks." If Mr. Torres were visiting his family for such lengths of time in Florida, that Florida address was his "usual abode" when he was served in Florida. *See State ex rel. Merritt v. Heffernan*, 142 Fla. 496, 195 So. 145 (1940). It would also be consistent with the affidavit of the Florida process server who said that Torres' mother remarked that Torres "would be home soon, and she would see to it that he received the papers." In any event, the burden was on Torres to prove that the place of substitute service was not his usual place of abode and his affidavit is inadequate for that purpose."

***Thompson v. State, Dept. of Revenue,* 867 So. 2d 603 (Fla. 1st DCA 2004).**

Facts:

The petition was served on Thompson's wife at her residence.

Thompson filed a motion to dismiss/quash for lack of service of process, stating that he was separated from his wife, that he has not resided at that address for over three years, and that he did not authorize anyone to accept service of process on his behalf.

Issue:

Did the trial court err in entering a non-final order denying his motion to quash service of process?

Holding:

The court reversed and remanded for an evidentiary hearing.

Reasoning:

Quoting from page 605:

"Thompson's motion and affidavit are based on the fact that the service did not comply with section 48.031 and was therefore legally deficient. *National Safety Associates, Inc. v. Allstate Insurance Co.,* 799 So. 2d 316, 317 (Fla. 2d DCA 2001). Thompson's affidavit makes a *prima facie* showing that he was not served at his usual place of abode by valid substituted service. *See, e.g., S.H. v. Department of Children and Families,* 837 So. 2d 1117, 1118 (Fla. 4th DCA 2003) (invalidating substituted service on father at mother's address, where mother's residence was not father's "usual place of abode" at the time of service); *Gonzalez v. Totalbank,* 472 So. 2d 861 (Fla. 3d DCA 1985) (invalidating substituted service when wife was separated from husband and not living at address where service was attempted). Having raised the issue of personal jurisdiction, Thompson's motion and accompanying affidavit placed the burden on the Department to establish the validity of service of process. *M.J.W.,* 825 So. 2d at 1041."

C. Ms. Duncan's Arguments

- During the week she lived at the halfway house, not at her sister's house.
- Service on a relative is not sufficient.
- Her more permanent address was the halfway house address. She had a room, etc., at the halfway house.
- *Heffernan* is an old case.
- In *Torres,* the court held that the defendant's mother's house was not the defendant's usual place of abode even though the mother indicated that the defendant would be home later.

D. The Plaintiff's Arguments

- Ms. Duncan stayed at her sister's house three nights a week.
- Ms. Duncan apparently received mail at her sister's house — the shoebox.
- Ms. Duncan listed her sister's address on her driver's license.
- In *Heffernan,* the court held that the apartment was the defendant's usual place of abode even though the defendant had left the apartment and was on a train back to his permanent residence.

- In *Torres*, the defendant had a permanent residence where he had lived for twelve years. He was just visiting his mother.

E. Mini-Conclusion

We may be able to prove that Ms. Duncan was not served at her usual place of abode.

Second Element: Any Person Residing Therein Who Is 15 Years of Age or Older

A. Specific Rules

Excerpt from Pages 1035-36 in *Magazine v. Bedoya,* 475 So. 2d 1035
(Fla. App. 3 Dist., 1985):

"First, Ms. Oakford's six-week stay at Magazine's residence was long enough that she may properly be regarded as "a person residing therein" under section 48.031(1). *Compare Sangmeister v. McElnea*, 278 So. 2d 675 (Fla. 3d DCA 1973) (four month visit establishes residing therein requirement) *with Gamboa v. Jones,* 455 So. 2d 613 (Fla. 3d DCA 1984) (ten-day visit **1036* does not meet the requirement of residency).[1]"

Cite checked: Still good law. Only negative citing reference is a Minnesota case.

B. Application

Ms. Webster is 32 and lives in the house. Thus, the only dispute is whether the house is Ms. Duncan's usual place of abode.

Third Element: Informing the Person of their Contents

A. Specific Rules

Courts do not seem to set out any specific rules for this element.

B. Description of Analogous Cases

1. Cases in Which the Court Held That the Element Was Met:

Excerpts from Page 1035 in *Magazine v. Bedoya,* 475 So. 2d 1035
(Fla. 3d DCA 1985):

"His mother-in-law's testimony that she did not know exactly what the papers were overcame the presumption of valid service by demonstrating that she was not informed of the contents thereof. We disagree.

Second, there was no evidence that Ms. Oakford was not informed of the contents of the papers served. Consequently, Magazine has failed to show, by clear and convincing evidence, that the service was defective.[2] Accordingly, the order denying his motion is affirmed.

Cite checked: Still good law. Only negative citing reference is a Minnesota case.

2. Cases in Which the Court Held That the Element Was Not Met:

Excerpt from Page 559 in *Bache, Halsey, Stuart, Shields, Inc. v. Mendoza,* 400 So. 2d 558 (Fla. App. 1981).

"[2] Section 48.031(1), Florida Statutes (1979) permits service of original process to be made by leaving copies with any person fifteen years or more who resides at the usual place of abode of the person to be served and "informing the person of their contents." The deputy sheriff did not recall explaining to Mrs. Mendoza the contents of the papers he left. Mrs. Mendoza testified at her deposition that service consisted solely of a knock on the door, a man saying "Mendoza," and delivery of papers, the contents of which she did not understand. Under these circumstances, we find no compliance with section 48.031(1), and we affirm the trial court's order setting aside default judgment.

Cite checked: Still good law.

C. Ms. Duncan's Arguments

The process server never told Ms. Webster that he was handing her a summons and complaint. He told her only that Ms. Duncan needed to go to court.

D. The Plaintiff's Arguments

Telling Ms. Webster that Ms. Duncan had to go to court is the equivalent of telling her that he was handing her a summons and complaint.

Distinguish *Bache.* In that case the process server could not recall telling Mrs. Mendoza anything.

E. Mini-Conclusion

Court will probably decide that the process server's statement was sufficient.

In recording your research notes, keep in mind that, most of the time, no one but you will see your notes. Thus, you can use whatever format you choose. For instance, you can choose to use a numbering system or you can choose to use bullets, and you can choose to write out case briefs for the analogous cases or you can choose a more informal format. Use what works best for you and for the particular problem that you have been asked to research. Just make sure that you record information accurately, that you have included citations for the information you have pasted into your notes or recorded, and that you keep track of which cases you have cite checked.

Although a completed template is a good start, you need to do more; in fact, you need to do a lot more. Before you begin writing, you need to make sure that you understand the big picture, that you have done a sophisticated analysis of the applicable statutes and cases, and that you have synthesized the applicable statutes and cases.

§ 7.1.1 Make Sure You Understand the Big Picture

Start by taking a step back. Can you place the issue that you were asked to research into the bigger picture? For instance, in our example case, do you understand how service of process relates to jurisdiction and how jurisdiction relates to whether the court had the power to enter a default judgment? If you don't, don't panic. The law is complicated, and neither professors nor employers expect first-, second-, or even third-year students to have a complete understanding of how the system works. However, both professors and employers expect students to look for answers and, when they can't find them, that they will ask questions. Thus, when you have a question about the big picture, try to find the answer in secondary sources, for example, on a website or in a practice book or hornbook. If these sources do not answer your question, ask questions. Instead of losing the respect of those you work with, you will, more likely than not, gain their respect. In fact, our experience has been that it is the students who ask questions, not those who don't, who get job offers.

§ 7.1.2 Make Sure You Understand the Statute

Once you understand the big picture, make sure you understand the statute. In particular, make sure you understand the "elements," or requirements, and that you have located any applicable statutory definitions and any sections that explain the statute's purpose. If the statute is a complicated one, take the time to diagram the statute.

In our example problem, Fla. Stat. §48.031 (2004) reads as follows:

> Service of original process is made by delivering a copy of it to the person to be served with a copy of the complaint, petition, or other initial pleading or paper or by leaving the copies at his or her usual place of abode with any person residing therein who is 15 years of age or older and informing the person of their contents. Minors who are or have been married shall be served as provided in this section.

The rules for citing Florida statutes are set out in Appendices 1 and 2 in the *ALWD Citation Manual* and in Table 1 in *The Bluebook*. To make a section symbol using Word, select "Insert," then "Symbols," and then "Special Characters." To save time, create a "hot key" for the section symbol.

P R A C T I C E
POINTER

In diagramming this statute, you determine that service can be accomplished in either of two ways: by delivering a copy of the summons, complaint, petition, or other initial pleading or paper to the person to be served *or* by leaving a copy of those documents at the person's usual place of abode with a person who resides there who is 15 years old or older and by informing the person with whom the documents are left of their contents.

Sample Diagram

Service of original process is made by delivering a copy of "it" with a copy of the complaint, petition, or other initial pleading or paper

    (1) to the person being served

or

    (2) by leaving the copies at

        a. his or her usual place of abode
        b. with any person residing therein
        c. who is 15 years of age or older *and*
        d. informing the person of their contents.

In diagramming a statute, pay particular attention to the and's and or's. For example, note that there is an "or" between the (1) and the (2) but that there is an "and" between the "c" and the "d." While you can accomplish service of process either by delivering the summons to the person being served or by leaving it at his or her usual place of abode, if you leave it at the person's usual place of abode, you must leave the summons with a person who is residing therein, that person must be 15 years old or older, *and* you must inform the person with whom you leave the documents of their contents.

In addition, in diagramming the statute, pay close attention to pronouns. For instance, in our example statute, what does the "it" refer to?

> Service of original process is made by delivering a copy of *it* to the person to be served with a copy of the complaint, petition, or other initial pleading or paper.

Finally, make sure that you understand what each modifier modifies. In our example statute, what does the phrase "residing therein" modify?

> Service of original process is made by delivering a copy of it to the person to be served with a copy of the complaint, petition, or other initial pleading or paper or by leaving the copies at his or her usual place of abode with any person *residing therein* who is 15 years of age or older and informing the person of their contents.

Finally, as you read statutes, keep in mind that some ambiguities are the result of poor drafting and that some ambiguities are intentional. Also keep in mind that, as a result of this poor drafting or intentional ambiguity, it may be difficult or even impossible to determine, at least from the statutory language, what the legislative body intended when it enacted the statute. Don't despair. You will often be able to use these ambiguities to make an argument on behalf of your client.

§ 7.1.3 Make Sure You Understand the General and Specific Rules

In addition to reading the statute carefully, also read carefully those portions of the cases that are relevant to the issue you were asked to research. For more on legal reading, see Chapter 4.

Begin by focusing on the cases that have set out general rules — for example, the cases that have listed the elements, the cases that have set out the rules relating to the burden of proof, and the cases that have explained the policies underlying the statute. For example, in researching the sample problem, we found several cases that set out the rules relating to the burden of proof.

Burden of Proof   EXAMPLE

(1) Excerpt from Page 605 in *Thompson v. State, Dept. of Revenue,* 867 So. 2d 603 (Fla. 1st DCA 2004).

"The burden of proof to sustain the validity of service of process is upon the person who seeks to invoke the jurisdiction of the court and, without proper service of process, the court lacks personal jurisdiction over the defendant. *M.J.W. v. Department of Children and Families,* 825 So. 2d 1038, 1041 (Fla. 1st DCA 2002).

[4] [5] "[A] process server's return of service on a defendant which is regular on its face is presumed to be valid absent clear and convincing evidence presented to the contrary." *Telf Corp. v. Gomez,* 671 So. 2d 818 (Fla. 3d DCA 1996). Although simple denial of service is not sufficient, *id.* at 819, Thompson's motion and affidavit are based on the fact that the service did not comply with section 48.031 and was therefore legally deficient. *National Safety Associates, Inc. v. Allstate Insurance Co.,* 799 So. 2d 316, 317 (Fla. 2d DCA 2001). Thompson's affidavit makes a *prima facie* showing that he was not served at his usual place of abode by valid substituted service. *See, e.g., S.H. v. Department of Children and Families,* 837 So. 2d 1117, 1118 (Fla. 4th DCA 2003) (invalidating substituted service on father at mother's address, where mother's residence was not father's "usual place of abode" at the time of service); *Gonzalez v. Totalbank,* 472 So. 2d 861 (Fla. 3d DCA 1985) (invalidating substituted service when wife was separated from husband and not living at address where service was attempted). Having raised the issue of personal jurisdiction, Thompson's motion and accompanying affidavit placed the burden on the Department to establish the validity of service of process. *M.J.W.,* 825 So. 2d at 1041. Accordingly, the cause is reversed and remanded for an evidentiary hearing to determine whether the attempted service of Thompson pursuant to section 48.031, Florida Statutes (2003), was valid. *See Venetian Salami, 554 So. 2d at 502-03; Mowrey Elevator of Florida, Inc. v. Automated Integration,* 745 So. 2d 1046, 1047-48 (Fla. 1st DCA 1999).

REVERSED and REMANDED."

Cite checked — still good law. No citing references for these points of law.

(2) Excerpt from Pages 818-819 in *Telf Corp. v. Gomez,* 671 So. 2d 818 (Fla. 3d DCA 1996).

"We affirm the order of the trial court denying appellants' respective motions to quash service of process. It has well been established that a process server's return of service on a defendant which is regular on its face is presumed to be valid absent clear and convincing evidence presented to the contrary. *Florida Nat'l Bank v. Halphen,* 641 So. 2d 495 (Fla. 3d DCA 1994); *Lazo v. Bill Swad Leasing Co.,* 548 So. 2d 1194 (Fla. 4th DCA 1989); ***819** Slomowitz v. Walker,* 429 So. 2d 797 (Fla. 4th DCA 1983); *Brugh v. Savings & Profit Sharing Pension Fund of United Ins. Co. of Am.,* 211 So. 2d 613 (Fla. 1st DCA 1968). Further, a defendant may not impeach the validity of the summons with a simple denial of service, but must present "clear and convincing evidence" to corroborate his denial. *Halphen,* 641 So. 2d at 496; *Jefferson Bank & Trust v. Levy,* 498 So. 2d 450 (Fla. 3d DCA 1986)."

Cite checked — *National Safety* declined to extend rule to case in which return was not regular on its face.

(3) Excerpt from Page 1035 in *Magazine v. Bedoya,* 475 So. 2d 1035 (Fla. 3d DCA 1985).

"A presumption of valid service arises from evidence of a return of service which is regular on its face. *Klosenski v. Flaherty,* 116 So. 2d 767 (Fla.1959). The party challenging the service must overcome that presumption by clear and convincing evidence. *Montano v. Montano,* 472 So. 2d 1377 (Fla. 3d DCA 1985); *Slomowitz v. Walker,* 429 So. 2d 797 (Fla. 4th DCA 1983)."

Cite check — Still good law.
Only citing reference is a Minn. case.

The rules for citing Florida Cases are set out in Appendices 1 and 2 in the *ALWD Citation Manual* and in Table 1 in *The Bluebook.* Note that neither *ALWD Citation Manual* nor *The Bluebook* use superscript. Thus, you may want to turn off the "Autocorrect" function that turns "1st" into "1st."

P R A C T I C E
POINTER

If all of the cases set out the same rule, all you need to do is make sure that you understand that rule. If, however, different cases set out different rules, you need to determine which of those rules governs. To do this, begin by cite checking the cases. If one or more of the cases have been reversed or overruled on the point of law for which you are looking at the case, discard those cases. They are no longer good law. If the remaining cases, that is, the cases that are still good law, set out the same rule, use that rule. If, however, there is still a discrepancy, try to resolve that discrepancy by looking to see if different rules apply in different types of cases (For example, is there a different rule in child custody cases than there is in contract cases?), whether different divisions apply different rules (For example, does the 1st DCA apply one rule and the 3d DCA apply a different rule?), or whether the rule seems to be evolving.

In our example case, all of the cases seem to set out the same rule of law. Although it takes some careful reading to determine what that rule is, the rule seems to be as follows:

1. The party who is seeking to invoke the jurisdiction of the court (the plaintiff) has the burden of proving that the service was valid.
2. If, however, the "return of service" is regular on its face, service is presumed to be valid.
3. Thus, if "the return of service" is regular on its face, the party challenging the validity of the service (the defendant) must present clear and convincing evidence that the service is invalid.

When you are not sure what a particular word or phrase means, take a few minutes to look up the definition. For example, if you are not sure what the phrase "return of service" means, look up that  phrase. If you are online, the easiest way to find a definition is to go to Google.com and, using the "Advanced Search" option, type in the word "definition" and the phrase "return of service." When you do, you will be taken to a site like *Legal-Explanations.com*, which provides plain English definitions of legal terms. In this instance, *Legal-Explanations.com* sets out the following definition for "return of service": "n. Written confirmation from a process server under oath that declares that the legal documents were served (such as a summons and complaint)."

Thus, in our example problem, because the return is regular on its face, Ms. Duncan would have to present clear and convincing evidence that the service was not valid.

If several cases set out the same rule, you will usually want to cite a recent case from the jurisdiction's highest court as authority for that rule. For example, in our sample case, you would want to cite to a recent Florida Supreme Court case. If  there is not a recent case from the jurisdiction's highest court, you can cite to an older case from the jursidiction's highest court and then to a more recent decision from an intermediate court of appeals. The exception to this "rule" is when the rule is known by the name of the case that announced it. For example, if you are setting out the *Miranda* rule, you would cite to *Miranda v. Arizona*, 384 U.S. 436 (1966) and not to a more recent United States Supreme Court case.

Once you understand the general rules, turn your attention to the specific rules, that is, the rules that the courts apply in determining whether a particular element, or requirement, is met. For instance, in our example case, look at the rules that the courts apply in determining whether the service was made at the defendant's usual place of abode. Do all of the cases set out the same rule? If they do not set out the same rule, are some of the cases no longer good law? If all of the cases are still good law, is there a way of reconciling the various rules?

Analogous Case

Excerpt from page 605 in *Thompson v. State, Dept. of Revenue*
867 So. 2d 603 (Fla. 1st DCA 2004).

"Turning to the merits, "[s]ection 48.031 expressly requires that substituted service be at the person's usual place of abode." *Shurman v. Atlantic Mortgage & Investment Corp.,* 795 So. 2d 952, 954 (Fla. 2001). The requirement "usual place of abode" means "the place where the defendant is actually living at the time of service." *Id., citing State ex rel. Merritt v. Heffernan,* 142 Fla. 496, 195 So. 145, 147 (1940)."

Cite checked — still good law.
No citing references for these points of law.

Excerpt from Page 586 in *Torres v. Arnco Const., Inc.,* 867 So. 2d
583 (Fla. 5th DCA 2004).

"In *State ex. rel. Merritt v. Heffernan,* 142 Fla. 496, 195 So. 145, 147 (1940), the Florida Supreme Court defined the term "usual place of abode" as the place where the defendant "is actually living at the time of service." The word "abode" means "one's fixed place of residence for the time being when service is made." *Id.* If a person has more than one residence, he must be served at the residence in which he is actually living at the time of service. *Id.* The Florida Supreme Court noted later in *Shurman v. Atlantic Mortg. & Inv. Corp.,* 795 So. 2d 952, 954 (Fla. 2001), that courts have frequently invalidated substituted service of process in cases where the defendant was not actually living at the place where service was made, even though process might have been delivered to a relative. *See, e.g., Alvarez v. State Farm Mut. Auto. Ins. Co.,* 635 So. 2d 131 (Fla. 3d DCA 1994); *Stern v. Gad,* 505 So. 2d 531 (Fla. 3d DCA 1987)."

Excerpt from Page 954 in *Shurman v. Atlantic Mortg. & Inv.
Corp.,* 795 So. 2d 952 (Fla. 2001).

"Going one step further, "usual place of abode" is the place where the defendant is actually living at the time of the service. The word "abode" means one's fixed place of residence for the time being when the service is made. Thus, if a person has several residences, he must be served at the residence in which he is actually living at the time service is made."

And in *Mygatt v. Coe,* 63 N.J.L. 510, 512, 44 A. 198, 199, the following pertinent statement appears:

"The statute does not direct service to be made at the "residence" of the defendant, but at his "dwelling house" or "usual place of abode," which is a much more restricted term. As was said in *Stout v. Leonard,* 37 N.J.L. 492, many persons have several residences, which they permanently maintain, occupying one at one period of the year and another at another period. Where such conditions exist, a summons must be served at the dwelling house in which the defendant is living at the time when the service is made. *Heffernan,* 195 So. at 147. *See also Milanes v. Colonial Penn Ins. Co.,* 507 So. 2d 777, 778 (Fla. 3d DCA 1987); *Panter v. Werbel-Roth Securities, Inc.,* 406 So. 2d 1267, 1268 (Fla. 4th DCA 1981); *Hauser,* 341 So. 2d at 532."

Cite checked: No cases have cited *Torres.*

Question

Do each of these cases set out the same rule? If they don't, what should you do?

Once you understand the big picture and have a good understanding of both the general and specific rules, it is time to start writing. As you do this writing, keep two things in mind. First, writing a memo is usually a multi-step process. If you want to do a good job, you will need to do a first draft, a second draft, and maybe even a third or fourth draft of your first draft. Thus, do not put off writing the first draft until the night before the final draft is due. Second, most of the time drafting a memo involves more than recording completely formed ideas and arguments. Most law students and attorneys find that they rethink their analysis and synthesis as they write. Thus, do not be surprised if, part way through writing the first draft, that you have one of those "aha!" moments in which you see the issue, the law, or an argument in a completely different light.

The rest of this chapter walks you through the process of writing the first draft of your first memo. Although we discuss the sections in the order in which they appear in a formal memo, you do not have to write the sections in order. For example, many law students and attorneys find that it works better to write the first draft of the discussion section before they write the first draft of the statement of facts, issue statement, and brief answer.

§ 7.2 Drafting the Heading

The heading is the easiest section to write. It consists of only four entries: the name of the person to whom the memo is addressed, the name of the person who wrote the memo, the date, and an entry identifying the client and the issue or issues discussed in the memo. Although the first three entries are self-explanatory, the fourth needs some explanation.

In some firms, the memo is filed only in the client's file. For such firms, the "Re:" entry can be quite general.

Sample Heading   EXAMPLE 1

To: Christina Galeano

From: Legal Intern

Date: September 12, 2006

Re: Elaine Duncan, Case No. 06-478

In other firms, the memo is filed not only in the client's file but also in a "memo bank" — that is, a computer or paper file in which all memos are filed by topic. In these offices, the "Re:" section serves two purposes. Within the client's file, it distinguishes the memo from any other memos that may have been or will be written, and in the memo bank, it provides either the database for a word search or topic categories under which the memo will be filed. To serve this last purpose, the heading should include the key terms.

Sample Heading

> To: Christine Galeano
>
> From: Legal Intern
>
> Date: September 12, 2006
>
> Re: Elaine Duncan, Case No. 06-478
>   Service of Process, Usual Place of Abode; Notification of
>   Contents

If you are working on a case in which there will be a number of different memos, use the "Re" entry to distinguish the memo that you have written from other memos that are already in the file or that might be added to the file at a later date.

P R A C T I C E

§ 7.3 Drafting the Statement of Facts

Just as every case starts with a story, so does every memo. Before you set out the issues, the law, and the arguments, tell the attorney who did what when.

§ 7.3.1 Decide What Facts to Include

In a typical statement of facts, there are three types of facts: the legally significant facts, the emotionally significant facts, and the background facts. In addition, the writer usually identifies those facts that are unknown.

a. Legally Significant Facts

A legally significant fact is a fact that a court would consider in deciding whether a statute or rule is applicable or in applying that statute or rule. For instance, in our example case, the legally significant facts are those facts that the court would consider in determining whether service of process was valid. More specifically, the legally significant facts are the facts that the court would consider in determining whether the summons was left at the defendant's usual place of abode, whether the summons was left with a person residing therein who is 15 years old or older, and whether the process server notified the person being served of the contents of the documents.

You can use either of two techniques to determine whether a fact is legally significant. Before you write the discussion section, you can prepare a two-column chart in which you list the elements in the first column and the facts that relate to those elements in the second column. See Chart 7.2.

Chart 7.2	Chart Listing Elements and the Facts That the Court Would Consider in Deciding Whether the Element Is Met

Element	Facts that the court would consider in deciding whether element is met
Usual place of abode	Ms. Webster told the process server that "Elaine isn't here today."
	On February 1, 2006, Ms. Duncan entered an inpatient drug treatment program in Miami. She remained in the program until March 27, 2006, when she moved into a residential treatment house for recovering addicts.
	During April, May, and June 2006, Ms. Duncan was a full-time resident at the halfway house. She had a bedroom in the house, ate her meals there, and had some of her possessions there.
	Beginning in July 2006, Ms. Duncan began spending less time at the halfway house and more time with her sister, Elizabeth Webster.
	During July and August 2006, Ms. Duncan spent weeknights at the halfway house and Friday, Saturday, and Sunday nights at her sister's house. Because she was spending time at her sister's house, she moved some of her clothing and personal effects into her sister's house.
	When Ms. Duncan renewed her driver's license in August 2006, she listed her sister's address as her address.
	From April and May 2006, Ms. Duncan put the halfway house address on employment applications. However, her driver's license showed her sister's address as her address.
	Her voter registration shows the address where she lived before entering the treatment program.
	Since August 1, 2006, Ms. Duncan has worked. On September 1, 2006, Ms. Duncan moved into her own apartment.
	The return on the service of process appears to be in order.
Person residing therein who is 15 years old or older	Ms. Webster lives in the house where the summons was left.
Informing person of contents	Ms. Webster is 32. [These facts have been omitted.]

Question

In our sample problem, what facts would the court consider in deciding whether the process server informed the person who was served of the contents of the summons and complaint?

The second technique is used after the discussion section has been completed. To ensure that you have included all of the legally significant facts in your statement of facts, go through your discussion section checking to make sure that each of the facts that you used in setting out the arguments is in your statement of facts. If you used a fact in the arguments, that fact is legally significant and should be included in the statement of facts. (Remember, writing a memo is a recursive process. Even though you may write the statement of facts first, you will need to revise it after you have completed the discussion section.)

b. Emotionally Significant Facts

An emotionally significant fact is one that, while not legally significant, may affect the way the judge or jury decides the case. For example, while it is not legally significant that Ms. Duncan was in a drug treatment program, that fact may affect the way the judge views her. Thus, that fact is an emotionally significant fact and should be included in the statement of facts. In addition, while it is not legally significant that Ms. Duncan was applying for jobs and obtained one, that fact may also affect the way in which the judge views her and should, therefore, be included in the statement of facts.

Question

Is the fact that Ms. Duncan listed the halfway house address on employment applications a legally significant fact? An emotionally significant fact?

c. Background Facts

In addition to including the legally and emotionally significant facts, also include those facts that are needed to tell the story and that provide the context for the legally and emotionally significant facts.

d. Unknown Facts

Sometimes you are not given all of the facts needed to analyze an issue. For instance, because the attorney did not know the law, he or she did not ask the right questions, or the documents containing the unknown facts are in the possession of the opposing party. If the unknown facts go to the heart of the issue, try to obtain them before writing the memo. In contrast, if the unknown facts are less important, go ahead and write the memo, but tell the attorney, either in the statement of facts or in the discussion section, what facts are unknown.

You may not realize a fact is unknown until you have read the cases. For instance, in our example problem, at the time that she interviewed Ms.

Duncan, the attorney did not ask Ms. Duncan whether the process server had tried to serve her at the halfway house or on any other occasions. However, now that you have read *Torres v. Arnco Constr., Inc.*, you know that this fact is potentially significant.

Question

In the Duncan case, what other facts would you like to know? Are any of those unknown facts ones that you need to know before you can write the memo?

§7.3.2 Select an Organizational Scheme

As a general rule, begin your statement of facts with an introductory sentence or paragraph that identifies the parties and the issue. Then present the facts using one of three organizational schemes: a chronological organizational scheme, a topical organizational scheme, or a combination of the two, for example, a scheme in which you organize the facts by topic and then, within each topic, present the facts in chronological order.

The facts themselves usually dictate which organizational scheme will work best. If the case involves a series of events related by date, then the facts should be presented chronologically. If, however, there are a number of facts that are not related by date (for example, the description of several different pieces of property) or a number of unrelated events that occurred during the same time period (for example, four unrelated crimes committed by the defendant over the same two-day period), the facts should be organized by topic.

In our example case, the facts can be presented using either a scheme that is primarily chronological or a scheme that is primarily topical. See Examples 1 and 2.

As a general rule, do not set out the facts using bullet points. Instead, use sentences and paragraphs. In addition, as a general rule do not refer to the parties by just their first names.

P R A C T I C E
POINTER

Statement of Facts with Facts Presented in Chronological Order   EXAMPLE 1

Elaine Duncan has contacted our office asking for assistance in overturning a default judgment. You have asked me to determine whether the service of process was valid.

On February 1, 2006, Ms. Duncan entered an inpatient drug treatment program in Miami, Florida. She remained in the program until March 27, 2006, when she moved into a residential treatment house for recovering addicts.

During April, May, and June 2006, Ms. Duncan was a full-time resident at the halfway house. She had a bedroom in the house, ate her meals there, and had some of her possessions there. In addition, when she applied for jobs in May and June, she listed the halfway house address as her address.

Beginning in July 2006, Ms. Duncan began spending less time at the halfway house and more time with her sister, Elizabeth Webster, who is 32. During July and August 2006, Ms. Duncan usually spent weeknights at the halfway house and Friday, Saturday, and Sunday nights at her sister's house. Because she was spending time at her sister's house, Ms. Duncan moved some of her clothing and personal effects into her sister's house. When she renewed her driver's license in August 2006, Ms. Duncan listed her sister's address as her address.

On Wednesday, July 26, 2006, a process server went to Ms. Webster's house and asked for Elaine Duncan. When Ms. Webster told the process server that "Elaine isn't here today," the process server handed the summons to Ms. Webster and told her that Ms. Duncan "needed to go to court."

Ms. Webster will testify that she never gave the summons to her sister. Because she thought that the papers related to some of Ms. Duncan's unpaid bills, she simply put the summons in a shoebox in the kitchen with a stack of Ms. Duncan's other mail. Ms. Duncan says she never received the summons and, as a result, did not respond. The return of service is regular on its face.

Ms. Duncan has been employed since August 1, 2006, and she has lived in her own apartment since September 1, 2006. Her voter's registration card lists the address that she lived at before she entered the treatment program.

There is nothing in the record that indicates whether the plaintiff tried to personally serve Ms. Duncan or whether it tried to serve her at the halfway house.

EXAMPLE 2   ## Statement of Facts with Facts Organized by Topic

You have asked me to determine whether the service of process on one of our clients, Elaine Duncan, is valid.

During the past six months, Ms. Duncan has lived in three places. From February 1, 2006, until March 27, 2006, Ms. Duncan was a patient in an inpatient drug treatment program in Miami, Florida. On March 27, 2006, she moved into an halfway house for recovering addicts. During April, May, and June, Ms. Duncan was a full-time resident at the halfway house. She had a bedroom in the house, ate her meals there, and had some of her possessions there. In addition, Ms. Duncan listed the halfway house address on job applications.

Beginning in July 2006, Ms. Duncan began spending more time at her sister's house. During July and August 2006, Ms. Duncan spent weeknights at the halfway house and Friday, Saturday, and Sunday nights at her sister's house. Because she was spending time at her sister's house, Ms. Duncan moved some of her clothing and personal effects into her sister's house. When she renewed her driver's licence in August 2006, Ms. Duncan listed her sister's address as her address.

On Wednesday, July 26, 2006, a process server went to Ms. Duncan's sister's house and asked for Elaine Duncan. When Ms. Duncan's sister, Ms. Webster, told the process server that "Elaine isn't here today," the process server handed the summons to Ms. Webster and told her that Ms. Duncan "needed to go to court."

Ms. Webster, who is 32, will testify that she never gave the summons to her sister. Because she thought that the paper related to some of Ms. Duncan's unpaid bills, she simply put the summons in a shoebox in the kitchen with a stack of Ms. Duncan's other mail. Ms. Duncan says she never received the summons and complaint, and as a result, she did not respond. The return of service is regular on its face. There is nothing in the record that indicates whether the plaintiff tried to personally serve Ms. Duncan or whether he tried to serve her at the halfway house.

Question

Is one example better than the other example? Why or why not?

If you are using a chronological organizational scheme, try to start the sentence that follows your introduction with a date. In addition, start many but not all of the following sentences with dates.

In contrast, if you are using a topical organizational scheme, try to use topic sentences that identify the topics. Do not, however, include law or argue the facts.

---

§7.3.3 Present the Facts Accurately and Objectively

In writing the statement of facts for an objective memorandum, present the facts accurately and objectively. Do not include facts that are not in your file, and do not set out legal conclusions, misstate facts, leave out facts that are legally significant, or present the facts so that they favor one side over the other. In the following example, the author has violated all of these "rules."

Poor Statement of Facts   EXAMPLE

Hoping to obtain a default judgment against Ms. Duncan, the plaintiff had the sheriff serve the summons and complaint at Ms. Duncan's sister's house, not at the halfway house where Ms. Duncan was actually living. Although Ms. Duncan occasionally visited her sister at her sister's house, she did not keep any of her personal belongings at her sister's house.

In the first sentence, the author violates the first two rules. First, she sets out facts that are not in the record when she states that the plaintiff hoped to get a default judgment and when she states that the plaintiff had a sheriff serve Ms. Duncan at her sister's house, not at the halfway house. Second, she sets out a legal conclusion when she states that the defendant was actually living at the halfway house. Because a person's usual place of abode is the place where the defendant is actually living, in the context of this case, the statement that the defendant was actually living in the halfway house is a legal conclusion. In the second sentence, the author violates the last three rules. The author misstates the facts when she states that Ms. Duncan did not keep any personal belongings at her sister's house; she leaves out legally significant facts when she does not include the fact that Ms. Duncan used her sister's address when she renewed her driver's license; and she presents the facts in a light favorable to her client when she states that Ms. Duncan only occasionally visited her sister.

§ 7.3.4 Checklist for Critiquing the First Draft of the Statement of Facts

A. Content

- The writer has included all of the legally significant facts.
- When appropriate, the writer included emotionally significant facts.
- The writer included enough background facts that a person not familiar with the case can understand what happened.
- The writer has identified the unknown facts.
- The writer presented the facts accurately.
- The writer presented the facts objectively.
- The writer has not included legal conclusions in the statement of facts.

B. Organization

- The writer has included an introductory sentence or paragraph that identifies the parties and the nature of the dispute.
- The writer has used one of the conventional organizational schemes: chronological, topical, or a combination of chronological and topical.

§ 7.4 Drafting the Issue Statement, or Question Presented

The issue statement, also called the question presented, establishes the memo's focus: it identifies the applicable statute or common law rule; it sets out the legal question; and it summarizes the facts that will be significant in deciding that question.

§ 7.4.1 Decide How Many Issue Statements You Should Have and the Order in Which They Should Be Listed

By convention, you should have the same number of issue statements as "parts" to the discussion section. Accordingly, if you have three issue statements — whether service of process was adequate, whether the statute of limitations has run, and whether the defendant is entitled to judgment as a matter of law — you should also have three parts to the discussion section, one corresponding to each of the three issues. If, however, you have only one issue statement — for example, whether service of process is valid — your discussion section will have only one part.

As a general rule, do not treat each element as a separate issue. For example, in our example case, do not treat usual place of abode as one issue, person residing therein who is 15 or older as a second issue, and informing about the contents as a third issue.

P R A C T I C E

POINTER

Convention also dictates that in a multi-issue memo you list the issues in the same order in which you discuss those issues in the discussion section. The first issue statement will correspond to the first section of the discussion section, the second will correspond to the second section, and so on.

§ 7.4.2 Select a Format

The two most common formats for an issue statement are the "under-does-when" format and the "whether" format. This chapter discusses the under-does-when format, and Chapter 10 discusses the whether format.

The under-does-when format is easier to use because the format forces you to include all the essential information. After the word "under," insert a reference to the applicable law; after the verb (for example, "does," "is," or "may"), insert the legal question; and after "when," insert the most important of the legally significant facts:

Under [insert reference to applicable law],
does/is/may [insert legal question]
when [insert the most important legally significant facts]?

a. Reference to Applicable Law

If it is to provide the reader with useful information, the reference to the rule of law cannot be too specific or too general. For example, in our sample problem, a reference to just the statute would be too specific: very few attorneys would know that Fla. Stat. § 48.031 (2004) deals with service of process. Similarly, a reference to "Florida law" is too broad: hundreds of cases are filed each year in which the issue is governed by Florida law.

Reference to the Rule of Law is Too Specific   EXAMPLE 1

Under Fla. Stat. § 48.031 (2004), . . .

EXAMPLE 2   **Reference to the Rule of Law is Too General**

Under Florida law, . . .

EXAMPLE 3   **Appropriate References**

Under Florida's service of process statute . . .
Under Flordia's service of process statute, Fla. Stat. § 48.031 (2004), ...

If you identify the "topic" in your statement of the legal question, you can refer to the statute by number in your reference to the rule of law. For example, in some instances the following format works well:

P R A C T I C E

Under Fla. Stat. § 48.031 (2004), was the service of process valid when . . .

---

b. The Legal Question

After identifying the applicable law, set out the legal question. In doing so, make sure that your statement of the legal question is neither too narrow nor too broad. If stated too narrowly, your statement of the legal question will not cover all of the issues and subissues; if stated too broadly, the question does not serve its function of focusing the reader's attention on the real issue.

EXAMPLE 1   **Legal Questions That Are Too Narrow**

- was the summons left at Ms. Duncan's usual place of abode. . . .
- was the summons left at the place where Ms. Duncan was actually living. . . .
- did the process server inform Ms. Webster about the contents of the summons. . . .

EXAMPLE 2   **Legal Questions That Are Too Broad**

- was the defendant entitled to a default judgment. . . .
- were Ms. Duncan's rights violated. . . .

EXAMPLE 3   **Legal Questions That Are Properly Framed**

- was service valid . . .
- was Ms. Duncan properly served . . .

- was service at Ms. Duncan's sister's house valid. . . .
- was the substituted service on the defendant's sister at the sister's house valid. . . .

Question

What are the pros and cons of each of the options set out in Example 3? For example, what are the pros and cons of saying "was service left at the defendant's usual place of abode with a person residing therein who was 15 years old or older and was that person notified of the contents of the summons and complaint" versus saying "was service valid?"

c. Legally Significant Facts

In our legal system, questions are always decided in the context of specific facts. As a consequence, you need to include in your issue statement those facts that the court will consider in answering the legal question.

In Example 1 set out below, the author has not included enough facts: while he has included the facts that the court would consider in deciding whether the process server informed the person served of the contents of the documents, he has not included facts that the court would consider in deciding whether the summons was left at Ms. Duncan's usual place of abode with a person 15 or older residing therein.

Author Has Not Included Enough Facts   EXAMPLE 1

Under Flordia's service of process statute, Fla. Stat. § 48.031 (2004), was the service valid when the process server told Ms. Webster that Ms. Duncan "needed to go to court"?

In contrast, in Example 2, the author has included too many facts. As a result, the issue statement is too long, and many attorneys would not take the time to read through it.

Author Has Included Too Many Facts   EXAMPLE 2

Under Florida's service of process statute, was substituted service on Ms. Duncan's sister at the sister's house valid when (1) Ms. Duncan was a patient in an inpatient drug treatment program in Miami from February 1, 2006, until March 27, 2006; (2) Ms. Duncan moved into a halfway house for recovering addicts on March 27, 2006; (3) during April, May, and June 2006, Ms. Duncan was a full-time resident at the halfway house, where she had a bedroom, where she ate her meals, and where she had some possessions; (4) during April and May 2006, Ms. Duncan listed the halfway house address on job applications; (5) beginning in July 2006, Ms. Duncan began spending less time at the halfway house and more time at her sister's home; (6) during July and August 2006, Ms. Duncan usually spent weeknights at the halfway house and Friday, Saturday, and Sunday nights at her sister's house; (7) when Ms. Duncan renewed her driver's license in August 2006, she listed her sister's address as her address; (8) on July 26, 2006, a process server went to Ms. Webster's house and asked for Elaine Duncan; (9) when Ms. Webster told the process server that "Elaine isn't here today," the process server handed the summons to Ms. Webster and told her that Ms. Duncan "needed to go to court"; and (10) Ms. Webster is 32 years old and lives at the house where she received the summons?

Examples 3 and 4 are much better: they include the key facts without going into too much detail.

EXAMPLE 3   ## Good Example

Under Florida's service of process statute, was Ms. Duncan properly served when (1) service was made on Ms. Duncan's 32-year-old sister on a Wednesday at Ms. Duncan's sister's house; (2) during the month when service was made, Ms. Duncan spent weeknights at a halfway house where she had a room, ate meals, and kept belongings and spent Friday, Saturday, and Sunday nights at her sister's house, where she had some belongings; (3) Ms. Duncan listed the halfway house address on job applications but her sister's address on her driver's license; (4) the process server told Ms. Duncan's sister that Ms. Duncan needed to go to court; and (5) Ms. Duncan's sister did not give the summons to Ms. Duncan, and Ms. Duncan states that she did not receive notice?

EXAMPLE 4   ## Good Example

Under Florida's statute authorizing substituted service of proces, was service on the defendant's adult sister at the sister's house valid when the defendant spent weeknights at a halfway house and Friday, Saturday, and Sunday nights at her sister's house; when the service was made on a weekday; when the process server told the defendant's sister that the defendant "needed to go to court"; and when the defendant states that she did not receive notice?

Question

Do you like Example 3 or Example 4 better? Why?

§ 7.4.3 Make Your Issue Statement Easy to Read

It is not enough to include the right information in your issue statement. You must also present that information in such a way that your issue statement is easy to read. The "under-does-when" format helps you write a readable issue statement by forcing you to use the three slots in a sentence:

$$\underline{\hspace{4cm}}, \quad \underline{\hspace{3cm}}, \quad \underline{\hspace{5cm}}.$$
introductory phrase or clause   main clause   modifiers/dependent clauses

The reference to the rule of law goes into the introductory phrase or clause; the legal question goes into the main clause; and the key facts go into the list of modifiers or dependent clauses at the end of the sentence. There are, however, some other things that you can do to make your issue statement easier to read. First, avoid having more than one introductory phrase or clause. Second, in drafting the main clause, try to use strong subjects and verbs. Third, in listing the facts, use parallel constructions for all the items in your list. Finally, if there are more than a few items in your list of facts, use enumeration or start each item in the list with the same word — for example, start each item in your list with "that" or "when."

§ 7.4.4 Checklist For Critiquing the First Draft of the Issue Statement

A. Content

- The reference to the rule of law is neither too broad nor too narrow.
- The legal question is properly focused.
- The most significant of the legally significant facts have been included.
- Legal conclusions have not been set out as facts.

B. Format

- The writer has used one of the conventional formats — for example, the "under-does-when" format.

§ 7.5 Drafting the Brief Answer

The brief answer serves a purpose similar to that served by the formal conclusion: it tells the attorney how you think a court will decide an issue and why. It is not, however, as detailed as the formal conclusion.

§ 7.5.1 Include a Brief Answer for Each Issue Statement

As a general rule, include a separate brief answer for each issue statement. In addition, start each of your brief answers with a one- or two-word short answer. The words that are typically used are "probably," and "probably not." After this one- or two-word answer, briefly explain your answer.

§ 7.5.2 Keep Your Brief Answer Short

In writing your brief answer, keep a couple of things in mind. First, remember your audience and purpose. You are writing to an attorney who needs an objective evaluation of the client's case. Second, make sure that you answer the question you set out in your issue statement and that you match the style you used in your issue statement. For example, if in setting out the legal question, you asked whether Ms. Duncan was properly served, then your short answer should answer that question. In addition, if in writing your issue statement you personalized the issue statement by using the parties' names, you should personalize the brief answer. In contrast, if you wrote a more generic issue statement, you should write a more generic brief answer. Third, be specific. Tell the attorney which elements you or the other side will or will not be able to prove. Finally, make sure that you get the burden of proof right. If you have personalized your issue statement and your client has the burden of proof, talk about what your client can and cannot prove. If, however, the other side has the burden of proof, talk about what it can and cannot prove. In contrast, if you wrote a more generic issue statement, talk about what the court will and will not conclude. While some attorneys will want you to discuss all of the elements, others will want you to discuss only the disputed elements.

EXAMPLE 1   ## Personalized Issue Statement and Brief Answer

Issue

Under Florida's service of process statute, was Ms. Duncan properly served when (1) service was made on Ms. Duncan's 32-year-old sister on a Wednesday at Ms. Duncan's sister's house; (2) during the month when service was made, Ms. Duncan spent weeknights at a halfway house where she had a room, ate meals, and kept belongings and spent Friday, Saturday, and Sunday nights at her sister's house, where she had some belongings; (3) Ms. Duncan listed the halfway house address on job applications but her sister's address on her driver's license; (4) the process server told Ms. Duncan's sister that Ms. Duncan needed to go to court; and (5) Ms. Duncan's sister did not give the summons to Ms. Duncan, and Ms. Duncan states that she did not receive notice?

Brief Answer

Probably not. Because the summons and complaint were given to Ms. Duncan's adult sister at the sister's house, Ms. Duncan will have to concede that the service was made on a person 15 years old or older who was living at the house at which the service was made. In addition, because the process server told Ms. Duncan's sister that Ms. Duncan needed to go to court, Ms. Duncan cannot meet her burden of proving that the person served was not informed of the contents of the documents. However, because Ms. Duncan was not actually living at her sister's house on the day that service was made, she can probably meet her burden of proving that her sister's house was not her usual place of abode.

EXAMPLE 2   ## Generic Issue Statement and Brief Answer

Issue

Under Florida's statute authorizing substituted service of proces, was service at the defendant's adult sister's house valid when the defendant spent weeknights at a halfway house and Friday, Saturday, and Sunday nights at her sister's house; the service was made on a Wednesday; the process server told the defendant's sister that the defendant "needed to go to court"; and the defendant states that she did not receive notice?

Brief Answer

Probably not. The court will conclude that the service was made on a person 15 years old or older living at the place where service was made and that the process server informed the person served of the contents of the documents. In addition, the court will probably conclude that the service was not made at the defendant's usual place of abode because the defendant was not actually living at the house on the day service was made.

Question

Which of the above formats do you prefer? Why?

§ 7.5.3 Checklist for Critiquing the First Draft of the Brief Answer

A. Content

- The writer has predicted but not guaranteed how the issue will be decided.
- The writer has briefly explained his or her prediction — for example, the writer has explained which elements will be easy to prove and which will be more difficult and why.

B. Format

- A separate brief answer has been included for each issue statement.
- The answer begins with a one- or two-word short answer. This one- or two-word short answer is then followed by a short explanation.

§ 7.6 Organizing the Discussion Section

In reading the discussion section, attorneys expect to see certain types of information, and they expect to see that information presented in a particular order.

These expectations are not born of whim. Instead, they are based on conventional formats, which are themselves based on the way attorneys think about legal questions. In analyzing a legal problem, most attorneys begin with the law. What is the applicable statute or common law rule? Most attorneys then apply that law to the facts of the client's case. Are both sides likely to agree on the conclusion, or will the application of the law be in dispute?

If the application is in dispute, most attorneys look to see how the law has been applied in similar cases. Because our system is a system based on precedent, the courts usually decide similar, or analogous, cases in a like manner.

Most attorneys then consider the arguments that each side is likely to make. What types of factual arguments are the opposing sides likely to make? What types of arguments based on the analogous cases are the sides likely to make? Given the purpose and policies underlying the statute or rule, what types of policy arguments might each side make?

Finally, most attorneys make a prediction. Given the facts, rules, cases, and arguments, how will a court decide each element?

The discussion section reflects this process. It contains the same components — rules, analogous cases, arguments, and mini-conclusions — in the same order. At its simplest, and at its best, the discussion section analyzes the problem, walking the attorney step-by-step through the law, cases, and arguments to the probable outcome.

§ 7.6.1 Select a Template

Just as there are standard house plans, there are standard plans for discussion sections. While builders have blueprints for ramblers, two-story homes, and split levels, attorneys have templates for problems involving an analysis of elements, for problems that require the balancing of competing interests, and for issues of first impression — that is, issues that have not yet been decided by the courts. In this chapter and in Chapter 10 we discuss one of those templates — the template for an elements analysis. In this chapter, we show you how to use that template to organize a memo involving a statute, and in Chapter 10 we show you how to use the template to organize a memo that involves a common law rule. Chapter 13 shows you how to organize a memo that involves a question of first impression and that involves, at least in part, the balancing of competing interests.

When you use the template for an elements analysis, begin the discussion section with an introductory section in which you set out the general rules. In this introductory section, introduce and set out the applicable statute or common law rule, explain who has the burden of proof and what the burden is, and set out any other rules that apply to all of the elements. In addition, if you expect that one or both of the parties will make policy arguments, explain the policies underlying the statute or common law rule. Typically, you will end the introductory section by doing one of two things. If you are going to discuss both the disputed and undisputed elements in separate subsections, end your introductory section with a roadmap that tells the attorney which elements the party with the burden of proof can or cannot prove or, if you are using a more generic writing style, that tells the attorney which elements are and are not likely to be in dispute. In the alternative, if you decide to raise and dismiss the undisputed elements at the end of your introductory section, raise and dismiss the undisputed element or elements, and then end the introductory section with a roadmap that lets your reader know how the rest of your discussion section is organized.

An element is undisputed if both sides are likely to agree that the element is either met or not met. In contrast, an element is in dispute if one side will argue that the element is met and the other side will argue that the element is not met.

P R A C T I C E

After the introductory section, discuss the elements. If you are using the first option set out above and are discussing both the disputed and undisputed elements in separate subsections, discuss the elements in the order that you listed them in your introductory section. What you include in your discussion of each of these elements will depend on whether the element is or is not in dispute. If an element is not likely to be in dispute, identify the element, set out any rules that the courts may apply in determining whether that element is met, and then apply those rules to the facts of your case. If, however, the element will be in dispute, your discussion will be much longer. In addition to setting out any rules that the courts apply in determining whether the disputed element is met, provide the attorney with the examples of how those rules have been applied in similar or analogous cases, and set out and evaluate each side's arguments.

Chart 7.3 provides you with a template for discussing a problem that requires an elements analysis. Note that the template is the same template that you used to record your research notes.

Chart 7.3   **Standard Template for an Elements Analysis**

Discussion

Introductory section that sets out the general rules:

- If one or both sides will make a policy argument, describe the policies underlying the statute or rule. (Occasionally it works well to describe the policies before introducing the statute.)
- Introduce and set out the applicable statute(s).
- Explain which side has the burden of proof and what that burden is.
- Set out any other rules that apply to all of the elements.
- End the section (1) by raising and dismissing the undisputed elements and by providing the attorney with a roadmap for the rest of your discussion or (2) by providing the attorney with a roadmap for the rest of the discussion. (You will then discuss all of the elements in order.)

Note: In the following material, we assume that you have picked the second option and, after the roadmap, you discussed all of the elements in order.

A.   First Element

- If the first element is not likely to be in dispute, simply set out and apply the applicable rule.
- If the first element is likely to be in dispute, set out the following information:
  1. Specific rules for the first element
  2. Examples of how specific rules have been applied in analogous cases
  3. Arguments
  4. Mini-conclusion for the first element

B.   Second Element

- If the second element is not likely to be in dispute, simply set out and apply the applicable rule.
- If the second element is likely to be in dispute, set out the following information:
  1. Specific rules for second element
  2. Examples of how the specific rules have been applied in analogous cases

3. Arguments
4. Mini-conclusion for second element

C. Third Element

- If the third element is not likely to be in dispute, simply set out and apply the applicable rule.
- If the third element is likely to be in dispute, set out the following information:
  1. Specific rules for the third element
  2. Examples of how specific rules have been applied in analogous cases
  3. Arguments
  4. Mini-conclusion for third element

D. Fourth Element

- If the fourth element is not likely to be in dispute, simply set out and apply the applicable rule.
- If the fourth element is likely to be in dispute, set out the following information:
  1. Specific rules for fourth element
  2. Examples of how specific rules have been applied in analogous cases
  3. Arguments
  4. Mini-conclusion for fourth element

§ 7.6.2 Modify the Template So That It Works for Your Problem

Just as a builder may need to modify a standard blueprint so that the house fits on the lot and satisfies the buyer's preferences, you may need to modify the standard template so that it works for your problem and your reader. For example, if a statute has only two elements, you will need only two subsections. Likewise, if the statute has five elements, you will need five subsections.

In our example problem, we initially identified four elements: (1) whether the summons was left at Ms. Duncan's usual place of abode; (2) whether the summons was left with a person who was 15 years old or older; (3) whether the person with whom the summons was left was residing therein; and (4) whether the process server informed the person served of the contents. See pages 87-88. In reading the cases, however, we observed that most courts treat what we labeled as the second and third elements as one element: the service must be made on a person 15 years or older residing therein. Because combining these two elements in this way makes sense (the two elements are closely related and neither is likely to be in dispute) and will save room, we decide to do what the courts have done and treat these two elements as a single element. See Chart 7.4.

Frequently, there is more than one way to list the elements. In these situations, the safest approach is to list the elements in the same way that the majority of the courts has listed them.

Chart 7.4   **Revised Template**

Template for an Elements Analysis

Discussion

Introductory section that sets out the general rules:

- Set out policies underlying Fla. Stat. § 48.031.
- Introduce and set out Fla. Stat. § 48.031.
- Explain which side has the burden of proof and what that burden is.
- Set out any other rules that apply to all of the elements.
- End with a roadmap that tells the attorney that Ms. Duncan should concede that the second element is met and that she will not be able to prove the third element. However, she may be able to prove that the service was not at her usual place of abode.

A.   Usual Place of Abode (disputed element)

1. Specific rules
2. Examples of how specific rules have been applied in analogous cases
3. Arguments *— parties re' rule &*
4. Mini-conclusion *its application*

B.   Age and Residing Therein (undisputed element)

1. Set out applicable rules *& apply facts*
2. Apply applicable rules

C.   Informing of Contents (disputed element)

1. Specific rules
2. Examples of how specific rules have been applied in analogous cases
3. Arguments
4. Mini-conclusion

§ 7.7   Drafting the Introductory, or General Rule, Section

As you learned in section 7.6, you will usually begin your discussion section with an introductory section in which you set out not only the general rule but also the rules relating to the burden of proof. In addition, depending on the problem, you may also include other rules that apply to all of the elements and a sentence or paragraph in which you explain the policies underlying the general rule. Finally, you will usually include a roadmap that tells the attorney which elements are and are not in dispute. You may also choose to raise and dismiss the undisputed elements.

§ 7.7.1 Decide What Information You Need and Want to Include in the Introductory Section

The first step is to list the information that you want to include in your introductory section. In preparing this list, keep two things in mind. First, remember your audience. If the attorney for whom you are preparing the memo knows little or nothing about the area of law, provide the attorney with an overview of the area of law, distinguishing closely related doctrines and defining key terms. If, however, the attorney knows the area of law, do not start at square one. Second, distinguish between general rules, which are rules that apply to all of the elements, and specific rules, which are rules that apply to only one of the elements. Include only general rules in your introductory section. Save the specific rules for the discussion of the element to which they apply.

In our service of process problem, we can presume that the attorney will have taken civil procedure as a law student and will, therefore, know the basics. Thus, in drafting the introductory section, we will not need to explain the difference between personal service and substituted service or define those terms. We will, however, want to set out the applicable portion of the statute, the rules relating to the burden of proof, the policies underlying the statute, and the fact that the courts have said that the statute should be narrowly construed to assure service. In addition, at the end we will want to include a roadmap.

§ 7.7.2 Order the Information

The next step is to put the items on your list in order. In most instances, you will want to set out more general information before more specific information. Thus, when drafting your general rule section, you will usually want to use an inverted pyramid: broad rules first, narrower rules next, and exceptions last. See section 23.3.

More general information

More specific information

Exceptions

In our example problem, the most general information is the policies that underlie the statute. The next most general information is the statute itself, and the most specific information is the rule relating to the burden of proof.

Thus, in our example problem we want to present the information in the following order.

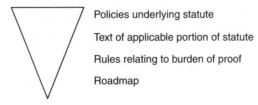

Policies underlying statute

Text of applicable portion of statute

Rules relating to burden of proof

Roadmap

The approach is similar when there is more than one applicable statutory section. Instead of listing the statutes in the order in which they appear in the code, set out the more general statutory sections first. For example, set out the statutory section that explains the purpose of the statute before the statutory section that has the rule, and set out the statutory section that has the rule before the statutory section containing definitions.

If you are not sure how to order the information in your introductory section, look at the cases. Because most courts set out more general information before more specific information, you can use the courts' opinions as a guide.

P R A C T I C E
POINTER

---

§ 7.7.3. Prepare the First Draft

In preparing the first draft, do not do what the author of Example 1 did, which is to string together a series of quotations, at least some of which set out the same rules using slightly different language.

Poor Draft: The Author Has Simply Strung Together a Series of Quotations

EXAMPLE 1

Discussion

"The purpose of service of process is to advise the defendant that an action has been commenced and to warn the defendant that he or she must appear in a timely manner to state such defenses as are available." *Torres v. Arnco Constr., Inc.*, 867 So. 2d 583 (Fla. 5th DCA 2004) *citing Shurman v. Atlantic. Mortg. & Inv. Corp.*, 795 So. 2d 952 (Fla. 2001); *Abbate v. Provident Nat'l Bank,* 631 So. 2d 312 (Fla. 5th DCA 1994). "It is well settled that the fundamental purpose of service is "to give proper notice to the defendant in the case that he is answerable to the claim of plaintiff and, therefore, to vest jurisdiction in the court entertaining the controversy." *Shurman,* 795 So. 2d 952, 953-54 (Fla. 2001) *citing State ex rel. Merritt v. Heffernan,* 142 Fla. 496, 195 So. 145, 147 (1940). Therefore, "a judgment entered without due service of process is void." *Torres,* 867 So. 2d at 586."

The statute specifically states:

Service of original process is made by delivering a copy of it to the person to be served with a copy of the complaint, petition, or other initial pleading or paper or by leaving the copies at his or her usual place of abode with any person residing therein who is 15 years of age or older and informing the person of their contents. Minors who are or have been married shall be served as provided in this section.

Fla. Stat. § 48.031(1)(a) (2004).

"The statutes regulating service of process are to be strictly construed to assure that a defendant is notified of the proceedings." *Torres*, 867 So. 2d at 586. "Indeed, because statutes authorizing substituted service are exceptions to the general rule requiring a defendant to be served personally, due process requires strict compliance with their statutory requirements." *Id.*

"[A] process server's return of service on a defendant which is regular on its face is presumed to be valid absent clear and convincing evidence presented to the contrary." *Telf Corp. v. Gomez,* 671 So. 2d 818 (Fla. 3d DCA 1996). "The simple denial of service is not sufficient." *Id.* at 819.

Thus, because Ms. Duncan is challenging the validity of the service, she will have the burden of proof. Ms. Duncan should concede that the summons was left with a person who is 15 years old or older residing therein. In addition, although the court will probably decide that Ms. Duncan's sister was informed of the contents of the documents, Ms. Duncan may be able to prove that the summons was not left at her usual place of abode.

Question

Why is it a bad idea to just cut and paste the rules that you set out in your research notes into your introductory section?

Instead of just cutting and pasting the rules from your research notes into your first draft, take the time to sort through the rules. Then draft your introduction, setting out each rule clearly and concisely.

While some attorneys will want you to paraphrase the rules that you draw from the cases, other attorneys will want you to use quotations. Thus, before you do your first draft, check with your supervising attorney to see which style he or she prefers.

PRACTICE
POINTER

EXAMPLE 2   **Better Draft: Author Has Set Out Each Rule Only Once**

Discussion

The fundamental purpose of service of process is to give defendants notice of claims that have been filed against them and to provide them with an opportunity to defend their rights. *Shurman v. Atlantic Mortg. & Inv. Corp.,* 795 So. 2d 952, 953-54 (Fla. 2001). Because it is important that litigants receive notice of actions against them, courts strictly construe and enforce statutes governing service of process. *Id.* at 954. In this case, the applicable portion of the statute reads as follows:

Service of original process is made by delivering a copy of it to the person to be served with a copy of the complaint, petition, or other initial pleading or

> paper or by leaving the copies at his or her usual place of abode with any person residing therein who is 15 years of age or older and informing the person of their contents. Minors who are or have been married shall be served as provided in this section.

Fla. Stat. § 48.031(a)(1) (2004).

Although the party seeking to invoke the jurisdiction of the court has the burden of proving that service was proper, if the return is regular on its face, the courts presume that the service was valid. *Thompson v. State, Dept. of Revenue,* 867 So. 2d 603, 605 (Fla. 1st DCA 2004); *Magazine v. Bedoya,* 475 So. 2d 1035, 1035 (Fla. 3d DCA 1985). In such instances, the party challenging the service has the burden of presenting clear and convincing evidence that the service was invalid. *Id.*

In this case, Ms. Duncan will have to concede that the summons was left with a person 15 years or older who was residing at the house where the summons and complaint were served. In addition, it is unlikely that Ms. Duncan will be able to prove that her sister was not informed of the contents of the documents. Ms. Duncan may, however, be able to present clear and convincing evidence that the summons was not left at her usual place of abode.

You do not, however, have to set out the entire statute. If only part of the statute is applicable, set out only that part.

Better Draft: Author Has Quoted Only the Applicable Portion of the Statute

Discussion

The fundamental purpose of service of process is to give defendants notice of claims that have been filed against them and to provide defendants with an opportunity to defend their rights. *Shurman v. Atlantic Mortg. & Inv. Corp.,* 795 So. 2d 952, 953-54 (Fla. 2001). Because it is important that litigants receive notice of actions against them, courts strictly construe and enforce statutes governing service of process. *Id.* at 954.

In Florida, substituted service can be made by leaving the copies at defendant's "usual place of abode with any person residing therein who is 15 years of age or older and informing the person of their contents." Fla. Stat. § 48.031(a)(1) (2004).

Although the party seeking to invoke the jurisdiction of the court has the burden of proving that service was proper, if the return is regular on its face, the courts presume that the service was valid. *Thompson v. State, Dept. of Revenue,* 867 So. 2d 603, 605 (Fla. 1st DCA 2004); *Magazine v. Bedoya,* 475 So. 2d 1035, 1035 (Fla. 3d DCA. 1985). In such instances, the party challenging the service has the burden of presenting clear and convincing evidence that the service was invalid. *Id.*

In this case, Ms. Duncan will have to concede that the summons was left with a person 15 years or older who was residing at the house where the summons and complaint were served. In addition, it is unlikely that Ms. Duncan will be able to prove that her sister was not informed of the contents of the documents. Ms. Duncan may, however, be able to present clear and convincing evidence that the summons was not left at her usual place of abode.

If your quotation has fifty words or more, you need to set it out as a block quote, indenting five spaces on the left and five spaces on the right margins and dropping the quotation marks. In contrast, if the quote has fewer than fifty words, you may include it in the text of your sentence. See Rules 47.4 and 47.5 in the *ALWD Citation Manual* and Rule 5.1 in *The Bluebook*. If you use Word, you can determine how many words are in your quote by highlighting the quoted language, selecting "Tools," and then selecting "Word Count."

§7.7.4 Include a Citation to Authority for Each Rule You Set Out

You must include a citation to authority for each rule that you set out in your memo. This authority may be a constitutional provision, a statute, a regulation, a court rule, or a case.

In choosing an authority, you should always choose mandatory, or binding, authority over persuasive authority. See pages 26-27 in Chapter 2. For example, in choosing a case, choose cases from your jurisdiction over cases from other jurisdictions. In addition, you will usually want to choose decisions from higher courts over decisions from lower courts and more recent decisions over older decisions. The exception might be when the decisions of the jurisdiction's highest court — for example, your state's highest court — are quite old and there are more recent decisions from your state's intermediate court of appeals. If the decisions from both your state's highest court and intermediate court are mandatory authority, you may choose to cite the more recent decision from the state intermediate court of appeals. Although there may be times when you want to list more than one case to show the attorney that the rule is well established, avoid long string cites. Compare Example 1 above with Examples 2 and 3.

Do not cite unpublished decisions as authority for a rule. Instead, cite a published decision — for example, the case or cases that the unpublished decision cited as authority for the rule.

Question

In Examples 2 and 3 above, did the author cite to mandatory or persuasive authorities?

§ 7.8 Raising and Dismissing the Undisputed Elements

More often than not, one or more of the elements will not be in dispute. Although you cannot ignore these undisputed elements, you do not need to devote much space to them.

§ 7.8.1 Decide Where to Put Your Discussion of the Undisputed Elements

While some attorneys choose to raise and dismiss the undisputed elements at the end of their introductory section, others choose to discuss all of the elements in order. Compare the following examples. In Example 1 the author has raised and dismissed the undisputed element in her roadmap at the end of her introductory section. In contrast, in Example 2 the author has raised and dismissed the undisputed element in its own subsection.

EXAMPLE 1

Undiputed Elements Raised and Dismissed at the End of the Introductory Section

In this case, Ms. Duncan will have to concede that the summons and complaint were left with a person 15 years or older who was residing at the house where the summons and complaint were served. Ms. Duncan's sister is 32 years old, and she was served at her house. Ms. Duncan may, however, be able to present clear and convincing evidence that the summons and complaint were not left at her usual place of abode or that her sister was not informed of the contents.

EXAMPLE 2

Undisputed Elements Raised in Separate Subsections

A. Usual Place of Abode...

B. Person 15 Years Old or Older Residing Therein

In addition to leaving the summons at the defendant's usual place of abode, the process server must leave the summons with a person 15 years old or older residing therein. If the court concludes that Ms. Duncan's sister's house was Ms. Duncan's usual place of abode, Ms. Duncan should concede that the summons was left with a person residing therein who is at least 15 years old: Ms. Webster is 32 years old, and the summons and complaint were left with her at her house.

C. Notified of Contents . . .

Question

Which of the above approaches do you prefer? Why?

§ 7.8.2 Prepare the First Draft of Your Discussion of the Undisputed Elements

In most instances, your discussion of an undisputed element will be very short. You will identify the element, set out any applicable specific rules, and apply those rules to the facts of your case. Typically, you will not include descriptions of analogous cases. Compare the following examples.

EXAMPLE 1 | **Poor Draft of Undisputed Element: Author Has Set Out Conclusion Without Setting Out Facts That Support That Conclusion**

Ms. Duncan should concede that the second element, that the summons and complaint be left with a person 15 years or older residing therein, is met.

EXAMPLE 2 | **Poor Draft of Undisputed Element: Author Has Gone Into Too Much Detail on Undisputed Element**

For substitute service of process to be valid at a defendant's "usual place of abode," the summons must be left with a person residing therein who is 15 years of age or older. Fla. Stat. § 48.031 (2004). Although the statute does not specify the period of time an individual must occupy a home to be regarded as "residing therein," the courts do not require extended habitation. *Compare Magazine v. Bedoya*, 475 So. 2d 1035 (Fla. 3d DCA 1985) (six-week stay long enough to establish residency) *with Gamboa v. Jones*, 455 So. 2d 613 (Fla. 3d DCA 1984) (ten-day visit not sufficient to establish residency). Because she is 32, Ms. Webster satisfies the age requirement. From the facts given, it is unclear how long Ms. Webster has lived at the home in question; however, the memo indicated that she was served at "her house." Thus, unless other facts are presented, Ms. Webster appears to be the owner and primary resident of the house, and she has lived there long enough to establish residency. Therefore, the "residing therein" requirement is met.

Better Draft of Undisputed Element

EXAMPLE 3

In addition to leaving the summons at the defendant's usual place of abode, the process server must leave the summons with a person 15 years old or older residing therein. If the court concludes that Ms. Duncan's sister's house was Ms. Duncan's usual place of abode, Ms. Duncan should concede that the summons was left with a person residing therein who is at least 15 years old: Ms. Webster is 32 years old, and the summons and complaint were left with her at her house.

Better Draft of Undisputed Element

EXAMPLE 4

In this case, Ms. Duncan will have to concede that the summons and complaint were left with a person 15 years or older who was residing therein: the summons was left with Ms. Duncan's 32-year-old sister, who lives at the house where the summons was left.

Better Draft of Undisputed Element

EXAMPLE 5

A court will find that the second element is met. Because the summons was left with Ms. Duncan's 32-year-old sister, the age requirement is met. In addition, because Ms. Duncan's sister lives at the house where the summons was left, the "residing therein" requirement is met.

Question

Which example do you like better? Example 3? Example 4? Example 5? Why?

While some elements are clearly not in dispute and some are clearly in dispute, there will be elements that fall somewhere in between these two categories.

P R A C T I C E
POINTER

```
              ×
──────────────────────────────
  Not in dispute      In dispute
```

When you have an element that falls into this "in between" cateogry, you will usually do more than raise and dismiss the element but less than a full analysis. Alert the attorney to the fact that one side might have a weak argument, set out that argument, explain why the argument is weak, and then move on. For a more detailed discussion of "in between" elements, see page 240 in Chapter 10.

§ 7.9 Discussing the Disputed Elements

You will usually want to create a separate subsection for each of your disputed elements. Include a subheading that identifies the element and then set out the following information:

(1) the specific rules for that element;
(2) cases that illustrate how those specific rules have been applied;
(3) each side's arguments; and
(4) your prediction about how the court is likely to decide the element.

Although there are a number of different ways in which this information can be presented, this chapter shows you how to present this information using what we call "the script format." Like the under-does-when format for issue statements, the script format forces you to include all of the essential information in your discussion of a disputed element, and it forces you to give appropriate weight to each side's arguments. In Chapters 10 and 13 we show you how to use more integrated formats.

We call the format described in this section the "script format" because, when you use this format you are, in essence, setting out the script for the oral arguments relating to the disputed element: the party with the burden of proof presents its arguments; the other side presents its arguments; and the court decides whether the element is or is not met. Note that the script format involves inductive rather than deductive reasoning. Instead of beginning your discussion of a disputed element by setting out your conclusion, you set out your conclusion at the end.

---

§ 7.9.1 Set Out the Specific Rules

Begin your discussion of a disputed element by setting out the rules that relate to that element. For example, if the courts apply a particular test in determining whether the element is or is not met, set out that test. Similarly, if the courts have defined any terms, set out those definitions.

In drafting your specific rule section, use the same process you used in drafting the introductory section. Begin by listing all of the information you want to include in your specific rule section, and then order that information, setting out more general information before more specific information. Finally, draft the specific rule paragraph or paragraphs.

In drafting these paragraphs, keep the following in mind. First, include only those rules that apply to the element that you are currently discussing. Do not repeat general rules that you set out in your introductory section, and do not set out rules that apply to other elements. Second, avoid cutting and pasting all of the rules from your research notes. Instead, determine what the rules are, and then set out each rule once, using clear and concise language. Finally, remember to include a citation to authority for each rule you set out. Compare the following examples, both of which are examples of the specific rule paragraph for the "usual place of abode" element.

Poor Draft of Specific Rule Paragraph: Writer Has Simply Cut and Pasted Rules from Research Notes into Draft

EXAMPLE 1

The Florida courts have defined "usual place of abode" as "the fixed place of residence for the time being when the service is made." *Shurman v. Atlantic Mortg. & Inv. Corp.*, 795 So. 2d 952, 953-54 (Fla. 2001). "If a person has more than one residence, a summons must be served at the residence at which the defendant is actually living at the time of service." *Id.* at 954. As the Florida Supreme Court noted in *Shurman,* "the courts have frequently invalidated substituted service of process in cases where the defendant was not actually living at the place where service was made, even though process might have been delivered to a relative." *Torres v. Arnco Constr., Inc.*, 867 So. 2d 583, 586 (Fla. 5th DCA 2004).

Better Draft of Specific Rule Paragraph: Writer Has Identified the Rules and Then Set Out Each Rule Once Using Language That is Clear and Concise

EXAMPLE 2

If a defendant has more than one residence, the defendant's usual place of abode is the place where the defendant was actually living at the time of service. *Shurman v. Atlantic Mortg. & Inv. Corp.*, 795 So. 2d 952, 953-54 (Fla. 2001). It is not enough that the summons and complaint are left with a relative. *Torres v. Arnco Constr., Inc.*, 867 So. 2d 583, 586 (Fla. 5th DCA 2004).

Question

Why is Example 2 better than Example 1?

§ 7.9.2 Describe the Analogous Cases

When an element is in dispute, most attorneys want to see not only the specific rules but also examples of how those specific rules have been applied in analogous cases. Thus, if an element is in dispute and there are analogous cases, you will usually want to include descriptions of some of those cases.

In drafting the analogous case section, always keep in mind why you are including cases. Do not include analogous cases just to prove to the attorney that you located and read the cases; the analogous case section is not there to prove that you did a lot of work. Instead, include analogous case descriptions because the case descriptions will help the attorney understand the rules or because either your side or the other side is likely to use the cases to support its position.

a. Identify the Analogous Cases

The first step is to identify the potentially analogous cases. If you have used the template set out on page 102, these cases will be listed under the heading "analogous cases." If, however, you did not use a template to record research results, you will need to go back through your cases, identifying those cases in which the court not only set out the specific rules but also applied those rules.

In our example problem, we identified five analogous cases: a 1940 Florida Supreme Court case, a 2001 Florida Supreme Court Case, and three Florida District Court of Appeals cases. See pages 106-112.

In looking for analogous cases, look first for cases from your jurisdiction. If you do not find any, you can then look for analogous cases from other jurisdictions. However, before deciding to use an out-of-state case, make sure that the other state's specific rules are the same as your state's specific rules.

P R A C T I C E

---

b. Sort the Cases

Once you have identified the analogous cases, sort those cases — for example, put the case or cases in which the court held that the elements were met in one stack and the cases in which the court held that the element was not met in a different stack.

EXAMPLE   **Case List**

Cases in which element was met	Cases in which element not met
State ex rel. Merritt v. Heffernan	*Alvarez v. State Farm Mut. Auto. Ins.*
	Shurman v. Atl. Mortg. & Inv. Corp.
	Torres v. Arnco Constr., Inc.
	Thompson v. State, Dept. of Revenue

---

c. Analyze and Synthesize the Cases

It is at this step that the real work begins. Because you want to do more than provide the attorney with "book reports" on the cases you have located and read, you need to analyze each of the cases and then synthesize the group.

Analysis requires you to read the cases carefully and critically, identifying the issue that was before the court, the standard of review that the court applied, the facts that the court considered, the court's holding, and the court's reasoning.

The standard of review is the standard that an appellate court uses in reviewing a trial court's decision. If the standard of review is *de novo*, the appellate court does not defer to the trial court. Instead, the appellate court reviews the issue on the merits, and can substitute its judgment for the judgment of the trial court. In contrast, if the standard of review is abuse of discretion, the appellate court defers to the trial court. When the standard of review is abuse of discretion, the appellate court will overturn the trial court only when the trial court abused its discretion. In general, the standard of review is *de novo* when the issue is an issue of law — for example, whether the trial court properly instructed the jury. In contrast, the standard of review is usually abuse of discretion if the issue is an issue of fact — for example, whether a particular expert is qualified. For more on the *de novo* standard of review and some of the other standards of review, see Chapter 18.

Once you have analyzed the cases, synthesize them. What do the cases in which the courts have held that the element is met have in common? What do the cases in which the courts have held that the element is not met have in common? What do the cases in which the courts have discussed a particular part of the rule have in common?

One way of doing this analysis and synthesis is to prepare a chart for each set of cases in which you identify the court, the date of the decision, the key facts, and the court's reasoning. Note that in the following examples, there is no column for the holding. This column is not necessary because the cases are grouped based on their "holdings." Example 1 contains the case in which the element was met, and Example 2 contains the cases in which the element was not met.

Just as it is unlikely that anyone other than you will see your research notes, it is unlikely that anyone other than you will see your charts. Thus, you should use the format and abbreviations that make sense to you. Do not waste time creating charts that "look nice."

Chart 7.5 — Case in Which Court Held That Service Was Made at the Defendant's Usual Place of Abode

Case	Court	Date	Facts	Reasoning
Merritt v. Heffernan	Florida Supreme Court	1940	▪ Wife served one hour after D left to go back to Minn. ▪ D had an office, voted, and paid taxes in Minn. ▪ D had moved family to Florida two months earlier. ▪ D had visited family twice "during season." ▪ Summons was left with D's wife and, apparently, D received actual notice.	▪ Ct acknowledges that D's permanent residence was in Minn. ▪ However, ct seems to think that it was more important that his family was in Florida, that D was on a train and not in Minn. at the time of service, and that the evidence suggested that D intended to return to Minn.

Chart 7.6 — Cases in Which Court Held That Service Was Not Made at the Defendant's Usual Place of Abode.

Case	Court	Date	Facts	Reasoning
Alvarez v. State Farm	Fla. 3d DCA	1994	▪ Service was left with D's cousin at cousin's residence. ▪ Affidavits, telephone bill, and marriage license established that D was not living with cousin at time of service and that she had not lived there for some time.	▪ Uncontradicted evidence established that D was not living at that address on the date of service or for some time before. Therefore, service of process was ineffective as a matter of law.
Shurman v. v. Atlantic Mortg. & Inv. Co.	Florida Supreme Court	2001	▪ Service left with D's wife. ▪ D had been incarcerated for at least 9 months.	▪ D was actually living at the prison. ▪ Substituted service, being in derogation of the common law, must be strictly construed. ▪ The expectation that D will normally receive notice of process served through a competent member of his household living at his place of abode does not prevail in the setting of familial disorganization frequently ensuing

				where the head of the household is committed to prison.
Torres v. Arnco Constr.	Fla. 5th DCA	2004	■ Summons left with D's mother. ■ D had resided in NY for 57 years and at NY address for 12 years. ■ NY neighbors verified that D lived in house but that he traveled a lot. ■ Mother said that D would be home soon.	■ Although standard of review is gross abuse of discretion, no live testimony. ■ P has the burden of proof. ■ P did not meet burden. ■ Mother's statement was ambiguous. ■ Dissent argues that D had burden of proof and that his statements were not sufficient. If Mr. Torres was visiting his family for such lengths of time in Florida, Florida address was his "usual abode" when he was served in Florida. It would also be consistent with the affidavit of the Florida process server who said that Torres's mother remarked that Torres "would be home soon, and she would see to it that he received the papers."
Thompson v. State, Dept. of Revenue	Fla. 1st DCA	2004	■ Service was made on D's wife. ■ Child support case. ■ In affidavit D stated that he has been separated from his wife, that he had not resided at that address for over three years, and that he did not authorize anyone to accept service of process on his behalf.	■ D's affidavit sufficient to establish *prima facie* case that he was not served at his usual place of abode. ■ Court cites other Fla. cases. ■ Having raised the issue of personal jurisdiction, D's motion and accompanying affidavit placed the burden on the Dept. to establish the validity of service of process.

In creating and examining your chart, you might discover

(1) that all of the cases in which the element is met have a particular fact or set of facts in common;
(2) that in all of the cases in which the element is met, the courts seem to focus on a particular policy underlying the rule;
(3) that different courts or different divisions of the same court seem to take a particular approach;
(4) that the rules seem to be evolving; or
(5) that the decisions seem to be result-oriented.

When you identify a common thread or, occasionally, the absence of a common thread, you have done synthesis.

d. Introduce the Cases

Do not ask the attorney to use his or her time figuring out why you included a description of a particular case or group of cases. Instead, introduce the case or group of cases. The type of introduction that you include will depend on the issue you are researching, the number of analogous cases you located, and what you discovered in analyzing and synthesizing each group of cases.

For instance, if you are using a case to illustrate part of a rule, a transition may be enough. In the following example, the writer uses the transition "for example" to introduce a case that illustrates the rule that, if the return is regular on its face, the court presumes that the service is valid unless the defendant presents clear and convincing evidence to the contrary.

EXAMPLE

Transition Introducing a Case That Illustrates the Application of a Particular Rule

Although the party seeking to invoke the jurisdiction of the court has the burden of proving that service was proper, if the return is regular on its face, the courts presume that the service was valid. *Thompson v. State, Dept. of Revenue,* 867 So. 2d 603, 605 (Fla. 1st DCA 2004); *Magazine v. Bedoya,* 475 So. 2d 1035, 1035 (Fla. 3d DCA 1985). For example, in a case involving a default judgment obtained by a bank, the District Court of Appeals held that the trial court had erred in overturning a default judgment because the return of service was regular on its face and the defendant did not "present 'clear and convincing evidence' to corroborate his denial of service." *Florida Nat'l Bank v. Halphen,* 641 So. 2d 495, 495 (Fla. 3d DCA 1994).

Similarly, if there is only one case that has interpreted and applied your statute or the disputed element, your introduction might set out that fact.

EXAMPLE

Using a Topic Sentence That Tells Attorney that there is Only One Case

The only case in which the Florida courts have discussed usual place of abode and held that the service was made at the defendant's usual place of abode is a 1940 case, *State ex rel. Merritt v. Heffernan,* 195 So. 145 (Fla. 1940). In *Heffernan,* the defendant's wife was served at the family's apartment in Florida. However, one hour before service was made, the defendant had left the apartment to return to . . .

In most instances, when you refer to a case by only one of the parties' names, use the plaintiff's name. For example, when you refer to *Thompson v. State, Dept. of Revenue,* 867 So. 2d 603, 605

(Fla. 1st DCA 2004), you would say "in *Thompson,*" and when you refer to *Magazine v. Bedoya,* 475 So. 2d 1035, 1035 (Fla. 3d DCA 1985), you would say "in *Magazine.*" There are, however, some exceptions to this general rule. When the plaintiff is the state, refer to the case using the defendant's name: "*State v. Smith*" becomes "in *Smith,*" and "*Commonwealth v. Jones*" becomes "in *Jones.*" In addition, if the courts typically refer to a case using the defendant's name, you should use that name. For instance, because the Florida courts refer to *State ex rel. Merritt v. Heffernan* as "*Heffernan,*" you should use "*Heffernan,*" not "*Merritt.*" For more on short cites, see Rule 12.21(b) in *the ALWD Citation Manual* and Rule 10.9 in *The Bluebook.*

The most sophisticated type of analysis is, however, principle-based analysis. When you do this type of analysis, you introduce a group of cases by setting out the principle that you are using the cases to illustrate. For example, if in analyzing and synthesizing the cases you determined that all of the cases had a particular fact in common, you would use this fact to introduce the group of cases. Likewise, if in analyzing and synthesizing the cases you determined that the courts gave considerable weight to one of the policies underlying the statute, you would use this policy to introduce the group of cases.

While in some instances everyone who reads a group of cases draws the same principle from those cases, in other instances different people may draw different principles. For instance, in working on our sample problem, students who analyzed the cases drew the following principles from the cases in which the courts held that service was not made at the defendant's usual place of abode.

Principle-Based Topic Sentence Used to Introduce Group of Analogous Cases

EXAMPLE 1

In most of the cases in which the courts have held that the summons was not left at the defendant's usual place of abode, the defendant had not lived at the house where service was made for a substantial period of time. *See, e.g., Shurman v. Atlantic Mortg. & Inv. Corp.,* 795 So. 2d 952 (Fla. 2001); *Alvarez v. State Farm Mut. Auto Ins. Co.,* 635 So. 2d 131, 132 (Fla. 3d DCA 1994).

Principle-Based Topic Sentence Used to Introduce Group of Analogous Cases

EXAMPLE 2

In cases in which the courts have held that substituted service was not made at the defendant's usual place of abode, service was made at the residence of a relative of the defendant, but the defendant produced evidence to show that he or she did not actually live with the relative at the time. *See, e.g., Shurman v. Atlantic Mortg. & Inv. Corp.*, 795 So. 2d 952 (Fla. 2001); *Alvarez v. State Farm Mut. Auto Ins. Co.*, 635 So. 2d 131, 132 (Fla. 3d DCA 1994).

EXAMPLE 3

Principle-Based Topic Sentence Used to Introduce Group of Analogous Cases

In the cases in which the courts have held that the service was not left at the defendant's usual place of abode, the defendant produced evidence that he or she was not living at the house where service was made. *See, e.g., Shurman v. Atlantic Mortg. & Inv. Corp.*, 795 So. 2d 952 (Fla. 2001); *Alvarez v. State Farm Mut. Auto Ins. Co.*, 635 So. 2d 131, 132 (Fla. 3d DCA 1994).

EXAMPLE 4

Principle-Based Topic Sentence Used to Introduce a Group of Analogous Cases

In the more recent cases, the courts have emphasized that the plaintiff has the burden of proving that the service was made at the defendant's usual place of abode. Therefore, if the defendant produced at least some evidence that he or she was not living at the house where the service was made, the court either held that the service was invalid or remanded the case for an evidentiary hearing. *See, e.g., Thompson v. State, Dept. of Revenue*, 867 So. 2d 603, 605 (Fla. 1st DCA 2004); *Torres v. Arnco Constr., Inc.*, 867 So. 2d 583 (Fla. 5th DCA 2004).

Questions

Why might different people draw different principles from the same group of cases? Is one of the preceding examples better than the other examples? Why or why not?

e. Draft Your Descriptions of the Cases

The last step is to draft the descriptions of the cases. In drafting these descriptions, remember why you are including case descriptions. You include case descriptions not to prove to your professor, the attorney you work for, or the client that you have located and read cases but to illustrate how the courts have applied a rule or set of rules or because you believe that either you or opposing counsel will use the cases that you describe to support an assertion.

If there are only two or three analogous cases, you might describe all of them. If, however, there are a number of cases, describe only representative cases. In selecting cases, use the following criteria:

- Select cases from your jurisdiction over cases from other jurisdictions.
- Select cases with published decisions over cases with unpublished decisions.
- Select cases that are more factually similar to your case over cases that are less factually similar.
- Select more recent cases over older cases.

- Select cases from higher courts over cases from lower courts.

In addition, most of the time you will be using the cases to see where your case falls along the continuum of decided cases. Is your case more like the cases in which the court held that the element was met or more like the cases in which the court held that the element was not met?

<u>Your Case</u>

Cases in which element met	Cases in which element not met

How much you say about a case will depend on the point that you are using the case to illustrate. If you are using the case to illustrate a small point, a sentence or even a clause or a phrase may be enough. In contrast, if you expect that one or both sides will rely heavily on a particular case, your description of that case will be longer. The bottom line is that you need to include only that information that is relevant to the rule or principle that you are using the cases to illustrate.

Compare the following examples. In Example 1, the case descriptions are very short because the author is using the cases to illustrate a small point. In contrast, in Example 2, the description is longer because the writer wants to use the case to illustrate several points and expects that both sides will use the case. In Example 3, the writer sets out two medium-length descriptions.

Short Descriptions of Two Cases

EXAMPLE 1

Although the statute does not specify how long the person who received the service must have been "residing therein," the courts do not require extended habitation. While in *Gamboa* the court determined that a ten-day visit was not sufficient to establish residency, *id.* at 64, in *Magazine*, the court determined that a six-week stay was sufficient, *id.* at 1035.

Longer Description in Which Author Sets Out Facts and Court's Holding and Reasoning

EXAMPLE 2

The only case in which the Florida courts have discussed usual place of abode and held that the service was made at the defendant's usual place of abode is a 1940 case: *State ex rel. Merritt v. Heffernan*, 195 So. 145 (Fla. 1940). In that case, the defendant's wife was served at the family's apartment in Florida. *Id.* at 146. However, one hour before service was made, the defendant had left the apartment to return to his permanent residence in Minnesota, where he had his office, voted, and paid taxes. *Id.* The court noted that many persons have several residences that they permanently maintain, occupying one at one period of the year and another during another period. *Id.* at 147. In such situations, the summons and complaint must be served at the dwelling house in which the defendant is living at the time when the service is made. *Id.* Although the defendant was on a train heading toward Minnesota at the time service was made, the court stated that he was not within the classification of persons who had at the time of service lost one place of residence and had not yet established another. *Id.* at 148. Instead, the court held that the defendant's then place of abode was the apartment in Florida. *Id.* at 147. The court also pointed out that the defendant had visited his family in Florida "twice during the season" and that there was no convincing proof that he did not intend to return to Florida. *Id.*

EXAMPLE 3

Two Descriptions in Which Author Sets Out Facts and Courts' Holdings and Reasoning

In contrast, in most of the cases in which the courts have held that the summons was not left at the defendant's usual place of abode, the defendant had not lived at the house where service was made for a substantial period of time. *See, e.g., Shurman v. Atlantic Mortg. & Inv. Corp.,* 795 So. 2d 952 (Fla. 2001); *Thompson v. State, Dept. of Revenue,* 867 So. 2d 603 (Fla. 1st DCA 2004). For example, in *Shurman,* the court held that the service had not been made at the defendant's usual place of abode when the summons was left with the defendant's wife at the family home but the defendant had been incarcerated for at least nine months. *Id.* at 955. Similarly, in *Thompson,* the court held that the summons had not been left at the defendant's usual place of abode when the summons was left with the defendant's wife at the family home. *Id.* at 605. In reaching its decision, the court relied on the defendant's affidavit, in which the defendant stated that he was separated from his wife, that he had not resided at that address for over three years, and that he did not authorize anyone to accept service of process on his behalf. *Id.* at 605. In both cases, the plaintiff did not present evidence contradicting the defendant's statements.

Occasionally, you will not need to include a full description of an analogous case. For example, you may not need to include a full description of a case if you are using the case to illustrate a single point or if you have already given full descriptions of one or two cases but want to tell the attorney about a third or fourth case or when you simply want to illustrate one aspect of a rule. In these situations you can use parentheticals.

EXAMPLE 1

Cases Described in Parentheticals

Although the statute does not specify the period of time an individual must occupy a home to be regarded as "residing therein," the courts do not require extended habitation. *Compare Magazine v. Bedoya,* 475 So. 2d 1035, 1035 (Fla. 3d, DCA 1985) (six-week stay sufficient to establish residency) *with Gamboa v. Jones,* 455 So. 2d 613, 614 (Fla. 3d DCA 1985) (ten-day visit not sufficient to establish residency).

EXAMPLE 2

Additional Cases Described in Parentheticals

In cases in which the courts have held that substituted service was not made at the defendant's usual place of abode, service was made at the residence of a relative of the defendant, but the defendant produced evidence to show that he or she did not actually live with the relative at the time. *See, e.g., Shurman v. Atlantic Mortg. & Inv. Corp.,* 795 So. 2d 952 (Fla. 2001); *Alvarez v. State Farm Mut. Auto Ins. Co.,* 635 So. 2d 131, 132 (Fla. 3d DCA 1994). For instance, in *Shurman,* the Florida Supreme Court held that service of process upon the defendant, who had been incarcerated for nine months, did not comply with section 48.031(1)(a) when service of process occurred at the defendant's wife's residence, which is where the defendant lived prior to incarceration. In that case, the court held that because the defendant was "actually living" in prison at the time of service, service at the his wife's residence was invalid. *Id.* at 955.

Similarly, in *Alvarez*, the defendant established by means of affidavits and supporting documentation, including a telephone bill and a marriage license, that she had not been living with her cousin for some time before process was served at her cousin's residence. *Id.* at 132; *accord Milanes,* 507 So. 2d at 778 (service of process on defendant's ex-wife at her residence was not service at the defendant's usual place of abode); *Gonzalez v. Totalbank,* 472 So. 2d 861, 864 (Fla. 3d DCA 1985) (service of process on defendant's wife at her residence not valid when wife was separated from husband and no longer living at address where service was attempted).

§ 7.9.3 Draft the Arguments

It is at this point in writing the memo that your role changes dramatically. No longer are you just a "reporter" telling the attorney what you found in doing your research. To do a good job presenting each side's arguments, you must become an advocate, using your training and mental resources to construct the arguments each side is likely to make. You must think like the plaintiff's attorney and then like the defendant's attorney.

When you use the script format, you write a "script" for the oral arguments on the issue. You begin by putting yourself in the shoes of the party with the burden of proof and set out the arguments that side might make. You then step into the other side's shoes and set out that side's arguments. Finally, you assume the role of the judge, predicting how the court would decide the element and how it would justify its decision. Thus, your "script" looks something like this:

"Script" for Arguments

EXAMPLE

- Party with the burden of proof's arguments
- Responding party's arguments
- Party with the burden of proof's rebuttal
- Court's decision + rationale

---

a. Identify Each Side's Arguments

The first step is to identify each side's arguments. If you used the template set out on pages 102-112 to do your research, start with the list of arguments that you set out there.

Chart 7.7   Identifying Arguments

Excerpt from Template

A. Usual Place of Abode

1. Specific rules
   [material not included]
2. Descriptions of analogous cases
   [material not included]
3. Arguments

Ms. Duncan's arguments

- During the week she lived at the halfway house, not at her sister's house.
- Service on a relative is not sufficient.
- Her more permanent address was the halfway house address. She had a room, etc., at the halfway house.
- *Heffernan* is an old case.
- In *Torres*, the court held that the defendant's mother's house was not the defendant's usual place of abode even though the mother indicated that the defendant would be home later.

The plaintiff's arguments

- Ms. Duncan stayed at her sister's house three nights a week.
- Ms. Duncan apparently received mail at her sister's house — the shoebox.
- Ms. Duncan listed her sister's address on her driver's license.
- In *Heffernan*, the court held that the apartment was the defendant's usual place of abode even though the defendant had left the apartment and was on a train back to his permanent residence.
- In *Torres*, the defendant had a permanent residence where he had lived for twelve years. He was just visiting his mother.

Do not, however, stop with the list that you came up with while research-ing the issue. Push yourself further, asking yourself whether the parties can make any of the other standard types of arguments. For example, can one or both of the parties make plain language arguments, arguments based on the analogous cases, or policy arguments?

Plain Language Arguments

A plain language argument is an argument in which you apply the plain language of a statute or rule to the facts of your case. For instance, in our example case, you would be making a plain language argument if you argued that, under the plain language of the statute, the service was not made at Ms. Duncan's *usual* place of abode because her sister's house was not the place where she "usually" lived. During the month in which service was made, Ms. Duncan spent four nights a week at the halfway house and only three nights a week at her sister's house. Similarly, you would be making a plain language argument if you argued that, under the plain language of the rule that the courts have set out, Ms. Duncan was not "actually living" at her sister's house because the summons and complaint were served on a weekday, and during the week Ms. Duncan lived at the halfway house. Note that a plain language argument has two components: a word or phrase from the statute or rule ("usual"/"actually living") and facts showing that that requirement is or is not met (four nights a week at the halfway house and three nights a week at sister's house/summons and complaint served on a weekday and on week-days Ms. Duncan lived at the halfway house).

To make sure you have considered all the plain language arguments, do two things. First, think about each word or phrase in the applicable part of the statute and the applicable rules, asking yourself what the plain meaning of that word or phrase requires. Second, go through each of your facts, asking yourself how each side might be able to use that fact.

Analogous Case Arguments

Under our system of law, judges usually decide similar cases in a like manner. Thus, if the analogous cases support the conclusion that you want the court to reach, you need to argue that your case is like the analogous cases, and therefore the court should reach the same result as the courts reached in those decisions. In contrast, if the analogous cases do not support the conclusion that you want the court to reach, you need to distinguish those cases. For example, in Ms. Duncan's case, Ms. Duncan will want to argue that her case is like *Thompson, Torres,* and *Alvarez,* and she will want to distinguish *Heffernan.* Conversely, the defendant will want to distinguish *Thompson, Torres,* and *Alvarez* and argue that its case is more like *Heffernan.*

To make sure you have considered all analogous case arguments, think about rules and principles that you drew from the cases and how each side might be able to use those rules or principles to support its position. In addition, go through the analogous cases one by one, thinking about how each side might be able to use each case.

In constructing analogous case arguments, ask yourself the following questions:

PRACTICE

- In what ways is the analogous case similar to your case?
- In what ways is it different?
- Is the case a relatively old case? If it is, how can each side use that fact?
- Is the case from an intermediate court of appeals or from the state's highest court? How can each side use that fact?
- Is the case well reasoned or poorly reasoned? How can each side use that fact?
- How have other cases used or distinguished the case?

Policy Arguments

In making a policy argument, look at the reasons why the legislature enacted a particular statute or a court adopted a particular rule, and use those underlying reasons to support your client's position. For example, in our sample case you could use the underlying reason that the service of process statutes were enacted — to ensure that defendants had notice of actions that had been filed against them — to argue that, in this case, service was invalid because Ms. Duncan never received notice.

When your issue is one that is governed by a statute, you may be able to find the policies underlying the statute in a "finding" or "purpose" section of the act of which your statute is a part, or a legislative history may tell you what the legislature intended when it enacted the statute. In addition, in applying statutes, the courts frequently set out what they believe are the policies underlying the statutes. Thus, to come up with policy arguments, look at the text of the statute, the statute's legislative history, and those parts of other courts' decisions that talk about the policies underlying the statute. Once you identify the various policies, determine how each side might be able to use those policies to support its position.

In situations in which the underlying reason for the statute is not explicitly laid out in the act, in the act's legislative history, or in court decisions, use common sense to determine why the statute was enacted. Ask yourself "what good was the legislature trying to promote" or "what harm was the legislature trying to prevent" when it enacted this statute. Those questions will help you articulate the policy underlying the statute.

At this initial stage, list all of the arguments (plain language, analogous case, and policy), no matter how weak they may seem. Later you can go through these arguments and weed out those that don't pass the "giggle" test — that is, those that you could not make to a court with a straight face.

P R A C T I C E

POINTER

A chart like the one set out in the next example can help you identify and keep track of the arguments that each side makes.

Chart 7.8   **Recording Possible Arguments**

Excerpt from Template

Element	Our Arguments	Other Side's Arguments
Usual Place of Abode (in dispute)	Plain language arguments:	Plain language arguments:
	Analogous case arguments:	Analogous case arguments:
	Policy arguments:	Policy arguments:
Age and Residing Therein (not in dispute)		
Informing of Contents (in dispute)	Plain language arguments:	Plain language arguments:
	Analogous case arguments:	Analogous case arguments:
	Policy arguments:	Policy arguments:

b. Order the Arguments

Once you have identified the arguments that each side can make, decide how you want to present those arguments. Once again, you have some choices. For example, you can organize the arguments by type. If you choose this organizational scheme, you will set out your plain language arguments in one paragraph or block of paragraphs, your analogous cases arguments in another paragraph or block of paragraphs, and your policy arguments in a third paragraph or block of paragraphs. Similarly, you would set out the other side's plain language arguments in one paragraph or block of paragraphs, its analogous case arguments in another paragraph or block of paragraphs, and its policy arguments in a third paragraph or block of paragraphs.

If you organize your arguments around types of arguments, you will usually set out the plain language arguments first, analogous case arguments second, and policy arguments third.

This ordering reflects the weight that courts typically give to the different types of arguments. If a court can decide an issue by applying the plain language of the statute or rule to the facts of the case, it will usually decide the issue based on the plain language. If, however, the court cannot decide the issue based on the plain language of the statute or rule, it will look to the cases to see how the cases have applied the statutory language. If the cases do not resolve the issue, the court will look to the policies underlying the statute.

Another way to organize the arguments is around the principles that you identified when you analyzed and synthesized the cases. If, for example, you determined that all of the cases in which the element is met have three factors in common, you could organize your arguments around those three factors. In setting out your arguments, you would discuss the first factor in one paragraph or block of paragraphs, the second factor in a second paragraph or block of paragraphs, and the third factor in a third paragraph or block of paragraphs. Similarly, in setting out the other side's arguments, you would discuss the first factor in one paragraph or block of paragraphs, the second factor in a second paragraph or block of paragraphs, and the third factor in a third paragraph or block of paragraphs. Within the paragraphs discussing these factors, you would set out any plain language, analogous case, or policy arguments that relate to that factor.

A third, and similar, approach is to organize your arguments around "lines of argument." For example, if you have a burden of proof argument and an argument on the merits, you could organize the arguments around these two lines of argument. In setting out these arguments, you would set out your arguments relating to your first line of argument in one paragraph or block of paragraphs and your arguments relating to the second line of argument in a second paragraph or block of paragraphs. You would then set out the other side's arguments, putting the other side's points relating to the first line of argument in one paragraph or block of paragraphs, and their points relating to the second line of argument in a second paragraph or block of paragraphs. In setting out these lines of argument, you would include the plain language, analogous cases, or policy arguments that relate to that line of argument.

For more on paragraph blocks, see section 22.6.

P R A C T I C E

POINTER

If you use the second approach, you will usually want to discuss the factors in the same order in which you set them out and illustrated them in your analogous case section. If you use the third approach, discuss threshold arguments first. Thus, if one argument builds upon another argument, set out the foundational argument first.

The following chart illustrates the differences between these three organizational schemes.

Chart 7.9	**Three Ways of Organizing the Arguments**	
	Excerpt from Template	
Arguments Organized by Type of Argument	**Arguments Organized by Principles, for Example, Common Factors**	**Arguments Organized by Lines of Argument**
Party with burden of proof's arguments	**Party with burden of proof's arguments**	**Party with buden of proof's arguments**
■ Plain language arguments ■ Analogous case arguments ■ Policy arguments	■ Arguments relating to first factor (include any plain language, analogous case, and policy arguments) ■ Arguments relating to second factor (include any plain language, analogous case, and policy arguments) ■ Arguments relating to third factor (include any plain language, analogous case, and policy arguments)	■ First line of argument (include any plain language, analogous case, and policy arguments) ■ Second line of argument (include any plain language, analogous case, and policy arguments)
Responding Party's Arguments	**Responding Party's Arguments**	**Responding Party's Arguments**
■ Plain language arguments ■ Analogous case arguments	■ Arguments relating to first factor (include any plain language, analogous case, and policy arguments)	■ First line of argument (include any plain language, analogous case, and policy arguments)

▪ Policy arguments	▪ Arguments relating to second factor (include any plain language, analogous case, and policy arguments)	▪ Second line of argument (include any plain language, analogous case, and policy arguments)
	▪ Arguments relating to third factor (include any plain language, analogous case, and policy arguments)	

Questions

What are the advantages and disadvantages of the three organizational schemes set out in Chart 7.9? Is there a fourth or fifth organizational scheme that might work?

c. Drafting the Arguments

In most instances, you should start your discussion of each side's arguments by setting out the side's general assertion. For example, in Ms. Duncan's case, start the "usual place of abode" arguments by stating that Duncan will argue that her sister's house was not her usual place of abode. Similarly, start your discussion of the other side's arguments by asserting that Ms. Webster's house was Ms. Duncan's usual place of abode or that it was one of her usual places of abode. In addition, if you are going to make a number of different arguments, you may want to alert the attorney to that fact.

Three Ways of Setting Out Ms. Duncan's General Assertion Relating to Usual Place of Abode   EXAMPLE 1

- Ms. Duncan will argue that her sister's house was not her usual place of abode.
- Ms. Duncan will argue that she was not actually living at Ms. Webster's house and that, therefore, Ms. Webster's house was not her usual place of abode.
- Ms. Duncan can make three arguments to support her assertion that her sister's house was not her usual place of abode. First, . . .

Three Ways of Setting Out the Defendant's General Assertion Relating to Usual Place of Abode   EXAMPLE 2

- In response, the defendant will argue that Ms. Webster's house was Ms. Duncan's usual place of abode.
- The defendant will counter by arguing that Ms. Duncan was actually living at her sister's house.
- The defendant can make three arguments to support its assertion that the service was made at Ms. Duncan's usual place of abode.

In addition to setting out your general assertion, also introduce and set out each of your sub-assertions. For example, if you are organizing the arguments around types of arguments, introduce each of these types of arguments, asserting that the plain language, the analogous cases, and/or the policies underlying the statute or rule support your general assertion. Likewise, if you are organizing your arguments around factors or lines of arguments, include a sentence introducing each of these sub-assertions.

EXAMPLE

Sentences Introducing Subassertions

- First, Ms. Duncan can argue the plain language of the statute supports her assertion that her sister's house was not her usual place of abode.
- The first factor supports Ms. Duncan's position: . . .
- Ms. Duncan can argue. . . . In the alternative, Ms. Duncan can argue . . . .

It is not, however, enough to just set out general assertions and subassertions. You also need to show the attorney how each side will support those assertions. One way to do this is to picture yourself standing in front of a judge. If you are making a plain language argument, what facts would you use, and how would you characterize those facts? If you are making an analogous case argument, what cases would you use, and how would you characterize and use those cases? If you are making an policy argument, what policies would you rely on, and how would you use those policies? Similarly, picture the other side presenting its arguments. How would its attorney use the facts, cases, and policies to support its position?

The following example is a poor draft because the author has not supported her assertions. For instance, in the first paragraph, the author asserts that Ms. Duncan's sister's house was not Ms. Duncan's usual place of abode because the treatment house was her usual place of abode. The author does not, however, back up this assertion with facts. For instance, she does not point out that Ms. Duncan had been a full-time resident of the halfway house for several months and that she was still spending four nights a week there. Similarly, although the author asserts that Ms. Duncan's case is more like *Torres* and *Alvarez* than it is like *Heffernan*, she does not support this assertion by comparing and contrasting the facts in those cases to the facts in Ms. Duncan's case. Finally, although the author sets out a rule relating to the burden of proof, she does not explain why or how that rule will produce a just result in this case.

P R A C T I C E

POINTER

While almost every attorney wants citations to authorities in the rule and analogous case sections of memos, not all attorneys want them in the argument sections. Thus, before you draft your memo, determine which approach the attorney you are working for prefers. Note that in the following samples we did not include citations: we did not include citations because, when citations are deleted, it is easier to see and critique the arguments.

Poor Draft: The Author Has Set Out Assertions But Has Not Supported Those Assertions

In this case, we can make three arguments to support our assertion that the summons and complaint were not left at Ms. Duncan's usual place of abode. First, we can argue that Ms. Duncan's sister's house was not Ms. Duncan's usual place of abode because the treatment house was Ms. Duncan's usual place of abode. Second, we can use the cases to support our position. Our case is more like *Torres* and *Alvarez* than *Heffernan*. Finally, we can argue that as a matter of public policy the party seeking to invoke the jurisdiction of the court has the burden of proving that the service was valid.

General assertion

First subassertion

Second sub-assertion

Third subassertion

In response, the defendant will argue that the summmons and complaint were left at Ms. Duncan's usual place of abode. The facts establish that Ms. Duncan was, in fact, living at her sister's house at the time the summons and complaint were served. Thus, this case is like *Merritt*. In addition, the defendant will distinguish cases like *Torres* and *Alvarez* on the basis that in those cases the defendant was not spending any time at the house where the service was made. Finally, the defendant can argue that the service was valid because the defendant's sister's house was the place where she was most likely to receive notice.

General assertion

First subassertion

Second sub-assertion

Third subassertion

The following example, while not perfect, is much better. In addition to setting out his assertions, the author has supported those assertions.

Improved Draft: Author Has Set Out Assertions and Support for Those Assertions

Ms. Duncan can make three arguments to support her assertion that her sister's house was not her usual place of abode. First, Ms. Duncan will argue that, under the plain language of the rule, her sister's house was not her usual place of abode. When a defendant has more than one residence, the service must be made at the place where the defendant was actually living at the time the summons and complaint were served. In this case, Ms. Duncan had more than one residence: during the week she lived at the halfway house and on weekends she visited her sister. Because the summons and complaint were served on a Wednesday, a weekday, the service was not made at the place where Ms. Duncan was actually living.

Ms. Duncan's general assertion

Ms. Duncan's first subassertion

Facts that support Ms. Duncan's first subassertion

Second, Ms. Duncan will argue that this case is more like *Torres* than *Heffernan*. Like Mr. Torres, who only visited his mother and who was not at his mother's house when service was

Ms. Duncan's second subassertion

Explanation of how
cases support
Ms. Duncan's
second sub-
assertion

made, Ms. Duncan only visited her sister and was not at her sister's house when the summons and complaint were served. However, while Mr. Torres's mother's statement that Mr. Torres "would be home soon" suggested that Mr. Torres would be returning to his mother's house that day, Ms. Duncan's sister told the process server that Ms. Duncan "isn't here today." In addition, while the plaintiff in *Torres* had tried on a number of occasions to serve Mr. Torres at his New York house, in our case we do not know whether the defendant tried to serve Ms. Duncan personally or at the halfway house.

Finally, *Heffernan* can be distinguished in two ways: (1) while Mr. Heffernan had been at his family's apartment only an hour before the summons and complaint were served, Ms. Duncan had not been at her sister's house for several days; and (2) while in *Heffernan* the summons and complaint were served on the defendant's wife, in our case the summons and complaint were served on Ms. Duncan's sister. It is also important to note that, since *Heffernan*, the courts have interpreted the service of process statutes more narrowly.

Ms. Duncan's third
subassertion

Finally, Ms. Duncan can argue that, as a matter of public policy, the court should hold that the summons was not left at Ms. Duncan's usual place of abode. The courts have repeatedly held that the service of process statutes should

Policies supporting
Ms. Duncan's third
subassertion

be strictly construed and that service on a relative is not, by itself, enough. *See, e.g., Shurman v. Atlantic Mortg. & Inv. Corp.*, 795 So. 2d 952, 953-54 (Fla. 2001). In addition, in this case, Ms. Duncan did not receive notice.

Plaintiff's main
assertion

Plaintiff's first sub-
assertion

In response, the plaintiff will argue that Ms. Duncan was served at one of her usual places of abode. In this case, Ms. Duncan was actually living at her sister's house at the time the summons and complaint were served. The courts have not required that the plaintiff be living at the house on the day on

Facts that support
plaintiff's first
subassertion

which the summons is served. Instead, they require only that the defendant be living there "at the time of service." Therefore, while Ms. Duncan may not have been at her sister's house on the day that the summons and complaint were served, she had been there the previous weekend, and she was there the following weekend. In addition, Ms. Duncan had possessions at her sister's house, and she listed her sister's address as her own address when she applied for a driver's license.

Plaintiff's second
subassertion

Thus, the plaintiff will argue that the facts in this case are much stronger than the facts in *Heffernan*. While in *Heffernan* Mr. Heffernan visited his family only "twice during the season," Ms. Duncan lived at her sister's house three days a week. In

Case that supports
plaintiff's second
subassertion

addition, while Mr. Heffernan had another permanent residence, Ms. Duncan was staying at a halfway house, which is by definition only a temporary residence. Finally, while in *Heffernan* there was no indication that Mr. Heffernan listed the Florida address on any documents, Ms. Duncan listed her sister's address on her driver's license. In addition, there is evidence indicating that Ms. Duncan received other types of mail at her sister's house.

The plaintiff will use these same facts to distinguish *Torres*. While in *Torres* Mr. Torres presented evidence establishing that his permanent residence was in New York, in our case Ms. Duncan did not have a permanent residence. In the five months before service, she had been an inpatient in a treatment facility, she had lived at the halfway house, and she had lived with her sister. The plaintiff can also distinguish *Shurman* and *Thompson*. While in *Shurman* and *Thompson* the record indicated that the defendants had not lived at the house where service had been made for months or years, in this case Ms. Duncan admits that she had stayed at her sister's house on the weekend before her sister was served.

> **Case that supports plaintiff's second subassertion**

Finally, the plaintiff will argue that, because the return was regular on its face, Ms. Duncan has the burden of proving, by clear and convincing evidence, that her sister's house was not her usual place of abode. In this instance, Ms. Duncan has not met that burden. In addition, when there is evidence that the defendant was in fact living at the house where service was made, the courts should not require plaintiffs to determine at which house the defendant was living on any particular day.

> **Plaintiff's third subassertion**
>
> **Policies supporting plaintiff's third sub-assertion**

Question

How else might the parties support their assertions?

§ 7.9.4 Predict How the Court Will Decide the Element

The final piece of information you need to include is your prediction about how a court would decide the element. Is it more likely that the court will find the element is met or more likely that it will find the element is not met?

In writing this section, you must once again change roles. Instead of playing the role of reporter describing the rules and analogous cases or the role of advocate making each side's arguments, you must play the role of judge. You must put yourself in the position of the particular court that would decide the issue — the trial court, appellate court, state court, federal court — and decide how that court is likely to rule.

At least initially, you may be uncomfortable making such predictions. How can a first-year law student predict how the court might rule? The good news is that with time and experience, you will get better and better at predicting how a court will decide a particular issue. In the meantime, read the statutes and cases carefully, and critically evaluate each side's arguments.

Careful reading and careful consideration of arguments, plus common sense, will help you make reliable predictions. Remember too that you are predicting, not guaranteeing, an outcome.

In setting out your conclusion, do two things: set out your prediction and briefly explain why you believe the court will decide the element as you have predicted. You do not have to include phrases like "I think" or "in my opinion."

In the first example below, the writer has set out his prediction but not his reasoning. In the second, the writer has set out both her prediction and her reasoning.

EXAMPLE 1

Poor Draft: The Writer Has Set Out the Prediction but Not the Reasoning

While both sides have strong arguments, the court will probably conclude that the summons was not left at Ms. Duncan's usual place of abode.

EXAMPLE 2

Better Draft: The Writer Has Set Out Both the Prediction and the Reasoning

While both sides have strong arguments, the court will probably conclude that the summons was not left at Ms. Duncan's usual place of abode. In the more recent cases, the courts have strictly construed the statute, holding that the service was not made at the defendant's usual place of abode when the defendant had a more permanent place of abode. Thus, because the halfway house was Ms. Duncan's more permanent residence, the court will probably conclude that it was Ms. Duncan's usual place of abode. In addition, the court may be influenced by two key facts: the record does not indicate that the plaintiff tried to serve Ms. Duncan at the halfway house, and Ms. Duncan states that she did not receive notice.

---

§ 7.9.5 Checklist for Critiquing the Discussion Section

A. Content

Introduction

- The writer has included a sentence or paragraph introducing the governing statute or common law rule.
- The writer has set out the general rule, quoting the applicable statutory sections and quoting or paraphrasing the common law rule.
- The writer has set out any other general rules.
- When appropriate, the writer has briefly described the policies underlying the statute or common law rule.
- The writer has included a roadmap.

- The writer has not included rules or information that the attorney does not need.
- The rules are stated accurately and objectively.
- For each rule stated, the writer has included a citation to authority.

Discussion of Undisputed Elements

- The writer has identified the element and, when there are specific rules, has set out those specific rules.
- The writer has applied the rules to the facts of the client's case, and has explained why the element is not in dispute.

Discussion of Disputed Elements

- For each disputed element, the writer has set out the specific rules, described cases that have interpreted and applied those rules, set out each side's arguments, and predicted how the court will decide the element.
- The author has included all of the applicable specific rules and set out those rules accurately and objectively.
- The author has introduced each group of analogous cases, telling the attorney what rule or principle the cases illustrate.
- The case descriptions illustrate the rule or principle and are accurate and objective.
- In setting out the arguments, the writer has set out both assertions and support for those assertions.
- The analysis is sophisticated: the writer has set out more than the obvious arguments.
- The writer has predicted each element will be decided and has given reasons to support those predictions.

B. Large-Scale Organization

- The writer has presented the information in the order in which the attorney expects to see it. For example, the writer begins the discussion section with an introductory section in which he or she sets out the general rules. The writer then walks the attorney through each of the elements, raising and dismissing the undisputed elements and doing a more complete analysis of the disputed elements.

§ 7.10 Drafting the Formal Conclusion

In a one-issue memo, the formal conclusion is used to summarize the analysis of that one issue. For example, in the Duncan case, the conclusion is used to tell the attorney why you believe the service of process was valid or invalid. Begin by setting out your answer to the question that you set out in your issue statement and then summarize your analysis of each element. Note that conclusions typically do not include case names and citations. Also note that the formal conclusion is a longer version of your brief answer.

EXAMPLE   ## Sample Conclusion

Conclusion

Because of the strong public policy in favor of ensuring that defendants receive notice of actions that have been filed against them, the court will probably hold that the substituted service of process was not valid.

Ms. Duncan will have to concede that her sister, Ms. Webster, is a person of suitable age and that Ms. Webster was residing at the house where the service was made. In addition, because the process server told Ms. Webster that Ms. Duncan needed to go to court, it seems unlikely that Ms. Duncan can prove by clear and convincing evidence that Ms. Webster was not informed of the contents.

Ms. Duncan may, however, be able to prove that the summons and complaint were not served at her usual place of abode. In the more recent cases, the courts have strictly construed the usual place of abode requirement, holding that the service was not made at the defendant's usual place of abode when the defendant had a more permanent place of abode. Thus, because the halfway house was Ms. Duncan's more permanent residence, the court will probably conclude that it was Ms. Duncan's usual place of abode. In addition, the court may be influenced by two key facts: the record does not indicate that the plaintiff tried to serve Ms. Duncan at the halfway house, and Ms. Duncan states that she did not receive notice.

While some attorneys will want you to stop at this point, others will want you to go one step further and offer strategic advice about what you think should be done next. What should the attorney tell the client? What action should the attorney take? Is this the type of case that the firm should, or wants to, handle? When you are asked to include this type of information in the conclusion, add a paragraph like the following.

EXAMPLE   ## Paragraph Setting Out Strategic Advice

Thus, because it appears that Ms. Duncan might win on the merits, I recommend that we move to quash the service of process and vacate the default judgment.

§ 7.10.1 Checklist for Critiquing the Conclusion

A. Content

- In a one-issue memorandum, the conclusion is used to predict how the issue will be decided and to summarize the reasons supporting that prediction.
- When appropriate, the writer includes not only the conclusion but also strategic advice.

B. Organization

- The information is organized logically.

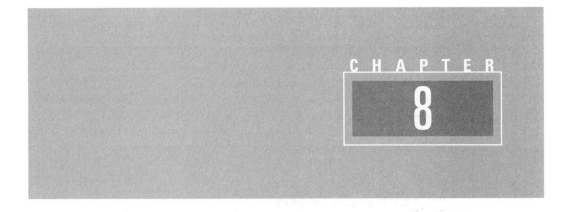

Revising, Editing, and Proofreading Memo 1

Yes, there are times when, because of time or money constraints, you will have to turn in a first draft of an in-house memo. You should not, however, get in the habit of doing so, and you should never submit a first draft to a court, to opposing counsel, or to your client. Unlike speaking, which disappears as soon as the words are spoken, written words remain: while well-written documents can enhance your reputation, poorly written ones can destroy it.

Whenever possible, do what we do in this chapter: treat revising, editing, and proofreading as three separate processes.

§ 8.1 Revise Your Draft

Revising is the process of "re-visioning" what you have written. During this re-visioning process, step back from your first draft and look at it through the eyes of your reader. Have you given the attorney all of the information that he or she needs? Have you presented that information in the order that the attorney expects to see it?

During the revising stage, you need to be willing to make major changes. If, in revising the draft, you realize that you did not need to include one part of your discussion, delete that part, no matter how many hours you spent drafting it. Similarly, if in revising the draft you realize that you did not research or discuss a major point, go back and do that research, analysis, and writing. Finally, if in revising your draft you realize that your organizational scheme just does not work, start over and reorganize a section or even the entire statement of facts or discussion section.

As a general rule, writers do a better job of revising when they print out a draft and lay out the pages side by side. Problems that were not apparent when you looked at your draft screen by screen may become apparent when you look at the draft in hard copy.

§8.1.1 Check Content

In revising a draft, look first at its content. If there are problems with content, solving those problems must be your first priority.

a. Have You Given the Attorney the Information He or She Needs?

In checking content, the first question to ask yourself is whether you have given the attorney the information that he or she requested. Did you research the assigned issue or issues? Did you locate all of the applicable statutes and cases? Did you identify and present the arguments that each side is likely to make? Did you evaluate those arguments and predict how the court is likely to rule?

In our example problem, the intern has given the attorney the information that she requested. The research is complete: the intern found not only the applicable statute but also the key cases. The discussion also begins at the right place. Because the attorney knew the basics, the intern did not need to explain the difference between personal service and substituted service. The discussion also stops where it should. The attorney did not ask whether Ms. Duncan could win on the merits. Instead, she asked whether the service of process was valid.

Last but not least, the intern included all of the pieces. She included both the general and specific rules and, when appropriate, descriptions of analogous cases. In addition, she applied those rules and cases to the facts of the client's case, anticipating the arguments that each side was likely to make and then evaluating those arguments and predicting how the court was likely to rule.

Thus, when the intern asks herself whether she has given the attorney the information he needs, the answer is yes. She knew the law, and in presenting that law, she used good judgment.

b. Check to Make Sure the Information Is Presented Accurately

In law, small errors can have serious consequences. The failure to cite check to make sure that a case is still good law, an omitted "not," or an "or" that should have been an "and," can make the difference between winning and losing, between competent lawyering and malpractice.

As a consequence, in writing a memo, you must exercise care. Because the attorney is relying on you, your research must be thorough. Make sure that you have located the applicable statutes and cases and have checked to make sure that those statutes and cases are still good law. In addition, make sure your analysis is sound. Did you read the statutes and cases carefully? Is the way in which you have put the pieces together sound? Finally, make sure you have presented the statutes and cases accurately and fairly. Did you correctly identify the issue in the analogous cases? Did you take a rule out of context? Did you misrepresent the facts or omit a key fact? Unless the attorney reads the statutes and cases you cite, he or she may not see an error until it is too late.

Questions

In the following example, the intern has made a number of mistakes. Can you identify them?[1] What would happen if the attorney relied on the statements in the following paragraph?

For substituted service of process to be valid, the process server must leave a copy of the summons at the defendant's usual place of abode with a relative who is 15 years or older who is residing therein. Fla. Stat. §48.031. In this case, the summons was left with a relative, Ms. Duncan's sister. In addition, Ms. Duncan is over the age of 15. However, we may be able to prove that Ms. Duncan's sister's house is not Ms. Duncan's usual place of abode. The Florida Supreme Court has held that a person's usual place of abode is the place where the person was actually living at the time that the service was made. *Thompson v. State, Dept. of Revenue*, 867 So. 2d 603, 605 (Fla. 2004). If the defendant has more than one residence, most courts have indicated that the summons can be served at either residence. *Milanes v. Colonial Penn. Ins. Co.*, 507 So. 2d 777, 778 (Fla. 3d DCA 1987).

EXAMPLE

---

§8.1.2 Check to Make Sure the Discussion Section Is Well Organized

The next step is to check the discussion section's large-scale organization. Has the information been presented in the order the attorney expects to see it?

One way to check large-scale organization is to prepare an after-the-fact outline. You can create this type of outline either by labeling the subject matter of each paragraph and then listing those labels in outline form or by summarizing what each paragraph says. See section 20.4.2.

---

1. In the first sentence, the author misstates the law: the current version of the statute states that service must be made on a person who is 15 years old or older, not on a relative who is 15 years old or older. In the fourth sentence, the author states that *Thompson* was decided by the Florida Supreme Court. In fact, it was decided by a District Court of Appeals. Finally, in the last sentence, the author states that most courts have stated that when the defendant has more than one residence, service can be made at either residence. There are no courts in Florida that have set out this rule.

§ 8.1.3 Check to Make Sure the Connections Are Explicit

Once you have revised for content and organization, look at your use of roadmaps, signposts, topic sentences, and transitions.

a. Roadmaps

A roadmap is just what the term implies: a "map" providing the reader with an overview of the document. While sometimes you will need to include a roadmap that outlines the steps in the analysis, at other times your statement of the rule or a list of the elements will be enough.

EXAMPLE

Roadmap Telling the Attorney Which Elements Will Be in Dispute and Which Elements Will Not Be in Dispute

In this case, Ms. Duncan will have to concede that the summons was left with a person 15 years or older who was residing at the house where the summons and complaint were served. In addition, it is unlikely that Ms. Duncan will be able to prove that her sister was not informed of the contents of the documents. Ms. Duncan may, however, be able to present clear and convincing evidence that the summons was not left at her usual place of abode.

Note that in the above example, the roadmap is substantive in nature. Instead of saying, "First I will discuss this and then I will discuss that," the writer has stated who can prove what. For more on roadmaps, see section 22.2.1.

b. Topic Sentences, Signposts, and Transitions

Topic sentences, signposts, and transitions serve the same function that directional signs serve on a freeway. They tell readers where they are, what to expect, and how the pieces are connected. See Chapter 24 and sections 21.2.2 and 22.5. While these directional signs may not be particularly important in some types of writing, they are essential in legal writing. Without them, the connections between paragraphs and between sentences may not be clear, making the analysis difficult to follow.

Compare Example 1 below, in which the writer has not included topic sentences, signposts, or transitions with Example 2. In Example 2, the topic sentences, signposts, and transitions are in boldface type.

EXAMPLE 1

Writer Has Not Included Topic Sentences, Signposts, or Transitions

When a defendant has more than one residence, the service must be made at the place where the defendant was actually living at the time the summons and complaint were served. Ms. Duncan had more than one residence: during the week she lived at the halfway house, and on weekends she visited her sister. Because the summons and complaint were served on a Wednesday, a weekday, the service was not made at the place where Ms. Duncan was actually living.

Like Mr. Torres, who only visited his mother and who was not at his mother's house when service was made, Ms. Duncan only visited her sister and was not at her sister's house when the summons and complaint were served. While Mr. Torres's mother's statement that Mr. Torres "would be home soon" suggested that Mr. Torres would be returning to his mother's house that day, Ms. Duncan's sister told the process server that Ms. Duncan "isn't here today." While the plaintiff in *Torres* had tried on a number of occasions to serve Mr. Torres at his New York house, we do not know whether the defendant tried to serve Ms. Duncan personally or at the halfway house. While Mr. Heffernan had been at his family's apartment only an hour before the summons and complaint were served, Ms. Duncan had not been at her sister's house for several days and, while in *Heffernan* the summons and complaint were served on the defendant's wife, in our case the summons and complaint were served on Ms. Duncan's sister. Since *Heffernan*, the courts have interpreted the service process statutes more narrowly.

The courts have repeatedly held that the service of process statutes should be strictly construed and that service on a relative is not, by itself, enough. *Shurman v. Atlantic Mortg. & Inv. Corp.*, 795 So. 2d 952, 953-54 (Fla. 2001). Ms. Duncan did not receive notice.

Writer Has Included Topic Sentences, Signposts, and Transitions   EXAMPLE 2

Ms. Duncan can make three arguments to support her assertion that her sister's house was not her usual place of abode. First, Ms. Duncan will argue that, under the plain language of the rule, her sister's house was not Ms. Duncan's usual place of abode. When a defendant has more than one residence, the service must be made at the place where the defendant was actually living at the time the summons and complaint were served. **In this case,** Ms. Duncan had more than one residence: during the week she lived at the halfway house and on weekends she visited her sister. Because the summons and complaint were served on a Wednesday, a weekday, the service was not made at the place where Ms. Duncan was actually living.

Second, Ms. Duncan will argue that this case is more like *Torres* than *Heffernan*. Like Mr. Torres, who only visited his mother and who was not at his mother's house when service was made, Ms. Duncan only visited her sister and was not at her sister's house when the summons and complaint were served. **However,** while Mr. Torres's mother's statement that Mr. Torres "would be home soon" suggested that Mr. Torres would be returning to his mother's house that day, Ms. Duncan's sister told the process server that Ms. Duncan "isn't here today." **In addition,** while the plaintiff in *Torres* had tried on a number of occasions to serve Mr. Torres at his New York house, **in our case** we do not know whether the defendant tried to serve Ms. Duncan personally or at the halfway house. ***Heffernan* can be distinguished in two ways: (1)** while Mr. Heffernan had been at his family's apartment only an hour before the summons and complaint were served, Ms. Duncan had not been at her sister's house for several days; and **(2)** while in *Heffernan* the summons and complaint were served on the defendant's wife, in our case the summons and complaint were served on Ms. Duncan's sister. **It is also important to note that,** since *Heffernan*, the courts have interpreted the service process statutes more narrowly.

Finally, Ms. Duncan can argue that, as a matter of public policy, the court should hold that the summons was not left at Ms. Duncan's usual place of abode. The courts have repeatedly held that the service of process statutes should be strictly construed and that service on a relative is not, by itself, enough. *Shurman v. Atlantic Mortg. & Inv. Corp.*, 795 So. 2d 952, 953-54 (Fla. 2001). **In addition**, in this case, Ms. Duncan did not receive notice.

c. Dovetailing

Another technique that you can use to make the connections between ideas clear is dovetailing. You use dovetailing when you refer back to a point made in the prior sentence or paragraph.

A   B   Reference to B   C

In the following two examples, the writer has used dovetailing to make clear the connections between the first and second sentences. The language that is in bold is the dovetail.

EXAMPLE 1   **Dovetailing Used to Connect First and Second Sentences**

During July and August 2006, Ms. Duncan usually spent weeknights at the half-way house, and Friday, Saturday, and Sunday nights at her **sister's house. Because she was spending time at her sister's house,** she moved some of her clothing and personal effects into her sister's house.

EXAMPLE 2   **Dovetailing Used to Connect First and Second Sentences**

Although the party seeking to invoke the jurisdiction of the court has the burden of proving that service was proper, the courts presume that the service was valid if the return is regular on its face. *Thompson v. State, Dept. of Revenue,* **867 So. 2d 603, 605 (Fla. 1st DCA 2004);** *Magazine v. Bedoya,* **475 So. 2d 1035, 1035 (Fla. 3d DCA. 1985). In such instances,** the party challenging the service has the burden of presenting clear and convincing evidence that the service was invalid. *Id.*

While in the above examples dovetailing was used to make clear the connections between sentences, in the next example it is used to make clear the connections between paragraphs. The first sentence in the second paragraph refers back to the information at the end of the first paragraph.

EXAMPLE 3   **Dovetailing Used to Connect Paragraphs**

Thus, the plaintiff will argue that the facts in this case are much stronger than the facts in *Heffernan.* While in *Heffernan,* Mr. Heffernan visited his family only "twice during the season," Ms. Duncan lived at her sister's house three days a week. In addition, while Mr. Heffernan had another permanent residence, Ms. Duncan was staying at a halfway house, which by definition is only a temporary residence. Finally, while in *Heffernan* there was no indication that Mr. Heffernan listed the Florida address on any documents, Ms. Duncan listed her sister's address on her driver's license.

The plaintiff will use these same facts to distinguish ***Torres.*** While in *Torres*, Mr. Torres presented evidence establishing that his permanent residence was in New York, in our case, Ms. Duncan did not have a permanent residence. In the five months prior to service, she had lived at a number of different addresses.

For more on dovetailing, see Section 23.3.

While roadmaps, topic sentences, signposts, transitions, and dovetailing are more important in legal writing than in many other types of writing, do not overuse them. For example, do not use dovetailing to connect all of your sentences or all of your paragraphs.

P R A C T I C E
POINTER

---

§ 8.2 Editing and Proofreading

Now the work is almost done. When you step back from the memo and look at it through the attorney's eyes, you are pleased with its content and organization. You do, however, still need to edit and proofread your memo.

Although some writers mistakenly believe that revising, editing, and proofreading are the same, they are not. While during the revision process you "re-vision" your creation, during the editing process you make that vision clearer, more concise, more precise, more accessible. Proofreading is different yet again. It is the search for errors. When you proofread, you are not asking yourself, "Is there a better way of saying this?" Instead, you are looking to see if what you intended to have on the page is in fact there.

Although the lines between revising and editing and between editing and proofreading blur at times, the distinctions among these three skills are important to keep in mind, if for no other reason than to remind you that there are three distinct ways of making changes to a draft and that the best written documents undergo all three types of changes.

§ 8.2.1 Edit Your Draft

Like revising, editing requires that you look at your work through fresh eyes. At this stage, however, the focus is not on the larger issues of content and organization but on sentence structure, precision and concision, grammar, and punctuation. The goal is to produce a professional product that is easy to read and understand. In this chapter, we focus on writing effective sentences and writing correctly. In Chapter 11, we focus on writing precisely and concisely.

A. Writing Effective Sentences

Most writers can substantially improve their sentences by following four simple pieces of advice about writing:

1. Use the actor as the subject of most sentences.
2. Keep the subject and verb close together.
3. Put old information at the beginning of the sentence and new information at the end.
4. Vary sentence length and pattern.

1. Use the Actor as the Subject of Most Sentences

By using the actor as the subject of most of your sentences, you can eliminate many of the constructions that make legal writing hard to understand: overuse of the passive voice, most nominalizations, expletive constructions, and many misplaced modifiers.

a. Passive Constructions

In a passive construction, the actor appears in the object rather than the subject slot of the sentence, or it is not named at all. For example, in the following sentence, although the jury is the actor, the word "jury" is used as the object of the preposition "by" rather than the subject of the sentence.

EXAMPLE 1 **Passive Voice**

A verdict was reached by the jury.

In the following example, the actor, "jury," is not named at all.

EXAMPLE 2 **Passive Voice**

A verdict was reached.

To use the active voice, simply identify the actor (in this case, the jury) and use it as the subject of the sentence.

EXAMPLE: **Active Voice**

The jury reached a verdict.

Now read each of the following sentences, marking the subject and verb or verb unit in the main clause and deciding whether the writer used the actor as the subject of the sentence. If the writer did not use the actor as the subject of the sentence, decide whether the sentence should be rewritten. As a general rule, the active voice is better unless the passive voice improves the flow of sentences or the writer wants to de-emphasize what the actor did. For more on the effective use of the active and passive voice see section 24.1.

First Draft

In contrast, in most of the cases in which the courts have held that the summons was not left at the defendant's usual place of abode, the house at which service was made had not been lived in by the defendant for a substantial period of time. *See, e.g., Shurman v. Atlantic Mortg. & Inv. Corp.*, 795 So. 2d 952 (Fla. 2001); *Alvarez v. State Farm Mut. Auto Ins. Co.*, 635 So. 2d 131, 132 (Fla. 3d DCA 1994). For example, in *Shurman*, it was held that the service had not been made at the defendant's usual place of abode when the summons was left with the defendant's wife at the family home but the defendant had been incarcerated for at least nine months. *Id.* at 955.

Sentence 1: First Draft

In contrast, in most of the cases in which the courts have held that the summons was not left at the defendant's usual place of abode, the <u>house</u> at which service was made <u>had not been lived in</u> by the defendant for a substantial period of time.

In writing Sentence 1, the writer used the passive voice. Instead of using the actor (the defendant) as the subject of the sentence, the writer has used the word "house." Because the writer did not have a good reason for using the passive voice, we recommend rewriting the sentence using the active voice.

Sentence 1: Rewrite

In contrast, in most of the cases in which the courts have held that the summons was not left at the defendant's usual place of abode, the <u>defendant had not lived</u> in the house where the summons was served for a substantial period of time.

Sentence 2: First Draft

For example, in *Shurman*, <u>it</u> <u>was</u> held that the service had not been made at the defendant's usual place of abode when the summons was left with the defendant's wife at the family home but the defendant had been incarcerated for at least nine months.

Like Sentence 1, Sentence 2 is written in the passive voice. Instead of using the actor as the subject of the sentence, the writer has used an expletive construction (it was). Because the writer did not have a good reason for using the passive voice, we have rewritten it.

Sentence 2: Rewrite

For example, in *Shurman*, the <u>court</u> <u>held</u> that the service had not been made at the defendant's usual place of abode when the summons was left with the defendant's wife at the family home but the defendant had been incarcerated for at least nine months.

Be sure to distinguish between the passive voice and past tense. A sentence written in the past tense may or may not use the passive voice.

P R A C T I C E

For more on the active and passive voice, see Section 24.1

b. Nominalization

You create a nominalization when you turn a verb or an adjective into a noun. Although there are times when you will want to use a nominalization, overuse of nominalizations can make your writing harder to read and understand. In the following sentence, "presumption" is a nominalization.

EXAMPLE   **First Draft**

If the return is regular on its face, there is a **presumption** that the service is valid.

To improve this sentence, identify the real actor (in this case, the courts) and then, in the verb, specifically state what action that actor has taken or will take. Note that "presumption" becomes "presume."

EXAMPLE: **Rewrite**

If the return is regular on its face, the courts **presume** that the service is valid.

---

c. Expletive Constructions

In an expletive construction, phrases such as "it is" or "there are" are used as the subject and verb of the sentence. Although it is sometimes necessary to use such a construction (note the use of an expletive construction in this paragraph), such a construction gives the reader almost no information. Therefore, whenever possible, use a concrete subject and verb — that is, a subject and verb that describe something the reader can "see" in his or her mind. See also sections 24.2 and 25.2.4.

First Draft
EXAMPLE

However, if the return is regular on its face, <u>there</u> <u>is</u> a presumption that the service is valid.

<u>It</u> <u>is</u> Ms. Duncan's argument that....

Rewrites
EXAMPLE

If the return is regular on its face, the <u>courts</u> <u>presume</u> that the service is valid.

<u>Ms. Duncan</u> <u>will argue</u> that....

Note that expletive constructions and nominalizations often go hand in hand. Because you use an expletive construction, you are forced into using a nominalization: If the return is regular on its face, <u>there</u> <u>is</u> a **presumption** that the service is valid.

P R A C T I C E

d. Dangling Modifiers

A dangling modifier is a modifier that does not reasonably modify anything in the sentence. For example, in the following sentence, the modifying phrase "Applying this test" does not reasonably modify anything in the sentence. It is not "it was held" that is doing the applying.

First Draft
EXAMPLE

Applying this test, it was held that the summons and complaint were not left at the defendant's usual place of abode.

The dangling modifier can be eliminated if the actor is used as the subject of the sentence.

EXAMPLE	**Rewrite**

Applying this test, the **court** held that the summons and complaint were not left at the defendant's usual place of abode.

Now the phrase "Applying this test" modifies something in the sentence: the court. For more on dangling modifiers, see section 27.6.2.

2. Keep the Subject and Verb Close Together

Researchers have established that readers cannot understand a sentence until they have located both the subject and the verb. In addition, readers have difficulty remembering the subject if it is separated from the verb by more than seven or eight words: if there are more than seven or eight words between the subject and verb, most readers read the sentence twice, once to find the verb and then a second time to find the subject.

The lesson to be learned from this research is that, as a writer, you should try to keep your subject and verb close together. In the following examples, the subject and verb are underlined.

EXAMPLE 1	**First Draft**

In such instances, the <u>burden</u> of presenting clear and convincing evidence that the service was invalid <u>is</u> on the party challenging the service.

EXAMPLE 2	**Rewrites**

In such instances, the <u>party</u> challenging the service <u>has</u> the burden of presenting clear and convincing evidence that the service was invalid.

In such instances, the <u>defendant</u> <u>has</u> the burden of presenting clear and convincing evidence that the service was invalid.

For more on subject-verb distance, see section 24.4.

3. Put Old Information at the Beginning of the Sentence and New Information at the End

Sentences, and the paragraphs they create, make more sense when the old information is placed at the beginning and the new information is placed at the end. When this pattern is used, the development progresses naturally from left to right without unnecessary backtracking.

Old Information Is at the Beginning of the Sentence, and New Information Is at the End

The only Florida case in which the summons was left with a relative with whom the defendant was visiting is *Torres*. *Id.* at 585. In that case, the plaintiff tried, for more than a month, to serve Mr. Torres at the New York apartment where Mr. Torres had lived for twelve years. *Id.* Although all attempts at service were unsuccessful, the New York process server indicated in his affidavit that he had "verified" with a neighbor that "Mr. Torres lived at the New York address, but that he was often out of town, and was expected to return in two weeks." *Id.* Because the server could not serve the defendant in New York, the plaintiff served Mr. Torres's mother at her residence in Florida. In his affidavit, the Florida process server stated that Mr. Torres's mother told him that "he (presumably Mr. Torres) would be home soon." *Id.* Mr. Torres stated that he never received notice. In holding that the service was not valid, the court noted that while the standard of review was gross abuse of discretion, the trial court had not heard live testimony, and the plaintiff had the burden of establishing that the service was valid. *Id.* at 587. The court then went on to note that the evidence tended to support Mr. Torres's position that his usual place of abode was in New York and that Mr. Torres's mother's statement that Mr. Torres would be home soon was, at best, ambiguous. *Id.*

In the paragraph set out above, the first sentence acts as a topic sentence, telling the attorney that there is only one Florida case that has facts similar to the facts in the client's case. That first sentence ends with a reference to the new information, which is the name of the case: *Torres*. In the second sentence, the name of the case is now the old information, so the second sentence begins with a reference back to that old information. The second sentence then ends with new information: that the plaintiff had tried on a number of occasions to serve the defendant in New York. In the third sentence, the old information is that the plaintiff had tried to serve the defendant in New York. Thus, the author uses this old information to start the third sentence, and puts the new information, that the neighbor had told the process server that the defendant was out of town, at the end of the third sentence.

Question

Analyze the rest of the sentences in the paragraph. In those sentences did the author put the old information at the beginning of the sentence and the new information at the end?

d. Vary Sentence Length and Pattern

Even if writing is technically correct, it is not considered good if it is not pleasing to the ear. Read the following example aloud.

All the Sentences Are About the Same Length and Use the Same Pattern

A process server went to Ms. Webster's house on Wednesday, July 26, 2006. The process server asked for Elaine Duncan. Ms. Webster told the process server that "Elaine isn't here today." The process server then handed the summons and complaint to Ms. Webster. The process server told Ms. Webster that Ms. Duncan "needed to go to court."

In the above example, the writing is not pleasing because the sentences are similar in length and all follow the same pattern. Although short, uncomplicated sentences are often better than long, complicated ones, the use of too many short sentences results in writing that sounds choppy and sophomoric. As the following example illustrates, the passage is much better when the writer varies sentence length and pattern.

EXAMPLE

Writer Has Varied the Length of the Sentences and the Sentence Pattern

On Wednesday, July 26, 2006, a process server went to Ms. Webster's house and asked for Elaine Duncan. When Ms. Webster told the process server that "Elaine isn't here today," the process server handed the summons to Ms. Webster and told her that Ms. Duncan "needed to go to court."

For more on sentence construction see Chapter 24.

B. Writing Correctly

For a moment, imagine that you have received the following letter from a local law firm.

EXAMPLE:

> Dear Student:
> Thank you for submitting an application for a position as a law clerk with are firm. Your grades in law school are very good, however, at this time we do not have any positions available. Its possible, however, that we may have a opening next summer and we therefore urge you to reapply with us then.
>
> Sincerely,
>
> Senior Partner

No matter how bad the market is, most students would not want to be associated with a firm that sends out a five-line letter containing three major errors and several minor ones. Unfortunately, the reverse is also true. No matter how short-handed they are, most law firms do not want a law clerk who has not mastered the basic rules of grammar and punctuation. Most firms cannot afford a clerk who makes careless errors or one who lacks basic writing skills.

Consequently, at the editing stage you need to go back through your draft and correct errors. Look first for the errors that potentially affect meaning (misplaced modifiers, misspellings, incorrect use of "which" and "that") and for errors that educated readers are likely to notice (incomplete sentences, comma splices, incorrect use of the possessive, lack of parallelism). Then look for the errors you know from past experience you are likely to make.

§ 8.2.2 Proofreading

Most writers learn the importance of proofreading the hard way. A letter, brief, or contract goes out with the client's name misspelled, with an "or" where there should have been an "and," or without an essential "not." At a minimum, these errors cause embarrassment; at worst, they result in a lawsuit.

To avoid such errors, treat proofreading as a separate step in the revising process. After you have finished revising and editing, go back through your draft and look not at content, organization, or sentence style, but for errors. Have you written what you intended to write?

Proofreading is most effective when it is done on hard copy several days (or, when that is not feasible, several hours) after you have finished editing. Force yourself to read slowly, focusing not on the sentences but on the individual words in the sentences. Is a word missing? Is a word unnecessarily repeated? Are letters transposed? You can force yourself to read slowly by covering up all but the line you are reading, by reading from right to left, or by reading from the bottom of the page to the top.

You can also use a free website, *readmeplease.com*, to help you proofread. This website will "read" your draft to you. Because the program reads each word, you can use it to check for double words, missing words, and wrong words.

Also, force yourself to begin your proofreading by looking at the sections that caused you the most difficulty or that you wrote last. Because you were concentrating on content or were tired, these sections probably contain the most errors.

Finally, when you get into practice, do not rely on just your spelling and grammar checkers. Instead, make it a habit to have a second person proofread your work. Not only will such a person see errors that you missed, he or she is also less likely than you to "read in" missing words.

§ 8.2.3 Citations

As a legal writer, you have an extra burden. In addition to editing and proofreading the text, you must also edit and proofread your citations to legal authorities. At the editing stage, focus on selection and placement of citations. Is the authority you cited the best authority? Did you avoid string cites (the citing of multiple cases for the same point)? Have you included a citation to authority for every rule stated? Did you include the appropriate signal? Have you over- or under-emphasized the citation? (You emphasize a citation by placing it in the text of a sentence; you de-emphasize it by placing it in a separate citation sentence.)

In contrast, at the proofreading stage, focus on the citation itself. Are the volume and page numbers correct? Are the pinpoint cites accurate? Have you included the year of the decision and any subsequent history? Is the spacing correct?

§ 8.3 Reviewing the Final Draft of the Memo

At long last, we are at the end of the process. We have researched, drafted, revised, edited, and proofread and, finally, we have finished the memo. Although the following memo is not a perfect one, it represents a good work product for a first-year law student. Thus, take a few minutes to read through it, noting what the author did well and what the author might do better.

EXAMPLE

Memo

To: Christine Galeano

From: Legal Intern

Date: September 12, 2006

Re: Elaine Duncan, Case No. 06-478
        Service of Process, Usual Place of Abode; Notification of Contents

Statement of Facts

Elaine Duncan has contacted our office asking for assistance in overturning a default judgment. You have asked me to determine whether the service of process was valid.

On February 1, 2006, Ms. Duncan entered an inpatient drug treatment program in Miami, Florida. She remained in the program until March 27, 2006, when she moved into a residential treatment house for recovering addicts.

During April, May, and June 2006, Ms. Duncan was a full-time resident at the halfway house. She had a bedroom in the house, ate her meals there, and had some of her possessions there. In addition, when she applied for jobs in May and June, she listed the halfway house address as her address.

Beginning in July 2006, Ms. Duncan began spending less time at the halfway house and more time with her sister, Elizabeth Webster, who is 32. During July and August 2006, Ms. Duncan usually spent weeknights at the halfway house and Friday, Saturday, and Sunday nights at her sister's house. Because she was spending time at her sister's house, Ms. Duncan moved some of her clothing and personal effects into her sister's house. When she renewed her driver's license in August 2006, Ms. Duncan listed her sister's address as her address.

On Wednesday, July 26, 2006, a process server went to Ms. Webster's house and asked for Elaine Duncan. When Ms. Webster told the process server that "Elaine isn't here today," the process server handed the summons to Ms. Webster and told her that Ms. Duncan "needed to go to court."

Ms. Webster will testify that she never gave the summons to her sister. Because she thought that the paper related to some of Ms. Duncan's unpaid bills, Ms. Webster simply put the summons in a shoebox in the kitchen with a stack of Ms. Duncan's other mail. Ms. Duncan says she never received the summons and, as a result, she did not respond. The return of service is regular on its face.

Ms. Duncan has been employed since August 1, 2006, and she has lived in her own apartment since September 1, 2006. Her voter's registration card lists the address that she lived at before she entered the treatment program.

There is nothing in the record that indicates whether the plaintiff tried to personally serve Ms. Duncan or whether it tried to serve her at the halfway house.

Issue

Under Florida's service of process statute, was Ms. Duncan properly served when (1) service was made on Ms. Duncan's 32-year-old sister on a Wednesday at Ms. Duncan's sister's house; (2) during the month when service was made, Ms. Duncan spent weeknights at a halfway house where she had a room, ate meals, and kept belongings and spent Friday, Saturday, and Sunday nights at her sister's house where she had some belongings; (3) Ms. Duncan listed the halfway house address on job applications but her sister's address on her driver's license; (4) the process server told Ms. Duncan's sister that Ms. Duncan needed to go to court; and (5) Ms. Duncan's sister did not give the summons to Ms. Duncan, and Ms. Duncan states that she did not receive notice?

Brief Answer

Probably not. Because the summons and complaint were given to Ms. Duncan's adult sister at the sister's house, Ms. Duncan will have to concede that the service was made on a person 15 years or older who was living at the house at which the service was made. In addition, because the process server told Ms. Duncan's sister that Ms. Duncan needed to go to court, Ms. Duncan cannot meet her burden of proving that the person served was not informed of the contents of the documents. However, because Ms. Duncan was not actually living at her sister's house on the day that service was made, she can probably meet her burden of proving that her sister's house was not her usual place of abode.

Discussion

The fundamental purpose of service of process is to give defendants notice of claims that have been filed against them and to provide defendants with an opportunity to defend their rights. *Shurman v. Atlantic Mortg. & Inv. Corp.*, 795 So. 2d 952, 953-54 (Fla. 2001). Because it is important that litigants receive notice of actions against them, courts strictly construe and enforce statutes governing service of process. *Id.* at 954.

In Florida, substituted service can be made by leaving the copies at defendant's "usual place of abode with any person residing therein who is 15 years of age or older and informing the person of their contents." Fla. Stat. § 48.031(a)(1)(2004).

Although the party seeking to invoke the jurisdiction of the court has the burden of proving that service was proper, if the return is regular on its face, the courts presume that the service was valid. *Thompson v. State, Dept. of Revenue,* 867 So. 2d 603, 605 (Fla. 1st DCA 2004); *Magazine v. Bedoya,* 475 So. 2d 1035, 1035 (Fla. 3d DCA 1985). In such instances, the party challenging the service has the burden of presenting clear and convincing evidence that the service was invalid. *Id.*

In this case, Ms. Duncan will have to concede that the summons was left with a person 15 years old or older who was residing at the house where the summons and complaint were served. In addition, it is unlikely that Ms. Duncan will be able to prove that her sister was not informed of the contents of the documents. Ms. Duncan may, however, be able to present clear and convincing evidence that the summons was not left at her usual place of abode.

A. "Usual Place of Abode"

If a defendant has more than one residence, the defendant's usual place of abode is the place where the defendant was actually living at the time of service. *Shurman v. Atlantic Mortg. & Inv. Corp.*, 795 So. 2d 952, 953-54 (Fla. 2001). It is not enough that the summons and complaint are left with a relative. *Torres v. Arnco Constr., Inc.*, 867 So. 2d 583, 586 (Fla. 5th DCA 2004).

The only case in which the Florida courts have discussed usual place of abode and held that the service was made at the defendant's usual place of abode is a 1940 case: *State ex rel. Merritt v. Heffernan*, 195 So. 145 (Fla. 1940). In that case, the defendant's wife was served at the family's apartment in Florida. *Id.* at 146. However, one hour before service was made, the defendant left the apartment to return to his permanent residence in Minnesota, where he had his office, voted, and paid taxes. *Id.* The court noted that many persons have several residences that they permanently maintain, occupying one at one period of the year and another during another period. *Id.* at 147. In such situations, the summons and complaint must be served at the dwelling house in which the defendant is living at the time when the service is made. *Id.* Although the defendant was on a train heading toward Minnesota at the time service was made, the court stated that he was not within the class of persons who had at the time of service lost one place of residence and had not yet established another. *Id.* at 148. Instead, the court held that the defendant's then place of abode was the apartment in Florida. *Id.* at 147. The court also pointed out that the defendant had visited his family in Florida "twice during the season" and that there was no convincing proof that he did not intend to return to Florida. *Id.*

In contrast, in most of the cases in which the courts have held that the summons was not left at the defendant's usual place of abode, the defendant had not lived at the house where service was made for a substantial period of time. *See, e.g., Shurman v. Atlantic Mortg. & Inv. Corp.*, 795 So. 2d 952 (Fla. 2001); *Alvarez v. State Farm Mut. Auto. Ins. Co.*, 635 So. 2d 131 (Fla. 3d DCA 1994). For example, in *Shurman*, the court held that the service had not been made at the defendant's usual place of abode when the summons was left with the defendant's wife at the family home but the defendant had been incarcerated for at least nine months. *Id.* at 955. Similarly, in *Thompson*, the court held that the summons had not been left at the defendant's usual place of abode when the summons was left with the defendant's wife at the family home. *Id.* at 605. In reaching its decision, the *Thompson* court relied on the defendant's affidavit, in which the defendant stated that he was separated from his wife, that he had not resided at that address for over three years, and that he did not authorize anyone to accept service of process on his behalf. *Id.* In both cases, the plaintiff did not present evidence contradicting the defendant's statements.

Ms. Duncan can make three arguments to support her assertion that her sister's house was not her usual place of abode. First, Ms. Duncan will argue that, under the plain language of the rule, her sister's house was not her usual place of abode. When a defendant has more than one residence, the service must be made at the place where the defendant was actually living at the time the summons and complaint were served. In this case, Ms. Duncan had more than one residence: during the week she lived at the halfway house, and on weekends she visited her sister. Because the summons and complaint were served on a Wednesday, a weekday, the service was not made at the place where Ms. Duncan was actually living.

Second, Ms. Duncan will argue that this case is more like *Torres* than *Heffernan*. Like Mr. Torres, who only visited his mother and who was not at his mother's house when service was made, Ms. Duncan only visited her sister and was not at her sister's house when the summons and complaint were served. However, while Mr. Torres's mother's statement that Mr. Torres "would be home soon" suggested that Mr. Torres would be returning to his mother's house that day, Ms. Duncan's sister told the process server that Ms. Duncan "isn't here today." In addition, while the plaintiff in *Torres* had tried on numerous occasions to serve Mr. Torres at his New York house, in our case we do not know whether the defendant tried to serve Ms. Duncan personally or at the halfway house. *Heffernan* can be distinguished in two ways: (1) while Mr. Heffernan had been at his family's apartment only an hour before the summons and complaint were served, Ms. Duncan had not been at her sister's house for several days; and (2) while in *Heffernan* the summons and complaint were served on the defendant's wife, in our case the summons and complaint were served on Ms. Duncan's sister. It is also important to note that, since *Heffernan*, the courts have interpreted the service of process statutes more narrowly.

Finally, Ms. Duncan can argue that, as a matter of public policy, the court should hold that the summons was not left at Ms. Duncan's usual place of abode. The courts have repeatedly held that the service of process statutes should be strictly construed and that service on a relative is not, by itself, enough. *Shurman v. Atlantic Mortg. & Inv. Corp.*, 795 So. 2d 952, 953-54 (Fla. 2001). In addition, in this case, Ms. Duncan did not receive notice.

In response, the plaintiff will argue that Ms. Duncan was served at one of her usual places of abode. The courts have not required that the defendant be living at the house on the day on which the summons was served. Instead, they require only that the defendant be living there "at the time of service." Therefore, while Ms. Duncan may not have been at her sister's house on the day that the summons and complaint were served, she had been there the previous weekend, and she was there the following weekend. In addition, Ms. Duncan had possessions at her sister's house, and she listed her sister's address as her own address when she applied for a driver's license.

Thus, the plaintiff will argue that the facts in this case are much stronger than the facts in *Heffernan*. While in *Heffernan* Mr. Heffernan visited his family only "twice during the season," Ms. Duncan lived at her sister's house three days a week. In addition, while Mr. Heffernan had another permanent residence, Ms. Duncan was staying at a halfway house, which is, by definition, only a temporary residence. Finally, while in *Heffernan* there was no indication that Mr. Heffernan listed the Florida address on any documents, Ms. Duncan listed her sister's address on her driver's license. In addition, there is evidence indicating that Ms. Duncan received other types of mail at her sister's house.

The plaintiff will use these same facts to distinguish *Torres*. While in *Torres*, Mr. Torres presented evidence establishing that his permanent residence was in New York, in our case, Ms. Duncan did not have a permanent residence. In the five months before service, she had been an inpatient in a treatment facility; she had lived at the halfway house; and she had lived with her sister. The plaintiff can also distinguish *Shurman* and *Thompson*. While in *Shurman* and *Thompson* the record indicated that the defendants had not lived at the house where service had been made for months or years, in this case, Ms. Duncan admits that she had stayed at her sister's house on the weekend before her sister was served.

Finally, the plaintiff will argue that, because the return was regular on its face, Ms. Duncan has the burden of proving, by clear and convincing evidence, that her sister's house was not her usual place of abode. In this instance, Ms. Duncan has not met that burden. In addition, when there is evidence that the defendant was in fact living at the house where service was made, the courts should not require plaintiffs to determine which house the defendant was living at on any particular day.

While both sides have strong arguments, the court will probably conclude that the summons was not left at Ms. Duncan's usual place of abode. In the more recent cases, the courts have strictly construed the statute, holding that the service was not made at the defendant's usual place of abode when the defendant had a more permanent place of abode. Thus, because the halfway house was Ms. Duncan's more permanent residence, the court will probably conclude that it was Ms. Duncan's usual place of abode. In addition, the court may be influenced by two key facts: the record does not indicate that the plaintiff tried to serve Ms. Duncan at the halfway house, and Ms. Duncan states that she did not receive notice.

B. "Person 15 Years Old or Older Residing Therein"

In addition to leaving the summons at the defendant's usual place of abode, the process server must leave the summons with a person 15 years old or older residing therein. If the court concludes that Ms. Duncan's sister's house was Ms. Duncan's usual place of abode, Ms. Duncan should concede that the summons was left with a person residing therein who is at least 15 years old: Ms. Webster is 32 years old, and the summons and complaint were left with her at her house.

C. "Informed of Contents"

[Analysis is omitted.]

Conclusion

Because of the strong public policy in favor of ensuring that defendants receive notice of actions that have been filed against them, the court will probably hold that the substituted service of process was not valid.

Ms. Duncan will have to concede that her sister, Ms. Webster, is a person of suitable age and that Ms. Webster was residing at the house where the service was made. In addition, because the process server told Ms. Webster that Ms. Duncan needed to go to court, it seems unlikely that Ms. Duncan would be able prove, by clear and convincing evidence, Ms. Webster was not informed of the contents.

Ms. Duncan may, however, be able to prove that the summons and complaint were not served at her usual place of abode. In the more recent cases, the courts have strictly construed "usual place of abode," holding that the service was not made at the defendant's usual place of abode when the defendant had a more permanent place of abode. Thus, because the halfway house was Ms. Duncan's more permanent residence, the court will probably conclude that it was Ms. Duncan's usual place of abode. In addition, the court may be influenced by two key facts: the record does not indicate that the plaintiff tried to serve Ms. Duncan at the halfway house, and Ms. Duncan states that she did not receive notice.

§ 8.4 Reflecting on the Lawyering Process

Researching and writing a memo is more than an academic exercise. Most memos are written in response to a client's request, and the client would not have contacted the attorney unless the issue was of some importance. Thus, in writing a memo, you need to think not only about the legal issues but also about the people who raised them.

One place to start is by examining our assumptions. For example, in working on the service of process issue, what assumptions did you make about the underlying cause of action? Did you assume that the plaintiff was suing Ms. Duncan for breach of contract? To obtain damages for injuries sustained in an accident? For divorce? To terminate her parental rights? Similarly, how did you picture Ms. Duncan? How old is she? Is she married? Does she have children? What is her education? What type of work does she do? What is her income? What is her race or ethnicity? Why did she begin using drugs? What will she be doing five or ten years from now? What is her relationship to the rest of her family?

Next, think about how your assumptions may have affected the way you viewed the case. Should the rules for service of process be different depending on the nature of the underlying cause of action? For instance, should the plaintiff's burden be higher in a divorce action than in a contract action, in actions to terminate parental rights, or to recover damages for injuries? Why or why not? In addition, is the firm that you work for more or less likely to take the case depending on Ms. Duncan's personal characteristics? Why or why not? Would Ms. Duncan's personal characteristics have any effect on how the judge would rule on the service of process issue? Why or why not? If there is a characteristic that you think would make the judge view Ms. Duncan more sympathetically, would you try to get that information before the judge? Why or why not?

Researching and Writing a Memo Involving State Common Law

Introduction: The Assignment

Assume that you work for a small firm in Lubbock, Texas. Several weeks after you start working, your supervising attorney hands you the following memo and asks you to determine whether an organization called Doctors and Nurses Who Care (DNWC) has obtained a right to Mr. Garcia's land through adverse possession.

To: Legal Intern

From: Supervising Attorney

Date: October 16, 2006

Re: Michael Garcia; Adverse Possession of Property in Washington State

- One of our long-time clients, Michael Garcia, has contacted our office regarding property that he owns in Washington State. Mr. Garcia is worried that an organization may have obtained title to this property through adverse possession.
- Mr. Garcia inherited the Washington property from his grandfather, Eduardo Montoya, in 1992.
- Mr. Montoya purchased the land in 1951. He and his family used the land every summer from 1951 until the late 1980s, when he became ill.
- When Mr. Montoya's family used the property, family members camped on the site and used a small dock for swimming, fishing, and boating.
- Mr. Garcia visited the property in the fall of 1992 but moved to Lubbuck not long after that visit. He did not visit the property from 1993 until last August.
- The group that has been using Mr. Garcia's land since 1990 is called Doctors and Nurses Who Care (DNWC).
- DNWC has owned the five-acre parcel that is just to the north of Mr. Garcia's property since 1989. DNWC uses its property for summer camps for children who suffer from serious illnesses and disabilities. In a typical summer, DNWC runs two one-week camps for children with cancer, two one-week camps for children who are blind, two one-week camps for children who are autistic, and two one-week camps for children with diabetes.
- DNWC maintains and uses the campsites, the fire area, the outhouse, and the dock, all of which are on Mr. Garcia's property.
- During the summer of 1994, DNWC posted a "No Trespassing" sign on the dock, and the sign is still there.
- Most of the time the children stay in cabins located on DNWC property. However, DNWC uses Mr. Garcia's property for campouts. One night each week, one group of about ten children will camp out in tents on Mr. Garcia's property, the next night another group of ten will camp out on his property, and so on. Thus, DNWC uses Mr. Garcia's land four or five nights a week for eight weeks each summer.
- During these campouts, the children pitch and stay in tents and cook over a fire.
- Mr. Garcia has paid all of the taxes and assessments.
- In about February 1994, Mr. Garcia received a letter from DNWC asking whether it could continue using his land for campouts. Mr. Garcia was busy and never responded to the letter.
- Last August, Mr. Garcia visited the property with the intent of spending a few days camping on the lake. When he got there, he discovered that there were children and their counselors on the property.
- Mr. Garcia went to the camp's headquarters and talked to the director, Dr. Liu, who was very nice. However, Dr. Liu told

Mr. Garcia that it was his understanding that the land belonged to DNWC.

- Mr. Garcia did not spend the night at the property that night, but he did spend the next night there after the children left. No one from DNWC asked him to leave.
- Although over the years the land around the lake has become more and more developed, the area on which the camp is located is still relatively undeveloped. Most of the property owners use their land only during the summer.

Because I am not familiar with Washington State law, would you please research this issue for me? Under Washington State law, may DNWC claim title to Mr. Garcia's land through adverse possession? I need your memo by the end of the week.

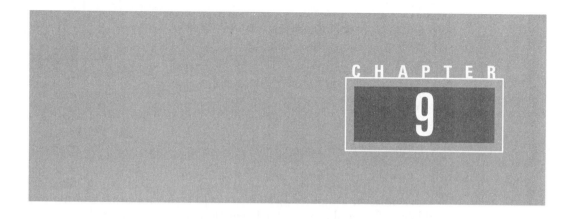

Researching Issues Governed by Common Law

lthough much of the law is now enacted law, there are still some issues that are governed by common law. Therefore, in addition to knowing how to research issues governed by statutes and ordinances, you also need to know how to research issues governed by common law.

§ 9.1 Are All Cases the Same?

The answer to this question is no. In fact, cases fall into two categories. In one category are the cases that set out, interpret, and apply the common law, and in the other category are the cases that interpret and apply enacted law.

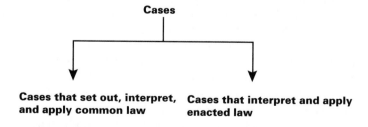

The following example shows how common law rules are created and the relationship between common law rules, enacted law, and the cases that interpret and apply enacted law.

Assume for the moment a blank slate. You are in a state with no common law rules and no statutes, ordinances, or regulations. The first case that your state's courts hear is *In re Marriage of Adamson*.

Case 1: *In re Marriage of Adamson*

In *Adamson*, a mother asks the court to grant her custody of her two children, a 2 year-old son and a 4 year-old daughter. Because there are no common law rules or statutes governing custody, the court must make its own law. After considering the community's norms and the facts of the case, the court grants the mother's request for custody on the grounds that young children should be with their mothers.

Case 2: *In re Marriage of Brown*

Not long after the court decides *Adamson*, another mother requests custody of her children, a 4 year-old son and a 14 year-old daughter. Unlike the situation ia *Adamson*, in this situation the slate is not blank. There is now precedent. In deciding *Brown*, the court will be guided by the court's decision in *Adamson*. The reasoning in *Adamson* (that young children should be with their mothers) is now a common law rule that the court applies in *Brown*.

Applying the common law rule set out in *Adamson*, the court grants the mother custody of her 4 year-old son. There is, however, no rule that deals with 14 year-old daughters. Thus, the court is once again in the position of creating its own common law rule. This time the court rules that teenage daughters should remain with their mothers and grants the mother custody of her daughter.

Case 3: *In re Marriage of Carey*

In the next case, *In re Marriage of Carey*, a mother with a history of abusing alcohol asks the court to grant her custody of her two daughters, who are 5 and 12. In deciding this case, the court applies both the common law rule set out in *Adamson*, that young children should be with their mothers, and the common law rule set out in *Brown*, that teenage daughters should remain with their mothers, and grants the mother custody of both daughters. In granting the mother custody, the court interprets the rules set out in *Adamson* and *Brown* and decides that those common law rules apply even if the mother has a history of abusing alcohol.

As *Adamson*, *Brown*, and *Carey* illustrate, in a common law system, the court's reasoning in one case becomes a common law rule that is applied in the next case. Of course, not all the rules announced in earlier cases are applied in all subsequent cases. For instance, if Case 4, *In re Marriage of Davidson*, involves the custody of a 1 year-old girl whose mother does not have a history of alcohol abuse, the court would apply only the rule announced in *Adamson*; it would not need to consider the additional common law rules set out in *Brown* and *Carey*. Nor does each case need to add to the existing law. The court could decide *Davidson* without creating any new rules.

Continuing with our example, assume that a few years after the court decides *In re Marriage of Carey*, the legislature enacts a statute that sets out the rules for determining child custody issues. In enacting such a statute, the legislature can do one of two things: it can enact or "codify" the common law rule, or it can abolish the common law rule and create its own statute-based rule. If the legislature enacts or codifies the common law rule, the cases that were decided before the statute was enacted are still good law, and the courts can use them in deciding how to interpret and apply the statute. If, however, the legislature abolishes the common law rule, the cases that were decided before the statute was enacted are, most likely, no longer good law.

In our example, the legislature decides to abolish the common law rules that favor mothers. Under the new statute, the courts must grant custody "in accordance with the best interests of the children." In determining what is in the best interests of the children, the courts must consider a variety of factors, including "the parents' wishes; the children's wishes; the interaction and interrelationship of the child with parents and siblings; the child's adjustment to his or her home, school, and community; and the mental and physical health of all of the individuals involved."

Because this statute abolished the common law rules set out in *Adamson*, *Brown*, and *Carey*, these cases are, to the extent that they contradict the statute, no longer good law. Thus, when Case 5, *In re Marriage of Edwards*, comes before the court, the court applies the statute and not the rules from *Adamson*, *Brown*, and *Carey*.

The application of a statute is not always clear, however. For example, assume that in *Edwards* the mother contends that she should be given custody not because the children are young but because she has always been their primary caretaker. Although the statute does not specifically address this argument, the court agrees with the mother, reasoning that because the mother has always been the primary caretaker, it would be in the children's best interest to remain with her.

Because the court's reasoning in *Edwards* (that it is in the best interests of the children to remain with the parent who has been their primary caretaker) is not inconsistent with the statute, that reasoning can be used by the courts in subsequent cases. In deciding Case 6, *In re Marriage of Forino*, the court will apply not just the statute but also the reasoning announced in *Edwards*. Similarly, in deciding Case 7, *In re Marriage of Gonzales*, the court will consider not only the statute and the reasoning in *Edwards*, but also the reasoning in *Forino*. Although the "rules" created in *Edwards* and *Forino* create precedent, these cases do not, at least technically, fall into the category of cases that we call the common law. Instead, they fall into the second category. They are simply cases that interpret and apply enacted law.

§ 9.2 Developing a Research Plan

Before electronic research became common, the tools that attorneys used to research issues governed by state and federal statutes were very different from the tools they used to research common law issues. When they researched an issue that was governed by a statute, attorneys used an annotated code to find the cases that had interpreted and applied the statute. See Chapter 6, page 86. In contrast, when attorneys researched a common law issue, they used a digest to find both the common law rule and the cases that had interpreted and applied that common law rule. While digests are still an excellent finding tool, today many lawyers use fee-based services such as LexisNexis, Loislaw, VersusLaw, and Westlaw to find cases that outline and apply common law doctrines.

Research Plan for an Issue Governed by Common Law

Jurisdiction:	[Enter the name of the applicable state.][1]
Type of Law:	Common law
Preliminary Issue Statement:	[Put your first draft of the issue statement here.]

Step 1:   Spend thirty to sixty minutes doing background reading on the Internet, in a state practice manual or book, in a hornbook or *Nutshell,* or in a legal encyclopedia.

Step 2:   Locate the cases from your jurisdiction that set out and apply the common law rules.

Step 3:   Cite check the cases that you plan to use to make sure that they are still good law.

Step 4:   If appropriate, locate cases from other jurisdictions, law review articles, or other commentaries that might be on point.

Question

How is the research plan for an issue governed by common law the same or different from the research plan for an issue governed by a statute? Compare this research plan with the one on page 74.

§ 9.3 Sources for Researching Problems Governed by State Common Law

The chart on page 201 lists some, but not all, of the sources you can use in researching an issue governed by common law. Because the names of the sources vary by state, we have listed the sources using generic labels, not specific names. You can, however, find the names of your state's practice books using your library's electronic card catalog, and you can find the names of your state's reporters using Appendix 1 of the *ALWD Citation Manual* or Table 1 in *The Bluebook.* Finally, note that not all states have all the sources that are listed.

---

1. Technically there is no federal common law.

§ 9.3.1 Background Reading

a. The Internet

Sometimes you can do your background reading on the Internet. For example, in some states, there are law firms that post plain English explanations of common law doctrines. One of the easiest ways to find these types of websites is to use the "Advanced Search" Option on Google. Simply type in the name of your state and terms that describe the doctrine. Remember, however, that information on websites may not be accurate or up to date. Thus, use the websites to familiarize yourself with the doctrine and not as authority.

b. Practice Manuals and Books

Although sometimes you can find good information about a common law doctrine on a free Internet site, most of the time the best source is a state practice manual or book. These manuals will usually provide a short history of the common law rule or doctrine, the general rules, and citations to key cases.

Chart 9.1	**Sources for Researching Issues Governed by Common Law**
Background Reading	▪ The Internet ▪ State practice manuals and practice books ▪ Hornbooks ▪ *Nutshells* ▪ Legal encyclopedias
Finding Tools	▪ State practice manuals and practice books ▪ State digests ▪ Regional digests ▪ Fee-based services such as LexisNexis, Loislaw, VersusLaw, and Westlaw ▪ Free Internet sites such as FindLaw.com, lexisone.com, or a state government website
Cases	▪ State reporter containing decisions from the state's highest appellate court ▪ State reporter containing decisions from the state's intermediate appellate court ▪ West regional reporter containing decisions from the state's highest appellate court and the state's intermediate appellate court ▪ Fee-based services such as LexisNexis, Loislaw, VersusLaw, and Westlaw ▪ Free Internet sites such as FindLaw.com, lexisone.com, or a state government website
Cite Checking	▪ KeyCite® ▪ *Shepard's*®

Secondary Authorities	▪ *American Law Reports* (for example, A.L.R.3d, A.L.R.4th, and A.L.R.5th)
	▪ Law review articles

In addition, if there are any statutes that affect the common law doctrine, the manual will usually provide you with cross-references to those statutes. Some examples of state practice manuals are *Trawick's Florida Practice and Procedure, Illinois Law and Practice*, and *Washington Practice*. While some practice books are only available in book form, increasingly they are being added to fee-based services. For instance, the West practice books are on Westlaw, and many state bar publications are on Loislaw.

c. Hornbooks and *Nutshells*

Hornbooks and *Nutshells* are also good sources for background reading. Like practice manuals, these books provide you with a short history of the common law rule and with the general rules. In addition, they usually include descriptions and citations to cases. However, unlike a state practice manual, which lists cases from a single state, hornbooks set out citations to cases from a variety of states. Most hornbooks are available only in book form. To find them in your library, use your library's electronic card catalog or ask a librarian.

d. Legal Encyclopedias

If one is available, you can also do background reading in a legal encyclopedia. While a few states have their own legal encyclopedias, most states do not. Thus, you will need to use a more general encyclopedia — for example, *American Jurisprudence Second* (Am. Jur. 2d) or *Corpus Juris Secundum* (C.J.S.) You can find encyclopedias in book form in your law library or on fee-based services such as LexisNexis and Westlaw.

See Exercise 9A in the *Practice Book.*

§9.3.2 Finding Tools

While at one point digests were the best way to find cases setting out and applying common law rules, today there are a number of other good ways to find cases.

a. Practice Manuals and Books

If you do your background reading in a practice manual or book, you can use that practice manual to find cases. More likely than not, the practice manual will cite cases that set out the common law rule and that explain who has the burden of proof and what that burden is. To find the cases cited in the practice manual, use the citation to locate the cases in the book version of a state or regional reporter; use the "Find by citation" option to find the cases on a fee-based service such as LexisNexis, Loislaw, VersusLaw, or Westlaw; or use a free Internet site if your state's cases are on that site.

b. Digests

Digests are subject indexes for both common law cases and cases that interpret and apply enacted law. Each digest is divided into a number of topics, with those topics divided into subtopics and, sometimes, subsubtopics. Under these topic headings are notes of decision summarizing cases that discuss the particular topic.

West publishes a number of digests, including state digests, which contain headnotes from every case published in the corresponding state reporters; regional digests, which contain headnotes from every case published in the corresponding regional reporter; and federal digests, which can be used to find cases published in the *Supreme Court Reporter*, the first, second, and third series of the *Federal Reporter*, and the first and second series of the *Federal Supplement*. In addition, West publishes a number of specialty digests — for example, the *Bankruptcy Digest*, the *Military Justice Digest*, and the *Education Law Digest*.

Digests published by West use West's Key Number System. The system works as follows. Through the years, West has created a series of topics and within those topics, "Key Numbers" for each point of law. This set of topics and Key Numbers is West's Key Number System.

When a court publishes an opinion, it sends a copy of its opinion to West, which assigns the case to an editor. The editor, who is an attorney, identifies each point of law discussed in the court's opinion, writes a single sentence summarizing that point of law, and then assigns that summary a topic and Key Number. These summaries are used in two ways. First, West uses them as headnotes for the case. In West publications, these headnotes are placed at the beginning of the case, after the name of the case but before the court's opinion. Second, these summaries are placed in the appropriate digests under their assigned topic and Key Number.

Because the headnotes are written by the company that publishes the reporter and not by the court, you may never cite to a headnote as authority. Instead, you must cite to that part of the court's opinion **P R A C T I C E**  from which the publishing company took the point of law summarized in the headnote. Similarly, you may not cite to the notes of decision presented in a digest. Instead, you must read and cite to the case from which that note of decision was drawn.

---

c. Fee-Based Services

There are a number of ways to find cases using LexisNexis, Loislaw, VersusLaw, and Westlaw. If, during your background reading, you located a case that is on point, you can use that case to find additional cases. For example, if you are using Westlaw, you can identify the headnotes that are on point and then use either the Key Numbers associated with those cases to do a Key Number search or use the "Most Frequently Cited Cases" option.

In the alternative, you can select your state's caselaw database (use a database that contains all your state's published decisions) and then construct a Boolean (terms or connector) search that includes a word or phrase that describes the common law doctrine (for example, "false imprisonment," "battery," or "nuisance") and a word that the courts are likely to have used in setting out the general rules or burden of proof (for example, "prove," "establish," "elements," or "factors"). Once you have found and analyzed the general rules, you can then run additional searches for cases that have interpreted or applied a specific element or factor.

d. Free Internet Sites

There are a growing number of free Internet sites that provide access to the official versions of state cases. Two of the most commonly used sites are *FindLaw.com* and *lexisone.com*. In addition, a growing number of states are establishing government websites that include some, if not all, of that state's published opinions. Finally, some state bar associations now offer their members free or low-cost use of "Casemaker," a database that provides attorneys with access to the official copy of their state's cases. Although the search engines on these sites may not be as sophisticated as the search engines on the fee-based sites, most of them allow at least some form of terms and connectors searching.

See **Exercise 9B** in the *Practice Book*.

§ 9.3.3 Cases

The cases setting out, interpreting, and applying common law rules are in the same reporters as the cases that interpret and apply enacted law. In publishing a case, neither the courts nor the publishing companies distinguish between the two categories of cases. Instead, all the cases are grouped together, organized not by type of case or by topic but by the date of the decision.

In some states, decisions are reproduced in both the state's reporter or reporters and in a regional reporter. For example, you can find the Virginia Supreme Court's decisions in both *Virginia Reports* (Va.) and in *Southeastern Reporter* (S.E., S.E.2d), and you can find the Virginia Court of Appeals' decisions in both the *Virginia Court of Appeals Reports* (Va. App.) and *Southeastern Reporter* (S.E., S.E.2d). In contrast, in Maine, recent decisions of the Maine Supreme Court are published only in the *Atlantic Reporter* (A. or A.2d). Maine does not have its own official or state reporter.

You can use Appendix 1 in the *ALWD Citation Manual* and Table 1 in *The Bluebook* to find the names of the reporter or reporters in which a particular state's cases are published.

P R A C T I C E

See **Exercise 9C** in the *Practice Book*.

§ 9.3.4 Other Authorities

Although most of the time you will be able to answer a client's question using your state's cases, occasionally you will need or want to go beyond those cases and look at cases from other states to see what others have said about the issue you have been asked to research. For example, you may want to do this additional type of research if your case involves an issue that has not been dealt with in your state, if different divisions within your state's intermediate appellate court system have taken different approaches, or if the case is particularly complicated or important.

a. *American Law Reports*

One of the easiest ways to find cases from other states is to use *American Law Reports* (A.L.R.). While originally A.L.R. served as a reporter, today most researchers use it for its annotations. Each annotation deals with a specific topic and lists cases by result and by jurisdiction.

Annotations dealing with state issues are found in A.L.R., A.L.R.2d, A.L.R.3d, A.L.R.4th, and A.L.R.5th. Annotations dealing with federal issues are found in A.L.R. Fed.

A.L.R.	1919-1948
A.L.R.2d	1948-1965
A.L.R.3d	1965-1980
A.L.R.4th	1980-1991
A.L.R.5th	1992-current
A.L.R. Fed.	1969-current

A.L.R. is available both in book form and on LexisNexis and Westlaw. The books have subject indexes.

Because you want the most current information, look first for annotations published in A.L.R.4th, A.L.R.5th, and A.L.R. Fed. In addition, if you are using the book version, be sure to check the pocket parts for more recent cases.

P R A C T I C E

---

b. Law Reviews and Journals

If you are looking for an in-depth discussion of a particular common law issue or for a critique of a case that has set out, interpreted, or applied a common law rule, consider looking for a law review article. Law reviews and journals publish articles written by law school professors, judges, practitioners, and law students. While most law reviews and journals are published by law schools, some are published by organizations.

The easiest way to find a law review article is to do a search on a fee-based service such as LexisNexis or Westlaw. After signing in, select the "Journals and Law Reviews" database, and then construct a search using terms that describe the common law issue.

§ 9.4 Example Showing How to Research a Common Law Issue

Now that you have a research plan and know at least some of the sources, it is time to do the research.

Step 1: Background Reading

Although you studied adverse possession during your first-year property class, you are not familiar with Washington's adverse possession laws. For example, you do not know whether adverse possession claims are still governed by common law or whether the common law rules have been replaced by a statute. Thus, you decide to begin your research by doing background reading.

Because your firm does not own any Washington practice books, you have two choices: either look for a free Internet site that discusses adverse possession in Washington, or use your firm's Westlaw subscription to see if it has a Washington practice book. Because you want to keep costs down, you look first for a free website. Using Google's "Advanced Search" option[2], you construct a search. In particular, you look for a website that contains the phrase "adverse possession" and the word "Washington." Exhibit 9.1, which is on the CD, shows you how to complete the search boxes, and Exhibit 9.2 shows you the search results.[3] Both of these exhibits due on the CD that came with this book.

Several of these sites provide useful information. For example, the first two links lead you to a website that sets out the text of Washington statutes that deal with adverse possession, and the third site provides you with a quick summary of the rules relating to adverse possession. See Exhibits 9.3 and 9.4.

Google indents entries when the indented entry leads you to the same website as the entry set out above the indented entry.

P R A C T I C E

POINTER

Because the websites that you located using Google provide only general information, you decide to spend the money and do a Westlaw[4] search. Because you do not know what Washington materials are on Westlaw, you sign on and, when the welcome screen appears, you click on the link to "My Westlaw." See Exhibit 9.5.

---

2. To use Google, go to *www.Google.com*. When the search screen appears, click on the link to the advanced search option. When you do, a screen like the one in Exhibit 9.1 will appear.

3. Because Google is constantly updated, your screens may not look the same as the screens set out on the CD.

4. Although this example shows how to do the research using Westlaw, you can do the same research using LexisNexis and other fee-based services.

When the "My Westlaw" page appears, scroll through the list of options until you come to the list of jurisdictions. Select "Washington," scroll to the bottom of the page and click on "Next," and, when the next screen appears, click on "Save." See Exhibit 9.6.

When you return to your welcome screen, you now have a tab for Washington. When you click on this tab, you get a screen with a search window and a list of all the Westlaw databases that contain Washington materials.[5] See Exhibit 9.7. Scrolling through the list of Washington databases, you discover that the *Washington Practice* series is available online. Thus, you select that book/database and then scroll back to the top of the screen to the search box. See Exhibit 9.8.

In constructing your search, you have several options. You could construct a broad search and look for any document in *Washington Practice* that contains the phrase "adverse possession." In the alternative, you could construct a narrower search and look for documents that contain both the term "adverse possession" and, in the same paragraph, a word that would indicate that the section contains a general discussion of adverse possession.

In this instance, the first alternative, searching for any document in the "Washington Practice Series" database that contains the term "adverse possession" retrieves eighty nine documents that contain that term. See Exhibits 9.9 and 9.10.

Because this first search retrieves so many documents, you decide to narrow your search by adding terms that the *Washington Practice* authors may have used in a section that provides general information about Washington's adverse possession law. In doing background reading on other topics, you have noticed that the sections that contain general information are often labeled "general," "overview," "summary," or "introduction." Because you do not know which of these words the author of your source might have used, you list all four, using an "or"[6] to connect them. You then connect this list of words to the phrase "adverse possession" using the connector "/s," which means "within the same sentence." This search will retrieve any document in the database that contains the phrase "adverse possession" within the same sentence as any one of the words in your list. See Exhibit 9.11. For more on constructing Westlaw searches, see the tutorials at *http://lscontent.westlaw.com/research/ppts/*.

In constructing your search, keep in mind that fee-based services such as Westlaw process the information in a search in a specified order. For example, Westlaw processes the information within parentheses first, treating the information within the parentheses as a single unit. It then processes the connectors in the following order: " ", space (or), +n, /n, +s, /s, +p, /p, & (and).

P R A C T I C E
POINTER

---

5. Because West updates Westlaw on a regular basis, your screens may not look like the screens in this book.
6. You do not need to include the "or." In both LexisNexis and Westlaw, a space is treated as an "or."

Your search retrieves thirteen documents. See Exhibits 9.11 and 9.12.

Although the titles of the first three documents, "Civil Procedure" (the first two) and "Rules Practice," indicate that these documents are not directly on point, the title of the next ten documents, "Real Estate — Property Law," suggests that they are on point. When you select the fourth entry, you find the information, set out in Exihibit 9.13.

At this point, you stop researching and spend thirty to forty five minutes reading section 8.1 of Volume 17 and some of the following sections. These sections lead you both to the statute that sets out the statutory period and to cases that are on point.

Step 2: Locating cases

Before you begin looking for cases, make a "shopping list." Although your lists will vary from issue to issue, in a case that involves an elements analysis, shop for the following types of information.

Shopping List

General Rules
1. Cases setting out the policies underlying the doctrine
2. Cases listing the elements
3. Cases explaining who has the burden of proof and what that burden is

First Element
1. Cases setting out the test that the courts apply in determining whether this element is met
2. Cases in which the court held that this element was met
3. Cases in which the court held that this element was not met

Second Element
1. Cases setting out the test that the courts apply in determining whether this element is met
2. Cases in which the court held that this element was met
3. Cases in which the court held that this element was not met

Third Element
1. Cases setting out the test that the courts apply in determining whether this element is met
2. Cases in which the court held that this element was met
3. Cases in which the court held that this element was not met

[Repeat for other elements.]

Once you have created your list, work through it, systematically looking for the information you need. One way to keep track of what you have found is to cut and paste information that you find into a template like the one set out on the following page.

Chart 9.2　Template for Research Notes

Introduction

1. Cases setting out the policies underlying the doctrine of adverse possession
2. Cases listing the elements of adverse possession
3. Cases explaining who has the burden of proof and what that burden is

A. Actual Possession

1. Cases setting out the test that the courts use in determining whether the claimant had actual possession
2. Cases in which the court held that the claimant had actual possession
3. Cases in which the court held that the claimant did not have actual possession
4. DNWC's arguments
5. Mr. Garcia's arguments

B. Open Possession

1. Cases setting out the test that the courts use in determining whether the claimant had open possession
2. Cases in which the court held that the claimant had open possession
3. Cases in which the court held that the claimant did not have open possession
4. DNWC's arguments
5. Mr. Garcia's arguments

C. Notorious Possession

1. Cases setting out the test that the courts use in determining whether the claimant's possession was notorious
2. Cases in which the court held that the claimant's possession was notorious
3. Cases in which the court held that the claimant's possession was not notorious
4. DNWC's arguments
5. Mr. Garcia's arguments

[The rest of the template has been omitted.]

There are a number of ways to find cases: you can find them (1) using citations to cases that you located while doing your background reading, (2) using one case to find other cases, (3) doing a "terms and connectors" search, and (4) using a digest.

1. Finding the Cases You Located During Your Background Reading

The easiest way to find cases is to look up cases that were cited in the source in which you did your background reading. For example, in our sample problem, look up the cases listed in the *Washington Practice* sections that you read that appear to contain the types of information that are on your shopping list. For example, look up the cases that appear to set out the general rules.

In this instance, you decide to start by looking up one of the cases that was cited for the general rule, *Chaplin v. Sanders*, 100 Wn.2d 853, 857, 676 P.2d 431 (1984). There are several ways to find a copy of this case. If you have the book version *of Washington Reports, Second Series*, or *Pacific Reporter, Second Series*, in your office, you can find a copy of the court's opinion in *Chaplin v. Sanders* in both sets. To find a copy of the opinion in *Washington Reports, Second Series*, locate volume 100 and then turn to page 853; to find a copy in the *Pacific Reporter, Second Series*, find volume 676 and then turn to page 431. Although the text of the opinion will be the same in both sources, the editorial features will be different. Because *Washington Reports, Second Series*, is Washington's official reporter, its headnotes were written by attorneys working for the company that publishes *Washington Reports*.[7] In contrast, because *Pacific Reporter, Second Series*, is published by West, its headnotes were written by the West editors using West's Key Number system.

In the alternative, you can find *Chaplin v. Sanders* using Westlaw or another fee-based service — for example, LexisNexis, Loislaw, or VersusLaw. To find *Chaplin v. Sanders* using Westlaw, go to one of the *Washington Practice* footnotes in which it is cited and click on the link. To find the case on another fee-based service, copy down the *Chaplin v. Sanders* citation, and then use that citation to find the case.

You can also find copies of Washington cases on free websites. For example, the Municipal Research and Service Center website, *mrsc.org*, has the full text of Washington Supreme Court decisions decided after 1938 and all of the Washington Court of Appeals' published decisions. In addition, *FindLaw.com* has recent Washington Supreme Court and Court of Appeals decisions.

Compare Exhibits 9.14 through 9.20. Exhibit 9.14 sets out the Washington Supreme Court's decision in *Chaplin v. Sanders* as the opinion appears in the book version in *Washington Reports, Second Series*, and Exhibit 9.15 sets out the text of the opinion as it appears in the book version of *Pacific Reporter, Second Series*. Exhibits 9.16 through 9.20 set out the opinion as it appears in fee-based and free online sources: Exhibit 9.16 shows the first page of the opinion as it appears on Westlaw; Exhibit 9.17 shows the first page of the opinion as it appears on LexisNexis; Exhibit 9.18 shows the first page of the opinion as it appears on Loislaw; and Exhibit 9.19 shows the first page of the opinion as it appears on *mrsc.org*. As Exhibit 9.20 illustrates, FindLaw.com has only recent cases. For older cases it provides a link to *mrsc.org*.

Question

How are the editorial features in the book, fee-based, and free sources the same and how are they different?

---

7. At different times, the *Washington Reports* has been published by different publishing companies.

You can use the same technique and sources to find other cases. For example, you can use the citations in sections 8.9 and 8.10 of Volume 17 of *Washington Practice* to find cases that discuss actual possession, the citations in sections 8.11-8.16 to find cases dealing with "hostility," and the citations in section 8.19 to find cases dealing with "exclusive." Finally, you can use the same technique to find the statutory section that sets out the statute of limitations.

To see the table of contents for the *Washington Practice series*, select the "Table of Contents" option from the toolbar and then "State Secondary Sources." Select "Washington," then "*Washington Practice*," and then "Real Estate." Under Real Estate, select "Adverse Possession." See Exhibits 9.21-9.26.

On Westlaw, the page breaks are marked using an asterisk followed by a page number. For example, the text following "*2" would be on page 2 in the reporter, and the text following

P R A C T I C E
POINTER

"*434" would be on page 434 in the reporter. If there are parallel cites, the text following "*2" would be on page 2 of the official reporter and the material following "**330" would be on page 330 in the unofficial reporter.

---

2. Using One Case to Find Other Cases

Having found one case, you can use that case to find other cases.

(a) Look Up the Cases That the Court Cites as Authority.   One way to find cases is to look up the cases that the court cites as authority. For example, in our example problem you could look up cases that were cited in *Chaplin*. However, the *Chaplin* decision is relatively old and, in it, the Washington Supreme Court overruled more than fifty other adverse possession cases. As a consequence, a better strategy would be to locate more recent cases.

(b) Cite Check the Case.   To find more recent cases, cite check the case that you have found and look for cases that have cited it as authority. To find cases that have cited *Chaplin v. Sanders*, use either KeyCite, which is on Westlaw, or *Shepard's*, which is on LexisNexis.

When you KeyCite *Chaplin v. Sanders*, you find that it has been cited in 204 documents. See Exhibit 9.27. Although you could look at all of these citing references, a better strategy is to use the "Limit KeyCite Display" function to locate cases that have cited *Chaplin* for a specific point. To do this, identify the headnote or headnotes that are on point.

For example, headnote 1 sets out the general rule and lists the elements. See Exhibit 9.28. Thus, to find other, more recent cases that have set out the general rule, scroll up and check the box next to headnote 1. Note that the number in parentheses after each headnote number tells you the number of documents that have cited your case — here *Chaplin* — for the point of law set out in that headnote. See Exhibit 9.29. Thus, thirty three documents have cited

Chaplin for the point of law set out in headnote 1 in the *Pacific Reporter* version of the case.

Keep in mind that the headnotes are not the same in the *Washington Reports* and *Pacific Reporter* versions of the cases: the *Washington Reports* headnotes are written and/or approved by Washington's Reporter of Decisions, and the *Pacific Reporter* headnotes are written by attorneys who work for West. For example, in *Chaplin*, the *Washington Reports* version of the case has two headnotes while the *Pacific Reporter* version of the case has eight. Because KeyCite is a West product, it uses the *Pacific Reporter* headnote numbers. Thus, when you use the "Limit KeyCite Display" function, make sure you are using the West headnote numbers, not the *Washington Reports* headnote numbers.

P R A C T I C E
POINTER

When we look at the list of documents that cite *Chaplin* for the point of law set out in headnote 1 of the *Pacific Reporter* version of the case, we see that five cases have four stars, which means that the citing cases "examined" or spent at least one paragraph discussing *Chaplin* for the point of law set out in headnote number 1. Of these five cases, the citations tell us that one, *ITT Rayonier*, is a Washington Supreme Court decision (if only the name of the state appears in the parenthetical, the case is a decision by that state's highest appellate court) and that the other four are decisions from Washington's intermediate court of appeals, the Washington Court of Appeals, which has three divisions. From the citations we can tell that four of these Washington Court of Appeals decisions were published and one, the one that has only a WL cite, is unpublished.

Because we are more interested in decisions from higher courts than we are decisions from lower courts, we look first at the *ITT Rayonier* case. If we need additional cases, we look at the more recently published Washington Court of Appeals decisions. If these decisions set out different rules or seem to apply the rules in different ways, we choose cases from the division of the Court of Appeals in which our case would be heard over cases from other divisions of the Court of Appeals.

(c) Use West's Key Number and "Most Cited Cases" Option. Another way to find cases is to use the headnotes to find additional cases that deal with the same point of law. For instance, instead of using the "Limit KeyCite" display to find other cases that have cited *Chaplin* for the point of law set out in headnote 1 of the *Pacific Reporter* version of the case, we can go to headnote 1 and click on the link to "Most Cited Cases." See Exhibit 9.30. This link takes us to the screen that allows us to create a custom digest for the point of law that was set out in headnote 1 of the *Pacific Reporter* version of *Chaplin*, which is the point of law that West has assigned the topic heading "Adverse Possession," and within that topic heading the key number 13. The shortcut reference for this point of law is 20k13: the "20" is the number that West has assigned to the topic heading "Adverse Possession;" the "k" is the abbreviation for Key Number, and the "13" is the key number. See Exhibit 9.28.

We can use the screen set out in Exhibit 9.31 to create a custom digest. In particular, we can use this screen to change the order in which the cases appear (most frequently cited cases first or more recent cases first), to select a jurisdiction, and to add additional search terms. In this instance, we choose the most frequently cited option and "Washington," and we do not add any search terms. When we click on "search," the screen set out in Exhibit 9.32 appears. This screen lists sixty nine Washington cases that have at least mentioned the point of law set out in 20k13. Note that not all of these cases will have cited *Chaplin*. While the "Limit Citing References" function takes you to cases that have cited the case you are KeyCiting, the "Most Frequently Cited" cases function takes you into the West digest for the jurisdiction that you selected and identifies cases that discuss your selected topic and Key Number. In other words, the "Most Cited References" function identifies all of the cases within a particular jurisdiction that have a headnote with your selected Key Number while the "Limit Citing References" function identifies only those cases that have that Key Number and that cited the case that you are KeyCiting.

You can also click on the headnote number. Although you will retrieve the same list of cases that you would retrieve if you clicked on "Most Cited Cases," those cases will be listed in a different order.

P R A C T I C E

Question

Compare the list of cases that you get when you click on the Key Number with the list of cases that you get when you click on "Most Cited Cases." How are the cases that you retrieve when you click on the KeyNumber ordered?

Once you find a case, you can find the relevant portion of this case by using the "Locate in Full Result" option to search for one of the terms that was set out in the headnote, or you can maximize the screen and scroll through the headnotes until you find the headnote that lists the elements. For example, to find the relevant language in *ITT Rayonier*, we click on the link to *ITT Rayonier* and when the case appears, we scroll through the headnotes until we find the headnote that sets out the general rule, headnote 1. See Exhibit 9.33. When we click on the headnote number, which in this instance is "[1]," we are taken to that place in *ITT Rayonier* where the court sets out the general rule. See Exhibit 9.34.

When you find a particularly useful case, download the case or email it to yourself. Although you may still have to pay the initial printing charge, you will have a copy of the case for your file and you can email the case to other attorneys in your office at no additional charge.

3. Finding Cases Using a "Terms and Connectors" Search

You can also find cases using a "terms and connectors" search. In constructing your search, begin by selecting your search terms. As a general rule, select as your first search term a term or set of terms that describes the area of law. For example, in the Garcia case, use the term "adverse possession" as your first search term. Then add search terms that will retrieve the types of information that are on your shopping list. For instance, if you need cases that discuss "open and notorious" possession, add "open and notorious" as a search term. Once you have selected your search terms, select your connectors. Is it enough that the two terms appear anywhere in the case, or should they be in the same paragraph? In the same sentence? Unfortunately, there is no formula you can use to select connectors; instead, you need to make an educated guess about where the terms are likely to appear in a court's opinion. In this instance, you decide on a middle approach and use "/p," which means within the same paragraph. Finally, select your database. Because you want Washington cases, you select the "Washington State Cases" database. See Exhibit 9.35.

Unfortunately, this search retrieves 172 documents. See Exhibit 9.36. A quick review of the search results reveals that the search retrieved not just those cases that contain a discussion of actual possession but also every case that lists the elements. Thus, to find cases that contain a more in-depth discussion of "open and notorious," you need to add additional search terms. The question, of course, is which search terms.

In the Garcia case, you have several options. You could add words that the courts use in discussing open and notorious possession. For instance, in doing your background reading in *Washington Practice*, you learned that possession is open and notorious if the landowner had actual notice of the adverse possessor's use of the land. Thus, to find cases that set out and apply this test for "open and notorious," select "Edit Search," and add key language from this test: "actual use." See Exhibit 9.37. When you add the term "actual use" to your other search terms using a "/p" as your connector, your search retrieves only four documents, and all of these documents not only list "open and notorious" as an element but also set out and apply the actual use test. See Exhibit 9.38. Note, however, that because this search is narrow, more likely than not, it does not retrieve some of the key cases. In the alternative, you can add words that describe the facts of your case that are relevant to whether the possession was actual; for example, you could add "knew" in an attempt to retrieve cases in which the landowner knew about the adverse possessor's use of the land. Unfortunately, until you try some searches, you will not know which, if any, of these searches will retrieve cases that are on point. In this instance, a search for cases that contain the words "adverse possession" and "open and notorious" and the word "knew" in the same paragraph retrieves fifteen documents. See Exhibits 9.39 and 9.40.

To retrieve cases that contain the word "knew" or the word "know," use "kn*w" as your search term. The "*" is a universal character and will retrieve words with any letter in the "*" slot.

P R A C T I C E

POINTER

As this set of searches demonstrates, it can be difficult to construct a "terms and connectors" search that retrieves only those cases that contain a discussion of one element. If you include just the word naming the element, your search will retrieve too many cases; in contrast, if you add additional terms, your search may not retrieve all of the cases that are on point.

4. Using a Digest to Locate Cases

To find cases using the book version of a digest, locate the digest that indexes cases from your jurisdiction and then select the digest volume that contains the applicable topic. For instance, in the Garcia case, select either the *Washington Digest* or the *Pacific Digest* and look up the topic "Adverse Possession." Then use the table of contents at the beginning of the Adverse Possession section to identify those subtopics that deal with actual possession. For a copy of the material from the *Washington Digest*, see Exhibit 9.41.

When you turn to section B, you find the list of Key Numbers shown in Exhibit 9.42. Read through the headnotes and select the Washington cases that appear to be most on point and look up those cases in either the applicable official reporter — for example, *Washington Reports, Second Series*, or *Washington Appellate Reports*; in the regional reporter — for example, *Pacific Reporter*; or on a fee-based or free website.

To find the online version of the digests, sign on to Westlaw. When the "Welcome" screen appears, locate the "More" menu, which is just to the right of the "Key Search" link on the tab menu bar. See Exhibit 9.42. When the pull-down menu appears, click on "Key Numbers and Digest." See Exhibit 9.43. Scroll through the list until you find the heading "Adverse Possession." See Exhibit 9.44. When you click on the "+," you see the expanded version of the table of contents for "Adverse Possession." See Exhibit 9.45. If you click on the "+" that is next to "1. Nature and Requisites" and then "B — Actual Possession," you find the same list as the list set out in Exhibit 9.42. See Exhibit 9.46.

In reading the cases, note that sometimes the courts discuss several elements at once. For example, they may discuss "open and notorious" or "open and visible" together. This is common.

Because the elements are so closely related, the courts will sometimes analyze them together. Sometimes you can do the same thing in your memo or brief. If the analysis for two elements is essentially the same, you may be able to analyze them together.

Step 3: Cite Checking the Cases That You Plan to Use in Your Memo or Brief

Before using a case in your memo or brief, cite check it to make sure that it is still good law. It is not enough to rely on your preliminary status checks. (See Chapter 4.) You can *shepardize*™ or KeyCite each of the cases that you plan to use by checking the cases one at a time or by using a service such as WestCheck.

Step 4: Locating Other Authorities

In some cases, you will want to look for an A.L.R. annotation or a law review article that discusses your topic and that provides you with insight into the arguments that each side might make. Do not, however, take this extra step unless you need to. For example, in the Garcia case there is no need to look for commentary, and you do not have the time and the client does not have the money for such an "optional" search.

CHAPTER 10

Drafting Memo 2

The good news is that writing the second memo is usually easier than writing the first one. The bad news is that writing any memo is a lot of work. If, however, you completed the template as you did your research, you have a good start on the first draft.

§ 10.1 Understanding What You Have Found

Presume that your completed template looks like the one set out in Chart 10.1. Although you have cut and pasted the general and specific rules into your template, you have written your own "case briefs" for the cases you think you may want to use as analogous cases, and, as you thought of them, you jotted down arguments that each side might make.

Although it may seem like it is easier to paste the cases into your template without reading them, in the end, this strategy almost always backfires. Thus, read and analyze as you go, copying the rules

PRACTICE
POINTER

into your template but "briefing" the analogous cases and thinking carefully and creatively about the arguments that each side is likely to make.

Chart 10.1   Research Notes for Memo 2

Issue: **Whether the DNWC has obtained a right to Mr. Garcia's land through adverse possession?**

Type of Law: **State common law and statutes**

Jurisdiction: **Washington**

Introductory Section

General Rules

- *ITT-Rayonier, Inc. v. Bell*, 112 Wn.2d 754, 774 P.2d 6 (1989)

  Quote from pages 757-58
  "In order to establish a claim of adverse possession, there must be possession that is: (1) open and notorious, (2) actual and uninterrupted, (3) exclusive, and (4) hostile. *Chaplin v. Sanders*, 100 Wash.2d 853, 857, 676 P.2d 431 (1984). Possession of the property with each of the necessary concurrent elements must exist for the statutorily prescribed period of 10 years. RCW 4.16.020."

  "Where the facts in an adverse possession case are not in dispute, whether the facts constitute adverse possession is for the court to determine as a matter of law."

- *Chaplin v. Sanders*, 100 Wn.2d 853, 676 P.2d 431 (1984)

  Quote from page 857
  "In order to establish a claim of adverse possession, the possession must be: 1) exclusive, 2) actual and uninterrupted, 3) open and notorious and 4) hostile and under a claim of right made in good faith."

- *Riley v. Andres*, 107 Wn. App. 391, 27 P.3d 618 (2001)

  Quote from page 395
  "To claim title to property by adverse possession, a party must possess the property for 10 years in a manner that is actual, uninterrupted, open and notorious, exclusive, and hostile."

- RCW 4.16.020. Actions to be commenced within ten years — Exception

  "The period prescribed for the commencement of actions shall be as follows: Within ten years:
  (1) For actions for the recovery of real property, or for the recovery of the possession thereof; and no action shall be maintained for such recovery unless it appears that the plaintiff, his or her ancestor, predecessor or grantor was seized or possessed of the premises in question within ten years before the commencement of the action."

Burden of Proof

- ***ITT Rayonier, Inc. v. Bell***, 112 Wn.2d 754, 774 P.2d 6 (1989)

Quote from pages 757-58
"As the presumption of possession is in the holder of legal title, *Peeples v. Port of Bellingham*, 93 Wash.2d 766, 773, 613 P.2d 1128 (1980), *overruled on other grounds, Chaplin v. Sanders, supra*, the party claiming to have adversely possessed the property has the burden of establishing the existence of each element. ****758*** *Skansi v. Novak*, 84 Wash. 39, 44, 146 P. 160 (1915), *overruled on other grounds, Chaplin v. Sanders, supra*."

Other General Rules

- ***Chaplin v. Sanders***, 100 Wn.2d 853, 676 P.2d 431 (1984)

Quote from page 863
"[A]dverse possession is a mixed question of law and fact. Whether the essential facts exist is for the trier of fact; but whether the facts, as found, constitute adverse possession is for the court to determine as a matter of law." *Peeples v. Port of Bellingham, supra* at 771, 613 P.2d 1128.

Policies Underlying Doctrine

- ***Chaplin v. Sanders***, 100 Wn.2d 853, 676 P.2d 431 (1984)

Quote from pages 859-60
"The doctrine of adverse possession was formulated at law for the purpose of, among others, assuring maximum utilization of land, encouraging the rejection of stale claims and, most importantly, quieting titles. 7 R. Powell, *Real Property* ¶ 1012[3] (1982); C. Callahan, *Adverse Possession* 91-94 (1961). Because the doctrine was formulated at law and not at equity, it was originally intended to protect both those who knowingly appropriated the land of others and those who honestly entered and held possession in full belief that the land was their own. R. Powell, at ¶ 1013 [2]; C. Callahan, at 49-50; 3 Am.Jur.2d *Advancements* § 104 (1962). Thus, when the original purpose of the adverse possession doctrine is considered, it becomes apparent that the claimant's motive in possessing the land is irrelevant and no inquiry should be made into his guilt or innocence. *Accord, Springer v. Durette*, 217 Or. 196, 342 P.2d 132 (1959); *Agers v. Reynolds*, 306 S.W.2d 506 (Mo.1957); *Fulton v. Rapp*, 59 Ohio Law Abs. 105, 98 N.E.2d 430 (1950); *see also* Stoebuck, *The Law of Adverse Possession in Washington*, 35 Wash. L. Rev. 53, 76-80 (1960)."

1.   Open and Notorious

A. Specific Rules

Riley v. Andres, 107 Wn. 391, 27 P.3d 618 (2001)

Quote from page 396:
"A claimant can satisfy the open and notorious element by showing either (1) that the title owner had actual notice of the adverse use throughout the statutory period or (2) that the claimant used the land such that any reasonable person would have thought he owned it."

Anderson v. Hudak, 80 Wn. App. 398, 907 P.2d 305 (1995)

Quote from pages 404-05:
"The open and notorious requirement is met if (1) the true owner has actual notice of the adverse use throughout the statutory period, or (2) the claimant uses the land so any reasonable person would assume that the claimant is the owner."

B. Analogous Cases

Element Met:

Riley v. Andres, 107 Wn. App. 391, 397, 27 P.3d 618 (2001)

Facts:
The claimants planted trees and shrubs and maintained land up to the point where the title owners' landscaping began. In particular, the claimants watered and pruned the plants, spread beauty bark, and pulled weeds.

Holding:
Although the court set out the two-part test listed above, it applied a slightly different test. It began by stating that a party who claims by adverse possession must show that its use is that of a true owner. It then states that the landscaping was the typical use of land of that character.

Element Not Met:

Anderson v. Hudak, 80 Wn. App. 398, 907 P.2d 305 (1995)

Facts:
The claimant (Anderson) planted a row of trees on a fifteen-foot strip of land that she thought belonged to her. There was, however, no evidence establishing that she did anything else on the land.

Holding:
The court stated that there was no evidence establishing that any of the true owners had actual notice of her possession of the trees. In addition, the court stated that the evidence was insufficient to establish that Anderson had used the land so that any reasonable person would assume that the claimant was the owner. Thus, the appellate court held that there was insufficient evidence to support the trial court's finding that Anderson's possession was open and notorious. *Id.* at 405.

C. DNWC's Arguments

Letter provided Mr. Garcia with actual knowledge that DNWC was using his land.

The way in which DNWC used the land would have led any reasonable person to assume that it owned the land. In fact, DNWC director seemed to think that DNWC owns the land.

Our case is more like *Riley* than *Anderson*. DNWC did more with the land than the Rileys did, and the court held that the Rileys' use of the land was sufficient to establish that their use was open and notorious.

D. Garcia's Arguments

It does not appear as if Garcia has an argument on actual notice. A court would probably find that the letter gave Mr. Garcia actual notice. However, even if the letter is not enough to establish actual notice, DNWC's acts are probably enough to establish that a reasonable person would have thought that it owned the land.

2. Actual and Uninterrupted

A. Specific Rules

[The rest of the template is not shown.]

§ 10.1.1 Make Sure You Understand the Big Picture

Now that you have completed the template, take a step back and make sure that you see the big picture. For instance, in our example case, do you understand the policies underlying the doctrine of adverse possession? Historically, why did the courts create the doctrine? Why have most state legislatures left the common law rules intact, only enacting statutes that set out the time for which the common law elements must be met?

§ 10.1.2 Make Sure You Understand the Common Law Rule and Any Applicable Statutes

In addition to making sure that you understand the big picture, make sure that you understand the common law rule. If the common law rule is complicated, diagram it using the same techniques that you would use to diagram a complicated statute. See pages 113–114. If the common law rule is not complicated, simply read the rule carefully, making sure that you know how many elements there are and whether those elements are connected by an "and" or an "or." Finally, make sure that you understand the relationship between the common law rule and any statutes that might apply. For example, in our sample problem, make sure that you understand the relationship between the common law rule, which lists the elements, and the statutes, which list the time periods for which the elements must be met.

§ 10.1.3 Make Sure You Understand the Burden of Proof

Because the determining factor in many cases is the burden of proof, make sure that you know which side has the burden of proof and what that burden of proof is. While in most civil cases it is the plaintiff who has the burden of proof, that is not true in adverse possession cases. In adverse possession cases, the party claiming the property through adverse possession has the burden of proof regardless of whether it was the party that filed the action claiming title to the land through adverse possession or whether it was the true owner who filed an action to quiet title. There is only one exception: if the claimant proves that it used the land as if the land were its own, then the true owner has the burden of proving that use was permissive.

§ 10.1.4 Make Sure You Understand the Specific Rules and the Cases That Have Interpreted and Applied Them

Finally, make sure you understand the law. For some areas of law, this part of the process is easy: the courts have set out, clearly and concisely, the rules that they apply in determining whether a particular element is met, and the courts apply those rules consistently. In other areas of law, however, the process is more complicated. In some instances, different courts set out different rules, or the courts set out one rule but seem to apply a different one. In other instances, it can be difficult to distinguish between the test for one element and the test for another element. A prime example of this type of situation is adverse possession: in many states, the tests for actual possession, open and notorious, and hostile are very similar.

To make sure that you understand the specific rules and the cases that have interpreted and applied them, look first at that section of the template in which you have set out the specific rules for a particular element. In discussing that element, do all of the courts set out the same rule? If they do, you have the rule. If, though, different courts seem to be setting out different rules, your job is more difficult. Begin by re-reading the specific rules. Are the courts setting out the same rule using different language, or are they setting out different rules? If the courts are setting out the same rules using different language, you have the rule. If, though, the courts are setting out different rules, you need to try to reconcile the rules.

Are the courts doing what the Washington Supreme Court did in *Chaplin v. Sanders* and overruling or abandoning one rule and adopting a new one? If they are, you need to determine which rule applies in your client's case. In the alternative, do different divisions of the same court apply different rules, or do the courts apply different rules in different types of situations? For instance, does Division I of the Washington Court of Appeals apply one rule and Division II a different rule, or do all of the divisions apply one rule when the land is in a rural area and another rule when the land is in an urban area?

Once you have figured out the specific rules, look at how those courts have applied the rules in the analogous cases. Do the courts apply the rules they set out? If they do not, what is the difference between the rules they set out and the rules they apply? Also look at the issue that was before the court. Was the issue whether the trial court erred in granting summary judgment? If it was, the appellate court will review the issue *de novo* and apply the same test that the trial court applied in deciding whether to grant or deny the motion. A decision that the trial court erred does not mean that the other side wins; instead, in most instances, it means that the appellate court will remand the case for a trial on the merits. In contrast, if the issue is whether there was sufficient evidence to support the jury's verdict, then the appellate court's review is much more limited. If there is sufficient evidence to support the jury's verdict, the appellate court may not substitute its judgment for the judgment of the jury.

After you have analyzed all of the elements, compare them, making sure that you understand the difference between the specific rules for each of the elements. An easy way to do this part of the analysis is to make a chart in which you compare the specific rule for each element. See Chart 10.2.

Chart 10.2   Chart Comparing Specific Rules

Open and Notorious	Actual and Uninterrupted	Exclusive	Hostile
The open and notorious requirement is met if (1) the true owner has actual notice of the adverse use throughout the statutory period, <u>or</u> (2) the claimant uses the land so any reasonable person would assume that the claimant is the owner. *Riley v. Andres*, 107 Wn. App. 391, 396, 27 P.3d 618 (2001).	The Washington courts have not set out a test for actual possession. 17 *Wash. Prac., Real Estate: Property Law* § 8.10 (2d ed.) In discussing "uninterrupted," the courts have held that the claimants' use was "continuous" even though they used the property only during the summer. The requisite possession requires such possession and dominion as ordinarily marks the conduct of owners in general in holding, managing, and caring for property of a like nature and condition.	"While possession of property by a party seeking to establish ownership of it by adverse possession need not be absolutely exclusive," "the possession must be of a type that would be expected of an owner . . ." *ITT-Rayonier*, 112 Wn.2d 754, 758, 774 P.2d 6 (1989).	"The 'hostility/claim of right' element of adverse possession requires only that the claimant treat the land as his own as against the world throughout the statutory period. The nature of his possession will be determined solely on the basis of the manner in which he treats the property. His subjective belief regarding his true interest in the land and his intent to dispossess or not dispossess another is irrelevant to this determination. Under this analysis, permission to occupy the land, given by the true title owner to the claimant or his predecessors in interest, will still operate to negate the element of hostility. The traditional presumptions still apply to the extent that they are not inconsistent with this ruling."

If you have trouble distinguishing the test used for
one element from the test used for another element,
look for a case, a law review article, or a practice
book that explains how the elements are the same
and how they are different.

§ 10.2 Drafting the Heading

You learned in Chapter 7 that drafting the heading is easy: just complete the
"To," "From," "Date," and "Re" blocks. If the memo will only be filed in the
client's file, the "Re" entry can be quite general. If, however, the memo will be
filed not only in the client's file but also in a "Memo Bank," the "Re" block
should be more specific. Include words that will allow other individuals to
locate the memo.

To: Supervising Attorney

From: Your name

Date: November 1, 2006

Re: Michael Garcia
            Adverse Possession; Washington law

Question

If this memo is going to be placed in both the client's file and a searchable
memo bank, what other words might you want to include in the "Re" slot?

§ 10.3 Drafting the Statement of Facts

In drafting the statement of facts for this chapter's sample memo, use the same
process that you used in drafting the statement of facts for the sample problem
set out in Chapter 7: (1) identify the legally significant, emotionally significant, background, and unknown facts; (2) select an organizational scheme;
and (3) present the facts accurately and objectively.

§ 10.3.1 Decide What Facts to Include

To identify the legally significant facts, create a chart similar to the one
set out on page 121. In the first column list the elements, and in the second
column list the facts that the court would consider in determining whether
those elements are met. See Chart 10.3.

Chart 10.3	Chart Listing Elements and the Facts that the Count Would Consider in Deciding Whether the Element is Met.
Elements	**Facts that the court would consider in deciding whether the element is met**
Open and Notorious Actual and Uninterrupted Exclusive Hostile	

Questions

What facts would the court considered in deciding whether DNWC's possession was open and notorious? actual and uninterrupted? exclusive? hostile?

Are there any other facts that might be emotionally significant? If you think that there are, what are those facts and do they help or hurt Mr. Garcia's case?

To identify the emotionally significant facts, think about which facts might influence a judge's or a jury's decision. In our example case, is the fact that the claimant is a group of doctors and nurses that is running a camp for sick and disabled children likely to influence the jury's or the judge's decision? If it is, then you should include that fact in the statement of facts. Similarly, is the fact that the land has been in Mr. Garcia's family for more than fifty years something that will influence the judge's or the jury's decision? If it is, you should include that fact in your statement of facts.

Finally, identify the facts that you need to tell the story and the unknown facts. If you cannot analyze the issue without the unknown facts, ask your supervising attorney for permission to obtain those facts. If, however, you can analyze the issue without the unknown facts, do so.

Question

In our example problem, do you need to know whether Mr. Garcia's grandfather gave DNWC permission to use the land? Why or why not?

§ 10.3.2 Select an Organizational Scheme

Once you have decided which facts need to be included, select an organizational scheme. As you learned in Chapter 7, the two most common organizational schemes are chronological and topical.

If you use a chronological organizational scheme, set out the facts in date order: start the story with Mr. Garcia's grandfather buying the land in question, and end with Mr. Garcia's visit to the property. In contrast, if you use a topical organizational scheme, set out the facts relating to the Garcia property in one paragraph or block of paragraphs, the facts relating to DNWC's property and DNWC's use of the Garcia property in a second paragraph or block of paragraphs, and the facts relating to the dispute in a third paragraph or block of paragraphs. In all instances, start the statement of facts with a paragraph in which you identify the parties and the issue. For more on paragraphs and paragraph blocks, see Chapter 22.

Statement of Facts Written Using a Chronological Organizational Scheme

Michael Garcia has contacted our office regarding property that he owns in Washington State. Mr. Garcia is concerned that the organization that owns the property next to his, Doctors and Nurses Who Care (DNWC), may be able to claim title to his property through adverse possession.

Mr. Garcia's property is on Lake Chelan in eastern Washington State. Mr. Garcia's grandfather, Eduardo Montoya, purchased the two-acre waterfront parcel in 1951, and the family used the land every summer from 1951 until Eduardo Montoya became ill in the late 1980s. When it used the land, the family would camp on the site and use a small dock for swimming, fishing, and boating.

In 1989, DNWC purchased the five-acre parcel that adjoins Mr. Montoya's property. Since 1990, DNWC has used its land as a summer camp for children with serious illnesses or disabilities. In a typical summer, DNWC runs two one-week camps for children with cancer, two one-week camps for children who are blind, two one-week camps for autistic children, and two one-week camps for children with diabetes.

Most of the time the children stay in cabins located on DNWC property. However, DNWC uses the Garcia property for "campouts." One night each week, one group of about ten children will camp out in tents on Mr. Garcia's property; the next night another group of ten will camp out on his property, and so on. Thus, DNWC has been using the Garcia property four or five nights a week for eight weeks each summer since 1990. During these campouts, the children pitch and stay in tents, cook over a fire, and use the dock. To facilitate these campouts, DNWC has maintained the campsite, the fire area, the outhouse, and the dock.

In 1992, Mr. Garcia's grandfather died and left the property to him. Although Mr. Garcia spent one weekend at the property in the fall of 1992, he moved to Texas in 1993 and did not visit the property again until last August. He has, however, continued to pay all of the taxes and assessments.

In February 1994, DNWC sent Mr. Garcia a letter asking him whether it could continue using his land for campouts. Mr. Garcia was busy and did not respond to the letter. Sometime during the summer of 1994, DNWC posted a "No Trespassing" sign on the dock, and the sign is still there.

Last August Mr. Garcia visited the property with the intention of spending a few days camping on the lake. When he got there, he discovered children and their counselors on the property.

After discovering the children on his land, Mr. Garcia went to DNWC's camp headquarters and talked to the director, Dr. Liu. However, Dr. Liu told Mr. Garcia that it was his understanding that the land belonged to DNWC. Although Mr. Garcia did not spend that night on the property, he did spend the next night there after the children left. DNWC did not ask him to leave.

Although over the years the land around the lake has become more and more developed, the area in which the camp is located is still relatively undeveloped. Most of the property owners use their land only during the summer.

Statement of Facts Written Using a Topical Organizational Scheme   EXAMPLE 2

Michael Garcia has contacted our office regarding property that he owns in Washington State. Mr. Garcia is concerned that the organization that owns the property next to his, Doctors and Nurses Who Care (DNWC), may be able to claim title to his property through adverse possession.

Mr. Garcia's property is located on Lake Chelan in eastern Washington State. Mr. Garcia's grandfather, Eduardo Montoya, purchased the two-acre waterfront parcel in 1951. From 1951 until Eduardo Montoya became ill in the late 1980s, the family used the land every summer. The family would camp on the site and use a small dock for swimming, fishing, and boating. In 1990, Mr. Garcia's grandfather died and left the property to Mr. Garcia. Although Mr. Garcia spent one weekend on the property in 1992, he moved to Texas in 1993 and did not visit the property from 1992 until last August. He has, however, continued to pay all of the taxes and assessments.

DNWC purchased the five-acre parcel that is to the north of Mr. Garcia's property in 1989. Since 1990, DNWC has used its land for a summer camp for children who suffer from serious illnesses and disabilities. In a typical summer, DNWC runs two one-week camps for children with cancer, two one-week camps for children who are blind, two one-week camps for children with autism, and two one-week camps for children with diabetes. While normally the children stay in cabins located on DNWC property, DNWC uses Mr. Garcia's property for "campouts." For example, on one night of the week, one group of about ten children will camp out in tents on Mr. Garcia's property, the next night another group of ten will camp out on his property, and so on. During these campouts, the children pitch and stay in tents and cook over a fire. To facilitate these campouts, DNWC has maintained the campsites, the fire area, the outhouse, and the dock. In the summer of 1994, DNWC posted a "No Trespassing" sign on the dock, and the sign is still there.

In February 1994, DNWC sent a letter to Mr. Garcia asking him if it could continue using his land for campouts. Mr. Garcia was busy and never responded to the letter.

Late last August, Mr. Garcia visited the property with the intention of spending a few days camping on the lake. When he got there, he discovered children and their counselors on the property. Upon making this discovery, Mr. Garcia went to DNWC's camp headquarters and talked to the director, Dr. Liu, who was very nice. However, Dr. Liu told Mr. Garcia that the land belonged to DNWC. Although Mr. Garcia did not spend that night on his property, he did spend the next night there after the children had gone. DNWC did not ask him to leave.

While the land around the lake has become more and more developed, the area in which the camp is located is still relatively undeveloped. Most of the property owners only use their land during the summer.

Questions

1. What "clues" did the authors of these two examples give their readers about the organizational scheme that they were using?

2. Does one of the organizational schemes work better than the other? Why or why not?

§ 10.3.3 Present the Facts Accurately and Objectively

Finally, in writing the statement of facts, make sure that you present the facts accurately and objectively. Do not set out facts that are not in your case file; do not set out legal conclusions; and do not present the facts in a light that favors your client or the other side.

Questions

In the following list, has the author set out the facts accurately and objectively? Why or why not?

1. Since 1992, the property has been used exclusively by DNWC.
2. Although Mr. Garcia did not respond to the letter because he was busy, if he had responded to the letter, he would have given DNWC permission to use his land for campouts.
3. DNWC has used the Garcia land for only 32 days a year.

§ 10.4 Drafting the Issue Statement

In Chapter 7, we showed you how to draft the issue statement, or question presented, using the "under-does-when" format. See section 7.4. When you use that format, you set out a reference to the applicable rule of law after the "under," the legal question after the verb, and the key facts after the "when."

Although the "under-does-when" format is the easiest format to use, some attorneys prefer the more traditional "whether" format. When you use the "whether" format, begin your issue statement with the word "whether" and then set out the legal question and the key facts. Although you do not need to include a reference to the rule of law, you may incorporate one into your statement of the legal question.

Compare the following examples. In the first example, the writer wrote the issue statement using the "under-does-when" format, and in the second and third examples, the writer wrote the issue statement using the "whether" format.

EXAMPLE 1   **Issue Statement Written Using the "Under-Does-When" Format, the Parties' Names, and Enumeration**

Issue

Under Washington common law, has Doctors and Nurses Who Care (DNWC) obtained a right to Mr. Garcia's land through adverse possession when (1) DNWC has used the land for campouts several nights a week for eight weeks each summer since 1990; (2) to facilitate these campouts, DNWC has maintained the campsites, fire area, outhouse, and dock; (3) in 1994, DNWC sent a letter to Mr. Garcia asking him if it could continue using the land for campouts, but Mr. Garcia did not respond to the letter; and (4) Mr. Garcia has paid the taxes but did not visit the land from 1993 until August 2006?

Issue Statement Written Using the "Whether" Format, the Parties' Names, and Enumeration

EXAMPLE 2

Issue

Whether Doctors and Nurses Who Care (DNWC) has obtained a right to Mr. Garcia's land through adverse possession when (1) DNWC has used the land for campouts several nights a week for eight weeks each summer since 1990; (2) to facilitate these campouts, DNWC has maintained the campsites, fire area, outhouse, and dock; (3) in 1994, DNWC sent a letter to Mr. Garcia asking him if it could continue using the land for campouts, but Mr. Garcia did not respond to the letter; and (4) Mr. Garcia has paid the taxes but did not visit the land from 1993 until August 2006.

You could also write the issue statement without referring to the parties by name.

Issue Statement Written Using the "Whether" Format but Not the Names of the Parties or Enumeration

EXAMPLE 3

Issue

Whether a claimant may obtain a right to land through adverse possession when the claimant used the disputed land for campouts several nights a week for eight weeks each summer since 1990; when the claimant has maintained the campsites, fire area, outhouse, and dock; when the claimant sent a letter to the title owner asking him if it could continue using the land for campouts but the title owner did not respond to the letter; and when the title owner has paid the taxes but did not visit the land for more than ten years.

At first, some writers are bothered by the fact that issue statements written using the "whether" format are incomplete sentences. If you are one of those writers, remember that the "whether" is shorthand for "The question is whether. . . ."

PRACTICE
POINTER

Note that a question mark is used with the "under/does/when" format and a period is used with the "whether" format.

P R A C T I C E
POINTER

§ 10.5 Drafting the Brief Answer

As we explained in Chapter 7, the brief answer answers the question asked in the issue statment. By convention, most brief answers begin with a one- or two-word answer, which is followed by a one-, two-, or three-sentence explanation.

In writing the brief answer, think about what you would tell the attorney if he or she stopped you in the hallway and asked you for a quick answer.

Attorney: Has DNWC obtained a right to Mr. Garcia's property through adverse possession?

You: It looks as if it may have. DNWC can easily prove that its possession was open and notorious, actual and uninterrupted, and exclusive. In addition, it looks like DNWC can prove that its possession was hostile. It has been using the property as if it were its own and, because Mr. Garcia did not respond to the letter asking for permission, DNWC has a good argument that its use was not permissive.

EXAMPLE: **Brief Answer**

Brief Answer

Probably. DNWC can easily prove that its possession was open and notorious, actual and uninterrupted, and exclusive. In addition, DNWC can probably prove that its possession was hostile: it used the land as a true owner would have used it and, although initially it may have been using the property with either Mr. Garcia's grandfather's or Mr. Garcia's permission, it appears that it has been using the property without permission since 1994. Because all of the elements are met for the statutory period, which is ten years, DNWC has a right to the land through adverse possession.

Before you include a brief answer, check with your supervising attorney to see if he or she wants one in the memo.

P R A C T I C E
POINTER

§ 10.6 Drafting the Discussion Section

As you learned in writing your first memo, drafting the discussion section is a multistage process involving planning, drafting, revising, editing, and proofreading. In this chapter, we walk you through the process again, showing you how to write the introductory section, how to raise and dismiss the undisputed elements, and how to organize the discussion of the disputed elements using both the script format and an integrated format.

In this section we review this process and then show you how to write the discussion of a disputed element using an integrated format.

§ 10.6.1 Select a Template

The first step is to select a template. In this case, we start with the standard template for a common law problem that requires an elements analysis. See Chart 10.4.

The standard template for a problem governed by a common law rule that requires an elements analysis is the same as the standard template for a problem governed by a statute that requires an elements analysis. Compare the template chart set out on pages 135-136 with the following template.

P R A C T I C E
POINTER

Chart 10.4	**Standard Template for a Problem Governed by a Common Law Rule That Requires an Elements Analysis ("script" format)**

Discussion

Introductory section that sets out the general rules:

- If one or both sides will make a policy argument, describe the policies underlying the common law rule.
- Introduce and set out the applicable common law rule.
- Explain which side has the burden of proof and what that burden is.
- Set out any other rules that apply to all of the elements.
- End with a roadmap that tells the attorney which elements are and are not likely to be in dispute.

A. First Element

1. If first element is not likely to be in dispute, simply set out and apply applicable rule.

2. If first element is likely to be in dispute, set out the following information.
    a. Specific rules
    b. Examples of how specific rules have been applied in analogous cases
        ■ Case or cases in which element was met
        ■ Case or cases in which element was not met
    c. Arguments
        ■ Arguments that element is met
        ■ Arguments that element is not met
    d. Mini-conclusion

B. Second Element

1. If second element is not likely to be in dispute, simply set out and apply applicable rule.
2. If second element is likely to be in dispute, set out the following information.
    a. Specific rules
    b. Examples of how specific rules have been applied in analogous cases
        ■ Case or cases in which element was met
        ■ Case or cases in which element was not met
    c. Arguments
        ■ Arguments that element is met
        ■ Arguments that element is not met
    d. Mini-conclusion

C. Third Element

1. If third element is not likely to be in dispute, simply set out and apply applicable rule.
2. If third element is likely to be in dispute, set out the following information.
    a. Specific rules
    b. Examples of how specific rules have been applied in analogous cases
        ■ Case or cases in which element was met
        ■ Case or cases in which element was not met
    c. Arguments
        ■ Arguments that element is met
        ■ Arguments that element is not met
    d. Mini-conclusion

[If there are more than three elements, add additional subsections.]

§ 10.6.2 Modify the Template So It Works for Your Problem

Because templates are just that, use common sense and, when appropriate, modify the template so that it works for your problem. For instance, in our example problem, there are four elements: (1) open and notorious, (2) actual and uninterrupted, (3) exclusive, and (4) hostile. Thus, we need to add a fourth subsection.

When different courts list the elements in different ways, give the attorney that information. For example, in introducing the elements include a sentence like the following: "While in some cases the Maine courts  have listed five elements, [cite], in other cases they have listed nine elements, [cite]." Then tell the attorney which approach you are taking and why. "Because the more recent cases list nine elements, this memo lists and discusses nine elements."

Of the four elements that the Washington courts list, two are not likely to be in dispute. More likely than not, DNWC can prove that its possession of Mr. Garcia's land was open and notorious and exclusive. In contrast, one element, "hostile," will be in dispute: while DNWC will argue that its use of Mr. Garcia's land was hostile, Mr. Garcia will argue that DNWC's letter asking him to donate his land to DNWC negates a finding that DNWC's possession was hostile. The last element, actual and uninterrupted, falls somewhere between the "not in dispute" and the "in dispute" categories. Although DNWC will probably be able to prove this element, we need to do more than just set out and apply the specific rule.

A copy of the modified template is set out below.

Chart 10.5　Modified Template

Discussion

Introductory section that sets out the general rules:

- Use policy to introduce the common law rule.
- Set out the common law rule.
- Explain which side has the burden of proof and what that burden is.
- Set out any other rules that apply to all of the elements.
- End with a roadmap that tells the attorney which elements are and which are not likely to be in dispute.

A. Open and Notorious

- Set out the specific rule for open and notorious.
- Apply the specific rule for open and notorious.

B. Actual and Uninterrupted

- Set out the specific rule for actual and uninterrupted.
- Briefly describe analogous cases.
- Explain why DNWC's arguments are stronger than Mr. Garcia's arguments.

C. Exclusive

- Set out the specific rule for exclusive.
- Apply the specific rule for exclusive.

D. Hostile

   1. Set out specific rules for hostile.
   2. Provide attorney with examples of how specific rules have been applied in analogous cases.
       - Case or cases in which claimant's possession was hostile
       - Case or cases in which claimant's possession was not hostile
   3. Arguments
       - DNWC's arguments
       - Mr. Garcia's arguments
   4. Mini-conclusion

§ 10.7 Draft the Introductory, or General Rule, Section

The process of drafting the introductory section of a memo governed by a common law rule is the same as the process that you used in drafting the introductory section for a problem governed by a statute: decide what information you want to include; order that information; and then present that information clearly, concisely, and objectively, including a citation to authority for each rule.

§ 10.7.1 Decide What Information You Need in the Introductory Section

You will usually include the following information in your introductory section:

- The applicable common law rule
- Any statutory sections that apply
- The rules relating to the burden of proof
- Any other rules that apply to all of the elements
- A roadmap telling the attorney which elements are likely to be in dispute and which elements are not likely to be in dispute

In addition, you may explain the history of the common law rule and/or the policies underlying that rule and, if you choose, you may raise and dismiss the undisputed elements. Thus, we go back to our research template and pull the following information. See Chart 10.6.

Chart 10.6   **Research Notes**

- Common law rule
  ***ITT Rayonier, Inc. v. Bell*, 112 Wn.2d 754, 774 P.2d 6 (1989)**

  Quote from pages 757-58
  "In order to establish a claim of adverse possession, there must be possession that is: (1) open and notorious, (2) actual and uninterrupted, (3) exclusive, and (4) hostile. *Chaplin v. Sanders,*

100 Wn. 2d 853, 857, 676 P.2d 431 (1984). Possession of the property with each of the necessary concurrent elements must exist for the statutorily prescribed period of 10 years. RCW 4.16.020."

- Applicable statute: RCW 4.16.020

"Within ten years"
"(1) For actions for the recovery of real property, or for the recovery of the possession thereof; and no action shall be maintained for such recovery unless it appears that the plaintiff, his or her ancestor, predecessor or grantor was seized or possessed of the premises in question within ten years before the commencement of the action."

- Rules relating to the burden of proof
  ***ITT Rayonier, Inc. v. Bell*, 112 Wn.2d 754, 774 P.2d 6 (1989)**

Quote from pages 757-58
"As the presumption of possession is in the holder of legal title, *Peeples v. Port of Bellingham,* 93 Wash.2d 766, 773, 613 P.2d 1128 (1980), *overruled on other grounds, Chaplin v. Sanders, supra,* the party claiming to have adversely possessed the property has the burden of establishing the existence of each element. *Skansi v. Novak,* 84 Wash. 39, 44, 146 P. 160 (1915), *overruled on other grounds, Chaplin v. Sanders, supra.*"

- Other general rules
  ***Chaplin v. Sanders*, 100 Wn.2d 853, 676 P.2d 431 (1984)**

Quote from page 863
"[A]dverse possession is a mixed question of law and fact. Whether the essential facts exist is for the trier of fact; but whether the facts, as found, constitute adverse possession is for the court to determine as a matter of law. *Peeples v. Port of Bellingham, supra* at 771, 613 P.2d 1128."

- Policies underlying common law rule
  ***Chaplin v. Sanders*, 100 Wn.2d 853, 676 P.2d 431 (1984)**

Quote from pages 859-60
"The doctrine of adverse possession was formulated at law for the purpose of, among others, assuring maximum utilization of land, encouraging the rejection of stale claims and, most importantly, quieting titles. 7 R. Powell, *Real Property* ¶ 1012[3] (1982); C. Callahan, *Adverse Possession* 91-94 (1961). Because the doctrine was formulated at law and not at equity, it was originally intended to protect both those who knowingly appropriated the land of others and those who honestly entered and held possession in full belief that the land was their own. R. Powell, at ¶ 1013 [2]; C. Callahan, at 49-50; 3 Am. Jur. 2d *Advancements* § 104 (1962). Thus, when the original purpose of the adverse possession doctrine is considered, it becomes apparent that the claimant's motive in possessing the land is irrelevant and no inquiry should be made into his guilt or innocence. *Accord, Springer v. Durette,* 217 Or. 196, 342 P.2d 132 (1959); *Agers v. Reynolds,* 306 S.W.2d 506 (Mo. 1957); *Fulton v. Rapp,* 59 Ohio Law Abs. 105, 98 N.E.2d 430 (1950); *see also* Stoebuck, *The Law of Adverse Possession in Washington,* 35 Wash. L. Rev. 53, 76-80 (1960)."

§ 10.7.2 Order the Information

In drafting the introductory section, you will usually want to set out more general rules before more specific rules. In our example problem, the most general rules are the policies underlying the doctrine of adverse possession. Thus, you set those out first. Then set out the common law rule, the statutory period, the rules relating to the burden of proof, the other general rules, and the roadmap.

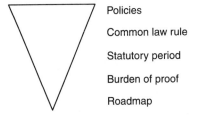

Policies

Common law rule

Statutory period

Burden of proof

Roadmap

If you are not sure what information is more general and what information is more specific, look at the cases. In most cases, the courts set out more general rules before more specific rules.

P R A C T I C E

---

§ 10.7.3 Prepare the First Draft

In drafting the introductory section, do not just string together the quotations from the research template. Instead, make sure that you understand the rules, and then present those rules clearly and concisely. Note that while some attorneys believe you should quote the rules, other attorneys prefer close paraphrases.

Whichever approach you use, make sure you include a citation to authority for each rule that you set out. In most situations, this citation should be to mandatory authority — that is, authority that will be binding on the court hearing the case. If one is available, try to cite a decision from the jurisdiction's highest court. If there are no decisions from the jurisdiction's highest court, cite to a relatively recent decision from the jurisdiction's intermediate court of appeals. Do not cite unpublished decisions and, except in unusual circumstances, do not cite out-of-state cases or secondary authorities as authority for a rule. Finally, as a general rule, do not include a long string of citations. One or two citations to mandatory authority are almost always sufficient.

First Draft of Introductory Section

Discussion

The doctrine of adverse possession arose to assure maximum use of the land, to encourage the rejection of stale claims, and to quiet titles. *Chaplin v. Sanders*, 100 Wn.2d 853,[1] 859-60, 676 P.2d 431 (1984); *see also* William B. Stoebuck, *The Law of Adverse Possession in Washington*, 35 Wash. L. Rev. 53, 53 (1960).

For a claimant to establish adverse possession, the possession must be: (1) actual and uninterrupted, (2) open and notorious, (3) exclusive, and (4) hostile for the statutory period. *ITT Rayonier, Inc. v. Bell*, 112 Wn.2d 754, 757, 774 P.2d 6 (1989); *Chaplin v. Sanders*, 100 Wn.2d 853, 857, 676 P.2d 431 (1984). In this case, the applicable statutory period is set out in RCW 4.16.020(1).

> (1) For actions for the recovery of real property, or for the recovery of the possession thereof and no action shall be maintained for such recovery unless it appears that the plaintiff, his or her ancestor, predecessor or grantor was seized or possessed of the premises in question within ten years before the commencement of the action.

The party claiming to have adversely possessed the property has the burden of establishing the existence of each element. *ITT Rayonier*, 112 Wn.2d at 757. In addition, adverse possession is a mixed question of law and fact. *Chaplin*, 100 Wn.2d at 863. Whether the essential facts exist is for the trier of fact to decide; but whether the facts, as found, constitute adverse possession is for the court to determine as a matter of law. *Id.*

In this case, DNWC can easily prove that their possession was open and notorious and exclusive. In addition, they can probably prove that their possession is actual and uninterrupted. The only element that they may not be able to prove is that their possession was hostile.

Comments

The writer uses the policies underlying the doctrine of adverse possession to introduce the general rule.

The writer sets out the common law rule.

The writer quotes all of RCW 4.16.020(1).

The writer tells the attorney who has the burden of proof.

The writer sets out the other general rules.

The writer tells the attorney which elements DNWC can easily prove and which elements it might have more trouble proving.

---

1. Because this case would be litigated in the Washington courts, the author has used the Washington citation rules. For a copy of the Washington Style Sheet, see *http://www.courts.wa.gov/appellate_trial_courts/supreme/?fa=atc_supreme.style*.

Although this draft of the introductory section is good, there are several things that the writer can do to make it better. First, the writer can delete unnecessary information. Although in most cases you will want to quote the applicable statutory sections, you do not need to quote RCW 4.16.020(1). Because RCW 4.16.020(1) sets out the time period and not the test itself, you just need to tell the attorney that, in this case, the statutory period is ten years.

Second, the writer can present the same information more concisely. Instead of setting out the burden of proof in a separate sentence, the writer can do what most courts have done: incorporate the burden of proof into the sentence listing the elements. Third, the writer can correct the grammatical and punctuation errors. Because DNWC is an organization, the proper pronouns are "it" and "its," not "they" and "their." In addition, do not use a colon to introduce a list unless the material that precedes the list could stand by itself as a complete sentence.

EXAMPLE 2   **Second Draft of Introductory Section**

Comments	Discussion
The writer uses the policies underlying the doctrine of adverse possession to introduce the general rule.	The doctrine of adverse possession arose to assure maximum use of the land, to encourage the rejection of stale claims, and to quiet titles. *Chaplin v. Sanders*, 100 Wn.2d 853, 859-60, 676 P.2d 431 (1984); *see also* William B. Stoebuck, *The Law of Adverse Possession in Washington*, 35 Wash. L. Rev. 53, 53 (1960).
The writer incorporates the burden of proof into the sentence listing the elements. In addition, the writer deletes the incorrect colon.	To establish title through adverse possession, the claimant must prove that its possession was (1) exclusive, (2) actual and uninterrupted, (3) open and notorious, and (4) hostile for the statutory period. *ITT Rayonier, Inc. v. Bell*, 112 Wn.2d 754, 757, 774 P.2d 6 (1989); *Chaplin v. Sanders*, 100 Wn.2d 853, 857, 676 P.2d 431 (1984). In this case, the statutory period is ten years. RCW 4.16.020(1).
The writer sets out the other general rules.	Adverse possession is a mixed question of law and fact. *Chaplin*, 100 Wn.2d at 863. Whether the essential facts exist is for the trier of fact to decide; but whether the facts, as found, constitute adverse possession is for the court to determine as a matter of law. *Id.*
The writer tells the attorney which elements DNWC can easily prove and which element it might have more trouble proving.	In this case, DNWC can easily prove that its possession was open and notorious and exclusive. In addition, it can probably prove that its possession is actual and uninterrupted. The only element that it may not be able to prove is that its possession was hostile.

§ 10.8 Raising and Dismissing the Undisputed Elements

An element is not in dispute if the party that has the burden of proof can easily prove that the element is met or if the party that has the burden of proof cannot prove that the element is met. When an element falls into this category, simply set out the applicable rules and apply them to your facts.

Raising and Dismissing Undisputed Element   EXAMPLE

A. Open and Notorious

A claimant can satisfy the open and notorious element by showing either (1) that the title owner had actual notice of the adverse use throughout the statutory period or (2) that the claimant used the land in such a way that any reasonable person would have thought that the claimant owned it. *Riley v. Andres*, 107 Wn. App. 391, 396, 27 P.3d 618 (2001).

In this case, DNWC can prove both that Mr. Garcia had actual notice of its adverse use and that any reasonable person would have thought that DNWC owned the land. To prove that Mr. Garcia had actual knowledge of DNWC's use of the land, DNWC can offer a copy of the letter that it sent to Mr. Garcia in 1994 asking for continuing permission to use his land for campouts. To prove that a reasonable person would have thought that DNWC owned the land, DNWC will point out that it not only used the land for campouts but also maintained the campsites, fire area, outhouse, and dock and that it posted a "No Trespassing" sign.

> **The writer has used a subheading to identify the element.**
>
> **The writer has paraphrased the rule, changing the "he" in the original quote to the gender neutral "claimant."**
>
> **The writer has used a topic sentence to tell the attorney that DNWC can prove this element under either test. The writer then sets out the facts that DNWC would use to prove that Mr. Garcia had actual knowledge and that a reasonable person would have thought that DNWC owned the land.**

In setting out rules, the emphasis should be on the rule, not on the name of the case or cases from which the rule is drawn. The easiest way to do this is to put the citation not in the sentence in which you set out the rule but in a separate citation sentence following the rule. Compare the following two examples:

P R A C T I C E

Poor Example   EXAMPLE 1

In *Riley v. Andres*, 107 Wn. App. 391, 396, 27 P.3d 618 (2001), the court stated that a claimant can satisfy the open and notorious element by showing either (1) that the title owner had actual notice of the adverse use throughout the statutory period or (2) that the claimant used the land such that any reasonable person would have thought that the claimant owned it.

EXAMPLE 2   **Good Example**

A claimant can satisfy the open and notorious element by showing either (1) that the title owner had actual notice of the adverse use throughout the statutory period or (2) that the claimant used the land such that any reasonable person would have thought that the claimant owned it. *Riley v. Andres*, 107 Wn. App. 391, 396, 27 P.3d 618 (2001).

Question

How would you use the information set out in the research template to raise and dismiss "exclusive"? Prepare a draft of the discussion and then compare your draft to the draft set out on page 280.

§ 10.9 Discussing Elements That Fall in Between the "Not in Dispute" and the "In Dispute" Categories

While in many instances all of the elements will fall into the "not in dispute" or the "in dispute" categories, there will be times when an element falls somewhere in between.

—————————————————————   x   —————————————————————

Element not in dispute   Element in dispute

     When an element falls into this "in between" category, spend more time discussing the element than you would if the element was not in dispute but not as much time as you would spend if it was in dispute.

     In this chapter's example problem, "actual and uninterrupted" falls into this "in between" category. Because the courts have not set out a test for "actual," the writer provides the attorney with examples showing the types of cases in which the courts have held that a claimant had actual possession and the types of cases in which the courts have held that the claimant did not have actual possession. Similarly, in discussing "interrupted," the writer provides the attorney with two brief case descriptions and then explains why Mr. Garcia's argument is weak.

Draft of Element That Is in the "In Between" Category

B. Actual and Uninterrupted

Although the Washington courts have not set out a test for actual possession, the cases illustrate the types of acts that are needed to establish actual possession. 17 *Wash. Prac., Real Estate: Property Law* § 8.10 (2d ed.)

> The writer uses a subheading to identify the elements. The writer tells the attorney that the courts have not set out a specific rule.

The courts have held that claimants had actual possession of rural land when the claimants built a fence and cultivated or pastured up to it, *Faubion v. Elder*, 49 Wn.2d 300, 301 P.2d 153 (1956); cleared the land, constructed and occupied buildings, and planted orchards, *Metro. Bldg. Co. v. Fitzgerald*, 122 Wash. 514, 210 P. 770 (1922); or cleared and fenced the land, planted an orchard, and built a road, *Davies v. Wickstrom*, 56 Wash. 154, 105 P. 454 (1909).

> The writer describes cases in which the courts have held that the claimants had actual possession.

In contrast, the courts have held that the claimants did not have actual possession of rural land when they maintained a fence intended to be a cattle fence, not a line fence, *Roy v. Goerz*, 26 Wn. App. 807, 614 P.2d 1308 (1980); erected two signboards and a mailbox and ploughed weeds, *Slater v. Murphy*, 55 Wn.2d 892, 339 P.2d 457 (1959); or occasionally used the land for gardening, piling wood, and mowing hay, *Smith v. Chambers*, 112 Wash. 600, 192 P. 891 (1920). *See generally*, 17 *Wash. Prac., Real Estate: Property Law* § 8.10 (2d ed.)

> The writer describes cases in which the courts have held the claimants did not have actual possession.

If DNWC had only used the land for occasional campouts, it would have been difficult for it to prove that it had actual possession. However, in addition to using the land for campouts, DNWC maintained the campsites, the fire area, the outhouse, and the dock, and it posted a "No Trespassing" sign. Because DNWC maintained permanent structures and posted the "No Trespassing" sign, more likely than not a court will hold that it had actual possession.

> The writer raises and dismisses "actual."

In addition, DNWC's use and maintenance of the campsites, fire area, outhouse, and dock are probably enough to establish that its possession was uninterrupted. In all of the cases in which the claimants maintained and used permanent structures, the courts have held that the use was uninterrupted. In addition, in *Howard v. Kunto*, 3 Wn. App. 393, 477 P.2d 210 (1970), the court held that the claimants' use was continuous even though they only used the property during the summer. As the court noted in that case, "the requisite possession requires such possession and dominion 'as ordinarily marks the conduct of owners in general in holding, managing, and caring for property of like nature and condition.'" *Id.* at 397. Thus, while Mr. Garcia might be able to argue that DNWC's use of the land was not uninterrupted because it only used the land during the summer months, this argument is a weak one. Because the land is recreational land, DNWC's use of the land during the summer is consistent with how the owners of similar land hold, manage, and care for their property.

> The writer raises and dismisses "uninterrupted."

Question

In this first paragraph, the writer cites a practice book as authority. Is this an appropriate use of a secondary source? Why or why not?

§ 10.10 Discussing the Disputed Elements Using the Script Format

In this section we review the script format by showing you how to write the discussion of "hostile" using that format. In the next section we show you how to write the same discussion using a more integrated format.

Because this section introduces several new techniques — for example, how to integrate case descriptions into the arguments and how to use parentheticals — you should read this section before reading section 10.11.

§ 10.10.1. Set Out the Specific Rules

In researching "hostile," we learned that, before 1984, the Washington courts considered the claimant's subjective intent in determining whether the claimant's possession was hostile. However, in 1984 the Washington Supreme Court overruled these pre-1984 cases and held that the claimant's subjective intent is irrelevant. Thus, under current Washington law, a claimant's use is hostile if the claimant uses the property as a true owner would have used it. There is, though, an exception to this rule. Even if the claimant used the property as a true owner would have used it, the claimant's use is not hostile if the claimant used the land with the owner's permission. This permission may be express or implied.

In setting out these rules, we follow the principle that we set out earlier: set out more general rules before more specific rules and exceptions. Thus, we set out the more general rules, which are the rules about using the property as a true owner would use it, before setting out the rules relating to the exception, which are the rules relating to permission. The amount of time we spend on each set of rules depends, however, on the facts of the client's case. If there are no facts indicating that the true owner gave the claimant permission, we would not need to spend very much time discussing the rules relating to permission. If, however, there are facts that suggest that the true owner might have given permission, we would go into more detail in setting out those rules. Because in our sample problem there are facts that indicate that the owner might have given permission, we take the second approach.

Setting Out Specific Rules

D. Hostile

While prior to 1984 the Washington courts considered the claimant's subjective intent in determining whether its use of the land was hostile, since 1984 the claimant's subjective intent has been irrelevant. *Chaplin*, 100 Wn.2d at 860-61, 676 P.2d 431 (1984) (overruling cases in which the courts had considered the claimant's subjective intent). Thus, under current Washington law, the claimant must prove only that it used the land as if it were its own for the statutory period. *Id.; Miller v. Anderson*, 91 Wn. App. 822, 828, 964 P.2d 365 (1998). If the claimant proves that it used the land as if it were its own, the use was hostile unless the true owner can prove that it gave the claimant permission to use the land. *Id.*	**Writer has included a subheading identifying the element.**
	The writer has given the attorney an important piece of information: that pre-1984 cases are no longer good law if they considered the claimant's subjective intent. The writer then sets out the current rule.
	The writer introduces the exception.
Permission can be express or implied. *Miller v. Anderson*, 91 Wn. App. at 829; *see Granston v. Callahan*, 52 Wn. App. 288, 759 P.2d 462 (1988). An inference of permissive use arises when it is reasonable to assume that the use was permitted. *Id.* If there was permission, the party claiming adverse possession bears the burden of proving that permission terminated because either (1) the servient estate has changed hands through death or alienation or (2) the claimant has asserted a hostile right. *Id.*	**Because the facts of Garcia's case suggest that DNWC's use was permissive, the writer sets out the rules relating to permission in some detail.**

Question

In the example set out above, the writer did not use a signal to introduce *Miller v. Anderson* but did use a signal ("*see*") to introduce *Granston v. Callahan*. Why did the writer not include a signal for *Miller* but did include one for *Callahan*? See Rule 44 in the *ALWD Citation Manual* and Rule 1.2 in *The Bluebook*.

§ 10.10.2 Describe the Analogous Cases

When an element is in dispute, you will usually want to provide the attorney with examples that show how the courts have applied the specific rules in analogous cases. For instance, in our example case, you want to provide examples of the cases in which the courts have held that the claimant was using the land as if it were the claimant's own land and examples of cases in which the court has held that the claimant's use was permissive.

In writing the first memo (see Chapter 7), we set out these case descriptions in a separate analogous case section. Although this option often works well, sometimes you will want to take a different approach and integrate descriptions of the analogous cases into the arguments or describe the case in a parenthetical following the citation to the case rather than in the text.

In deciding whether to put the cases in a separate analogous case section or to integrate them into the arguments, consider the following factors: (1) whether the descriptions are short or long; (2) whether both sides will use the same cases; and (3) whether you will use the same cases for more than one line of argument. It usually works better to put the case descriptions into a separate analogous case description if the case descriptions are long, both sides will use the same cases, and the cases will be used for more than one line of argument. In contrast, it may work better to integrate the case descriptions into the arguments if the descriptions are short, only one side will use a particular case, or the case relates to only one line of argument. For instance, if a case is being offered only as additional support for a proposition or to illustrate a single point, a parenthetical is appropriate.

a. Setting Out the Cases in a Separate Analogous Case Section

In our example problem, you can describe the analogous cases in either a separate analogous case section, or you can integrate the descriptions into the arguments. When you describe the analogous cases in a separate analogous case section, your outline looks like this:

1. Specific rules
2. Descriptions of analogous cases
3. Party with burden of proof's arguments
4. Responding party's arguments
5. Mini-conclusion

When you set out the analogous cases in a separate analogous case section, make sure you do more than provide the attorney with briefs of the cases you have read. Instead of just describing cases, use the cases to illustrate a particular point or set of points. For example, use the cases to illustrate the types of fact situations in which the courts have held that a particular element was met or was not met, to illustrate the types of reasoning the courts have used in deciding whether a particular element is met or is not met, or to show the evolution of a rule. As a general rule, start each paragraph or block of paragraphs with a topic sentence that tells the attorney what point or points you are using the cases to illustrate, and then tailor your case descriptions so they illustrate the point or points you set out in your topic sentence.

Writing a memo is not an academic exercise in which you get points for including particular types of information. Consequently, do not include case descriptions just to include case descriptions.

PRACTICE POINTER

Include them only if they will help the attorney understand how the courts apply a particular rule or set of rules or because you think that one or both sides will try to use a particular case or group of cases to support their arguments. In addition, present your case descriptions in such a way that the attorney does not have to guess why you included the descriptions.

Separate Analogous Case Section

In deciding whether a claimant was using the land as if it were its own, the courts consider whether the claimant made improvements to the land, whether the claimant maintained the property, and whether the claimant used the land on a regular basis. *See, e.g., Chaplin v. Sanders*, 100 Wn.2d 853, 855-56, 676 P.2d 431 (1984); *Timberlane Homeowners Ass'n, Inc. v. Brame*, 79 Wn. App. 303, 310-11, 901 P.2d 1074 (1995). For example, in *Chaplin*, the court held that the claimants were using the land as if it were their own when the claimants built a road across the disputed land, cleared and maintained the disputed land, installed utility lines, and used the area for recreational activities. *Id.* at 855-56. Similarly, in *Timberlane*, the court held that claimants had used land belonging to the homeowners' association as if it was their own when they built and maintained a fence and a concrete patio and the claimants' children played on the land. *Id.* at 310-11.

> Writer uses a topic sentence to introduce the first group of cases.

> Description of first analogous case: writer sets out the court's holding and the key facts.

> Description of second analogous case: writer sets out the court's holding and the key facts.

In contrast, in deciding whether the claimants' use was permissive, the courts consider whether the parties are related or have a friendly relationship, whether the improvements benefited both the claimants' and the title owners' property, and whether the title owner allowed the claimant to use the land as a neighborly accommodation. *See, e.g., Granston*, 52 Wn. App. at 294-95; *Miller v. Jarman*, 2 Wn. App. 994, 471 P.2d 704 (1970). For instance, in *Granston*, the court held that the claimants' use was permissive because the original owners of the two parcels were brothers who worked together to build driveways, walkways, and other improvements that benefited both properties. *Id.* at 294-95. Likewise, in *Miller*, the court held that the use was permissive because the title owners had allowed the claimants, who were their neighbors, to use their driveway as a neighborly accommodation. *Id.* at 255.

> Writer uses a topic sentence to introduce the second group of cases.

> Description of first analogous case: writer sets out the court's holding and the key facts.

> Description of second analogous case: writer sets out the court's holding

---

P R A C T I C E   POINTER

When your topic sentence sets out the principle that you have drawn from a group of cases, you will usually need to include the signal "*see*" or "*see, e.g.*" The "*see*" tells the attorney that you have drawn an inference from the group of cases, and the "*e.g.*" tells the attorney that the cases you have cited are representative of or merely examples of many authorities. *See* Rule 45.3 in the *ALWD Citation Manual* and Rule 1.2 in *The Bluebook*.

---

b. Integrating the Descriptions of the Analogous Cases into the Arguments

When you integrate the descriptions of the analogous cases into the arguments, your outline for the discussion of a disputed element looks like this:

1. Specific rules
2. Party with the burden of proof's arguments including descriptions of the analogous cases
3. Responding party's arguments, including descriptions of the analogous cases
4. Mini-conclusion/prediction

The key to successfully integrating case descriptions into the arguments is keeping the case descriptions short. You must, however, make sure that you do not misrepresent the issue before the court, the rule that the court applied, the key facts, or the court's holding and reasoning. In addition, remember to include citations to authority.

EXAMPLE   ## Case Descriptions Integrated into the Arguments

Writer sets out DNWC's first assertion.	DNWC will argue that its use of Mr. Garcia's land was hostile because DNWC used the land as if it were its own. As in *Chaplin*, in which the Washington Supreme Court held that the claimants had used the disputed land as if it were their own when they built a road across the disputed land, cleared and maintained the disputed land, installed utility lines, and used the area for recreational activities, *id.* at 855-56, in our case, DNWC used the land as if it were its own when it maintained the campsites, the fire area, the outhouse, and the dock; when it used the land for campouts; and when it posted a "No Trespassing" sign on the dock.
The writer describes an analogous case.	
The writer compares the facts in the analogous case to the facts in the client's case.	

Question

What are the pros and cons of putting the case descriptions into a separate analogous case section? What are the pros and cons of integrating the analogous case descriptions into the arguments?

c. Using Parentheticals

While sometimes you will need to use several sentences or even several paragraphs to describe a case, at other times a phrase or a clause is all that is needed. In these latter instances, instead of describing the case in text, you may use a parenthetical.

As a general rule, you will want to set a case out in text when it is one of your key cases. For example, in our example case, you would want to describe *Granston* and *Crites* in text. In the following example, the author describes the first two cases in text and a third case in a parenthetical.

Using Parentheticals

In deciding whether the claimants' use was permissive, the courts consider whether the parties are related or have a friendly relationship, whether the improvements benefited both the claimants' and the title owners' property, and whether the title owners allowed the claimants to use the land as a neighborly accommodation. *See, e.g., Granston*, 52 Wn. App. at 294-95; *Crites v. Koch*, 49 Wn. App. 171, 177, 741 P.2d 1005 (1987). For instance, in *Granston*, the court held that the claimants' use was permissive because the original owners of the two parcels were brothers who worked together to build driveways, walkways, and other improvements that benefited both properties. Similarly, in *Crites*, the court held that the claimant's use of his neighbor's farmland to turn around his equipment and to access another part of his land was not hostile because all of the parties agreed that it was common for farmers to park equipment on their neighbors' fields and to use their neighbors' land. *Id.* at 177. In addition, the parties agreed that such use was recognized as neighborly courtesy, whether or not permission was expressly granted. *Id.; accord, Miller v. Jarman*, 2 Wn. App. 994, 471 P.2d 704 (1970) (holding the claimants' use was permissive because the title owners had allowed the claimants, who were their neighbors, to use their driveway as a neighborly accommodation).

> **The writer uses a topic sentence to introduce the group of cases.**
>
> **The writer sets out the description of the first case in text.**
>
> **The writer sets out description of the second case in text.**
>
> **The writer describes a third case in a parenthetical following the citation to the third case.**

In using parentheticals, keep several "rules" in mind. First, if you are going to compare or contrast the facts in an analogous case to facts in your case, describe the analogous case in text, not in a parenthetical. Second, keep your parentheticals short. If you cannot give the attorney the information that he or she needs in a word, phrase, or clause, do not use a parenthetical. Third, make sure that in trying to present the information concisely, you do not mislead the attorney.

Although there is no set format for parentheticals, most take one of the following forms.

word or phrase	(built a road)
participial phrase (verb with "–ing" ending)	(holding that the claimants, who had built and maintained a road, had used the land as if were their own)
clause	(Court held that the claimants had used the land as if it were their own when they built and maintained a road.)

As a general rule, do not capitalize the first word of the parenthetical when using only a word, phrase, or participial phrase. Do, however, capitalize the first word when using a complete clause or sentence. In addition, if you use one form for one parenthetical, use the same form for the other parentheticals in the same string of citations.

§ 10.10.3 Draft the Argument

a. Identify Each Side's Arguments

The first step is to identify each side's arguments. In arguing that its possession was hostile, what arguments can DNWC make? In arguing that DNWC's possession was not hostile, what arguments can Mr. Garcia make?

Unfortunately, there is no easy way of identifying each side's arguments. There are, however, some techniques that sometimes help.

Begin by asking yourself which of the standard arguments the parties can make. Can they make plain language arguments — that is, arguments in which they apply the plain language of the specific rules to the facts of the case? Can they make analogous case arguments, arguing that their case is similar to a particular case or set of cases or distinguishing a particular case or set of cases? Can they make policy arguments? Given the policies underlying the doctrine of adverse possession, is this a case in which the court should decide that DNWC's use was hostile?

If you get stuck making a particular type of argument — for example, a plain language argument, look again at the cases and see (1) whether the parties made a plain language argument and (2) if they did, how they constructed their arguments. Similarly, if you are having trouble comparing and contrasting the analogous cases, see how the courts have compared and contrasted those cases. Borrowing arguments is not only okay but expected.

b. Select an Organizational Scheme

As you saw in Chapter 7, when you use the script format, you present the arguments in the same order that they would be presented to the judge. Thus, in most instances, you set out the moving party's argument first and the responding party's arguments second. In addition, sometimes you will set out the moving party's rebuttal.

Script Format

Moving Party's Arguments

- Argument 1
- Argument 2
- Argument 3

Responding Party's Arguments

- Argument 1
- Argument 2
- Argument 3
- Argument 4

Moving Party's Rebuttal

While sometimes each side will have the same number of arguments, at other times one side will have fewer (or more) arguments.

P R A C T I C E

POINTER

In setting out the party's arguments, you have several options: you may organize the arguments by type — for example, you may set out a party's plain language arguments in one paragraph or block of paragraphs, its analogous case arguments in a second paragraph or block of paragraphs, and its policy arguments in a third paragraph or block of paragraphs. In the alternative, you may organize the arguments around sub-assertions. For instance, in our example case, in one block of paragraphs you may set out all of DNWC's arguments relating to using the land as a true owner would have used it and in a separate block of paragraphs all of its arguments relating to whether that use was permissive.

If you organize the arguments by type of argument, begin the section in which you summarize the moving party's arguments by setting out its assertion. Then set out the moving party's plain language arguments, its analogous case arguments, and its policy arguments. End by setting out the responding party's assertion, its plain language arguments, its analogous case arguments, and its policy arguments.

Outline for Arguments Organized by Type of Argument

EXAMPLE 1

Script Format for a Disputed Element

Moving Party's Arguments

- Main assertion
- Plain language arguments

- Analogous case arguments
- Policy arguments

Responding Party's Arguments

- Main assertion
- Plain language arguments
- Analogous case arguments
- Policy arguments

The types of arguments that a party can make will vary from case to case. While sometimes both sides will be able to make plain language, analogous case, and policy arguments, at other times a party may be able to make only one or two of these types of arguments. For instance, in our example case, both sides can make plain language and analogous case arguments, but they cannot make policy arguments.

PRACTICE POINTER

EXAMPLE 2

Draft of Arguments When Arguments Organized by Type

The writer sets out DNWC's main assertions

DNWC can argue that its use of Mr. Garcia's land was hostile because DNWC treated Mr. Garcia's land as its own and because it did not have either express or implied permission to use the land.

The writer introduces and sets out DNWC's plain language argument.

DNWC can argue that the facts of the case support its assertion that it was using the land as its own and that it did not have Mr. Garcia's permission to use the land. For more than ten years, DNWC maintained the campsites, the fire area, the outhouse, and the dock; it used the land for campouts; and it posted a "No Trespassing" sign. In addition, although it wrote a letter requesting permission to use the land, Mr. Garcia did not respond to the letter.

The writer introduces and sets out DNWC's analogous case arguments.

Thus, DNWC will argue that this case is more like *Chaplin* and *Timberlane* than it is *Granston* and *Miller*. Like the claimants in *Chaplin* and *Timberlane*, DNWC maintained the disputed land and used the disputed land on a regular basis. In contrast, unlike the claimants in *Granston*, who were related to the title owner, there is no evidence that any of DNWC's members are related to Mr. Garcia. In addition, unlike *Miller*, in which there was evidence that the title owner allowed the claimants to use the land as a neighborly accommodation, there is nothing in this case that indicates that Mr. Garcia was allowing DNWC to use his land as a neighborly accommodation. While there does not appear to be an antagonistic relationship between DNWC and Mr. Garcia, there is nothing to suggest a close relationship.

In contrast, Mr. Garcia can argue that DNWC was not using the property as if it were its own or, even if it was, it was using the land with his implied permission.

> The writer sets out Mr. Garcia's assertion.

Mr. Garcia will argue that the facts do not support a conclusion that DNWC was using the land as if it were its own. Although DNWC maintained and used the campsites, fire area, outhouse, and dock, it did not build any new structures. In addition, although it used the land, DNWC did so for only a few days a week for only a few weeks a year. Finally, in this case, DNWC asked for permission to continue to use the land. In its February 2004 letter to Mr. Garcia, DNWC asked Mr. Garcia if it could continue using the land. Although Mr. Garcia did not specifically grant permission, he did not revoke permission. Thus, it is reasonable to assume that DNWC was using the land with Mr. Garcia's implied permission.

> The writer introduces and sets out Mr. Garcia's plain language arguments.

Mr. Garcia may also use the cases to support his assertions. In both *Chaplin* and *Timberlane*, the claimants made major improvements to the land: in *Chaplin*, the claimants built a new road, cleared and maintained the land, and installed power lines, and in *Timberlane* the claimants built a new fence and a new patio. In contrast, in this case, DNWC did not build any new structures. Rather, it only maintained existing structures. In addition, as in *Miller,* in this case Mr. Garcia allowed DNWC to use the land as a neighborly accommodation. Just as it is not uncommon for farmers to allow other farmers to use their land to turn around their vehicles, it is not uncommon for landowners to allow charitable organizations to make occasional use of their land.

> The writer introduces and sets out Mr. Garcia's analogous case arguments.

In response, DNWC can argue that even if its initial use was permissive, that permission ended. If Mr. Garcia's grandfather gave DNWC permission to use his land, that permission would have terminated when he died. *See Granston*, 52 Wn. App. at 294-95. Likewise, even if DNWC had Mr. Garcia's implied permission to use the land, that permissive use ended in 1994 when, after not receiving a response from Mr. Garcia, DNWC posted a "No Trespassing" sign on the dock and continued to use the property as if it were its own.

> The writer sets out DNWC's rebuttal.

As we noted in Chapter 7, different attorneys have different views on whether you need or should include citations to authority in the argument section when you have already  described and cited the cases in a separate analogous case section. When you have already described the cases in a separate analogous case section, some attorneys would tell you not to repeat the citations, and others would tell you to repeat them. All attorneys, however, would agree that if you are mentioning a case for the first time, you need to include a citation to the authority. Thus, if you are integrating your case descriptions into the arguments, you will always need to include citations, including, when possible, pinpoint cites.

If you organize your arguments around subassertions, set out your main assertion, your first subassertion, your support for your first subassertion, your second subassertion, your support for your second subassertion, and so on. In supporting your subassertions, set out any plain language, analogous case, and policy arguments that relate to that subassertion.

EXAMPLE 3   **Arguments Organized Around Subassertions**

Script Format for a Disputed Element

Moving Party's Arguments

- Main assertion
- First subassertion
- Arguments relating to first subassertion
- Second subassertion
- Arguments relating to second subassertion

Responding Party's Arguments

- Main assertion
- First subassertion
- Arguments relating to first subassertion
- Second subassertion
- Arguments relating to second subassertion

EXAMPLE 4   **Draft of Arguments When Arguments Organized by Type of Argument**

The writer sets out DNWC's main assertion.	DNWC can argue that its use of Mr. Garcia's land was hostile because it treated Mr. Garcia's land as its own and because, since 1994, it did not have either express or implied permission to use the land.
The writer sets out DNWC's first subassertion and its support for its first subassertion.	DNWC will begin by arguing that it was using the land as if the land were its own. Like the claimants in *Chaplin* and *Timberlane*, DNWC maintained the disputed land. It maintained not only the campsites and fire area but also the outhouse and the dock. In addition, like the claimants in *Chaplin* and *Timberlane*, DNWC used the property on a regular basis by holding campouts on the land several nights a week for eight weeks every summer.
The writer sets out DNWC's second subassertion and its support for that subassertion.	DNWC will also argue that its use was not permissive. Unlike *Granston*, in which the parties were related, in this case there is no evidence that any of DNWC's members are related to Mr. Garcia. In addition, unlike the farmers in *Crites*, who allowed other farmers to use their land to turn around their equipment or to access their own land, owners of recreational property do not typically allow their neighbors to use their land on a regular and repeated basis through the summer months.

In contrast, Mr. Garcia will argue that DNWC was not using the property as if it were its own or, even if it was, it was using the land with his implied permission. Garcia will argue that the facts do not support a conclusion that DNWC was using the land as if it were its own. Although DNWC maintained the campsites, fire area, outhouse, and dock, it did not build any new structures. In addition, although it used the land, it did so for only a few days a week for a few weeks a year. Thus, the facts in this case can be distinguished from the facts in *Chaplin* and *Timberlane.* While in both of those cases, the claimants made substantial improvements to the land — for example, by building a road or by building a fence and a patio — in this case DNWC did not build anything new.

The writer sets out Garcia's main assertion.

The writer sets out Garcia's first subassertion and his support for that subassertion.

In the alternative, Mr. Garcia can argue that even if DNWC was using the land as if it were its own, it was doing so with his permission. In its 1994 letter to Mr. Garcia, DNWC acknowledged that it was using the land with Mr. Garcia's permission, and it requested permission to continue using the land. Because Mr. Garcia did not revoke his permission, it is reasonable to assume that DNWC used the land with Mr. Garcia's implied permission. Consequently, this case is more similar to *Crites* than it is to *Lingvall.* As in *Crites,* in which the title owner allowed the claimants to use his land as a neighborly accommodation, in this case Mr. Garcia allowed DNWC to use his land as a neighborly accommodation. In addition, unlike *Lingvall,* in which there was an antagonistic relationship between the parties, in this case there was not.

The writer sets out Garcia's second subassertion and his support for that subassertion.

In response, DNWC may argue that even if the initial use was permissive, that permission ended. If Mr. Garcia's grandfather gave DNWC permission to use his land, that permission would have terminated when he died. *See Granston,* 52 Wn. App. at 294-95. Likewise, even if DNWC had Mr. Garcia's implied permission to use the land, that permissive use ended in 1994 when, after not receiving a response from Mr. Garcia, DNWC posted a "No Trespassing" sign on the dock and continued to use the property as if it were its own.

The writer sets out DNWC's rebuttal.

§ 10.10.4 Predict How the Court Will Decide the Element

When you use the script format, the last section is a mini-conclusion in which you predict how the court is likely to decide the element. Will the court decide that the moving party has or has not met its burden of proof?

In setting out the mini-conclusion, provide not only the answer but also the reasoning. Why will the court decide that the moving party has or has not met its burden?

EXAMPLE 1   **The Writer Has Set Out the Conclusion but Not the Reasoning**

The writer sets out the conclusion.   In this case, the court is likely to hold that DNWC's use of Mr. Garcia's land was hostile. DNWC used the land as if it were its own, and it did so without Mr. Garcia's permission.

EXAMPLE 2   **The Writer Has Set Out the Conclusion and the Reasoning**

The writer sets out the reasoning.   In this case, DNWC appears to have the stronger arguments. Although DNWC has the burden of proof, it will probably be able to prove that it used the Garcia land as if it were its own when it maintained and used the campsites, the fire area, the outhouse, and the dock during the peak season. In addition, it will probably be able to prove that its use was not permissive. Although it is possible that initially DNWC was using the land with Mr. Garcia's grandfather's permission, that permission ended when Mr. Garcia's grandfather died and left the property to Mr. Garcia. In addition, even though DNWC asked for permission to continue using the property, Mr. Garcia never responded to that request. DNWC indicated its hostile intent when it posted the "No Trespassing" sign and continued to use the property as its own. Finally, it seems unlikely that a court would conclude that Mr. Garcia allowed DNWC to use his land as a neighborly accommodation. Although it may be common for farmers to allow neighboring farmers to use their land to turn around their vehicles, it is uncommon for an owner of recreational land to allow a neighbor to use the owner's land through the peak season.

The writer sets out the conclusion/ prediction.   Thus, because DNWC used the property as its own, the court will probably hold that it has proved that its use was hostile.

---

§ 10.11 Organizing the Discussion Section Using an Integrated Format

When you use an integrated format for a disputed element, you include the same information that you include when you use the script format: specific rules, descriptions of analogous cases, both sides' arguments, and a mini-conclusion. You simply "package" the information differently. You present the information in a different order and from a different perspective.

§ 10.11.1 Use Deductive Rather Than Inductive Reasoning

When you use the script format, you use a form of inductive reasoning. Instead of setting out your conclusion near the beginning, you set it out at the end. You set out the specific rules first, the analogous cases and arguments second, and your conclusion last. In contrast, when you use an integrated format, you use a form of deductive reasoning. You set out your conclusion near the beginning and then explain how you reached that conclusion.

Script Format **Inductive Reasoning**	**Integrated Format** **Deductive Reasoning**
Specific Rules	Specific Rules
Descriptions of Analogous Cases[2]	Descriptions of Analogous Cases[3]
Moving Party's Arguments	Mini-Conclusion/Prediction[4]
▪ First Argument ▪ Second Argument ▪ Third Argument	Reasoning
Responding Party's Arguments	▪ First Reason (summarize and evaluate each side's arguments) ▪ Second Reason (summarize and evaluate each side's arguments) ▪ Third Reason (summarize and evaluate each side's arguments)
▪ First Argument ▪ Second Argument ▪ Third Argument	
Rebuttal (if any)	
Mini-Conclusion/Prediction	

§ 10.11.2 Present the Information from a Judge's Perspective

When you use the script format, you assume the perspective of a script writer and describe the action as it unfolds. For example, when you get to the arguments, you summarize the moving party's arguments, the responding party's arguments, the moving party's rebuttal, and then the court's decision. In contrast, when you use one of the integrated formats, you assume the role of the judge who has heard each side's arguments and is now setting out his or her decision and its reasoning. Thus, when you use an integrated format, you set out your conclusion and then your reasoning,

---

2. You can also integrate your descriptions of the analogous cases into the arguments. See pages 258-259.

3. You can also integrate your descriptions of the analogous cases into the reasoning. See pages 259-261.

4. You can also put your mini-conclusion/prediction before the paragraph or block of paragraphs in which you set out the specific rules.

which incorporates each side's arguments and your evaluation of those arguments.

§ 10.11.3 Make Sure You Give Appropriate Weight to Each Side's Arguments

The advantage of the script format is that the format forces you to give appropriate weight to each side's arguments. Even though you may think that one side's arguments are weaker than the other side's arguments, you have to set out the weaker side's arguments. The disadvantage of the script format is that the discussion is usually longer, and the format may result in a discussion that feels as if the writer is working through a list of arguments.

The advantage of the integrated format is that the discussion of the disputed element is shorter and, when done well, the analysis may appear to be more sophisticated. The disadvantage is that it can be difficult to write a good integrated discussion. It can be difficult to give appropriate weight to each side's arguments, and it can be difficult to write sentences that are easy to read and understand.

The discussion of a disputed element written using the integrated format should contain the same information as a discussion of that element written using the script format. If you are leaving out information, you are doing something wrong.

P R A C T I C E

---

§ 10.11.4 Write the Specific Rule Section

The specific rule section is the same regardless of whether you use the script format or the integrated format. Set out more general rules before more specific rules and exceptions, do more than just string together a series of quotations, and include a citation to authority for each rule you set out. The following example illustrates that the specific rule section is the same regardless of whether you use the script format or an integrated format.

Specific Rule Paragraph

Script   Integrated

D. Hostile

While prior to 1984 the Washington courts considered the claimant's subjective intent in determining whether its use of the land was hostile, since 1984 the claimant's subjective intent has been irrelevant. *Chaplin v. Sanders*, 100 Wn. 2d 853, 860-61, 676 P.2d 431 (1984) (overruling cases in which the courts considered the claimant's subjective intent). Thus, under current Washington law, the claimant must prove only that it used the land as if it were its own for the statutory period. *Id; Miller v. Anderson*, 91 Wn. App. 822, 828, 964 P.2d 365 (1998). If the claimant proves that it used the land as if it were its own, the use was hostile unless the true owner can prove that it gave the claimant permission to use the land. *Id.*

Permission can be express or implied. *Miller v. Anderson*, 91 Wn. App. at 829, *citing Granston v. Callahan*, 52 Wn. App. 288, 759 P.2d 462 (1988) (case dealt with a prescriptive easement, not adverse possession). The courts infer that the use was permissive when, under the circumstances, it is reasonable to assume that the use was permitted. *Id.* If there was permission, the party claiming adverse possession bears the burden of proving that permission terminated because either (1) the servient estate changed hands through death or alienation, or (2) the claimant has asserted a hostile right. *Id.*

D. Hostile

While prior to 1984 the Washington courts considered the claimant's subjective intent in determining whether its use of the land was hostile, since 1984 the claimant's subjective intent has been irrelevant. *Chaplin*, 100 Wn.2d 853, 860-61, 676 P.2d 431 (1984) (overruling cases in which the courts had considered the claimant's subjective intent). Thus, under current Washington law, the claimant must prove only that it used the land as if it were its own for the statutory period. *Id; Miller v. Anderson*, 91 Wn. App. 822, 828, 964 P.2d 365 (1998). If the claimant proves that it used the land as if it were its own, the use was hostile unless the true owner can prove that it gave the claimant permission to use the land. *Id.*

Permission can be express or implied. *Miller v. Anderson*, 91 Wn. App. at 829, *citing Granston v. Callahan*, 52 Wn. App. 288, 759 P.2d 462 (1988) (case dealt with a prescriptive easement, not adverse possession). The courts infer that the use was permissive when, under the circumstances, it is reasonable to assume that the use was permitted. *Id.* If there was permission, the party claiming adverse possession bears the burden of proving that permission terminated because either (1) the servient estate changed hands through death or alienation, or (2) the claimant has asserted a hostile right. *Id.*

In setting out citations to authority, you may use parentheticals to provide the attorney with additional information about the cases. For instance, in the preceding example, the writer used a parenthetical to tell the attorney that, in *Chaplin*, the Washington Supreme Court overruled those cases in which the courts had considered the claimant's subjective intent in determining whether the claimant's use was hostile. Similarly, the writer used a parenthetical to tell the attorney that, while the *Miller* court cited *Granston* as authority, *Granston* involved a prescriptive easement, not adverse possession. See Rule 46 in the *ALWD Citation Manual* and Rule B5.1.4 in *The Bluebook*

§ 10.11.5 Describe the Analogous Cases

In describing the analogous cases, you have the same choices you had when you used the script format: you may set out the analogous cases in a separate analogous case section, or you may integrate the case descriptions into the arguments. In addition, when appropriate you may describe a case in a parenthetical following the citation to the cases. See pages 246-248. When you set out the analogous cases in a separate analogous case section, that section is the same regardless of whether you use the script or the the integrated format.

EXAMPLE   **Analogous Cases Described in a Separate Analogous Case Section**

Script	Integrated
In deciding whether a claimant was using the land as if it were its own, the courts consider whether the claimant made improvements to the land, whether the claimant maintained the property; and whether the claimant used the land on a regular basis. *See, e.g., Chaplin*, 100 Wn.2d at 855-56; *Timberlane Homeowners Ass'n, Inc. v. Brame* 79 Wn. App 303, 310-11, 901 P.2d 1074 (1995). For example, in *Chaplin*, the court held that the claimants were using the land as if it were their own when the claimants built a road across the disputed land, cleared and maintained the disputed land, installed utility lines, and used the area for recreational activities. *Id.* at 855-56. Similarly, in *Timberlane*, the court held that claimants had used land belonging to the homeowners' association as if it	In deciding whether a claimant was using the land as if it were its own, the courts consider whether the claimant made improvements to the land, whether the claimant maintained the property, and whether the claimant used the land on a regular basis. *See, e.g., Chaplin*, 100 Wn.2d at 855-56; *Timberlane Homeowners Ass'n, Inc. v. Brame* 79 Wn. App. 303, at 310-11, 901 P.2d 1074 (1995) For example, in *Chaplin*, the court held that the claimants were using the land as if it were their own when the claimants built a road across the disputed land, cleared and maintained the disputed land, installed utility lines, and used the area for recreational activities. *Id.* at 855-56. Similarly, in *Timberlane*, the court held that claimants had used land belonging to the homeowners' association as if it was

was their own when they built and maintained a fence and a concrete patio and the claimants' children played on the land. *Id.*

In deciding whether the claimants' use was permissive, the courts consider whether the parties are related or have a friendly relationship, whether the improvements benefited both the claimants' and the title owners' property, and whether the title owners allowed the claimants to use the land as a neighborly accommodation. *See, e.g., Granston v. Callahan*, 52 Wn. App. 288, 759 P.2d 462 (1988); *Miller v. Jarman*, 2 Wn. App. 994, 471, P.2d 704 (1970). For instance, in *Granston*, the court held that the claimants' use was permissive because the original owners of the two parcels were brothers who worked together to build driveways, walkways, and other improvements that benefited both properties. *Id.* at 294-95. Likewise, in *Miller*, the court held that the use was permissive because the title owners had allowed the claimants, who were their neighbors, *Id.* at 294. In contrast, in *Lingvall v. Bartmess*, 97 Wn. App. 245, 256, 982 P.2d 690 (1999), the court held that the antagonistic relationship between two brothers negated a finding that the claimant's use of the land was permissive.

their own when they built and maintained a fence and a concrete patio and the claimants' children played on the land. *Id.*

In deciding whether the claimants' use was permissive, the courts consider whether the parties are related or have a friendly relationship, whether the improvements benefited both the claimants' and the title owners' property, and whether the title owners allowed the claimants to use the land as a neighborly accommodation. *See, e.g., Granston v. Callahan*, 52 Wn. App. 288, 759 P.2d 462 (1988); *Miller v. Jarman*, 2 Wn. App. 994, 471, P.2d 704 (1970). For instance, in *Granston*, the court held that the claimants' use was permissive because the original owners of the two parcels were brothers who worked together to build driveways, walkways, and other improvements that benefited both properties. *Id.* at 294-95. Likewise, in *Miller*, the court held that the use was permissive because the title owners had allowed the claimants, who were their neighbors, to use their driveway as a neighborly accommodation. *Id.* at 294. In contrast, in *Lingvall v. Bartmess*, 97 Wn. App. 245, 256, 982 P.2d 690 (1999), the court held that the antagonistic relationship between two brothers negated a finding that the claimant's use of the land was permissive.

Remember to introduce each group of cases. For example, include a topic sentence that tells the attorney what principle or point you are using a group of cases to illustrate. In addition, use a

P R A C T I C E

transition to tell the attorney whether a second case illustrates the same or a, different point from the first case.

---

§ 10.11.6 Set Out your Mini-Conclusion/ Prediction

The first subsection that is different is the mini-conclusion. In the script format, the mini-conclusion comes after the arguments and contains both your evaluation of each side's arguments and your prediction about how you think the court will decide the disputed element. In contrast, in an integrated format, the mini-conclusion is near the beginning of your discussion of the disputed element and is much shorter. Although you set out your prediction, you integrate your evaluation of the arguments into the presentation of the arguments. Rather than work inductively from arguments to conclusion, you announce conclusions first and then show how they are supported by the arguments.

EXAMPLE   ## Mini-Conclusion

Script	Integrated
(Mini-conclusion is set out at the very end, after arguments.)	(Mini-conclusion is set out before arguments.)

In this case, DNWC appears to have the stronger arguments. Although DNWC has the burden of proof, it will probably be able to prove that it used the Garcia land as if it were its own when it maintained and used the campsites, the fire area, the outhouse, and the dock during the peak season. In addition, it will probably be able to prove that its use was not permissive. Although it is possible that initially DNWC was using the land with Mr. Garcia's grandfather's permission, that permission terminated when Mr. Garcia's grandfather died and left the property to Mr. Garcia. In addition, even though DNWC asked for permission to continue using the property, Mr. Garcia never responded to that request, and DNWC did an act that indicated its hostile intent when it posted the "No Trespassing" sign and continued to use the property as its own. Finally, it seems unlikely that a court would conclude that Mr. Garcia allowed DNWC to use his land as a neighborly accommodation. Although it may be common for farmers to allow neighboring farmers to use their land to turn around their vehicles, it is common for owners of recreational land to allow neighbors to use their land

In this case, the court will probably conclude that DNWC has met its burden of proving that its use of the Garcia land was hostile.

First, the court will probably conclude that DNWC has met its burden of proving that it used the land as if it were its own. [Rest of the analysis goes here.]

Second, the court will probably conclude that DNWC's use of the Garcia land was not permissive. [Rest of the analysis goes here.]

through the peak season. Thus, because
DNWC used the property as its own and
did an act that would have terminated the
permission, the court will probably hold
that it has proven that its use was hostile.

When you use the integrated format, you can use your mini-conclusion as
a roadmap for your reasoning. Compare the following two examples.

Mini-Conclusion

Integrated (no roadmap)

[Mini-conclusion is set out before
arguments.]
 In this case, the court will probably
conclude that DNWC has met its burden
of proving that its use of the Garcia land
was hostile.
 First, the court will probably
conclude that DNWC has met its burden
of proving that it used the land as if it
were its own. [Rest of the analysis goes
here.]
 Second, the court will probably
conclude that DNWC's use of the Garcia
land was not permissive. [Rest of the
analysis goes here.]

Integrated (roadmap)

[Mini-conclusion is set out before
arguments.]
 In this case, the court will probably
conclude that DNWC's use of the Garcia
land was hostile for two reasons: (1)
DNWC was using the land as if it were
its own and (2) DNWC's use of the
Garcia land was not permissive.
 First, the court will probably
conclude that DNWC has met its burden
of proving that it used the land as if it
were its own. [Rest of the analysis goes
here.]
 Second, the court will probably
conclude that DNWC's use of the Garcia
land was not permissive. [Rest of the
analysis goes here.]

---

§ 10.11.7 The Arguments

When you set out the arguments using the script format, you organize the
arguments by party. Set out all of the party with the burden of proof's arguments and then all of the responding party's arguments. In contrast, when you
use an integrated format, you organize the arguments by the reasons supporting your mini-conclusion. You set out the mini-conclusion and then the first
reason, the second reason, and so on.

EXAMPLE 1 ## Script vs. Integrated Format

<table>
<tr><td align="center">**Script Format**
(arguments organized by party)</td><td align="center">**Integrated Format**
(arguments organized by reasons)</td></tr>
<tr><td>**Moving Party's Arguments**</td><td>**Mini-Conclusion**</td></tr>
<tr><td>• Moving party's general assertion</td><td>**Reason 1**</td></tr>
<tr><td>• Moving party's first subassertion and support for that subassertion
• Moving party's second subassertion and support for that subassertion</td><td>• Integrated discussion of moving and responding parties' arguments</td></tr>
<tr><td>**Responding Party's Arguments**</td><td>**Reason 2**</td></tr>
<tr><td>• Responding party's first subassertion and support for that subassertion
• Responding party's second subassertion and support for that subassertion</td><td>• Integrated discussion of moving and responding parties' arguments</td></tr>
<tr><td>**Mini-Conclusion**</td><td>**Reason 3**</td></tr>
<tr><td></td><td>• Integrated discussion of moving and responding parties' arguments</td></tr>
</table>

The following example shows how to set out the same arguments using the two different formats.

EXAMPLE 2 ## Same Arguments Presented Using the Script and Integrated Formats

Script	**Integrated**
DNWC can argue that its use of Mr. Garcia's land was hostile because it treated his land as its own and because, since 1994, it did not have either express or implied permission to use the land.	In the Garcia case, the court will probably conclude DNWC's use of Mr. Garcia's land was hostile.
DNWC will begin by arguing that it was using the land as if the land were its own. Like the claimants in *Chaplin* and *Timberlane*, DNWC maintained the disputed land. DNWC will point out that it maintained not only the campsites and fire area but also the outhouse and the dock. In addition, like the claimants in	First, the court will probably conclude that DNWC used Mr. Garcia's land as if it were the true owner. Although DNWC did not build any new structures on Mr. Garcia's land, it maintained the campsites, the fire area, the outhouse, and the dock. In addition, although DNWC did not use the property year-round, it did use the property during the summer, which is how a

Chaplin and *Timberlane*, DNWC used the property on a regular basis by holding campouts on the land several nights a week for eight weeks every summer.

DNWC will also argue that its use was not permissive. Unlike *Granston*, in which the parties were related, in this case there is no indication that any of DNWC's members are related to Mr. Garcia. In addition, unlike the farmers in *Crites*, who allowed other farmers to use their land to turn around their equipment or to access their own land, owners of recreational property do not typically allow their neighbors to use their land throughout the summer months.

In contrast, Mr. Garcia can argue that DNWC was not using the property as if it were its own or, even if it were, it was using the land with his implied permission.

Mr. Garcia will argue that the facts do not support a conclusion that DNWC was using the land as if it were its own.

Although DNWC maintained the campsites, fire area, outhouse, and dock, it did not build any new structures. In addition, although it used the land, it did so for only a few days a week and a few weeks a year. Thus, the facts in this case can be distinguished from the facts in *Chaplin* and *Timberlane*. While in both of those cases, the claimants made substantial improvements to the land — for example, by building a road or building a fence and a patio — in this case DNWC did not build anything new.

In the alternative, Mr. Garcia can argue that even if DNWC was using the land as if it were its own, it was doing so with his permission. In its 1994 letter to Mr. Garcia, DNWC acknowledged that it was using the land with Mr. Garcia's permission, and it requested permission to continue using the land. Because Mr. Garcia did not revoke his permission, it is reasonable to assume that DNWC used the land with Mr. Garcia's implied permission. Thus, this case is more similar to *Crites* than it is to *Lingvall*. As

typical owner would have used the land. Thus, this case is similar to *Chaplin* and *Timberlane*, in which the claimants maintained and used the disputed land as a true owner would have used the land. While in *Chaplin* and *Timberlane* the claimants built new structures (in *Chaplin*, the claimants built a road and, in *Timberlane*, they built a fence and a patio), the courts have held that the claimant does not have to do everything that a title owner might do.

Second, the court will probably conclude that DNWC's use of Mr. Garcia's land was not permissive. Unlike *Granston*, in which the parties were related and had a close relationship, there is no evidence that the members of DNWC are related to Mr. Garcia. In addition, unlike *Crites*, in which the parties agreed that they typically allowed their neighbors to use their land to turn around their equipment or to access the other parts of their own land, typical owners of recreational land do not allow neighboring property owners to use their land several days a week during the peak season.

While Mr. Garcia can argue that the letter that DNWC sent to him establishes that DNWC's use of the land was permissive, the court will probably reject this argument. First, the court will conclude that if Mr. Garcia's grandfather gave DNWC permission to use his land, that permission terminated when his grandfather died. In addition, the court will probably conclude that even if DNWC used Mr. Garcia's land with Mr. Garcia's implied permission from the time of his grandfather's death until DNWC sent the letter in February of 1994, that permission terminated in the summer of 1994 when DNWC posted the "No Trespassing" sign and continued to use the property as its own.

in *Crites*, in which the title owner allowed the claimants to use his land as a neighborly accommodation, in this case Mr. Garcia allowed DNWC to use his land as a neighborly accommodation. In addition, unlike *Lingvall*, in which there was an antagonistic relationship between the parties, in this case there was not.

In response, DNWC can argue that even if its initial use was permissive, that permission terminated. If Mr. Garcia's grandfather gave DNWC permission to use his land, that permission would have terminated when he died. *See Granston*, 52 Wn. App. at 294-95. Likewise, even if DNWC had Mr. Garcia's implied permission to use the land, that permissive use ended in 1994 when, after not receiving a response from Mr. Garcia, DNWC posted a "No Trespassing" sign on the dock and continued to use the property as if it were its own.

Because the author included the citations for these cases when she described them in the analogous case section, she has not repeated the citations in the argument section. Check with your supervising attorney to see if he or she wants you to use this approach or if he or she wants you to repeat the citations.

P R A C T I C E
POINTER

Questions

Is there information in the script version of the discussion that is not in the integrated version? If there is, does that information need to be added to the integrated discussion? If it does, how would you rewrite the integrated discussion to include that information?

In using the integrated format, writers sometimes end up drafting discussions of the disputed elements that are conclusory. Instead of setting out and evaluating each side's arguments, the writer sets out only those arguments that support his or her conclusion. Compare the following examples.

Writer Sets Out Only the Winning Arguments and Neglects to Include the Losing Arguments

EXAMPLE

First, the court will probably conclude that DNWC used Mr. Garcia's land as if it were the true owner. DNWC maintained the campsites, the fire area, the outhouse, and the dock. In addition, DNWC used the land for eight weeks of the summer, which would be typical for that type of property. Thus, this case is similar to *Chaplin* and *Timberlane*, in which the claimants maintained and used the disputed land.

Writer Gives Appropriate Weight to Each Side's Arguments

EXAMPLE

First, the court will probably conclude that DNWC used Mr. Garcia's land as if it were the true owner. Although DNWC did not build any new structures on Mr. Garcia's land, it maintained the campsites, the fire area, the outhouse, and the dock. In addition, although DNWC did not use the property year-round, it did use the property during the summer, which is how a typical owner would have used the land. Thus, this case is similar to *Chaplin* and *Timberlane*, in which the claimants maintained and used the disputed land as a true owner would have used the land. While in *Chaplin* and *Timberlane* the claimants built new structures (in *Chaplin*, the claimants built a road and in *Timberlane* they built a fence and a patio), the courts have held that the claimant does not have to do everything that a title owner might do.

Writers who prefer the integrated format often do so because it avoids the ping pong back-and-forth effect of "the plaintiff will argue" and "the defendant will argue." Unfortunately, though, in avoiding the ping-pong back-and-forth language, some writers fail to give appropriate weight to both sides' arguments. It is, however, possible to include both sides' arguments without using the "the plaintiff will argue" and "the defendant will argue" language.

Strategy 1: Put One Side's Arguments in a Dependent Clause and the Other Side's Arguments in the Main Clause.

One of the easiest constructions is to put the weaker argument in a dependent clause and the stronger argument in the main clause. A dependent clause is a clause that begins with a word like "although," "even though," or "while." A main clause is a clause that can stand by itself as a complete sentence.

Although [weaker argument], [stronger argument] .

Strategy 1

EXAMPLE

Although DNWC did not build any new structures on Mr. Garcia's land, it maintained not only the campsites and the fire area but also the outhouse and the e dock. In addition, although DNWC did not use the property year-round, it did use the property during the summer, which is how a typical owner would have used the land.

The problem, of course, is that if you use this construction too often the writing becomes repetitive. Thus, you need to use other sentence constructions for setting out both sides' arguments on any given point.

Strategy 2: Use a "This and not That" Sentence Structure.

Another strategy that can work well is a "this and not that" sentence. When you use this strategy, remember to include a sentence that explains why your case is more like Case A than Case B.

EXAMPLE   **Strategy 2**

Thus, Mr. Garcia's case is more like *Granston* than *Lingvall*.

Strategy 3: Set Out One Side's Argument in One Sentence or Set of Sentences and the Other Side's Argument in a Second Sentence or Set of Sentences.

You do not have to set out both side's arguments in a single sentence. When the arguments are complicated, or long, set out one side's arguments in one sentence or set of sentences and the other side's arguments in a separate sentence or set of sentences.

EXAMPLE   **Strategy 3**

Mr. Garcia has paid all of the taxes and assessments on the disputed piece of property. Nevertheless, the courts have consistently found that payment of taxes and assessments is not enough to defeat an adverse possession claim.

EXAMPLE   **Strategy 3**

Some actions taken by DNWC and Mr. Garcia suggest that both sides knew the property was his. In about February 1994, DNWC wrote Mr. Garcia asking whether it could continue using his land for campouts. In August 2006, Mr. Garcia visited the property with the intent of spending a few days camping on the lake. When he discovered there were children and their counselors on the property, he went to the camp's headquarters and talked to the director. Arguably, these actions suggest that Mr. Garcia was asserting his rights as an owner; however, other actions suggest that DNWC was successfully asserting its adverse claim. First, when Mr. Garcia did not respond to DNWC's, letter, DNWC put up a "No Trespassing" sign. There is no evidence that Mr. Garcia had ever put up a "No Trespassing" sign, nor is there evidence that he removed DNWC's "No Trespassing" sign. Second, when Mr. Garcia found children and counselors on the property, he did not tell them to leave. Instead he was the one who left, returning only the following evening after they had gone.

Strategy 4: Use the "Plaintiff Will Argue, Defendant Will Argue" Language.

It is also not wrong to include an occasional "the plaintiff will argue" or "the defendant will respond." Just make sure to organize the arguments around the lines of the argument, not each side's assertions.

Strategy 4   EXAMPLE

We can argue that the letter that DNWC sent to Mr. Garcia establishes that DNWC's use of the land was permissive. However, the court will probably reject this argument on the ground that even though Mr. Garcia did not respond, DNWC continued using his land for more than ten years.

§ 10.12 Some Final Words About the First Draft

If you are finding writing the first draft difficult, stop and ask yourself the following questions:

1. Do I understand the issue that I was asked to research?
2. Do I understand the law?
3. What information does the attorney need?
4. Am I presenting the information in the order that the attorney expects to see it?
5. What is the point that I am trying to make in this paragraph, this sentence, or this clause or phrase?

If you do not understand the issue or the law, step back from the writing process until you do. Depending on the circumstances, you may need to do more research and reading; you may need to talk to the attorney who assigned the project, double-checking the assignment, summarizing the parts of the law that you have figured out, and asking questions about the parts of the law that you do not understand; or you may need to find someone to just listen to you as you talk. If you choose this last option, make sure that you do not disclose any privileged information.

If you understand the issue and the law but are not sure what to include in the memo or how to order the information, make decisions based on who your audience is, what your audience expects, and what makes sense in your particular situation. For example, if the conventional formats work, use them. If, however, they do not work, abandon them and do what works. Just keep in mind that the content and organization need to make sense not just to you but also to those who will be reading and using your memo.

Finally, if you get stuck on a particular paragraph or sentence, try speaking the following sentence: "The point that I want to make in this [paragraph]/ [sentence] is _____." Once you can say the point, try writing that point, putting the actor in the subject slot and the action in the verb slot. In the alternative, remember that this is just the first draft. Thus, at this point, your paragraphs and sentences do not need to be perfect. The key is to get a draft. Once you produce that draft you can do what we do in the next chapter, which is to revise, edit, and proofread.

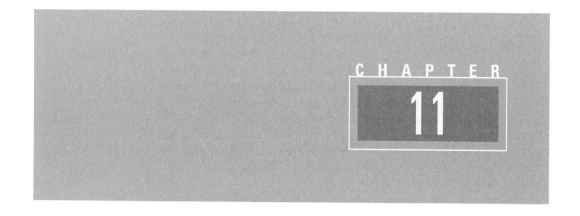

Revising, Editing, and Proofreading Memo 2

s you learned in writing your first memo, your first draft should not be your last draft. Because so much is at stake for the client, the firm, and for you, take the time to revise, edit, and proofread your memo.

§ 11.1 Revising for Content and Organization

In revising the draft, focus first on content and organization. Begin by checking the memo's content. Have you given the attorney the information that he or she needs to evaluate the case? If you did not, add that information. Did you include information that the attorney does not need? If you did, delete it. Did you present the information accurately and objectively? If you have misstated a rule or misrepresented a case, correct those errors.

Next, check the large-scale organization. Did you present the information in the order that the attorney expects to see it? For example, did you follow your modified template, starting with an introductory section and then walking the attorney through the elements one by one? In walking the attorney through the disputed elements, did you use one of the standard organizational schemes: for example, did you use the script format or an integrated format? In setting out the specific rules, did you set out more general rules before more specific rules and exceptions? If you did not do all of these things, stop and make the necessary revisions.

Finally, check your small-scale organization. Have you used roadmaps, signposts, topic sentences, and transitions? One way to check the small-scale organization is to look at the first sentence of each paragraph. Does that sentence accurately identify the topic of that paragraph? Is there a transition that tells the attorney how that paragraph is related to the prior paragraphs? For more on small-scale organization, see Chapter 21.

Also, check to make sure that the discussion of the various elements are "coherent." See pages 174-177. For example, make sure you have repeated key terms and phrases. What terms and phrases are in the specific rules? Do those same terms and phrases appear in the descriptions of the analogous cases? In the arguments? In the mini-conclusion? In the following example, note how the writer has repeated the key terms and phrases, which are "actual notice" and "used the land such that any reasonable person would have thought that the claimant owned it." The references to "actual notice" are in bold, and the references to "used the land such that any reasonable person would have thought that the claimant owned it" are underlined.

EXAMPLE   **Author Has Created Coherence by Repeating Key Terms**

A claimant can satisfy the open and notorious element by showing either (1) that the title owner had **actual notice** of the adverse use throughout the statutory period or (2) that the claimant <u>used the land such that any reasonable person would have thought that the claimant owned it</u>. *Riley v. Andres,* 107 Wn. App. 391, 396, 27 P.3d 618 (2001).

In this case, DNWC can prove both that Mr. Garcia had **actual notice** of its adverse use and <u>that any reasonable person would have thought that DNWC owned the land</u>. To prove that Mr. Garcia had **actual notice** of DNWC's use of the land, DNWC can point to the letter that it sent to Mr. Garcia in 1994 asking for continuing permission to use his land for campouts. To prove that <u>a reasonable person would have thought that DNWC owned the land,</u> DNWC will point out that it not only used the land for campouts but also maintained the campsites, fire area, outhouse, and dock. In addition, it posted a "No Trespassing" sign.

---

§ 11.2 Editing Your Draft

In Chapter 5, we set out four "rules" that help you write effective sentences: (1) use the actor as the subject of most of your sentences; (2) keep your subject and verb close together; (3) put old information at the beginning of the paragraph and new information at the end; and (4) vary sentence length and patterns. You should apply those same rules to this second memo. In particular, pay attention to the sentences that tend to be more difficult to write: the sentence setting out the issue; the sentences setting out complex rules; and, when you use an integrated format, the sentences in which you set out the reasons that support your conclusion.

In this chapter, we add two more recommendations: (5) make sure that your writing is concise and (6) make sure that your writing is precise.

§ 11.2.1 Write Concisely

Although writing sentences with strong subject-verb units eliminates much unnecessary language, you also need to edit out such throat-clearing expressions as "it is expected that . . ." and "it is generally recognized that . . ." and redundancies like "combined together" and "depreciate in value" (see sections 25.2.5 and 25.2.7). In the following example, the first draft has eighty six words, and the revised draft has sixty five words.

First Draft (86 Words)   EXAMPLE

It is generally recognized that a claimant can satisfy the "open and notorious" element by showing one of two things. The claimant can show either (1) that the title owner had real and actual notice of the adverse nature of the claimant's use of the land throughout the statutory period or (2) that the claimant used the land in such a way that any reasonable person would have thought or believed that the claimant owned it. *Riley v. Andres,* 107 Wn. App. 391, 396, 27 P.3d 618 (2001).

Revised Draft (65 Words)   EXAMPLE

A claimant can prove that its possession was open and notorious by showing either (1) that the title owner had actual notice of the adverse use throughout the statutory period or (2) that the claimant used the land in such a way that any reasonable person would have thought that the claimant owned it. *Riley v. Andres,* 107 Wn. App. 391, 396, 27 P.3d 618 (2001).

In this second example, the writer reduced the number of words by 25 percent by doing some simple editing. Writers using the same technique throughout a draft can get a 10-page draft down to 7-1/2 pages. For more on writing concisely, see section 25.2.

§ 11.2.2 Write Precisely

If conciseness is the first hallmark of excellent legal writing, precision is the second. Make sure that you use correct terms, that you use those terms consistently, that subjects and verbs are paired correctly, and that in making your arguments you compare or contrast similar things.

a. Select the Correct Term

In the law, many words have specific meanings. For example, the words "held," "found," and "ruled" have very different meanings. In most instances, use "holding" to refer to the appellate court's answer to the issue raised on appeal. In contrast, use "found" to refer to the trial court's or jury's finding of fact and "ruled" when talking about the court's ruling on a motion or objection.

Compare Examples 1, 2, and 3. In Example 1, the writer used "held" incorrectly because the writer is not setting out the court's holding. In contrast, in Example 2, the writer used "held" correctly because the writer is setting out the court's holding. Similarly, in Example 3, the writer used "found" correctly because the writer is describing the court's findings of fact. Finally, in Example 4, the writer used "ruled" correctly.

| EXAMPLE 1 | **"Held" Used Incorrectly** |

For example, in *Chaplin,* the court **held** that the claimants had built a road across the disputed land, cleared and maintained the disputed land, installed utility lines, and used the disputed land for recreational activities.

| EXAMPLE 2 | **"Held" Used Correctly** |

For example, in *Chaplin*, the court **held** that the claimants had used the disputed land as their own when they built a road across the disputed land, cleared and maintained the disputed land, installed utility lines, and used the disputed land for recreational activities. *Id.* at 864.

| EXAMPLE 3 | **"Found" Used Correctly** |

For example, in *Chaplin,* the court **found** that the claimants had built a road across the disputed land, cleared and maintained the disputed land, installed utility lines, and used the disputed land for recreational activities.

| EXAMPLE 4 | **"Ruled" Used Correctly** |

The court **ruled** that the evidence was inadmissible.

b. Use Terms Consistently

In addition to making sure that you use the correct term, also make sure that you use terms consistently. If something is an "element," continue to refer to it as an element. Do not switch and suddenly start calling it a "factor" or a "requirement."

| EXAMPLE 1 | **Inconsistent Use of Terms** |

To prove adverse possession, the claimant must prove five **elements**: that its possession was (1) exclusive, (2) actual and uninterrupted, (3) open and notorious, and (4) hostile for the statutory period. *ITT Rayonier, Inc. v. Bell*, 112 Wn.2d 754, 757, 774 P.2d 6 (1989); *Chaplin v. Sanders,* 100 Wn.2d 853, 857, 676 P.2d 431 (1984). In this case, the statutory period is ten years. RCW 4.16.020(1). Whether a particular **factor** is met is a mixed question of law and fact. *Chaplin,* 100 Wn.2d at 863. Whether the essential facts exist is for the trier of fact to decide; but whether the facts, as found, satisfy the **requirement** is for the court to determine as a matter of law. *Id.*

| EXAMPLE 2 | **Consistent Use of Terms** |

To prove adverse possession, the claimant must prove five **elements**: that its possession was (1) exclusive, (2) actual and uninterrupted, (3) open and notorious, and

(4) hostile for the statutory period. *ITT Rayonier, Inc. v. Bell,* 112 Wn.2d 754, 757, 774 P.2d 6 (1989); *Chaplin v. Sanders,* 100 Wn.2d 853, 857, 676 P.2d 431 (1984). In this case, the statutory period is ten years. RCW 4.16.020(1). Whether a particular **element** is met is a mixed question of law and fact. *Chaplin,* 100 Wn.2d at 863. Whether the essential facts exist is for the trier of fact to decide; but whether the facts, as found, satisfy the **element** is for the court to determine as a matter of law. *Id.*

c. Make Sure the Subjects and Verbs Go Together

In addition to making sure that you have selected the right word and used it consistently, also make sure that the subjects of your sentences go with the verbs and objects. For instance, while courts "state," "find," "rule," and "hold," they do not "argue." It is the parties who present arguments. See section 25.1.6. In the following sentence the subject and verb do not go together.

Subject and Verb Mismatch   EXAMPLE 1

While a **court** can **argue** that DNWC was not using the land as if it were its own, this argument is not a strong one.

Subject and Verb Go Together   EXAMPLE 2

While Mr. Garcia can **argue** that DNWC was not using the land as if it were its own, this argument is not a strong one.

---

d. Compare or Contrast Similar Facts

In setting out the arguments, you will often want to show how your case is similar to or different from other cases. For instance, you will want to compare or contrast the facts in your case to the facts in another case. In making this comparison, make sure that you are comparing apples with apples and oranges with oranges. For example, do not compare a case name to a party or a party to a fact. In the following example, the author has not compared similar things. She compared a whole case (*Granston*) to a person (Mr. Garcia).

Author Has Not Compared Similar Things   EXAMPLE 1

Unlike *Crites*, in which the title owner allowed the claimants to use his land as a neighborly accommodation, **Mr. Garcia** did not allow DNWC to use his land as a neighborly accommodation.

Author Has Compared Similar Things   EXAMPLE 2

Unlike *Crites*, in which the title owner allowed the claimants to use his land as a neighborly accommodation, **in this case**, Mr. Garcia did not allow DNWC to use his land as a neighborly accommodation.

Remember that when a name is italicized the
reference is to the court's decision. When the name
is not italicized, the reference is to a person. Thus,
in the following sentence, *"Crites"* is a reference to

the court's decision in *Crites v. Koch,* and the reference to "Crites" is a reference
to the plaintiff, Mr. Crites.
"In *Crites,* the court held that Koch allowed Crites to use his land as a neighborly
accommodation."

For more on writing precisely, see section 25.1.

§ 11.3 Proofreading the Final Draft

The final step in the process is to proofread your draft, checking for spelling
errors, grammatical and punctuation errors, typographical errors, and citation
errors. The easiest way to proofread is to print out a copy of your memo and
read through it word by word, spending the most time on the sections that you
worked on last or when you were the most tired. For an alternative, use a
program like the free version of *readplease.com,* which reads your writing
aloud.

§ 11.4 The Final Draft

Critique the final draft of the memo using the following checklist.

§ 11.4.1 Checklist of Critiquing Final Draft of Memo

Checklist for Critiquing an Objective Memo

I. Statement of Facts

    A. *Content*

- The writer has included all of the legally significant facts.
- When appropriate, the writer included emotionally significant facts.
- The writer included enough background facts that a person who is not
  familiar with the case can understand what happened.
- The writer has identified the unknown facts.
- The writer presented the facts accurately.
- The writer presented the facts objectively.
- The writer has not included legal conclusions in the statement of
  facts.

B. Organization

- The writer has included an introductory sentence or paragraph that identifies the parties and the nature of the dispute.
- The writer has used one of the conventional organizational schemes: chronological, topical, or a combination of chronological and topical.

II. Issue Statement

A. Content

- The reference to the rule of law is neither too broad nor too narrow.
- The legal question is properly focused.
- The most significant of the legally significant facts have been included.
- Legal conclusions have not been set out as facts.

B. Format

- The writer has used one of the conventional formats, for example, the "under-does-when" format or the "whether" format.

III. Brief Answer

A. Content

- The writer has predicted but not guaranteed how the issue will be decided.
- The writer has briefly explained his or her prediction; for example, the writer has explained which elements will be easy to prove and which will be more difficult to prove and why.

B. Format

- A separate brief answer has been included for each issue statement.
- The answer begins with a one- or two-word short answer. This one- or two-word short answer is then followed by a short explanation.

IV. Discussion Section

A. Content

Introduction
- The writer has included a sentence or paragraph introducing the governing statute or common law rule.
- The writer has set out the general rule, quoting the applicable statutory sections or quoting or paraphrasing the common law rule.
- The writer has set out any other general rules.
- When appropriate, the writer has briefly described the policies underlying the statute or common law rule.
- The writer has included a roadmap.
- The writer has not included rules or information that the attorney does not need.

- The writer has set out the rules accurately and objectively.
- The writer has included a citation to authority for each rule.

Discussion of Undisputed Elements
- The writer has identified the element and, when there are specific rules, set out those specific rules.
- The writer has applied the rules to the facts of the client's case, explaining why the element is not in dispute.

Discussion of Disputed Elements
- For each disputed element, the writer has set out the specific rules, described cases that have interpreted and applied those rules, set out each side's arguments, and predicted how the court will decide the element.
- The writer has included all of the applicable specific rules and set out those rules accurately and objectively.
- The writer has introduced each group of analogous cases, telling the attorney what rule or principle the cases illustrate.
- The case descriptions illustrate the rule or principle and are accurate and objective.
- In setting out the arguments, the writer has set out both assertions and support for those assertions.
- The analysis is sophisticated: the writer has set out more than the obvious arguments.
- The writer has predicted how each element will be decided and given reasons to support those predictions.

B. Large-Scale Organization

- The writer has presented the information in the order in which the attorney expects to see it. For example, the writer begins the discussion section with an introductory section in which he or she sets out the general rules. The writer then walks the attorney through each of the elements, raising and dismissing the undisputed elements and doing a more complete analysis of the disputed elements.

V. Conclusion

A. Content

- In a one-issue memorandum, the conclusion is used to predict how the issue will be decided and to summarize the reasons supporting that prediction.
- When appropriate, the writer includes not only the conclusion but also strategic advice.

B. Organization

- The information is organized logically.

VI. Writing

- The paragraph divisions are logical, and the paragraphs are neither too long nor too short.

- The writer has used signposts, topic sentences, transitions, and dove-tailing to make clear the connections between ideas.
- When appropriate, the writer has used the actor as the subject of the sentence, and the subject and verb are close together.
- The writer has varied the length of the sentences and the sentence patterns so that each sentence flows smoothly from the prior sentence.
- The writing is concise and precise.
- The writing is grammatically correct and correctly punctuated.

VII.　Citation

- The writer has included citations to authority for each rule and for each analogous case.
- The writer has used the proper citation forms.

Final Draft of Memo

EXAMPLE

To:　　　　Supervising Attorney

From:　　　Writer's Name

Date:　　　November 1, 2006

Re:　　　　Michael Garcia
　　　　　　Adverse possession; Washington law

Statement of Facts

Michael Garcia has contacted our office regarding property that he owns in Washington State. Mr. Garcia is concerned that the organization that owns the property next to his, Doctors and Nurses Who Care (DNWC), may be able to claim title to his property through adverse possession.

Mr. Garcia's property is on Lake Chelan, which is in the eastern part of Washington State. Mr. Garcia's grandfather, Eduardo Montoya, purchased the two-acre waterfront parcel in 1951, and the Montoya family used the land every summer from 1951 until Eduardo Montoya became ill in the late 1980s. When it used the land, the family would camp on the site and use a small dock for swimming, fishing, and boating.

In 1989, Doctors and Nurses Who Care (DNWC) purchased the five-acre parcel that adjoins Mr. Montoya's property. Since 1990, DNWC has used its land as a summer camp for children with serious illnesses or disabilities. In a typical summer, DNWC runs two one-week camps for children with cancer, two one-week camps for children who are blind, two one-week camps for autistic children, and two one-week camps for children with diabetes.

Most of the time the children stay in cabins located on DNWC property. However, DNWC uses Mr. Garcia's property for "campouts." One night each week, one group of about ten children will camp out in tents on Mr. Garcia's property; the next night another group of ten will camp out on the property, and so on. Thus, DNWC has been using the Garcia property four or five nights a week for eight weeks each summer since 1990. During these campouts, the children pitch and stay in tents, cook over a fire, and use the dock. To facilitate these campouts, DNWC has maintained the campsites, the fire area, the outhouse, and the dock.

In 1992, Mr. Garcia's grandfather died and left the property to Mr. Garcia. Although Mr. Garcia spent one weekend at the property in the fall of 1992, he moved to Texas in 1993 and did not visit the property until last August. He has, however, continued to pay all of the taxes and assessments.

In February 1994, DNWC sent Mr. Garcia a letter asking him whether it could continue using his land for campouts. Mr. Garcia was busy and did not respond to the letter. Sometime during the summer of 1994, DNWC posted a "No Trespassing" sign on the dock, and the sign is still there.

Last August, Mr. Garcia visited the property with the intent of spending a few days camping on the lake. When he got there, he discovered children and their counselors on the property. After discovering the children on his land, Mr. Garcia went to DNWC's camp headquarters and talked to the director, Dr. Liu. Dr. Liu told Mr. Garcia that it was his understanding that the land belonged to DNWC. Although Mr. Garcia did not spend that night at the property, he did spend the next night there after the children left. DNWC did not ask him to leave.

Although over the years the land around the lake has become more and more developed, the area in which the camp is located is still relatively undeveloped. Most of the property owners use their land only during the summer.

Issue

Whether Doctors and Nurses Who Care (DNWC) has obtained a right to Mr. Garcia's land through adverse possession when (1) it has used the land for campouts several nights a week for eight weeks each summer since 1990; (2) to facilitate these campouts, DNWC has maintained the campsites, fire area, outhouse, and dock; (3) in 1994, DNWC sent a letter to Mr. Garcia asking him if it could continue using the land for campouts, but Mr. Garcia did not respond to the letter; and (4) Mr. Garcia has paid the taxes, but did not visit the land from 1993 until August 2006.

Brief Answer

Probably. DNWC can easily prove that its possession was open and notorious, actual and uninterrupted, and exclusive. In addition, DNWC can probably prove that its possession was hostile: it used the land as a true owner would have used it and, although initially it may have been using the property with either Mr. Garcia's grandfather's or Mr. Garcia's permission, it appears that it has been using the property without permission since 1994. Because all of the elements are met for the statutory period, which is ten years, DNWC has a right to the land through adverse possession.

Discussion

The doctrine of adverse possession arose to assure maximum use of the land, to encourage the rejection of stale claims, and to quiet titles. *Chaplin v. Sanders,* 100 Wn.2d 853, 859-60, 676 P.2d 431 (1984); *see also* William B. Stoebuck, *The Law of Adverse Possession in Washington,* 35 Wash. L. Rev. 53, 53 (1960).

To establish title through adverse possession, the claimant must prove that its possession was (1) exclusive, (2) actual and uninterrupted, (3) open and notorious, and (4) hostile for the statutory period. *ITT Rayonier, Inc. v. Bell,* 112 Wn.2d 754, 757, 774

P.2d 6 (1989); *Chaplin v. Sanders,* 100 Wn.2d at 857. In this case, the statutory period is ten years. RCW 4.16.020(1).

Adverse possession is a mixed question of law and fact. *Chaplin,* 100 Wn.2d at 863. Whether the essential facts exist is for the trier of fact to decide, but whether the facts, as found, constitute adverse possession is for the court to determine as a matter of law. *Id.*

In this case, DNWC can easily prove that its possession was open and notorious and exclusive. In addition, it can probably prove that its possession is actual and uninterrupted. The only element that it may not be able to prove is that its possession was hostile.

A. Open and Notorious

A claimant can satisfy the open and notorious element by showing either (1) that the title owner had actual notice of the adverse use throughout the statutory period or (2) that the claimant used the land such that any reasonable person would have thought that the claimant owned it. *Riley v. Andres,* 107 Wn. App. 391, 396, 27 P.3d 618 (2001).

In this case, DNWC can prove both that Mr. Garcia had actual notice of its adverse use and that any reasonable person would have thought that DNWC owned the land. To prove that Mr. Garcia had actual knowledge of DNWC's use of the land, DNWC can offer a copy of the letter that it sent to Mr. Garcia in 1994 asking for continuing permission to use his land for campouts. To prove that a reasonable person would have thought that DNWC owned the land, DNWC will point out that it not only used the land for campouts but also maintained the campsites, fire area, out-house, and dock and posted a "No Trespassing" sign.

B. Actual and Uninterrupted

Although the Washington courts have not set out a test for actual possession, the cases illustrate the types of acts that are needed to establish actual possession. 17 *Wash. Prac., Real Estate: Property Law* § 8.10 (2d ed.)

The courts have held that the claimants had actual possession of rural land when the claimants built a fence and cultivated or pastured up to it, *Faubion v. Elder,* 49 Wn.2d 300, 301 P.2d 153 (1956); cleared the land, constructed and occupied buildings, and planted orchards, *Metro. Bldg. Co. v. Fitzgerald,* 122 Wash. 514, 210 P. 770 (1922); or cleared and fenced the land, planted an orchard, and built a road, *Davies v. Wick-strom,* 56 Wash. 154, 105 P. 454 (1909).

In contrast, the courts have held that the claimants did not have actual possession of rural land when they maintained a fence intended to be a cattle fence and not a line fence, *Roy v. Goerz,* 26 Wn. App. 807, 614 P.2d 1308 (1980); erected two signboards and a mailbox and plowed weeds, *Slater v. Murphy,* 55 Wn.2d 892, 339 P.2d 457 (1959); or occasionally used the land for gardening, piling wood, and mowing hay, *Smith v. Chambers,* 112 Wash. 600, 192 P. 891 (1920). 17 *Wash. Prac., Real Estate: Property Law* § 8.10 (2d ed.)

If DNWC had used the land only for occasional campouts, it would have been difficult for it to prove that it had actual possession. However, in addition to using the land for campouts, DNWC maintained the campsites, the fire area, the outhouse, and the dock, and it posted a "No Trespassing" sign. Because DNWC maintained permanent structures and posted the "No Trespassing" sign, more likely than not a court will hold that it had actual possession.

In addition, DNWC's use and maintenance of the campsites, fire area, outhouse, and dock are probably enough to establish that its possession was uninterrupted. In all of the cases in which the claimants maintained and used permanent structures, the courts have held that the use was uninterrupted. In addition, in *Howard v. Kunto*, 3 Wn. App. 393, 477 P.2d 210 (1970), the court held that the claimants' use was continuous even though the claimants used the property only during the summer. As the court noted in that case, "the requisite possession requires such possession and dominion 'as ordinarily marks the conduct of owners in general in holding, managing, and caring for property of like nature and condition.'" *Id.* at 397. Thus, while Mr. Garcia might be able to argue that DNWC's use of the land was not uninterrupted because DNWC used the land only during the summer months, this argument is a weak one. Because the land is recreational land, DNWC's use of the land only in the summer is consistent with how the owners of similar land hold, manage, and care for their property.

C. Exclusive

To establish that its possession was exclusive, the claimant must show that its possession was "of a type that would be expected of an owner...." *ITT Rayonier*, 112 Wn.2d 754, 758, 774 P.2d 6 (1989). Therefore, while sharing possession of the land with the true owner will prevent a claimant from establishing that its possession was exclusive, sharing possession with a tenant or allowing occasional use by a neighbor does not. *Id.*

In this case, Mr. Garcia has stated that he did not visit the property between 1992 and 2006. Thus, during that period DNWC did not share the property with the true owner. Although DNWC "shared" its use of Mr. Garcia's land with its campers, this fact should not prevent a court from finding that its possession was exclusive. Because the campers used the Garcia land under DNWC's supervision, they are analogous to tenants.

D. Hostile

While prior to 1984, the Washington courts considered the claimant's subjective intent in determining whether its use of the land was hostile, since 1984 the claimant's subjective intent has been irrelevant. *Chaplin,* 100 Wn. 2d at 860-61 (overruling cases in which the courts had considered the claimant's subjective intent). Consequently, under current Washington law, the claimant must prove only that it used the land as if it were its own for the statutory period. *Id.; Miller v. Anderson*, 91 Wn. App. 822, 828, 964 P.2d 365 (1998). If the claimant proves that it used the land as if it were its own, the use was hostile unless the true owner can prove that it gave the claimant permission to use the land. *Id.*

Permission can be express or implied. *Miller v. Anderson*, 91 Wn. App. at 829; *Granston v. Callahan*, 52 Wn. App. 288, 759 P.2d 462 (1988) (case dealt with a prescriptive easement, not adverse possession). The courts infer that the use was permissive when, under the circumstances, it is reasonable to assume that the use was permitted. *Id.* If there was permission, the party claiming adverse possession bears the burden of proving that permission terminated because either (1) the servient estate changed hands through death or alienation or (2) the claimant has asserted a hostile right. *Id.*

In deciding whether a claimant was using the land as if it were its own, the courts consider whether the claimant made improvements to the land, whether the claimant maintained the property, and whether the claimant used the land on a regular basis.

See, e.g., Chaplin, 100 Wn.2d at 855-56; *Timberlane Homeowners Ass'n, Inc., v. Brame*, 79 Wn. App. 303, 310-11, 901 P.2d 1074 (1995). For example, in *Chaplin*, the court held that the claimants were using the land as if it were their own when the claimants built a road across the disputed land, cleared and maintained the disputed land, installed utility lines, and used the area for recreational activities. *Id.* at 855-56. Similarly, in *Timberlane*, the court held that claimants had used land belonging to the homeowners' association as if it was their own when they built and maintained a fence and a concrete patio and the claimants' children played on the land. *Id.* at 310-11.

In deciding whether the claimants' use was permissive, the courts consider whether the parties are related or have a friendly relationship, whether the improvements benefited both the claimants' and the title owners' property, and whether the title owners allowed the claimants to use the land as a neighborly accommodation. For instance, in *Granston*, the court held that the claimants' use was permissive because the original owners of the two parcels were brothers who worked together to build driveways, walkways, and other improvements that benefited both properties. *Id.* at 294-95. Likewise, in *Miller v. Jarman*, 2 Wn. App. 994, 998-99, 471 P.2d 704 (1970), the court held that the use was permissive because the title owners had allowed the claimants, who were their neighbors, to use their driveway as a neighborly accommodation. In contrast, in *Lingvall v. Bartmess*, 97 Wn. App. 245, 256, 982 P.2d 690 (1999), the court held that the antagonistic relationship between two brothers negated a finding that the claimant's use of the land was permissive.

In the Garcia case, the court will probably conclude DNWC's use of Mr. Garcia's land was hostile.

First, the court will probably conclude that DNWC used Mr. Garcia's land as if it were the true owner. Although DNWC did not build any new structures on Mr. Garcia's land, it maintained the campsites, the fire area, the outhouse, and the dock. In addition, although DNWC did not use the property year-round, it did use the property during the summer, which is how a typical owner would have used the land. Thus, this case is similar to *Chaplin* and *Timberlane,* in which the claimants maintained and used the disputed land as a true owner would have used the land. While in *Chaplin* and *Timberlane* the claimants built new structures (in *Chaplin*, the claimants built a road and, in *Timberlane*, they built a fence and a patio), the courts have held that the claimant does not have to do everything that a title owner might do.

Second, the court will probably conclude that DNWC's use of Mr. Garcia's land was not permissive. Unlike *Granston*, in which the parties were related and had a close relationship, there is no evidence that the members of DNWC are related to Mr. Garcia. In addition, unlike *Crites*, in which the parties agreed that they typically allowed their neighbors to use their land to turn around their equipment or to access the other parts of their own land, the typical owner of recreational land does not allow a neighboring property owner to use its land several days a week during the peak season.

While Mr. Garcia can argue that the letter that DNWC sent to him establishes that DNWC's use of the land was permissive, the court will probably reject this argument. First, the court will conclude that if Mr. Garcia's grandfather gave DNWC permission to use his land, that permission terminated when his grandfather died. *See Granston*, 52. Wn. App. at 294-95. In addition, the court will probably conclude that even if DNWC used Mr. Garcia's land with Mr. Garcia's implied permission from the time of his grandfather's death until DNWC sent the letter in February of 1994, that permission terminated in the summer of 1994 when DNWC posted the "No Trespassing" sign and continued to use the property as its own.

Conclusion

More likely than not, DNWC will be able to establish title to Mr. Garcia's land through adverse possession.

To prove that its possession was open and notorious, DNWC only needs to show that Mr. Garcia had actual notice of its use of his land throughout the statutory period or that it used his land in such a way that any reasonable person would have thought that it owned this land. In this case, DNWC can use a copy of the letter that it sent to Mr. Garcia to prove that he had actual notice, and it can show that its use of the land for campouts was such that any reasonable person would have thought that DNWC owned the land.

To prove that its possession was actual and uninterrupted, DNWC need only show that it actually used the land and that its use was consistent with how the true owner might have used the land. The case law suggests that DNWC's maintenance of the campsites, fire area, outhouse, and dock was sufficient to establish actual possession. In addition, although DNWC used the land only during the summer months, the court is likely to find that such use was uninterrupted because most owners of recreational land use their land only during certain seasons.

To prove that its use of the land was exclusive, DNWC will have to show that it did not share the land with anyone else. Although we could try to argue that DNWC's use was not exclusive because it allowed campers to use the land, this argument is weak because the campers used the land under DNWC's supervision.

Finally, to prove that its use was hostile, DNWC will have to prove that it used the land as if it were its own and that it did not do so with Mr. Garcia's permission. DNWC's maintenance and use of the property is probably sufficient to establish that it used Mr. Garcia's land as if it were its own. In addition, DNWC will be able to prove that its use was not permissive. Even if DNWC's initial use of the property was with Mr. Garcia's grandfather's permission, that permission terminated when Mr. Garcia's grandfather died. In addition, although in its 1994 letter DNWC asked Mr. Garcia for permission to continue using the land, DNWC has a strong argument that it did a hostile act that terminated permission when, even after Mr. Garcia did not respond, DNWC continued maintaining and using the property and posted the "No Trespassing" sign.

Because all of these elements have been met for the statutory period, which is ten years, DNWC has established a right to title to the land through adverse possession.

§ 11.5 Reflecting on the Lawyering Process

Assume for a minute that you have determined that there is a 90 percent chance that DNWC will be able to prove that it has possession of Mr. Garcia's land through adverse possession. Also assume that you would charge Mr. Garcia about $20,000 to litigate this case. If you were the attorney advising Mr. Garcia, what would you recommend? What factors would you ask him to consider? What other options might you suggest? For example, would you suggest that he donate his land to DNWC? What factors might change your advice? What would you do if Mr. Garcia rejected your advice?

Researching and Writing a Memo Involving Federal Law

Introduction: The Assignment

In this part, Part 3, we tackle a slightly different project. Instead of showing you how to research and write a memo for an attorney, we show you how to research and write a prehearing memo for a judge. Thus, as you read through the next three chapters, assume that you are working as a law clerk for a United States District Court judge in the Northern District of Illinois, which is in the Seventh Circuit, and that the judge has given you the following assignment.

To: Law Clerk

From: District Court Judge

Date: June 15, 2006

Re: United States v. Tamil Welfare and Human Rights Committee, et al.

The United States has charged the Tamil Welfare and Human Rights Committee (TWHRC) and some of its members under 18 U.S.C. § 2339B, which makes it illegal to provide material support to a Foreign Terrorist Organization (FTO). The facts are as follows:

- Tamil Welfare and Human Rights Committee (TWHRC) is a non-profit organization based in Illinois. In December 2005, the TWHRC provided tsunami warning equipment to the Liberation Tigers of Tamil Eelam (LTTE).
- The system included monitoring devices, communications equipment, and sirens.
- The LTTE was formed in 1976 with the goal of achieving self-determination for the Tamil residents of Tamil Eelam, which is in the northern and eastern provinces of Sri Lanka.
- In 1997, then Secretary of State Madeline Albright designated the LTTE as a "foreign terrorist organization" under the Antiterrorism and Effective Death Penalty Act (AEDPA), 62 Fed. Reg. 52,649-51.[1]

Before I rule on the parties' proposed jury instructions, I need to determine what type of "intent" the current version of 18 U.S.C. § 2339B requires. The government wants a jury instruction that states that a defendant violates 18 U.S.C. § 2339B if it knowingly provides material support to a group that has been designated as a foreign terrorist organization. In contrast, the defendants want an instruction that states that the government must prove (1) that the defendants knowingly provided material support to a foreign terrorist organization and (2) that the defendants intended that the terrorist group would use the communications equipment to further the terrorist group's illegal activities. Thus, please research the intent issue for me and prepare a memo summarizing both sides' arguments and setting out your recommendation.

---

1. No, this is not a typographical error. The designation does in fact appear on pages 52,649 through 52,651 in volume 62 of the *Federal Register*.

CHAPTER 12

Researching Issues Governed by Federal Statutes and Regulations

The issue that the judge has asked you to research is the type of issue that most attorneys love. Not only does it involve interesting legal analysis, but it also involves interesting social and political questions. Thus, as you research the issue, look not only at what the statute says, but also at what Congress intended when it enacted the statute, how other courts have interpreted and applied the statute, and how the court's decision might affect both the government and its efforts to prevent terrorism and individuals who want to provide humanitarian aid to individuals who may have connections to terrorist organizations.

Because most judges have access to either LexisNexis or Westlaw, the focus of this chapter is on electronic sources. If, however, you do not have access to LexisNexis or Westlaw, you can do most of the research using book sources and free websites.

§ 12.1 Creating a Research Plan for Issues Governed by Federal Statutes

If the judge had asked you to research a federal statute, determining whether all of the elements were met, your research plan would be the same as the research plan for issues governed by state statutes. You would do background reading; you would locate primary authorities — for example the applicable federal statutes and regulations and the cases interpreting those statutes and regulations; you would cite check both the statute and the cases; and, if appropriate, you would look at additional primary and secondary sources. Thus, when you have been asked to research an issue governed by federal statutes and regulations that involves an elements analysis, your research plan would look like the one set out below.

Research Plan No. 1 for Researching an Issue Governed by a Federal Statute That Involves an Elements Analysis

Jurisdiction: Federal

Type of Law: Enacted law

Preliminary Issue Statement: [Put your first draft of the issue statement here.]

Step 1.   If you are unfamiliar with the area of law, spend thirty-sixty minutes familiarizing yourself with the area of law by looking for information on the Internet, in a practice book, in a hornbook, in a *Nutshell*, in a legal encyclopedia, or in another secondary source.

Step 2.   Locate, read, and analyze the applicable *United States Code* sections, the applicable *Code of Federal Regulations* sections, and cases that have interpreted or applied the applicable statutory sections and regulations.

Step 3.   Cite check the statutes, regulations, and cases to make sure that they are still good law.

Step 4.   If appropriate, locate and read additional primary and secondary authorities.

In this instance, however, the issue that the judge has asked you to research does not involve a traditional elements analysis. Instead of asking you to identify 2339B's elements and then determine whether the government can prove each of those elements, the judge has asked you to look at a single element: 2339B's *mens rea* requirement. In addition, instead of asking you to research an element in which there is a well-established rule, the judge has asked you to research an issue of first impression. Although courts in the Ninth and Fifth Circuits have decided cases in which 18 U.S.C. § 2339B's *mens rea* requirement was at issue, there are no United States Supreme Court or Seventh Circuit Court of Appeals decisions that are on point.

As a consequence, the research for this problem is different from the research that we did for the service of process and adverse possession problems in three ways: (1) while both the service of process and adverse possession problems involved issues governed by state law, this problem involves an issue governed by federal law; (2) while both the service of process and adverse possession problems required you to do a traditional elements analysis, this problem involves only one element, 18 U.S.C.'s *mens rea* requirement; and (3) while both the service of process and adverse possession problems required you to apply well-established rules of law to a particular fact situation, this memo deals with an issue of first impression.

Because this problem involves a different type of analysis, the research plan is different. Compare the research plan set out below with the research plans set out above and the research plans set out on page 74 in Chapter 6 the research plan set out on page 200 in Chapter 9.

Research Plan for a Federal Issue Involving an Issue of First Impression

Jurisdiction:	Federal
Type of Law:	Federal Statutes
Preliminary Issue Statement:	What type of intent is required under section 2339B of the AEDPA?

Step 1.   Spend thirty-sixty minutes on Google looking for and reading "articles" that describe or discuss the AEDPA and, in particular, 18 U.S.C. § 2339B.

Step 2.   Locate and read mandatory authority — for example, the text of 18 U.S.C. § 2339B and any Seventh Circuit Court of Appeals or United States Supreme Court decisions that have discussed the type of intent required under 18 U.S.C. § 2339B.

Step 3.   If there is no mandatory authority, identify the types of arguments each side will make and the authorities that they will use to support those arguments. For example, identify the plain language, the legislative history, the case law, and the policy arguments that each side may make and the authorities that they may use to support those arguments.

Step 4.   Cite check statutes and cases to make sure that they are still good law.

While the research plans for the two types of federal research are different, the sources are, for the most part, the same.

§ 12.2 Sources for Federal Statutory Research

When you research an issue governed by a federal statute or by federal statutes and regulations, you will use some or all of the following sources:

Chart 12.1	Sources for Researching an Issue Governed by Federal Statutes and Regulations

	Federal Law
Background Reading	▪ The Internet ▪ Practice books ▪ Hornbooks ▪ *Nutshells* ▪ Legal encyclopedias
Session Laws (statutes in order enacted)	▪ *Statutes at Large*
Codes (statutes organized by topics)	▪ *United States Code* (U.S.C.) ▪ *United States Code Annotated* (U.S.C.A.) ▪ *United States Code Service* (U.S.C.S.)
Regulations	▪ *Code of Federal Regulations* (C.F.R.)
Cases Interpreting and Applying Statutes	▪ *Federal Supplement* (F. Supp, F. Supp. 2d or F. Supp. 3d) (decisions from the United States District Courts) ▪ *Federal Reporter* (F. or F.2d or F.3d) (decisions from the United States Court of Appeals) ▪ *United States Reports* (U.S.) (decisions from the United States Supreme Court) ▪ *Supreme Court Reporter* (S. Ct.) (decisions from the United States Supreme Court) ▪ *Supreme Court Reporter, Lawyer's Edition* (L. Ed. or L. Ed. 2d) (decisions from the United States Supreme Court)
Legislative History	▪ Summaries ▪ Compiled legislative histories ▪ Original source materials, for example, copies of bills, transcripts from House and Senate Hearings, House and Senate Committee Reports, and the *Congressional Record*
Cite Checking	▪ KeyCite® ▪ *Shepard's*®
Secondary Authorities	▪ Law review articles ▪ Treatises ▪ Loose-leaf services ▪ *American Law Reports, Federal* (A.L.R. Fed.)

§ 12.2.1 Sources for Background Reading

a. The Internet

For many issues governed by federal statutes, the best place to do your background reading is the Internet. If you know the name of the act, select a instance, if you are looking for information about the AEDPA, go on to Google or a similar search engine, select the "Advanced Search" option, and search for websites that contain the phrase "Antiterrorism and Effective Death Penalty Act" or the acronym AEDPA and at least one of the following words or phrases: "overview," "summary," or "introduction."

Although LexisNexis and Westlaw have databases that deal with federal acts, there is a charge for using these databases. Thus, look first for information on a government website. If you do not  find anything there, then look on LexisNexis, Westlaw, or one of the other fee-based services.

When the list of websites appears, quickly review it, looking for websites that will provide you with a summary of the federal act that you have been asked to research.

Google is even easier to use if you add the Google toolbar. To add it, go to *google.com* and then select "View" and then "Toolbars." When the pull-down menu appears, click on "Google." Once the toolbar  appears, you can click on the highlighter to turn the highlighting function off and on.

b. Practice Manuals

Although most law firms, agencies, and courts have book copies of their state's practice manuals, they may not have book copies of federal practice manuals. Instead, they may purchase loose-leaf services for the areas of law in which they practice and rely on fee-based services like LexisNexis, Loislaw, VersusLaw, or Westlaw for their other needs. For example, a tax attorney might purchase a book copy of the *Tax Planning Desk Book* by Louis S. Goldberg and rely on LexisNexis for everything else.

c. Hornbooks and *Nutshells*

Hornbooks and *Nutshells* are one-volume books that provide the reader with an overview of an area of law. For example, the hornbook *Intellectual Property: The Law of Copyrights, Patents, and Trademarks* provides the reader with an overview of the various topics in intellectual property law. Similarly, the shorter, one-volume *Intellectual Property: Unfair Competition in a Nutshell* provides the reader with an overview of the law relating to unfair competition.

Note that most hornbooks and *Nutshells* deal with areas of law, not specific federal acts. Thus, as a general rule, use a hornbook or a *Nutshell* when you want to do background reading on an area of law and use the Internet when you want to do background reading on a specific act.

You can use your library's electronic card catalog to find hornbooks and *Nutshells.* You can also ask law librarians and practitioners for recommendations.

P R A C T I C E
POINTER

---

d. Legal Encyclopedias

At one point, the book versions of legal encyclopedias were the source of choice for background reading. When asked to research an issue in an area of law that they did not know, attorneys would go to one of the two legal encyclopedias, *American Jurisprudence* (Am. Jur.) or *Corpus Juris Secundum* (C.J.S.), and read its summary of the law.

Like the book versions of other more general encyclopedias, the book versions of legal encyclopedias are used less and less often. They are expensive to buy and update and take lots of space to store. Thus, if the office in which you work has a current legal encyclopedia, by all means use it. If, however, your office does not have a book version, use an electronic version, which is on LexisNexis and Westlaw, or use the Internet, a practice book, or a hornbook or *Nutshell*.

See Exercise 12A in the *Practice Book.*

§ 12.2.2 Sources for Federal Statutes and Regulations

Federal statutes come in three forms: you can find the text of a particular federal act in the session laws, in the unannotated code, and in two annotated codes.

a. Session Laws

Statutes at Large sets out federal statutes in the order in which they were enacted. At the end of each Congress, the statutes enacted during that Congress are collected and arranged, not by topic, but by date. For instance, statutes enacted during the 106th Congress will be set out in date order in one set of volumes; the statutes enacted during the 107th Congress will be set out in date order in another set of volumes; and so on. Therefore, to find a session law, you need to know the number of the Congress during which the statute was enacted and the statute's number. Typically, the only time that you will use session laws is when you are doing a legislative history.

b. Unannotated Codes

Statutes are "codified" when they are arranged, not in chronological, order, but by topic. Consequently, in a code all of the statutes relating to a particular topic will be placed together. For instance, in the *United States Code*, all of the federal statutes relating to interstate highways are placed under one title, all of the statutes relating to endangered species are placed under another title, and all of the statutes relating to Social Security benefits are placed under yet another title. The decision about where to place a particular statute is made not by Congress itself but by attorneys who work for the Office of the Law Revision Counsel.

The unannotated code for federal statutes is the *United States Code* (U.S.C.). It is published by the United States Printing Office, and it is the official version of the United States statutes. You can find a book copy of the *United States Code* in most law libraries and larger public libraries. In addition, you can also find free copies of the *United States Code* on a number of sites, including the Office of the Law Revision Counsel's website (*http://uscode.house.gov/lawrevisioncounsel.php*), the Government Printing Office's website (*www.gpoaccess.gov/uscode/index.html*), and on *FindLaw. com*. Use an unannotated code when all you need, or want, is the text of the particular statute or when you want to see the relationship among several different sections.

The Office of the Law Revision Counsel's website *http://uscode.house.gov/lawrevisioncounsel.php*, is searchable and has tables listing sections that have been affected by new legislation.

**P R A C T I C E
POINTER**

---

c. Annotated Codes

An annotated code is a code that contains not only the text of the statutes but also historical notes, cross-references to other sources published by the same publisher, and notes of decision. Thus, an annotated code is both a primary authority because it sets out the law itself and a finding tool because you can use it to find other primary authorities (for example, cases that have interpreted and applied the statute) and secondary authorities (for example, practice books and treatises that discuss the statute).

For federal statutes, there are two annotated codes. The *United States Code Annotated* (U.S.C.A.) is published by West and is available both in book form and on Westlaw, and the *United States Code Service* (U.S.C.S.) is published by LexisNexis and is available both in book form and on LexisNexis.

You should use an annotated code when you are interested not only in the text of the statute but also in how the courts have interpreted and applied the statute.

All of your citations to federal statutes should be to the U.S.C., not to the U.S.C.A. or the U.S.C.S. The only time that you should cite to the U.S.C.A. or the U.S.C.S. is when the material that you are citing appears in one of those sources but not in the U.S.C. See Rule 14.1 in the *ALWD Citation Manual* and Rule 12.2.1 in *The Bluebook.*

See Exercise 12B in the *Practice Book.*

d. Federal Regulations

In enacting a statute, Congress often grants an administrative agency the power to promulgate regulations. When agencies follow the proper procedures for promulgating these regulations, the regulations have the effect of law and are therefore primary authority.

For most agencies, the procedures for promulgating regulations are set out in the Administrative Procedure Act. This Act, which is codified at 5 U.S.C. §§ 551 *et seq.*, requires (1) that notice of a proposed regulation be published in the *Federal Register*, (2) that there be time for comment and hearings, and (3) that the enacted version of the regulation be published initially in the *Federal Register* and permanently in the *Code of Federal Regulations.*

You can find book copies of the *Code of Federal Regulations* (C.F.R.) in most law libraries and in many larger public libraries. In addition, you can find copies of the C.F.R. on a number of free Internet sites. For instance, you can find the entire text of the C.F.R. on the Government Printing Office's website, *http://www.gpoaccess.gov/cfr/*, and on *FindLaw.com*. In addition, you can find selected C.F.R. sections on agency websites. For example, you can find the regulations that relate to the Social Security Act on the Social Security Administration's website, *http://www.ssa.gov/regulations/*; and you can find regulations that relate to our national parks on the Department of Interior's website, *http://www.cr.nps.gov/linklaws.htm.*

There are also a number of free websites that provide access to all or part of the *Federal Register*. For example, you can find the complete text of the *Federal Register* on the Government Printing Office's website, *http://www.gpoaccess.gov/fr/*, and selected portions on *FindLaw.com*. In addition, *www.regulations.gov* not only lists proposed regulations but also provides a vehicle for commenting on those proposed regulations.

See Exercise 12C in the *Practice Book.*

§ 12.2.3 Sources for Cases That Have Interpreted or Applied a Federal Statute or Regulation

a. Finding Tools

When the statute and any applicable regulations answer your question, you do not need to look for cases that interpreted or applied the statute.

However, when the statute and its applicable regulations are ambiguous, you will usually want to find cases that have interpreted the statute and regulations. There are at least three ways to find these cases.

Not all statutes have corresponding regulations. For example, there are no regulations for criminal statutes.

P R A C T I C E

One of the easiest ways to find these cases interpreting a federal statute is to use the notes of decision following the statutory sections. As soon as a federal court issues a published decision, the court sends an electronic copy of the decision to the publishing companies (for example, LexisNexis and West). Attorneys who work for these companies read the decisions and write one-sentence summaries of each point of law set out in the decisions. In addition to using these one-sentence summaries as headnotes at the beginnings of the cases, if a summary relates to a particular statute, the publishing company will place that summary in the notes of decision for that particular statute in the versions of the annotated code that that publishing company publishes. For example, the notes of decision that West attorneys draft are placed not only at the beginnings of the cases in the reporters published by West but also in the notes of decision that follow the text of the statutes in the *United States Code Annotated* and Westlaw.

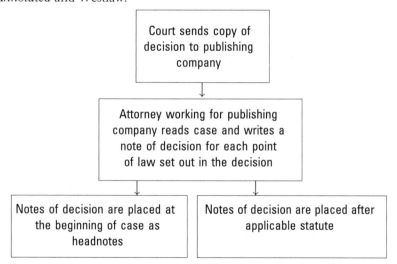

If there are relatively few cases that have discussed a particular statute, these notes of decision will be set out by court and date after the statute. (Notes of decision from higher courts will be set out before notes of decision from lower courts, and notes of decision from more recent cases will be listed before notes of decision from older cases.) If, however, there are a number of cases that have discussed a particular statute, the notes of decisions will be organized by subtopics and then, within those topics, by court and date. Your job as a legal researcher is to select the topics that appear to be on point and then to read through the notes of decision under those topics, identifying the cases that appear to be most on point. Once you identify the cases that appear to be most on point, you then need to locate and read the relevant portions of those cases.

Because the notes of decision are written by attorneys who work for the publishing companies and not the courts, the notes are finding tools and not something that you can rely on or cite to in a memo or a brief.

P R A C T I C E
POINTER

You can also find cases that have discussed a particular statute by looking at the list of citing references for that statute, by doing a "terms and connectors" search on LexisNexis, Loislaw, VersusLaw, or Westlaw, or by using a federal digest.

See Exercise 12D in the *Practice Book*.

b. Reporters

Federal cases are published in a number of different reporters, which are sets of books that set out the text of court decisions, not by topic, but in the order in which the cases were decided. The following chart shows the reporters in which decisions from the United States Supreme Court, the United States Courts of Appeals, and the United States District Courts are published. There are also specialized reporters — for example, the *Bankruptcy Reporter, Reports of States' Tax Courts*, and the *Military Justice Reporter*.

Chart 12.2   **Federal Reporters**

Court	Name of Reporter	Abbreviation	Coverage Dates
United States Supreme Court (appellate court)	*United States Reports*	U.S.	1789 to date
	Supreme Court Reporter	S. Ct.	1882 to date
	Supreme Court Reporter, Lawyer's Edition	L. Ed.	1879 to 1956
	Supreme Court Reporter, Lawyer's Edition, Second Series	L. Ed. 2d	1956 to date
United States Court of Appeals (appellate court)	*Federal Reporter*	F.	1889 to 1924
	Federal Reporter, Second Series	F.2d	1924 to 1993
	Federal Reporter, Third Series	F.3d	1993 to date
United States District Court (trial court)	*Federal Supplement*	F. Supp.	1932 to 1998
	Federal Supplement, Second Series	F. Supp. 2d	1998 to date
	Federal Supplement, Third Series	F. Supp. 3d	
	Federal Rules Decisions (contains district court decisions interpreting and applying the *Federal Rules of Civil Procedure*)	F.R.D.	1938 to date

Although all United States Supreme Court opinions are reported, or published, not all district court and court of appeals opinions are reported. Many courts do not allow citations to unreported opinions. To determine whether you can cite unreported opinions, check your local court rules.

Both the *Supreme Court Reporter* and the *Supreme Court Reporter, Lawyer's Edition*, are unofficial reporters published by private publishing companies. (The *Supreme Court Reporter* is published by West, and the *Supreme Court Reporter, Lawyer's Edition*, is published by LexisNexis.) While the text of an opinion is the same in all three reporters, the headnotes and other "editorial features" are different.

Although most federal courts have book copies of the federal reporters, most law firms do not. Therefore, if you are working for the court, you can find a copy of federal decisions in both book and online sources. If, however, you are working for a law firm, you will probably have to use online sources. While most of the time you will use a fee-based service like LexisNexis, Loislaw, VersusLaw, or Westlaw, you can find the text of many federal opinions on free Internet sites. For example, many of the federal courts now publish copies of their opinions on their official court websites. To find links to these websites, go to *www.uscourts.gov*. In addition, you can find the full text of United States Supreme Court decisions decided since 1893 on *FindLaw.com*. For instance, to find a free copy of the United States Supreme Court's decision in *Brown v. Board of Education*, go to *FindLaw.com*, select "Cases and Codes," and then "United States Supreme Court decisions."

There are three ways to find information in FindLaw's United States Supreme Court database: (1) you can search using a case's citation; (2) you can search using a party's name; and (3) you can search the full text of United States Supreme Court decisions using a terms and connectors search.

Although FindLaw's databases for the United States Court of Appeals and District Court decisions are not as large as its database for Supreme Court decisions, it does have a number of the more recent cases. For instance, you can find the text of all recent United States Court of Appeals decisions and some recent United States District Court decisions.

See Exercise 12E in the *Practice Book*.

§ 12.2.4 Sources for Legislative Histories

When you research legislative history, you are looking for the documents that were created as part of the process of enacting or amending a piece of legislation. The following chart summarizes the steps that a bill goes through when it is introduced in the United States House of Representatives and the documents that would be produced at each step. The steps and the documents are the same for a bill that is introduced in the United States Senate.

Chart 12.3   **How a House Bill Becomes Law**

Steps	Documents
1. A member of the House of Representatives introduces the bill.	Bill; Reference in *Congressional Record*
2. The bill is referred to a committee. The committee may then refer the bill to a subcommittee. (Most bills die in committee.)	Hearings; Committee Print
3. If the bill does not die in committee, the committee submits its report on the bill to the House.	Committee Report
4. The bill is presented to the House for debate, amendments, and a vote.	Reference in *Congressional Record*; Engrossed Bill[1]
5. If the bill is approved, it is sent to the Senate. The Senate repeats steps 1-4.	Reference in *Congressional Record*; Engrossed Bill
6. If the Senate passes the bill, it returns the bill, with any amendments, to the House. The House then approves the amendments, determines that the amendments are unacceptable, or creates a Conference Committee to create a compromise bill.	Reference in *Congressional Record*; Conference Committee Report; Enrolled Bill
7. If both the House and Senate pass the same version of the bill, the bill is sent to the President for signature. If the President signs the bill, it becomes law.	Presidential Statement; Public Law

1. An "Engrossed Bill" is the official copy of a bill or joint resolution that has been passed by the House or Senate.

Because legislative histories take so long to compile, when you are asked to do a history, look first to see whether someone else has already compiled one.

a. Summaries

If all you need is a summary of a statute's legislative history, look for a case or a law review article that summarizes the statute's legislative history. If you find a summary, you can use the citations set out in that summary to locate the original documents. For example, if the case or article refers to a committee report, use the citation to the report to locate the report using free Internet sources.

Although you can do a separate search for these summaries, most often you will run across them during the course of your research. Thus, it is often best to postpone doing a legislative history until you have read a number of cases.

P R A C T I C E

b. Compiled Legislative Histories

A compiled legislative history is a book, a notebook, a file folder, or a website that sets out some or all of the documents created during the process of enacting a particular piece of legislation. Unlike summaries, which simply summarize the legislative history, these compiled histories include copies of the original documents. For example, a compiled legislative history may have the marked-up copy of the bill, transcripts of hearings, copies of committee reports, excerpts from the floor debate, and the President's statement.

The following list sets out some of the best sources for compiled legislative histories:

> *United States Code and Administrative News* (U.S.C.A.A.N.) (in book form and on Westlaw)
> Nancy Johnson, *Sources of Compiled Legislative Histories* (2000, Fred B. Rothman & Co., now William S. Hein & Co) (book).
> *Union List of Legislative Histories*, 7th Edition (2000) (see *http://www.llsdc.org/sourcebook/about-union-histories.htm*)
> LexisNexis and Westlaw legislative histories databases, including the Arnold and Porter databases on Westlaw.

See Exercise 12F in the *Practice Book*.

c. Sources for Assembling Your Own Legislative History

If you cannot find a compiled legislative history, you will need to compile your own. For instructions on how to compile a legislative history for a federal statute, see *Federal Legislative History Research: A Practitioner's Guide to Compiling the Documents and Sifting for Legislative Intent* by Richard J. McKinney and Ellen A. Sweet, which is at *http://www.llsdc.org/sourcebook/fed-leg-hist.htm*, or the Law Librarians' Society of Washington, D.C.'s website, which is at *http://www.llsdc.org/sourcebook/fed-leg-hist.htm*.

§ 12.2.5 Sources for Additional Secondary Authority

a. Law Reviews and Law Journals

It comes as no surprise that law reviews and law journals publish articles about the law. What is surprising is that most, but not all, are edited by law students. Some of these journals are general in nature, publishing articles on a wide range of topics. (See, for example, the *Maine Law Review* and the *Stanford Law Review*.) Others deal with specific areas of the law — for instance, environmental law or international law. (See, for example, *Journal of Environmental Law and Litigation* and *Harvard International Law Journal*.) In addition, some organizations and groups also publish law reviews. For example, the Legal Writing Institute publishes a journal titled *Legal Writing*. While most law review articles are written by law school professors, law reviews also publish articles written by judges and practitioners and notes and comments written by law students.

Use law reviews when you are looking for information about a new area of law or a new issue in an established area of law. You can find law review articles in the book versions of the individual law reviews themselves and online on LexisNexis and Westlaw. In addition, some law schools have begun putting copies of their law reviews on their own websites, and some are beginning to offer electronic subscriptions.

b. *American Law Reports, Federal*

American Law Reports (A.L.R.) was first published in 1919 to compete against West's National Reporter System. Unlike West's National Reporter System, which publishes every reported state and federal decision, A.L.R. is selective: it publishes only "significant" cases and annotations that discuss the issues raised in those cases.

Although few attorneys ever used A.L.R. as a source of case law, they did use the annotations. These annotations, which are researched and written by attorneys, collect and summarize cases that have discussed a particular issue. The annotations that deal with federal issues are set out in A.L.R. Fed.

You can find a book copy of the A.L.R. in your law library or the electronic version on LexisNexis and Westlaw. In the book copy, you can find annotations using the subject index; online, you can find annotations using a "terms and connectors" search.

c. Looseleaf Services

Historically, looseleaf services were what their name suggests: a service that provided information in "looseleaf" notebooks that were updated by taking out a page and replacing it with a new page. Today, most looseleaf services are available both in book form and on fee-based services like LexisNexis or Westlaw.

Although each looseleaf service is different, most deal with specialized areas of law. For example, there are looseleaf services that deal with federal tax issues, with federal benefits issues (for example, Social Security), and with many federal issues (for example, environmental issues). Most looseleaf services provide a wide range of up-to-date information about these specialized areas. For example, many of them set out the text of the applicable statutes and regulations, the text of proposed legislation and regulations, and summaries of relevant court and administrative decisions.

To determine which looseleaf services are in your library, check your library's electronic catalog or ask a law librarian. To determine which looseleaf services are available on a particular fee-based service, check the service's directory or ask your service's representative.

Because looseleaf services are expensive, they may not be included in your basic LexisNexis or Westlaw service package. You can, however, access them for an additional fee.

P R A C T I C E

See Exercise 12G in the *Practice Book*.

§ 12.3 Researching the *Mens Rea* Issue

Research plan in hand, it is time to do the research itself.

Step 1: Do Background Reading

Unless you already have a good working knowledge of the AEDPA and section 2339B, spend thirty to sixty minutes doing background reading either on the Internet or in law reviews.

a. Use Google to Locate Information About the AEDPA and 2339B

The easiest, and cheapest, way to get an overview of the AEDPA is to use the Internet. Go to Google and, using the "Advanced Search" option, look for websites that contain the phrase "Antiterrorism and Effective Death Penalty Act" and one of the following words: "overview," "summary," or "introduction." See Exhibits 12.1 and 12.2, which are on the CD that came with this book.

Although most government websites use the full name of the act, some do not. Therefore, you may also want to include the act's initials as an additional search term. For instance, in our example, you might want to search for "Antiterrorism and Effective Death Penalty Act" or AEDPA.

P R A C T I C E

When you look at the first four or five websites, you discover two things. First, you learn that the AEDPA deals primarily with federal *habeas corpus* law, not with humanitarian aid to terrorist organizations. Second, you learn that, because of the political nature of the AEDPA, many of the websites are sponsored by special interest groups. Thus, you decide to try another, narrower Google search. To find websites that discuss the particular portion of the AEDPA that you have been asked to analyze, you search for websites that contain "2339B." To find more "neutral" sites, you search for sites that contain the domain name "edu." To see this new search and its results, see Exhibits 12.3 and 12.4 on the CD.

To search a single domain, use the "Domain" box that is on Google's "Advanced Search" screen.

P R A C T I C E
POINTER

Many of the websites that this second search retrieved are on point. For example, the first and second links take you to the text of the statute, the third link takes you to a PowerPoint presentation prepared by Professor William C. Banks of Syracuse University College of Law, and the fourth and fifth links take you to reports prepared for Congress. Because these sites appear to be on point, spend time exploring and reading them. In doing so, always note who posted the information and the date that the site was last updated.

b. Look for Law Review Articles That Discuss the AEDPA and Section 2339B

When the issue you have been asked to research involves a cutting edge and/or controversial subject, you may be able to find a law review article that provides you with background information. The easiest way to find these articles is to go on to LexisNexis or Westlaw and run a search in the journals and law reviews database. Start by searching for articles that contain "2339B." If that search retrieves a large number of documents, add search terms. For example, you can add search terms that are designed to recover articles that contain a summary of 2339B by adding words like "summary," "overview," or "introduction," or you can add search terms that are designed to recover articles that deal with the intent requirement and material support by adding the words "intent" and "material support."

Questions

What search terms and connectors would you use to find law review articles that provide background information about 2339B? Design a series of searches and then test them. Which search or searches retrieve an article that provides background information about 2339B?

c. If Your Background Reading Indicates That There Is No Mandatory Authority, Create a Research Template

If the websites and/or law review articles indicate that there is a United States Supreme Court decision or a Seventh Circuit Court of Appeals decision that answers the issue you have been asked to research, locate and read that case. If the case is on point, you have your answer, and you can stop your research and begin writing your memo.

Question

Why can you stop your research if you find a United States Supreme Court or Seventh Circuit Court of Appeals decision that is on point?

If, however, the websites and/or law review articles indicate that there is neither a United States Supreme Court nor a Seventh Circuit Court of Appeals decision that is on point, create a research template and begin to fill in your template. Although there are a number of ways to organize the information that you find, the following template works well.

Chart 12.4   **Research Template**

I. Mandatory Authority (federal statutes, United States Supreme Court decisions, and Seventh Circuit Court of Appeals decisions)

   A.   Text of statute
   B.   United States Supreme Court cases
   C.   Seventh Circuit Court of Appeals cases

II. Arguments and Support for Those Arguments

   A.   Plain language arguments
   B.   Legislative history arguments
   C.   Arguments based on cases from other circuits and district court decisions
   D.   Policy arguments

Step 2: Locating Mandatory Authority

Start your search for mandatory authority by finding the applicable version of the statute, which in our sample problem is the version of 18 U.S.C. § 2339B that was in effect in December 2005, the date when the TWHRC provided the tsunami warning system to the LTTE. After you find the applicable version of the statute, look for United States Supreme Court and Seventh Circuit Court of Appeals decisions.

a. Locate the Applicable Version of the Statute

At least in theory, you can find the current version of a federal statute in a book source — for example, the book version of the U.S.C., the book version of the U.S.C.A., or the book version of the U.S.C.S. Unfortunately, though, it usually takes months (if not years) to update these book sources. Consequently, if there is a chance that the statute has been amended during the last two or three years, a book source is not a good choice. Many of the free websites are not much better. It can take some time for even reliable websites like *Thomas.loc.gov* and *FindLaw.com* to update their sites. Therefore, if you need the most recent version of a statute, the most reliable sources are LexisNexis and Westlaw. To find a copy of 18 U.S.C. § 2339B on Westlaw, log on to Westlaw, and then type "18 U.S.C. 2339B" in the "Find by Citation" box. See Exhibit 12.5 and 12.6, which are on the CD.

Question

How can you find a copy of 18 U.S.C. § 2339B using LexisNexis?

When you use the "Find by Citation" box, you do not need to include the "§" symbol.

Once you have located the statute, do three things: (1) check the status of the statute; (2) check to see when the website was last updated; and (3) read and analyze the statute.

1. Check the Status

If you look at the top of the main textbox, you will see a yellow flag just to the left of the citation. This flag, which has been inserted by West editors, tells you that one or more courts have held that section 2339B is unconstitutional or has been preempted and/or that there is legislation pending that would affect section 2339B. When you look at the textbox that is on the left part of the screen, you see that in this instance, the yellow flag is there for both reasons: one or more courts have held that section 2339B is unconstitutional, and there is legislation pending that would affect section 2339B.

To find out more, click on the "History" link. When you do, a screen appears that tells you that in two cases, *Humanitarian Law Project v. Dept. of Justice* and *United States v. Sattar*, the courts held that a prior version of 2339B was unconstitutional. See Exhibit 12.7 on the CD. In addition, the screen tells you that there are two bills pending before the 109th Congress that would affect 2339B. Both pieces of information provide you with leads you will need to track down.

Question

Is the information that you find on LexisNexis the same as the information that you find on Westlaw? Why or why not?

2. *Check to See When the Website Was Last Updated*

To find out when the website was last updated, pull up the full version of the statute (click on the link to the full text of the statute) and then scroll to the very end of the statute. On Westlaw, there will be a statement telling you the date and public law number through which the website is current. See Exhibit 12.8 on the CD.

Question

Which site was updated more recently, LexisNexis or Westlaw?

3. *Read and Analyze the Statute*

The next step is to read and analyze the statute, including any applicable cross-references and any relevant additional material. Thus, read and analyze section 2339B; section 2339A, which is referred to in section 2339B and which sets out the definition of "material support"; and the findings, which are set out after section 2339B but that are not part of 2339B. Note that these findings were not codified — that is, they were not placed into a particular section of the *United State Code*. Consequently, if you cite to them, use the public law number, which is set out immediately above the text of the findings. For the screen setting out the findings, see Exhibit 12.9. on the CD.

Question

Has 18 U.S.C. § 2339B or the definition of "material support" set out in 18 U.S.C. § 2339A been amended since this book was written? How can you find out?

The links in the left window provide you with tools that you can use to find information within a particular statute. See Exhibit 12.10 on the CD. For example, the "Table of Contents" link allows

P R A C T I C E

you to place a particular section into a larger context, see Exhibit 12.11; the "Versions" link lets you track amendments, see Exhibit 12.12; and the "Outline" link allows you to find particular information within a single statutory section, see Exhibit 12.13. on the CD.

Question

Does LexisNexis provide you with links to similar types of information? For example, does LexisNexis have a table of contents link? A versions link? A section outline? Does it have links that are not on Westlaw?

Although section 2339B specifically requires that the government prove (1) that the individual knowingly provided material support or resources to a terrorist organization and (2) that the individual knew the organization had been designated as a terrorist organization or had engaged or engages in terrorist activities, section 2339B does not talk about intent. Because the statute does not mention intent to further the terrorist organization's illegal activities, the government will argue that it does not have to prove intent. In contrast, the defendants will argue that without an intent requirement the statute is unconstitutional. The text of 18 U.S.C. § 2239B is set out below.

> Whoever knowingly provides material support or resources to a foreign terrorist organization, or attempts or conspires to do so, shall be fined under this title or imprisoned not more than 15 years, or both, and, if the death of any person results, shall be imprisoned for any term of years or for life. To violate this paragraph, a person must have knowledge that the organization is a designated terrorist organization (as defined in subsection (g)(6)), that the organization has engaged or engages in terrorist activity (as defined in section 212(a)(3)(B) of the Immigration and Nationality Act), or that the organization has engaged or engages in terrorism (as defined in section 140(d)(2) of the Foreign Relations Act.

Because the statute is ambiguous, the next step is to look for mandatory authority — that is, United States Supreme Court or Seventh Circuit Court of Appeals decisions that have decided, or at least discussed, the issue.

4. Locate United States Supreme Court and Seventh Circuit Court of Appeals Decisions

Although there are other ways to locate Supreme Court and Seventh Circuit cases, the easiest way is to cite check section 2339B, looking for United States Supreme Court and Seventh Circuit cases that have cited 18 U.S.C. § 2339B. To do this using Westlaw, click on the "Citing References" link. See Exhibit 12.14. on the CD. When you click on the link, you retrieve the list set out in Exhibit 12.15. Scroll through the list, looking for United States Supreme Court cases (the citation will be to "U.S.," "S.Ct." or "L. Ed. 2d") or Seventh Circuit cases (the cite will be to F.2d or F.3d, and there will be a reference to the 7th Cir.).

Question

How would you find United States Supreme Court and Seventh Circuit Court of Appeals decisions using the version of *Shepard's*® that is on LexisNexis?

On the date that we ran the search, there were no United States Supreme Court decisions that cited 18 U.S.C. § 2339B, and only one Seventh Circuit

case, *Boim v. Quranic Literacy Inst. & Holy Land Found. for Relief & Dev.*,
291 F.3d 1000, (7th Cir. 2002). If it is on point, the Seventh Circuit decision
is mandatory authority. Thus, you click on the link to *Boim*, which takes you
to headnote 7, which is the first place in *Boim* where there is a citation to
2339B.

You read headnote 7, and then, because the headnote is confusing and is
not authority, you click on the headnote 7 link, which takes you to that part of
the court's opinion from which the West editors drew headnote 7. When you
read that part of the Seventh Circuit's opinion, you find that the case, while
not directly on point, provides some insight into how the Seventh Circuit
might interpret 2339B. Therefore you take the time to read and cite
check *Boim*.

Question

Why is *Boim* not directly on point? Is *Boim* a 2339A or a 2339B case? If *Boim* is
a 2339A case, why do the parties and the court talk about 2339B?

Step 3: Locate Persuasive Authority

In the absence of mandatory authority, each side will make its best arguments about the type of intent required under section 2339B: the government
will do its best to persuade the court that section 2339B does not require proof
that the TWHRC intended to further LTTE's illegal activities, and the
TWHRC will argue that it does.

When a statute is involved, parties can typically make four types of arguments: plain language arguments, legislative history arguments, analogous
case arguments, and policy arguments. Although you could research these
arguments one at a time, an easier and more efficient approach is to "borrow"
these arguments from cases, law review articles, and other commentaries.

a. Locate Cases from Other Circuits and from District Courts That Discuss Section 2339B and Intent

As a general rule, start your search for persuasive authorities by looking for
cases from other jurisdictions that have discussed the issue. While decisions
from the other circuits' courts of appeals may not be mandatory authority,
most district court judges give court of appeals decisions considerable weight.
In addition, look for district court decisions from your own circuit and from
other circuits. Although district court decisions can never be mandatory
authority, many district court judges give considerable weight to well-
researched and reasoned district court decisions.

Questions

Why are decisions from other circuit courts of appeals persuasive rather than
mandatory authority? Why are district court decisions always persuasive
authority?

Not surprisingly, there are several ways to find these decisions. One way is to work your way through the list of citing references, looking first at the cases listed under the subheading "knowledge and intent." This approach leads you to one case, *United States v. Al-Arian*, a 2004 decision by the United States District Court for the Middle District of Florida. See Exhibit 12.16, which is on the CD.

A second approach is to look at the notes of decision that are set out after 18 U.S.C. § 2339B. To find these notes of decision, go back to the full text version of 2339B, and then scroll down until you find the "table of contents" for the notes of decision. See Exhibit 12.17. on the CD. Because the heading "Knowledge and intent" seems to be on point, click on the link to 3B. When you do, you are taken to the section of the notes of decision set out in Exhibit 12.18. On the date that we looked at subsection 3B, the only case that was listed was *United States v. Al-Arian*, the same case that was listed under the heading "Knowledge and intent" in the list of citing references.

Question

Does the current version of LexisNexis or Westlaw contain any additional citations to cases?

A third option is to do a "terms and connectors" search using 2339B and the word "intent" as search terms. If you connect these two terms with a "/p," which means within the same paragraph, and run your search in the federal cases database, you retrieve fifteen documents. See Exhibits 12.19 and 12.20 on the CD. Note that four of these documents are citations to *Boim* and *Al-Arian*, cases that we have already identified as being potentially useful, and that one of the cases, *United States v. Tabatatai*, is an unpublished opinion. See Exhibit 12.21. on the CD.

Because twelve is a manageable number of documents, the next step is to read at least some of the cases. In doing so, start with the most recent cases that appear to be on point. For example, in our sample problem, start with the Middle District of Florida's most recent decision, *Al-Arian*, and then, based on what you see in that case, move to other cases — for example, to cases that are cited both in *Al-Arian* and that are on the search results list.

Question

Why do you want to read the more recent cases first?

The first thing that you note when you look at these cases is that the courts' opinions are long and the analyses are complicated. You need, therefore, to approach the reading of the cases in a way that is efficient and sound. There are several strategies that can work when used appropriately.

Strategy 1: Before Reading a Case, Check the Case's Status

If the case has a red flag, find out why. The easiest way to do this is to skim the relevant portions of the case or cases that reversed or overruled the case that has the red flag. Although you may be able to use information and arguments from the red flagged case (at this point, all of the cases are persuasive, not mandatory authority), you also do not want to waste time. For example, in our example problem, some of the key cases are the *Humanitarian Law Project* cases. One of these cases, *Humanitarian Law Project v. Dept. of Justice*, 352 F.2d 382 (9th Cir. 2003), is one of the documents that our "terms and connectors" on the CD search retrieved. See Exhibit 12.22. However, the case has a red flag. When you pull up the full version of the case and click on the links to "Full History" and "Direct History-Graphical View," you find more than a dozen decisions, many of which are many pages long. See Exhibits 12.23 and 12.24 on the CD. Although you will want and need to read some of these decisions, you do not need to read all of them. Start with the most recent decision, *Humanitarian Law Project v. U.S. Dept. of Justice*, 393 F.3d 902 (9th Cir. 2004), and then work your way back through the decisions until you have a good feel for the approach that the Ninth Circuit has taken.

Strategy 2: Read the Relevant Portions of the Case and Then Decide Whether You Need to Read the Entire Case

When a decision is long, read the relevant portions of the case, and then decide whether you need to read the entire case. For example, if there is a summary or syllabus at the beginning of the case, read that first to identify the issue that was before the court. (If there is no summary or syllabus, skim the first part of the court's opinion until you find the court's statement of the issue.) If the issue suggests that the case may have useful information, identify the headnotes that are most on point, and then use those headnote numbers to locate the relevant portion or portions of the opinion. If these portions contain information that you think you can use, read the entire opinion. Skim those portions that are not directly on point and read carefully those that are.

For example, when you click on the link to the most recent decision in *Al-Arian*, you find the screen set out in Exhibit 12.25 on the CD.

When you scroll down, you will find a section titled "Background" and a section titled "Holding." See Exhibit 12.26. A quick reading of these two sections indicates that *Al-Arian* is directly on point: the issue before the court was what type of intent section 2339B requires. Thus, you scroll down a bit further, looking for the headnote or headnotes that are most on point. In this instance, the West headnote most on point is headnote 1. See Exhibit 12.27 on the CD. When you click the link on the "[1]," you are taken to the portion of the court's opinion that is set out in Exhibit 12.28.

Strategy 3: If a Case or Series of Cases Are Particularly Complex, Read Someone Else's Summary of the Cases Before Reading Them Yourself

If a case or series of cases is particularly complex, start by reading another court's or commentator's summary of the case or series of cases. For example, before tackling the *Humanitarian Law Project* cases, look for a recent case, law review article, or even a website that summarizes the cases. Although these summaries are not substitutes for reading the cases, you can use them to guide your reading. For example, on the day that we googled "Humanitarian Law Project," we found a number of websites that summarized the *Humanitarian Law Project* cases. As you read these websites, keep in mind that many of the sites are sponsored by special interest groups, including the Humanitarian Law Project itself.

Finally, as you read the cases, keep your research template at hand and fill in arguments and support for those arguments as you come across them. For example, as you are reading *Al-Arian*, take notes on the plain language arguments that it sets out and the rules of statutory construction that it cites as authority. Similarly, in reading *United States v. Hammond*, take notes on the legislative history arguments that the parties made and the portions of the *Congressional Record* that are cited as authority.

b. Research 2339B's Legislative History

While some judges want to know a statute's legislative history, other judges give little or no weight to such histories. See Michael H. Koby, *The Supreme Court's Declining Reliance on Legislative History: The Impact of Justice Scalia's Critique*, 36 Harv. J. on Legis. 369 (1999). Thus, before you spend time doing a legislative history, check with your judge to see if she wants you to do one.

In this instance, the judge does want to know section 2339B's legislative history. In particular, she wants to know about statements that were made when section 2339B was initially enacted, about amendments to the statute, and about statements that were made during the amendment process.

As you learned in section 12.2, there are three ways to find a statute's legislative history: (1) you can find references to legislative history documents in a case, a law review article, or other secondary source and then look up those cases; (2) you can find a compiled legislative history; or (3) you can compile your own legislative history.

1. Locating Documents Cited in Another Source

On page 402 of *Humanitarian Law Project v. U.S. Dept. of Justice*, 352 F.3d 382 (9th Cir. 2003), the court makes the following statement.

> The one statement in the Congressional Record that refers to an intent requirement in § 2339B was made by Senator Hatch, who co-sponsored AEDPA. In introducing the Conference Report to the Senate, Senator Hatch stated: "[t]his bill also includes provisions making it a crime to *knowingly provide material support to the terrorist functions* of foreign groups designated by a Presidential finding to be engaged in terrorist activities. I am convinced we have crafted a narrow but effective designation provision which meets these obligations while safeguarding the freedom to associate, which none of us would willingly give up." 142 Cong. Rec. S3354 (daily ed., April 16, 1996) (statement of Sen. Hatch) (emphasis added).

To find this statement, go to *www.GPOAccess.gov* and click on "Congressional Record." See Exhibit 12.29. Because you are looking for a statement that was made in 1996, select "Simple Search." See Exhibit 12.30. When the next screen appears, select "Congressional Record Vol. 142" and type the page number — in this instance, S3354 — in the search box. See Exhibit 12.31. When the text of the *Congressional Record* appears, scroll down until you find the relevant language. See Exhibit 12.32.

In the alternative, use *Thomas.loc.gov* or the *Congressional Record* databases on LexisNexis or Westlaw.

2. Using the Public Law Number, Look for a Compiled Legislative History for the 1996 Version of Section 2339B in Either the Book or the Electronic Version of U.S.C.C.A.N.

To find the public law number, go to the end of section 2239B and find the historical notes. See Exhibit 12.34 on the CD. Then go on to Westlaw, select the "Welcome" screen, and then, in the "Search these databases" box, type "USCCAN-Rep." See Exhibit 12.35 on the CD. When the search number appears, type in the public law number. See Exhibit 12.36. Browse through the documents that this search retrieves, looking for information that may indicate what Congress intended when it enacted the AEDPA. See Exhibit 12.37.

3. Construct Your Own Legislative History

For new pieces of legislation, such as the December 17, 2004, amendments, you will need to construct your own legislative history. To do this, cite check section 2339B to locate the public law number for the December 17, 2004, amendments. See Exhibit 12.38 on the CD. Go to *Thomas.loc.gov* and, under "Legislation," select "Public Laws." See Exhibit 12.39 on the CD. When the next screen appears, select the 108th Congress, the range that would include Public Law 108-458, and then "search." See Exhibit 12.40 on the CD. When the next screen appears, click on the various links, and scan the documents that you find, looking for relevant information. (Keep in mind that the Act was a large one that covered a number of different topics, most of which are not relevant to the issue that you have been asked to research.) See Exhibit 12.41.

c. Locate Law Review Articles That Discuss 18 U.S.C. § 2339B

To find law review articles that discuss 18 U.S.C. § 2339B and the intent requirement, use the "Find by Citation" box to look up articles that are cited after the text of 2339B or that are cited in the cases or run a search in Westlaw's or LexisNexis's law review databases. The screen shot in Exhibit 12.42 shows you how you can use the "Welcome" screen on your "Federal" tab to locate Westlaw's "Journals and Law Reviews" database. Once you have selected the database, construct a search that is likely to retrieve law review articles that discuss the intent requirement under section 2339B.

1. A.L.R. Fed.

You should also look for A.L.R. annotations that discuss section 2339B. To find the ALR database, go to the "Welcome" screen and, in the box titled "Search these databases," type in "ALR". Once you are in the ALR database, construct and run your search.

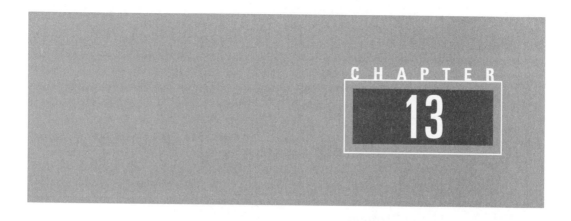

Drafting a Prehearing Memo

I n some ways, it is a crazy system. What sane person would ask someone who is just days out of law school to research and analyze a case that is before a trial court or appellate court and then make a recommendation about how the case should be decided? That is, however, exactly what we ask judicial clerks to do. Most state and federal appellate court judges have one or more law clerks who research the law and then draft a document that not only summarizes the law and each side's arguments but that also sets out the law clerk's recommendation.

Students who work for judges for course credit during law school are usually called judicial externs. In contrast, recent graduates who work for judges for pay are usually called judicial clerks.

P R A C T I C E
POINTER

Different courts use different names for these documents. While in some courts these documents are called "bench memos," in other courts they are called "prehearing memoranda" or "report and recommendation." In addition, the formats vary from court to court and even from judge to judge. In surveying state and federal judges, we found a number of different formats, including the following:

EXAMPLE 1	**List of Sections**

- Heading
- Introduction
- Statement of the Case (includes factual background and procedural history)
- Discussion (or Legal Analysis)
- Conclusion

EXAMPLE 2	**List of Sections**

- Heading
- Nature of the Case
- Statement of Facts and Procedural History
- Issue Statements and Short Answers
- Rules and Analysis
- Recommendation

EXAMPLE 3	**List of Sections (used for memos written for motion calendar)**

- Caption
- Motions Presented
- Issues
- Background and Procedural History
- Plaintiff's Argument
- Defendant's Argument
- Discussion
- Conclusion

Because different judges prefer different formats, ask one of your judge's more experienced law clerks what format your judge prefers. For the purposes of this chapter, we discuss the sections that are set out in Examples 1 and 2.

§ 13.1 Drafting the Heading or the Caption

Most headings and captions have the following information:

(1) The case name and number;
(2) If the case is scheduled for oral argument, the date of the oral argument; and
(3) The name of the judge or judges who will be hearing or deciding the case.

In addition, some headings contain the name of the requesting judge, the law clerk's name, and the date the memo is submitted.

Sample Heading

Case Name:	United States v. Tamil Welfare and Human Rights Committee, et al.
Case Number:	05-1111
Trial Date:	March 15, 2006

If you include a caption, that caption will usually be a modified version of the caption in the actual case.

§ 13.2 Drafting the Introduction or the Nature of Case Section

A good introduction or nature of the case section identifies the issue that you were asked to research and each side's position. It may also include your recommendation. For instance, in the example problem, you would indicate that you had been asked to research the intent issue, and you would set out the government's position, the defendant's position, and your recommendation.

Sample Introduction

Before ruling on each side's proposed jury instructions, you have asked me to determine what type of intent 18 U.S.C. § 2339B requires. The government argues that it needs to prove only that the defendants knowingly provided material support or resources to a foreign terrorist organization. In contrast, the defendants argue that the government must prove both that the defendants knowingly provided material support or resources to a foreign terrorist organization and that they did so with the intent to further the foreign terrorist organization's illegal activities. The most recent amendments suggest that Congress did not intend to require proof of intent to further the foreign terrorist organization's illegal activities. Such a reading of the statute may, however, make the statute unconstitutional under either the First or the Fifth Amendments.

§ 13.3 Drafting the Statement of Facts and Procedural History

The Statement of Facts and Procedural History should give the judge two types of information: it should set out the underlying facts that are relevant to the issue or issues that you have been asked to research, and it should summarize the judicial proceedings. In other words, use the Statement of Facts and Procedural History sections to tell the judge what happened before the case was filed in the courts and what has happened since the case was filed. Note that some judges want the underlying facts first and then the procedural history but that other judges want the procedural history first and then the facts. In addition, note that some judges want the facts and procedural history in a single section without subheadings but that other judges want them divided into two subsections with one subsection labeled "Facts" and the other labeled "Procedural History."

When you have been asked to research a narrow issue — for example, an issue relating to one of the jury instructions, the judge may not want you to include a procedural history. Thus, instead of adopting a "blind" fill-in-the-blank approach, use common sense and tailor your memo so that it works for your particular audience (your judge) and your particular purpose (the issue that you have been asked to research).

P R A C T I C E
POINTER

The "rules" for drafting the Statement of Facts and Procedural History are the same as the rules for drafting the statement of facts in an objective memo to an attorney: (1) include all of the legally significant facts; (2) include enough background facts so that the judge can understand what happened, when it happened, and why and how it happened; (3) if appropriate, include emotionally significant facts; and (4) if appropriate, include unknown facts. In deciding whether it is appropriate to include emotionally significant and unknown facts, consider the nature of the case and your judge's preferences.

Because the example case involves a legal question, not a question of fact, the statement of the facts can be very short. The only legally significant fact is that the TWHRC wants to provide a tsunami warning system, which falls within the definition of "communications equipment," to a group that has been designated as a foreign terrorist organization.

Question

Do you agree that the only legally significant fact is that the TWHRC provided a tsunami warning system to a group that has been designated as a foreign terrorist organization? Why or why not?

Because you have been asked to research a very narrow issue (an issue related to a particular jury instruction), you do not need to include a procedural history. Compare the following two examples.

EXAMPLE 1   ### Short Statement of Facts and Procedural History

In December 2005, the Tamil Welfare and Human Rights Committee (TWHRC) provided tsunami warning equipment to the Liberation Tigers of Tamil Eelam (LTTE), which has been designated as a foreign terrorist organization (FTO) by the State Department. Under the government's proposed jury instruction, the government would have to prove only that the defendants knowingly provided material support or resources to an FTO. In contrast, under the defendants' proposed jury instructions, the government would have to prove both that the defendants knowingly provided material support to an FTO and that the defendants provided this material support with the intent to further the FTO's illegal activities.

Longer Statement of Facts and Procedural History

EXAMPLE 2

Facts

In 1997, then Secretary of State Madeline Albright designated the Liberation Tigers of Tamil Eelam (LTTE) as a foreign terrorist organization (FTO) under the Antiterrorism and Effective Death Penalty Act (AEDPA). The LTTE is an organization that seeks self-determination for the Tamil residents of Tamil Eelam, who live in the northern and eastern provinces of Sri Lanka. In December 2005, the Tamil Welfare and Human Rights Committee (TWHRC), a nonprofit organization based in Illinois, donated a tsunami warning system to the LTTE.

Procedural History

The United States has charged the TWHRC and some of its members under 18 U.S.C. § 2339B with providing material support or resources to an FTO. Under the government's proposed jury instructions, the government would have to prove only that the defendants knowingly provided material support to an FTO. In contrast, under the defendants' proposed jury instructions, the government would have to prove both that the defendants knowingly provided material support to an FTO and that the defendants provided this material support with the intent to further the FTO's illegal activities.

Question

Which version is a judge likely to prefer? Why?

§ 13.4 Drafting the Issue Statements and Short Answer

While some judges do not want a formal issue statement or short answer, others do. Of the judges who want formal issue statements and short answers, some want you to set out the issue statements and short answers in separate sections, and some want you to combine the issue statements and short answers. Thus, before writing this section, ask a more experienced law clerk what format your judge prefers.

§ 13.4.1 Drafting the Issue Statement

The issue statement for an issue that involves the application of a well-established rule to a particular set of facts is different from the issue statement for an issue that involves only a question of law. When the issue involves the application of a well-established rule, use one of the conventional formats. For example, use the "under-does-when" format and set out a reference to the rule of law, the legal question, and then the key facts. See section 7.4.2 on page 127. In the alternative, use the "whether" format, and set out the legal question and then the key facts. See section 10.3.

When, however, the issue that you have been asked to research is an issue of law, you do not need to include facts in your issue statement. Instead, simply set out the legal question and, when you can, the options.

In Example 1, the clerk has used a modified version of the "under-does-when" format and, in Example 2, the clerk has used a modified version of the "whether" format.

Issue Statement Using a Modified "Under-Does-When" Format

Under 18 U.S.C. § 2339B, does the government have to prove only that the defendant knew that it was providing material support or resources to a group that has been designated as a foreign terrorist organization, or must the government also prove that the defendant provided the material support or resources with the intent to further the foreign terrorist organization's illegal activities?

Issue Statement Using a Modified "Whether" Format

Whether 18 U.S.C. § 2339B requires the government to prove only that the defendant knew that it was providing material support or resources to a group that has been designated as a foreign terrorist organization, or whether 18 U.S.C. § 2339B requires the government to prove both that the defendant knew that it was providing material support or resources to a group that has been designated as a foreign terrorist organization and that it provided that support with the intent to further the foreign terrorist organization's illegal activities.

It is not "wrong," however, to refer to the parties by name or to include some of the key facts. For example, you could also write the issue statement as the clerk does in Example 3. Note that in Example 3 the clerk does not use either the "under-does-when" format or the "whether" format.

Issue Statement That Includes Some of the Key Facts

To convict the members of the TWHRC of providing material support or resources to a foreign terrorist organization in violation of 18 U.S.C. § 2339B, must the government prove only that the TWHRC provided a tsunami warning system to the LTTE knowing that the LTTE has been designated as a foreign terrorist organization, or must the government also prove that the TWHRC provided the tsunami warning system to the LTTE with the intent to further the LTTE's illegal activities?

Question

Which one of the above examples do you think that a judge would prefer? Why?

§ 13.4.2 Drafting the Short Answer

If the judge wants you to include a short answer, write something that is similar to the brief answers you wrote for the attorneys in the service of process and adverse possession memos. If the judge wants you to include your recommendation, do so. Otherwise, do not.

Short Answer That Does Not Include a Recommendation   `EXAMPLE 1`

This case presents an issue of first impression: while the courts in the Ninth and Eleventh Circuits have ruled on the issue, the Seventh Circuit has not. The better approach seems to be the approach taken by the Ninth Circuit, which has held that the government needs to prove only that the defendant knew it was providing material support to an organization that has been designated as an FTO. The Ninth's Circuit approach is more consistent with the statute's plain language and legislative history than the approach taken by a district court in the Eleventh Circuit, and the Ninth Circuit's approach is sound as a matter of public policy because, once a party makes a donation to a terrorist group, it cannot control how the terrorist group uses that donation.

Short Answer That Includes a Recommendation   `EXAMPLE 2`

I recommend that the court adopt the approach taken by the Ninth Circuit and hold that the government must prove only that the defendant knew it was providing material support to an organization that has been designated as a FTO. This approach gives effect to Congress's intent as evidenced by the statute's legislative history and by the recent amendments and is sound as a matter of public policy because, once a party makes a donation to a terrorist group, it cannot control how the terrorist group uses that donation.

---

§ 13.5 Organizing the Discussion Section

While both the service of process problem and the adverse possession problem involved an elements analysis, this chapter's problem does not. Although 18 U.S.C. § 2339B sets out a series of elements, the judge has asked you to discuss only one of those elements, the *mens rea* requirement. In addition, while the service of process and adverse possession problems involved well-established areas of law, this problem involves an issue of first impression. While the Ninth Circuit Court of Appeals and the United States District Court for the Middle District of Florida have interpreted 18 U.S.C. § 2339B, no Seventh Circuit court has.

Because the issue that you have been asked to research does not involve an elements analysis, the organizational plan that we used in the service of process and the adverse possession problems does not work. Instead, we need to use one of the organizational plans for issues of first impression. Under the first of these plans, the organizing principle is the different ways of interpreting the statute or the majority and minority approaches to a particular issue: you introduce the issue, you set out the law and arguments that support one approach, you set out the law and arguments that support the second approach, and then you conclude by evaluating the merits of the two approaches.

EXAMPLE

Generic Research Plan Using the Differing Approaches as the Organizing Principle

Introduction

- Introduce "rule" that the court has been asked to interpret — for example, the statute that the court has been asked to interpret.
- Briefly describe approaches.

Part I: Approach 1

- Introduce approach.
- Set out reasons courts have given for adopting this approach.
- Set out other reasons that support the adoption of this approach.

Part I: Approach 2

- Introduce approach.
- Set out reasons courts have given for adopting this approach.
- Set out other reasons that support the adoption of this approach.

Part III: Evaluation

- Critique and evaluate the two approaches.
- Recommend approach and reasons that support recommendation.

While most often the courts will split, taking two different approaches, sometimes there are more than two approaches. If the courts have taken three, four, or five different approaches, include subsections for each approach. In addition, distinguish the various approaches, setting out the reasons the courts have given for adopting each approach, setting out other reasons that support the adoption of each approach, and critiquing and evaluating each approach.

P R A C T I C E
POINTER

If you use this first organizational plan for the example problem, your outline for the discussion or rules and analysis section would look like the outline set out in the next example.

Outline for Example Problem

Introduction

- Introduce 18 U.S.C. § 2339B.
- Briefly describe the statute's legislative history and amendments.
- Briefly describe approaches.

Part I: Ninth Circuit's approach in *Humanitarian Law Project* Cases

- Introduce the Ninth's Circuit's approach.
- Set out reasons the Ninth Circuit gave in the *Humanitarian Law Project* cases.
  - Plain language arguments?
  - Legislative history arguments?
  - Arguments based on case law?
  - Policy arguments?
- Set out other reasons that support the adoption of the Ninth Circuit's approach.
  - Plain language arguments?
  - Legislative history arguments?
  - Arguments based on case law?
  - Policy arguments?

Part II: United States District Court for the Middle District of Florida's Approach in *Al-Arian*

- Introduce the United States District Court for the Middle District of Florida's approach.
- Set out reasons the District Court gave in *Al-Arian*.
  - Plain language arguments?
  - Legislative history arguments?
  - Arguments based on case law?
  - Policy arguments?
- Set out other reasons that support the adoption of the Middle District of Florida's approach.
  - Plain language arguments?
  - Legislative history arguments?
  - Arguments based on case law?
  - Policy arguments?

Part III: Evaluation

- Critique and evaluate the two approaches.
- Recommend one of the approaches and summarize reasons that support the recommendation.

A second plan organizes the arguments by type. After introducing the two approaches, the clerk sets out and critiques any plain language arguments, legislative history arguments, arguments based on the case law, and policy arguments that the parties might make.

Generic Research Plan Using Types of Arguments as the Organizing Principle

Introduction

- Introduce the "rule" that the court has been asked to interpret — for example, the statute that the court has been asked to interpret.
- Briefly describe the possible approaches.
- Include a roadmap that identifies the types of arguments that parties are likely to make.

I. Plain Language Arguments

- Set out and critique the plain language arguments using an integrated format.[1]

II. Legislative History Arguments

- Set out and critique the legislative history arguments using an integrated format.

III. Analogous Case Arguments

- Set out and critique arguments based on the case law using an integrated format.

IV. Policy Arguments

- Set out and evaluate the policy arguments using an integrated format.

You will not always set out all four types of arguments. For example, if your problem involved the interpretation of a constitutional provision rather than a statute, there would not be any legislative history arguments. Similarly, if there are no cases, either in your jurisdiction or any other jurisdiction, that discuss the issue or related issues, you would not have any analogous case arguments. In addition, you may not always set out the arguments in the order in which they are listed in the generic organizational plan. Although in general courts look to the plain language of a statute before they consider other arguments, if there is another argument that is determinative, start your discussion with that argument.

---

1. See section 10.11 on pages 254-268.

When we modify the generic research plan so that it works with the example problem, our outline looks like the one set out below.

Generic Research Plan Using Types of Arguments as the Organizing Principle

Introduction

- Introduce 18 U.S.C. § 2339B.
- Briefly describe the two approaches.
  - Government has to prove only that the defendant knew that it was providing material support to a group that has been designated as a foreign terrorist organization.
  - Government has to prove both that the defendant knew that it was providing material support to a group that has been designated as a foreign terrorist organization and that the defendant intended to further the foreign terrorist organization's illegal activities.
- Include a roadmap that identifies the types of arguments that parties are likely to make.

I. Plain Language Arguments

- Set out the plain language of 18 U.S.C. § 2339B.
- Set out and evaluate both sides' plain language arguments.

II. Legislative History Arguments

- Summarize 18 U.S.C. § 2339B's legislative history.
- Set out and evaluate both sides' legislative history arguments.

III. Analogous Case Arguments

- Summarize the facts and the court's holding and reasoning in the *Humanitarian Law Project* cases.
- Summarize the facts and the court's holding and reasoning in *Al-Arian.*
- Summarize any Seventh Circuit cases that suggest how the Seventh Circuit deals with issues like this one.
- Set out and evaluate both sides' analogous case arguments.

IV. Policy Arguments

- Set out and evaluate both sides' policy arguments.

V. Weigh the Relative Merits of the Plain Language, Legislative History, Analogous Cases, and Policy Arguments

- Critically evaluate the various arguments.

Depending on the issue, there may also be other ways to organize the discussion. Therefore, before deciding on an organizational scheme, think about other possible organizational schemes. Is there another scheme that might work better than the ones set out above? If there is, use it. However, make sure that the organizational scheme you choose works not just for you, the clerk, but also for your reader, the judge or judges for whom you are writing the memo.

If a court in another jurisdiction has discussed the issue that you have been asked to analyze, look at how that court organized its opinion. If that court's opinion was easy for you to follow, think about adopting its organizational plan. If, however, you found the other court's opinion confusing, determine whether it was the organizational scheme that was the culprit. If it was, pick a different plan.

---

§ 13.6 Drafting the Discussion or Analysis: The Introductory Section

Most of the time you will want to start your discussion or analysis section with an introductory section. When the issue is one of first impression, use this section to tell the judge that the issue is one of first impression and to provide the judge with the background information that he or she will need to understand the issue and to evaluate the various approaches and arguments.

In deciding what information to include, think about your reader. How much does your judge know about this area of law? If the judge knows very little, you may need to place the issue into a larger context. For instance how, does your issue fit with related issues and doctrines? Why and when was the statute enacted? If, however, the judge knows the area of law, your introductory section can be much shorter: just provide the judge with the information he or she needs to understand the issue you were asked to research and analyze. In other words, give the judge what he or she needs, nothing less and nothing more.

You are not expected to be a mind reader. Thus, when you get an assignment, ask questions. Is the judge familiar with the area of law? Does your judge like a lot of background information, or does he or she prefer a "quick and dirty" approach? If you do not feel comfortable asking the judge these questions, ask one of the judge's more experienced clerks.

Thus, different judges might prefer one of the following versions of the introductory section to the other versions.

Sample Introduction

EXAMPLE 1

In response to the Oklahoma City bombing, Congress enacted the Antiterrorism and Effective Death Penalty Act of 1996, Pub. L. No. 104-132, 110 Stat. 1214 (1996) (AEDPA), to combat terrorist financing and support. *See* 142 Cong. Rec. S3352 (daily ed. Apr. 16, 1996) (statement of Sen. Hatch). The AEDPA authorizes the Secretary of State to designate an organization as a foreign terrorist organization (FTO), *see* 8 U.S.C. § 1189(a) (West, Westlaw current through Pub L. No. 109-4), and prohibits the provision of material support to these designated FTOs. *See* 18 U.S.C. § 2339B(a)(1) (Westlaw current through P.L. No. 109-4).

Under the current version of § 2339B,

> **[w]hoever knowingly provides material support or resources to a foreign terrorist organization**, or attempts or conspires to do so, shall be fined under this title or imprisoned not more than 15 years, or both, and, if the death of any person results, shall be imprisoned for any term of years or for life.

18 U.S.C. § 2339B(a)(1) (emphasis added).

The term "material support or resources" (material support) is defined in § 2339B's sister statute, 18 U.S.C. § 2339A (Westlaw current through P.L. No. 109-4). Section 2339A defines "material support or resources" as follows:

> (1) the term **"material support or resources" means** any property, tangible or intangible, or service, including currency or monetary instruments or financial securities, financial services, lodging, training, expert advice or assistance, safehouses, false documentation or identification, **communications equipment**, facilities, weapons, lethal substances, explosives, personnel (1 or more individuals who may be or include oneself), and transportation, except medicine or religious materials;
>
> (2) the term "training" means instruction or teaching designed to impart a specific skill, as opposed to general knowledge.

18 U.S.C. § 2339A(b)(1) (emphasis added).

Congress enacted § 2339A two years prior to enacting § 2339B as part of the Violent Crime Control and Law Enforcement Act of 1994, Pub. L. No. 103-322, 108 Stat. 1796, 2022 (1994). Unlike § 2339B, § 2339A criminalizes the provision of material support only when the defendant knows or intends that the support will be used by the recipient to further its terrorist agenda. (The recipient need not be designated an FTO.) The relevant wording of the current version of Section 2339A follows:

> **Whoever provides material support or resources** or conceals or disguises the nature, location, source, or ownership of material support or resources, **knowing or intending that they are to be used in preparation for, or in carrying out [terrorist activities].** . . .

18 U.S.C. § 2339A(a) (emphasis added).

On its face, § 2339B does not require that the provider of material support know or intend that the support would further the FTO's unlawful ends. Instead, section 2339B requires only that the defendant know that the recipient of the support was an FTO or that the recipient had engaged in terrorist activities.

In this case, TWHRC argues that the statute requires proof that a person not only provided material support to an FTO but also intended to further the FTO's unlawful ends. Although it can make plain language, legislative history, and arguments based on the case law, TWHRC's strongest argument is a policy argument. In response, the defendants argue that the plain language of the statute, its legislative history, and the Ninth Circuit's decision establish that Congress did not intend that the statute require proof of intent. In addition, the defendants have a strong policy argument.

EXAMPLE 2

Sample Introduction

In 1994, Congress enacted what is now 18 U.S.C. § 2339A as part of the Violent Crime Control and Law Enforcement Act of 1994, Pub. L. No. 103-322, § 120005, 108 Stat 1796 (1994). Section 2339A makes it a crime to provide "material support or resources" knowing or intending that they will be used "in preparation for, or in carrying out" crimes of terrorism. 18 U.S.C. § 2339A (2000). "Material support or resources" is defined very broadly. The current definition reads as follows:

> (1) the term "material support or resources" means any property . . . or service, including currency or monetary instruments . . . , lodging, training, expert advice or assistance, . . . *communications equipment*, facilities, weapons, lethal substances, explosives, personnel (1 or more individuals who may be or include oneself), and transportation, except medicine or religious materials.

18 U.S.C.A. § 2339A (West, Westlaw through P.L. No. 109-4) (emphasis added).

In 1996, Congress enacted 18 U.S.C. § 2339B as part of the Antiterrorism and Effective Death Penalty Act (AEDPA). Like § 2339A, § 2339B made it a crime, punishable by a ten-year sentence, to knowingly provide "material support or resources"; unlike § 2339A, § 2339B encompassed a broad range of behavior, criminalizing all knowing provisions of material support to any organization that had been designated as a "foreign terrorist organization" by the Secretary of State, whether the provider intended that the support be used for terrorist purposes or for humanitarian (or any other) purposes. Section 2339B uses the same broad definition of "material support or resources" as § 2339A.

In 2001, Congress enacted the USA PATRIOT Act of 2001, increasing the prison term to fifteen years and adding a life sentence if any death resulted from the violation. Pub. L. No. 107-56, § 810(d), 115 Stat. 272 (2001). Two years later, the Ninth Circuit Court of Appeals struck down portions of § 2339B on First and Fifth Amendment grounds. *See Humanitarian Law Project v. U.S. Dept. of Justice*, 352 F.3d 382, 403 (9th Cir. 2003), *vacated by* 393 F.3d 902 (9th Cir. 2004) (*Humanitarian* 2003). In response, Congress enacted the Intelligence Reform and Terrorism Prevention Act of 2004, which clarified the definition of "material support or resources" and made the intent requirement more explicit. Pub. L. No. 108-458, § 6603, 118 Stat. 3638 (2004). The relevant portion of the current version of § 2339B reads as follows:

> § 2339B. Providing Material Support or Resources to Designated Foreign Terrorist Organizations
>
> (a) Prohibited activities.
> (1) Unlawful conduct. Whoever knowingly provides material support or resources to a foreign terrorist organization, or attempts or conspires to

do so, shall be fined under this title or imprisoned not more than 15 years, or both, and, if the death of any person results, shall be imprisoned for any term of years or for life. *To violate this paragraph, a person must have knowledge that the organization is a designated terrorist organization . . . , that the organization has engaged or engages in terrorist activity . . . , or that the organization has engaged or engages in terrorism. . . .*
* * *
(g) Definitions. As used in this section —
(4) the term "material support or resources" has the same meaning given that term in section 2339A (including the definitions of "training" and "expert advice or assistance" in that section); . . .
     (i) Rule of construction. *Nothing in this section shall be construed or applied so as to abridge the exercise of rights guaranteed under the First Amendment to the Constitution of the United States.*

18 U.S.C.A. § 2339B (West, Westlaw through Pub. L. No. 109-3) (emphasis added).

This memo analyzes the plain language of § 2339B, its legislative history, the cases from other jurisdictions that have interpreted § 2339B, and each side's policy arguments.

Questions

What organizational scheme did each clerk use? Did both clerks set out more general information before more specific information? Did they organize the information around topics? Did they set out the information in chronological order? Which organizational scheme works better? Why?

§ 13.7 The Discussion or Analysis: Identifying, Setting Out, and Evaluating the Arguments

Regardless of how you decide to organize the arguments (majority/minority, plaintiff/defendant, or type of argument) you need to provide the judge with a thorough but concise summary and evaluation of each side's arguments. In doing so, your analysis needs to be sophisticated, and your writing needs to be clear, precise, and engaging.

§ 13.7.1 Identify the Arguments

When you work for a judge, the bar is raised about as high as it can go. Even when the attorneys' analysis is not sophisticated, yours needs to be.

Start by making sure that you have identified all of the arguments. Although in civil cases your judge may not want you to make an independent evaluation of the case, in criminal cases most judges want you to alert them to arguments that the parties missed. One way to make sure that you have identified all of the possible arguments is to consider all of the "standard moves" using a chart like the one set out on page 326.

Finally, think outside the box. Are there other ways to approach the issue? Other arguments that could be made? Assumptions that need to be challenged?

Chart 13.1	**Identify Arguments Each Side Can Make**	
	TWHRC's Arguments	**Government's Arguments**
Plain language arguments		
Legislative history arguments		
Analogous history arguments		
Policy arguments		
Constitutional concerns		

§ 13.7.2 Identifying and Presenting Plain Language Arguments

The canons of statutory construction state that the courts should begin their analysis of a statute by looking at the statute's language. If that language is unambiguous, the analysis stops there. The courts simply apply the statute's "plain language." If, however, the statute's language is ambiguous or would produce an absurd result — for example, a statute that is unconstitutional on its face — the courts continue their analysis, looking at the statute's legislative history, at how other courts have applied the statute or similar statute, and at the policies underlying the statute.

The canons of statutory construction can, however, be a double-edged sword. *See, e.g.,* Karl Llewellyn, *Remarks on the Theory of Appellate Decision and the Rules or Canons About How Statutes are to be Construed,* 3 Vand. L. Rev. 395 (1950).

P R A C T I C E
POINTER

Because courts usually begin their analysis by looking at the language used in the statute, you will usually start your discussion or analysis of the arguments by setting out any plain language arguments that the parties may have. If you have organized your arguments by approach or by party, start by telling the judge whether the statute's plain language supports that approach or that party's arguments. If, however, you are organizing the arguments as we have chosen to do — by type — set out your plain language first, setting out and evaluating both sides' plain language arguments. In doing so, make sure that your analysis is objective and sophisticated and that your writing is clear and concise.

Compare the following examples. While in the first example, the clerk provides the judge with the basic information, the analysis is not particularly sophisticated. The second and third examples are better.

EXAMPLE 1

Clerk Provides the Judge with Basic Information but the Analysis Is Not Particularly Sophisticated

A. Plain Language Arguments

In interpreting a statute, the courts look first at the plain language of the statute.

> The clerk refers to one of the applicable canons of statutory construction but does not include a citation to authority.

In this case, § 2339B's plain language establishes that Congress did not want to require proof of specific intent to further the terrorist activities of an FTO. Neither the original nor the amended version of § 2339B includes language requiring the government to prove that the defendant intended to further an FTO's terrorist activities. Instead, the plain language requires only two things: (1) that the defendant knowingly provide material support and (2) that the defendant knows that the group has been designated as an FTO.

> The clerk sets out her conclusion.
> The clerk includes some support for her conclusion. The analysis is, however, very basic.

EXAMPLE 2

A. Plain Language Arguments

In interpreting a statute, the courts look first to the statute's plain language. *Boim v. Quranic Literacy Inst.*, 291 F.3d 1000, 1009 (7th Cir. 2002). Unless that language is ambiguous or its application would produce an absurd result, the analysis ends with the statute's plain language. *Id.*

> Instead of setting out only one of the applicable canons of statutory construction, the clerk sets out two. Because the clerk works for a judge in the Seventh Circuit, the clerk cites a Seventh Circuit Court of Appeals case as authority.

In this case, the government will argue that § 2339B is not ambiguous. While § 2339B requires proof that the person knew that he or she was providing material support or resources to a group that has been designated as an FTO, the statute does not require proof that the person intended to further the foreign terrorist organization's illegal activities.

> Although the clerk presents the arguments using the script format, the focus is on the two competing canons of statutory construction: the government uses the

first canon to support its position, and the TWHRC uses the second canon to support its position.

Note how the clerk has used boldface to emphasize the key terms in the statute. The clerk has also added a parenthetical following the cite (emphasis added) to let the judge know that he has added the bold.

(a) Prohibited activities.

(1) Unlawful conduct. **Whoever knowingly provides material support or resources to a foreign terrorist organization**, or attempts or conspires to do so, shall be fined under this title or imprisoned not more than 15 years, or both.... To violate this paragraph, **a person must have knowledge that the organization is a designated terrorist organization..., that the organization has engaged or engages in terrorist activity..., or that the organization has engaged or engages in terrorism....**

18 U.S.C. § 2339B (Westlaw current through Pub. L. No. 109-94 approved Oct. 26, 2005) (emphasis added).

The clerk uses a topic sentence to let the judge know that he is moving from the government's argument to TWHRC's arguments. Note that in setting out TWHRC's arguments, the clerk tells the judge (1) that the TWHRC is asking for alternative forms of relief and (2) which of these forms the TWHRC prefers.

The TWHRC will respond by arguing that a plain language interpretation of § 2339B produces an absurd result: a statute that is unconstitutional. Thus, the TWHRC will argue that this court has two choices: either it can hold that 18 U.S.C. § 2339B is unconstitutional, or it can apply the rule set out by the United States Supreme Court in cases like *Jones v. United States,* 526 U.S. 227 (1999) and *United States v. X-Citement Video,* 513 U.S. 64 (1994) and interpret the statute in such a way as to avoid constitutional difficulties. While TWHRC's first choice would be for the court to hold that the statute is unconstitutional, its second choice would be for the court to read an intent requirement into the statute: to obtain a conviction the government would have to prove that the person intended to further the FTO's illegal activities.

While in this example the clerk's analysis is more sophisticated, he has not evaluated each side's arguments or reached a conclusion. While the clerk does not need to put that evaluation and conclusion in this subsection, he does need to put it somewhere — for example, at the end of the discussion/analysis section or in the conclusion/recommendation.

Analysis Is More Sophisticated

EXAMPLE 3

A. Plain Language Arguments

The plain language of § 2339B indicates that the government does not have to prove that the defendant intended to further the FTO's illegal activities.

The clerk begins the plain language arguments subsection with a mini-conclusion.

The current version of § 2339B requires only that a person knowingly provide material support or resources to an FTO with the "knowledge that the organization is a designated terrorist organization" or that the organization has engaged in terrorist activity. 18 U.S.C. § 2339B (Westlaw current through Pub. L. No. 109-94 approved Oct. 26, 2005). Although the court could interpret this phrase to mean that the person must *know* or believe that the organization is likely to use such support to further its terrorist activities, such an interpretation is tenuous at best.

In setting out the plain language arguments, the clerk uses an integrated approach. For example, in this paragraph the clerk sets out both an argument that supports the government's position and an argument that supports the TWHRC's position. Note that the clerk evaluates the TWHRC's argument, saying that it is "tenuous at best."

Three facts support the conclusion that Congress did not want to require the government to prove that the defendant intended to further the FTO's illegal activities. First, in enacting section 2339B's sister statute, section 2339A, Congress included the language "knowing or intending."

The clerk uses this paragraph to introduce three arguments that support the government's position and to set out the first of those three arguments.

18 U.S.C. § 2339A

(a) **Offense.** — Whoever provides material support or resources or conceals or disguises the nature, location, source, or ownership of material support or resources, **knowing or intending** that they are to be used in preparation for, or in carrying out, a violation of. . . .

Note that the clerk introduces the statutes, has edited out irrelevant language, and has highlighted the key terms.

In contrast, in enacting 18 U.S.C. § 2339B, Congress did not include the "knowing or intending" language.

18 U.S.C. § 2339B

(a) Prohibited activities.

(1) Unlawful conduct. **Whoever knowing-lyprovides material support or resources to a foreign terrorist organization**, or attempts or conspires to do so, shall be fined under this title or imprisoned not more than 15 years, or both.... To violate this paragraph, **a person must have knowledge that the organization is a designated terrorist organization . . . , that the organization has engaged or engages in terrorist activity . . . , or that the organization has engaged or engages in terrorism. . . .**

The clerk uses a signpost ("second") to let the judge know that he is moving from the first of the three arguments to the second of the three arguments.	Second, although Congress amended § 2339B in 2004 to clarify the knowledge requirement, it did not add an intent requirement. Pub. L. No. 108-458, § 6603(C). Instead, Congress inserted the following language:
Although this second argument is, arguably, a legislative history argument, the clerk has placed it in her plain language section. When appropriate, you can cross reference or even combine your discussion of the plain language and analogous case arguments.	To violate this paragraph, a person must have knowledge that the organization is a designated terrorist organization (as defined in subsection (g)(6)), that the organization has engaged or engages in terrorist activity (as defined in section 212(a)(3)(B) of the Immigration and Nationality Act), or that the organization has engaged or engages in terrorism (as defined in section 140(d)(2) of the Foreign Relations Authorization Act, Fiscal Years 1988 and 1989). Pub., L. No. 108-458, § 6603(C)
The clerk uses a signpost ("Third,") to let the judge know that he is moving from the second argument to the third and last argument.	Third, in enacting § 2339B, Congress found that "foreign terrorist organizations that engage in terrorist activity are so tainted by their criminal conduct that **any contribution** to such an organization facilitates that conduct." Pub. L. No. 104-132, § 301(a)(7) (emphasis added). This finding strongly suggests that Congress did not want to require proof of intent.
In the topic sentence for this paragraph, the clerk uses the word "however" to alert the judge to the fact that he is moving to an argument that supports TWHRC's position. The clerk sets out one of the possible contingencies. Although the clerk sets out his conclusion at the very beginning and in the first paragraph, evaluates one of the TWHRC's arguments, he does not explain why, taken as a whole, the government's arguments are stronger than the TWHRC's arguments.	The United States Supreme Court has stated, however, that, when possible, the courts should interpret statutes to avoid constitutional difficulties. *United States v. X-Citement Video*, 513 U.S. 64, 73 (1994). *See also* 18 U.S.C. § 2339B(i) (2000), which states that "[n]othing in this section shall be construed or applied so as to abridge the exercise of rights guaranteed under the First Amendment to the Constitution of the United States." Thus, if § 2339B is unconstitutional without an intent requirement, the court could read an intent requirement into the statute.

Question:

How would you revise Examples 2 and 3 to make them better?

§ 13.7.3 Identifying, Setting Out, and Evaluating Legislative History Arguments

Most judges fall into one of two camps: they like to know a statute's legislative history and they give at least some weight to it, or they think that legislative histories are useless because it is impossible to infer Congress's intent from statements made during hearings or on the floor. Thus, before spending too much time on legislative history, check with your judge to see what he or she wants you to include.

In setting out the legislative history, you have several options: you can present the legislative history as a history, describing the events in the order in which they occurred, or you can set out that part of the legislative history that supports one reading of the statute and then the legislative history that supports the other reading of the statute. Compare the following examples.

Analysis Is Weak   EXAMPLE 1

When introducing the bill that included the language that now makes up § 2339B, Senator Hatch stated,

In this example, the clerk jumps feet first into the statute's legislative history.

This bill also includes provisions making it a crime to knowingly provide material support to the terrorist functions of foreign groups designated by a Presidential finding to be engaged in terrorist activities. [N]othing in the Constitution provides the right to engage in violence against fellow citizens or foreign nations. Aiding and financing foreign terrorist bombings is not constitutionally protected activity.... I have to believe that honest donors to any organization want to know if their contributions are being used for such scurrilous terrorist purposes. We are going to be able to tell them that after this bill ... I am convinced we have crafted a narrow but effective designation provision which meets these obligations while safeguarding the freedom to associate, which none of us would willingly give up.

The clerk begins the legislative history section by setting out a long quote from the *Congressional Record*. However, because the clerk has not introduced the quotation or highlighted the key language, the judge does not know why the clerk included the quotation or what to look for in reading it. For example, which approach does this quotation support? The government's position? TWHRC's position?

142 Cong. Rec. S3354 (daily ed. April 16, 1996).

Unexpectedly, the clerk moves from Senator Hatch's statement to a discussion of the amendments. The clerk ends this subsection by setting out his conclusion. Although the conclusion is a reasonable one, the clerk does not state how he got from the legislative history to his conclusion. For example, what is it in Senator Hatch's statement that may support the TWHRC's position?

Section 2339B has been amended twice since it became law; the first amendment increased the penalties associated with violation of the statute, and the second amendment clarified the definitions of training and personnel, as well as adding language to clarify the general intent requirement. 18 U.S.C. § 2339B (Westlaw current through Pub. L. No. 109-94 approved Oct. 26, 2005).

Although Senator Hatch's statement may support the TWHRC's argument, Congress's failure to amend the statute to require proof of specific intent is evidence that Congress does not want to require proof of intent.

EXAMPLE 2:   ## Analysis Is More Sophisticated

B. Legislative History Arguments

The clerk begins this subsection both with a subheading that tells the judge that this subsection contains the legislative history arguments and with a topic sentence that connects this subsection to the prior subsection and then sets out the clerk's conclusion. (All in 30 words, which includes the subheading.)

Like the plain language, 2339B's legislative history suggests that Congress did not intend to require proof that the defendant intended to further the FTO's illegal activities.

The clerk sets out the legislative history using a chronological organizational scheme. In doing so, the clerk integrates a description of the history with a discussion and evaluation of each side's arguments. For example, note the sentence that begins with "Although Senator Hatch's

In introducing the Senate Conference Report on the AEDPA, Senator Hatch, who cosponsored the bill, stated, "[t]his bill also includes provisions making it a crime to knowingly provide material support *to the terrorist functions* of foreign groups designated . . . to be engaged in terrorist activities." 142 Cong. Rec. S3354 (daily ed. April 16, 1996) (statement of Sen. Hatch) (emphasis added). Although Senator Hatch's statement seems to imply that Congress only wanted to prohibit contributions that are intended to further an FTO's terrorist functions, Senator Hatch immediately went on to say, "I am convinced we have crafted a narrow but effective designation provision which meets these obligations while safeguarding the freedom to associate, which none of us would willingly give up." *Id.* This second sentence alters the context in which the first sentence should be interpreted, making it less likely that Senator Hatch was speaking about scienter and more likely that he was speaking about the distinction between punishing mere association with an FTO (which would likely abridge a right granted by the First Amendment) and punishing the conduct of providing material support to an FTO (which would have fewer constitutional implications). These statements do, however, provide evidence that Congress had intended to craft a statute that did not criminalize an overly broad range of behavior and did not abridge any constitutionally protected rights.

統statement. . . ." In this sentence the clerk sets out the weaker argument in the dependent clause, and then sets out and evaluates the stronger argument in the main independent clause. Also note that the clerk does not include a long quote. Instead, he simply quotes the key phrases.

On the same day that Senator Hatch made his comments, Senator Snowe said, "[T]his bill . . . will cut off the ability of terrorist groups . . . to raise huge sums in the United States for supposedly 'humanitarian' purposes, where in reality a large part of those funds go toward conducting terrorist activities." 142 Cong. Rec. S3380 (daily ed. April 16, 1996) (statement of Sen. Snowe). This statement can be interpreted at least two ways. On the one hand, this statement provides some evidence that Congress intended to cut off **all** support from the United States to FTOs, regardless of the ostensible purpose of the donation. On the other hand, this comment could also be read as evidence that Congress intended to prohibit only support for terrorist activities that was cloaked behind a fraudulent façade of humanitarianism. It is not clear from Senator Snowe's statement whether Congress intended to criminalize only those donations of support that in reality go toward conducting humanitarian activities.

In this paragraph, the clerk juxtaposes Senator Hatch's statement with the recent amendment. Implicit in the author's discussion in both the prior paragraph and this paragraph is the clerk's determination that the arguments based on Senator Hatch's statement are weak.

The Congressional statement of findings and purpose regarding § 2339B provides some clarification on this last point: "foreign organizations that engage in terrorist activity are so tainted by their criminal conduct that **any contribution** to such an organization facilitates that conduct." Antiterrorism and Effective Death Penalty Act of 1996, Pub. L. No. 104-132, § 301, 110 Stat 1214 (1996) (emphasis added). This finding provides unequivocal evidence that Congress did in fact intend to criminalize all donations made to FTOs, regardless of the intent of the donor or of the actual use to which the support would be put. Supporting this interpretation, the House Conference Report for the Comprehensive Antiterrorism Act of 1995 (a predecessor of the AEDPA) provides further evidence of Congress's

In this paragraph, the clerk provides the judge with an integrated discussion of whether Congress could have intended to deviate from standard practice and enact a criminal statute that does not require proof of specific intent. The clerk sets out TWHRC's argument and then, without labeling it as such, the government's response.

approach to controlling contributions to terrorist organizations:

> There is no other mechanism, other than an *outright prohibition on contributions*, to effectively prevent such organizations from using funds raised in the United States to further their terrorist activities abroad.... The prohibition is absolutely necessary to achieve the government's compelling interest in protecting the nation's safety from the very real and growing terrorist threat.

H.R. Rep. No. 104-383 at 45 (emphasis added).

In conclusion, the *Congressional Record* contains some support for a holding that § 2339B has a scienter requirement. However, less equivocal evidence in the record supports a holding that to convict under § 2339B, the government would need only to prove that the defendants knew they were providing material support to an organization that they knew had been designated as an FTO.

§ 13.7.4 Identifying, Setting Out, and Evaluating Arguments Based on Case Law

If the issue that you have been asked to research is an issue of first impression, there are, by definition, no controlling cases. The only cases will be cases from other jurisdictions or cases that discuss analogous statutes or issues.

If there are cases from other jurisdictions, you will usually want to tell the judge about those cases. In doing so, your focus will not be on the facts of those cases; rather, your focus will be on the rule that the courts in the other jurisdictions applied. What rule did the court apply, and why did it apply that rule rather than some other rule? If you note a problem with the court's reasoning, alert your judge to that problem.

In the following example, Example 1, the clerk has forgotten why he is describing the court's decision in *Al-Arian*: instead of focusing on what the court did and why, the clerk devotes most of the description to a summary of the facts, which in this particular situation is of little use or interest to the judge.

Poor Analogous Case Description

EXAMPLE 1

C. Analogous Case Arguments

The TWHRC will ask the court to take the approach that the United States District Court for the Middle District of Florida took in *United States v. Al-Arian*, 308 F. Supp. 2d 1322 (M.D. Fla. 2004). In that case, the government filed criminal charges against members of the Palestinian Islamic Jihad-Shiqaqi Faction (the PIJ), who purportedly operated and directed fundraising and other organizational activities in the United States for almost twenty years. The PIJ is a foreign organization that uses violence, principally suicide bombings, and threats of violence to pressure Israel to cede territory to the Palestinian people.

> **The clerk's heading and topic sentence are good: the heading tells the judge the topic, and the topic sentence tells the judge that the clerk is setting out the TWHRC's arguments.**

Count 1 of the indictment alleged a wide ranging pattern of racketeering activity beginning in 1984 and lasting through February 2003, including murder, extortion, and money laundering. The indictment detailed some 256 overt acts, ranging from soliciting and raising funds to providing management and organizational and logistical support for the PIJ. The overt act section of the indictment detailed numerous suicide bombings and attacks by PIJ members causing the deaths of over 100 people, including two United States citizens, and injuries to over 350 people, including seven United States citizens.

> **In this paragraph the clerk sets out the facts, which are, we agree, interesting. Unfortunately, this is not the information the judge needs. While the judge needs a quick summary of the facts, the focus needs to be on the court's reasoning.**

In its decision, the court concluded that to convict a defendant under Section 2339B(a)(1), the government had to prove beyond a reasonable doubt that the defendant knew that (a) the organization was an FTO or had committed unlawful activities that caused it to be so designated and (b) what he was furnishing was "material support." In addition, the court concluded that the government also had to prove that the defendant had a specific intent that the support would further the illegal activities of an FTO. *See Al-Arian*, 329 F. Supp. at 1297.

> **Although the clerk tells the judge what the court concluded, he does not tell the judge why the court reached the conclusion that it reached. For example, the clerk does not tell the judge why the *Al-Arian* judge rejected the Ninth Circuit's approach.**

In Example 2, the law clerk has done a better job giving the judge the information that he or she needs.

Better Example

EXAMPLE 2

While the court's decision in *United States v. Al-Arian*, 329 F. Supp. 2d 1294 (M.D. Fla. 2004), supports the defendants' position, the court's reasoning is no longer sound.

> **The clerk begins her description of the analogous cases by telling the judge the court's reasoning in *Al-Arian* is no longer sound.**

The clerk then describes *Al-Arian*. In doing so, her focus is not on the facts of the case but on the district court's reasoning.

In *Al-Arian*, the United States District Court for the Middle District of Florida read an intent requirement into 18 U.S.C. § 2339B. *Id.* In concluding that the government had to prove that the defendants intended to further the FTO's illegal activities, the court stated that "where a statute is susceptible of two constructions, by one of which grave and doubtful constitutional questions arise and by the other of which such questions are avoided, our duty is to adopt the latter." *Id.* at 1299 (quoting *Jones v. United States*, 526 U.S. 227, 239 (1999)).

The clerk evaluates the district court's reasoning in *Al-Arian*, explaining why, given the recent amendment, the district court's reasoning is no longer sound.

Although the version of § 2339B that the Florida court interpreted may have been susceptible to a construction requiring specific intent, the amended version is not. Before Congress amended § 2339B, there were multiple ways to interpret the statute. The statute could have been read as providing for a strict liability offense. Alternatively, it could have been read to require knowledge that the organization was a designated FTO or knowledge of the organization's conduct to give rise to its designation as an FTO. Finally, it is even feasible that the statute implied that the person providing material support must at least know or believe that the FTO was likely to use such support for terrorist activities, which seems to be the construction accepted by the Florida court. However, the recent amendment makes it clear that, in order to violate the statute, a person must only have knowledge of the organization's designation or the activities that gave rise to the designation. At the time of the amendment, Congress had the opportunity to adopt the holding of *Humanitarian II* or *Al-Arian*. Congress chose to adopt the approach taken in *Humanitarian II*.

While in our example problem there were cases from other jurisdictions that were on point, you may come across a situation in which there are no cases, either in your jurisdiction or in any other jurisdiction. In such situations, include a sentence telling the judge that there are no cases that are on point.

EXAMPLE

Sentence Telling the Judge That There Are No Cases on Point

To date, there are no reported cases involving [include reference to statute].

In other situations you may be asked to work on a case in which one of the parties has cited a case that you have determined is not on point. When this happens, tell the judge that the case is not on point and explain why.

EXAMPLE

Sentence Telling the Judge That Case Is Not on Point

Although the plaintiffs use *Smith v. Jones* to support their argument, that case is not on point. While the present case involves a criminal statute, *Smith* involved a civil statute. Similarly, although the defendants cite *United States v. Morgan* as authority, that case applied a statute that has since been repealed.

---

§ 13.7.5 Identifying, Setting Out, and Evaluating Policy Arguments

When a case involves an issue of first impression, the most persuasive arguments are often policy arguments. Thus, identify each side's policy arguments, and then briefly summarize them. In doing so, look both at what would be "just" in the case that is currently before the court and at the bigger picture. In future cases, what rule would be the best rule?

D. Policy Argument

In deciding how to interpret § 2339B, the court should consider two types of policy arguments: (1) the United States' interest in protecting its citizens from terrorism versus the United States' interest in providing individuals with humanitarian aid and (2) constitutional issues.

(1) Protecting Citizens from Terrorism vs. Providing Humanitarian Aid

While the public policy of "protecting the nation's safety from the very real and growing terrorist threat" is compelling and should not be undermined, that policy is not absolute: it must be balanced against the goals of encouraging humanitarian charitable donations and not punishing innocent conduct.

A. The Medicine Exemption

While the list of items and services that constitute prohibited "material support" is long and broad, Congress chose not to prohibit donations of "medicine or religious material" to FTOs. 18 U.S.C. § 2339A (2000). While this exemption might be interpreted as to allow the donation of humanitarian aid in general, the legislative history behind the medicine exemption indicates that it was not intended to apply so broadly. First, the medicine exemption is not a clear indicator of a legislative intent to allow humanitarian aid as a matter of policy because the amendment that added the medicine exemption to § 2339A was passed by only one vote in committee. H.R. Rep. No. 104-383 at 73. Furthermore, the report from that committee states, " 'Medicine' should be understood to be limited to the medicine itself, and does not include the vast array of medical supplies." H.R. Rep. No. 104-518 at 114, 1996 U.S.C.C.A.N. (110 Stat 1214) 947. Thus, the medicine exemption was not intended to be a general-purpose humanitarian aid exemption.

Congress's actual intent behind the medicine exemption is more difficult to infer. Because it is relatively easily sold, donated medicine could certainly be converted to nonhumanitarian use. Thus, the medicine exemption would appear to provide a bad-faith medicine donor with a potential route around § 2339B's prohibitions. However, because Congress has not done away with the exemption on any of the occasions it has amended § 2339A, Congress seems content to live with this potential loophole.

Even if the medicine exemption was not intended to allow groups to provide humanitarian aid to FTOs, it could be interpreted as evidence that, as a matter of policy, § 2339B should not prohibit humanitarian aid given without any intent to further an FTO's terrorist agenda. A narrow interpretation of the medicine exemption would, in fact, create the absurd situation where it would be permissible to donate Viagra to an FTO, but a felony to donate band-aids; permissible to donate Prozac, but a felony to donate water purification tablets.

In addition, the court might allow the donation of humanitarian aid on policy grounds because groups designated as FTOs "often do much more than commit terrorist acts. They also undertake important and worthwhile charitable, humanitarian, educational, or political activities." Randolph N. Jonakait, *The Mens Rea for the Crime of Providing Material Resources to a Foreign Terrorist Organization*, 56 Baylor L. Rev. 861, 873 (2004). If the court holds that § 2339B has no scienter requirement, charitable giving that ought to be encouraged by a rich country like the United States "will have taken on previously unknown risks" because donors who seek only to support an FTO's humanitarian agenda could be subjected to criminal penalties. *Id.*

On the other hand, any broadening of the medicine exemption would conflict with Congress's intent to make an outright prohibition on contributions from the United States to FTOs and interfere with Congress's larger goal of combating terrorism. *See* H.R. Rep. No. 104-383 at 45. In addition, any exemption for humanitarian aid would be extremely difficult to administer so as to ensure that the humanitarian aid was not subverted to further the FTO's terrorist agenda:

> [T]errorist organizations do not maintain organizational structures or "fire-walls" to prevent resources donated for humanitarian purposes from being used to commit or support terrorist acts . . . even if funds or goods raised for charitable purposes are in fact so used, the addition of such items to the coffers of terrorist groups frees funds raised from other sources for use in facilitating terrorist acts. Thus, humanitarian support, however well-intentioned, increases the resources that a terrorist organization can devote to terrorist ends.

Brief for the Appellees/Cross-Appellants at 16-17, *Humanitarian Law Project v. U.S. Dept. of Justice*, 352 F.3d 382 (9th Cir. 2003) (No. 02-55082).

As a matter of policy, the government recognizes that any material support, training, or donations made to an FTO are "dangerous quite apart from the specific intent of the donor." *Id.* at 9-10. In other words, a humanitarian intent on the part of the donor does not restrict an FTO's use of the donated goods to peaceful purposes.

Congress's stated policy of preventing all contributions to FTOs is certainly undermined by the medicine exemption, and it may be that the medicine exemption cannot be completely reconciled with the policy behind the antiterrorism statutes. But the mere fact that § 2339B is not completely consistent between its language and the policies it seeks to further is not grounds for effectively abandoning those policies by creating a loophole as large as the one that would be created if the court interprets the medicine exemption broadly. Even so, without creating a large loophole, the court should interpret the policies behind § 2339B as allowing only those humanitarian donations that would not serve to further an FTO's terrorist agenda.

B. Constitutional Issues

The policy that "wrongdoing must be conscious to be criminal" is fundamental to our justice system. *Morissette v. United States,* 342 U.S. 246, 252 (1952). The courts have long required proof of some kind of criminal intent to "protect those who were not blameworthy in mind from conviction." *Id.* The latest amendment to § 2339B (to violate the statute, a person must "have knowledge that the organization is a designated terrorist organization"), 18 U.S.C. § 2339(B) purports to adhere to this concept because, to be convicted, defendants must have known that they provided material support to an organization and must have known that the organization was an FTO (or had engaged in or engages in acts of terrorism). *See, e.g., Humanitarian II,* 352 F.3d at 399; Jonakait, *supra,* at 875. This interpretation of the statute, however, leads to absurd results insofar as it means that a cab driver could be guilty for giving a ride to an FTO member if the cab driver knew that the person was a member of an FTO or that the person was a member of an organization that had engaged in terrorist activity. *United States v. Al-Arian,* 329 F. Supp. 2d 1294, 1337-38, *modification denied,* 329 F. Supp. 2d 1294 (M.D. Fla. 2004).

To avoid similar problems of absurdity, some courts have held that statutes should not be interpreted "so as to sweep within a crime otherwise significant innocent activities." *Staples v. United States,* 511 U.S. 600, 610 (1994) (quoting *Liparota v. United States,* 471 U.S. 419, 426 (1985)); *see also United States v. X-Citement Video,* 513 U.S. 64, 69 (1994); Jonakait, *supra,* at 876-77. Accordingly, "the Supreme Court and [the Ninth] circuit have construed Congress' [sic] inclusion of the word 'knowingly' to require proof of knowledge of the law and an intent to further the proscribed act." *Humanitarian 2003,* 352 F.3d at 399.

Finally, make sure that your writing is concise and precise and that you have not made any grammatical, punctuation, or citation errors. See Chapters 14, 27, and 28.

14

Revising, Editing, and Proofreading a Prehearing Memo

ne of the greatest compliments that you can receive as a judicial extern or judicial clerk is to have the judge incorporate your analysis, your language, or — best of all — both into an order or opinion. To increase the chances of this happening, make sure that you leave enough time to revise, edit, and proofread the prehearing memos you submit.

§ 14.1 Revising

We end this book, Book 2, where we started: with a discussion of audience and purpose. In revising a prehearing memo, start by thinking about your audience and your purpose. In particular, ask yourself the following questions.

a. Did You Answer the Question the Judge Asked?

If the judge asked you to research a particular issue, make sure that you researched that issue. Similarly, if the judge asked you to write a more general prehearing memo, make sure you did that.

b. Did You Give the Judge the Information He or She Needs — Nothing More and Nothing Less?

Never forget that judges are busy. As a conscientious extern or clerk, you will want to be thorough, but temper the "overly thorough" impulse with some common sense about just how much you should put in the prehearing memo. As a general rule, do not discuss every possible issue and subissue, every possible argument, and every case the parties may cite. Instead, give the judge the information that he or she needs and then stop.

c. Did You Use the Format and Tone the Judge Prefers?

As we noted at the beginning of Chapter 13, different judges prefer different formats. For example, different judges will want you to include different sections in your memo, to order those sections in various ways, or to use a particular set of labels for the sections. In addition, while some judges will want you to use a formal writing style, others will want a more informal memo.

d. Did You Use an Organizational Scheme That Makes Sense Not Only to You But Also to the Judge?

Most first drafts are "writer-based": the writer sets out the material in an order that makes sense to him or her. While sometimes the writer's organization scheme will also make sense to the intended reader, that is not always the case. Therefore, after finishing the first draft, step back and look at your draft from your reader's point of view. Is the organizational scheme that you selected one that makes sense not only to you but also to the judge? If it doesn't, revise your draft. Remember: you are writing for the judge, not for yourself.

e. Have You Included Reader-Friendly Roadmaps, Signposts, and Transitions?

Once you have the right information in the right order, make sure you have included enough roadmaps, signposts, and transitions so the judge can easily follow your analysis. For example, in the following example, the clerk uses the rule as a roadmap.

EXAMPLE   **Rule That Serves as Roadmap**

In determining whether 18 U.S.C. § 2339B requires specific or general intent, the courts first look to the plain language of the statute. *Boim v. Quranic Literacy Inst. and Holy Land Found. for Relief and Dev.*, 291 F.3d 1000, 1009 (7th Cir. 2002). If the plain language of the statute is ambiguous or would produce an absurd result, the courts then look at the statute's legislative history, the policies underlying the statute, and how other jurisdictions have interpreted the statute. *See id.*

Questions

After reading the roadmap set out above, what do you expect to see? Do you expect to see a discussion of the plain language of the statute? What do you expect to see after the discussion of the statute's plain language?

§ 14.2 Editing

Once you are confident about the large- and small-scale organization, double check your sentences to make sure they are easy to read and understand. As part of your sentence check, make sure your writing is both precise and concise.

§ 14.2.1 Write Effective Sentences

As you learned on pages 178-184 in Chapter 8, you can usually improve your writing by following four simple rules.

1. Use the actor as the subject of most sentences.
2. Keep the subject and verb close together.
3. Put old information at the beginning of the sentence and new information at the end.
4. Vary sentence lengths and patterns.

Most readers would agree that the following paragraph, which is taken from the end of the court's decision in *Al-Arian*, is well written. In addition to including a good topic sentence and good transitions, Judge Moody used the actor as the subject of most of the sentences, the subjects and verbs are close together, old information is at the beginning of the sentence and new information is at the end, and there is a good mix of shorter and longer sentences and different sentence patterns. In the example, the subject of each sentence is in bold, the verb is underlined, and the number of words in the sentence is set out in the parenthetical at the end of each sentence. In the margin, there is a note saying whether the sentences were written in active or passive voice.

Excerpt from *Al-Arian*   EXAMPLE

"This **Court** <u>does</u> not <u>believe</u> this burden is that great in the typical case. (14) Often, such an **intent** <u>will be easily inferred</u>. (8) For example, a **jury** <u>could infer</u> a specific intent to further the illegal activities of a FTO when a defendant knowingly provides weapons, explosives, or lethal substances to an organization that he knows is a FTO because of the nature of the support. (43) Likewise, a **jury** <u>could infer</u> a specific intent when a defendant knows that the organization continues to commit illegal acts and the defendant provides funds to that organization knowing that money is fungible and, once

Active voice
Passive voice
Active voice

Active voice

Active voice   received, the donee can use the funds for any purpose it chooses. (47) That is, by its nature, **money** <u>carries</u> an inherent danger for furthering the illegal aims of an organization.

Active voice   (18) **Congress** <u>said</u> as much when it found that FTOs were 'so tainted by their criminal conduct that any contribution to such an organization facilitates that conduct.' (26) Pub. L. No. 104-132, § 301(a)(7)."

Questions

In the example set out above, was Judge Moody's decision to write the second sentence using the passive voice a good one? Why or why not? Did Judge Moody put old information at the beginning of sentences and new information at the end?

One of the best ways to check your sentences is to read your writing aloud. As you read, mark the sentences that are hard to read or that do not sound quite right. Then, after you have finished reading your draft, go back to those sentences and check first to see whether you have used the actor as the subject of the sentence and whether your subject and verb are close together.

In addition to following the four rules set out above, try to write sentences that not only start strong but also end strong. For example, while the following sentences start strong, they have weak endings.

EXAMPLE 1   ### Sentence Has a Strong Beginning but a Weak Ending

These freedoms are delicate and vulnerable, as well as supremely precious in our society.

EXAMPLE 2   ### Sentence Has a Strong Beginning but a Weak Ending

Because First Amendment freedoms need breathing space to survive, government may regulate in the area only with narrow specificity.

In Example 1, the sentence begins with a well-turned phrase. "These freedoms are delicate and vulnerable...." While some readers may also like the next phrase, "as supremely precious," other readers would say that the writer "goes over the top" when he uses the word "supremely." Almost all readers would agree that the last phrase, "in our society," dilutes the impact of the sentence. Instead of putting the most important point at the end of the sentence in the position of emphasis, the author added an unnecessary point. Similarly, in Example 2, the sentence starts with the effective use of personification: "Because the First Amendment needs breathing space to survive...." However, the author drops the personification and ends the sentence with a good, but poorly articulated, point. It seems almost as though the author gets tired of his own sentences before he finishes them. In your own writing, strive to finish strong.

§ 14.2.2 Use Language Precisely

In Chapter 11 we discussed the importance of using terms of art such as "held," "find," "element," and "factor" precisely. See pages 272-273. It is, however, just as important to use words that are specific to your statute or common law rule precisely.

Sometimes using words precisely is easy. For example, in discussing the "open and notorious" element of adverse possession, you know that you should use the term "open and notorious" and not synonyms that you find in a thesaurus. At other times and in other contexts, you may inadvertently and mistakenly start using slightly different words or phrases for key terms. For example, in our sample problem, instead of using the language of the statute, you may find yourself shortening the phrase "material support or resources" to "material support," or you may find that you start using completely different phrases, for example, "material assistance" or "humanitarian aid." While variations in phrasing do not always change the meaning of the statute, sometimes they do, and when they do, the writing is imprecise. For instance, "humanitarian aid" is a much narrower term than "material support or resources." That change in phrasing is not just a matter of variety in vocabulary; the change in phrasing changes the analysis.

The bottom line, then, is to use terms of art and statutory language precisely. Variety can be a good thing in writing, but you should know when and when not to use synonyms. When it comes to terms of art or statutory language, consistency is the virtue that will keep your writing precise.

Questions

What should you do if the statute uses one word or phrase and the courts use a different word or phrase? What should you do if some courts use one word or phrase and other courts use a different word or phrase?

§ 14.2.3 Edit Out the Extra Sentences, Clauses, Phrases, and Words

One judge we know has a hard and fast rule: no prehearing memo can be more than three single-spaced pages. Although at times it might seem impossible to comply with such a rule, in most cases, if you understand the issue, the law, and the arguments, you can get your memo down to just a couple of pages. However, to do so, you will have to make every sentence, every clause, every phrase, and every word count. Look, for instance, at the following excerpt from a bench memo written by an extern:

EXAMPLE 1:   **First Draft (128 words)**

The initial focus of statutory analysis is the plain meaning of the language of the statute itself. *Boim,* 291 F. Supp. 2d at 1009. As written, the plain meaning of 18 U.S.C. § 2339B does not require the government to demonstrate that a defendant possessed the *mens rea* of specific intent to support illegal terrorist acts. Instead, the defendant violates the statute only if he or she "knowingly provide[d] material support or resources to a foreign terrorist organization" with the "knowledge that the organization is a designated terrorist organization" or that the organization engages in terrorist activities. 18 U.S.C. § 2339B(a)(1). The language does not state a requirement that the defendant must intend for the material support to contribute directly to a criminal terrorist act by the FTO.

EXAMPLE   **Revised Draft: (90 words)**

In analyzing a statute, the courts look first at the plain meaning of the statute's language. *Boim,* 291 F. Supp. 2d at 1009. In the present case, 18 U.S.C. § 2339B does not require the government to prove that a defendant intended to support illegal terrorist acts. Instead, the government need only prove that the defendant "knowingly provide[d] material support or resources to a foreign terrorist organization" with the "knowledge that the organization is a designated terrorist organization" or that the organization engages in terrorist activities. 18 U.S.C. § 2339B(a)(1).

Question

What techniques did the author use to get the first draft, which was 128 words, down to 91 words? (Review section 25.2.)

§ 14.3 Revising and Editing for Style

In Chapters 8 and 11 we encouraged you to think of revising and editing as two separate processes: during the revising process, you re-vision what you have written, and during the editing process, you work on writing easy-to-read sentences and on using language that is both precise and concise. There are times, however, when an insight during the revising process leads you to the perfect word or phrase or when, during the editing process, the selection of a particular word or phrase allows you to see the issue and your analysis in a completely new, and more sophisticated, light. Do not ignore these opportunities.

In addition, when time permits, take the time to develop the perfect metaphor or to turn the perfect phrase. For a bit of inspiration and instruction, read the material in Chapter 26 on eloquence, and then use one or more of the techniques described in that chapter. Once you have tried a technique, step back from your writing and see if the technique that you used works. If it does, keep what you have written. If it does not, go back to your original draft.

Turning the perfect phrase or coming up with the perfect metaphor takes not only a good vocabulary and a storehouse of images, but also confidence and the willingness to take a chance. You need

to have confidence in your analysis, you need to have confidence in your ability to use language, and you need to be willing to risk the judge's red pen.

The following sentences are taken from first-year students' prehearing memos. Which examples work and why?

Excerpt from Prehearing Memo

EXAMPLE 1

The spike in prosecutions for violations of section 2339B was followed by an increase in judicial scrutiny. The level of intent required by the statute and the broad definition of "material support" were most commonly under the magnifying glass of the courts.

Excerpt from Prehearing Memo

EXAMPLE 2

Although facing an uphill battle with the plain and unambiguous text of the statute, the plaintiffs can draw the court's attention to statutory construction canons laid out by the United States Supreme Court, which state that statutes are to be interpreted in a manner that avoids constitutional difficulties.

Excerpt from Prehearing Memo

EXAMPLE 3

Indeed, the courts are often called upon to balance protecting the security of the Nation against protecting the very liberties upon which it was founded. However, despite powerful policy concerns that would urge the adoption of a limited *mens rea* requirement for section 2339B, the principle of personal guilt upon which the foundations of our notions of criminal liability are built cannot easily be set aside.

§ 14.4　Proofreading

Many judges have pet peeves. For some, it is the incorrect use of apostrophes, for others dangling modifiers, and for still others, typing "statue" instead of "statute." Therefore, while you should try to eliminate all of the grammar, punctuation, and typographical errors from your drafts, at a minimum make sure that you do not make an error that will trigger your judge's "hot button."

Here are ten common errors that annoy many judges:

1. Incorrect use of apostrophes (See section 28.4 and the Glossary of Usage).

"Its" is a pronoun.
"It's" is a contraction for "it is."

"John Jones's car" is the singular possessive.
"The Joneses' car" is the plural possessive.

2. Dangling modifiers (See section 27.6.2).

Incorrect:
Applying this rule, it is clear . . . .

Correct:
Applying this rule, the court concluded . . . .

3. Misplaced modifiers (See section 27.6.1).

Incorrect:
Hidden under his bed, the defendant had wrapped the weapon in an old pillow-case.

Correct:
The defendant had wrapped the weapon in an old pillowcase and hidden it under his bed.

4. Pronouns that do not agree with the noun (See section 27.4.2).

Incorrect:
The company claims that they did not violate the contract.

Correct:
The company claims that it did not violate the contract.

5. Lack of parallelism for items in a list (See section 27.7).

Incorrect:
A jury could infer specific intent to further an FTO's illegal activities when a defendant knowingly provides weapons, explosives, or knows the funds will be used to buy lethal substances.

Correct:
A jury could infer specific intent to further an FTO's illegal activities when a defendant knowingly provides weapons, explosives, or funds for lethal substances.

6. Comma splices (See section 28.6.1).

Incorrect:
The plaintiffs seek to support the humanitarian effort of the FTO, they do not seek to support the FTO's illegal activities.

Correct:
The plaintiffs seek to support the humanitarian effort of the FTO; they do not seek to support the FTO's illegal activities.

7. Typos that result from relying on Spellcheck (See section 29.1).

"trail" rather than "trial"
"judgement" rather than "judgment"

8. Overuse of "clearly" (See section 24.6.5).

First Draft:
The plain language of the statute clearly favors the government's interpretation of section 2339B's intent requirement.

Revised:
The plain language of the statute favors the government's interpretation of section 2339B's intent requirement.

First Draft:
Clearly, the facts illustrate that the plaintiff clearly intended to support humanitarian efforts, not terrorist activities.

Revised:
The facts illustrate that the plaintiff intended to support humanitarian efforts, not terrorist activities.

9. Incorrect or missing pinpoint citations (See Rule 12.5(b) in the *ALWD Citation Manual* and pages 7-9 in the Eighteenth Edition of *The Bluebook*).

Incorrect:
Two years later, the Ninth Circuit Court of Appeals struck down portions of section 2339B on First and Fifth Amendment grounds. *See Humanitarian Law Project v. U.S. Dept. of Justice*, 352 F.3d 382 (9th Cir. 2003), *vacated by* 393 F.3d 902 (9th Cir. 2004) (*Humanitarian 2003*).

Correct:
Two years later, the Ninth Circuit Court of Appeals struck down portions of section 2339B on First and Fifth Amendment grounds. *See Humanitarian Law Project v. U.S. Dept. of Justice*, 352 F.3d 382, 403 (9th Cir. 2003), *vacated by* 393 F.3d 902 (9th Cir. 2004) (*Humanitarian 2003*).

10. Incorrect or misusing citation signals (See Rule 45 in the *ALWD Citation Manual* and Rule 1.2 in the Eighteenth Edition of *The Bluebook*.

Incorrect:
Although facing an uphill battle with the plain and unambiguous text of the statute, the plaintiffs can draw the court's attention to statutory construction canons laid out by the United States Supreme Court, which state that statutes are to be interpreted in a manner that avoids constitutional difficulties. *Jones v. United States*, 526 U.S. 227, 233 (1999).

Correct:
Although facing an uphill battle with the plain and unambiguous text of the statute, the plaintiffs can draw the court's attention to statutory construction canons laid out by the United States Supreme Court, which state that statutes are to be interpreted in a manner that avoids constitutional difficulties. *See, e.g., Jones v. United States*, 526 U.S. 227, 233 (1999).

§ 14.5 Reflecting on the Process

The AEDPA problem set out in this Part, Part 3 of Book 2, raises the same issue that is raised each time the President nominates a judge for a position on the United States Supreme Court, the United States Court of Appeals, or the United States District Court. How far should a judge go in interpreting the Constitution or a federal statute? For example, in this case did Judge Moody go too far in reading an intent requirement into 18 U.S.C. § 2339B? Should the Ninth Circuit have held that the statute, as amended, is unconstitutional? What is the right balance between being an activist judge and a strict constructionist?

The AEDPA problem also raises another issue. What is your role as a judicial extern or a judicial clerk? For example, does your particular judge want you to play the role of the devil's advocate, testing his or her values, assumptions, and analysis, or does your judge want you to play the role of a scribe, accepting his or her decision and reasoning without questioning it? Depending on the role that the judge wants you to play, what would you do if you think that the judge's decision is biased or his or her reasoning is flawed?

§ 14.6 Sample Memos

By now we hope you know that there is almost always more than one way to analyze an issue, more than one way to organize a discussion section, and more than one way to craft a particular paragraph or sentence. The three sample memos that are set out on the CD that came with this book illustrate this point. All three memos were written by first-year law students and all are good.

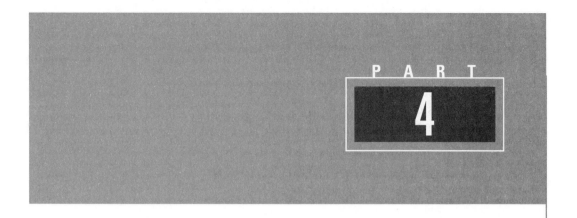

Drafting Letters to Clients

Introduction: The Assignment

In the first three parts of this book, Book 2, we described the process of researching, drafting, and revising, editing, and proofreading an objective memorandum. In this part, we tackle a slightly different but perhaps even more common type of legal writing: letters to clients.

As an attorney, you will write many different types of letters to clients. You will, for example, write letters confirming that you have agreed to represent a particular individual and the fee agreement, letters updating your client about the status of his or her case, and letters like the ones that we describe in the next two chapters: opinion letters that explain the law and your client's options.

For the purposes of the next two chapters assume that you are an attorney in Austin, Texas, and that you represent Mary Corner, who has just purchased a restaurant in a historic building in the Austin Historic District. On September 11, 2006, Ms. Corner filed an application for a permit to install two six feet by four feet painted signs on the front of her new restaurant, the Corner Café, which is located in the corner of a building that has been designated as a Historic Landmark. One sign would be on the north side of the building, and the other sign would be on the west side of the building. Each sign would extend eighteen inches above the roof line and would have a beige background and green lettering. At night, the signs would be lit by a small light installed under the sign. On October 2, 2006, the Historic Landmark Commission denied Ms. Corner's application and gave her fourteen days to appeal its decision. Ms. Corner wants to know whether she should appeal the Commission's decision.

CHAPTER 15

Researching Issues Governed by County and City Ordinances

I f you are like many law students, when you applied to law school you envisioned yourself working on the big issues: you saw yourself prosecuting or defending individuals charged with felonies, investigating major corporate scandals, or working to enforce treaties protecting the environment or basic human rights.

Although you may end up working on high-profile cases or issues of national or international importance, it is also likely that you will work on smaller, more local cases, cases that are governed not by federal or state statutes or international treaties but by county or city ordinances. While these cases may not make the front page of anything other than your local newspaper, they involve important issues, For, it is often county and city ordinances that determine what may and may not be built in a neighborhood, what a local business may and may not do, and what types of signs a business can post on the front of its business.

§ 15.1 Introduction to County and City Government

Most state constitutions give the state legislature the power to create counties and the people within the affected area the power to create a city. See, for example, section 2 of the Illinois Constitution and Article XI, section 3, of the Washington Constitution.

Although the process varies from state to state, in most states the people within the affected area may create a city by voting to incorporate. In general, cities operate under a charter. Like our federal and state constitutions, charters establish the form of government and set out the powers granted to the city.

Most counties and cities have three branches of government: a legislative branch (for example, a county or city council), which enacts legislation; an executive branch (for example, a county executive, mayor, or city manager), which enforces that legislation; and a court system (for example, a district or municipal court), which has limited jurisdiction.

§ 15.2 Creating a Research Plan for an Issue Governed by County or City Ordinances

Because many cases involving county or city ordinances involve either small amounts of money or are brought by individuals with limited resources, you will often need to research these issues quickly and inexpensively. Thus, the first research plan is designed to help you answer relatively simple questions in just an hour or two using free sources. There will, of course, be other cases in which you will need to do more thorough research. The second research plan is designed to help you research those issues.

Plan No. 1
Research Plan for Quickly and Inexpensively Researching an Issue Governed by a County or City Ordinance

Jurisdiction:	[Enter the name of the county or city.]
Type of Law:	Enacted law
Preliminary Issue Statement:	[Put your first draft of the issue statement here.]

Step 1:	Locate your county's or city's ordinances on the county's or city's website or on a free website that collects and publishes ordinances — for example, *FindLaw.com* or *Municode.com*.
Step 2:	Read and analyze the applicable section or sections and then apply the plain language of those sections to the facts of your case.

Plan No. 2
Research Plan for Doing More Thorough Research of an Issue
Governed by a County or City Ordinance

Jurisdiction:	[Enter the name of the county or city.]
Type of Law:	Enacted law
Preliminary Issue Statement:	[Put your first draft of the issue statement here.]

Step 1:   Locate your county's or city's ordinances on the county's or city's website or on a free website that collects and publishes ordinances — for example, *FindLaw.com* or *Municode.com.*

Step 2:   Read and analyze the applicable sections, determining whether the ordinance is constitutional, and/or identifying the elements, determining which elements appear to be in dispute. If none of the elements is likely to be in dispute, stop researching. If, however, one or more of the elements are likely to be in dispute, research the disputed elements using Steps 3-6.

Step 3:   Using free Internet websites, look for articles that discuss the area of law. Using those articles identify cases that may be on point.

Step 4:   Using free Internet sites, books, or fee-based services, locate copies of cases that are on point.

Step 5:   Before you decide to use a case, cite check the case to determine (1) whether the case is still good law and (2) whether there are any additional cases that discuss the same point. Look up and, if appropriate, cite check any additional cases that you locate through cite checking.

Step 6:   If appropriate, locate law review articles and other commentaries that might be on point.

§ 15.3 Sources for Researching Issues Governed by City and County Ordinances

In researching issues governed by city and county ordinances, you will usually be looking for one or more of the following documents.

a. Charters

In most cases, you will not need to find a copy of the county's or city's charter. For example, you will not need to find a copy of a charter when common sense tells you that the county or city had the power to enact a particular ordinance or to do a particular act.

There will, however, be times when you do need to find a copy of the charter. In these cases, look first on the county's or city's website. To do this, use a search engine like Google or Yahoo and type in the name of the city, the name of the state, and the word "charter." In the alternative, look for a website that collects and publishes charters for the counties or cities in your state or contact your county or city offices and ask the clerk to email you an electronic copy of the charter or to mail you a paper copy. There may be a fee for paper copies.

See Exercise 15A in the *Practice Book*.

b. Ordinances

Many cities and counties post copies of their ordinances on their official county or city webpage or with a free service like *FindLaw.com* or *Municode. com*. In addition, some fee-based services collect and publish copies of county and city codes. For example, you can find copies of many county and city ordinances on Loislaw, and you can find some county and city ordinances on LexisNexis and Westlaw. As a last resort, you can usually obtain paper copies of the ordinances from either the county or city clerk or at the local public library.

Because not all counties and cities update their materials on a regular basis, always check to make sure that the ordinances you find are the ordinances that govern. For example, if the cause of action arose in the past, make sure that you have the ordinances that were in effect at the time the cause of action arose. In contrast, if you are advising a client about what it may or may not do in the future, make sure that you know what the ordinances currently say and what changes have been proposed.

See Exercise 15B in the *Practice Book*.

c. Other County and City Documents

Sometimes you will need to find copies of other county and city documents. For example, you may want to find the minutes of a county or city council meeting to find out what the council intended when it adopted a particular ordinance; you may want to find the decisions of a county or city commission, department, or agency; or you might want to find a record that was filed with a county or city. Although you may be able to find some of this information on the county's, city's, commission's, or department's website, more likely than not you will have to obtain that information from the county or city itself.

§ 15.4 Researching the Signage Issue

The first step in researching the signage issue set out in the Introduction, which is on page 351, is to modify the research plan. Because the signage issue is more likely than not a relatively simple issue, we start with Plan 1, modifying it so that it works for this particular problem.

Modified Version of Plan No. 1

Jurisdiction: Austin, Texas

Type of Law: Enacted law

Preliminary Issue Statement: What types of business signs are allowed
                                               in the Austin Historic District?

Step 1:   Locate the Austin, Texas, ordinances dealing with business
             signs in the Austin Historic District using a free website.
Step 2:   Read and analyze the applicable section or sections and
             determine what types of business signs are allowed in the
             Austin Historic District.

With a research plan in mind, you begin your research by looking for a
free website that sets out the current version of the City of Austin ordinances.
One way to find such a site is to use the "Advanced Search" option[1] on
Google. See Exhibit 15.1, which is on the CD that came with this book.

When you want to find a city's official website, use
the phrase "city of" and the name of the city rather
than just the name of the city. To find ordinances,
use the word "ordinances" in your search.

Your search retrieves the list set out in Exhibit 15.2.[2] Because the first
link seems to set out Austin ordinances and seems to be reliable (the
URL "*www.ci.austin.tx.us/*" indicates that the site is some type of official
website), you click on that link. When you do, the page set out in Exhibit
15.3. appears.

When your Google search retrieves more than
one entry from the same website, the second entry
will be indented. See, for example, the URL entries
that are indented in Exhibit 15.2.

---

1. To find the "Advanced Search" option, go to *Google.com*. Near the top of the page you
will see the box that can be used to type in your search terms for regular searches. To the right of
that box is a list of options. Click on the "Advanced Search" option.
2. Because the Internet is constantly changing, the list that you retrieve may be different
from the list set out in Exhibit 15.2.

When you click on "City Codes or Ordinances" you are taken to the screen shown in Exhibit 15.4. This screen allows you to select the way in which you want to view the ordinances: either with frames or without frames. If you select the "Frames" option, you are taken to the screen set out in Exhibit 15.5.

The screen set out in Exhibit 15.5 provides you with both a wealth of information and a wealth of options. For example, the left pane provides you with a list of the titles, or parts, of the Austin Code, and the main pane tells you that, on the date we looked at the Code, the Code was current through June 2005. You can find a particular ordinance using either the information in the left pane or one of the search options set out in the toolbar near the top of the page.

Although the webpage provides a number of options, you decide to select the "Advanced Search" option. When you click on that option, the search screen set out in Exhibit 15.6 appears. After thinking again about the specific issue that you were asked to research, you decide to look for a section that contains either the word "sign" or "signage" and the phrase "historic district."

When you click on "Search," you are taken to the section of the Austin Code set out in Exhibit 15.7. Note that we selected "medium" for the results search option: the "medium" option provides a quick description of what is included in any particular code section.

The search results tell us that Chapter 25.10 sets out the sign regulations for the City of Austin. Quickly skimming the titles of the sections contained in this chapter, we see several sections that may be on point: section 25.10-101 seems to deal with signs allowed in all sign districts without an installation permit; section 25-10-103 deals with signs prohibited in all sign districts; and so on. If you click on any of these links, you are taken to the page shown in Exhibit 15.8.

Although you will want to read most of these sections, you start with the section that seems most on point: section 25-10-121, Historic Sign District Regulations. When you click on the link to this section, you are taken to the page set out in Exhibit 15.9.

Having found the applicable code sections, you now need to spend thirty to sixty minutes reading and analyzing those sections and any sections that they refer to. Once you have done that reading, you can begin the next step in the process: drafting the letter to the client. See Chapter 16.

Drafting, Revising, and Editing the Opinion Letter

Some clients love their attorney and recommend him or her to their business associates, friends, relatives, and people they meet at the gym and on the golf course. Unfortunately, other clients do not give their attorneys the same rave reviews.

As a new attorney, how do you make it more likely that you fall into the first and not the second category? While "by winning" seems like the obvious answer, it is not the only answer. Even though clients tend to like attorneys who win or who tell the clients what they want to hear better than attorneys who lose or who give them bad news, many clients are looking for more: they want an attorney who listens to them, who explains the law to them in language they can understand, who gives them good advice, and who does not make promises that are not kept. In addition, they want an attorney who is professional. They want someone who dresses professionally, who has a professional demeanor, and whose written documents look professional.

Thus, in writing a letter to a client, keep in mind that you are doing more than just telling the client what the law is or what you think your client should do. You are establishing a relationship with your client and building, or destroying, your professional reputation.

§ 16.1 Know Your Audience and Your Purpose

Before drafting a document, ask yourself two questions: Who is my audience? What is my purpose?

§ 16.1.1 The Audience for an Opinion Letter

Although the primary audience for an opinion letter is the client, there may be a secondary audience. The letter may be read not only by the client but also by an interested third party or, in some cases, by the other side. Consequently, in writing the letter, you must write for both the client and for anyone else who may read the letter.

In our example case, the primary audience for your opinion letter will be Mary Corner. Mary Corner may, however, show the letter to another small business owner, to friends and relatives, or even to a city official.

§ 16.1.2 The Purpose of an Opinion Letter

Assume for a moment that the audience is the client and no one else. In writing to that client, what is your purpose? Is it to inform? To persuade? To justify your bill? Should you be giving the client only your conclusions, or should you include the information that the client needs to reach his or her own conclusions?

Your role is determined, at least in part, by your state's Rules of Professional Conduct. For example, in Texas attorneys are bound by the following rule and comments.

EXAMPLE   **Texas Disciplinary Rules of Professional Conduct Rules**

1.03   Communication

(a) A lawyer shall keep a client reasonably informed about the status of a matter and promptly comply with reasonable requests for information.

(b) A lawyer shall explain a matter to the extent reasonably necessary to permit the client to make informed decisions regarding the representation.

Comment:

1. The client should have sufficient information to participate intelligently in decisions concerning the objectives of the representation and the means by which they are to be pursued, to the extent the client is willing and able to do so. For example, a lawyer negotiating on behalf of a client should provide the client with facts relevant to the matter, inform the client of communications from another party and take other reasonable steps to permit the client to make a decision regarding a serious offer from another party. A lawyer who receives from opposing counsel either an offer of settlement in a civil controversy or a proffered plea bargain in a criminal case should promptly inform the client of its substance unless prior discussions with the client have left it clear that the proposal will be unacceptable. See Comment 2 to Rule 1.02.

2. Adequacy of communication depends in part on the kind of advice or assistance involved. For example, in negotiations where there is time to explain a proposal the lawyer should review all important provisions with the client before proceeding to an agreement. In litigation a lawyer should explain the general strategy and prospects of success and ordinarily should consult the client on tactics that might injure or coerce others.... The guiding principle is that the lawyer should reasonably fulfill client expectations for information consistent with the duty to act in the client's best interests, and the client's overall requirements as to the character of representation.

Thus, under the Texas rules, your primary purpose in writing the letter would be to give Mary Corner the information that she needs to make an informed decision about whether to appeal the Historic Landmark Commission's decision.

Question

Given the rules set out above, can a secondary purpose of your letter be to persuade the client to take a particular course of action? Or to show the client that you have spent a lot of time researching the issue and that your bill is, therefore, reasonable?

§ 16.2 Prepare the First Draft of the Letter

Just as convention dictates the content and form of the objective memorandum, convention also dictates the content and form of the opinion letter. Most opinion letters have (1) an introductory paragraph identifying the issue and, most often, the attorney's opinion; (2) a summary of the facts on which the opinion is based; (3) an explanation of the law; (4) the attorney's advice; and (5) a closing sentence or paragraph. Note the similarities between the objective memorandum and the opinion letter.

Objective Memorandum	Opinion Letter
heading	name
	address
	file reference
	salutation
question presented	introductory paragraph
brief answer	opinion
statement of facts	summary of facts on which opinion is based
discussion section	explanation
conclusion	advice
	closing

§ 16.2.1 The Introductory Paragraph

In writing the introductory paragraph, you have two objectives to establish the appropriate relationship with your client and to define the issue or goal. In addition, you will often include substantive information. For example, when the news is favorable, you will almost always want to set out your opinion in the introductory paragraph.

Because the introductory paragraph is so important, avoid "canned" opening sentences. For instance, do not begin all of your letters with "This letter is in response to your inquiry of..." or "As you requested...." Instead of beginning with platitudes, begin by identifying the issue or goal. Compare the following examples.

EXAMPLE 1   **Canned Opening Sentence**

This letter is in response to your inquiry of September 10, 2006. The information that you requested is set out below.

EXAMPLE 2   **Better Opening Sentence**

I have now finished researching the rules relating to business signs in historic districts.

EXAMPLE 3   **Even Better Opening Sentence**

After our meeting yesterday, I researched the Austin ordinances governing signs in the Austin Historic District.

Because Example 1 could be used to open almost any letter, it subtly suggests to the reader that he or she is just one more client to whom the attorney is cranking out a response. Therefore, most successful attorneys avoid opening sentences like the one in Example 1 and, like the authors of Examples 2 and 3, they personalize their openings.

§ 16.2.2 Statement of the Issue

Although you need to identify the issue, you do not want to include a formal issue statement. In most instances, the "under-does-when" and the "whether" formats used in office memos are inappropriate in an opinion letter.

In deciding how to present the issue, keep in mind your purpose, both in including a statement of the issue and in writing the letter itself. You are including an issue statement because you want the client to know that you understand the issue and because you want to protect yourself. Consequently, you include a statement of the issue for both rhetorical and practical reasons. You use it to establish a relationship with the client and to limit your liability.

In the example case, there are a number of different ways and places to set out the issue: you can incorporate your issue statement into your introductory paragraph; you can combine your statement of the issue with your statement of your opinion; or you can set out the issue at the beginning of your explanation of the law.

Issue Statement Incorporated into the Introductory Paragraph

EXAMPLE 1

During our meeting on Monday, you asked me whether you should appeal the City's decision denying your request to install a sign above the entrance to your new restaurant, the Corner Café.

Issue Statement Combined with Your Opinion

EXAMPLE 2

I have completed my review of the ordinances governing business signs in the Austin Historic District. Based on this review, I recommend that you appeal the City's decision denying your request to install a sign above the entrance to your new restaurant, the Corner Café.

Issue Used to Introduce Explanation of the Law

EXAMPLE 3

[Introductory paragraph and facts go here.]

Before deciding whether to appeal the City's denial of your application for a permit to install a sign above the entrance to your new restaurant, you should consider the following ordinances and the procedures and costs that are involved in appealing a decision. [Explanation of the law goes here.]

---

§ 16.2.3 Opinion

When the client has asked for your opinion, set out your opinion in the letter. When the news is good, you will usually put your opinion in the introductory paragraph; having had his or her question answered, the client can then concentrate on the explanation. You may, however, want to use a different strategy when the news is bad. Instead of putting your opinion "up front," you may choose to put it at the end, in the hope that having read the explanation, the client will better understand the conclusion.

Whatever your opinion, present it as your opinion. Because you are in the business of making predictions and not guarantees, never tell clients that they will or will not win. Instead, present your opinion in terms of probabilities: "You have about a 25 percent chance of winning your appeal." "It is unlikely that you would win on appeal." "It is unlikely that the City Council will overturn the decision of the Historic Landmark Commission and grant your application for a permit."

§ 16.2.4 Summary of the Facts

There are two reasons for including a summary of the facts. As with the statement of the issue, the first is rhetorical: you want the client to know that you heard his or her story. The second is practical. You want to protect yourself. Your client needs to know that your opinion is based on a particular set of facts and that, if the facts turn out to be different, your opinion might also be different.

Just as you do not include all of the facts in the statement of facts written for an objective memorandum, you do not include all of the facts in an opinion letter. Include only those that are legally significant or that are important to the client. Because the letter itself should be short, keep your summary of facts as short as possible. For instance, in the example case, your statement of facts might look like this.

EXAMPLE   **Summary of Facts**

On September 11, 2006, you filed an application for a permit to install two six-foot by four-foot painted signs on the front of your new restaurant, the Corner Café, which is located in the corner of a building that has been designated as an Historic Landmark. Your signs would have a beige background and green lettering. At night, the signs would be lit by a small light installed under the sign. On October 2, 2006, the Historic Landmark Commission denied your application and gave you fourteen days to appeal its decision.

---

§ 16.2.5 Explanation

Under the rules of professional responsibility, you must give the client the information that he or she needs to make an informed decision. It is essential, therefore, that you give not only your opinion but also the basis for your opinion. The explanation section is not, however, just a repeat of the discussion section from an objective memorandum. It is usually much shorter and much more client-specific.

When the explanation requires a discussion of more than one or two issues, you will usually want to include a roadmap. See section 21.2.1. Having outlined the steps, you can then discuss each step in more detail. The amount of detail will depend on the question, the subject matter, and the client. Although there are exceptions, as a general rule, do not set out the text of ordinances or statutes or include specific references to cases. Instead, just tell the client what the ordinances, statutes, and cases say, without citations to authority.

After explaining the law, apply the law to the facts of your client's case. If a particular point is not in dispute, explain why it is not in dispute; if it is in dispute, summarize each side's arguments. The difference between the analysis in an objective memorandum and in an opinion letter is a difference in degree, not kind. In each instance, give the reader what he or she needs — nothing more and nothing less. For examples of explanations, see the sample letters set out at the end of this chapter.

§ 16.2.6 Advice

When there is more than one possible course of action, include an advice section in which you describe and evaluate each option. For example, if there are several ways in which your client could change its business operations to avoid liability, describe and evaluate each of those options. Similarly, if your client could choose negotiation over arbitration or arbitration over litigation, describe and evaluate each option. Having described the options, you can then advise the client as to which option you think would be in his or her best interest.

§ 16.2.7 Concluding Paragraph

Just as you should avoid canned openings, also avoid canned closings. Instead of using stock sentences, use the concluding paragraph to affirm the relationship that you have established with the client and to confirm what, if anything, is to happen next. What is the next step and who is to take it?

§ 16.2.8 Warnings

Some firms will want you to include explicit warnings. They will want you to tell the client that your opinion is based on current law and on the facts currently available and that your opinion might be different if the facts turn out to be different. Other firms believe that these warnings, when set out explicitly, set the wrong tone. Because practice varies, determine which approach your firm takes before writing the letter.

In writing your letter you can use the modified semi-block format, the full block (the date, the paragraphs, and the signature block are not indented), or the modified block (paragraphs are not indented but the date and signature block are). For examples of each format, see the sample letters at the end of this chapter and *Webster's Legal Secretaries Handbook* (2d ed. 1996).

§ 16.3 Revising, Editing, and Proofreading the Opinion Letter

It is not enough that the law be stated correctly and that your advice be sound. Your letter must be well written and the tone must be the one that you intend.

§ 16.3.1 Writing a Well-Written Letter

Like other types of writing, a well-written letter is well organized. As a general rule, you will want to present the information in the order listed above: an introductory paragraph in which you identify the issue and give your opinion followed by a summary of the facts, an explanation of the law, your advice, and a concluding sentence or paragraph. You will also want to structure each paragraph carefully, identifying the topic in the first sentence and making sure that each sentence builds on the prior one. Transitions are also important. Use them to keep your reader on track and to make the connections between ideas explicit.

Also take care in constructing your sentences. You can make the law more understandable by using concrete subjects and active verbs and relatively short sentences. When longer sentences are needed, manage those sentences by using punctuation to divide the sentences into shorter units of meaning.

Finally, remember that you will be judged by the letter you write. Although clients may not know whether you have the law right, they will know whether you have spelled their names correctly. In addition, many will notice other mistakes in grammar, punctuation, or spelling. If you want to be known as a competent lawyer, make sure that your letters provide the proof.

§ 16.3.2 Using an Appropriate Tone

In addition to selling competence, you are selling an image. As you read each of the following letters, picture the attorney who wrote it.

EXAMPLE   **Letter A**

Dear Mr. and Mrs. McDonald:

This letter is to acknowledge receipt of your letter of February 17, 2006, concerning your prospects as potential adoptive parents. The information that you provided about yourselves will need to be verified through appropriate documentation. Furthermore, I am sure that you are cognizant of the fact that there are considerably more prospective adoptive placements than there are available adoptees to fill those placement slots.

Nonetheless, I will be authorizing my legal assistant to keep your correspondence on file. One can never know when an opportunity may present itself and, in fact, a child becomes unexpectedly available for placement. If such an opportunity should arise, please know that I would be in immediate contact with you.

Very sincerely yours,

Kenneth Q. Washburn III
Attorney at Law

EXAMPLE   **Letter B**

Dear Bill and Mary,

Just wanted you to know that I got your letter asking about adopting a baby. I can already tell that you two would make great parents. But, as you probably know, there are far more "would be" parents out there than there are babies.

But I don't want you to lose hope. You might be surprised. Your future little one may be available sooner than you think. It has happened before! And you can be sure that I'll call you the minute I hear of something. Until then, I'll have Marge set up a file for you.

All the best,

Ken Washburn

Letter C

Dear Mr. and Mrs. McDonald:

Your letter about the possibility of adopting a baby arrived in my office yesterday. Although the information in your letter indicates that you would be ideal adoptive parents, I am sure that you realize that there are more couples who wish to adopt than there are adoptable babies. For this reason, you may have to wait for some time for your future son or daughter.

Even so, occasionally an infant becomes available for adoption on short notice. For this reason, I will ask my legal assistant to open a file for you so that we can react quickly if necessary. Because we do not know exactly when an infant will become available, I recommend that we begin putting together the appropriate documentation as soon as possible. In the meantime, please know that I will call you immediately if I learn of an available infant who would be a good match for you.

Sincerely,

Kenneth Washburn

Question

If you were "shopping" for an attorney, would you choose the author of Letter 1, Kenneth Q. Washburn III; the author of letter 2, Ken Washburn; or the author of Letter 3, Kenneth Washburn? Why?

§ 16.3.3 Checklist for Critiquing the Opinion Letter

I. Organization

- The information has been presented in a logical order: the letter begins with an introductory sentence or paragraph that is followed, in most instances, by the attorney's opinion, a summary of the facts, an explanation, the attorney's advice, and a concluding paragraph.

II. Content

- The introductory sentence identifies the topic and establishes the appropriate relationship with the client.
- The attorney's opinion is sound and is stated in terms of probabilities.
- The summary of the facts is accurate and includes both the legally significant facts and the facts that are important to the client.
- The explanation gives the client the information that he or she needs to make an informed decision.
- The options are described and evaluated.
- The concluding paragraph states who will do what next and sets an appropriate tone.

III. Writing

- The client can understand the letter after reading it once.
- When appropriate, the attorney has included roadmaps.
- The paragraph divisions are logical, and the paragraphs are neither too short nor too long.
- Signposts and topic sentences have been used to tell the client where he or she is in the explanation and what to expect next.
- Transitions and dovetailing have been used to make clear the connections between sentences.
- In most sentences, the writer has used the actor as the subject of the sentence.
- In most sentences, the subject and verb are close together.
- The writer has used the passive voice when he or she wants to emphasize what was done rather than who did it or when the passive voice facilitates dovetailing.
- In most sentences, the old information is at the beginning of the sentence and the new information is at the end.
- The writer has varied both sentence length and sentence structure so that each sentence flows smoothly from the prior sentence.
- The writing is concise: when appropriate, sentences have been reduced to clauses, clauses to phrases, and phrases to words.
- The writer has used language precisely: the writer has selected the correct term and used that term consistently.

§ 16.4 Sample Client Letters

EXAMPLE 1   **Sample Client Letter**

Confidential
Attorney-Client Communication

Mary Corner
101 Main Street
Austin, Texas 73344

Dear Ms. Corner:

During our meeting yesterday, you asked me whether you should appeal the Historic Landmark Commission's decision denying your request for a permit to install a sign above the entrance to your new restaurant, the Corner Café. To answer your question, I have reviewed the facts and the Austin ordinances on signs in the Historic Landmark districts.

You submitted your original application on September 11, 2006. In that application, you requested a permit that would have allowed you to install two six feet by four feet painted wood signs on the front of your building. One of the signs would have been installed on the north side of the building, and the other would have been installed on the west side of the building. Both signs would extend about eighteen inches above the top of the building and would be beige with green lettering. At night, the signs would be lit by a light installed under the signs. The Historic Landmark Commission denied your application on October 2, 2006, giving you fourteen days to appeal its decision to the City Council.

City of Austin ordinances prohibit certain types of signs in Historic Landmark districts. For example, the ordinances specifically prohibit roof signs and any sign, or any portion of a sign, that rotates. Although your sign would not rotate, it might fall within the definition of a roof sign, which is defined as a sign that is "installed over or on the roof of a building." In determining whether to grant a permit for other types of signs, the Historic Landmark Commission considers a number of other factors, including the following:

(1) the proposed size, color, and lighting of the sign;
(2) the material from which the sign is to be constructed;
(3) the proliferation of signs on a building or lot;
(4) the proposed orientation of the sign with respect to structures; and
(5) other factors that are consistent with the Historic Landmark Preservation Plan, the character of the National Historic Register District, and the purpose of historic landmark regulations.

If the Commission denied your application for a permit because your proposed signs fall within the definition of a roof sign, there is little or no chance that the City Council would overturn the Commission's decision. Our only hope would be to persuade the City Council that a sign that extends above the top of the building does not fall within the definition of a roof sign.

If, however, the Commission denied the permit for some other reason, the City Council might overturn the Commission's decision, particularly if your proposed signs are consistent in size, color, lighting, and material with other signs in the area and if there are not already a number of other signs on the building.

To preserve your right to appeal, I recommend that you file a notice of appeal within the time limits set out in the letter that you received from the Commission. I would then schedule a meeting with a member of the Commission to determine the reason that the Commission denied your application. If the Commission denied your application because your signs would extend beyond the roof line, the Commission may be willing to approve your application for a permit if you agree to change the size and/or locations of your signs so that they do not extend beyond the roof line. Similarly, if the Commission denied your application because of the signs' size, color, or lighting, you may be able to work with the Commission to modify your application so that your proposed signs meet the Commission's criteria. If, however, you cannot find out from the Commission why it denied your application or you cannot reach an agreement with the Commission about an application that would meet its criteria, you can then proceed with your appeal to the City Council.

Although you do not need an attorney to file an appeal with the City Council or to schedule meetings with the Commission, I would be glad to assist you with either or both actions. If you would like me to act on your behalf, please call me by Thursday, October 12, 2006, so that I can submit the appeal before the deadline. If you would like to file the appeal without my assistance, please see the instructions that are set out in the letter that you received from the Commission. In addition, you can request an appointment with a Commissioner by calling the following number: (512) 974-2680. If you have any further questions or concerns, please feel free to call me.

Very truly yours,

Your name

EXAMPLE 2 **Sample Client Letter**

Confidential
Attorney-Client Communication

July 30, 2006

Ms. Marian Walter
1234 Main Street
Wichita, KS 67218

File No. 0192002

Dear Ms. Walter:

Since our meeting on July 22, 2006, I have researched the law regarding your legal right to vacate your current location before the expiration of your lease. If you decide to move out before the end of your lease and your landlord, Valley Antiques, files a lawsuit to collect the unpaid rent, you can probably win the lawsuit. You should, however, consider some of your other options.

Because my opinion is based on the following facts, please contact me if I have left out a fact or misstated a fact.

In June 2005, you received a brochure advertising an "elegant antiques mall" that was certain to attract "the most discriminating clients." When you met with the leasing agent, Joann Carter, she told you that the mall would house antique stores and that the mall was designed to attract adults, not children. In August 2005, you signed a five-year lease. The lease stated that the remaining spaces would be rented to antique stores or other retail businesses.

Between August 2005 and November 2005, five other upscale antique stores moved into the mall. The landlord was, however, unable to rent the remaining eight spaces to antique dealers. As a result, between February and April 2006, the landlord leased four of the remaining spaces to other types of businesses. It leased one of the spaces to a video arcade and three others to secondhand stores. Since these stores moved into the mall, there have been children with skateboards in the mall area, and you have experienced a 20 percent decrease in profits. In addition to making oral complaints, on May 1, 2006, you sent a letter to the landlord notifying it that you believe that it violated the terms of your lease when it leased spaces in the mall to the video arcade and secondhand stores.

If you vacate the premises and default on the lease, Valley Antiques may file a lawsuit against you to recover the rent due for the remaining months of the lease. If this happens, you can argue that Valley Antiques "constructively evicted" you when it leased to the arcade and second-hand stores. A constructive eviction is different from an actual eviction. An actual eviction occurs when the landlord literally takes the premises away from the tenant; a constructive eviction occurs when the landlord interferes with a tenant's right to use the premises for their intended purpose. It would be up to the jury to decide whether the circumstances surrounding your case constitute constructive eviction.

To establish that you have been constructively evicted, you will need to prove four things. First, you must prove that Valley Antiques violated the lease agreement. Valley Antiques will argue that, under the lease, it had the right to lease to retail stores and an arcade and thrift shops are retail stores. Although the lease does allow Valley Antiques to lease to retail stores, you may argue that both parties understood the language in the lease to mean that Valley Antiques could lease to antique stores and other "upscale" retail establishments, for example, an upscale jewelry store or restaurant. Based on the language in the brochure and the statements made by the leasing agent, a jury should conclude that the landlord violated the lease by leasing the other spaces to the video arcade and secondhand stores.

Second, you must prove that when Valley Antiques leased the vacant spaces to a video arcade and secondhand stores, it substantially interfered with your ability to use your leased space. Although there have been cases in which the courts have found that a landlord substantially interfered with a tenant's use of its leased space when the landlord rented to an incompatible business, there are other cases in which the court found that the landlord did not substantially interfere. The key seems to be whether the landlord's act caused a loss of profits. Thus, to prove substantial interference, we will have to show that Valley Antiques caused your loss of profits when it leased the vacant spaces to the arcade and the secondhand stores. Even though we should be able to do this, Valley Antiques will try to prove that your losses are the result of other factors, such as the seasonal nature of your business, a general decline in business in the area, or your own business practices.

Third, you must prove that you gave Valley Antiques notice of the problem and an opportunity to correct it. You should be able to meet this requirement: in addition to making oral complaints, you also sent a letter, and you have given Valley Antiques several months to correct the problem.

Finally, you must prove that you vacated the premises within a reasonable amount of time after complaining to the landlord. If you vacate the premises by September 1, 2006, the jury will most likely find that you have met this requirement.

Although you should be able to prove that you have been constructively evicted, litigation is expensive and stressful, and there are no guarantees. As a result, you should consider some of your other options.

One option is to stay and pay rent. Although this option avoids the expense and stress of litigation, you may lose your right to claim that you have been constructively evicted. As I indicated earlier in this letter, one of the requirements for constructive eviction is that you move out within a reasonable time. In addition, if your loss in profits continues, it may be impractical to stay in business.

A second option would be to try to sublease your space to another business. Although your lease requires that you obtain Valley Antiques' approval before you sublet your space, the courts have said that a landlord cannot withhold approval except for good cause. The risk associated with this option is that you may be liable for unpaid rents if the new tenant fails to make payments.

A third option is to try to negotiate an early termination of the lease on the grounds that Valley Antiques has violated the lease by leasing to the arcade and secondhand stores. I can do this for you or, if you want to minimize your costs, you can do it on your own.

A fourth option would be to file a lawsuit against Valley Antiques for breach of contract. Although you should be able to win this lawsuit and recover your lost profits, such a lawsuit would be expensive and, once again, there are no guarantees.

Unfortunately, none of these options is very good. As a result, you need to balance your desire to move out of the mall against the potential costs. Although there is a good chance that your landlord will not sue you, under our state's statute of limitations, it has six years to file a lawsuit. Thus, you would have to live under the cloud of potential litigation for a number of years.

Please contact my office to schedule an appointment to talk in more detail about your options. I look forward to meeting with you.

Sincerely,

Attorney at Law

Sample Client Letter

Confidential
Attorney-Client Communication

November 18, 2006

Onlinebooks.com
6524 Industrial Parkway South
Tampa Bay, Florida 33607

Dear Ms. Brooks:
You have asked if Onlinebooks may ask job applicants whether they have back problems or have used more than five days of sick leave during

the past year. My research indicates that the Americans with Disabilities Act (ADA) prohibits the asking of such questions. You can, however, ask questions that will help you determine whether an applicant can perform the essential job requirements. Because my opinion is based on current law and my understanding of the facts, I have set out those facts so that you can review them for accuracy. Please note that a change in the facts might change my opinion.

Onlinebooks employs "pickers," that is, individuals who pick books off shelves, place them in a box, and then place the box on a conveyor belt. Pickers must be able to climb, reach, and lift boxes weighing up to thirty pounds. In the past, some of the individuals you have hired as pickers have not been able to do all parts of the job or have used substantial amounts of sick leave for back or other health problems. Thus, you want to ask job applicants about whether they have back problems and about how they use sick leave.

The ADA prohibits employers from discriminating against qualified job applicants who are disabled. More specifically, the ADA prohibits employers from asking applicants questions that are designed to "weed out" individuals who have a disability or who suffer from a chronic illness. As a result, Onlinebooks cannot ask job applicants about whether they have back problems or about their use of sick leave.

The ADA does not, however, prohibit an employer from asking job applicants whether they can, with or without reasonable accommodations, perform the essential functions of the job for which they are applying. Therefore, Onlinebooks may describe the essential functions of the job and then ask applicants whether they can perform those functions. For example, you may tell applicants that pickers must be able to climb, reach, and lift thirty-pound boxes and then ask them whether they can perform each of these tasks. In addition, Onlinebooks may ask applicants to demonstrate that they can do each of these tasks.

If an applicant asks for a reasonable accommodation, Onlinebooks must grant that accommodation unless doing so would impose an unreasonable burden on Onlinebooks. For example, if an applicant asks to be allowed to wear a back support or to use a handcart to move heavy boxes longer distances, you should grant the request unless doing so would create an unreasonable burden on the company. You would not, however, need to grant an employee's request to be exempted from carrying boxes weighing over, for example, ten pounds.

In addition, the ADA does not prohibit employers from asking applicants about their work histories. Thus, although you may not ask applicants how much sick leave they used in the last year, you may ask them about their attendance records. In doing so, you just need to make sure that the questions are designed to collect information about the applicants' work records, not to determine whether the individual is disabled or suffers from a chronic illness.

To summarize then, although you may not ask applicants whether they have back problems, you may ask them whether they can, with or without reasonable accommodations, perform the essential functions of the job. In addition, although you may not ask applicants about their use of sick leave, you may ask them about their attendance records as long as your questions are not designed to collect information about whether the person is disabled or suffers from a chronic illness.

If you have any additional questions, please feel free to contact me.

Sincerely,

Attorney at Law

Introduction to Persuasive Writing and Oral Advocacy

Introduction

The brief is one of the attorney's most powerful tools. In an age of crowded dockets, the attorney's voice is most clearly heard in the quiet of the judge's chambers. At the trial court level, a good brief can persuade the court to grant or deny a motion, to admit or refuse to admit evidence, or to give or not give a particular jury instruction. On appeal, a good brief can persuade the court to reverse or affirm a lower court's ruling, create a new rule or follow an old one, or change or continue an established policy. If the brief does not persuade, it is unlikely that the oral argument will.

Unfortunately, good briefs are hard to write. Writing one requires knowledge, insight, and hard work. You must understand both your audience and your purpose in writing to that audience; you must have mastered both the facts of your case and the law; and you must put all of the pieces together clearly, concisely, and persuasively.

In writing a brief you are not, however, starting from scratch. You will be using the research, analytical, and writing skills that you have already developed. In addition, you will be using the advocacy skills that you learned as a child and teenager. As the following example illustrates, most of us learned the "standard moves" of advocacy long before we came to law school.

Jon, a 17-year-old junior, wants to use his father's sports car for the junior prom. Because he knows that persuading his father will be difficult, Jon plans his strategy carefully. During the week before he makes his request, Jon is on his best behavior. He is easy to get along with, does his homework without being nagged, and even volunteers to mow the lawn.

When he finally approaches his father, he begins by setting the stage. He subtly reminds his father of how mature and reliable he has become and then begins talking about Sarah, his date for the prom, and about the importance of the event. Isn't Sarah beautiful and intelligent? Isn't your junior prom something you remember for the rest of your life?

He then poses the question. He isn't asking for himself; he is asking for Sarah. Wouldn't it be so much nicer for Sarah if he could take her to the prom in his father's sports car rather than the family's other car, which shows the effect of years of hauling kids from one event to another?

When his father doesn't immediately agree, Jon launches into his first argument. Although Jon's father has said that neither Jon nor his older brothers can drive the sports car, Jon knows that there have been exceptions to this family rule. Both of Jon's older brothers were allowed to drive the car to their proms. Thus, Jon's version of the rule is not that he and his brothers cannot drive the car but that they can drive the car only on prom nights.

Jon's father responds by distinguishing the cases. Both of Jon's brothers had excellent driving records, while Jon has had two speeding tickets. Therefore, the father's version is not that the teenagers can drive the sports car only on prom nights but that a teen can drive the car on prom night provided that he has a good driving record.

Instead of accepting defeat and walking away, Jon tries a couple of other approaches. He begins by conceding that in the past he did not have a good driving record. Recently, however, his driving record has been very good. In the last nine months, he has not had any tickets. Thus, his argument is that, in fact, he falls within the rule set out by his father. Because he currently has a good driving record, he should be allowed to use the sports car on prom night.

Jon also tries a couple of policy arguments. If his parents want to promote safe driving, he should be rewarded for his recent behavior. In addition, his parents can promote participation in social activities they approve of by allowing him to use the car. He also refers his father to the decision of the family's neighbors, the Morgans. Although the Morgans' son David has a worse driving record than Jon, the Morgans have told David that he can use their Lexus for the prom.

In making his argument to his father, Jon does many of the things that you will do as a trial attorney. He creates a favorable context for his argument; he presents the facts in the light most favorable to his client; he frames the issue carefully, asking his father for the car not for himself but for his girlfriend; and he makes factual arguments, arguments based on both "in state" and "out of state" cases, and policy arguments.

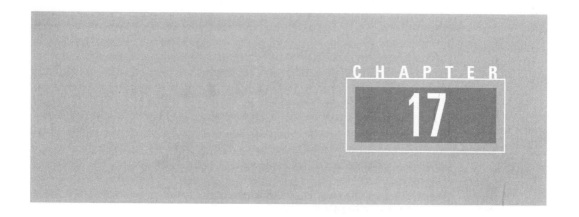

CHAPTER

17

Writing a Trial Brief

§ 17.1 Motion Briefs

Much of litigation is a motions practice. For example, as a trial attorney, you will file motions for temporary relief, to compel discovery, to suppress evidence, to dismiss, or for summary judgment. Although not all of these motions will be supported by briefs, many will.

§ 17.1.1 Audience

In writing a brief in support of or in opposition to a motion, your primary audience is the trial judge.

Sometimes you will know which judge will read your brief. Either the brief has been requested by a specific judge or you know which judge will hear the motion. At other times, though, you will not know which judge will read your brief. The motion will be read by whatever judge is hearing motions on the day that your motion is argued.

If you know which judge will read your brief, write your brief for that judge. Learn as much as you can about that judge, and then craft a brief that he or she will find persuasive. If you do not know which judge will read your brief, write a brief that will work for any of the judges who may hear your motion. Although a particular approach might work well with one judge, do not risk using that approach if it might offend other judges.

Whichever situation you find yourself in, keep the judge's schedule in mind. It is not uncommon for a judge hearing civil motions to hear twenty motions in a single day. If in each of these cases each party has filed a twenty-page brief, the judge would have 800 pages to read. Given this workload, it is not surprising that for most judges the best brief is the short brief. Know what you need and want to argue, make your argument, and then stop.

Also keep in mind the constraints placed on trial judges. Because trial judges must apply mandatory authority, they need to know what the law is, not what you think it should be. Whenever possible, make the easy argument: set out and apply existing law.

§ 17.1.2 Purpose

In writing to a trial judge, you have two goals: to educate and to persuade. You are the teacher who teaches the judge both the applicable law and the facts of the case. You are not, however, just a teacher. You are also an advocate. As you teach, you will be trying to persuade the court to take a particular action.

§ 17.1.3 Conventions

The format of a particular brief will vary from jurisdiction to jurisdiction and, even within a jurisdiction, from court to court. Consequently, you need to check the local rules. Is there a local rule that prescribes the types of information that should be included in the brief, the order in which that information should be presented, and the particular format? If there is no local rule, check with other attorneys or with the court clerk to see if there is a format that is typically used.

§ 17.2 *State v. Patterson*

In this chapter, our example case is *State v. Patterson*, a criminal case in which the defendant has filed a motion to suppress the identifications obtained at a show-up shortly after an assault and at a line-up held four days later. See the documents on pages 381-386.

§ 17.3 Developing a Theory of the Case

Good advocates do not just set out the facts and the law. Instead, they use the facts and the law to construct a compelling story.

A good story, or theory of the case, appeals both to the head and to the heart. The theory of the case puts together the law and the facts in a way that is legally sound and that produces a result that the court sees as just.

There are at least two ways of coming up with a good theory of the case. The first is to look at the case through your client's eyes. According to your client, what happened? Why did the other people involved do what they did? Why did your client act as he or she did? Why does your client think that what he or she did was legally right? Justified? Is there law that supports your client's view of what happened?

The second way is to look at the cases involving the same issue in which the court reached the result that you want the court to reach in your case. In

Form 9.28   **SEATTLE POLICE DEPARTMENT**   Case Number

CSS 21.122   02-49721

DATE 08-12-02   **TIME** 6:05 ·P.M.   **PLACE** Police Headquarters

STATEMENT OF: Beatrice Marie Martinez
_____

    My name is Beatrice Marie Martinez, and I live at 801
East Harrison #202, and my phone number is 329-9679. I
am 17 years old. Today, at 4:30 p.m. I left my apartment,
beginning my walk to work; Angelo's Restaurant at 5th &
Pike. I walked southbound on Harvard to Denny Way, then
westbound on Denny Way to Boylston. I again walked
southbound on Boylston, until I came to East Howell Street.
As I was walking westbound on East Howell Street, a red,
old station wagon was going eastbound, and it attracted my
attention because it slowed down and the driver was looking
at me. I didn't think much of it, and turned the corner,
now walking southbound in the 1700 block of Belmont. As I
turned the corner, I again saw the old red station wagon,
coming northbound on Belmont. As I came to an apartment building,
the station wagon pulled in front of me, blocking the sidewalk, and the driver kept looking at me. The driver jumped
out of the car, and shouted "Hey." I looked at him, and he
had what looked to me to be a .38, pointed at my stomach. I
stepped back, and heard someone else yell "Hey," and I ran
across the street and hid behind a wall. I also pushed
buttons, trying to get someone to let me inside the
apartment house. The man who appeared to be in his early 40s,
white, 165-170 lbs., 5'7-8 blondish brown hair, wearing
dark jacket, and glasses, jumped back into the station
wagon, and took off down the street. A man ran up, and took
me to his apartment to call police. The police came, and
took a report and were taking me home, when I saw the man,
walking in front of us. Police arrested him, and I again
went back to the apartment, at the request of the police. I
was brought downtown by the man who had the apartment, to
give this statement. This is a true and correct statement,
to the best of my knowledge.

STATEMENT
TAKEN BY: *Det. Al Yuen*   **SIGNED:** *Beatrice Martinez*

WITNESS: **WITNESS:**

Form 9.28   **SEATTLE POLICE DEPARTMENT**   Case Number

CSS 21.122   06-49721

DATE 08-14-06   **TIME** 6:47 P.M.   **PLACE** Police Headquarters

STATEMENT OF: Chester Joseph Clipse

   My name is Chester Joseph Clipse, I'm a 19 year old
white male. I live at 600 E. Olive St., Apt. 110. Today at
about 4:50 p.m., I was walking home, and as I approached my
apartment building, at Corner of E. Olive St. and Belmont,
I saw a man in a red dodge wagon driving up the street
slowly. He pulled into my parking stall, so I approached,
to see what he was doing. He approached a girl, who was on
the sidewalk, and she screamed. At this time, I saw the man
had a gun, and I yelled "Hey." He turned, and ran to his
car, putting the gun under his coat. The girl ran across
the street, and the guy backed out, and took off down the
street, northbound. At that moment, a meter maid came down
street, and I flagged him down, telling him what happened.
The meter maid took off after the man, and I took the girl
to my apartment house to get her off the street. I went
with officers and positively identified the car, which was
parked in the 600 Block of E. Howell. The driver was a white
man about late 30's or early 40's. He was about 5'9 or
5'10, and about 180-185 lbs. He had brown wavy hair, and
was wearing a green outfit. After the officers had left, I
saw him walking up the street, and I saw officers confront
him. The officers sent me back inside with the girl.
   This is a true and correct statement to the best of my
knowledge.

**STATEMENT
TAKEN BY:** Det. Al Yuen   **SIGNED:** Chester Clipse

WITNESS: **WITNESS:**

Form 9.28   **SEATTLE POLICE DEPARTMENT**   Case Number

CSS 21.122   06-49721

DATE 08-15-06   **TIME** 3:22 P.M.   **PLACE** Police Headquarters

STATEMENT OF: Dean Patterson

     On August 13-14, I worked my usual 11-7 shift as a
security guard. When I got home, I went to bed and slept
until about 1:00 p.m. At 2:30, my wife, a nurse at a nearby
hospital, received a call asking her to come to work at
3:00 p.m. She told them that she could come in and, at
about 3:00, I drove her to work. When I got back, I
couldn't find a parking spot in front of our building and
was forced to park almost a block away. Between 3:00 and
4:30 I did two loads of laundry, watched an old movie on
T.V., and talked on the phone with both a friend, Karen
Callendar, and my wife. I made my last trip to the laundry
room at about 4:30 p.m.. On my way back, I decided to check
my car to see how much gas I had. After I checked the gas,
I moved the car to a parking spot right in front of our
building. At about 5:00, I left the apartment and began
walking toward the hospital, where I planned to join my
wife at 5:15 for her dinner break. When I was about two
blocks from our apartment, I was stopped and arrested. The
gun that was found in my apartment is the gun that I was
issued by the security company that I work for.

STATEMENT
TAKEN BY: Det. Al Yuen   **SIGNED:** Dean Patterson

WITNESS: **WITNESS:**

**IN THE SUPERIOR COURT OF THE STATE OF WASHINGTON
FOR KING COUNTY**

STATE OF WASHINGTON,	)	
	)	
Plaintiff,	)	NO. 06-49721
	)	
vs.	)	INFORMATION
	)	
DEAN EUGENE PATTERSON,	)	
	)	
Defendant.	)	
	)	

I, Norm Mason, Prosecuting Attorney for King County, in
the name and by the authority of the State of Washington,
by this Information do accuse Dean Eugene Patterson of the
crime of assault in the second degree, committed as follows:

That the defendant Dean Eugene Patterson, in King
County, Washington, on or about August 14, 2006, did knowingly assault Beatrice Martinez, a human being, with a
weapon and other instrument or thing likely to produce
bodily harm, to-wit: a revolver;

Contrary to RCW 9A.36.021 (1)(C), and against peace and
dignity of the State of Washington.

Norm Mason

NORM MASON
Prosecuting Attorney

Michael T. Frankel

By Michael T. Frankel
MICHAEL T. FRANKEL
Assistant Chief Criminal Deputy
Prosecuting Attorney

Witnesses for state:

Chester Joseph Clipse
Beatrice Marie Martinez
Richard Edward Martin
Terry William Hindman
William P. Cox
Al Yuen
Roy Moran

Information

Line-Up Document

Form 9.3　　　　　　　　SHOW-UP IDENTIFICATION
CSS 21.53　　　　　　　　Seattle Police Department
Rev. 9-72　　　　　Criminal Investigation Division

Case Number: _06 - 49721_　　　　　　Date: _8-16-06_
　　　　　　　　　　　　　　　　　　　Time: _1400_

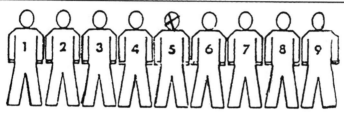

I have just witnessed a show-up consisting of _5_ person(s).

I identify the above number(s) _5_

the person(s) who _assaulted me_
　　　　　　　　　(robbed me, assaulted me, etc.)
on _August 14_　　_4:40_　　at _1700 Belmont_
　　(date)　　　　(time)　　　　　(address)

The person(s) I have indicated above have been identified
to me as: _____
　　Dean Patterson

Witness
　or
(Victim) _Beatrice Martinez_　_801 E. Harrison # 202_
　　　　(Signature)　　　　　(address)　　　　(phone)
　　　　　　　　　　　　　　　　　　_329-9679_
Statement taken by: _Det. Al Yuen_　Witness: _____

Show-up prepared by: _"　　　"_　　Location: _____

Photographs taken by: _Det. R. Reed_
　　　　　　　　　(name)　　　　　　(division)

Attorney present: _Terry Kellogg_
　　　　　　　　(name)

Waiver signed:　Yes _____　No _X_

Line-Up Document

Form 9.3	SHOW-UP IDENTIFICATION
CSS 21.53	Seattle Police Department
Rev. 9-72	Criminal Investigation Division

Case Number: _06 - 49721_

Date: _8-16-06_
Time: _1400_

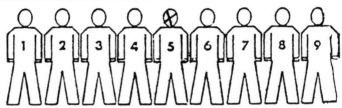

I have just witnessed a show-up consisting of ~~five~~ person(s).
I identify the above number(s) _no Id_

the person(s) who _____
                    (robbed me, assaulted me, etc.)
on _8-14-06_   _16:45_   at _600 East Olive Street_
   (date)   (time)   (address)

The person(s) I have indicated above have been identified
to me as: _____

(Witness)
or
Victim: _Chester Clipse, 600 East Olive Street_
         (Signature)   (address)   (phone)

Statement taken by: _Det. Al Yuen_ Witness: _____

Show-up prepared by: _"   "_ Location: _____

Photographs taken by: _Det. R. Reed_
                       (name)   (division)

Attorney present: _Jerry Kellogg_
                   (name)

Waiver signed: Yes _____ No _X_

those cases, what was the winning party's theory of the case? What legal arguments did that party make? How did it characterize what happened? What was the court's reaction? Did the trial court "buy" the winning party's theory of the case or come up with its own theory of the case?

In our case, Patterson says that he did not commit the crime. He was simply at the wrong place at the wrong time. At the time that crime was committed, Patterson was doing laundry, moving his car, and getting ready to meet his wife for dinner. Although Martinez has identified him as her assailant, she did so only because police pointed him out to her and suggested to her that he was the man who had assaulted her. In addition, Patterson does not match Martinez's and Clipse's description of the assailant. While both Martinez and Clipse told the police that the assailant was in his late 30s or early 40s, Patterson is only 22. In contrast, the State says that Patterson is the person who assaulted Martinez. Martinez has identified Patterson as her assailant, his car matches the one that Martinez and Clipse have described, and a gun was found in his apartment.

§ 17.4 The Caption

In many jurisdictions, motion briefs are printed on pleading, or numbered, paper. In addition, in many jurisdictions, the caption is set out on the first page beginning on about line 5. The parties' names are set out on the left-hand side, and the case number and the title of the document are set out on the right-hand side. See pages 422 and 432.

§ 17.5 The Statement of Facts

Never underestimate the importance of the facts. Particularly at the trial court level, it is the facts, not the law, that usually determine the outcome.

§ 17.5.1 Select the Facts

Like the statement of facts in an objective memo, the statement of facts in a motion brief contains three types of facts: background facts, legally significant facts, and emotionally significant facts.

a. Background Facts

Background facts play a different role in persuasive writing than they do in objective writing. In an objective statement of facts, the writer includes only those background facts that are needed for the story to make sense. In a persuasive statement of facts, you want to do more. You want to use background facts to create a favorable context. See section 17.5.3(a).

b. Legally Significant Facts

Because most courts require that the statement of facts be "fair," in writing the statement of facts you must include all of the legally significant facts, both favorable and unfavorable. Thus, in our example case both the State and the defendant must include all of the facts that will be relevant in determining whether the identifications obtained at the show-up and at the line-up should be suppressed and whether Martinez and Clipse should be allowed to make in-court identifications.

c. Emotionally Significant Facts

While you must include all of the legally significant facts, you do not need to include all of the facts that are emotionally significant. Although as a defensive move you may sometimes include an emotionally significant fact that is unfavorable, recharacterizing it or minimizing its significance, most of the time you will not. It is more common to include only those emotionally significant facts that favor your client.

The harder question is how to handle emotionally significant facts that are unfavorable to the other side. Should you sling mud, or should you take a higher road and omit any reference to those facts? The answer is that it depends: it depends on the fact, on the case, and on the attorney. If the fact's connection to the case is tenuous, most attorneys would not include it. If, however, the case is weak and the fact's connection is closer, many attorneys would include it, some using it as a sword, others using it much more subtly.

§ 17.5.2 Select an Organizational Scheme

In selecting an organizational scheme, consider two factors. First, decide which organizational scheme makes the most sense. Does it make more sense to use a chronological organizational scheme, a topical organizational scheme, or a topical organizational scheme with the facts within each topic set out in chronological order? Second, decide which organizational scheme will allow you to set out the facts in such a way that you are able to present your story and your theory of the case effectively.

In our example case, it makes sense to set out the facts in chronological order. In deciding whether to suppress the evidence, the trial judge will want to know what happened first, second, and third. A chronological organizational scheme will also allow each side to tell its story. The only difference will be that Patterson will start his story with his activities on the day in question, while the State will start its story where it started for the victim: with the assault.

§ 17.5.3 Present the Facts

In writing the statement of facts for an objective memo, you set out the facts accurately and objectively. You did not present the facts in the light most favorable to your client.

In writing the statement of facts for a motion brief, you still need to set out the facts accurately. One of the fastest ways to lose a case is to leave out legally significant facts or to misrepresent either the legally significant or emotionally significant facts. Being accurate does not mean, however, that you need to set out the facts objectively. You are permitted and, in fact, expected to present the facts in such a way that they support your theory of the case.

In presenting the facts, attorneys use a number of different techniques. They create a favorable context, they tell the story from their client's point of view, they emphasize the facts that support their theory of the case and de-emphasize those that do not, and they select their words correctly.

a. Create a Favorable Context

A court will view a fact differently depending on the context in which it is presented. Consider, for example, the following sentence:

He pulled out his gun and, at point-blank range, shot the woman in the head.   **EXAMPLE 1**

After reading this sentence, what is your reaction? Who is the "bad guy"? Who is the victim? For most, it is the gunman who is the bad guy. Having shot a woman at point-blank range, he is a cold-blooded killer who should be found guilty of murder. Now read the following sentence.

Pushing his young son out of harm's way, he pulled out his gun and, at point-blank range, shot the woman in the head.   **EXAMPLE 2**

Although the gunman has shot a woman, he is no longer a cold-blooded killer. He is a father shooting to save his son. The context has changed, and the gunman is no longer the bad guy. He and his son are the victims. Consider one final sentence.

Having stalked his victim for days, the gunman pushed his young son behind him, pulled out his gun and, at point-blank range, shot the woman in the head.   **EXAMPLE 3**

Do we still have a father shooting to save his son? The answer is no. Now we have a gunman who is worse than the cold-blooded killer in the first example: we have a stalker who shoots a woman in front of his own son. Another context, a different verdict.

As the preceding examples illustrate, one way to create a favorable context is to start the story where it favors your client. In the following example, Patterson uses this technique. Instead of starting his statement of facts with the assault or his arrest, he starts it by describing what he was doing on the day of the assault. By starting with these facts, he is able to start the story with facts that support his theory of the case: that he is an innocent pedestrian who happened to be in the wrong place at the wrong time. Note how the writer works in the fact that Patterson is married, that he has a job, and that he does nice things, for instance, he takes his wife to work, does the laundry, and arranges to meet his wife during her dinner break.

EXAMPLE 1

The First Three Paragraphs of the Defendant's Statement of Facts

At 7:30 on Monday morning, August 14, 2006, 22-year-old Dean Patterson finished his shift as a security guard and walked to his apartment. After having breakfast with his wife, Patterson went to bed and slept until about 1:00 p.m. At about 2:30 p.m., Patterson's wife received a phone call asking her to work at the local hospital, where she is employed as a nurse. She got ready, and Patterson dropped her off at the hospital at about 3:10. When he returned, Patterson could not find a parking place close to his apartment and had to park several blocks away.

At about 3:30, Patterson called his wife to find how long she would have to work. They had had plans to go to a movie that evening, and he wanted to know whether he should change those plans. At about 3:50, Patterson took a load of laundry to the apartment complex's laundry room. When he returned to his apartment, Patterson watched part of an old movie. At about 4:20, Patterson went back to the laundry room to put the clothes in the dryer. On his way back, he walked to where his car, an older model red station wagon, was parked to see if he needed to get gas. As he did so, Patterson noticed a parking spot much closer to his apartment and, after checking his gas gauge, moved his car to that spot. After parking his car, Patterson got out of the car and, because the driver's side door does not lock from the outside, walked to the passenger side to lock the doors. As he did so, he nodded to a parking enforcement officer who was driving by.

By this time, it was 4:30, and Patterson decided to phone his wife again. He arranged to meet her at 5:15 for her dinner break. Patterson picked up the laundry and then left the apartment a little before 5:00 to meet his wife.

The State also creates a favorable context. However, instead of starting its statement of facts by describing Patterson's actions, it begins the story where it started for the victim. In the first paragraph of its statement of facts, the State describes the assault and then the show-up and line-up.

EXAMPLE 2

The First Paragraph of the State's Statement of Facts

On Monday, August 14, 2006, Beatrice Martinez was assaulted with a deadly weapon. At a show-up held thirty to forty minutes after the attack, Martinez positively identified the defendant, Dean E. Patterson, as her assailant. Four days after the assault, Martinez picked Patterson out of a line-up, once again positively identifying him as her assailant.

b. Tell the Story from the Client's Point of View

One of the most powerful persuasive devices is point of view. In most cases, you will want to tell the story as your client would tell it.

One way of telling the story from your client's point of view is to make your client the "actor" in most of your sentences. Note how in the defendant's statement of facts, the writer has made Patterson or his wife the subject in most of the main clauses while, in the State's statement of facts, the writer has made Martinez the subject in most of the main clauses.

In the following examples, the subject of each sentence is in bold.

Excerpt from Defendant's Statement of Facts

At 7:30 on Monday morning, August 14, 2006, 22-year-old **Dean Patterson** finished his shift as a security guard and walked to his apartment. After having breakfast with his wife, **Patterson** went to bed and slept until about 1:00 p.m. At about 2:30 p.m., **Patterson's wife** received a phone call asking her to work at the local hospital where she is employed as a nurse. **She** got ready, and **Patterson** dropped her off at the hospital at about 3:10. When he returned, **Patterson** could not find a parking place close to his apartment and had to park several blocks away.

At about 3:30, **Patterson** called his wife to find how long she would have to work. **They** had had plans to go to a movie that evening, and **he** wanted to know whether he should change those plans. At about 3:50, **Patterson** took a load of laundry to the apartment complex's laundry room. When he returned to his apartment, **Patterson** watched part of an old movie. At about 4:20, **Patterson** went back to the laundry room to put the clothes in the dryer. On his way back, **he** walked to where his car, an older model red station wagon, was parked to see if he needed to get gas. As he did so, **Patterson** noticed a parking spot much closer to his apartment and, after checking his gas gauge, moved his car to that spot. After parking his car, **Patterson** got out of the car and, because the driver's side door does not lock from the outside, walked to the passenger side to lock the doors. As he did so, **he** nodded to a parking enforcement officer who was driving by.

By this time, **it** was 4:30, and **Patterson** decided to phone his wife again. **He** arranged to meet her at 5:15 for her dinner break. **Patterson** picked up the laundry and then left the apartment a little before 5:00 to meet his wife.

Excerpt from the State's Statement of Facts

On Monday, August 14, 2006, **Beatrice Martinez** was assaulted with a deadly weapon. At a show-up held thirty to forty minutes after the attack, **Martinez** positively identified the defendant, Dean E. Patterson, as her assailant. Four days after the assault, **Martinez** picked Patterson out of a line-up, once again positively identifying him as her assailant.

c. Emphasize the Facts That Support Your Theory of the Case, and De-emphasize Those That Do Not

In addition to presenting the facts from the client's point of view, good advocates emphasize those facts that support their theory of the case and de-emphasize those that do not. They do this by using one or more of the following techniques.

1. Airtime

Just as listeners remember best the songs that get the most airtime, readers remember best the facts that get the most words. Consequently, favorable facts should be given considerable "airtime," while unfavorable ones should be given little or no "play." In our example case, if Patterson is going to persuade the court that the identifications are unreliable, he needs to de-emphasize the fact that Martinez saw the car twice. Although he cannot omit the fact that the car drove by twice, he does not need to give this fact very much airtime. In contrast, if the State is going to persuade the court that Martinez's identifications are reliable, it needs to emphasize the fact that she saw the car twice. Thus, the State wants to give this fact as much airtime as possible. In the following examples, the relevant facts are in bold.

EXAMPLE 1   **Excerpt from the Defendant's Statement of Facts**

Martinez has stated that she was walking down Belmont **when a car that had driven by earlier** pulled in front of her. The man got out of his car, took one or two steps toward Martinez, and then pulled a gun from his pocket. As soon as she spotted the gun, Martinez screamed, looked away, and then, crying, ran across the street. The entire encounter was over in a second or two.

EXAMPLE 2   **Excerpt from the State's Statement of Facts**

As she was walking north on Belmont, Martinez observed an older model red station wagon with a chrome luggage rack as it passed slowly by her. Moments later, the same car came down the street again. This time, the driver pulled his car in front of Martinez, stopping his car so that it blocked her path. As Martinez watched, the driver got out of his car and walked toward her. The man then took a gun from his coat pocket and pointed it at Martinez. Martinez looked at the gun, looked back up at her assailant, and then, crying, ran back across the street to safety.

---

2. Detail

Just as readers tend to remember best those facts that get the most airtime, they also tend to remember best those facts that are described in detail. The more detail, the more vivid the picture; the more vivid the picture, the more likely it is that the reader will remember the particular facts. Thus, airtime and detail work hand in hand. In contrast, to de-emphasize unfavorable facts, good advocates describe them in general terms.

Look once again at the following examples, this time comparing the way in which the defendant and the State describe the assailant's car. By leaving out the description of the car, is the defendant setting out all of the legally significant facts? What inference does the State want the judge to draw?

EXAMPLE 1   **Excerpt from the Defendant's Statement of Facts**

Martinez has stated that she was walking down Belmont when **a car** that had driven by earlier pulled in front of her. The man got out of his car, took one or two steps toward Martinez, and then pulled a gun from his pocket. As soon as she spotted the gun, Martinez screamed, looked away, and then, crying, ran across the street. The entire encounter was over in a second or two.

Excerpt from the State's Statement of Facts

EXAMPLE 2

As she was walking north on Belmont, Martinez observed **an older model red station wagon with a chrome luggage rack** as it passed slowly by her. Moments later, the same car came down the street again. This time, the driver pulled his car in front of Martinez, stopping his car so that it blocked her path. As Martinez watched, the driver got out of his car and walked toward her. The man then took a gun from his coat pocket and pointed it at Martinez. Martinez looked at the gun, looked back up at her assailant, and then, crying, ran back across the street to safety.

3. *Positions of Emphasis*

Try the following experiment. Read section 24.6 of this book and then close the book and write down everything you can remember. If you are like most readers, the items on your list will be the information that appeared at the beginning and end of the section, at the beginning and end of a paragraph, or at the beginning and end of a sentence.

Because readers tend to remember best information that is placed in a position of emphasis (the beginning and end of a section, the beginning and end of a paragraph, and the beginning and end of a sentence), whenever possible, place the facts that you want to emphasize in one of these positions. Conversely, if you want to de-emphasize a fact, bury it in the middle. Place it in the middle of a sentence, in the middle of a paragraph, or in the middle of a section.

In the following examples, the defendant wants to emphasize that Martinez told the police that her assailant was in his mid-forties. As a consequence, he places that fact near the end of the paragraph. In contrast, because the State wants to de-emphasize that fact, it places it in the middle of a sentence in the middle of a paragraph.

Excerpt from the Defendant's Statement of Facts

EXAMPLE 1

Because she was upset, Martinez was able to give the police only a general description of her assailant. She described him as being a short, white male with blondish-brown hair who was wearing glasses and a dark jacket. In addition, **she told the police that her assailant was in his early 40s**. Patterson is 22.

Excerpt from the State's Statement of Facts

EXAMPLE 2

Martinez told the police that her assailant was a white male who was about 5'7" tall, that her assailant had wavy blondish-brown hair, **that her assailant appeared to be in his early 40s**, and that at the time of the assault, her assailant was wearing a dark jacket and glasses.

In the next set of examples, the defendant wants to de-emphasize that he owns an older model red station wagon while the State wants to emphasize that fact.

EXAMPLE 3   ## Excerpt from the Defendant's Statement of Fact

At about 3:50, Patterson took a load of laundry to the apartment complex's laundry room. When he returned to his apartment, Patterson watched part of an old movie. At about 4:20, Patterson went back to the laundry room to put the clothes in the dryer. On his way back, he walked to where his car, **an older model red station wagon**, was parked to see if he needed to get gas. As he did so, Patterson noticed a parking spot much closer to his apartment and, after checking his gas gauge, he moved his car to that spot. After parking his car, Patterson got out of the car and, because the driver's side door does not lock from the outside, he walked to the passenger side to lock the doors. As he did so, he nodded to a parking enforcement officer who was driving by.

EXAMPLE 4   ## Excerpt from the State's Statement of Fact

Later that day, **the police searched Patterson's car, an older model red station wagon with a chrome luggage rack**, and his apartment. In the apartment, they found a gun.

---

4. Sentence Length

Just as airtime and detail work together, so do positions of emphasis and sentence length. Because readers tend to remember information placed in shorter sentences better than information placed in longer sentences, good advocates place favorable facts in short sentences in a position of emphasis. For instance, in Example 1, not only did defense counsel place the favorable fact in a position of emphasis, but he also put that fact in a relatively short sentence. In Example 2, the State not only buried the information in the middle of the paragraph, it also placed the information in the middle of a long sentence.

EXAMPLE 1   ## Excerpt from the Defendant's Statement of Facts

Because she was upset, Martinez was able to give the police only a general description of her assailant. She described him as being a short, white male with blondish-brown hair who was wearing glasses and a dark jacket. In addition, she told police that her assailant was in his early 40s. **Patterson is 22**.

EXAMPLE 2   ## Excerpt from the State's Statement of Facts

Martinez told the police that her assailant was a white male who was about 5'7" tall, that her assailant had wavy blondish-brown hair, **that her assailant appeared to be in his early 40s**, and that at the time of the assault, her assailant was wearing a dark jacket and glasses.

In the following example, the State uses a short sentence at the end of a paragraph to emphasize that the police found a gun in Patterson's apartment.

Excerpt from the State's Statement of Facts

EXAMPLE 3

Later that day, the police searched Patterson's car, an older model red station wagon with a chrome luggage rack, and his apartment. **In the apartment, they found a gun**.

5. Active and Passive Voice

Good advocates use the active voice when they want to emphasize what the actor did and the passive voice when they want to draw the reader's attention away from the actor's actions. Consider the following examples.

Active Voice

EXAMPLE 1

Patterson assaulted Martinez.

Passive Voice

EXAMPLE 2

Martinez was assaulted.

Because the State wants to emphasize that it was Patterson who assaulted Martinez, the prosecutor would use the language in Example 1. In contrast, because the defendant states that he is not the person who assaulted Martinez, he would use the language set out in Example 2. See section 23.1 for more on the active and passive voice.

6. Dependent and Main Clauses

Another technique is to put favorable facts in the main clause and unfavorable facts in a dependent clause. Compare the following examples. While the defendant wants to emphasize the fact that Clipse was unable to make an identification and de-emphasize the fact that Martinez was able to make an identification, the State wants to do the opposite.

Excerpt from the Defendant's Brief

EXAMPLE 1

Later that day, the police searched Patterson's car and apartment. In the apartment, the police found the gun issued to Patterson by his employer. Four days later, the police held a line-up at the police station. **Although Martinez identified Patterson as the man who had approached her, Clipse did not pick Patterson out of the lineup.**

Excerpt from the State's Brief

EXAMPLE 2

A line-up was held four days later. **Although Clipse was unable to identify the man who had assaulted Martinez, Martinez identified Patterson as her assailant.**

d. Choose Your Words Carefully

Words are powerful. Not only do they convey information, but they also create images. Consider, for example, the labels that might be used to describe Mr. Patterson:

Mr. Dean Patterson
Dean Patterson
Patterson
Dean
the suspect
the accused
the defendant

While defense counsel would probably want to use "Mr. Patterson," "Dean Patterson," or "Patterson" in referring to her client, the prosecutor would want to use "the defendant." By using his name, defense counsel reminds the judge that her client is a real person. The title "Mr. Patterson" makes Patterson seem less like a person charged with a felony and more like an average respectable citizen. In contrast, by using the label "defendant" the State suggests that Patterson is guilty.

Other word choices can also subtly persuade the court. For instance, in the following paragraph the defendant wants to set up his argument that Officer Yuen's actions tainted the identifications. Thus, he uses words like "agreed" to suggest that Martinez's identification was prompted by Officer Yuen's questions, words like "questioned" to suggest that the officers' actions would have indicated to Martinez and Clipse that Patterson was guilty, and words like "watched" to remind the court that Martinez and Clipse may have been influenced by the officers' actions.

EXAMPLE   **Excerpt from the State's Statement of Facts**

Even though Martinez was unable to see the man's face, she **agreed** with the officer that the man looked like her assailant. At this point, Officer Yuen stopped the car, got out, and approached Patterson. As he was **questioning** Patterson, Officer Cox drove up with Clipse. While Martinez and Clipse **watched**, Officers Cox and Yuen **continued questioning** Patterson. Officer Cox then returned to Martinez and Clipse and walked them back to Clipse's apartment. While Officer Cox did so, Officer Yuen placed Patterson under arrest.

§ 17.5.4 Checklist for Critiquing the Statement of Facts

I. Organization

- The facts have been presented in a logical order (chronologically or topically).
- When possible, the facts have been presented in an order that favors the client.

II. Content

- The writer has included both the relevant procedural facts (procedural history) and the facts on which the case is based (statement of facts).
- All of the legally significant facts have been included.
- The emotionally significant facts that favor the client have been included.
- An appropriate number of background facts have been included.

III. Persuasiveness

- The writer has presented the facts so that they support the writer's theory of the case.
- The writer has presented the facts in a favorable context.
- The writer has presented the facts from the point of view that favors the client. (In telling the client's story, the writer has used the client as the subject of most sentences.)
- The writer has emphasized favorable facts and de-emphasized unfavorable ones.
  - Favorable facts have been given more airtime than unfavorable facts.
  - Favorable facts have been described in detail; unfavorable facts have been described more generally.
  - The positions of emphasis have been used effectively. When possible, favorable facts have been placed at the beginning and end of the statement of facts, at the beginning and end of a paragraph, and at the beginning and end of a sentence.
  - Short sentences and short paragraphs have been used to emphasize favorable facts; unfavorable facts have been placed in longer sentences in longer paragraphs.
  - Active and passive voices have been used effectively.
  - Favorable information has been emphasized by placing it in the main, or independent, clause; unfavorable facts have been placed in dependent, or subordinate, clauses.
- Words have been selected not only for their denotation but also for their connotation.

§ 17.6 Drafting the Issue Statement

§ 17.6.1 Select the Lens

The issue statement is the lens through which the judge views the case. Select the correct lens and you improve your chances that the court will see the case as you see it and decide the motion in your client's favor.

The difficulty, of course, is in selecting the lens. How do you select just the right one? Unfortunately, there is no easy answer. Because selecting the lens is, at least in part, a creative act, there is no foolproof formula.

There are, however, some strategies that you can try. First, think about your theory of the case. Given your theory, how should you frame the issue? Second, look at how the court framed the issues in cases that are similar to yours. In the cases in which the courts suppressed the evidence, how did the court frame the issue? Did the court focus on the defendant's rights? On the police's abuse of its power? On discrepancies in the testimony? On the unreliability of the witnesses? Then look at the cases in which the courts did not suppress the evidence.

Finally, brainstorm. From what other angles can you view the case? What other labels can you attach? Think outside the box.

§ 17.6.2 Select a Format

Most courts do not prescribe a format for an issue statement. Although you should have the same number of issue statements as you have main argumentative headings, you can state the issue using the under-does-when format, the whether format, or the multi-sentence format.

EXAMPLE 1   ### "Under-Does-When" Format

Under the Fourteenth Amendment, should the court grant the defendant's motion to suppress Martinez's show-up identification (1) when a police officer pointed out Patterson to Martinez, repeatedly asking the shaken Martinez whether Patterson looked like her assailant; (2) when, during the second or two that Martinez had to view her assailant, her attention was focused on his gun and not his face; and (3) when Martinez told the police that her assailant was in his early 40s and Patterson is only 22 years old?

EXAMPLE 2   ### "Whether" Format

Whether the court should grant the defendant's motion to suppress Martinez's show-up identification (1) when a police officer pointed out Patterson to Martinez, repeatedly asking the shaken Martinez whether Patterson looked like her assailant; (2) when, during the second or two that Martinez had to view her assailant, her attention was focused on his gun and not his face; and (3) when Martinez told the police that her assailant was in his early 40s and Patterson is only 22 years old.

EXAMPLE 3   ### Multi-Sentence Format

On August 14, 2006, a man jumped out of his car, approached Martinez, and pointed a gun at her. As soon as she saw the gun, Martinez screamed and, crying, ran across the street. Shortly after the assault, a police officer twice asked Martinez whether a pedestrian looked like her assailant. Although Martinez could not see the pedestrian's face, she agreed. The police then questioned the pedestrian, Dean Patterson, while Martinez and another witness watched. Both Martinez and the witness told the police that Martinez's assailant was in his late 30s or early 40s. Patterson is 22.

Under these circumstances, should the court suppress Martinez's show-up and line-up identifications and prevent Martinez and Clipse from making in-court identifications?

Although you may use any one of these formats, once you select a format, use it for each of your issue statements. Do not write one issue statement using the under-does-when format, a second issue statement using the whether format, and a third using the multi-sentence format. Also remember that you are not bound by opposing counsel's choices. You do not need to use the same format that he or she used, and you do not need to have the same number of issue statements. Do not let your opponent dictate your strategy.

§ 17.6.3 Make Your Issue Statement Subtly Persuasive

Your issue statement should be subtly persuasive. After reading it, the judge should be inclined to rule in your client's favor.

There are two techniques that you can use to make your issue statements persuasive. First, state the legal question so that it suggests the conclusion you want the court to reach. For example, if you want the court to grant the motion, ask whether the court should grant the motion. In contrast, if you want the court to deny the motion, ask whether the court should deny the motion. Second, include the facts that support your position and present those facts in the light most favorable to your client.

For example, in our example case, the defendant wants to state the legal question so that it suggests that the court should grant his motion to suppress. In contrast, the State wants to frame the question so that it suggests that the court should deny the defendant's motion.

The Defendant's Statement of the Legal Question

EXAMPLE

"Whether the court should grant the motion to suppress when . . . ."

The State's Statement of the Legal Question

EXAMPLE

"Whether the court should deny the motion to suppress when . . . ."

The defendant also wants to set out the facts so that they suggest that the police procedures were unnecessarily suggestive and that Martinez's identifications are unreliable. Accordingly, the defendant wants to set out the facts that establish that the procedure was suggestive. (Instead of allowing Martinez to identify Patterson independently, a police officer pointed out Patterson and repeatedly asked the shaken Martinez whether he looked like her assailant.) In addition, the defendant wants to set out facts that establish that Martinez had a limited opportunity to view her assailant and that her description was inaccurate. Note that in both instances the authors set out the facts related to the first part of the test first and then the facts related to the second part of the test.

EXAMPLE 1   ## The Defendant's Issue Statement

Under the Fourteenth Amendment, should the court grant the defendant's motion to suppress Martinez's show-up identification (1) when a police officer pointed out Patterson to Martinez, repeatedly asking the shaken Martinez whether Patterson looked like her assailant; (2) when, during the second or two that Martinez had to view her assailant, her attention was focused on his gun and not his face; and (3) when Martinez told the police that her assailant was in his early 40s and Patterson is only 22 years old?

While the defendant wants to set out the facts that indicate that the police procedures were unnecessarily suggestive and that Martinez's identifications are unreliable, the State wants to downplay the police officer's questions and emphasize instead that Martinez had a good opportunity to view her assailant.

EXAMPLE 2   ## The State's Issue Statement

Should the court deny the defendant's motion to suppress when the police merely asked the victim whether a pedestrian looked like her assailant and when the victim observed her assailant on two occasions for several seconds in broad daylight?

Thus, writing a persuasive issue statement is a three-step process. You must select the appropriate lens, choose a format, and then craft your issue statement so that it is subtly persuasive.

§ 17.6.4 Checklist for Critiquing the Issue Statement

I. Format

- There are the same number of issue statements as there are main argumentative headings.
- The attorney has used one of the conventional formats: under-does-when, whether, or multi-sentence.
- The same format has been used for each question presented.

II. Content

- The issue statement states the legal question and includes references to the legally significant facts. In addition, when appropriate, it also includes a reference to the rule of law.
- The legal questions have been framed so that they support the writer's theory of the case.

III. Persuasiveness

- The legal question has been framed so that it suggests an answer favorable to the client.

- Favorable facts have been emphasized, and unfavorable ones de-emphasized.
- Words have been selected for both their denotation and their connotation.

IV. Writing

- The judge can understand the issue statement after reading it through once.
- Punctuation has been used to divide the issue statement into manageable units of meaning.
- When appropriate, parallel constructions have been used.
- In both the main and subordinate clauses, the subjects and verbs are close together.
- The issue statement is grammatically correct, correctly punctuated, and proofread.

§ 17.7 Ordering the Issues and Arguments

§ 17.7.1 Present the Issues and Arguments in a Logical Order

In many cases, logic dictates the order of both the issues and, under each issue, the arguments. Threshold questions (for example, issues relating to whether the court has jurisdiction or to the statute of limitations) must be discussed before questions relating to the merits of the case. Similarly, the parts of a test must be discussed in order and, when one argument builds on another, the foundation argument must be presented first.

Although in our example case there is only one issue — whether the court should grant the defendant's motion to suppress — under that issue are several subissues. The court must decide (1) whether to suppress Martinez's show-up identification, (2) whether to suppress Martinez's line-up identification, and (3) whether to suppress any in-court identifications that Martinez or Clipse might make.

Logic dictates, at least in part, the order in which these three subissues should be discussed. Because an impermissibly suggestive show-up would taint the line-up and in-court identifications, you should discuss the show-up before the line-up and both the show-up and the line-up before the in-court identifications.

Logic also dictates the order of the arguments. Before it will suppress an identification, the court must find (1) that the police procedures were impermissibly suggestive and (2) that, under the totality of the circumstances, the resulting identifications are unreliable. Consequently, the defendant must discuss suggestiveness first.

In deciding whether an identification is reliable, the court considers five factors: (1) the witness's opportunity to see her assailant; (2) the witness's degree of attention; (3) the accuracy of the witness's description; (4) the witness's level of certainty; and (5) the length of time between the crime and the confrontation. Does logic dictate that these factors be discussed in any particular order?

§ 17.7.2 Decide Which Issues and Arguments Should Be Presented First

First impressions count. As a consequence, when logic does not dictate the order of your issues or arguments, put your strongest issues and your strongest arguments first. In addition, some attorneys like to end their brief with a strong argument. Although this strategy allows you to take advantage of the positions of emphasis, it also creates a risk. If the judge does not finish your brief, he or she may not see one of your strong arguments.

§ 17.8 Drafting the Argumentative Headings

§ 17.8.1 Use Your Argumentative Headings to Define the Structure of the Arguments

Just as posts and beams define the form of a building, argumentative headings define the form of the argument. When drafted properly, they provide the judge with an outline of the argument.

EXAMPLE   **Defendant's Argumentative Headings**

I. THE COURT SHOULD GRANT THE DEFENDANT'S MOTION TO SUPPRESS MARTINEZ'S SHOW-UP AND LINE-UP IDENTIFICATIONS AND MARTINEZ'S AND CLIPSE'S IN-COURT IDENTIFICATIONS.
> [Text]

A. Martinez's show-up identification should be suppressed because the police procedures were impermissibly suggestive and because Martinez's identification is unreliable.
> [Text]

1. The police procedures were impermissibly suggestive because the police officer repeatedly asked Martinez whether Patterson looked like her assailant and because the officers questioned Patterson in Martinez's presence.
> [Text]

2. Martinez's identification is unreliable because Martinez was able to view her assailant for only a few seconds, her attention was focused on the gun and not his face, and her description of her assailant does not match the description of Patterson.
> [Text]

B. Martinez's line-up identification should be suppressed because it was tainted by the show-up.

[Text]

C. <u>Martinez should not be permitted to make an in-court identification</u>
<u>because such an identification would be tainted by the impermissibly</u>
<u>suggestive show-up and the line-up.</u>

In addition to defining the structure of the argument, argumentative headings also act as locators. By using the headings and subheadings, a judge can locate a particular argument. Argumentative headings also help the writer. As a practicing attorney, you will seldom have large blocks of time available for writing. Instead, you will have to squeeze in an hour here and two hours there. If you prepare your argumentative headings first, you can use what time you have effectively and write the sections one at a time.

§ 17.8.2 Use Your Argumentative Headings to Persuade

In addition to using argumentative headings to define the structure of your argument, use the headings to persuade.

Begin your heading by setting out a positive assertion. If you want the court to grant your motion to suppress, make that assertion: "The court should grant the motion to suppress. . . ." In contrast, if you want the court to deny the motion to suppress, make that assertion: "The court should deny the motion to suppress. . . ."

Not Effective: Not a Positive Assertion   EXAMPLES

The court should not grant the motion to suppress. . . .

The court should not suppress Martinez's show-up identification. . . .

Effective: Positive Assertion   EXAMPLE

The court should deny the motion to suppress. . . .

The court should admit Martinez's show-up identification. . . .

After setting out your assertion, you will usually want to set out the facts or reasons that support your assertion. The most common format is as follows:

Assertion	because	facts or reasons that support your assertion
Martinez's line-up identification should be suppressed	because	it was tainted by the impermissibly suggestive show-up.

In those instances in which you do not set out the reasons in your heading, use subheadings or sub-subheadings to set out the reasons. Look again at the headings and subheadings in the defendant's argumentative headings. Although the writer has not included a "because" clause in the main heading, she has included them in the subheadings and sub-subheadings.

EXAMPLE 2   **Defendant's Argumentative Headings**

I.   THE COURT SHOULD GRANT THE DEFENDANT'S MOTION TO SUPPRESS MARTINEZ'S SHOW-UP AND LINE-UP IDENTIFICATIONS AND MARTINEZ'S AND CLIPSE'S IN-COURT IDENTIFICATIONS.

[Text]

A.   Martinez's show-up identification should be suppressed because the police procedures were impermissibly suggestive and because Martinez's identification is unreliable.

[Text]

1.   The police procedures were impermissibly suggestive because the police officer repeatedly asked Martinez whether Patterson looked like her assailant and because the officers questioned Patterson in Martinez's presence.

[Text]

2.   Martinez's identification is unreliable because Martinez was able to view her assailant for only a few seconds, her attention was focused on the gun and not his face, and her description of her assailant does not match the description of Patterson.

[Text]

B.   Martinez's line-up identification should be suppressed because it was tainted by the show-up.

[Text]

C.   Martinez should not be permitted to make an in-court identification because such an identification would be tainted by the impermissibly suggestive show-up and the line-up.

---

§ 17.8.3 Make Your Headings Readable

If the judge does not read your headings, they do not serve either of their functions: they do not provide the judge with an outline of your argument, and they do not persuade. To make sure that your headings are read by the judge, keep them short and make them easy to read. As a general rule, your headings should be no more than three typed lines.

In the following example, the writer has tried to put too much information in her heading. As a result, the heading is too long, and the sentence is difficult to understand.

Heading Is Too Long and Difficult to Understand

The police procedures were impermissibly suggestive because the witness viewed only one person, the police repeatedly asked the witness whether that person looked like her assailant, and the police questioned the person in front of the witness, and because the person was simply walking down the street and not trying to escape and the witness was not likely to die or disappear, there was no reason to conduct a one-person show-up.

The following heading is much better. Instead of trying to put her entire argument into her heading, the writer has included only her most important points.

Heading Is Shorter and Easier to Understand

1. The police procedures were impermissibly suggestive because the police officer repeatedly asked Martinez whether Patterson looked like her assailant and because the officers questioned Patterson in Martinez's and Clipse's presence.

§ 17.8.4 Follow the Conventions: Number, Placement, and Typefaces

By convention, you should have one, and only one, main argumentative heading for each issue statement. You set out the question in your issue statement and answer it in your main heading. Although subheadings and sub-subheadings are optional, if you include one, you should have at least two. You may, or may not, elect to include text between the main heading and the first subheading or between a subheading and the first sub-subheading.

Historically, only three typefaces were used. When briefs were prepared using typewriters, the main headings were set out using all capital letters, the subheadings were underlined, and the sub-subheadings were set out using regular typeface. Although many attorneys still use this system, others have adopted different systems, for example, setting out the main headings in bold rather than all capitals. Check with your local court and firm to see what is commonly done in your jurisdiction.

Typefaces for Main Heading, Subheadings, and Sub-subheadings

    I.   FIRST MAIN HEADING [Answers question set out in first issue statement.]
           [If appropriate, set out introductory paragraph and general rules here.]

        A.   First subheading
             [If appropriate, set out test here.]
           1.   First sub-subheading
               [Set out argument here.]
           2.   Second sub-subheading
               [Set out argument here.]

    B. <u>Second subheading</u>
      [Set out argument here.]

  II. SECOND MAIN HEADING [If you had two issue statements, answers question set out in the second issue statement.]

    A. <u>First subheading</u>
      [Set out argument here.]

    B. <u>Second subheading</u>
      [Set out argument here.]

    C. <u>Third subheading</u>
      [Set out argument here.]

---

§ 17.8.5 Checklist for Critiquing the Argumentative Headings

I. Content

- When read together, the headings provide the judge with an outline of the argument.

II. Persuasiveness

- Each heading is in the form of a positive assertion.
- Each assertion is supported, either in the main heading or through the use of subheadings.
- The headings are case-specific; that is, they include references to the parties and the facts of the case.
- Favorable facts are emphasized and unfavorable facts are de-emphasized or omitted if not legally significant.
- Favorable facts have been placed in the positions of emphasis.
- Favorable facts have been described vividly and in detail.
- Words have been selected both for their denotation and their connotation.

III. Conventions

- The writer has used the conventional typefaces for main headings, subheadings, and sub-subheadings.
- There is never just one subheading or just one sub-subheading in a section.

IV. Writing

- The judge can understand the heading after reading it through once. (Headings are not more than two or three lines long.)
- Punctuation has been used to divide the heading into manageable units of meaning.
- When appropriate, parallel constructions have been used.
- In both the main and subordinate clauses, the subject and verb are close together.
- The headings are grammatically correct, correctly punctuated, and proofread.

§ 17.9 Drafting the Arguments

Most of us have had arguments. As children, we fought with our parents over cleaning our rooms or over how late we could stay out. As adults, we have fought with friends, roommates, spouses, and partners over household chores, budgets, and world events.

Although most of us have had arguments, very few of us have been taught how to make arguments. We know how to express our anger and frustration; we do not know how to set out an assertion and then systematically walk our listener through our "proof." Even fewer of us have been taught how to set out our proofs persuasively.

It is, however, exactly these skills — the ability to set out an assertion, to walk your reader through your proof, and to present that proof persuasively — that you will need to develop if you are going to write an effective brief. Good advocates have the mental discipline of a mathematician. They think linearly, identifying each of the steps in the analysis, and then walk the judge through those steps in a logical order. They also have the creativity and insight of an advertising executive. They know their "market," and they know both the image they want to create and how to use language to create it. In short, they have mastered both the science and the art of advocacy.

§ 17.9.1 Identify Your Assertions and Your Support for Those Assertions

An argument has two parts: an assertion and the support for that assertion.

a. Setting Out Your Assertion

An assertion can take one of two forms. It can be procedural, setting out the procedural act you want the court to take, or it can be substantive, setting out the legal conclusion you want the court to reach.

Types of Assertions   `EXAMPLES`

Procedural:

> The court should grant the motion to suppress.

> The court should deny the motion to suppress.

Substantive:

> The police procedures were impermissibly suggestive.

> The witness's identification is reliable.

---

b. Supporting Your Assertion

Although your assertion is an essential part of your argument, it is not, by itself, an argument. How many judges would be persuaded by the following exchange?

Defense counsel:	Your Honor, the court should grant the Defendant's motion to suppress.
Prosecutor:	Your Honor, we respectfully disagree. The court should deny the motion.
Defense counsel:	No, Your Honor, the court should grant the motion.
Prosecutor:	No. The court should deny the motion.

An exchange in which the defendant asserts that the police procedures were impermissibly suggestive and the prosecutor asserts that they were not is equally unpersuasive. Standing alone, assertions do not persuade. They must be supported.

In law, that support can take one of several forms. You can support an assertion by applying a statute or common law rule to the facts of your case, by comparing or contrasting the facts in your case to the facts in analogous cases, or by explaining why, as a matter of public policy, the court should rule in your client's favor.

In the first example set out below, the defendant supports his assertion by applying the rule to the facts of his case. In the second example, the defendant supports his assertion by comparing the facts in his case to the facts in the analogous cases, and, in the third example, he supports his assertion using public policy.

EXAMPLE 1   **Defendant Supports His Assertion by Applying the Rules to the Facts of His Case**

Assertion:	The police procedures were impermissibly suggestive.
Support:	Rule: One-person show-ups are inherently suggestive. *See Neil v. Biggers*, 409 U.S. 188, 199, 93 S. Ct. 375, 34 L. Ed. 2d 401 (1972).[1] When the police present the witness with a single suspect, the witness usually infers that the police believe that the person being presented committed the crime. *Id.*
Application:	In this case, the police presented Martinez with a single suspect: Dean Patterson. In doing so, the police suggested to Martinez that Patterson was the man who had assaulted her.

EXAMPLE 2   **Defendant Supports His Assertion by Comparing the Facts in His Case with the Facts in an Analogous Case**

Assertion:	The police procedures were impermissibly suggestive.
Support:	Analogous case: In *State v. Booth,* 36 Wn. App. 66, 67-68, 671 P.2d 1218 (1983), the police brought the witness to the scene of the arrest and showed him a single suspect, who was sitting with his back to the witness in the back seat of the police car. The court held that the police procedures were impermissibly suggestive. *Id.* at 71.

---

1. Because this brief is being submitted to a Washington court, the writer has used the Washington citation rules.

Application: As in *Booth,* in our case the police showed the witness a single
suspect and asked her to identify him before she had an oppor-
tunity to see his face. The only difference between the two cases
is the identity of the person in the police car. While in *Booth* it was
the suspect who was in the car, in our case it was the witness.

The Defendant Supports His Assertion by Using Public Policy   EXAMPLE 3

Assertion: The police procedures were impermissibly suggestive.

Support: Policy: To protect the rights of defendants, the courts should suppress unreliable identifications.

Application: Because Martinez's identifications are unreliable, Patterson will
be denied his right to a fair trial if Martinez's show-up and line-up
identifications are admitted.

If there is only one argument that supports your assertion, make that
argument. If, however, you can make several different arguments, think
about whether you want to include all of those arguments. Will your brief
be more persuasive if you set out only one strong argument, or will it be more
persuasive if you set out three, four, or five arguments? Identifying the arguments is the science; deciding which arguments to include is the art.

§ 17.9.2 Select an Organizational Scheme

In making their arguments, most advocates use one of two types of reasoning: deductive or inductive. When you use deductive reasoning, you set out
your assertion and then the support for that assertion. In contrast, when you
use inductive reasoning, you set out your support first, and then walk the
judge through your support to your conclusion.

Deductive Reasoning:

Assertion: The identification is not reliable.

Support: The identification is not reliable because Martinez viewed her
assailant for only two or three seconds.

The identification is not reliable because Martinez's attention was
focused on the gun and not on her assailant's face.

The identification is not reliable because Martinez's description of
her assailant was inaccurate.

The identification is not reliable because, at least initially, Martinez
was not certain that Patterson was her assailant.

Inductive Reasoning:

Support: Martinez viewed her assailant for only two or three seconds.

Martinez's attention was focused on the gun and not on her
assailant's face.

Martinez's description of her assailant was inaccurate.

At least initially, Martinez was not certain that Patterson was her assailant.

Conclusion: Because Martinez viewed her assailant for only two or three seconds, because her attention was focused on the gun and not on her assailant's face, because her description of her assailant was inaccurate, and because, at least initially, she was not certain that Patterson was her assailant, Martinez's identification is not reliable.

If you use deductive reasoning, you will usually use a version of the following blueprint. Note the similarities between this blueprint and the blueprints that you used to organize the discussion section in your objective memo. Also note that the example shows two different ways of setting out the arguments. Under the first subheading, the assertion is set out first. Under the second subheading, the assertion is set out after the rules and the descriptions of the cases. You should use whichever format is, in your case, most likely to be effective.

EXAMPLE   **Blueprint for an Argument Set Out Using Deductive Reasoning**

    I. MAIN HEADING
       [Test set out in the light most favorable to your client.]

       A. <u>First subheading</u>
          1. Assertion
          2. Rules set out in the light most favorable to your client
          3. Descriptions of the analogous cases
          4. Your arguments
          5. Your response to your opponent's arguments

       B. <u>Second subheading</u>
          1. Rules set out in the light most favorable to your client
          2. Descriptions of the analogous cases
          3. Assertion
          4. Your arguments
          5. Your response to your opponent's arguments

When you use inductive reasoning, you will usually integrate the rules, the descriptions of the cases, and your response to the other side's arguments into each of your arguments.

EXAMPLE   **Blueprint for an Argument Set Out Using Inductive Reasoning**

    I. MAIN HEADING

       A. <u>First subheading</u>
          1. First argument
          2. Second argument
          3. Third argument

4. Fourth argument
5. Conclusion

B. <u>Second subheading</u>
   1. First argument
   2. Second argument
   3. Third argument
   4. Conclusion

There are also several other organizational schemes that you may use. For example, if, in your case, the facts are your best argument, start by setting out the facts. Then show how those facts are similar to the facts in cases in which the court reached the conclusion you want the court to reach.

Facts Set Out First   EXAMPLE

I. MAIN HEADING
[Test set out in the light most favorable to your client.]

A. <u>First subheading</u>
   1. Facts of your case
   2. Comparison of the facts in your case to the facts in analogous cases
   3. Courts' holdings in analogous cases
   4. Response to other side's arguments
   5. Conclusion

In the following example, defense counsel used this strategy in arguing that the show-up was impermissibly suggestive. Because none of the cases supported her position, defense counsel began her argument by setting out her assertion and the facts that support that assertion.

Excerpt from the Defendant's Brief   EXAMPLE

A. <u>The police procedures were unnecessarily suggestive because the police showed Martinez a single suspect, asked Martinez whether the suspect looked like her assailant, and questioned the suspect in front of Martinez.</u>

In this case, Officer Yuen's actions suggested to Martinez that he believed Patterson was her assailant.

While driving Martinez home, Officer Yuen pulled up behind Patterson and asked Martinez whether Patterson looked like her assailant. When Martinez did not respond, Officer Yuen repeated his question, asking "Does that look like your assailant?"

Although Martinez could not see Patterson's face, after hesitating, she agreed with Officer Yuen that Patterson looked like her assailant. At that point, Officer Yuen pulled up behind Patterson, got out of the police car, and began questioning him. A few minutes later, Officer Cox and Clipse arrived, and both Officer Yuen and Officer Cox questioned Patterson while Martinez and Clipse watched.

In contrast, if your best argument is an argument based on an analogous case, start by describing that case.

Excerpt from the State's Brief

A. <u>Merely asking the victim whether a pedestrian looks like her assailant does not make a permissible show-up impermissibly suggestive.</u>

There are no published Washington cases in which the courts have held that a show-up was impermissibly suggestive. Instead, in a Division I case, the court held that the show-up was not impermissibly suggestive when the police picked up the witness at a tavern and told him that they wanted to take him back to his apartment to see if he could identify his assailant. *State v. Rogers,* 44 Wn. App. 510, 515-16, 722 P.2d 1249 (1986). When the witness, an elderly individual who was not wearing his glasses, arrived back at his apartment, he identified the defendant when the defendant came out of the building. *Id.* There was a uniformed police officer in front of the defendant and another uniformed police officer following behind him. *Id.*

Similarly, in *State v. Booth,* 36 Wn. App. 66, 70-71, 671 P.2d 1218 (1983), the court held that the show-up was not impermissibly suggestive when the police asked the witness to accompany them to the place where the defendant had been arrested and the witness identified the defendant after seeing him in the back of a police car. *Id.* at 67-68; *accord State v. Guzman-Cuellar,* 47 Wn.2d 326, 734 P.2d 966 (1987) (show-up not impermissibly suggestive when the defendant was shown to three of the four eye-witnesses while he was in handcuffs standing next to a police car).

Although you want to set out the pieces of your argument in the order that the judge expects to see them, you also want to emphasize your best arguments. Therefore, instead of using a format mechanically, use it creatively to accomplish your purpose.

§ 17.9.3 Present the Rules in the Light Most Favorable to Your Client

Although the structure of the argument section is similar to the structure of the discussion section, the way in which you present the rules is very different. While in an objective memo you set out the rules objectively, in a brief you set them out in the light most favorable to your client. Without misrepresenting the rules, you want to "package" them so that they support your assertion.

To set out the rules in the light most favorable to your client, use one or more of the following techniques.

A. Create a favorable context.
B. State favorable rules as broadly as possible and unfavorable rules as narrowly as possible.
C. Emphasize favorable rules and de-emphasize unfavorable rules.
   1. Emphasize the burden of proof if the other side has the burden; de-emphasize the burden of proof if you have the burden.

2. Give favorable rules more airtime and unfavorable rules less airtime.

3. Place favorable rules in a position of emphasis and bury unfavorable ones.

4. Place favorable rules in short sentences or in the main clause, and place unfavorable rules in longer sentences or in dependent clauses.

D. Select your words carefully.

Compare the following examples, identifying the techniques that the authors used.

Objective Statement of the Rule

EXAMPLE 1

In deciding whether identification testimony is admissible, the courts apply a two-part test. Under the first part of the test, the defendant must prove that the police procedures were impermissibly suggestive. If the court finds that the procedure was impermissibly suggestive, the State then has the burden of showing that, under the totality of the circumstances, the reliability of the identification outweighs the suggestive police procedure. *Manson v. Braithwaite,* 432 U.S. 98, 108, 97 S. Ct. 2243, 53 L. Ed. 2d 140 (1977).

Rules Stated in the Light Most Favorable to the Defendant

EXAMPLE 2

The United States Supreme Court has developed a two-part test to ensure a criminal defendant the procedural due process guaranteed to every individual by the Fourteenth Amendment. *Manson v. Braithwaite,* 432 U.S. 98, 108, 97 S. Ct. 2243, 53 L. Ed. 2d 108 (1977).

Under the first part of the test, the defendant need show only that the identification that he seeks to suppress was obtained through the use of unnecessarily suggestive police procedures. *Id.* Once this has been established, the onus shifts to the State to prove that, under the totality of the circumstances, the witness's identification is so reliable that it should be admitted even though it was obtained through unnecessarily suggestive means. *Id.*

Rules Stated in the Light Most Favorable to the State

EXAMPLE 3

Identifications should not be kept from the jury unless the procedures used in obtaining the identifications were so suggestive and unreliable that a substantial likelihood of irreparable misidentification exists. *Simmons v. United States,* 390 U.S. 377, 384, 88 S. Ct. 967, 19 L. Ed. 2d 1247 (1968).

In deciding whether identification evidence is admissible, the courts employ a two-part test. Under the first part of the test, the defendant has the burden of proving that the identification evidence that he seeks to suppress was obtained through impermissibly suggestive procedures. *Manson v. Braithwaite,* 432 U.S. 98, 108, 97 S. Ct. 2243, 53 L. Ed. 2d 140 (1977). Only if the defendant satisfies this substantial burden is the second part of the test applied.

Even if the court determines that the police procedures were impermissibly suggestive, the evidence is admissible if, under the totality of the circumstances, the identifications are reliable. Due process does not compel the exclusion of an identification if it is reliable. *Id.*

Let's begin by comparing the opening sentences of all three examples. In Example 1, the writer simply states that the court applies a two-part test. There is no attempt to create a favorable context.

EXAMPLE 1   ## Objective Statement of the Rule

In deciding whether identification testimony is admissible, the courts apply a two-part test.

In contrast, in Examples 2 and 3, the writers package the rule, using policy to create a context that favors their respective clients. The key language is highlighted.

EXAMPLE 2   ## Rules Stated in the Light Most Favorable to the Defendant

The United States Supreme Court has developed a two-part test **to ensure a criminal defendant the procedural due process guaranteed to every individual by the Fourteenth Amendment.**

EXAMPLE 3   ## Rules Stated in the Light Most Favorable to the State

Identifications should not be kept from the jury unless the procedures used in obtaining the identifications were so suggestive and unreliable that a substantial likelihood of irreparable misidentification exists.

In addition to creating a favorable context, each of the advocates has focused on different parts of the rule and has emphasized those parts that support his or her assertion and de-emphasized those that do not. Compare the highlighted passages.

EXAMPLE 1   ## Objective Statement of the Rule

Under the first part of the test, **the defendant must prove** that the police procedures were impermissibly suggestive.

Rules Stated in the Light Most Favorable to the Defendant

EXAMPLE 2

Under the first part of the test, **the defendant need show** only that the identification that he seeks to suppress was obtained through the use of unnecessarily suggestive police procedures.

Rules Stated in the Light Most Favorable to the State

EXAMPLE 3

Under the first part of the test, **the defendant has the burden of proving** that the identification evidence he seeks to suppress was obtained through impermissibly suggestive procedures.

Similarly, both sides try to lead the court to the desired conclusions. Defense counsel presumes that the defendant will meet his burden; the State presents the second part of the test as an alternative. Even if the State loses on the first part of the test, it wins on the second. Once again, in excerpts from Examples 2 and 3 the key language is highlighted.

Rules Stated in the Light Most Favorable to the Defendant

EXAMPLE 2

Once this has been established, the onus shifts to the State to prove that, under the totality of the circumstances, the witness's identification is so reliable that it should be admitted even though it was obtained through unnecessarily suggestive means.

Rules Stated in the Light Most Favorable to the State

EXAMPLE 3

In deciding whether identification evidence is admissible, the courts employ a two-part test. Under the first part of the test, the defendant has the burden of proving that the identification evidence he seeks to suppress was obtained through impermissibly suggestive procedures. *Manson v. Braithwaite,* 432 U.S. 98, 113, 97 S. Ct. 2243, 53 L. Ed. 2d 140 (1977). **Only if the defendant satisfies this substantial burden is the second part of the test applied.**

Even if the court determines that the police procedures were impermissibly suggestive, the evidence is admissible if, under the totality of the circumstances, the identifications are reliable. Due process does not compel the exclusion of an identification if it is reliable. *Id.*

Finally, look at the words that each side uses:

Defendant	*State*
ensure	so suggestive
guaranteed	burden
onus shifts	substantial burden
so reliable	compel

Instead of using the language they saw in the cases or the first word that came to mind, each side selected its words carefully, with the goal of subtly influencing the decisionmaking process.

§ 17.9.4 Present the Cases in the Light Most Favorable to Your Client

When you use analogous cases to support your argument, present those cases in the light most favorable to your client. If a case supports your position, emphasize the similarities between the facts in the analogous case and the facts in your case. On the other hand, if a case does not support your position, emphasize the differences.

In our example case, both sides use *State v. Booth*, 36 Wn. App. 66, 671 P.2d 1218 (1983), a case in which the court held that the identification was reliable. The relevant portion of the court's opinion is set out below.

EXAMPLE   **Excerpt from *State v. Booth***

The facts provide several indicia of reliability. Ms. Thomas was driving slowly, it was a clear day, and she observed Booth for approximately 45 seconds. Her attention was greater than average because he had money in his hands and was running. In addition, her attention was particularly drawn to the car with Missouri plates because she had lived in Missouri. Finally, the identification took place 30 to 40 minutes later and was unequivocal. On the basis of these facts we find that reliability outweighed the harm of suggestiveness and the identification was properly admitted.

Because the court found that the identification was reliable, the defendant wants to distinguish *Booth*. As a consequence, in discussing opportunity to view, the defendant wants to emphasize that in *Booth* the witness viewed the defendant for almost a minute, while in our case the witness viewed her assailant for only a few seconds.

EXAMPLE   **Excerpt From the Defendant's Brief**

An identification will not be found to be reliable unless the witness had an adequate opportunity to view the defendant. This was the situation in *Booth*. In that case, a bystander was able to view the defendant for almost a minute. *Id.* at 71. Because she was able to view the defendant for an extended period of time under good conditions, the court concluded that her identification was reliable. *Id.* In contrast, in our case Martinez viewed her assailant for only two or three seconds.

Conversely, the State wants to emphasize the similarities between the facts in its case and the facts in *Booth*. Thus, it tries to minimize the amount of time that the witness had to view the defendant.

Excerpt from the State's Brief

The courts do not require that the witness have viewed the defendant for an extended period of time. For example, in *Booth,* the court found the witness's identification was reliable even though the witness had viewed the defendant for less than a minute. *Id.* at 71.

§ 17.9.5 Present the Arguments in the Light Most Favorable to Your Client

In addition to presenting the rules and analogous cases in the light most favorable to your client, you also want to set out the arguments in the light most favorable to your client. As a general rule, you will want to set out your own arguments first, give your own arguments the most airtime, and use language that strengthens your arguments and undermines the other side's arguments.

a. Present Your Own Arguments First

You will almost always set out your own arguments first. By doing so, you can take advantage of the position of emphasis, emphasizing your argument and de-emphasizing the other side's arguments.

The following example shows you what you do not want to do. By setting out the defendant's assertions, the State gives the defendant's arguments extra airtime. The court gets to read the defendant's argument in the defendant's brief and then again in the State's brief.

Excerpt from the State's Brief: Ineffective

The defendant argues that the police procedures were impermissibly suggestive because the police showed Martinez a single suspect, Patterson, and because they asked Martinez whether Patterson looked like her assailant.

It is our contention that the police procedures were not impermissibly suggestive. One-person show-ups are not per se impermissibly suggestive; if the show-up occurs shortly after the commission of the crime during a search for the suspect, it is permissible. *See State v. Booth,* 36 Wn. App. 66, 70-71, 671 P.2d 1218 (1983).

The following example is substantially better. Instead of starting its arguments by setting out the defendant's assertions, the State starts by setting out a favorable statement of the rule. It then sets out its own argument, integrating its responses to the defendant's arguments into its own arguments.

EXAMPLE 2   **Excerpt from the State's Brief: More Effective**

One-person show-ups are not per se impermissibly suggestive: a show-up is permissible if it occurs shortly after the commission of a crime during a search for the suspect. *See State v. Booth,* 36 Wn. App. 66, 70-71, 671 P.2d 1218 (1983).

In this case, the show-up occurred within forty-five minutes of the assault. It also occurred before the police officers had completed their investigation: Officer Yuen saw Patterson as he was leaving the crime scene to take Martinez home.

Under these circumstances, Officer Yuen would not have been doing his job if, upon seeing a man who matched the assailant's description, he had not asked Martinez whether the man looked like her assailant. The officer's question, "Is that the man?" was not enough to turn a permissible show-up into one that was impermissibly suggestive.

b. Give the Most Airtime to Your Own Arguments

Most of the time, you will want to give more airtime to your own arguments than you do to the other side's arguments. Your goal is to respond to or counter the other side's arguments without giving them too much airtime. Compare the following examples. In the first example, the State gives too much airtime to the defendant's age. In the second, the State counters the defendant's arguments without over-emphasizing them.

EXAMPLE 1   **Excerpt from the State's Brief: Ineffective**

On the whole, Martinez's description was accurate. When she was interviewed, Martinez told the police that her assailant was a white male, that he was approximately 5'7" tall, that he weighed between 165 and 170 pounds, that he had blondish-brown hair, that he was wearing a dark jacket, and **that he appeared to be in his early 40s. In fact, the defendant is 22.**

This discrepancy in age is insignificant. It is often difficult to guess a person's age: some people appear older than they are, while others appear younger. Thus, the court should give little weight to the fact that Martinez misjudged the defendant's age. On the basis of the other information Martinez gave to the police, the police were able to identify the defendant as the assailant.

EXAMPLE 2   **Excerpt from the State's Brief: More Effective**

Martinez was able to give the police a detailed description of her assailant. When she was interviewed, she told the police that her assailant was a white male with blondish-brown hair, that he was approximately 5'7" tall and weighed between 165 and 170 pounds, **that he appeared to be in his early 40s**, and that he was wearing a dark green jacket.

This description is accurate in all but one respect. **Although Martinez misjudged the defendant's age**, she accurately described his hair, his height and weight, and his clothing.

c. Use Language That Strengthens Your Arguments and Undermines the Other Side's Arguments

In setting out your own arguments, do not use phrases such as "We contend that...," "It is our argument that...," "We believe that...," or "We feel...." Just set out your assertions. The following examples from the defendant's brief demonstrate this.

Excerpt from the Defendant's Brief   EXAMPLE

Ineffective:

It is our contention that the police procedures were impermissibly suggestive.

More Effective:

The police procedures were impermissibly suggestive.

On the other hand, when it is necessary to set out the other side's argument, use an introductory phrase that reminds the court that the statement is just the other side's assertion or argument.

Excerpt from the Defendant's Brief   EXAMPLE

Although the State contends that Martinez's identification is reliable, she had only a second or two to view her assailant.

---

d. Use the Same Persuasive Techniques You Used in Setting Out the Facts, Issues, Rules, and Analogous Cases

Finally, when appropriate, use the same persuasive techniques that you used in writing the other parts of your brief. For instance, use the positions of emphasis to your best advantage. Place your best points at the beginning or end of a section or paragraph. In addition, whenever possible, put your strong points in short sentences or, in a longer sentence, in the main clause. Finally, select your words carefully. Choose words that convey not only the right denotation but also the right connotation.

Also remember that persuasive arguments are not written; they are crafted. On first drafts, concentrate on content and organization; on subsequent drafts, work on writing persuasively.

§ 17.9.6 Checklist for Critiquing the Argument

I. Content

- Has the author set out his or her assertions?
- Has the author supported his or her assertions?
  - If appropriate, has the author applied the applicable statute or common law rule to the facts of his or her case?
  - If appropriate, has the author compared and contrasted the facts in the analogous cases to the facts in his or her case?
  - If appropriate, has the author explained why, as a matter of public policy, the court should rule in his or her client's favor?
- Has the author cited to all of the relevant authorities?
- Are the author's statements of the rules and descriptions of the cases accurate?

II. Organization

- Has the author used one of the conventional organizational schemes — for example, deductive or inductive reasoning?
- Has the author used an organizational scheme that allows him or her to emphasize the strongest parts of his or her arguments?

III. Persuasiveness

Rules
- Has the author presented the rule in the light most favorable to his or her client?
  - Did the author create a favorable context?
  - Did the author state favorable rules as broadly as possible and unfavorable rules as narrowly as possible?
  - Did the author emphasize favorable rules and de-emphasize unfavorable ones?
  - Did the author select words both for their denotation and for their connotation?

Analogous Cases
- Has the author presented the cases in the light most favorable to his or her client?
  - Did the author create a favorable context?
  - Did the author state favorable holdings as broadly as possible and unfavorable holdings as narrowly as possible?
  - Did the author emphasize favorable facts and de-emphasize unfavorable ones?
  - Did the author select words both for their denotation and for their connotation?

Arguments
- Did the author present his own arguments first?
- Did the author give his or her own arguments the most airtime?

- Did the author use language that strengthens his or her arguments and weakens his or her opponent's arguments?

§ 17.10 The Prayer for Relief

The final section of the brief is the prayer for relief or the conclusion. In some jurisdictions, the prayer for relief is very short. The attorney simply sets out the relief that he or she wants.

Excerpt from the Defendant's Brief   EXAMPLE

Prayer for Relief

For the reasons set out above, the defendant respectfully requests that the Court grant the Defendant's motion and suppress Martinez's show-up and line-up identifications and any in-court identifications that Martinez or Clipse might make.

In other jurisdictions, the attorney sets out the relief that he or she is requesting and summarizes the arguments.

Excerpt from the Defendant's Brief   EXAMPLE

Conclusion

The Court should suppress Martinez's show-up identification because the police officer's questions were impermissibly suggestive and because, given Martinez's limited opportunity to view her assailant and the inaccuracies in her description, her identification is unreliable.

The court should also suppress Martinez's line-up identification and any in-court identifications that Martinez or Clipse might make. Both the line-up and the in-court identifications have been tainted by the impermissibly suggestive show-up.

---

§ 17.11 Signing The Brief

Before the brief is submitted to the court, it must be signed by an attorney licensed to practice law in the state. The following format is used in many jurisdictions.

Submitted this _____ day of _____, 200 ____.

_____

Attorney for the Defendant

EXAMPLE **Defendant's Brief**

THE SUPERIOR COURT OF KING COUNTY, WASHINGTON

STATE OF WASHINGTON,	)	Case No.: No. 06-01-2226
	)	
Plaintiff,	)	DEFENDANT'S BRIEF IN SUPPORT
	)	OF MOTION TO SUPPRESS
v.	)	
	)	
DEAN E. PATTERSON,	)	
	)	
Defendant.	)	
————————————————	)	

Statement of Facts

At 7:30 a.m. on Monday, August 14, 2006, 22-year-old Dean Patterson finished his shift as a security guard and walked to his apartment. After having breakfast with his wife, he went to bed and slept until about 1:00 p.m. At about 2:30 p.m., Patterson's wife received a phone call asking her to work at the local hospital where she is employed as a nurse. Patterson's wife got ready, and Patterson dropped her off at the hospital at about 3:10.

At about 3:30, Patterson called his wife to find how long she would have to work: they had had plans to go to a movie that evening, and he wanted to know whether he should change those plans. At about 3:50, Patterson took a load of laundry to the apartment complex's laundry room. When he returned to

1

1   his apartment, Patterson watched part of an old movie. At about 4:20, Patter-

2   son went back to the laundry room to put the clothes in the dryer. On his way

3   back, he walked to where his car, an older model red station wagon, was

4   parked to see if he needed to get gas. As he did so, Patterson noticed a park-

5   ing spot much closer to his apartment and, after checking his gas, moved his

6   car to that spot. After parking his car, Patterson got out of the car and, because

7   the driver's side door does not lock from the outside, walked to the passenger side

8   to lock the doors. As he did so, he nodded to a parking enforcement officer who

9   was driving by.

10   By this time, it was 4:30, and Patterson decided to phone his wife again. He

11   arranged to meet her at 5:15 for her dinner break. Patterson retrieved the laundry

12   and then left the apartment a little before 5:00 to meet his wife.

13   At about 4:30 p.m. on the same day, seventeen-year-old Beatrice Martinez

14   left her apartment to walk to work. As she was walking southbound on Belmont,

15   a car that had driven by earlier pulled in front of her. The man got out of his

16   car, took one or two steps toward Martinez, and then pulled a gun from his

17   pocket. As soon as she spotted the gun, Martinez screamed, looked away, and

18   then, crying, ran across the street. The entire encounter was over in three or

19   four seconds.

20   At about 4:50 p.m. Chester Clipse was walking home when he saw a man in a

21   red station wagon driving slowly down the street. When the man started to pull

22   into Clipse's parking stall, Clipse started to approach him to tell him that he could

23   not park there. As he did so, Clipse saw the man get out of his car and walk

24   toward a girl, who was on the sidewalk. He then heard the girl scream, and as

1   she screamed, Clipse saw that the man had a gun. Clipse yelled "hey," and the man

2   turned and ran to his car, putting the gun under his coat. As the girl ran across the

3   street, the man got back into his car, backed out, and drove away, traveling north-

4   bound on Belmont.

5   At the same time, a parking enforcement officer drove down the street. Clipse

6   flagged him down, told him what had happened, and described the car and the man.

7   The parking enforcement officer called 911 and then left to try to locate the car.

8   Because the girl was still crying, Clipse took her to his landlady's apartment. He then

9   went back outside and waited for the police.

10   When the police arrived, Clipse told Officers Yuen and Cox what had happened.

11   Clipse told the police that the man was white, about 5'10" tall, and about 180 to 185

12   pounds. He also told the officers that the man was wearing a green outfit and that he

13   was in his late 30s or early 40s.

14   While Clipse was talking to the police, Officer Cox received a radio mes-

15   sage indicating that the parking enforcement officer had located a car that

16   matched the one that Clipse had described. While Officer Cox took Clipse in his

17   car to see if Clipse could identify the car, Officer Yuen went inside to inter-

18   view Martinez.

19   Because she was still upset, Martinez was able to give Officer Yuen only a

20   general description of her assailant. She described him as being a short, white

21   male with blondish-brown hair who was wearing glasses and a dark jacket. In

22   addition, she told police that her assailant was in his early 40s.

23

24

1   After interviewing Martinez, Officer Yuen took the still shaken Martinez to

2   his car to take her home. When they had traveled less than a block, Officer

3   Yuen noticed a white male wearing dark-colored clothing. As he drove up

4   behind him, Yuen asked Martinez, "Is that the man?" When Martinez did not

5   immediately answer, Yuen asked the question again: "Is that the man who

6   assaulted you?"

7   Even though Martinez was unable to see the man's face, she agreed with the officer

8   that the man looked like her assailant. At this point, Officer Yuen stopped the car, got out,

9   and approached Patterson. As he was questioning Patterson, Officer Cox drove up with

10   Clipse. While Martinez and Clipse watched, Officers Cox and Yuen continued questioning

11   Patterson. Officer Cox then returned to Martinez and Clipse and walked them back to

12   Clipse's apartment. While he did so, Yuen placed Patterson under arrest.

13   Later that day, the police searched Patterson's car and apartment. In the apartment,

14   the police found the gun issued to Patterson by his employer. Four days later, the police held

15   a line-up. Although Martinez identified Patterson as the man who had approached her,

16   Clipse did not identify Patterson.

17   **Issue**

18   Under the Fourteenth Amendment, should the Court grant the dafendant's motion to

19   suppress Martinez's show-up and line-up identifications and Martinez's and Clipse's in-

20   court identifications when (1) a police officer pointed out Patterson to Martinez, repeat-

21   edly asking the shaken Martinez whether Patterson looked like her assailant, (2) the

22   police questioned Patterson in front of Martinez and Clipse, (3) during the second or two

23   that Martinez had to view her assailant, her attention was focused on his gun and not

24   his face, and (4) both Martinez's and Clipse's descriptions were inaccurate?

1   **Argument**

2   I. THE COURT SHOULD GRANT PATTERSON'S MOTION TO SUPPRESS MARTINEZ'S SHOW-UP AND LINE-UP IDENTIFICATIONS AND

3   MARTINEZ'S AND CLIPSE'S IN-COURT IDENTIFICATIONS.

4   The United States Supreme Court has developed a two-part test to ensure a

5   criminal defendant the procedural due process guaranteed to every individual by the

6   Fourteenth Amendment. *Manson v. Braithwaite*, 432 U.S. 98, 113, 97 S. Ct. 2243, 53 L. Ed.

7   2d 140 (1977).

8   Under the first part of the test, the defendant need show only that the

9   identification that he seeks to suppress was obtained through the use of un-

10   necessarily suggestive police procedures. *Id.* Once the defendant has estab-

11   lished that the procedure was suggestive, the onus shifts to the State to prove

12   that, under the totality of the circumstances, the witness's identification is so

13   reliable that it should be admitted even though it was obtained through suggestive

14   means. *Id.*

15   A. <u>Martinez's show-up identification should be suppressed because the police procedures were impermissibly suggestive and because Martinez's identifica-</u>

16   <u>tion is unreliable.</u>

17   The courts have repeatedly condemned the practice of showing a witness a

18   single suspect. *See, e.g., Stovall v. Denno*, 388 U.S. 293, 302, 87 S. Ct. 1967, 18 L. Ed. 2d

19   1199 (1967); *State v. Rogers*, 44 Wn. App. 510, 515, 722 P.2d 1349 (1986); *State v. Kraus*, 21 Wn.

20   App. 388, 391-92, 584 P.2d 946 (1978). Although such show-ups are not per se impermissibly

21   suggestive, they should be admitted only if the show-up occurred during the prompt

22   search for the suspect and if the State proves that the witness's identification is reliable.

23   *State v. Rogers*, 44 Wn. App. at 515.

24

1. The police procedures were unnecessarily suggestive because the police showed Martinez a single suspect, asked Martinez whether the suspect looked like her assailant, and questioned the suspect in front of Martinez.

In this case, Officer Yuen's actions suggested to Martinez that he believed that Patterson was her assailant. While driving Martinez home, Officer Yuen pulled up behind Patterson and asked Martinez whether Patterson looked like her assailant. When Martinez did not respond, Officer Yuen repeated his question, asking "Is that the man who assaulted you?"

Although Martinez could not see Patterson's face, after hesitating, she agreed with Officer Yuen that Patterson looked like her assailant. At that point, Officer Yuen pulled up behind Patterson, got out of the police car, and began questioning him. A few minutes later, Officer Cox and Clipse arrived, and both Officer Yuen and Officer Cox questioned Patterson while Martinez and Clipse watched.

Unlike *State v. Kraus*, 21 Wn. App. at 392, in which the show-up identification occurred during a prompt search for the robber, in this case the show-up did not occur while the police were searching for Martinez's assailant. Instead, it occurred while the officer was driving Martinez home. In addition, unlike *Stovall*, 388 U.S. at 302, in which the police held the show-up because they were concerned that the suspect might die, in this case, there were no exigent circumstances. In fact, because the police had located a car that matched the description of the one driven by the assailant, they could have identified the owner of the car and any individuals who had driven it and placed them in a line-up.

1   2.   Martinez's identification is unreliable because Martinez was able to view her
        assailant for only a few seconds, her attention was focused on the gun and
2   not his face, and her description of her assailant does not match the descrip-
        tion of Patterson.

3

4   The key inquiry in determining the admissibility of a witness's identification is

5   its reliability. *Manson v. Braithwaite*, 432 U.S. 98, 114, 97 S. Ct. 2243, 53 L. Ed. 2d 140

6   (1977). In determining whether an identification is reliable, the courts consider the wit-

7   ness's opportunity to view the person who committed the crime; the witness's degree of

8   attention, the time between the crime and the confrontation, the witness's level of

9   certainty, and the accuracy of the witness's prior description. *Neil v. Biggers*, 409

10   U.S. 188, 93 S. Ct. 375, 34 L. Ed. 2d 401 (1972); *State v. Booth*, 36 Wn. App. 66, 69,

11   671 P.2d 1218 (1983).

12   First, in this case, Martinez did not have a good opportunity to view her assailant.

13   Unlike the witness in *Rogers*, who was with his assailant for almost twenty minutes,

14   and the witness in *Booth*, who observed the robber for at least forty-five seconds,

15   Martinez was able to view her assailant for only a few seconds. During the pretrial

16   hearing, Martinez testified that she had seen her assailant for two or three seconds

17   before she turned and ran. Although Martinez testified that she had noticed the car

18   on a prior occasion, she did not testify that she had noticed the driver. In a similar

19   case, the court held that the witness had not had a good opportunity to view the

20   robber when the witness was with the robber for five to six minutes and viewed him

21   for two or three minutes. *State v. McDonald*, 40 Wn. App. 743, 747, 700 P.2d 327

22   (1985).

23

24

7

1   Second, Martinez's attention was not focused on her assailant. Unlike the witness in

2   *Booth*, whose attention was focused on the robber because he was running and carrying

3   money and got into a car with license plates from the witness's home state, Martinez's

4   attention was focused on the car and then on the gun that her assailant was holding. As

5   Martinez has testified, she looked at the gun, then glanced at the man holding it, and

6   then ran.

7   Third, although the show-up occurred within about forty-five minutes of the assault,

8   Martinez's level of certainty was low. The first time that Officer Yuen asked Martinez

9   whether Patterson was the man, she did not respond. In addition, the second time that

10   Officer Yuen asked her the same question, she said only that Patterson looked like him.

11   She did not say, "Yes, that is him."

12   Finally, Martinez's description was inaccurate. Although Martinez told the

13   police that her assailant was in his early 40s, Patterson is 22. While sometimes

14   an individual will believe that an individual is two, three, or even five years older

15   than the individual actually is, it is extremely uncommon for someone to be off by

16   twenty years.

17   In this case, Martinez identified Patterson as her assailant only because Officer

18   Yuen suggested to her that Patterson was the man who had assaulted her. In addition,

19   the State cannot prove that Martinez's identification is reliable. Martinez did not have

20   a good opportunity to view her assailant, her attention was not focused on her

21   assailant, her identification was uncertain, and her description was inaccurate. As

22   a consequence, Patterson's due process rights would be violated if Martinez's identi-

23   fication is admitted.

24

1   B.   Martinez's line-up identification should be suppressed because it was tainted
        by the show-up.

2

3   When the initial identification is obtained through impermissibly suggestive proce-

4   dures, subsequent identifications must also be suppressed unless the State can prove

5   that the subsequent identifications are reliable. *State v. McDonald*, 40 Wn. App. at 746.

6   In *McDonald*, the court reversed the defendant's conviction, concluding that the proce-

7   dures used at the line-up were impermissibly suggestive and that the State had not proved

8   that the witness's subsequent in-court identification was reliable.

9   Similarly, in this case the procedures were impermissibly suggestive, and the

10 State cannot prove that Martinez's subsequent identifications are reliable. See section

11 1A (2), *supra*. Martinez picked Patterson out of the line-up, not because she remem-

12 bered him as her assailant, but because the police had suggested to her that he was

13 her assailant.

14   C.   Martinez and Clipse should not be permitted to make an in-court identification
        because such an identification would be tainted by the impermissibly sugges-

15   tive show-up and the line-up.

16

17   Just as Martinez's line-up identification was tainted by the impermissibly sugges-

18 tive show-up, Martinez's and Clipse's in-court identifications have also been tainted.

19 Although the police did not ask Clipse whether Patterson looked liked the man who had

20 assaulted Martinez, Clipse watched as the police questioned Patterson. In addition,

21 Patterson was with Martinez, who may have told him that Officer Yuen believed that

22 Patterson was her assailant.

23

24

9

1   **Prayer for Relief**

2   For the reasons set out above, the Defendant respectfully requests that the Court

3 suppress Martinez's show-up and line-up identifications and that the Court not permit

4 Martinez or Clipse to make an in-court identification.

5   Dated this 23rd day of September, 2006.

6   _____

7   Attorney for Defendant
                             Washington Bar No. 00000

8

9

10

11

12

13

14

15

16

17

18

19

20

21

22

23

24

EXAMPLE   **State's Brief**

1

2

3

4

5   THE SUPERIOR COURT OF KING COUNTY, WASHINGTON

6   STATE OF WASHINGTON,   )   Case No.: No. 06-01-2226

)

7   Plaintiff,   )   STATE'S BRIEF IN OPPOSITION TO

)   DEFENDANT'S MOTION TO SUPPRESS

8   v.   )

)

9   DEAN E. PATTERSON,   )

)

10   Defendant.   )

             _____   )

11

12   **Statement of Facts**

13   On Monday, August, 14, 2006, Beatrice Martinez was assaulted with a deadly weapon.

14   At a show-up held thirty to forty minutes after the attack, Martinez identified the defendant,

15   Dean E. Patterson, as her assailant. Four days after the assault, Martinez picked Patterson

16   out of a line-up, once again identifying him as her assailant.

17   Ms. Martinez left her apartment at about 4:30 p.m. to walk to work at Angelo's, a

18   restaurant. As she was walking north on Belmont, Martinez observed an older model

19   red station wagon with a chrome luggage rack as it passed slowly by her. Moments

20   later, the same car came down the street again. This time, the driver pulled his car in

21   front of Martinez, stopping his car so that it blocked her path. As Martinez watched,

22   the driver got out of his car and walked toward her. The man then took a gun from his

23   1

24

1   coat pocket and pointed it at Martinez. Martinez looked at the gun, looked back up at

2   her assailant, and then, crying, ran back across the street to safety.

3   At about the same time, Chester Clipse was walking south on Belmont. As

4   he approached his apartment, Clipse saw a man in a red station wagon pull into his

5   parking stall. Clipse immediately started walking toward the man to tell him that he

6   could not park there. A moment later, Clipse saw the man get out of his car and approach

7   a girl, who had suddenly stopped. As Clipse watched, the man pulled out a gun and pointed it

8   at the girl.

9   Both Martinez and Clipse screamed, and the man turned and ran to his car, putting the

10   gun under his coat. As the girl ran across the street, the man got back into his car, backed

11   out, and drove away, traveling northbound on Belmont.

12   Clipse ran to the girl to make sure that she had not been hurt. As he was comforting her,

13   a parking enforcement officer drove up the street. Clipse stopped him, told him what had

14   happened, and gave him a description of the station wagon. The parking enforcement

15   officer called 911 and then left to search for the station wagon.

16   Clipse took Martinez into his landlady's apartment and then went back outside to wait

17   for the police. When the police arrived, Clipse told Officers Yuen and Cox what had hap-

18   pened. Clipse described the car and told the police that the man was white, that he was

19   about 5'10" tall and about 180 to 185 pounds, that he was in his late 30s or early 40s, and that

20   he was wearing a green outfit.

21   While Clipse was talking to the police, Officer Cox received a radio message indicating

22   that the parking enforcement officer had located a red station wagon. While Officer Cox

23   took Clipse in his car to see if Clipse could identify the car, Officer Yuen went inside to

24   interview Martinez.

2

1   Martinez told the police that her assailant was a white male who was about

2   5'7" tall and who weighed about 165-170 pounds, that her assailant had wavy

3   blondish-brown hair, that her assailant appeared to be in his early 40s, and that at the

4   time of the assault, her assailant was wearing a dark jacket and

5   glasses.

6   After interviewing Martinez, Officer Yuen offered to drive Martinez home, and

7   Martinez accepted the offer. When they were less than a block from the scene of

8   the assault, Officer Yuen saw a man matching the description given to him by Martinez.

9   Officer Yuen asked Martinez whether the man was her assailant. After getting a good

10   look at the man, Martinez answered "Yes."

11   Officer Yuen stopped the car and, after telling Martinez to stay in the car,

12   approached the man. As he was doing so, Officer Cox drove by and stopped. While

13   Officer Cox escorted Martinez and Clipse back to Clipse's apartment building, Officer

14   Yuen arrested the man, Dean Patterson.

15   Later that day, the police searched Patterson's car, an older model red station

16   wagon with a chrome luggage rack, and his apartment. In the apartment, they found

17   a gun.

18   A line-up was held four days later. Although Clipse was unable to identify the man who

19   had assaulted Martinez, Martinez identified Patterson as her assailant.

20   **Issue**

21   Should the Court deny the defendant's motion to suppress when the police

22   merely asked the victim whether a pedestrian was her assailant and when the

23   victim observed her assailant on two occasions for several seconds in broad

24   daylight?

Argument

I. THE COURT SHOULD DENY THE DEFENDANT'S MOTION TO SUPPRESS BECAUSE THE POLICE PROCEDURES WERE NOT IMPERMISSIBLY SUGGESTIVE AND THE VICTIM'S IDENTIFICATION IS RELIABLE.

Identifications should not be kept from the jury unless the procedures used in obtaining the identifications were so suggestive and unreliable that a substantial likelihood of irreparable misidentification exists. *See Simon v. United States*, 390 U.S. 377, 384, 89 S. Ct. 1127, 22 L. Ed. 2d 402 (1969).

In deciding whether identification evidence is admissible, the courts employ a two-part test. Under the first part of the test, the defendant has the burden of proving that the identification evidence that he or she seeks to suppress was obtained through impermissibly suggestive procedures. *Manson v. Braithwaite*, 432 U.S. 98, 113, 97 S. Ct. 2243, 5 L. Ed. 2d 140. Only if the defendant satisfies this substantial burden is the second part of the test applied. *Id.*

Even if the court determines that the police procedures were impermissibly suggestive, the evidence is admissible if, under the totality of the circumstances, the identifications are reliable. *Simmons v. United States*, 390 U.S. at 384. Due process does not compel the exclusion of an identification if it is reliable. *Id.*

A. <u>Merely asking the victim whether a pedestrian was her assailant does not make a permissible show-up impermissibly suggestive.</u>

There are no published Washington cases in which the courts have held that a show-up was impermissibly suggestive. In *State v. Rogers*, 44 Wn. App. 510, 511, 722 P.2d 1249 (1986), the court held that the show-up was not impermissibly

1   suggestive even though the police had picked up the witness at a tavern, told him that

2   they wanted to take him back to his apartment to see if he could identify his assailant,

3   and then presented the defendant to him while the defendant was standing between

4   two uniformed police officers. Similarly, in *State v. Booth*, 36 Wn. App. 66, 671 P.2d

5   1218 (1983), the court held that the show-up was not impermissibly suggestive

6   when the police asked the witness to accompany them to the place where the

7   defendant had been arrested and the witness identified the defendant after seeing

8   him in the back of a police car. *Id.* at 67-68; *accord State v. Guzman-Cuellar*, 47 Wn.2d

9   326, 734 P.2d 966 (1987) (show-up not impermissibly suggestive when the defendant

10   was shown to three of the four eyewitnesses while in handcuffs standing next to a

11   police car).

12   In our case, the show-up was not nearly as suggestive as the show-ups in

13   *Rogers, Booth,* or *Guzman-Cuellar.* Unlike the officers in *Rogers, Booth,* and *Guz-*

14   *man-Cuellar,* Officer Yuen did not ask Martinez to go with him to identify her assailant.

15   Instead, the show-up occurred "by accident" as he was taking Martinez home. In

16   addition, when Martinez made her identification, the defendant was not flanked by

17   police officers, sitting in the back of a patrol car, or in handcuffs standing next to a

18   police car.

19   If Officer Yuen had not asked Martinez whether the pedestrian looked like her

20   assailant, he would not have been doing his job. If he was going to protect others,

21   Officer Yuen needed to know whether the pedestrian was Martinez's assailant. The

22   officer's question, "Is that the man?" was not enough to turn a permissible show-up

23   into one that was impermissibly suggestive.

24

5

B. <u>Martinez's identification was reliable: she had observed her assailant on two occasions, her attention was focused on her assailant, and, except for her statement about her assailant's age, her description was accurate.</u>

Even if the police procedures were suggestive, the identification is admissible unless the procedures are "so impermissibly suggestive as to give rise to very substantial likelihood of irreparable misidentifications." *Simmons v. United States,* 390 U.S. 377, 384, 88 S. Ct. 967, 19 L. Ed. 2d 402 (1968). In deciding whether the identification is reliable, the courts consider the witness's opportunity to view the criminal at the time of the crime, the witness's degree of attention, the accuracy of the witness's description, the level of certainty demonstrated by the witness at the confrontation, and the length of time between the crime and the confrontation. *Neil v. Biggers,* 409 U.S. 188, 199-200, 93 S. Ct. 375, 34 L. Ed. 2d 401 (1972).

The courts do not require that the witness have viewed the defendant for an extended period of time. For example, in *Booth,* the court found the witness's identification reliable when the witness had viewed the defendant for less than a minute. Because the witness's attention had been drawn to the fleeing man and because she viewed him in broad daylight, the court found that the identification was reliable. Similarly, in our case, Martinez's attention had been drawn to her assailant. Shortly before the assault, Martinez watched as her assailant drove slowly by her. Consequently, when he drove by her again, her attention was focused on him. She watched as he drove his car in front of her, blocking her path. In addition, she watched as he got out of his car and walked toward her. Thus, although she looked at him for only two or three

6

1   seconds once he pulled out the gun, before that time, she had a good opportunity to

2   view him and her attention had been focused on him.

3   The courts also do not require that the witness's description be completely accu-

4   rate. In *State v. Kraus,* 21 Wn. App. 388, 584 P.2d 946 (1978), the court held that the

5   witness's identification was reliable despite the fact that the witness had stated that

6   the robber was wearing a dark jacket and the defendant was wearing a light-colored

7   jacket. Similarly, in *State v. Maupin,* 63 Wn. App. 887, 822 P.2d 355 (1992), the court

8   held that the witness's identification was reliable even though the witness was not able

9   to tell the police the rapist's race.

10   In this case, Martinez was able to give the police a detailed description of her

11   assailant. When she was interviewed, she told the police that her assailant was a

12   white male with blondish-brown hair that he was approximately 5'7" tall and weighed

13   between 165 and 170 pounds, that he appeared to be in his early 40s, and that he was

14   wearing a dark green jacket. This description is accurate in all but one respect.

15   Although Martinez misjudged the defendant's age, she accurately described his car,

16   his hair, his height and weight, and his clothing.

17   In addition, Martinez's identification occurred shortly after the assault, and Marti-

18   nez was certain in her identification. Although she did not answer Officer Yuen's

19   question the first time that he asked her, as soon as she got a better look at the

20   defendant, she identified him as her assailant. As she stated during the suppression

21   hearing, "Once I got a good look at him I was sure it was him."

22

23

24

C.   <u>Because the show-up was not impermissibly suggestive, the court should not suppress Martinez's line-up identification or prevent Martinez or Clipse from making in-court identifications.</u>

The Court should not suppress Martinez's line-up identification, nor should it prevent Martinez or Clipse from making an in-court identification. Because the show-up was not impermissibly suggestive, see subsection IA, it did not taint either the line-up or any potential in-court identifications.

Although Clipse may have seen the police talking with the defendant, such an act by itself is not enough to make a show-up impermissibly suggestive. *See State v. Guzman-Cuellar*, 47 Wn.2d 326, 734 P.2d 966 (1987); *State v. Rogers,* 44 Wn. App. 510, 722 P.2d 1249 (1986); *State v. Booth,* 36 Wn. App. 66, 671 P.2d 1218 (1983). In addition, like Martinez, Clipse had a good opportunity to view Martinez's assailant. His attention was drawn to the assailant because the man was pulling into his parking spot, and, except for his description of the assailant's age, Clipse's description was accurate.

Prayer for Relief

For the reasons set out above, the State respectfully requests that the Court deny the defendant's motion to suppress and admit Martinez's show-up and line-up identifications and permit Martinez and Clipse to make an in-court identification.

Dated this 28th day of September 2006.

_____
Assistant Prosecuting Attorney
Washington Bar No. 00000

Writing an Appellate Brief

I t is the stuff of movies and childhood fantasies. You are standing before the United States Supreme Court making an impassioned argument. You are arguing that the votes should, or should not, be recounted in the presidential election; that the defendant was, or was not, the victim of racial profiling; or that the government should, or should not, be allowed to restrict stem cell research.

While such high stakes oral advocacy is exciting and dramatic, in many cases the brief is as important, if not more important. Although Hollywood and John Grisham may be more inclined to write a scene depicting oral advocacy, in the real legal world it is frequently the brief that makes the difference.

In this chapter, we continue our discussion of written advocacy, which was begun in the last chapter on trial briefs, and take it to the next level: the appellate brief. Much of what we discussed about advocacy still applies, but now we show you how to write an appellate brief. More specifically, we introduce you to the rules on appeal; we show you how to review a record for error; we talk about how to develop a theory of the case; and we describe the process of drafting, revising, and editing an appellate brief. Then, in Chapter 19 we talk about oral advocacy, specifically how to prepare for and deliver an effective oral argument.

§ 18.1 Practicing Before an Appellate Court

§ 18.1.1 Types of Appellate Review

In most jurisdictions, court rules provide for two types of appellate review: an appeal as of right and discretionary review. For example, in Washington, Rule on Appeal 2.1(a) reads as follows:

RAP 2.1: Methods for Seeking Review of Trial Court Decision — Generally

(a) **Two Methods for Seeking Review of Trial Court Decisions.** The only methods for seeking review of decisions of the superior court by the Court of Appeals and by the Supreme Court are the two methods provided by these rules. The two methods are:

(1) Review as a matter of right, called "appeal"; and

(2) Review by permission of the reviewing court, called "discretionary review."

RAP 2.2 then lists the decisions of the superior court that may be appealed, and RAP 2.3 describes the conditions under which a court will grant discretionary review. As in many other jurisdictions, in Washington, final judgments, decisions determining actions, orders of public use and necessity, juvenile court dispositions, orders depriving a person of all parental rights, and orders of incompetency and commitment may be appealed as of right. Other decisions will be reviewed only if (1) the superior court has committed an obvious error that would render further proceedings useless; (2) the superior court has committed probable error and the decision of the superior court substantially alters the status quo or substantially limits the freedom of a party to act; or (3) the superior court has departed so far from the accepted and usual course of judicial proceedings or so far sanctioned such a departure as to call for review by an appellate court.

§ 18.1.2 Scope of Review

As a general rule, an appellate court will review only those errors listed in the notice of appeal or notice for discretionary review. For example, in Washington, RAP 2.4 provides as follows.

RAP 2.4: Scope of Review of a Trial Court Decision

(a) **Generally.** The appellate court will, at the instance of appellant, review the decision or parts of the decision designated in the notice of appeal or notice for discretionary review and other decisions in the case as provided in sections (b), (c), (d), and (e). The appellate court will, at the instance of the state, review those acts in the proceeding below which if repeated on remand would constitute error prejudicial to the state. The appellate court will grant a respondent affirmative relief by modifying the decision which is the subject matter of the review only (1) if the respondent also seeks review of the decision by the timely filing of a notice of appeal or a notice for discretionary review, or (2) if demanded by the necessities of the case.

In addition, as a general rule, appellate courts will review only those errors that were raised, or preserved, at trial. The only types of errors that can be raised for the first time on appeal are claims that the trial court lacked jurisdiction to hear the case, claims that the plaintiff failed to establish facts upon which relief can be granted, and some claims that the error was of constitutional magnitude.

RAP 2.5: Circumstances Which May Affect Scope of Review

(a) **Errors Raised for First Time on Review.** The appellate court may refuse to review any claim of error which was not raised in the trial court. However, a party may raise the following claimed errors for the first time in the appellate court: (1) lack of trial court jurisdiction, (2) failure to establish facts upon which relief can be granted, and (3) manifest error affecting a constitutional right. A party or the court may raise at any time the question of appellate court jurisdiction. A party may present a ground for affirming a trial court decision which was not presented to the trial court if the record has been sufficiently developed to fairly consider the ground. A party may raise a claim of error which was not raised by the party in the trial court if another party on the same side of the case has raised the claim of error in the trial court.

§ 18.1.3 The Notice of Appeal or Notice for Discretionary Review

The rules on appeal also set out the procedure for filing a notice of appeal or a notice for discretionary review. In Washington, Title 4 of the Rules on Appeal sets out the jurisdiction of each division of the state's court of appeals and the process for seeking direct review by the state's supreme court; Title 5 sets out the time limits for filing the notice, what the notice must contain, and where the notice must be filed; and Title 6 explains how the courts notify the parties about the acceptance of review.

Of particular importance to us for our example case (see section 18.3) are RAP 4.1(b)(2), which states that decisions by the Pierce County Superior Court are reviewed by Division II of the Washington Court of Appeals; RAP 5.2(a), which states that the notice of appeal must be filed not with the appellate court but in the trial court and that the notice must be filed within thirty days after entry of final judgment; and RAP 5.3, which states that the notice of appeal must be titled Notice of Appeal, must specify the party or parties seeking review, must designate the decision or part of the decision that the party wants reviewed, and must name the appellate court to which review is taken.

§ 18.1.4 The Record on Appeal

After filing the notice of appeal or notice for discretionary review, the next thing the appellant or petitioner must do is designate the record on appeal. He or she must identify those clerk's papers, portions of the report of proceedings, and exhibits that are relevant to the issues on review.

After identifying those portions of the trial record that are relevant, the appellant or petitioner must serve on all the parties, the clerk of the trial court, and the clerk of the appellate court a designation of clerk's papers and exhibits and make arrangements to have the relevant portions of the trial record transcribed. The responding party may then elect to supplement the record.

§ 18.1.5 Types of Briefs

The next step in the process is the preparation of the brief itself. As a general rule, the appellant or petitioner files its brief first. After reading the appellant's or petitioner's brief, the respondent then prepares and files its brief. The appellant or petitioner then has the opportunity to file a reply brief, which answers arguments made by the respondent in its brief. In some jurisdictions, the rules also permit a reply brief by the respondent, a brief by the appellant in a criminal case, and amicus briefs, which are briefs that are submitted by groups or individuals who have a strong interest in the subject matter of the case but who are not parties.

§ 18.2 Understanding Your Audience, Your Purpose, and the Conventions

Just as it was important to understand the audience and purpose of an objective memorandum, opinion letter, and trial brief, it is also important to understand the audience and purpose of an appellate brief. Without an understanding of your audience and your purpose in writing to that audience, you will not be able to make good decisions about what to include and exclude or about how to best present your arguments.

§ 18.2.1 Audience

The primary audience for an appellate brief is the panel of judges who will be deciding the appeal. This means that if you are seeking review in an intermediate court of appeals, you will usually be writing to three judges, and if you are seeking review in your state supreme court, you will be writing to nine justices. When you are writing for your intermediate court of appeals, you may or may not know who your judges will be. In many states, there are more than three judges on the court, and you are not told which judges will be on your panel until the day of oral argument. In contrast, when you are writing to your state supreme court, you will usually know who will be hearing your case.

Whether you know for sure which judges will be hearing your case, you should research your court before you begin to write. You can do this by reading recent decisions issued by the court or by talking with other attorneys who are familiar with the court. In addition, you can usually locate information about individual judges on your state court's homepage on the Internet. Often these pages will provide a photograph of each judge and information about his or her education and prior experience.

The judges are not, however, your only audience. In most appellate courts, each appeal is assigned to a particular judge, who then assigns the case to one of his or her law clerks. After reading the briefs and independently researching the issues, the clerk prepares a memo to the judge (usually called a "bench" memo) that summarizes the law and each side's arguments and, in some courts, recommends how the appeal should be decided. Because law clerks can shape how the judges view the appeal, they are some of your most significant readers.

Finally, you are also writing for your client and for opposing counsel. You want to write your brief in such a way that your client feels that his or her story is being told and that opposing counsel knows that he or she is up against a well-prepared, thoughtful, and vigorous advocate.

As you write, you also need to keep in mind that most appellate judges have substantial workloads. Many intermediate appellate judges hear between 100 and 150 cases a year, and write opinions in approximately one-third of those cases. If each party submits a fifty-page brief, each judge would have to read between 10,000 and 15,000 pages in the course of a year. Length is, therefore, an issue. Appellate judges want briefs that are brief.

Also keep in mind that appellate judges must work within certain constraints, the most significant of which is the standard of review. Although in some cases the court's review is *de novo*, in most cases the review is more limited: instead of deciding the case on its merits, the appellate court only reviews the trial court's decisions. The appellate court looks, for example, to see if the trial judge abused his or her discretion or if there is substantial evidence to support the jury's verdict. (For more on standard of review, see section 18.4.2(d).)

In addition, in some cases the appellate court is itself bound by mandatory authority. State intermediate courts of appeal are bound by the decisions of the state's supreme court, and both the state courts and the United States Courts of Appeals are bound by decisions of the United States Supreme Court interpreting and applying the United States Constitution.

§ 18.2.2 Purpose

In writing an appellate brief, your purpose is twofold: to educate and to persuade. In addition to explaining the underlying facts and the law, you must also explain what happened at trial and persuade the appellate court that the decision of the trial court was correct and should be affirmed, that the trial court's decision was wrong and should, therefore, be reversed, or that the case should be remanded to the trial court for further action.

§ 18.2.3 Conventions

Just as the process of bringing an appeal is governed by rules, so is the format of an appellate brief. These rules are usually quite specific and govern everything from the types of briefs that may be filed to the sections that must be included, the type of paper, and citation form. The following rules are representative.

RAP 10.3: Content of Brief

(a) **Brief of Appellant or Petitioner.** The brief of the appellant or petitioner should contain under appropriate headings and in the order here indicated:

(1) *Title Page.* A title page, which is the cover.

(2) *Tables.* A table of contents, with page references, and a table of cases (alphabetically arranged), statutes and other authorities cited, with references to the pages of the brief where cited.

(3) *Assignments of Error.* A separate concise statement of each error a party contends was made by the trial court, together with the issues pertaining to the assignments of error.

(4) *Statement of the Case.* A fair statement of the facts and procedure relevant to the issues presented for review, without argument. Reference to the record must be included for each factual statement.

(5) *Argument.* The argument in support of the issues presented for review, together with citations to legal authority and references to relevant parts of the record. The argument may be preceded by a summary.

(6) *Conclusion.* A short conclusion stating the precise relief sought.

(7) *Appendix.* An appendix to the brief if deemed appropriate by the party submitting the brief.

(b) **Brief of Respondent.** The brief of respondent should conform to section (a) and answer the brief of appellant or petitioner. A statement of the issues and a statement of the case need not be made if respondent is satisfied with the statement in the brief of appellant or petitioner. If a respondent is also seeking review, the brief of respondent must state the assignments of error and the issues pertaining to those assignments of error presented for review by respondent and include argument on those issues.

(c) **Reply Brief.** A reply brief should be limited to a response to the issues in the brief to which the reply brief is directed.

RAP 10.4: Preparation and Filing of Brief by Party

(a) **Typing or Printing Brief.** Briefs shall conform to the following requirements:

(1) One legible, clean, and reproducible copy of the brief must be filed with the appellate court. The brief should be printed or typed in black on 20-pound substance 8½- by 11-inch white paper. Margins should be at least 2 inches on the left side and 1½ inches on the right side and on the top and bottom of each page.

(2) The text of any brief typed or printed in a proportionally spaced typeface must appear in print as 12 point or larger type with 3 points or more leading between lines. The same typeface and print size should be standard throughout the brief, except that footnotes may appear in print as 10 point or larger type with 2 points or more leading between lines and quotations may be the equivalent of single spaced. Except for material in an appendix, the typewritten or printed material in the brief shall not be reduced or condensed by photographic or other means.

(3) The text of any brief typed or printed in a monospaced typeface shall be done in pica type or the equivalent at no more than 10 characters per inch. The lines must be double spaced, that is, there may be at most 3 lines of type per inch. Quotations and footnotes may be single spaced. Except for material in an appendix, the typewritten or printed material in the brief shall not be reduced or condensed by photographic or other means.

(b) **Length of Brief.** A brief of appellant, petitioner, or respondent, and a pro se brief in a criminal case should not exceed 50 pages. A reply brief should not exceed 25 pages. An amicus curiae brief, or answer thereto, should not exceed 20 pages. For the purpose of determining compliance with this rule appendices, the title sheet, table of contents, and table of authorities are not included. For compelling reasons the court may grant a motion to file an over-length brief.

(c) **Text of Statute, Rule, Jury Instruction, or the Like**. If a party presents an issue which requires study of a statute, rule, regulation, jury instruction, finding of fact, exhibit, or the like, the party should type the material portions of the text out verbatim or include them by copy in the text or in an appendix to the brief.

(d) **Motion in Brief**. A party may include in a brief only a motion which, if granted, would preclude hearing the case on the merits.

(e) **Reference to Party**. References to parties by such designations as "appellant" and "respondent" should be kept to a minimum. It promotes clarity to use the designations used in the lower court, the actual names of the parties, or descriptive terms such as "the employee," "the injured person," and "the taxpayer."

(f) **Reference to Record**. A reference to the record should designate the page and part of the record. Exhibits should be referred to by number. The clerk's papers should be abbreviated as "CP"; exhibits should be abbreviated as "Ex"; and the report of proceedings should be abbreviated as "RP." Suitable abbreviations for other recurrent references may be used.

(g) **Citations**. Citations must be in conformity with the form used in current volumes of the Washington Reports. Decisions of the Supreme Court and of the Court of Appeals must be cited to the official report thereof and should include the national reporter citation and the year of the decision. The citation of other state court decisions should include both the state and national reporter citations. The citation of a United States Supreme Court decision should include the United States Reports, the United States Supreme Court Reports Lawyers' Edition, and the Supreme Court Reporter. The citation of a decision of any other federal court should include the federal reporter citation and the district of the district court or circuit of the court of appeals deciding the case. Any citation should include the year decided and a reference to and citation of any subsequent decision of the same case.

(h) **Unpublished Opinions**. A party may not cite as an authority an unpublished opinion of the Court of Appeals.

In addition to the rules, there may be other, unwritten conventions governing the format of the brief. For example, attorneys may use a particular format for the table of authorities or for the questions presented, or there may be conventions regarding the capitalization of words like "court." Thus, in addition to reading and following the rules, always check with the court clerk and other attorneys to find out what is expected.

§ 18.3 Getting the Case: *State v. Strong*

It is your second year in law school, and you have been hired to work in the Office of Assigned Counsel in Tacoma, Washington. One of the cases the office is handling is *State v. Strong*. The facts of the case are as follows.

On May 17, 2005, Mr. Strong was standing on a street corner in Tacoma, Washington, in an area known for an unusually high incidence of illegal drug activity, when he was approached by Officer Thomas Hanson. Because he did not recognize Mr. Strong, Officer Hanson asked Mr. Strong his name and several questions about what he was doing in the area. Mr. Strong cooperated, giving the officer his name.

Officer Hanson then went back to his patrol car and drove about a block to a block and a half down a hill. He then stopped and ran a criminal history check using Mr. Strong's name and description. The check showed that Mr. Strong had prior arrests for drug-related crimes but no outstanding warrants. As he began to drive away, Officer Hanson glanced into his rearview mirror and saw Mr. Strong standing in the middle of the road, staring at his car. His suspicions aroused, Officer Hanson turned his car around and drove back toward Mr. Strong. As he did so, Mr. Strong began walking quickly toward an apartment complex and an adjacent wooded area. Because the area was dark, Officer Hanson turned on his spotlight so that he could see better. After Officer Hanson did so, Mr. Strong walked toward a tree, dropped what appeared to be a package under the tree, and then walked quickly away. Mr. Strong then slowed his pace, eventually stopping. Neither the record nor the findings of facts make it clear when Mr. Strong stopped or how far he walked.

Officer Hanson got out of his car, told Mr. Strong to stop walking, and retrieved the package from behind the tree. In the package he found half of a cola can containing what appeared to be crack cocaine. Officer Hanson read Mr. Strong his *Miranda* rights and formally placed him under arrest. During the search incident to arrest, Officer Hanson discovered a .38 caliber semi-automatic pistol and a Rolex watch on Mr. Strong. The substance in the cola can was later confirmed to be crack cocaine.

Before trial, Mr. Strong made a motion asking the trial court to suppress the can containing the cocaine, the gun, and the watch. The trial court denied the motion. Although Mr. Strong could have sought discretionary review of the trial court's denial of his motion, he chose not to do so because it would have been difficult to establish that the superior court committed an obvious error that would render further proceedings useless or that the superior court departed so far from the accepted and usual course of judicial proceedings as to call for immediate review by an appellate court. (See section 18.1.1 above.) As a result, the case proceeded to trial and, after a one-day trial, a jury found Mr. Strong guilty. One month later, a sentencing hearing was held, and Mr. Strong was sentenced.

Soon after the entry of judgment and sentence, Ms. Elder, Mr. Strong's attorney and your supervising attorney, met with Mr. Strong to explain his options. She described the appeals process, telling him how long he had to file an appeal (thirty days from the date of entry of judgment and sentence), how long it would take for his case to be heard by the court of appeals (about twelve to eighteen months), and the provisions for staying his sentence while his case was on appeal. In addition, she also explained that if he did not appeal or if his appeal was denied, his current convictions would be used in calculating his sentence on any future crimes.

After considering his options, Mr. Strong decided that he wanted to appeal. As a result, Ms. Elder prepared a notice of appeal and ordered a copy of the record.

§ 18.4 Preparing to Write the Brief

§ 18.4.1 Reviewing the Record for Error

Ms. Elder received her copy of the record on November 16. Several days later, she began reviewing it. Like most attorneys, Ms. Elder reviewed the record for error using a four-step process. She began by reviewing her trial notes, writing down the errors that she had identified during the trial. She then began a systematic review of the record, noting

- each motion that she made that was denied,
- each motion that the State made that was granted,
- each objection that she made that was overruled,
- each objection that the State made that was sustained,
- each request for a jury instruction that the she made that was denied, and
- each request for a jury instruction the State made that was granted.

For example, in going through the transcript for the sentencing hearing, Ms. Elder noted the following objection, which was overruled.

Excerpt from the Verbatim Report of Proceedings   EXAMPLE

State's Direct Examination of Officer Hanson: . . .

Q. Officer, why did you stop the defendant after he dropped the object behind the tree?

A. I believed he was trying to dispose of some type of contraband, narcotics or something, that he didn't want me to find in his possession.

Q. At the time that he dropped the item, you didn't know what it was. Is that correct?

A. No I didn't.

Q. How did you describe it in your report?

A. I'll have to review my notes. If I remember right, I described it as some type of package.

Q. And even if it wasn't a controlled substance, were you concerned that—

A. He could have been littering. It could have been—

Ms. Elder: Your Honor, once again I am going to object. Speculation at point.

Mr. Lion: Your Honor, the question was why this officer—

Ms. Elder: The officer has testified as to why he stopped him and to what he believed it was, as far as he knew. Speculation as to anything further about what it could have been is gratuitous and not relevant.

Mr. Lion: Your Honor, it has to do with this officer's basis for stopping someone—

The Court: Overruled.

Mr. Lion: Thank you.

As her third step, Ms. Elder looked for the other, less obvious types of errors.

- Were Mr. Strong's constitutional rights violated? (Was he read his *Miranda* rights? Was he represented by counsel at all significant stages in the process?)
- Was Mr. Strong tried within the appropriate time period? Was he given the right to confront the witnesses against him? Is his sentence cruel and unusual?
- Is the statute under which Mr. Strong was charged constitutional?
- Was there misconduct on the part of the judge, opposing counsel, or the jury?

Finally, Ms. Elder examines her own actions. Did she miss a defense or fail to object to a motion or a piece of evidence? If she did, Mr. Strong might be able to argue that he was denied effective assistance of counsel.

Having identified the potential errors, Ms. Elder can analyze them and decide which of them she should raise on appeal.

§ 18.4.2 Selecting the Issues on Appeal

As an appellate judge, whom would you find more credible: the attorney who alleges twenty-three errors or the one who alleges three?

Most appellate judges take the attorney who lists two, three, or four errors more seriously than the attorney who lists a dozen or more. Instead of describing the attorney who lists numerous errors as "thorough" or "conscientious," judges use terms such as "inexperienced," "unfocused," and "frivolous." When so many errors are listed, the appellate court is likely to think that the problem is not the trial court but the attorney bringing the appeal.

But how do you decide which errors to discuss in your brief? Once again, Ms. Elder uses a four-step process. She determines (a) whether there was in fact an error, (b) whether that error was preserved, (c) whether the error was harmless, and (d) the standard of review.

a. Was There an Error?

The first question is whether there was in fact an error. Does the Constitution, a statute, or case law allow you to make a credible argument that the trial judge's ruling was erroneous? In order to answer this question, you will usually need to do at least some research. For example, in *Strong*, Ms. Elder needed to do some preliminary research to determine whether a good faith argument could be made that the search was illegal under either the Fourth Amendment or the Washington Constitution. Because her research indicated that there was an argument under both the Fourth Amendment and the Washington Constitution, she continued with her analysis of those issues. In contrast, the other research she did was not as fruitful. After doing some preliminary research on sentencing, she determined that she could not make a good faith argument that the trial court erred in ruling that possession of a short firearm and possession of a controlled substance are not the same criminal conduct. As a result, Ms. Elder abandoned that issue. Without a good faith basis for raising the sentencing issue, she risked, at a minimum, annoying the court and, at worst, a potential Rule 11 action for making a frivolous claim.

b. Was the Error Preserved?

It is not enough that there was an error. Unless the error involves an issue of constitutional magnitude, that error must have been preserved. Defense counsel must have objected or in some other manner brought the alleged error to the attention of the trial court and given the trial court the opportunity to correct the error.

Thus, in *Strong*, if Ms. Elder had not filed a motion to suppress, she would not have been able to raise the admissibility of the evidence for the first time on appeal. Although the admissibility of the evidence affects an appellant's Sixth Amendment right to a fair trial, the Washington courts have held that it is not an error of constitutional magnitude. Having brought a motion to suppress, however, Ms. Elder did not need to do more to preserve the error.

c. Was the Error Harmless?

The next question is whether the error was harmless. As the courts have often said, an appellant is entitled to a fair trial, not a perfect one.

> The reversal of a conviction entails substantial social costs: it forces jurors, witnesses, courts, the prosecution, and the appellants to expend further time, energy, and other resources to repeat a trial that has already once taken place.... These societal costs of reversal and retrial are an acceptable and often necessary consequence when an error ... has deprived the appellant of a fair determination of the issue of guilt or innocence. But the balance of interest tips decidedly the other way when the error has had no effect on the outcome of the trial.
>
> William Rehnquist, *Harmless Error, Prosecutorial Misconduct, and Due Process: There's More to Due Process Than the Bottom Line*, 88 Colum. L. Rev. (1988).

In determining whether an error is harmless, most courts apply either the contribution test or the overwhelming untainted evidence test. Under the contribution test, the appellate court looks at the tainted evidence to determine whether that evidence could have contributed to the fact finder's determination of guilt. If it could have, reversal is required. The courts that apply the overwhelming untainted evidence test take a different approach: Instead of looking at the tainted evidence, they look at that which is untainted. If the untainted evidence is sufficient to support a finding of guilt, reversal is not required.

Thus, as an advocate, you need to weed out those errors that were harmless. Although the court may have acted improperly when it admitted a particular piece of evidence or testimony, more likely than not you do not have a case if that same evidence or testimony was properly elicited from another witness.

d. What Is the Standard of Review?

The last thing that you need to consider is the standard of review. In deciding whether there was an error, what standard will the appellate court apply? Will it review the issue *de novo*, making its own independent determination, or will it defer to the trial court, affirming the trial court unless the trial court's finding was clearly erroneous or the trial court judge abused his or her discretion?

As a general rule, an appellate court will review questions of law *de novo*. As a consequence, when the issue is whether the jury was properly instructed, the appellate court will make its own independent determination. The standard is different when the question is one of fact. In most circumstances, an appellate court will not disturb factual findings unless such findings are "clearly erroneous" or "contrary to law." Similarly, an appellate court will give great deference to the trial court judge's evidentiary rulings, and will not reverse the trial court unless the judge abused his or her discretion.

Because the rules set out above are general, you must research the standard of review. Sometimes this research will be easy. In one of its opinions, the court will state the standard that is to be applied. At other times, the research is much more difficult. Although the court decides the issue, it does not explicitly state what standard it is applying. In such cases, read between the lines. Although the court does not state that it is reviewing the issue *de novo*, is that in fact what the court has done?

Because very few issues are pure questions of law or pure questions of fact, you may be able to argue the standard of review. While the appellant will usually want to argue that the appellate court should review the question *de novo*, the respondent will usually want to argue that the appellate court should affirm unless the trial court's ruling was clearly erroneous or the trial court abused its discretion.

Having gone through these four steps, Ms. Elder is ready to select the issues on appeal. She decides to challenge the trial court's denial of her motion to suppress on the grounds that the seizure was unlawful under both the Fourth Amendment and the Washington Constitution. Because both issues raise questions of law, she will argue that the standard of review is *de novo*, a standard that favors her client.

§ 18.4.3 Preparing an Abstract of the Record

Before beginning her brief, Ms. Elder does one last thing: she creates an abstract of the record by going through the trial transcript and taking notes on each piece of relevant testimony. For each piece of relevant testimony, she notes the name of the individual who gave the testimony, she writes down the page number on which the testimony appears, and she summarizes the testimony. (RP is the abbreviation used by the Washington courts for the report of proceedings or trial transcript.)

EXAMPLE   **Excerpt from Ms. Elder's Abstract of the Record**

Direct Examination of Officer Hanson

RP 3   Officer Hanson has 440 hours of training at academy and 18 hours of training in narcotics identification

RP 4   Officer Hanson makes at least three to five drug-related arrests a week

RP 4   Area in which Strong was arrested has a high incidence of drug arrests

RP 6   Officer Hanson noticed Strong standing on corner — he testifies that at
         that time "nothing struck me as being suspicious" (line 19)

RP 6   Officer Hanson describes his initial conversation with Strong. He asked
         Strong his name and Strong replied

* * *

Although preparing such an abstract is time-consuming, it forces Ms. Elder to go through the record carefully, identifying each piece of relevant testimony. It also makes brief writing and preparation for oral argument easier. Instead of having to search through the entire record for the testimony she needs, Ms. Elder can refer to her abstract.

§ 18.4.4 Preparing the Record on Appeal

After having determined which issues she will raise on appeal, Ms. Elder goes back through the trial record and identifies those parts that she wants included as the record on appeal. She selects as clerk's papers (CPs) the Information, the Motion to Suppress, the Findings of Fact and Conclusions of Law and Order Denying the Motion to Suppress, the jury's Verdict Form, the Judgment and Sentence, and the Notice of Appeal. In addition, she includes the transcript of the evidentiary hearing on the motion to suppress. Because she was not assigning error to anything that happened during the trial, she does not have the trial record transcribed or transmitted. In addition, because there were no relevant exhibits, she does not have any of them designated as part of the record on appeal.

§ 18.5 Researching the Issues on Appeal

How an individual researches an issue depends in large part on that individual's familiarity with the area of law. In this case, Ms. Elder is an experienced criminal defense lawyer who has handled hundreds of motions to suppress and who, as a result, knows the law relating to searches and seizures very well. As a consequence, she is able to start her research with a case, *California v. Hodari D.*, a 1991 decision in which the United States Supreme Court set out a two-part test for determining when a seizure occurs. Ms. Elder rereads this case and then cite checks it.

Although Ms. Elder was able to start her research with a case, an individual who is less familiar with criminal law would have to take a different approach.

For an attorney unfamiliar with Washington's law on searches and seizures, the best place to start researching would be with a Washington practice book that specifically discusses searches and seizures in Washington. Such a source would provide the attorney with an overview of Washington law and point him or her to the key cases. If addition, the attorney might want to look for a law review or bar journal article that specifically discusses Washington's law on searches and seizures. In the alternative, an individual unfamiliar with search and seizure law might look for secondary sources that are not tailored to the specific state: for example, a hornbook, an ALR annotation, a law review article, or a treatise.

§ 18.6 Planning the Brief

Having spent about four hours researching the issues, Ms. Elder is ready to begin working on the brief. She does not, however, begin by putting fingers to the keyboard. Instead, she spends another two or three hours analyzing the facts and the law, developing a theory of the case, and selecting an organizational scheme.

§ 18.6.1 Analyzing the Facts and the Law

To write an effective brief, Ms. Elder must master both the facts of the case and the law. Specifically, she needs to know what each witness said, and did not say, at the evidentiary hearing and every finding of fact and conclusion of law that the court entered. In addition, she needs to read carefully all of the relevant cases and think not only about how she might be able to use them to support her argument but also about how the State might use them in its arguments.

Ms. Elder also needs to think about what relief she wants and the various ways in which she might persuade the court to grant that relief. Here, ends-means reasoning often works well. She starts with the conclusion that she wants the court to reach and then works backwards through the steps in the analysis.

EXAMPLE   **Defendant's Ends-Means Analysis**

- **Relief wanted:** Charges dismissed.
- **How to get charges dismissed:** Have appellate court reverse trial court.
- **How to get appellate court to reverse trial court:** Show that the seizure was illegal.
- **How to show that seizure was illegal:** Show that under Fourth Amendment there was a show of authority and that Strong submitted to that show of authority.
- **How to show that there was a show of authority:** Show that spotlight was a show of authority or that the spotlight combined with the officer's other actions was a show of authority.
- **How to show that spotlight was a show of authority:** Analogize spotlight to emergency light cases and headlight cases using *Stroud* and *Vandover* as authority or argue that a reasonable person in same circumstances would not feel free to leave.
- **How to show that spotlight combined with officer's other actions was a show of authority:** Use *Soto-Garcia* to argue that there was a progressive intrusion.

In contrast, the State's ends-means analysis would look like this.

EXAMPLE   **State's Ends-Means Analysis**

- **Relief wanted:** Jury verdict affirmed.
- **How to get jury verdict affirmed:** Show that the trial court did not err when it denied Strong's motion to suppress.

- **How to show that trial court did not err:** Show that the seizure was proper under the Fourth Amendment.
- **How to show that the seizure was proper under the Fourth Amendment:** Show that there was no show of authority or, if there was a show of authority, that Strong did not submit to it.
- **How to show that there was no show of authority:** Establish that there is no case law in Washington that says that a spotlight is a show of authority. In addition, distinguish spotlights from flashing emergency lights. In the alternative, establish that spotlight plus other actions was not a progressive intrusion. Distinguish *Soto-Garcia*.
- **How to show that appellant did not submit:** Use record to establish that after spotlight was turned on, Strong continued walking quickly away from the officer.

§ 18.6.2 Developing a Theory of the Case

Having thoroughly mastered both the facts and the law, Ms. Elder is ready to develop her theory of the case. At its simplest, a theory of the case is the legal theory that the attorney relies on in arguing the case to the court. A good theory of the case, however, goes beyond a legal theory or legal argument. It becomes the lens through which the attorney and, if the attorney is effective, the court views the case. For more on theory of the case, see section 17.3.

In *State v. Strong*, Ms. Elder can argue several different legal theories. She can argue that the seizure was illegal under the Fourth Amendment, permissible under the Fourth Amendment but illegal under the Washington Constitution, or illegal under both the Fourth Amendment and the Washington Constitution. In contrast, the State has fewer options. To win, it must establish that the seizure was legal under both the Fourth Amendment and the Washington Constitution.

In addition, Ms. Elder can choose from among several different lenses. She can keep a narrow focus and emphasize that Mr. Strong's rights were violated when the officer questioned him, ran a criminal history check on him, and then drove toward him while shining a spotlight on him. In the alternative, she can choose a wider focus and argue that this case is not just about Mr. Strong but about police officers who step over the line and by their own actions create situations that allow them to stop citizens like you and me. Or she can choose a completely different focus. Instead of challenging what the trial court did, she can challenge the United States Supreme Court. Will Washington follow the lead of the Supreme Court and adopt the *Hodari D.* test, a test that has been criticized by numerous commentators, or will Washington follow the lead of other states and, under an independent state analysis, reject *Hodari D.?*

The State has similar options. It can choose a narrow lens and emphasize that Mr. Strong is a convicted felon who was in a high crime area late at night with crack cocaine, or the State can choose a wider lens and emphasize the need to give police officers the tools they need to fight the war on drugs. Do we, as a society, want to make Officer Hanson wait until Mr. Strong commits a crime before we allow him to investigate? Isn't an ounce of prevention worth a pound of cure? Or the State can choose a different lens and argue that the *Hodari D.* test helps protect us as citizens by discouraging suspects from fleeing.

In choosing her theory of the case for *State v. Strong*, Ms. Elder keeps in mind that the theories that tend to work best are those that appeal to both the head and the heart. In deciding a case, judges want to make sure both that the law they are announcing and applying is sound and that the result is just. Judges are unlikely to adopt a rule if it produces, in the context of the case before them, an unjust result or a rule that is unsound.

§18.6.3 Selecting an Organizational Scheme

Because there has to be a one-to-one correspondence between the issue statements and main headings (see sections 18.11 and 18.14.3), the last thing that Ms. Elder does before she begins writing is to select an organizational scheme. Should she have one issue statement and therefore one main heading, two issue statements and therefore two main headings, or three or more issues and main headings? In addition, she needs to decide the order in which she wants to present the issues and arguments. Should she start with the federal constitutional analysis or the state constitutional analysis?

a. Deciding on the Number of Issues and Headings

In almost every case there is more than one way to organize the argument. You may choose to state the issue broadly, with one issue statement and one main heading, or you may choose to state the issues more narrowly, and have several issue statements and several main headings. For example, in *State v. Strong*, Ms. Elder has the following options.

EXAMPLE   **Option 1**

One Issue Statement:

> Did the trial court err in denying Mr. Strong's motion to suppress?

One Main Heading with Three Subheadings:

> I. THE TRIAL COURT ERRED IN DENYING MR. STRONG'S MOTION TO SUPPRESS.
>   A. There was a seizure under the Fourth Amendment.
>   B. There was a seizure under the Washington Constitution.
>   C. At the time of the seizure, Officer Hanson did not have an articulable suspicion that Mr. Strong was engaging in or about to be engaged in criminal conduct.

EXAMPLE   **Option 2**

Three Issue Statements:

> 1. Under the Fourth Amendment, did a seizure occur when Officer Hanson drove toward Mr. Strong, focusing his spotlight on him, and Mr. Strong, after walking out of the street and a few feet toward an apartment complex, dropped something behind a tree, turned, and stopped?
>
> 2. Did the trial court err when it ruled that Article I, section 7, of the Washington Constitution does not provide more protection than the Fourth Amendment?

3. Did Officer Hanson have an articulable suspicion that Mr. Strong was engaging in or about to be engaged in criminal conduct at the time Officer Hanson focused his spotlight on Mr. Strong when the only facts before the officer were that Mr. Strong was in a high crime area, Mr. Strong had a criminal history, and Mr. Strong walked to the middle of the road and watched the police car?

Three Main Headings:

I.   THERE WAS A SEIZURE UNDER THE FOURTH AMENDMENT.

II. EVEN IF THERE WAS NOT A SEIZURE UNDER THE FOURTH AMENDMENT, THERE WAS A SEIZURE UNDER THE WASHINGTON CONSTITUTION.

III. AT THE TIME OF THE SEIZURE, OFFICER HANSON DID NOT HAVE AN ARTICULABLE SUSPICION THAT MR. STRONG WAS ENGAGING IN OR ABOUT TO BE ENGAGED IN CRIMINAL CONDUCT.

Option 3

EXAMPLE

Two Issue Statements:

1. Under the Fourth Amendment, did a seizure occur when Officer Hanson drove toward Mr. Strong, focusing his spotlight on him, and Mr. Strong, after walking out of the street and a few feet toward an apartment complex, dropped something behind a tree, turned, and stopped?

2. Did the trial court err when it ruled that Article I, section 7, of the Washington Constitution does not provide more protection than the Fourth Amendment?

Two Main Headings, Each with Two Subheadings:

I.   UNDER THE FOURTH AMENDMENT, MR. STRONG WAS UNLAWFULLY SEIZED.

    A.   A seizure occurred because Mr. Strong submitted to a show of authority.

    B.   At the time of the seizure, Officer Hanson did not have an articulable suspicion that Mr. Strong was engaging in or about to be engaged in criminal conduct.

II. UNDER THE WASHINGTON CONSTITUTION, MR. STRONG WAS UNLAWFULLY SEIZED.

    A.   The Washington Constitution provides more protection than the Fourth Amendment.

    B.   At the time of seizure, Officer Hanson did not have an articulable suspicion that M. Strong was engaging in or about to be engaged in criminal conduct.

Because we are still in the planning stage, the issue statements and argumentative headings are not in their final form. See section 18.11 for more on drafting the issue statements and section 18.14 for more on drafting the argumentative headings.

In selecting one option over others, first consider your theory of the case. Does one option allow you to present your theory better than the others?

Second, determine how closely related the issues are. The more closely related they are, the more likely it is that you will want to treat them as one issue; the less closely related they are, the more likely it is that you should treat them as separate issues. For example, if all of your issues relate, as they do in *State v. Strong*, to a single motion to suppress, you will probably want to treat them as one issue. If, however, they are unrelated — for example, one relates to a motion to suppress, another to a jury instruction, and the third to the sentence that was imposed — you will usually want to treat them as separate issues. Third, consider which option will allow you to divide your arguments into the most manageable chunks. You do not want to have one fifty-page argument or fifty one-page arguments. Finally, consider which option will allow you to present your arguments most concisely, with the least repetition.

Although in the *Strong* case any of the three options would work, Ms. Elder chooses the second option. Although the issues are closely related, she wants to emphasize that Mr. Strong is entitled to relief on either of two grounds: the Fourth Amendment or the Washington Constitution. The second option emphasizes this fact without unnecessarily repeating the articulable suspicion argument.

b. Ordering the Issues and Arguments

In many cases, logic dictates the order of your issues and arguments. Threshold questions — for example, issues relating to subject matter jurisdiction, service of process, and the statute of limitations — must be discussed before questions relating to the merits of the case. Similarly, the parts of a test should usually be discussed in order and, when one argument builds on another, the foundation argument must be put first.

When logic does not dictate the order of your issues and arguments, you will usually want to start with your strongest argument. By doing so, you ensure that the judges will read your strongest argument and that your strongest argument is in a position of emphasis. You can then go through the rest of your issues and arguments in the order of their strength, or you can begin and end with strong issues and arguments and bury your weaker arguments in the middle.

In the *Strong* case, logic does not dictate the ordering of the issues or the arguments. Given the law, the appellant can present either the Fourth Amendment or the Article 1, Section 7, argument first.

Having thoroughly analyzed the facts and the law, developed a theory of the case, and selected an organizational scheme, Ms. Elder is now ready to begin preparing the brief. Although Ms. Elder did not draft the sections in order — for the purpose of this chapter, we discuss the sections in the order that they appear in the brief.

§ 18.7 Preparing the Cover

The first page of your brief is the title page, or cover. As in most other jurisdictions, in Washington the cover is governed by court rules, which specify the color of paper that should be used, the information that should be included, and the format. (See Form 5 of the Washington Rules on Appeal.) The briefs at the end of the chapter show the correct format for briefs submitted to the Washington courts.

§ 18.8 Preparing the Table of Contents

The second page of your brief should be the table of contents. Once again, the rules specify the information that should be included and the format that should be used. (See Form 6 of the Washington Rules on Appeal and the sample briefs at the end of this chapter.)

§ 18.9 Preparing the Table of Authorities

Immediately following the table of contents is the table of authorities. In this section, list each of the cases, constitutional provisions, statutes, rules, and other authorities cited in the brief. As a general rule, cases are listed first, in alphabetical order, followed by constitutional provisions, statutes, court rules, and secondary authorities. (See Form 6 of the Washington Rules on Appeal and the sample briefs at the end of this chapter.)

In listing the authorities, use the citation form prescribed by your court rules (your jurisdiction may or may not have adopted the *ALWD Citation Manual* or the *Bluebook*) and include references to each page in the brief where the authority appears. Both LexisNexis and Westlaw have programs that you can use to check your citations and prepare the table of authorities.

§ 18.10 Drafting the Assignments of Error

In some states, including Washington, the Rules on Appeal require the appellant to set out assignments of error.

RAP 10.3(a)

(a) **Brief of Appellant or Petitioner.** The brief of the appellant or petitioner should contain . . .

(3) *Assignments of Error.* A separate concise statement of each error a party contends was made by the trial court.

RAP 10.3(g)

(g) **Special Provision for Assignments of Error.** A separate assignment of error for each instruction which a party contends was improperly given or refused must be included with reference to each instruction or proposed instruction by number. A separate assignment of error for each finding of fact a party contends was improperly made or refused must be included with reference to the finding or proposed finding by number. The appellate court will only review a claimed error which is included in an assignment of error or clearly disclosed in the associated issue pertaining thereto.

The Washington courts have held that such assignments of error are jurisdictional. This means that if an assignment of error is not included, the court need not consider the issue, even if the issue is argued in the brief.

The format of such assignments of error is simple. Each begins with the assertion "The trial court erred when . . ." and then identifies the procedural act that the appellant claims was error.

EXAMPLE

Format for Assignment of Error

The trial court erred when it denied Mr. Strong's Motion to Suppress.

There need not be the same number of assignments of error as there are issues. One assignment of error could raise a number of issues, or a number of assignments of error could give rise to a single issue. Unless the respondent is counter-appealing, the respondent should not include assignments of error in its brief.

§ 18.11 Drafting the Issues Pertaining to Assignments of Error

While the assignments of error are neutral statements of the errors that the appellant claims occurred at trial, the issues pertaining to the assignments of error, or questions presented, are not. Both the appellant and the respondent want to use the issues pertaining to the assignments of error section of the brief to present their theories of the case to the court.

Look, for example, at the following issue statements from *Hishon v. King & Spaulding*, a case in which the United States Supreme Court was asked to decide whether law firms were subject to federal civil rights laws prohibiting discrimination in employment on the basis of sex, race, religion, or national origin.

EXAMPLES

Petitioner's Statement of the Issue

Whether King and Spaulding and other large institutional law firms that are organized as partnerships are, for that reason alone, exempt from Title VII of the Civil Rights Act of 1964, and are free (a) to discriminate in the promotion of associate lawyers to partnership on the basis of sex, race or religion; and (b) to discharge those associates whom they do not admit to partnership based on reasons of sex, race or religion under an established "up-or-out" policy.

Respondent's Statement of the Issues

1. Whether law partners organized for advocacy are entitled to constitutionally protected freedom of association.
2. Whether Congress intended through Title VII of the Civil Rights Act of 1964 to give the Equal Employment Opportunity Commission, a politically appointed

advocacy agency engaged in litigation, jurisdiction over invitations to join law firm partnerships.

The petitioner's issue statement sets out its theory of the case: in this case the issue is whether law firms are free to discriminate on the basis of sex, race, religion, or national origin. Similarly, the respondent's issue statements set out its theory. To the respondent, this is not a case about discrimination. Instead, it is a case about whether the partners in a law firm are entitled to their constitutionally protected right of freedom of association and about whether members of a politically appointed advocacy agency have the right to determine who is invited to join a law firm.

§ 18.11.1 Select a Format

Most court rules do not prescribe the format that should be used for the issue statement. They allow you to state the issue using the under-does-when format, the whether format, or a multi-sentence format.

"Under-Does-When" Format

EXAMPLE

Under the Fourth Amendment, did a seizure occur when Officer Hanson drove toward Mr. Strong, focusing his spotlight on him, and Mr. Strong, after walking out of the street and a few feet toward an apartment complex, dropped something behind a tree, turned, and stopped?

"Whether" Format

EXAMPLE

Whether a seizure occurred under the Fourth Amendment when Officer Hanson drove toward Mr. Strong, focusing his spotlight on him, and Mr. Strong, after walking out of the street and a few feet toward an apartment complex, dropped something behind a tree, turned, and stopped.

Multisentence Format

EXAMPLE

On the evening of May 17, 2001, William Strong was standing on a corner talking with an acquaintance when Officer Hanson approached him and began questioning him. After receiving answers to his questions, Officer Hanson returned to his marked police car, drove a short distance, and then stopped and ran a criminal history check. After completing this check, Officer Hanson looked in his rearview mirror and saw Mr. Strong standing in the road, looking in his direction. Officer Hanson immediately turned his car around and, accelerating, drove toward Mr. Strong, focusing his spotlight on him. Mr. Strong walked quickly out of the road, toward an apartment complex, and then, after dropping something behind a tree, turned and stopped. Under these circumstances, was Mr. Strong seized at the time Officer Hanson focused the spotlight on him?

Although you may use any format, once you select a format, use it for each of your issues. Do not write one issue using the under-does-when format and another using the whether format. Also remember that you are not bound by your opponent's choices. You do not need to use the format that he or she used, and you do not need to have the same number of issues. Select the format that works best for you.

§ 18.11.2 Make the Issue Statement Subtly Persuasive

A good issue statement is subtly persuasive. It subtly suggests the conclusion you want the court to reach and provides support for that conclusion.

In writing the issue statements for an appellate brief, you can use three techniques to make your statements subtly persuasive: (1) you can state the question so that it suggests the conclusion you want the court to reach; (2) you can emphasize the facts that support your theory of the case, and (3) you can emphasize or de-emphasize the standard of review.

a. State the Question So That It Suggests the Conclusion You Want the Court to Reach

Begin by framing the legal question so that it suggests the conclusion you want the court to reach. For example, in writing the issue statement for *State v. Strong*, Ms. Elder frames the question so that it suggests that a seizure occurred under the Fourth Amendment. In contrast, the State frames the question so that it suggests that the trial court acted properly when it denied Mr. Strong's motion to suppress. In reading the following examples, note first how each side frames the question so that it suggests the conclusion it wants the court to reach. Then note that, while the State refers to what the trial court did, Ms. Elder does not. While the State wants to remind the appellate court that the trial court denied the motion, Ms. Elder wants to present the issue as a constitutional issue.

EXAMPLE **Appellant's Statement of the Legal Question**

Under the Fourth Amendment, did a seizure occur when . . .

EXAMPLE **Respondent's Statement of the Legal Question**

Was the trial court's denial of defendant's motion to suppress proper when . . .

---

b. Emphasize the Facts That Support Your Theory of the Case

In addition to stating the question so that it suggests a favorable conclusion, you also want to emphasize the facts that support your theory of the case. For instance, in the following example, Ms. Elder has emphasized the facts that suggest there was a seizure by setting out those facts in detail and by using vivid language. In addition, instead of referring to her client as the defendant, she refers to him by name.

Defendant's Issue Statement

Under the Fourth Amendment, did a seizure occur when Officer Hanson turned his police car around and drove toward Mr. Strong, accelerating and focusing his spotlight on him?

In contrast, in drafting its issue statement, the State emphasizes the facts that support its theory of the case. It sets out the facts that it will rely on in arguing that the officer had an articulable suspicion and describes the spotlight using only general terms.

State's Issue Statement

Did the trial court properly deny defendant's motion to suppress when, after noting that the defendant was standing in the middle of the road staring at his car, Officer Hanson turned around and drove north on Chicago Avenue, illuminating the area with his spotlight only after the defendant walked quickly off the road toward a dark, wooded area?

c. Emphasize or De-emphasize the Standard of Review

Another way to make your issue statement subtly persuasive is to use the standard of review to your advantage. As a general rule, if the standard of review favors your client, include a reference to it in your issue statement; if it does not, do not include a reference to the standard of review in your issue statement.

Defendant's Statement of the Issue: Standard of Review Not Emphasized

Did the trial court err when it ruled that Officer Hanson had an articulable suspicion that Mr. Strong was engaging in or was about to be engaged in criminal conduct when . . . ?

The State's Statement of the Issue: Standard of Review Emphasized

Did the trial court act within its discretion when it ruled that Officer Hanson had an articulable suspicion that the defendant was engaging in or was about to engage in criminal conduct when . . . ?

§ 18.11.3 Make Sure the Issue Statement Is Readable

An issue statement that is not readable is not persuasive. Thus, during the revising process, check your issue statement to make sure a judge can understand it after reading it once. First, look at the length of your issue statement. If your issue statement is more than four or five lines long, try to shorten it. The longer the statement, the more difficult it becomes to read. Second, make sure that you have presented the information in manageable "chunks." One way to make a long issue statement easier to read is to use the three slots in a sentence:

introductory phrase or clause	main clause	modifier

Finally, make sure your statement of the issue does not contain any grammatical errors. In particular, make sure that your subject and verb agree and that, in listing the facts, the items are parallel. See sections 27.4.1 and 27.7.

See section 17.6.4 for a checklist for critiquing the issue statements.

§ 18.12 Drafting the Statement of the Case

Over and over again, judges emphasize the importance of the facts. At both the trial and appellate court levels, judges want to know what the facts are and how the law should be applied to them.

Because the facts are so important, good advocates spend considerable time crafting their statement of the case. They think carefully about which facts they want to include, how those facts should be organized, and how the facts can be presented in the light most favorable to their client.

§ 18.12.1 Check the Rules

Just as there are rules governing the cover, tables, and statement of issues, there is also a rule governing the statement of the case. RAP 10.3(a)(4) sets out the rule for the appellant's brief, and RAP 10.3(b) sets out the rule for the respondent's brief.

RAP 10.3(a) Brief of Appellant or Petitioner

(4)*Statement of the Case.* A fair statement of the facts and procedure relevant to the issues presented for review, without argument. Reference to the record must be included for each factual statement.

RAP 10.3(b) Brief of Respondent

The brief of respondent should conform to section (a) and answer the brief of appellant or petitioner. A statement of the issues and a statement of the case need not be made if respondent is satisfied with the statement in the brief of appellant or petitioner.

Thus, in *State v. Strong*, Ms. Elder needs to include both a procedural history and a statement of the facts in her statement of the case. While the rules do not require the respondent to include a statement of the case, most prosecutors include one. Just as defense counsel wants the opportunity to present the facts in the light most favorable to his or her client, the prosecutor wants the opportunity to present the facts in the light that supports the State's position.

§ 18.12.2 Draft the Procedural History

Almost always, attorneys set out the procedural history first, using it to set the stage for the statement of facts and establishing that the case is properly before the appellate court. As a general rule, you will want to include the following facts in your procedural history: (1) a statement describing the nature of the action, (2) a description of any relevant motions and their disposition, (3) a statement telling the court whether the case was heard by a judge or by a jury, (4) the date that final judgment was entered, and (5) the date the notice of appeal or the petition for review was filed. For example, in *State v. Strong*, the procedural history would look something like this.

Procedural History From Appellant's Brief

EXAMPLE

William Strong was charged with one count of Possession of a Controlled Substance under RCW 69.50.401(d), one count of Unlawful Possession of a Firearm under RCW 9.41.040(1), and one count of Possession of Stolen Property in the Second Degree under RCW 9A.56.160. CP 1. After an evidentiary hearing, the trial court denied Mr. Strong's Motion to Suppress. RP 4.

The case went to trial, RP 8, and on September 8, 2006, a jury found Mr. Strong guilty on all three counts. CP 5. Judgment and sentence were entered on September 24, 2006. RP 15. Mr. Strong filed his notice of appeal on October 16, 2006. CP 18.

Notice that each statement is supported by a reference to the rule. CP stands for Clerk's Paper — that is, a document filed with the trial court; RP stands for report of proceedings — that is, the transcript from a hearing or trial.

§ 18.12.3 Select the Facts

Like the statement of facts in an objective memo and motion brief, the statement of facts in an appellate brief contains three types of facts: legally significant facts, emotionally significant facts, and background facts.

a. Legally Significant Facts

Because the court rules require that the statement of the case be "fair," in writing the statement of facts you must include all of the legally significant facts, both favorable and unfavorable. Thus, in *Strong*, the parties must include all of the facts that will be relevant in determining whether there was a seizure. Ms. Elder must include the fact that Mr. Strong walked away from the officer, that he walked quickly, and that he dropped some type of "package" behind a tree. Similarly, the prosecutor must include the fact that the officer accelerated as he drove toward Mr. Strong, that he shone his spotlight on Mr. Strong, and that Mr. Strong stopped before being ordered to do so by the officer.

b. Emotionally Significant Facts

While you must include all of the legally significant facts, you do not need to include all of the facts that are emotionally significant. Although as a defensive move you may sometimes include an emotionally significant fact that is unfavorable, recharacterizing it or minimizing its significance, most of the time you will not. It is more common to include only those emotionally significant facts that favor your client.

The harder question is how to handle emotionally significant facts that are unfavorable to the other side. Should you sling mud, or should you take a higher road and omit any reference to those facts? The answer is that it depends: it depends on the fact, on the case, and on the attorney. If the case is strong and the fact's connection to the case is tenuous, most attorneys would not include the fact. If, however, the case is weak and the fact's connection is closer, many attorneys will include it; some using it as a sword, others using it much more subtly.

c. Background Facts

Background facts play a different role in persuasive writing than they do in objective writing. In an objective statement of facts, the writer includes only those facts that are needed for the story to make sense. In a persuasive statement of facts, you want to do more. You want to use background facts to create a favorable context.

§ 18.12.4 Select an Organizational Scheme

After selecting the facts, the next step is to select an organizational scheme. Should the facts be presented chronologically, topically, or in an organizational scheme that combines the two?

Unlike an objective statement of facts, in which the only selection criterion was logic, in writing a persuasive statement of facts there are two criteria: you want to select a scheme that is logical and that allows you to present the facts in an order most favorable to your client.

In *Strong*, because the sequence of events is important, logic dictates that the facts be presented chronologically. In addition, a chronological scheme allows both defense counsel and the prosecutor to present the facts in a favorable context. By starting with the initial encounter, defense counsel can start with something favorable: "When approached by Officer Hanson, Mr. Strong was standing on a corner with a woman watching an encounter between Officer Hanson and another individual." Similarly, the State can start with something favorable: "At the time he approached Mr. Strong, Officer Hanson had just finished responding to a call in a high crime area."

§ 18.12.5 Present the Facts in the Light Most Favorable to the Client

Although the rules require that the statement of facts be fair, they do not require that it be objective. As an advocate, you want to present the facts in the light most favorable to your client. To do so, use the following techniques.

Techniques You Can Use in Writing a Persuasive Statement of Facts

    a. Create a Favorable Context.
    b. Tell the Story from the Client's Point of View.
    c. Emphasize the Facts That Support Your Theory of the Case and De-Emphasize Those That Do Not.
        1. Airtime
        2. Detail
        3. Positions of Emphasis
        4. Sentence Length
        5. Sentence Construction
        6. Active and Passive Voice
    d. Choose Your Words Carefully.

a. Create a Favorable Context

One way to create a favorable context is to start the story where it favors your client. Look again at the examples in Chapter 17. In the first example, the defendant starts his statement of facts where his story started: with his activities on the day of the assault.

The First Three Paragraphs of the Defendant's Statement of Facts in *State v. Patterson*   EXAMPLE 1

At 7:30 on Monday morning, August 14, 2006, 22-year-old Dean Patterson finished his shift as a security guard and walked to his apartment. After having breakfast with his wife, Patterson went to bed and slept until about 1:00 p.m. At about 2:30 p.m., Patterson's wife received a phone call asking her to work at the local hospital, where she is employed as a nurse. She got ready, and Patterson dropped her off at the hospital at about 3:10. When he returned, Patterson could not find a parking place close to his apartment and had to park several blocks away.

At about 3:30, Patterson called his wife to find how long she would have to work. They had had plans to go to a movie that evening, and he wanted to know whether he should change those plans. At about 3:50, Patterson took a load of laundry to the apartment complex's laundry room. When he returned to his apartment, Patterson watched part of an old movie. At about 4:20, Patterson went back to the laundry room to put the clothes in the dryer. On his way back, he walked to where his car, an older model red station wagon, was parked to see if he needed to get gas. As he did so, Patterson noticed a parking spot much closer to his apartment and, after checking his gas gauge, moved his car to that spot. After parking his car, Patterson got out of the car and, because the driver's side door does not lock from the outside, walked to the passenger side to lock the doors. As he did so, he nodded to a parking enforcement officer who was driving by.

By this time, it was 4:30, and Patterson decided to phone his wife again. He arranged to meet her at 5:15 for her dinner break. Patterson picked up the laundry and then left the apartment a little before 5:00 to meet his wife.

In contrast, the State starts its statement of facts where the story started for the victim. In the first paragraph of its statement of facts, the State describes the assault and then the show-up and line-up.

EXAMPLE 2

EXAMPLE 2 **The First Paragraph of the State's Statement of Facts in *State v. Patterson***

On Monday, August 14, 2006, Beatrice Martinez was assaulted with a deadly weapon. At a show-up held thirty to forty minutes after the attack, Martinez positively identified the defendant, Dean E. Patterson, as her assailant. Four days after the assault, Ms. Martinez picked Patterson out of a line-up, and once again positively identified him as her assailant.

Although the differences are more subtle, context is equally important in *State v. Strong*. Ms. Elder starts the story where it started for Mr. Strong: with his activities on the night in question. She then goes on to describe Officer Hanson's actions from Mr. Strong's point of view.

EXAMPLE 1 **First Paragraph of Appellant's Statement of Facts**

On the evening of May 17, 2006, William Strong was standing on the corner of Lincoln and Chicago in Tacoma talking to a friend when Officer Hanson approached him and began questioning him. RP 18. Standing only a foot or two from Mr. Strong, Officer Hanson asked Mr. Strong to identify himself and to explain what he was doing in the area. RP 18. Mr. Strong willingly answered Officer Hanson's questions, telling him that his name was William Strong. RP 19.

In contrast, the prosecutor starts the story where it started for Officer Hanson and tells that story from Officer Hanson's point of view.

EXAMPLE 2 **First Paragraph of the Respondent's Statement of Facts**

At about 10:40 p.m. on May 17, 2006, Officer Hanson was called to the corner of Lincoln and Chicago to investigate a report of drug activity. RP 12. After completing his investigation, RP 13, Officer Hanson noticed the defendant, an individual he did not recognize, standing on the corner. RP 17. Because he makes a point to meet the people in his patrol area, Officer Hanson initiated a social contact. RP 18.

Note the last sentence in the second example. Even within the paragraph, the prosecutor is using context to his advantage. He uses the clause, "Because he makes a point to meet the people in his patrol area" to create a favorable context for the fact that Officer Hanson initiated a contact with Mr. Strong. The inference he wants the reader to draw is that Officer Hanson is a conscientious police officer.

b. Tell the Story from the Client's Point of View

One of the most powerful persuasive devices is point of view. As a general rule, you will want to present the facts from your client's point of view. You can do this by telling the story as your client would tell it and by using your client as the actor in most sentences. Look again at the following examples. In the first example, the first paragraph from Mr. Strong's brief, the story is told as Mr. Strong would tell it, and he is the actor in both the first and third sentences. In contrast, in the second example, the first paragraph of the respondent's brief, the story is told as Officer Hanson would tell it, and Officer Hanson is the actor in all three sentences. In each sentence, the subject of the sentence is in boldface type.

First Paragraph of Appellant's Statement of Facts   `EXAMPLE 1`

On the evening of May 17, 2006, **William Strong** was standing on the corner of Lincoln and Chicago in Tacoma talking to a friend when Officer Hanson approached him and began questioning him. RP 18. Standing only a foot or two from Mr. Strong, **Officer Hanson** asked Mr. Strong to identify himself and to explain what he was doing in the area. RP 18. **Mr. Strong** willingly answered Officer Hanson's questions, telling him that his name was William Strong. RP 19.

First Paragraph of the Respondent's Statement of Facts   `EXAMPLE 2`

At about 10:40 p.m. on May 17, 2006, **Officer Hanson** was called to the corner of Lincoln and Chicago to investigate a report of drug activity. RP 12. After completing his investigation, RP 13, **Officer Hanson** noticed the defendant, an individual he did not recognize, standing on the corner. RP 17. Because he makes a point to meet the people in his patrol area, **Officer Hanson** initiated a social contact. RP 18.

---

c. Emphasize Those Facts That Support Your Theory of the Case and De-emphasize Those That Do Not

In addition to presenting the facts from the client's point of view, good advocates emphasize those facts that support their theory of the case and de-emphasize those that do not. They do this by using one or more of the following techniques.

1. Airtime

Just as listeners remember best the songs that get the most airtime, readers remember best the facts that get the most words. Consequently, if you want the judges to remember a fact, give that fact as much airtime as possible. For example, in *State v. Strong*, Ms. Elder wants the judges to remember that Officer Hanson approached Mr. Strong and questioned him. As a result, she gives these facts as much airtime as possible. In contrast, the State wants to de-emphasize these facts. In the following examples, the facts related to the initial encounter are in bold.

First Paragraph of Appellant's Statement of Facts   `EXAMPLE 1`

On the evening of May 17, 2006, William Strong was standing on the corner of Lincoln and Chicago in Tacoma talking to a friend when **Officer Hanson approached** him and began questioning him. RP 18. Standing only a foot or two from Mr. Strong, Officer Hanson asked Mr. Strong to identify himself and to explain what he was doing in the area. RP 18. Mr. Strong willingly answered Officer Hanson's questions, telling him that his name was William Strong. RP 19.

EXAMPLE 2   ## First Paragraph of the Respondent's Statement of Facts

At about 10:40 p.m. on May 17, 2006, Officer Hanson was called to the corner of Lincoln and Chicago to investigate a report of drug activity. RP 12. After completing his investigation, RP 13, Officer Hanson noticed the defendant, an individual he did not recognize, standing on the corner. RP 17. Because he makes a point to meet the people in his patrol area, **Officer Hanson initiated a social contact.** RP 18.

---

2. Detail

Just as readers tend to remember best those facts that get the most airtime, they also tend to remember best those things that are described in the most detail. Thus, if you want the judges to remember a particular fact, use detail in setting out that fact. Use concrete subjects, action verbs, and adjectives and adverbs to create a vivid picture. In contrast, if you want to de-emphasize a particular fact, use more general language. In the following examples, compare the ways in which the attorneys describe the criminal history check and the spotlight.

EXAMPLE 1   ## Excerpt from Appellant's Brief

After questioning Mr. Strong, Officer Hanson returned to his patrol car, got into the car, and drove about a block and a half down a hill. RP 6. He then ran a criminal history check, **which showed that Mr. Strong had prior arrests but that there were no outstanding warrants.** RP 7. Officer Hanson then looked in his rearview mirror and saw that Mr. Strong had walked to the middle of the street and was looking in his direction. RP 8. Officer Hanson immediately turned his car around and began driving toward Mr. Strong. RP 8. As Mr. Strong began moving toward the side of the street, Officer Hanson accelerated, **turned on his spotlight, and focused the spotlight on Mr. Strong.** RP 9-10.

EXAMPLE 2   ## Excerpt from Respondent's Brief

Officer Hanson then got into his car and began to leave the area. RP 6. **After driving about one and a half blocks, Officer Hanson stopped and ran a criminal history check on the defendant. RP 7. The check showed that the defendant had a long criminal history, including numerous arrests for drug-related crimes.** RP 7.

After he completed the criminal history check, Officer Hanson once again began to drive away. RP 8. As he did so, he glanced in his rearview mirror and saw that the defendant had walked into the center of the street and was staring, for what seemed an unusually long period of time, at the police car. RP 8. Because the defendant's behavior seemed suspicious, Officer Hanson turned his car around and began driving back toward the defendant. RP 8. The defendant immediately moved from the middle of the street toward a dark, wooded area. RP 9-10. **So that he could see better, Officer Hanson turned on his spotlight, illuminating the area.** Instead of stopping, the defendant continued to walk quickly away from Officer Hanson toward the wooded area. RP 10.

Note first the way in which the attorneys deal with the criminal history check. Ms. Elder uses few words and generic language. "Mr. Strong had prior arrests." In contrast, the prosecutor gives the fact considerably more airtime (the phrase "criminal history check" appears three times) and describes the history in as much detail as the record allowed. Similarly, the parties handle the spotlight differently. Although both sides give the fact about the same amount of airtime, Ms. Elder's description is more vivid than the prosecutor's.

3. Positions of Emphasis

Another technique that can be used to emphasize favorable facts is to place those facts in positions of emphasis. Because readers remember better those things that they read first and last, favorable facts should be placed at the beginning and end of the statement of the case, at the beginning and end of paragraphs, and at the beginning and end of sentences. Unfavorable facts should be buried in the middle: in the middle of the statement of facts, in the middle of a paragraph, in the middle of a sentence. See pages 393-394 and section 24.6.3.

Look again at the examples from the Patterson case set out in Chapter 17. In the first example, defense counsel wants to emphasize that the victim, Beatrice Martinez, told the police that her assailant was in his 40s. Thus, he puts that fact at the end of the paragraph. On the other hand, because the State wants to de-emphasize that fact, the prosecutor buries it in the middle of a sentence in the middle of a paragraph.

Excerpt from the Defendant's Statement of Facts

EXAMPLE 1

Because she was upset, Ms. Martinez was able to give the police only a general description of her assailant. She described him as being a short, white male with blondish-brown hair who was wearing glasses and a dark jacket. In addition, **she told police that her assailant was in his early 40s.**

Excerpt from the State's Statement of Facts

EXAMPLE 2

Ms. Martinez told the police that her assailant was a white male who was about 5'7" tall, **that her assailant had wavy blondish-brown hair, that her assailant appeared to be in his early 40s,** and that at the time of the assault, her assailant was wearing a dark jacket and wire-rim glasses.

In *State v. Strong,* the attorneys use the same technique. Ms. Elder has placed a favorable fact, that Officer Hanson questioned Mr. Strong, in a position of emphasis at the beginning of the paragraph and buried the unfavorable fact, that Mr. Strong has a criminal history, in the middle of the paragraph. In addition, she has ended the paragraph with a favorable fact: that Officer Hanson focused a spotlight on Mr. Strong.

EXAMPLE 3   ## Excerpt from Appellant's Brief

After questioning Mr. Strong, Officer Hanson returned to his patrol car, got into the car, and drove about a block and a half down a hill. RP 6. He then ran a criminal history check, **which showed that Mr. Strong had prior arrests** but that there were no outstanding warrants. RP 7. Officer Hanson then looked in his rearview mirror and saw that Mr. Strong had walked to the middle of the street and was looking in his direction. RP 8. Officer Hanson immediately turned his car around and began driving toward Mr. Strong. RP 8. As Mr. Strong began moving toward the side of the street, Officer Hanson accelerated, turned on his spotlight, and **focused the spotlight on Mr. Strong**. RP 9-10.

In the next example, the prosecutor divided what had been one paragraph into two paragraphs so that he could take better advantage of the positions of emphasis. The prosecutor has put favorable facts at the beginning and the end of each paragraph. He has started the first paragraph by stating that Mr. Strong had begun to leave the area and ended it with the fact that Mr. Strong had numerous arrests for drug-related crimes. In the second paragraph, the prosecutor has started the paragraph with another reference to the criminal history check and ended it with the defendant walking quickly away. Although the prosecutor would have liked to bury the unfavorable fact in the middle, he could not do so without interrupting the flow of the story. As a result, the unfavorable fact is not in the middle but near the end of the paragraph.

EXAMPLE 4   ## Excerpt from Respondent's Brief

Officer Hanson then got into his car and began to leave the area. RP 6. After driving about one and a half blocks, Officer Hanson stopped and ran a criminal history check on the defendant. RP 7. The check showed that the defendant **had a long criminal history, including numerous arrests for drug-related crimes**. RP 7.

After he completed the criminal history check, Officer Hanson once again began to drive away. RP 8. As he did so, he glanced in his rearview mirror and saw that the defendant had walked into the center of the street and was staring, for what seemed an unusually long period of time, at the police car. RP 8. Because the defendant's behavior seemed suspicious, Officer Hanson turned his car around and began driving back toward the defendant. RP 8. The defendant immediately moved from the middle of the street toward a dark, wooded area. RP 9-10. So that he could see better, Officer Hanson turned on his spotlight, illuminating the area. **Instead of stopping, the defendant continued to walk quickly away from Officer Hanson toward the wooded area.** RP 10.

4. Sentence Length

Because readers tend to remember information placed in shorter sentences better than information placed in longer sentences, good advocates place favorable facts in short sentences in a position of emphasis. For instance, in the following example, defense counsel has buried the unfavorable fact, that Mr. Strong dropped a "package," in a long sentence in the middle of the paragraph and has put the favorable fact, that Mr. Strong stopped, in a short sentence at the end of the paragraph. See pages 393-395 and section 24.5. The favorable facts are in bold and the unfavorable facts are in italics.

Excerpt from Appellant's Brief　　　　　EXAMPLE

As the patrol car came toward him, Mr. Strong walked quickly off the road. RP 11, 12. He then walked two or three steps toward an apartment complex, *dropped what appeared to Officer Hanson to be a package behind a tree,* and then turned and walked two or three steps back toward Officer Hanson. RP 11, 12. **Mr. Strong then stopped**. RP 12.

---

5. Sentence Construction

If you want to emphasize a fact, place it in the main clause in a relatively short sentence. If you want to de-emphasize a fact, place it in a dependent or subordinate clause in a relatively long sentence. In the following example, Ms. Elder has placed the facts that she wants to emphasize (that Officer Hanson turned his car around and began driving toward Mr. Strong, and that Officer Hanson accelerated, turned on his spotlight, and focused the spotlight on Mr. Strong) in main clauses and the fact that she wants to de-emphasize (that Mr. Strong began to move to the side of the road) in a subordinate clause at the beginning of a relatively long sentence. Once again, the favorable facts are in bold and the unfavorable ones in italics.

Excerpt from Appellant's Brief　　　　　EXAMPLE

Officer Hanson immediately turned his car around and began driving toward Mr. Strong. *As Mr. Strong began moving toward the side of the street,* **Officer Hanson accelerated, turned on his spotlight, and focused the spotlight on Mr. Strong.**

---

6. Active and Passive Voice

Good advocates use the active voice when they want to emphasize what the actor did and the passive voice when they want to draw the reader's attention away from the actor's actions. In our example case, Ms. Elder wants to emphasize that Officer Hanson approached Mr. Strong. Therefore, in setting out this fact, she uses the active voice, making Officer Hanson the actor.

EXAMPLE   **Active Voice**

Officer Hanson approached Mr. Strong and began questioning him.

In contrast, the State wants to de-emphasize the fact that Officer Hanson approached Mr. Strong. Thus, it sets out this fact using the passive voice.

EXAMPLE   **Passive Voice**

Strong was approached by Officer Hanson.

See page 395 and section 24.1 for more on the active and passive voice.

d. Choose Your Words Carefully

Because words create powerful images, select your words carefully. In addition to selecting the word that conveys the right meaning, select the word that creates the right image. Consider, for example, the labels that might be used to describe Mr. Strong:

Mr. Strong
William Strong
Strong
William
Willie
the defendant
the accused

While Ms. Elder would probably want to use "Mr. Strong," "William Strong," or "Strong" in referring to her client, the prosecutor would want to use "the defendant." By using Mr. Strong's name, Ms. Elder makes her client a real person. The title "Mr. Strong" makes Strong seem less like a convicted felon and more like an average citizen. In contrast, by using the labels "defendant" or "the accused," the State de-humanizes Mr. Strong and suggests that he is guilty.

Note that in many jurisdictions the rules state that the parties should not use the labels "appellant" or "respondent."

RAP 10.4 . . .
(e) **Reference to Party.** References to parties by such designations as "appellant" and "respondent" should be kept to a minimum. It promotes clarity to use the designations used in the lower court, the actual names of the parties, or descriptive terms such as "the employee," "the injured person," and "the taxpayer."

Also consider the words that can be used to describe what Mr. Strong and Officer Hanson said. Although all of the following words convey essentially the same information, their connotations are very different.

Words That Have Essentially the Same Meaning but Different Connotations

EXAMPLE

Says	Makes a statement
Alleges	Makes a controversial charge or statement without presentation of proof
Asserts	States or expresses positively
Affirms	States or expresses positively but with less force than asserts
Declares	Carries the approximate force of asserts but suggests a more formal statement
Claims	Maintains a position in the face of an argument
Maintains	Declares to be true
Avers	Declares in a positive or dogmatic manner
Argues	Implies intent to persuade an adversary through debate

While Ms. Elder would use words like "stated," "asserts," or "affirms" in describing Mr. Strong's statements, she would use words like "says," "claims," or "maintains" when talking about what Officer Hanson said. Conversely, the prosecutor would use words like "alleges," "claims," "maintains," or "argues" in describing Mr. Strong's statements and words like "stated," "asserts," or "affirms" in describing Officer Hanson's statements.

In addition, in writing her statement of facts, Ms. Elder chose words that create images consistent with her theory of the case. Look at the words and phrases below that are in boldface type:

Excerpt from Appellant's Brief

EXAMPLE

Officer Hanson immediately turned his car around and began driving toward Mr. Strong. As Mr. Strong began moving toward the side of the street, Officer Hanson **accelerated**, turned on his **spotlight**, and **focused** the **spotlight** on Mr. Strong.

Because she wanted to establish that Officer Hanson's actions were a show of authority, Ms. Elder used the clause, "Officer Hanson immediately turned his car around and began driving toward Mr. Strong" rather than "Officer Hanson turned and began driving north on Chicago," the word "accelerated" rather than the clause "increased his speed," the word "spotlight" rather than just "light," and the word "focused" instead of "turned." In addition, because she wanted to establish that Mr. Strong submitted to Officer Hanson's show of authority, Ms. Elder chose to say that "Mr. Strong began moving toward the side of the street" rather than "Mr. Strong began walking quickly away from Officer Hanson."

e. Be Subtly Persuasive

Most beginning attorneys make one of two mistakes. They either present the facts objectively or, in an attempt to be persuasive, they go over the line and include arguments in their statement of facts, setting out facts that are not supported by the record, or using purple prose.

Excerpt from Appellant's Brief

Officer Hanson's action constitutes a show of authority. While Mr. Strong was standing in front of his apartment complex talking to a friend, Officer Hanson approached him and began interrogating him. He demanded his name and questioned him about what he was doing. RP 4. Although Mr. Strong cooperated fully, Officer Hanson would not give up. RP 5. Hoping to find that there was a warrant for Mr. Strong's arrest, Officer Hanson went back to his car, drove a short distance away, and then stopped and ran a criminal history check. RP 7. Although the check did not reveal any outstanding warrants, Officer Hanson turned his car around, and, increasing his speed, drove directly toward Mr. Strong, capturing him in the blinding glare of his high-powered spotlight. RP 10, 11.

Most judges would not find this version of the statement of the facts persuasive. Instead of setting out facts, in the first sentence the author sets out a legal conclusion. Although a sentence like this one belongs in the argument section of the brief, it does not belong in the statement of facts. In addition, the second and fourth sentences contain facts that are not in the record. Nothing in the record indicates that Mr. Strong was standing in front of his own apartment house or that Officer Hanson ran the criminal history check because he hoped to find that there was an outstanding warrant for Mr. Strong's arrest. Finally, the author has gone too far in trying to present the facts in a light favorable to Mr. Strong. Instead of creating a favorable context, words like "interrogating," "capturing," "blinding glare," and "high-powered spotlight" make the judge wary. For more on purple prose, see section 26.1.

For a checklist for critiquing the statement of facts, see section 17.5.4.

§ 18.13 Drafting the Summary of the Argument

The summary of the argument is what the title implies: a summary of the advocate's argument. Although some courts do not require one (the Washington rules state that the "argument *may* be preceded by a summary"), a summary can be a useful tool. For those judges who read the entire brief, it provides an overview of the arguments and the authorities that support those arguments; for those judges who do not read everything, it sets out the key points.

You may want to write two drafts of your summary of the argument. By preparing a first draft before you write the argument section, you will force yourself to focus. If you understand your arguments, you should be able to set out each of them in a paragraph or two. If you can't, more thinking and outlining are needed.

Preparing a second draft after you have written the argument section is equally useful. This version can serve as a check on your arguments: when strung together, the opening sentences of your paragraphs or paragraph blocks should provide the judges with a summary of the argument. If they don't, it is the argument section itself, not the summary, that needs work.

The most common problem attorneys have with the summary of the argument is length. They write too much. The summary of the argument should be no more than one or two pages long, with one or two paragraphs for each argument. Citations to authority should also be kept to a minimum. Although you may want to refer to key cases and statutes, the focus should be on the arguments, not the citations. Another common problem is that attorneys do not make clear the connections between their arguments. Use transitions to make clear when one argument is a continuation of another argument and when an argument is an alternative argument.

§ 18.14 Drafting the Argumentative Headings

Argumentative headings serve two functions in an appellate brief. They provide the court with an outline of the argument and they help persuade.

§ 18.14.1 Use the Argumentative Headings to Provide the Court with an Outline of the Argument

When properly drafted, the argumentative headings provide the court with an outline of your arguments. By reading the headings set out in the table of contents, the judges can see your assertions, your support for those assertions, and relationships between your various assertions and arguments.

Argumentative headings also serve several other purposes. They help the judges by dividing the argument into manageable sections and by acting as locators, which allow the judges to locate a particular part of the argument quickly. In addition, these headings help the attorney. Because attorneys like Ms. Elder seldom have large blocks of time available for writing, the brief must usually be written in sections. By drafting the headings first, an attorney can write one section or subsection at a time, and put the pieces together at the end.

§ 18.14.2 Use the Argumentative Headings to Persuade

Good attorneys use argumentative headings in the same way good politicians use sound bites — to catch their readers' attention and to persuade their readers to see the issue as they see it.

Most good argumentative headings have four characteristics: (1) they are framed as positive assertions, (2) they set out both the assertion and the support for that assertion, (3) they are as specific as possible, and (4) they are easy to read and understand. In addition, in a good argumentative heading, the writer uses the same persuasive techniques that he or she used in drafting the issue statements and statement of facts.

a. Write Your Headings as Positive Assertions

If a heading is to be persuasive, it needs to be in the form of a positive assertion. For example, in *State v. Strong*, Ms. Elder does not want to begin her main heading with the following negative assertion.

EXAMPLE 1   **Negative Assertion**

The trial court did not act properly when it denied Mr. Strong's motion to suppress.

Instead, she wants to turn this negative statement into a positive one:

EXAMPLE 2   **Positive Assertion**

The trial court erred when it denied Mr. Strong's motion to suppress.

Similarly, the State wants to start its main heading with a positive assertion:

EXAMPLE 3   **Negative Assertion**

The trial court did not err when it denied the defendant's motion to suppress.

EXAMPLE 4   **Positive Assertion**

The trial court properly denied the appellant's motion to suppress.

---

b. Provide Support for Your Assertions

By itself, though, an assertion does not make a very good sound bite. Thus, as a general rule you will also want to support your assertions. For example, instead of just stating that the trial court erred when it denied Mr. Strong's motion to suppress, Ms. Elder needs to support that assertion:

EXAMPLE   **Positive Assertion Plus Support for Assertion**

The trial court erred when it denied Mr. Strong's motion to suppress because the spotlight was a show of authority, and Mr. Strong submitted.

Similarly, instead of just saying that the trial court acted properly when it denied Mr. Strong's motion to suppress, the prosecutor would want to add a supporting statement:

EXAMPLE   **Positive Assertion Plus Support for Assertion**

The trial court acted properly when it denied the defendant's motion to suppress because the spotlight was not a show of authority and, even if it was, the defendant did not submit.

As the above examples illustrate, one of the most common patterns for an argumentative heading is the following.

Assertion + because/when + support for assertion

How general or specific your support is will depend on how you have organized your argument. If you have a main heading without any subheadings, your support should be as specific as possible. If, however, you have a main heading with subheadings and sub-subheadings, your main heading can be quite general. The sub-subheadings will provide the more specific support. The following examples show three different ways of setting out and supporting a positive assertion.

Main Heading but No Subheadings; Support Set Out in the Form of Key Facts

EXAMPLE 1

   I. UNDER THE FOURTH AMENDMENT, A SEIZURE OCCURRED WHEN OFFICER HANSON DROVE TOWARD MR. STRONG, ACCELERATING AND TURNING HIS SPOTLIGHT ON HIM, AND MR. STRONG TOOK A FEW STEPS AND STOPPED.

Main Heading but No Subheadings; Support Set Out in the Form of Legal Conclusions

EXAMPLE 2

   I. UNDER THE FOURTH AMENDMENT, THE TRIAL COURT ERRED WHEN IT DENIED MR. STRONG'S MOTION TO SUPPRESS BECAUSE THE SPOTLIGHT WAS A SHOW OF AUTHORITY, AND MR. STRONG SUBMITTED.

Main Heading and Subheadings

EXAMPLE 3

   I. THE TRIAL COURT ERRED WHEN IT DENIED MR. STRONG'S MOTION TO SUPPRESS BECAUSE THE SPOTLIGHT WAS A SHOW OF AUTHORITY, AND MR. STRONG SUBMITTED TO THE SHOW OF AUTHORITY.

      A. <u>The spotlight was a show of authority because a reasonable person would not have felt free to leave.</u>

      B. <u>Mr. Strong submitted to the show of authority when he did not leave the area lighted by the spotlight and stopped before being ordered to do so by the officer.</u>

---

c. Make the Headings as Specific as Possible

As a general rule, make your headings case specific. Instead of writing statements that are so broad that they could apply to a number of different cases, write statements that talk specifically about the parties and facts in your case.

Compare the following examples.

EXAMPLE   **Too General**

- The trial court erred when it denied defendant's motion to suppress.
- The trial court erred when it denied defendant's motion to suppress because there was a show of authority and the defendant submitted.
- The seizure was proper.
- The seizure was proper because the officer had an articulable suspicion.

EXAMPLE   **More Specific**

- The trial court erred when it denied Mr. Strong's motion to suppress because the spotlight was a show of authority, and Mr. Strong submitted when, after taking a few steps, he turned and stopped.
- The seizure was proper because, after seeing the defendant drop a package behind the tree, Officer Hanson had an articulable suspicion that the defendant was engaged in or was about to engage in criminal conduct.

d. Make Your Headings Readable

A heading that is not readable is not persuasive. For example, even though the following heading is in the proper form, it is not persuasive because very few judges would read it.

EXAMPLE   **Argumentative Heading Is Too Long**

THE TRIAL COURT ERRED IN DENYING MR. STRONG'S MOTION TO SUPPRESS BECAUSE, UNDER THE TOTALITY OF THE CIRCUMSTANCES, A SEIZURE OCCURRED WHEN OFFICER HANSON, AFTER QUESTIONING MR. STRONG, DROVE AWAY, RAN A CRIMINAL HISTORY CHECK, AND THEN, AFTER SEEING MR. STRONG STANDING IN THE MIDDLE OF THE ROAD, DROVE BACK TOWARD MR. STRONG, SPOTLIGHTING HIM, AND, MR. STRONG, AFTER WALKING TOWARD AN APARTMENT COMPLEX AND DROPPING AN ITEM BEHIND A TREE, TURNED AND STOPPED BEFORE BEING TOLD TO DO SO BY THE OFFICER.

In addition to keeping your headings short — usually no more than two or three lines long — use sentence constructions that make the headings easier to read. Use parallel constructions (see section 27.7) and, when appropriate, repeat the words that highlight the parallel structure (for example, "that" or "because"). Finally, when appropriate, use commas, semicolons, and colons to divide the sentence into more manageable units of meaning.

e. Use the Same Persuasive Techniques You Used in Drafting the Issue Statements and Statement of Facts

In drafting their argumentative headings, good advocates use many of the same persuasive techniques that they use in drafting their issue statements and statements of facts. When possible, they create a favorable context, they set out the facts from the client's point of view, they give more airtime to favorable facts than to unfavorable facts, they describe favorable facts in more detail than unfavorable facts, they take advantage of the positions of emphasis, and they choose their words carefully.

In the following example, Ms. Elder has created a favorable context ("after questioning Mr. Strong"), has presented the facts from Mr. Strong's point of view ("drove toward Mr. Strong, focusing his spotlight on him"), has taken advantage of the position of emphasis by putting her most favorable fact at the end, and has chosen her words carefully.

Appellant Has Used Persuasive Techniques Effectively   EXAMPLE

    A. <u>A show of authority occurred when, after questioning Mr. Strong, Officer Hanson turned his car around and, accelerating, drove toward Mr. Strong, focusing his spotlight on him.</u>

---

§ 18.14.3 Use the Conventional Formats for Headings

Although seldom set out in rules, in most jurisdictions there are conventions governing the number, type, and typeface for argumentative headings. For example, as we noted in section 17.8.4, convention dictates that you should have a main heading for each of your issue statements. Thus, if you have one issue you should have one main heading; if you have two issues, two main headings; and so on. The issue sets out the question, and the heading gives your answer to that question.

In addition to main headings, you may also use subheadings and sub-subheadings and, rarely, sub-sub-subheadings. There are, however, some things to keep in mind if you use additional headings. First, if you include one subheading, you need to have at least two at that same level. As a consequence, if you find that you have only one subheading in a section, either delete that heading or add at least one additional heading. Second, while you are not required to put text between the main heading and the first subheading, it is usually a good idea to do so. As a general rule, use this space to set out the general rule and a roadmap for that section of your brief. Finally, keep in mind the typefaces that attorneys use for the various levels of headings. The formats provide the judges with signals about where they are in the argument.

The following example shows one way of using headings. Note that following convention, all capital letters have been used for the main headings and underlining for the subheadings.

Typefaces for Argumentative Headings   EXAMPLE

    I. FIRST MAIN HEADING [corresponds to first issue statement]
       [Introduce and set out the general rule.]
       [Provide your reader with a roadmap for your argument.]

    A. <u>First subheading</u>
       [Introduce and set out the specific rules.]
       1. <u>First sub-subheading</u>
          [Set out your argument.]
       2. Second sub-subheading
          [Set out your argument.]
    B. <u>Second subheading</u>
       [Set out your argument.]
    C. <u>Third subheading</u>
       [Set out your argument.]

II. SECOND MAIN HEADING [corresponds to second issue statement]
    [Introduce and set out the general rule.]
    [Provide your reader with a roadmap for your argument.]
    A. <u>First subheading</u>
       [Set out your argument.]
    B. <u>Second subheading</u>
       [Set out specific rules.]
       1. First sub-subheading
          [Set out your argument.]
       2. Second sub-subheading
          [Set out your argument.]

See section 17.9.6 for a checklist for critiquing the argumentative headings.

§ 18.15 Drafting the Arguments

A brief is only as good as its argument section. An argument section that is well written persuades; one that is not, does not.

§ 18.15.1 Knowing What You Need, and Want, to Argue

If your arguments are to be focused, you must know what you need, and want, to argue. You may not just throw out a number of assertions, rules, and cases and hope that the court will make sense of them for you.

Therefore, before you begin to write, you need to determine what type of argument you are making. Are you asking the court to adopt a new rule? To apply an existing rule? To determine whether the trial court abused its discretion or whether there is sufficient evidence to support a jury's verdict? The following decision tree can help you decide what type of arguments you need to make.

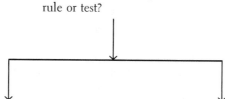

Are you asking the appellate court to apply an existing rule or test or to adopt a new rule or test?

If you are asking the appellate court to apply an exisiting rule or test, is the standard of review *de novo* or something more deferential?

If you are asking the appellate court to adopt a new rule or test, you need to establish (1) that the appellate court is not bound by mandatory authority, (2) that the rule that you are advocating is a better rule than the rule your opponent is advocating, and (3) that under your rule, you win. In addition, in the alternative, you may want to argue that you are entitled to relief under the rule that your opponent is advocating.

If the standard of review is *de novo*, you need to set out the rule or test and then walk the court through it, showing why each part is or is not met.

If the standard of review is more deferential, for example, abuse of discretion, you need to show the appellate court why the trial court did or did not abuse its discretion.

§ 18.15.2 Selecting an Organizational Scheme

Once you have determined what type of argument you want to make, you then need to select the organizational scheme that will work best for that argument.

If you are asking the court to adopt a new rule or test, you will usually use a version of the blueprint set out in section 13.5. You will start by establishing that there is no existing rule or test, then persuade the court that the rule or test you are proposing is "better" than the rule or test being proposed by your opponent, and end by applying your proposed rule or test to the facts of your case. In addition, sometimes you will argue in the alternative: even if the court adopts the rule or test being advocated by opposing counsel, you still win under that test.

Organizational Scheme for Issues of First Impression

- Introduction establishing that the issue is one of first impression
- Assertion setting out proposed rule

- Arguments relating to why the court should adopt your proposed rule rather than the rule being proposed by your opponent
- Application of your proposed rule to the facts of your case
- If appropriate, alternative argument asserting that even under the rule being proposed by your opponent you win

If you are asking the court to apply an existing rule or test, you have more options. You can use the blueprint for a problem involving an elements analysis (see pages 53-56 in Chapter 5), setting out the rule or test first, the descriptions of analogous cases second, your arguments third, and your conclusion last. You can use the traditional format but integrate your discussion of the analogous cases into your arguments; or you can break with tradition and begin with the facts. You can also vary each of these organizational schemes by adding an assertion or a set of assertions at the beginning or, when the rule or test requires you to analyze a series of elements or factors, by dividing your argument into subsections, each with its own rules, descriptions of analogous cases, and arguments.

Options for Organizing the Argument Section When the Problem Involves an Elements Analysis

Option 1: Traditional Format

I. ARGUMENTATIVE HEADING
- Favorable statement of the rule
- Descriptions of analogous cases
- Your argument, including your response to your opponent's arguments
- Conclusion

Option 2: Traditional Argument but Descriptions of Cases Integrated into Argument

I. ARGUMENTATIVE HEADING
- Favorable statement of the rule
- Your argument, including cases and facts that support your position and your response to your opponent's arguments
- Conclusion

Option 3: Traditional Format with Assertion at the Beginning

I. ARGUMENTATIVE HEADING
- Assertion
- Favorable statement of the rule
- Descriptions of analogous cases
- Your argument, including your response to your opponent's arguments
- Conclusion

Option 4: Nontraditional Format: Facts Presented First

I. ARGUMENTATIVE HEADING
- Legally and emotionally significant facts
- Comparison of facts in client's case to facts in analogous cases
- Conclusion

Option 5: Nontraditional Format with Assertion at the Beginning and Then Key Facts

I. ARGUMENTATIVE HEADING
- Assertion
- Legally and emotionally significant facts
- Comparison of facts in client's case to facts in analogous cases
- Conclusion

Option 6: Traditional Format with Each Element or Factor Discussed in Separate Subsections and Descriptions of Analogous Cases Integrated into Arguments

I. ARGUMENTATIVE HEADING
- Favorable statement of the general rule
  - A. First Element
    - Favorable statement of specific rule
    - Your argument including description of analogous cases and facts that support your position and your response to your opponent's arguments
    - Mini-conclusion
  - B. Second Element
    - Favorable statement of specific rule
    - Your argument including description of analogous cases and facts that support your position and your response to your opponent's arguments
    - Mini-conclusion
  - C. Third Element
    - Favorable statement of specific rule
    - Your argument, including description of analogous cases and facts that support your position and your response to your opponent's arguments
    - Mini-conclusion

General Conclusion

For more on the different options, see section 17.9.2.

Although there is always a temptation to use the organizational scheme with which you are most comfortable, as an advocate this is a temptation you need to resist. If you are to persuade the court, you need to pick the scheme that allows you to emphasize the strongest parts of your argument. For example, if the rule strongly favors your client, you will usually want to select an organizational scheme that allows you to put the rule at the beginning, in the position of emphasis. Conversely, if the facts are very favorable, you will usually want to use an organizational scheme that allows you to put them at the beginning. At other times, when there are a number of steps to the analysis, it works best to select an organizational scheme that allows you to begin your argument with your assertions, set out in the order that you discuss them.

The following examples set out three different ways of organizing the same argument. Read through each of the examples, determining which scheme works best.[1]

EXAMPLE 1   ### Excerpt from Defendant's Brief

Argumentative Heading (a subheading)

C. When Officer Hanson spotlighted Mr. Strong, he did not have an articulable suspicion that Mr. Strong was engaged in or was about to engage in criminal behavior.

Favorable statement of the rule

A seizure is unlawful if an officer cannot point to specific and articulable facts giving rise to a reasonable suspicion that the person seized was engaged in or was about to be engaged in criminal activity. *Terry v. Ohio,* 392 U.S. 1, 21-22, 88 S. Ct. 1868, 20 L. Ed. 2d 889 (1968); *State v. Pressley,* 64 Wn. App. 591, 595, 825 P.2d 749 (1992). Although the courts look at the totality of the circumstances in determining whether the facts were sufficient to support a finding that the officer had an articulable suspicion, the courts have repeatedly held that the fact that the person was in a high crime area or an area known for drug trafficking is not sufficient to establish articulable suspicion. *State v. Gleason,* 70 Wn. App. 13, 18, 851 P.2d 731 (1993); *State v. Soto-Garcia,* 68 Wn. App. 20, 26, 841 P.2d 1271 (1992); *State v. Pressley,* 64 Wn. App. 591, 597 825 P.2d 749

Description of analogous cases

(1992). For example, in *Gleason,* the court found that an officer did not have an articulable suspicion that the defendant was engaged in or about to be engaged in criminal activity when the officer saw the defendant leave an apartment complex where narcotics were known to be sold. *Id.* at 17-18. Similarly, in *Soto-Garcia,* the court held that the officer did not have an articulable suspicion that the defendant was engaged in or about to be engaged in criminal activity when the defendant was seen walking late in the evening in an area known for cocaine trafficking. *Id.* at 26. In contrast, in *Pressley,* the court held that the officer did have an articulable suspicion when the defendants were in a high crime area, had their hands chest high, one of the defendants was pointing to an object in her hand and the other was staring at it, and, when the officer approached, the woman with the object in her hand said, "Oh shit" and closed her hand. *Id.* at 597.

---

1. Because the following examples were taken from a brief written for a Washington court, we have used the Washington citation rules. Some of these rules differ from the rules set out in *The Bluebook* and the *ALWD Citation Manual.*

As in *Gleason* and *Soto-Garcia*, in this case the only fact before the officer was that Mr. Strong was in an area known for drug trafficking. Unlike the defendants in *Pressley*, Mr. Strong was not huddled with another individual pointing at his hand and when he was approached by the officer he did not close his hand or say, "Oh shit." Rather, when he was approached by the officer, he answered all of the officer's questions. Walking into the middle of the street, looking at a police car, and walking out of the street are not acts that are illegal or that indicate that an individual is about to engage in criminal conduct.

Appellant's arguments

Appellant's response to the State's argument

Because Officer Hanson did not have an articulable suspicion that Mr. Strong was engaging in or was about to be engaged in criminal conduct at the time he spotlighted Mr. Strong, the seizure was illegal, and the evidence must be suppressed.

Conclusion

Excerpt from Defendant's Brief

EXAMPLE 2

C. <u>The seizure was illegal because Officer Hanson did not have an articulable suspicion that Mr. Strong was engaged in or was about to be engaged in criminal conduct.</u>

Argumentative Heading (subheading) *option 3*

At the time Officer Hanson spotlighted Mr. Strong, he did not have an articulable suspicion that Mr. Strong was engaged in or was about to engage in criminal conduct.

Assertion

A seizure is unlawful if an officer cannot point to specific and articulable facts giving rise to a reasonable suspicion that the person seized was engaged in or was about to be engaged in criminal activity. *Terry v. Ohio,* 392 U.S. 1, 21-22, 88 S. Ct. 1868, 20 L. Ed. 2d 889 (1968); *State v. Pressley,* 64 Wn. App. 591, 595, 825 P.2d 749, 751 (1992). Although the courts look at the totality of the circumstances in determining whether the facts were sufficient to support a finding that the officer had an articulable suspicion, the courts have repeatedly held that the fact that the person was in a high crime area or an area known for drug trafficking is not sufficient to establish articulable suspicion. *State v. Gleason,* 70 Wn. App. 13, 18, 851 P.2d 731 (1993); *State v. Soto-Garcia,* 68 Wn. App. 20, 26, 841 P.2d 1271 (1992); *State v. Pressley,* 64 Wn. App. 591, 597, 825 P.2d 749 (1992).

Favorable statement of the rule

In this case, the only facts before Officer Hanson at the time he spotlighted Mr. Strong were that Strong was in a high crime area; that Strong had cooperated with Officer Hanson, giving him his name and answering his questions; that after Officer Hanson left, Strong walked to the middle of the road; and that when Officer Hanson began driving toward Strong,

Appellant's argument including facts and cases that support appellant's position

Strong moved out of the road and toward an apartment complex. In factually similar cases, the courts have held that such facts are not sufficient to support a finding of articulable suspicion. For example, in *Gleason*, the court held that an officer did not have an articulable suspicion that the defendant was engaged in or about to be engaged in criminal activity when the officer saw the defendant leave an apartment complex where narcotics were known to be sold. *Id.* at 18, P.2d at 734. Similarly, in *Soto-Garcia*, the court held that the officer did not have an articulable suspicion that the defendant was engaged in or about to be engaged in criminal activity when the defendant was seen walking late in the evening in an area known for cocaine trafficking. *Id.* at 26, 841 P.2d at 1274.

Appellant's response to State's argument

An articulable suspicion exists only when the defendant is engaged in activities that strongly suggest criminal conduct. Thus, in *Pressley*, the court based its decision that the officer had an articulable suspicion on the fact that not only were the two women in a high crime area but that they had their hands chest high, one of the women was pointing to an object in her hand and the other was staring at it, and, when the officer approached, the woman with the object in her hand said, "Oh shit" and closed her hand. *Id.* at 597, 825 P.2d at 752. Because similar facts are not present in this case, Officer Hanson did not have an articulable suspicion, and the evidence should be suppressed.

EXAMPLE 3   **Excerpt from Defendant's Brief**

Argumentative Heading (subheading)

C. The seizure was illegal because Officer Hanson did not have an articulable suspicion that Mr. Strong was engaged in or was about to be engaged in criminal conduct.

Legally significant facts

At the time he spotlighted Mr. Strong, the only facts before Officer Hanson were that Strong was in a high crime area; that Strong had cooperated with Officer Hanson, giving him his name and answering his questions; that after Officer Hanson left, Strong walked to the middle of the road; and that when Officer Hanson began driving toward Strong, Strong began walking out of the road toward an apartment complex.

Assertion

Description of analogous cases conduct

In similar cases, the courts have held that these types of facts are not sufficient to support a finding that at the time of the seizure the officer had an articulable suspicion that the defendant was engaged in or was about to be engaged in criminal conduct. For example, in *State v. Gleason,* the court held that an officer did not have an articulable suspicion that the defendant was engaged in or about to be engaged in criminal activity when the officer saw the defendant leave an apartment complex where narcotics were known to be sold. *Id.* at 18. Similarly, in *State v. Soto-Garcia,* the court held that the officer did not have an articulable suspicion that the defendant was engaged in or about to be engaged in criminal activity when the defendant was seen walking late in the evening in an area known for cocaine trafficking and answered the officer's questions about why he was in the area. *Id.* at 26.

Argument

Thus, for the court to find that the officer had an articulable suspicion, the State must show more than that the defendant was in a high crime area. It must be able to point to specific facts that indicate that the defendant is engaging in or is about to engage in criminal conduct. Unlike *State v. Pressley,* in which the women were not only in a high crime area but one of them had something in her hand and the other was pointing to it and said, "Oh, shit" when the officer approached, *id.* at 597, in this case there are no facts indicating that the defendant was about to engage in criminal activity. Walking to the middle of the street, watching a police car, and walking out of the street are not illegal and do not provide evidence that the defendant was about to engage in criminal activity.

Response to State's argument

Because the State has not been able to meet its burden, the seizure was illegal, and the evidence must be suppressed.

Conclusion

---

§ 18.15.3 Presenting the Rules, Descriptions of Analogous Cases, and Arguments in the Light Most Favorable to Your Client

Although the organizational schemes for an argument in a brief are similar to the organizational schemes for the discussion of an issue in an objective memorandum, the method of presentation is different. While in an objective memorandum you present the rules, cases, and arguments as objectively as possible, in a brief you want to present them in the light most favorable to your client.

a. Present the Rule in the Light Most Favorable to Your Client

Good advocacy begins with a favorable statement of the rule. Although you do not want to misstate a rule, quote a rule out of context, or mislead a court, you do want to present the rule in such a way that it favors your client. There are a number of ways in which you can do this. You can present the rule in a favorable context, you can state the rule broadly or narrowly, you can state the rule so that it suggests the conclusion you want the court to reach, and you can emphasize who has the burden of proof.

The following example sets out an objective statement of a rule.

<table>
<tr><td>EXAMPLE 1</td><td>

Objective Statement of the Rule

In determining whether a stop was justified, the courts examine the totality of the circumstances to determine whether there were specific and articulable facts that, taken together with reasonable inferences from those facts, suggest that the defendant was engaged in or was about to be engaged in criminal activity. *State v. Glover,* 116 Wn.2d 509, 513, 806 P.2d 760 (1991).

</td></tr>
</table>

In the next example, Ms. Elder has rewritten the objective statement of the rule so that the rule is presented in a light more favorable to her client. Instead of beginning her statement of the rule with a neutral statement, she begins it with a statement that supports the conclusion she wants the court to reach: that the seizure was unlawful. She then emphasizes that it is the State that has the burden of proving that the officer relied on specific and articulable facts. In the second sentence, Ms. Elder de-emphasizes the fact that the courts look at the totality of the circumstances by putting that part of the rule in a dependent clause in the middle of the paragraph. She then ends her statement of the rule with a favorable statement from the courts: that the courts have repeatedly held that the fact that the person is in a high crime area or an area known for drug trafficking is not sufficient to establish an articulable suspicion.

<table>
<tr><td>EXAMPLE 2</td><td>

Appellant's Statement of the Rule

A seizure is unlawful if the State cannot prove that the officer had specific and articulable facts giving rise to a reasonable suspicion that the person seized was engaged in or about to be engaged in criminal activity. *State v. Glover,* 116 Wn.2d 509, 513, 806 P.2d 760 (1991). Although the courts look at the totality of the circumstances in determining whether the facts were sufficient to support a finding that the officer had an articulable suspicion, the courts have repeatedly held that the fact that the person was in a high crime area or an area known for drug trafficking is not sufficient to establish an articulable suspicion. *State v. Gleason,* 70 Wn. App. 13, 18, 851 P.2d 731 (1993); *State v. Soto-Garcia,* 68 Wn. App. 20, 26, 841 P.2d 1271 (1992); *State v. Pressley,* 64 Wn. App. 591, 597, 825 P.2d 749 (1992).

</td></tr>
</table>

Similarly, the prosecutor has rewritten the neutral statement of the rule so that the rules are presented in a light that is more favorable to his position. In the following example, the prosecutor starts his statement of the rule by creating a favorable context: "Because officers need to be able to question individuals suspected of committing a crime. . . ." He then states the rule as broadly as possible: "a *Terry* stop is permitted whenever an officer has a reasonable and articulable suspicion that an individual is or is about to be engaged in a criminal activity." The prosecutor also ends his statement of the rule with a favorable statement: that the officer need only have the ability to reasonably surmise from the information at hand that a crime is in progress or has occurred. Finally, the prosecutor has chosen his words carefully. Look, for example, at his use of the phrase "reasonably surmise."

Respondent's Statement of the Rule

EXAMPLE 3

Because officers need to be able to question individuals suspected of committing a crime, a *Terry* stop is permitted whenever an officer has a reasonable and articulable suspicion that an individual is or is about to be engaged in criminal activity. *State v. Glover,* 116 Wn.2d 509, 513, 806 P.2d 760 (1991). In making these stops, the officer does not need to have the level of information necessary to justify an arrest; he or she need only have the ability to reasonably surmise from the information at hand that a crime is in progress or has occurred. *State v. Kennedy,* 107 Wn.2d 1, 6, 726 P.2d 445 (1986).

For additional examples, see section 17.9.3.

b. Present the Cases in the Light Most Favorable to Your Client

Just as you want to present the rules in a light favorable to your client, you also want to present the cases in a favorable light. The first step in this process is to determine whether you need to include descriptions of analogous cases. If you do, the second step is to determine how much you need to say about each case, and the final step is to determine how you can present each case in a light favorable to your client.

Step 1: Decide Whether You Need to Include Descriptions of Analogous Cases

Do not include descriptions of analogous cases just to include descriptions of analogous cases. Include them because (a) they provide support for your assertion, (b) you need to distinguish cases your opponent has used to support his or her assertion, or (c) even though the case does not support your assertion and has not been cited by your opponent, as an officer of the court you are obligated to bring the case to the court's attention. Remember, you can use a case as authority for a rule without setting out its facts, holdings, and rationale.

Step 2: Decide How Much You Need to Say About an Analogous Case

How much you say about a case depends on how you want to use that case. If the case is the centerpiece of your argument, you will usually describe the case in detail, setting out the facts, the court's holding, and the court's reasoning. You will then build your argument around this case, comparing the facts in your case to the facts in the analogous case and arguing for the same result. See Example 1, set out below. In contrast, if the case illustrates a relatively minor point, you will usually say far less about the case, maybe only setting out the holding and one or two facts. In these situations, you can either set out the court's holding and the key facts in text or in a parenthetical following the citation to the case. See Example 2 below.

EXAMPLE 1   ### Case Is Centerpiece of Argument

The facts in our case are significantly different from the facts in *California v. Hodari D.* In *Hodari D.,* two officers were on routine patrol when, rounding a corner in an unmarked car, they saw four or five youths huddled around a small red car parked at the curb. When the youths saw the police car, they panicked and began to run. Hodari and one companion ran west through an alley; the others ran south. Seeing the youths run, the officers became suspicious and gave chase. While one of the officers remained in the car, the other ran north along 63rd, then west on Foothill Boulevard, and then south on 62nd, getting ahead of Hodari. Because Hodari was looking over his shoulder and not where he was going, he did not see the officer until the officer was almost upon him. When he did see the officer, Hodari tossed what appeared to be a small rock. A moment later, the officer tackled Hodari. *Id.* at 626.

Unlike Hodari, who ran several blocks, Mr. Strong walked only from the center of the road to the side of the road and then a few steps toward an apartment complex. As Officer Hanson testified, Strong "walked maybe ten or twelve feet." RP 43. In addition, unlike Hodari, who did not stop until he was tackled by the police officer, Mr. Strong stopped before being told to do so by Officer Hanson.

EXAMPLE 2   ### Case Used to Illustrate One Important, but Minor, Point

The courts have consistently held that a seizure does not occur when an officer uses a device to see what he or she could see unaided in other circumstances. For example, in *State v. Rose,* the court held that a seizure did not occur when an officer used a flashlight to look through an unobstructed window. *Id.* at 397; *accord, State v. Young,* 28 Wn. App. 412, 416-17, 624 P.2d 725 (1981) (holding that a search did not occur when an officer used a flashlight to look through a car's windows).

Step 3: Present the Case in the Light Most Favorable to Your Client

Just as there are a number of techniques you can use to present a rule in the light most favorable to your client, there are a number of techniques you can use to present a case in a favorable light. You can describe the facts of the case using general or specific terms; you can state the court's holding broadly or narrowly; and you can emphasize or de-emphasize particular material through your use of the positions of emphasis, sentence length and sentence construction, and your choice of words.

In the following example, Ms. Elder describes two favorable cases. Because she wants the court to find that her case is like these two cases, she describes the facts using general rather than specific terms, and she states the holding broadly rather than narrowly.

Descriptions of Cases That Support the Defendant's Argument

In factually similar cases, the courts have held that such facts are not sufficient to support a finding of articulable suspicion. For example, in *Gleason,* the court held that an officer did not have an articulable suspicion that the defendant was engaged in or about to be engaged in criminal activity when the officer saw the defendant leave an apartment complex where narcotics were known to be sold. *Id.* at 18, 851 P.2d at 734. Similarly, in *Soto-Garcia,* the court held that the officer did not have an articulable suspicion that the defendant was engaged in or about to be engaged in criminal activity when the defendant was seen walking late in the evening in an area known for drug trafficking. *Id.* at 26, 841 P.2d at 1274.

In contrast, in the next paragraph, Ms. Elder wants to distinguish an unfavorable case. As a consequence, she describes the facts in more detail and states the holding more narrowly.

Description of a Case That Does Not Support the Defendant's Argument

An articulable suspicion exists only when the defendant is engaged in activities that strongly suggest criminal conduct. Thus, in *Pressley* the court based its decision that the officer had an articulable suspicion not only on the fact that the two women were in a high crime area but also on evidence establishing that they had their hands chest high, one of the women was pointing to an object in her hand and the other was staring at it, and, when the officer approached, the woman with the object in her hand said, "Oh, shit" and closed her hand. *Id.* at 597, 825 P.2d at 752.

For additional examples, see section 17.9.3.

There are also several things that you do not want to do in presenting analogous cases. First, and probably most important, do not organize your arguments around individual cases. For example, do not use the following organizational scheme.

Poor Organizational Scheme

  I. ARGUMENTATIVE HEADING
      Favorable statement of rule
      A. Description of Case A
          Comparison of the facts in your case to the facts in Case A
      B. Description of Case B
          Comparison of the facts in your case to the facts in Case B
      C. Description of Case C
          Comparison of the facts in your case to the facts in Case C
      Conclusion

Instead, organize your arguments around assertions or legal principles, using the cases only as support for those assertions or to illustrate how those legal principles have been applied.

EXAMPLE 2   ## Better Organizational Scheme

I. ARGUMENTATIVE HEADING
    Favorable statement of rule
    A. Assertion 1
        Description of Case A
        Description of Case B
        Argument using Case A and Case B
    B. Assertion 2
        Description of Case C
        Argument using Case C
    Conclusion

Second, avoid starting a paragraph with a citation to a case. Because you are using the cases to illustrate an assertion or a principle, start the paragraph with a topic sentence that sets out the principle you are using the case to illustrate or with a transition that tells the judges that you are presenting an example or illustration.

EXAMPLE 1   ## Poor Opening

In *State v. Gleason,* the court held that a seizure occurred when the officer walked toward the defendant, asked him whether he could talk to him, asked him why he was there, and then demanded his identification. Although a reasonable person might have felt free to leave after the initial request, a reasonable person would not have felt free to ignore the officer's demand for identification. *Id.* at 18, 851 P.2d at 374. Similarly, in *State v. Soto-Garcia,* the court held that a seizure occurred when an officer approached the defendant on the street, asked him some questions, checked his identification, and then asked him if he had cocaine and if he could search him. *Id.* at 25, 841 P.2d at 1273.

EXAMPLE 2   ## Better Opening

Courts look at the officer's conduct in determining whether a reasonable person would feel free to leave. *State v. Gleason,* 70 Wn. App. 13, 18, 851 P.2d 731 (1993); *State v. Soto-Garcia,* 68 Wn. App. 20, 26, 841 P.2d 1271 (1992). In *Gleason,* the court found that a seizure occurred when the officer walked toward the defendant, asked him whether he could talk to him, asked the defendant why he was there, and then demanded his identification. *Id.* at 18. Although a reasonable person might have felt free to leave after the initial request, a reasonable person would not feel free to ignore the officer's demand for identification. *Id.* Similarly, in *Soto-Garcia,* the court held that a seizure occurred when an officer approached the defendant on the street, asked him some questions, checked his identification, and then asked him if he had cocaine and if he could search him. *Id.* at 25. Under these circumstances, a reasonable person would not feel free to leave. *Id.*

Third, avoid the temptation to include case description after case description. As a general rule, it is better to include one or two carefully selected cases than four, five, or six cases. Your brief will be shorter, something that will please almost every judge, and your preparation for oral argument will be easier. (Remember, for every case you cite, you need to know that case, inside and out, for oral argument.) When it is important to cite more than one or two cases, set out the best case or cases in text and then reference the other cases using parentheticals. See pp. 246–248.

Finally, remember that if you describe a case you need to use that case in your argument. Don't leave cases hanging, hoping the judge will figure out why you included the case in your brief.

c. Present the Arguments Effectively

It is not enough, however, to present the rules and cases in a light favorable to your client. If you are to persuade a judge, you must also use those rules and cases effectively.

d. Make Clear How the Rules and Cases Apply to Your Case

One of the most common mistakes that attorneys make in writing a brief is that they do not make explicit the connections between the parts of their argument. They set out an assertion but do not connect it to the rule; they set out the rule but do not connect it to the descriptions of analogous cases; and they set out descriptions of analogous cases but do not connect the facts and holdings in those cases to their case. Look, for instance, at the following example. Although all of the pieces are there, those pieces have not been connected. In particular, the writer has not used the language of the rule — that is, "a show of authority occurs when a reasonable person would not feel free to leave" in describing the analogous cases, and he has not explicitly compared the facts in the analogous cases to the facts in *Strong*.

Ineffective Argument   EXAMPLE 1

A show of authority occurs when a reasonable person would not feel free to leave. *California v. Hodari D.,* 499 U.S. 621, 626, 111 S. Ct. 1547, 113 L. Ed. 2d 690 (1991). In *State v. Vandover,* the court held that a seizure occurred when an officer followed a car and then turned on his emergency lights. *Id.* at 757. In *State v. DeArman,* the court held that a seizure occurred when an officer pulled up behind a parked vehicle and turned on his emergency lights. *Id.* at 1248. In our case, a seizure occurred when Officer Hanson approached Mr. Strong and turned on his light.

The following version is better. Note how the phrase, "show authority" appears in the statement of the rule, the descriptions of the analogous cases, and in the argument.

Better Argument   EXAMPLE 2

A **show of authority** occurs when a reasonable person would not feel free to leave. *California v. Hodari D.,* 499 U.S. 621, 626, 111 S. Ct. 1547, 113 L. Ed. 2d 690 (1991).

For example, in *State v. Vandover,* the court held that there was a **show of authority** when an officer began following the defendant's car and turned on his emergency lights because, under these circumstances, a reasonable person would not feel free to leave. *Id.* at 757. Similarly, in *State v. DeArman,* the court held that there was a **show of authority** when an officer pulled up behind a parked vehicle and turned on his emergency lights. As the court stated, "under these circumstances a reasonable person would not feel free to terminate the encounter." *Id.* at 624. Just as the officers in *Vandover* and *DeArman* approached the defendants and turned on their lights, Officer Hanson approached Mr. Strong and turned on his light. Thus, there was a **show of authority** because, under the circumstances, a reasonable person would not have felt free to leave.

e. Don't Ignore the Weaknesses That Are Inherent in Your Argument

Another error that attorneys commonly make is that they do not deal with the "weaknesses" in their argument. Although sometimes this strategy works, more often it does not. Even if the opposing party does not notice the problems, the court will.

For example, in the example set out above, the writer does not deal with the fact that in the two analogous cases the lights were the officers' emergency lights while in *Strong* the light was a spotlight. By not dealing with this distinction in his own argument, the writer opens the door to an argument like the following one.

EXAMPLE   **Excerpt from Respondent's Brief**

Neither of the cases that Defendant relies on is on point. While in *Vandover* and *DeArman* the officers turned on their flashing emergency lights, in our case Officer Hanson turned on his spotlight.

Instead of ignoring problems, the better strategy is to deal with the problems up front.

EXAMPLE   **Rewrite of Appellant's Argument**

A show of authority occurs when a reasonable person would not feel free to leave. *California v. Hodari D.,* 499 U.S. 621, 626, 111 S. Ct. 1547, 113 L. Ed. 2d 690 (1991). For example, in *State v. Vandover,* the court held that there was a show of authority when an officer began following the defendant's car and turned on his emergency lights because, under these circumstances, a reasonable person would not feel free to leave. *Id.* at 757. Similarly, in *State v. DeArman,* the court held that there was a show of authority when an officer pulled up behind a parked vehicle and turned on his emergency lights. As the court stated, "under these circumstances a reasonable person would not feel free to terminate the encounter." *Id.* at 624. Although both *Vandover* and *DeArman* involved emergency lights and not spotlights, the courts' reasoning applies here. Just as a reasonable person would not feel free to leave when an officer pulls up behind him and turns on emergency lights, a person would not feel free to leave when an officer turns his car around and, driving toward that person, focuses his spotlight on that person. Thus, just as there was a show of authority in *Vandover* and *DeArman,* there was also a show of authority in this case.

---

f. Don't Overlook Good Arguments

Finally, sometimes attorneys miss their strongest argument. For example, in *Strong,* the defendant's strongest argument is that the show of authority resulted from a combination of events: the initial contact, the driving toward the defendant, and the spotlight. Compare the following example to the earlier examples.

Author Includes All of Defendant's Arguments

EXAMPLE

The first prong of the test, show of authority, is met whenever an officer's actions would indicate to a reasonable person that he or she is not free to leave or terminate the encounter. *California v. Hodari D.,* 499 U.S. 621, 626, 111 S. Ct. 1547, 113 L. Ed. 2d 690 (1991). In deciding whether this prong is met, the courts do not look at a single action. Instead, they look at the totality of the circumstances to see whether the officer focused his attention on a particular individual or whether there has been a progressive intrusion into an individual's privacy. *See, e.g., State v. Soto-Garcia,* 68 Wn. App. 20, 26, 841 P.2d 1271 (1992); *State v. Vandover,* 63 Wn. App. 754, 756, 822 P.2d 784 (1992).

In this case, Officer Hanson focused his attention on Mr. Strong. He stopped and questioned Mr. Strong, ran a criminal history check on Mr. Strong, and then turned his car around and drove toward Mr. Strong, accelerating and focusing his spotlight on him. Under similar circumstances, the courts have found that such actions are a show of authority. For example, in both *Vandover* and *State v. DeArman,* 54 Wn. App. 621, 624, 774 P.2d 1247, 1248 (1989), the court held that a seizure occurred when an officer pulled up behind a vehicle and turned on his emergency lights. Although these two cases involved emergency lights and not spotlights, in each instance the officers focused their attention on a particular individual, indicating to that individual that he was not free to leave or terminate the encounter.

In addition, Officer Hanson progressively intruded into Mr. Strong's privacy. Although a reasonable person might have felt free to terminate the initial encounter, he would not feel free to leave when Officer Hanson drove toward him and turned his spotlight on him. As the court found in *Soto-Garcia,* while an individual may feel free to terminate an initial encounter, he may not feel free to leave if an officer continues questioning him. "Considering all of the circumstances . . . , the atmosphere created by Tate's [the officer's] progressive intrusion into Soto-Garcia's privacy was of such a nature that a reasonable person would not believe that he or she was free to end the encounter." *Id.* at 25, 841 P.2d at 1274.

Thus, there was a show of authority under either rule. There was a show of authority because Officer Hanson focused his attention on Mr. Strong or, in the alternative, because Officer Hanson progressively intruded into Mr. Strong's privacy.

Although adding the additional arguments makes the brief longer, in this instance doing so is a good choice. Because both her "focused attention" and "progressive intrusion" arguments are legally sound, Ms. Elder substantially increases her chances of getting a reversal by arguing in the alternative.

g. Respond to Your Opponent's Arguments but Do Not Emphasize Them

As the respondent, you need to address your opponent's arguments without emphasizing them. There are several ways in which you can do this. First, avoid starting your argument by repeating your opponent's argument. Instead, begin by setting out your own positive assertion, by setting out the rule in a light favorable to your client, or by setting out the facts that support your position.

In the following examples, Example 1 sets out the appellant's arguments, and Examples 2 and 3 show two different ways in which the respondent might respond to those arguments. Example 2 is poor because the State begins its argument by repeating the defendant's arguments. Example 3 is better because the State begins its arguments by making its own case.

EXAMPLE 1   **Appellant's Argument**

C.   When Officer Hanson turned the spotlight on Mr. Strong, he did not have an articulable suspicion that Mr. Strong was engaged in or was about to be engaged in criminal conduct.

A seizure is unlawful if an officer cannot point to specific and articulable facts giving rise to a reasonable suspicion that the person seized was engaged in or about to be engaged in criminal activity. *State v. Pressley,* 64 Wn. App. 591, 595, 825 P.2d 749, 752 (1992). Although the courts look at the totality of the circumstances in determining whether the facts were sufficient to support a finding that the officer had an articulable suspicion, the courts have repeatedly held that the fact that the person was in a high crime area or an area known for drug trafficking is not sufficient to establish articulable suspicion. *State v. Gleason,* 70 Wn. App. 13, 16, 851 P.2d 731 (1993); *State v. Soto-Garcia,* 68 Wn. App. 20, 26, 841 P.2d 1271 (1992); *State v. Pressley,* 64 Wn. App. 591, 597, 825 P.2d 749 (1992).

For example, in *Gleason,* the court held that an officer did not have an articulable suspicion that the defendant was engaged in or about to be engaged in criminal activity when the officer saw the defendant leave an apartment complex where narcotics were known to be sold. *Id.* at 17-18. Similarly, in *Soto-Garcia,* the court held that the officer did not have an articulable suspicion that the defendant was engaged in or about to be engaged in criminal activity when the defendant was seen walking late in the evening in an area; known for cocaine trafficking. *Id.* at 26. In contrast, in *Pressley,* the court held that the officer did have an articulable suspicion when the defendants were in a high crime area; the defendants had their hands chest high; one of the defendants was pointing to an object in her hand and the other was staring at it; and, when the officer approached, the woman with the object in her hand said, "Oh, shit" and closed her hand. *Id.* at 597.

As in *Gleason* and *Soto-Garcia,* in this case the only fact before the officer was that Mr. Strong was in an area known for drug trafficking. Unlike the defendants in *Pressley,* Mr. Strong was not huddled with another individual pointing at his hand, and when he was approached by the officer, he did not close his hands or say, "Oh, shit."

Rather, when he was approached by the officer, he answered all of the officer's questions. Walking into the middle of the street, looking at a police car, and walking out of the street are not acts that are illegal or that indicate that an individual is or is about to be engaged in criminal conduct.

Because Officer Hanson did not have an articulable suspicion that Mr. Strong was engaged in or about to be engaged in criminal conduct at the time he spotlighted Mr. Strong, the seizure was illegal, and the evidence must be suppressed.

Poor Response to Defendant's Argument

EXAMPLE 2

C. The search was legal because, at the time he turned on his spotlight, Officer Hanson had an articulable suspicion that the defendant was engaged in or about to be engaged in criminal conduct.

Defendant argues that when Officer Hanson turned on his spotlight he did not have an articulable suspicion that Mr. Strong was engaged in or about to be engaged in criminal conduct. In particular, defendant argues that this case is more like *State v. Gleason,* 70 Wn. App. 13, 851 P.2d 731 (1993), and *State v. Soto-Garcia,* 68 Wn. App. 20, 841 P.2d 1271 (1992), than it is like *State v. Pressley,* 64 Wn. App. 591, 825 P.2d 749 (1992).

Although Officer Hanson did testify that one of the facts he considered was the fact that the defendant was in a high crime area late at night, there were other facts. Thus, this case is less like *Gleason* and *Soto-Garcia* and more like *Pressley.* Although Mr. Strong did not say "Oh, shit" when Officer Hanson approached, he did walk to the middle of the road and then back toward a wooded area.

Better Response to Defendant's Argument

EXAMPLE 3

C. The seizure was legal because, at the time he turned on his spotlight, Officer Hanson had an articulable suspicion that the defendant was engaged in or about to be engaged in criminal conduct.

A stop is lawful if, at the time of the stop, the officer can point to specific and articulable facts giving rise to a reasonable suspicion that the person seized was engaged in or about to be engaged in criminal activity. *State v. Pressley,* 64 Wn. App. 591, 595, 825 P.2d 749, 752 (1992).

In this case, Officer Hanson was able to point to specific and articulable facts. Unlike *Gleason* and *Soto-Garcia,* in which the only facts before the officers were that the defendants were in high crime areas, in this case there are a number of other facts indicating that the defendant was engaged in or about to be engaged in criminal conduct. For example, after Officer Hanson drove away, the defendant walked to the center of the road and stood there, apparently watching Officer Hanson for what Officer Hanson described as an unusually long time. Then, after Officer Hanson turned his car around, the defendant began walking quickly toward a wooded area, and bent down and dropped something behind a tree. Thus, this case is more like *Pressley.* Just as the defendant in *Pressley* engaged in conduct that appeared suspicious to an experienced police officer, so too did the defendant in this case.

See section 17.9.6 for a checklist for critiquing the argument section.

§ 18.16 Drafting the Conclusion or Prayer for Relief

The final section of the brief is the conclusion or the prayer for relief. In most jurisdictions this section is short. Unlike the conclusion in an objective memorandum, you do not summarize the arguments. Instead, you simply set out the relief you are requesting. For example, as the appellant you usually ask the court to reverse or remand, and if you are the respondent you usually ask the court to affirm or remand. Sometimes you will ask for a single type of relief; at other times you will ask for different types of relief for different errors or for alternative forms of relief. To determine what type of relief you can request, read cases that have decided the same or similar issues and look to see what type of relief the parties requested and what type of relief the court granted.

In our example case, Ms. Elder asks the court to reverse or, in the alternative, to reverse and remand. While it is possible that the court would reverse, holding that evidence should have been suppressed and without that evidence there was insufficient evidence to convict, the court could also remand the case and leave the decision to the State as to whether the case is to be retried without the suppressed evidence. In contrast, the State asks the appellate court to affirm the trial court's decision.

§ 18.17 Preparing the Signature Block

Before submitting your brief to the court, you must sign it, listing your name and, in most jurisdictions, your bar number. The format typically used is as follows:

> Respectfully submitted, this _____
> day of _____, 2006
>
> _____
> Name of attorney
> Attorney for [Appellant or Respondent]

§ 18.18 Preparing the Appendix

Most jurisdictions allow the parties to attach one or more appendices to their briefs. Such appendices should be used not to avoid the page limits but to set out information that a judge would find useful but that might not be readily available. For example, if one of your issues requires the court to interpret the language of a particular statute or set of statutes, you may set out the text of the statute or statutes in an appendix. Similarly, if an issue requires the court to look carefully at the language of a case, particularly an out-of-state case or a recent case, you may set out a copy of the case in an appendix.

§ 18.19 Revising, Editing, and Proofreading

It is impossible to state strongly enough the importance of revising, editing, and proofreading your brief. In both criminal and civil cases, your client is depending on you to make his or her best case to the court.

Unfortunately, many of the briefs that are submitted to the courts are not well written. As judge after judge has complained, many briefs are too long. Instead of setting out their two or three best arguments, many attorneys make two or three times that many arguments. In addition, in many briefs, the attorneys don't clearly state either their position or the relief they are requesting. In fact, in many instances, it appears that the attorneys don't understand either the law or their own arguments. Finally, some briefs are so poorly written that even the most easygoing judges become distracted by the long, hard-to-read sentences, dangling modifiers, comma splices, and misuses of the possessive.

Because she wants to do the best that she can for her clients, Ms. Elder spends almost as much time revising, editing, and proofreading her brief as she does researching the issues and preparing the first draft. After completing the first draft, she sets it aside for a day or two while she works on other projects. When she comes back to the brief, she looks first at the arguments she has made, asking herself the following questions. Has she identified all of the issues? For each issue, has she made clear her position and what relief she is requesting? Has she provided the best support for each of her assertions? Has she included issues, arguments, or support that is not necessary?

When she is happy with the content, Ms. Elder then rereads her brief, trying to read it as a judge would read it. Is the material presented in a logical order? Has she made clear the connections between arguments and parts of arguments? Is each argument, paragraph block, paragraph, and sentence easy to read and understand? At this stage, Ms. Elder also works more on writing persuasively. She checks to make sure that she has presented the rules, cases, and facts in a light favorable to her client and that she has used persuasive devices effectively.

Ms. Elder then tries to put the brief down for at least a short period of time so that she can, once again, come back to it with "fresh eyes." This time, she works primarily on two things. She begins by looking at her writing style. Are there places where she could make her writing more eloquent? See Chapter 26. She then goes back through the brief, revising for conciseness and precision, and making sure that her writing is correct. In particular, she looks for the types of mistakes that she knows she has a tendency to make. Finally, she goes back through her brief, checking her citations and adding page numbers to her table of contents and table of authorities.

While this process is time-consuming, and thus expensive, Ms. Elder finds that the process pays off in a number of ways. First, and most important, she does a good job of representing her client. Because her briefs are well written, her clients get a fair hearing from the court. Second, because she has worked at it, through the years she has become both a better and a faster writer. Finally, she has protected and enhanced one of her most important assets: her reputation. Because her briefs are well written, judges tend to take them and her more seriously.

Note: In the following example briefs, the brief writers have cited according to the rules set out in the Washington Rules on Appeal. When you write your own brief, be sure to consult your own state's rules.

Appellant's Brief

No. 05-1-00468-1

COURT OF APPEALS,
DIVISION II,
OF THE STATE OF WASHINGTON

State of Washington, Respondent,

v.

William Dennis Strong, Appellant.

BRIEF OF APPELLANT

Susan Elder
Attorney for Appellant
Office of Assigned Counsel
100 Main Street
Tacoma, Washington 98402

Table of Contents

Table of Authorities

A. Table of Cases

Washington Cases

Other Cases

A.   Assignments of Error

Assignments of Error

1. The trial court erred in denying Mr. Strong's Motion to Suppress. CP 5.

2. The trial court erred in entering Conclusion of Law No. 2: "Under the Fourth Amendment, no seizure occurred until the deputy asked the defendant to stop." CP 5.

3. The trial court erred in entering Conclusion of Law No. 3: "Article I, Section 7, of the Washington Constitution provides no greater protection than the Fourth Amendment." CP 6.

4. The trial court erred in entering Conclusion of Law No. 4: "At the time the officer told the defendant to stop, the deputy had an articulable suspicion that the defendant was engaging in or about to be engaged in criminal conduct." CP 6.

5. The trial court erred in entering Conclusion of Law No. 4: "Following the retrieval of the charred soda can, the officer had probable cause to arrest the defendant." CP 6.

6. The trial court erred in entering judgment and sentence. CP 18-19.

Issues Pertaining to Assignments of Error

1. Under the Fourth Amendment, did a seizure occur when Officer Hanson drove toward Mr. Strong, focusing his spotlight on him, and Mr. Strong, after moving out of the street and a few feet toward an apartment complex, dropped something behind a tree, turned, and stopped? (Assignments of Error 1, 2, 5, and 6.)

2. Did the trial court err when it ruled that Article I, Section 7, of the Washington Constitution does not provide more protection than the Fourth Amendment? (Assignments of Error 1, 3, 5, and 6.)

3. Did Officer Hanson lack an articulable suspicion that Mr. Strong was engaged in or about to be engaged in criminal conduct when, at the time Officer Hanson focused the spotlight on Mr. Strong, the only facts before Officer Hanson were that Mr. Strong was in a

high crime area, that Mr. Strong had a criminal history, and that Mr. Strong walked to the middle of the road and watched the police car? (Assignments of Error 1, 4, 5, and 6.)

B.   Statement of the Case

Procedural History

William Strong was charged with one count of Possession of a Controlled Substance under RCW 269.50.401(d), one count of Unlawful Possession of a Firearm under RCW 9.41.040(1), and one count of Possession of Stolen Property in the Second Degree under RCW 9A.56.160. CP 1. After an evidentiary hearing, the trial court denied Mr. Strong's Motion to Suppress. RP 4.

The case went to trial, RP 8, and a jury found Mr. Strong guilty on all three counts. CP 10. Judgment and sentence were entered on September 26, 2005. CP 18-19. Mr. Strong filed his notice of appeal on October 17, 2005. CP 20.

Statement of Facts

On the evening of May 17, 2005, William Strong was standing on the corner of Lincoln and Chicago in Tacoma, Washington, talking to a friend when Officer Hanson approached him and began questioning him. RP 4. Standing only a foot or two from Mr. Strong, Officer Hanson asked Mr. Strong to identify himself and to explain what he was doing in the area. RP 5. Mr. Strong willingly answered Officer Hanson's questions, telling him his name. RP 5.

After questioning Mr. Strong, Officer Hanson returned to his patrol car, got in the car, and drove about a block and a half down a hill. RP 6. He then ran a criminal history check, which showed that Mr. Strong had prior arrests but that there were no outstanding warrants. RP 7. Officer Hanson then looked in his rearview mirror and saw that Mr. Strong had walked to the middle of the street and was looking in his direction. RP 8. Officer Hanson immediately turned his car around and began driving toward Mr. Strong. RP 8. As Mr. Strong began moving toward the side of the street, Officer Hanson accelerated, turned on his spotlight, and focused the spotlight on Mr. Strong. RP 9-10.

As the patrol car came toward him, Mr. Strong walked quickly out of the road. RP 11, 12. He then walked two or three steps toward an apartment complex, dropped what appeared to Officer Hanson to be a package behind a tree, and then turned and walked two or three steps back toward Officer Hanson. RP 11, 12. He then stopped. RP 12.

At that point, Officer Hanson told Mr. Strong, who was already stopped, to stop. Officer Hanson got out of his police car, walked to the tree, and picked up a soda can with a charred bottom. RP 13. Believing that the material inside the can was a controlled substance, Officer Hanson arrested Mr. Strong. RP 13-15. Mr. Strong did not resist arrest. RP 17.

C. Summary of Argument

Mr. Strong was illegally seized when Officer Hanson drove toward Mr. Strong, focusing his spotlight on him.

A seizure occurred under the Fourth Amendment because there was a show of authority to which Mr. Strong submitted. Officer Hanson focused his attention on Mr. Strong when he approached him and questioned him. He then progressively intruded into Mr. Strong's affairs when he ran a criminal history check on Mr. Strong and, after turning his car around, accelerated and drove toward Mr. Strong, shining his spotlight on him. Although Mr. Strong walked quickly to the side of the road, he did not flee. Instead, he stayed within the area illuminated by the spotlight and stopped before being ordered to do so.

In the alternative, a seizure occurred under Article 1, Section 7, of the Washington Constitution. In this case, only one of the six *Gunwall* factors is in dispute, and that factor, preexisting state law, is met because the Washington courts have consistently applied an objective rather than a subjective test in determining when a seizure occurs. In addition, an independent state analysis establishes that in cases like this one the courts have found that Article I, Section 7, of the Washington Constitution provides more protection than the Fourth Amendment: Washington citizens have an expectation that police officers will not progressively intrude into their personal affairs. Finally, under the *Mendenhall* test, a seizure occurred because a reasonable person would not have felt tree to leave or terminate the encounter.

Whether the court applies the Fourth Amendment or Article I, Section 7, the seizure was unreasonable because, at the time Officer Hanson focused his spotlight on Mr. Strong, he did not have an articulable suspicion that Mr. Strong was engaged in or about to be engaged in criminal conduct. At that point, the only facts before Officer Hanson were that Mr. Strong was in a high crime area, had a criminal history, and was standing in the middle of the street watching the police car.

D. Argument

I. UNDER THE FOURTH AMENDMENT, A SEIZURE OCCURRED WHEN OFFICER HANSON DROVE TOWARD MR. STRONG, ACCELERATING AND FOCUSING HIS SPOTLIGHT ON HIM.

Because this case involves only issues of law, the standard of review is *de novo. See State v. Thorn*, 129 Wn.2d 347, 351, 917 P.2d 108, 111 (1996).

Before 1991, the United States Supreme Court applied an objective test in determining whether a seizure occurred: a seizure occurred when a reasonable person would not feel free to leave or terminate an encounter. *See, e.g., Florida v. Bostick*, 501 U.S. 429, 111 S. Ct. 2386, 115 L. Ed. 2d 389 (1991); *United States v. Mendenhall*, 446 U.S. 544, 100 S. Ct. 1870, 64 L. Ed. 2d 497 (1980). In 1991, the United States Supreme Court modified this test, adding a subjective component. *California v. Hodari D.*, 499 U.S. 621, 628, 111 S. Ct. 1547, 113 L. Ed. 2d 690 (1991). *See also* 3 Wayne LaFave, *Search and Seizure* § 9.3 (3d ed. 1996) (criticizing

Hodari D. and its policy implications). Under the test set out in *Hodari D.,* a seizure occurs either when the police use physical force or when a citizen actually submits to a show of authority. *Hodari D.,* 499 U.S. at 628. Although Officer Hanson did not use physical force, he did make a show of authority to which Mr. Strong submitted.

A.   <u>A show of authority occurred when, after questioning Mr. Strong, Officer Hanson turned his car around and, accelerating, drove toward Mr. Strong, focusing his spotlight on him.</u>

A show of authority occurs whenever an officer's actions would indicate to a reasonable person that he or she is not free to leave or terminate an encounter. *California v. Hodari D.,* 499 U.S. 621, 628, 115 S. Ct. 1547, 113 L. Ed. 2d 690 (1991). In deciding whether this test is met, the courts do not look at a single action. Instead, they look at the totality of the circumstances to see whether the officer focused his attention on a particular individual or whether there was a progressive intrusion into an individual's privacy. *See, e.g., State v. Soto-Garcia,* 68 Wn. App. 20, 24, 841 P.2d 1271, 1274 (1992); *State v. Vandover,* 63 Wn. App. 754, 756, 822 P.2d 784, 785 (1992).

In the case before the court, Officer Hanson focused his attention on Mr. Strong. Officer Hanson stopped and questioned Mr. Strong, RP 4-5, ran a criminal history check on him, RP 7, and then turned his car around and drove toward Mr. Strong, accelerating and shining his spotlight on him, RP 9-10. Under similar circumstances, the courts have found that such actions are a show of authority. *See, e.g., State v. Stroud,* 30 Wn. App. 392, 395, 634 P.2d 316, 318 (1981); *State v. Vandover,* 63 Wn. App. 754, 756, 822 P.2d 784, 785 (1992); *State v. DeArman,* 54 Wn. App. 621, 624, 774 P.2d 1247, 1248 (1989). For example, in *Stroud,* the court held that the use of emergency lights and high beam headlights constituted a show of authority. Similarly, in both *Vandover* and *DeArman,* the court held that a seizure occurred when an officer pulled up behind a vehicle and turned on his emergency lights.

Although both of these cases involved emergency lights and not spotlights, in each instance the officers focused their attention on a particular individual, indicating to that individual that he was not free to leave or terminate the encounter.

In addition, Officer Hanson progressively intruded into Mr. Strong's privacy. Although a reasonable person might have felt free to terminate the initial encounter, he would not have felt free to leave once Officer Hanson drove toward him, focusing the spotlight on him. As the court found in *Soto-Garcia*, a case in which a police officer confronted an individual, questioned him, ran an identification check, and then asked him if he had cocaine, an individual may not feel free to leave if the officer continues questioning him. "Considering all of the circumstances . . . , the atmosphere created by [the officer's] progressive intrusion into Soto-Garcia's privacy was of such a nature that a reasonable person would not believe that he or she was free to end the encounter." *Id.* at 25.

Thus, there was a show of authority under either rule. There was a show of authority because Officer Hanson focused his attention on Mr. Strong or, in the alternative, because Officer Hanson progressively intruded into Mr. Strong's privacy.

B.   Mr. Strong submitted to the show of authority when he did not leave the area lighted by the spotlight and stopped before being ordered to do so.

An individual submits to a show of authority when he or she stops or stays within the area controlled by a police officer. *See United States v. Wilson*, 953 F.2d 116 (4th Cir.1991). For example, in a case in which an officer drove up behind the defendant's vehicle and turned on his emergency lights, the court held that the defendant had been seized at the time the police officer turned on his lights even though the defendant, who had been stopped at a stoplight, drove through the intersection and did not stop until a short time later. *DeArman*, 54 Wn. App. at 624. Similarly, in *Wilson*, the court held that the defendant had submitted even though he continued walking toward his destination. *Id.* at 126.

Like the defendants in *DeArman* and *Wilson*, Mr. Strong stayed within the area controlled by the police officer. Although he took several steps after Officer Hanson turned on his spotlight, he never left the area being spotlighted by Officer Hanson, and he stopped before being told to do so. Thus, the facts in this case are very different from the facts in *Hodari D.* and *Brower v. Inyo County*, 489 U.S. 593, 596, 109 S. Ct. 1378, 103 L. Ed. 2d 628 (1989). Unlike Hodari, who ran several blocks, and Brower, who led the police on a twenty-mile car chase. Mr. Strong took only a few steps. While both *Hodari D.* and *Brower* involved fleeing suspects, this case does not.

Because Mr. Strong did not flee, he should not be denied the protections granted to him under the Fourth Amendment. While he did not immediately stop, he submitted to the officer's authority by stopping shortly after walking to the side of the road and by staying within the area being spotlighted.

II. UNDER ARTICLE I, SECTION 7, THE PROPER TEST IS THE TEST SET OUT IN *UNITED STATES V. MENDENHALL*.

Even if the court determines that no seizure occurred under the Fourth Amendment, a seizure occurred under Article I, Section 7, of the Washington Constitution.

In determining whether the Washington Constitution provides more protection than the United States Constitution, Washington courts do a three-part analysis. First, they analyze the factors set out in *State v. Gunwall*, 106 Wn.2d 54, 720 P.2d 808 (1986), to determine whether an independent state analysis is warranted. Second, if the *Gunwall* factors indicate that an independent state analysis is warranted, the courts do an independent analysis, determining whether the Washington Constitution provides more protection than the United States Constitution. *Id.* Finally, if the courts find that the Washington Constitution provides more protection, the courts determine what test is appropriate under the Washington Constitution and then apply that test. *Id.*

A. Under *State v. Gunwall,* an independent state analysis is warranted because all six *Gunwall* factors are satisfied.

In determining whether an independent state analysis is warranted, the courts consider six nonexclusive factors: (1) the textual language of the Washington Constitution, (2) significant differences between the texts of parallel provisions in the Washington and United States Constitutions, (3) state constitutional and common-law history, (4) preexisting state law, (5) differences in structure between the Washington and United States Constitutions, and (6) whether the issue relates to matters of particular state interest or local concern. *State v. Gunwall,* 106 Wn.2d 54, 61-62, 720 P.2d 808 (1986). The Washington Supreme Court has previously held that factors one, two, three, five, and six are met in cases involving the interpretation of Article I, Section 7. *See State v. Boland,* 115 Wn.2d 571, 576-77, 800 P.2d 1112 (1990) (holding that factors one, two, three, and five are met); *State v. Johnson,* 128 Wn.2d 431, 446, 909 P.2d 293, 302 (1996) (holding that factor six is met). In addition, in the context of this case, factor four, preexisting state law, is also met.

In the other cases, the courts have found that factor four is met when Washington's preexisting law differs from federal law. For example, in *Gunwall,* the court held that factor four was met when there were preexisting state statutes protecting telephonic and electronic communications. *Id.* at 65. Similarly, in *Boland* the court held that factor four was met when there was a preexisting local ordinance governing the placement of garbage cans. *Id.* at 576.

In this case, the preexisting state law also differs from the standard set out in *Hodari D.* While in *Hodari D.* the Supreme Court set out a subjective standard, looking to see whether the defendant did in fact submit, the Washington courts apply an objective standard, looking to see whether a reasonable person would have felt free to leave. *See, e.g., State v. Thorn,* 129 Wn.2d 347, 917 P.2d 108 (1996); *State v. Mennegar,* 116 Wn.2d 304, 787 P.2d 1247 (1990); *State v. Soto-Garcia,* 68 Wn. App. 20, 841 P.2d 1271 (1992); *State v. Elwood,* 52 Wn. App. 70, 757 P.2d 547 (1988). Because the tests applied by the federal and state courts are different, the fourth factor is met, and an independent state analysis is warranted.

B.   <u>An independent state analysis indicates that Article I, Section 7 provides more protection than the Fourth Amendment.</u>

The Washington courts have consistently held that Article I, Section 7, provides more protection than the Fourth Amendment.

In one line of cases, the Washington courts have held that this protection extends to an individual's property. For example, while the Fourth Amendment does not protect garbage placed in a can on the curb outside an individual's home, Article I, Section 7, does. *State v. Boland,* 115 Wn.2d 571, 800 P.2d 1112 (1990). Likewise, while the Fourth Amendment does not protect an individual's property stored in a jail lock box or in a locked container in a car, such property is protected under Article I, Section 7. *State v. Stroud,* 106 Wn.2d. 144, 720 P.2d 436 (1986).

In addition, in a second line of cases, the Washington courts have held that this additional protection extends to an individual's person. Under Article I, Section 7, police may not use thermal detection devices in the course of warrantless surveillance of an individual, *State v. Young,* 123 Wn.2d 173, 186, 867 P.2d 593, 599 (1994), or stop all vehicles at mandatory check points without warrants justifying the stops or without individualized suspicion of criminal activity, *Seattle v. Mesianai,* 110 Wn.2d 454, 457, 755 P.2d 775, 777 (1988).

More important though, the Washington courts have always applied an objective test in determining whether a seizure occurred. To protect the rights of all citizens, the courts have looked at whether a reasonable person would have felt free to leave and not whether a particular individual did or did not submit. *See, e.g., State v. Thorn*, 129 Wn.2d 347, 917 P.2d 108 (1996).

Because the Washington courts have consistently held that Article I, Section 7, provides more protection than the Fourth Amendment and because the Washington courts have consistently applied an objective rather than a subjective test in determining whether a seizure occurred, the court should hold that Article I, Section 7, provides more protection in this case. As the Washington Supreme Court states in *State v. Johnson*, the Washington Constitution protects "those privacy interests which the citizens of this state have held, and should be entitled to hold, safe from governmental trespass. . . ." *Id.* at 446, 909 P.2d at 302 (citing *State v. Boland*, 115 Wn.2d 573, 800 P.2d 1112 (1990)).

C.   Under Article I, Section 7, the correct test is an objective test: whether a reasonable person would feel free to leave or terminate the encounter.

The Washington courts should continue to apply the objective test set out in *United States v. Mendenhall*. 446 U.S. 544, 100 S. Ct. 1870, 64 L. Ed. 2d 497 (1980): a seizure occurs if a reasonable person would not have felt free to leave or terminate the encounter. This is the test that was applied by the Washington courts before the Supreme Court's decision in *Hodari D.; see, e.g., State v. Mennegar*, 116 Wn.2d 304, 787 P.2d 1247 (1990), and the test that the Washington courts have continued to apply after *Hodari D.; see, e.g., State v. Thorn*, 129 Wn.2d 347, 917 P.2d 108 (1996). In addition, this test is more consistent with public policy. As Professor LaFave has noted, the test set out in *Hodari D.* encourages police officers to "turn a hunch into a reasonable suspicion by inducing conduct justifying the suspicion." 3 Wayne LaFave, *Search and Seizure* 130 (1996).

As noted in Subsection IA, in this case an individual would not have felt free to leave or terminate the encounter. Officer Hanson both focused his attention on Mr. Strong and progressively intruded into his affairs when, after questioning Mr. Strong, he ran a criminal history check on Mr. Strong and then turned his car around and drove directly toward Mr. Strong, shining his spotlight on him.

   III.   UNDER BOTH THE FOURTH AMENDMENT AND ARTICLE I, SECTION 7, THE SEIZURE WAS ILLEGAL BECAUSE OFFICER HANSON DID NOT HAVE AN ARTICULABLE SUSPICION THAT MR. STRONG WAS ENGAGED IN OR ABOUT TO BE ENGAGED IN CRIMINAL CONDUCT.

At the time he spotlighted Mr. Strong, the only facts before Officer Hanson were that Mr. Strong was in a high crime area, RP 4; that Mr. Strong stood in the middle of the road apparently looking at Officer Hanson, RP 8; and that when Officer Hanson began driving toward Mr. Strong, Mr. Strong began walking from the middle of the road to the side of the road, RP 9-10.

In similar cases, the courts have held that these types of facts are not sufficient to support a finding that at the time of the seizure the officer had an articulable suspicion that the defendant was engaging in or about to engage in criminal conduct. *State v. Gleason*, 70 Wn. App. 13, 851 P.2d 731 (1993); *State v. Soto-Garcia*, 68 Wn. App. 20, 841 P.2d 1271 (1992). In *Gleason*, the court held that an officer did not have an articulable suspicion that the defendant was engaged in or about to be engaged in criminal activity when the officer saw the defendant leave an apartment complex where narcotics were known to be sold. *Id.* at 17. Similarly, in *Soto-Garcia*, the court held that the officer did not have an articulable suspicion that the defendant was engaged in or about to be engaged in criminal activity when the defendant was seen walking late in the evening in an area known for cocaine trafficking and answered the officer's questions about why he was in the area. *Id.* at 26.

Thus, for the court to find that the officer had an articulable suspicion, the State must show more than that the defendant was in a high crime area. It must be able to point to specific facts that indicate that the defendant is engaged in or about to be engaged in criminal conduct. Unlike *State v. Pressley*, 64 Wn. App. 591, 597, 528 P.2d 749 (1992), in which the women were not only in a high crime area but one of them had something in her hand and the other was pointing to it and said, "Oh, shit" when the officer approached, in this case there are no facts indicating that Mr. Strong was about to engage in criminal activity. Walking to the middle of the street, watching a police car, and walking out of the street are not illegal and do not provide evidence that Mr. Strong was about to engage in criminal activity.

Because the State has not been able to meet its burden, the seizure was illegal and the evidence must be suppressed.

E. Conclusion

For the reasons set out above, Mr. Strong respectfully requests that the Court of Appeals find that the trial court erred in denying his motion to dismiss and remand the case to the trial court for further proceedings.

Respectfully submitted this 23rd day of January, 2006.

_____
Susan Elder
WSBA No. 0000
Attorney for Appellant

RESPONDENT'S BRIEF

No. 05-1-00468-1

COURT OF APPEALS,
DIVISION II,
OF THE STATE OF WASHINGTON

State of Washington, Respondent,

v.

William Dennis Strong, Appellant.

BRIEF OF RESPONDENT

Samuel Lion
Attorney for Respondent
Pierce County Prosecutor's Office
900 Tacoma Avenue
Tacoma, Washington 98402

Table of Contents

Table of Authorities

A. Table of Cases

Washington Cases

Other Cases

B. Constitutional Provisions

C. Statutes

A. Statement of the Issue

Whether the trial court properly denied the defendant's motion to suppress, concluding (a) that no seizure occurred under the Fourth Amendment until Officer Hanson asked the defendant to stop, (b) that, under the circumstances of this case, Article I, Section 7, of the Washington Constitution does not provide more protection than the Fourth Amendment, and (c) that at the time he asked the defendant to stop, Officer Hanson had an articulable suspicion that the defendant was engaged in or about to be engaged in criminal conduct. (Appellant's Assignments of Error 1-6)

B. Statement of the Case

Procedural History

The defendant, William D. Strong, was charged under RCW 69.40.401(d) with possession of cocaine, under RCW 9A.56.160 with unlawful possession of stolen property in the second degree, and under RCW 9.41.040(1) with unlawful possession of a firearm. CP 1. The defendant filed a motion asking the court to suppress both the cocaine and the Rolex watch. CP 3. After an evidentiary hearing, Judge Johnson denied the motion. CP 13-16.

The case went to trial, RP 3, and on September 16, 2005, the jury entered a verdict of guilty, CP 18. Judgement and Sentence were entered on September 26, 2005. CP 18-19. Defendant's Notice of Appeal was timely filed on October 17, 2005. CP 20.

Statement of Facts

At about 11:00 p.m. on May 17, 2005, Officer Hanson was on patrol in the McChord gate area of Tacoma, an area known for its unusually high level of drug activity and drug arrests. RP 4. After responding to a call at the corner of Lincoln and Chicago Avenues, Officer Hanson saw the defendant standing on the corner. RP 4. Because he did not recognize him, Officer Hanson followed his usual procedure and approached him, initiating a social contact. RP 5.

1

After talking with the defendant for one or two minutes, Officer Hanson returned to his car and drove one or two blocks down a hill. RP 6. He then ran a criminal history check on the defendant, using the name that the defendant had given him. RP 7. While the check did not indicate that there were any outstanding warrants, it did show that the defendant had an extensive criminal history, including arrests for selling controlled substances. RP 7.

After he completed his check, Officer Hanson began to drive away. RP 8. As he did so, he looked in his rearview mirror and noticed the defendant standing in the middle of the road, staring at him. RP 8. When the defendant continued to stand in the road, Officer Hanson turned his car around and began driving back up the hill. RP 9. As he did so, the defendant began to walk quickly out of the road toward a dark, wooded area. RP 9, 11.

Because it was difficult to see, Officer Hanson turned on his spotlight, illuminating the general area. RP 9-11. The defendant ignored the spotlight and continued walking. RP 11. As Officer Hanson watched, the defendant walked behind a tree and dropped what appeared to be a package. RP 11. He then turned and continued walking a few steps before stopping. RP 12.

As the defendant stopped, Officer Hanson stopped his vehicle and asked the defendant to stop. RP 12. Officer Hanson then walked behind the tree and picked up half a soda can that was charred on the bottom. RP 13. After inspecting the substance inside the can, Officer Hanson determined that the substance was cocaine. RP 14-15.

After reading the defendant his rights, Officer Hanson placed him under arrest. During a search incident to the arrest, Officer Hanson found a Rolex watch in the defendant's pocket. RP 16. A subsequent investigation established that the watch was stolen. RP 17.

Officer Hanson has had more than ten years of experience, has made numerous drug arrests, and has had extensive training in the identification of controlled substances. RP 2-3.

2

C. Argument

I. THE TRIAL COURT PROPERLY DENIED THE DEFENDANT'S MOTION TO SUPPRESS THE COCAINE AND STOLEN ROLEX WATCH.

A. <u>The trial court correctly concluded that a seizure did not occur until Officer Hanson asked the defendant to stop and the defendant stopped.</u>

Under the Fourth Amendment a seizure does not occur until an officer uses physical force or the suspect submits to an officer's show of authority. *California v. Hodari D.,* 499 U.S. 621, 629, 111 S. Ct. 1547, 113 L. Ed. 2d 690 (1991). In this case, Officer Hanson did not use any physical force. RP 17. In addition, he did not exercise his authority until, after seeing the defendant drop something behind a tree, he ordered the defendant to stop.

The courts have repeatedly held that officers have the right to approach individuals and ask them questions, *United States v. Mendenhall,* 446 U.S. 544, 553, 100 S. Ct. 1870, 64 L. Ed. 2d 497 (1980); *Terry v. Ohio,* 392 U.S. 1, 9, 100 S. Ct. 1870, 64 L. Ed. 2d 497 (1968). Thus, there was no show of authority when Officer Hanson approached the defendant and asked him his name.

In addition, there was no show of authority when Officer Hanson turned his car around and drove back up the hill or when he turned on his spotlight. While the Washington courts have not specifically dealt with this issue, the Oregon courts have held that the use of a spotlight does not constitute a show of authority. For example, in *State v. Deptuch,* 95 Or. App. 54, 767 P.2d 471 (1989), the court held that there was no show of authority when an officer drove up next to the defendant's vehicle and shone a spotlight into the vehicle.

A show of authority has only been found in those circumstances in which officers use a siren, emergency lights, or a gun. *Compare State v. Nettles,* 70 Wn. App. 706, 711, 855 P.2d 699, 702 (1993), *review denied,* 123 Wn.2d 1010 (1994), with *State v. Stroud,* 30 Wn. App. 392, 396, 334 P.2d 316, 318 (1981), *review denied,* 96 Wn.2d 1025 (1982). In *Nettles,* the court concluded that there was no show of authority when, after driving by the defendant twice, the officer pulled her car over and parked and told the defendant and his companion that she would like to speak to them and asked them to come to her car. *Id.* at 711. In contrast, in *Stroud* the court concluded that there was a show of authority when two officers pulled up behind a legally parked car and turned on both their flashing light and their high beam headlights. *Id.* at 396.

In this case, Officer Hanson did not turn on his siren or his emergency lights or pull his gun. RP 10. He simply turned his car around and drove back up the hill. RP 8. He used his spotlight not to signal to the defendant to stop but to illuminate the area. RP 10. As the Washington Supreme Court has stated, an officer may use light to illuminate what he or she could see if it were daylight. *State v. Rose,* 128 Wn.2d 388, 396, 909 P.2d 280,289 (1996).

In addition, Officer Hanson did not focus his attention on the defendant or progressively intrude into his affairs. Unlike *State v. Soto-Garcla,* 68 Wn. App. 20, 841 P.2d 1271 (1992), a case in which the officer questioned the defendant for an extended period of time, taking the defendant's identification back to his patrol car and asking the defendant whether he had any cocaine on his person, in this case, Officer Hanson asked the defendant only one or two questions. Officer Hanson then left the area and drove a block to a block and a half away. RP 6. Although the defendant could also have left the area, he chose not to. Instead, he followed Officer Hanson. After Officer Hanson left, the defendant walked to the middle of the street and stood there, watching Officer Hanson. RP 8. Had the defendant not followed Officer Hanson and stood in the middle of the street for an unusually long period of time, Officer Hanson would have driven away after completing the criminal history check. RP 15.

In the alternative, even if the spotlight was a show of authority, the defendant did not submit to it. After Officer Hanson turned on the spotlight, the defendant continued walking quickly toward the dark, wooded area. RP 10. As Officer Hanson testified, "When he saw me turn around and come back up the street, he also turned and started heading toward the wooded area at a fast pace." RP 11.

Although the defendant did not run, he did flee. It was not until after the defendant dropped the cocaine behind the tree that he turned back toward the officer and began to stop. RP 11. Up until that time, he was not under Officer Hanson's control and could have, at any time, run into the wooded area.

> B.   <u>The trial court correctly concluded that the Washington Constitution does not provide more protection than the Fourth Amendment.</u>

An independent state analysis is not warranted in this case because the fourth *Gunwall* factor, preexisting state law, is not met. *See State v. Gunwall,* 106 Wn.2d 54, 720 P.2d 808 (1986). In the alternative, even if the fourth *Gunwall* factor is met, the Washington Constitution does not provide more protection than the Fourth Amendment, and there was no seizure under the test suggested by the defendant.

> 1.   <u>The fourth *Gunwall* factor is not met in this case.</u>

For the fourth *Gunwall* factor to be met, there must be preexisting state law that differs from the federal law. *See, e.g., State v. Boland,* 115 Wn.2d 571, 576-77, 800 P.2d 1112, 1115 (1990) (concluding that there was a preexisting local ordinance governing the collection of garbage); *State v. Gunwall,* 106 Wn.2d 54, 65, 720 P.2d 808 (1986) (concluding that there were preexisting state statutes protecting telephonic and electronic communications). In this case, there is no preexisting local ordinance or state statute. Instead, the Washington courts have always followed the lead of the federal courts. When the United States Supreme Court announced the *Mendenhall* test, the Washington courts adopted it. *See, e.g., State v. Stroud,* 30 Wn. App. at 396. Similarly, when the United States Supreme Court modified the *Mendenhall* test in *Florida v. Bostick,* 501 U.S. 429, 111 S. Ct. 2382, 115 L. Ed. 2d 389 (1991), the Washington courts followed the Supreme Court's lead, also adopting the *Bostick* test. *See, e.g., State v. Thorn,* 129 Wn.2d 347, 352, 917 P.2d 108, 111 (1996); *State v. Nettles,* 70 Wn.2d at 708.

Because there is no preexisting municipal ordinance or state law and because the Washington courts have always followed the lead of the federal courts, the fourth *Gunwall* factor is not met, and an independent state analysis is not warranted.

2. <u>In the alternative, even if an independent state analysis is warranted, Article I, section 7, does not grant more protection than the Fourth Amendment.</u>

While the Washington courts have held that Article I, section 7, provides more protection than the Fourth Amendment in a limited number of circumstances, all of those cases involved either a defendant's property or a defendant in his home or car. *See, e.g., State v. Young,* 123 Wn.2d 173, 186, 867 P.2d 593 (1994) (Officers used a thermal detection device to perform warrantless surveillance of the defendant's home); *State v. Boland,* 115 Wn.2d 571, 576, 800 P.2d 1112 (1990) (Officers removed garbage from the defendant's trash can and took it to police headquarters); *Seattle v. Mesianai,* 110 Wn.2d 454, 457, 755 P.2d 775 (1988) (officers stopped all motorists as part of sobriety checkpoint program); *State v. Stroud,* 106 Wn.2d 144, 152, 720 P.2d 436, 441 (1986) (Officers searched unlocked glove compartment and several unlocked containers). There are no cases in which the Washington courts have held that Article I, Section 7, provides more protection than the Fourth Amendment for activities conducted within public view.

In fact, the Washington courts have repeatedly held that an individual does not have an expectation of privacy in objects in public view or for activities done within public view. *See, e.g., State v. Kennedy,* 107 Wn.2d 1, 726 P.2d 445 (1986); *State v. Seagull,* 95 Wn.2d 898, 901, 632 P.2d 44 (1981). In *Kennedy,* the court held that an individual has no expectation of privacy in a weapon clearly visible inside a parked car, and in *Seagull,* the court held that no reasonable expectation of privacy exists when an object is in plain view of someone standing in a public area. Similarly, the court has held that a defendant does not have an expectation of privacy in a public bathroom in which the toilets are exposed. *State v. Berber,* 48 Wn. App. 583, 589, 740 P.2d 863, 867 (1987).

In this case, the defendant chose to act, not within the privacy of his home, but on a public street. Under such circumstances, Article I, Section 7, does not provide more protection than the Fourth Amendment.

3. <u>No seizure occurred under the *Mendenhall* test because, like the defendant, a reasonable person would have felt free to leave or terminate the encounter.</u>

Even if the court adopts the *Mendenhall* test, no seizure occurred in this case. As discussed in section IA, there was no show of authority until Officer Hanson told the defendant to stop. A spotlight is not a show of authority, and Officer Hanson did not turn on his siren or emergency lights or pull his gun. In addition, the defendant's own conduct indicates that under the circumstances a reasonable person would feel free to leave. After Officer Hanson turned on his spotlight, the defendant continued walking away from Officer Hanson toward a wooded area. RP 11-12.

C.   At the time that he told the defendant to stop, Officer Hanson had an articulable suspicion that the defendant was engaged in or about to be engaged in criminal conduct.

Because officers need to be able to question individuals suspected of committing a crime, a *Terry* stop is permitted whenever an officer has a reasonable and articulable suspicion that an individual is engaged in or about to be engaged in criminal activity. *See Terry v. Ohio,* 392 U.S. 1, 21-22, 100 S. Ct. 1870, 64 L. Ed. 2d 497 (1968); *State v. Glover,* 116 Wn.2d 509, 513, 806 P.2d 760, 762 (1991). In making these stops, the officer does not need to have the level of information necessary to justify an arrest; he or she need only have the ability to reasonably surmise from the information at hand that a crime is in progress or has occurred. *State v. Kennedy,* 107 Wn.2d 1, 6, 726 P.2d 445 (1986).

At the time that he told the defendant to stop, Officer Hanson had an articulable suspicion that the defendant was engaged in or about to be engaged in criminal conduct. After Officer Hanson drove away, the defendant walked to the center of the street and stood there, staring at Officer Hanson's car for an unusually long period of time. RP 8. Then, when Officer Hanson turned his car around and began driving back up the hill, the defendant walked quickly to the side of the road toward a dark, wooded area, walked behind a tree, and dropped something behind the tree. RP 11-12. Thus, Officer Hanson did not base his decision to stop the defendant merely on the fact that the defendant was in a high crime area or on the fact that he had a criminal history. Instead, Officer Hanson based his decision on conduct, which in light of his experience and training, indicated that the defendant was attempting to dispose of contraband.

D. Conclusion

For the reasons set out above, the State respectfully requests that the Court affirm the trial court's judgment.

Submitted this 17th day of March, 2006.

_____

Samuel Lion
Attorney for the State
Bar No. 999999

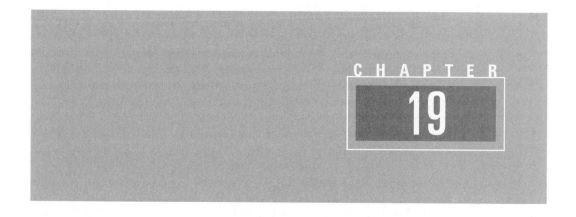

Oral Advocacy

O ral argument. For some, it is the part of practice they most enjoy; for others, it is the part they most dread.

Whichever group you fall into, oral argument is probably not what you expect. It is not a speech, a debate, or a performance. Instead, when done right, it is a dialogue between the attorneys, who explain the issues, law, and facts, and the judges, who ask questions not because they want to badger the attorney or because they want to see how much he or she knows but because they want to make the right decision.

§ 19.1 Audience

In making an oral argument, who is your audience? At the trial court level, the audience is the trial judge who is hearing the motion; at the appellate level, it is the panel of judges hearing the appeal. In both instances, the audience is extremely sophisticated. Although an eloquent oral argument is more persuasive than an oral argument that isn't eloquent, form seldom wins out over substance. If you don't have anything to say, it doesn't matter how well you say it.

At oral argument, the court can be either "hot" or "cold." The court is hot when the judges come prepared to the oral argument. The judges have studied the briefs and, at least in some appellate courts, have met in a pre-oral argument conference to discuss the case. In contrast, a cold court is not as prepared. The judge or judges are not familiar with the case, and if they have read the briefs, they have done so only quickly.

As a general rule, hot courts are more active than cold courts. Because they have studied the briefs, they often have their own agenda. They want to know more about point A, or they are concerned about how the rule being advocated might be applied in other cases. As a consequence, they often take more control over the argument, directing counsel to discuss certain issues and asking a number of questions. A cold court is usually comparatively passive. Because the judges are not as familiar with the case, most of their questions are informational. They want counsel to clarify the issue, supply a fact, or explain in more detail how the law should be applied.

§ 19.2 Purpose

In making your oral argument, you have two goals: to educate and to persuade. You want to explain the law and the facts in such a way that the court rules in your client's favor.

§ 19.3 Preparing for Oral Argument

The key to a good oral argument is preparation. You must know what you must argue to win, you must know your case, and you must have practiced both the text of your argument and your responses to the questions the court can reasonably be expected to ask.

§ 19.3.1 Deciding What to Argue

In making your argument, you will have only a limited amount of time. Depending on the case and the court, you will be granted ten, fifteen, or thirty minutes to make your points, answer the judge or judges' questions, and, if you are the appellant, to make your rebuttal. Because time is so limited, you will not be able to make every argument that you made in your brief. You must be selective.

In selecting the issues and arguments that you will make, choose those that are essential to your case. Don't spend your time on the easy argument if, to get the relief you want, you must win on the hard one. Make the arguments that you must make to win.

Also anticipate the arguments that the other side is likely to make. Although you don't want to make the other side's arguments, try to integrate your responses into your argument. Similarly, anticipate the court's concerns and decide how they can best be handled.

§ 19.3.2 Preparing an Outline

Do not write out your argument. If you do, you will either read it, or perhaps worse yet, memorize and recite it. Neither is appropriate. A dialogue does not have a predetermined text. Instead, prepare either a list of the points you want to cover or an outline.

Because it is difficult to predict how much of the time will be spent answering the court's questions, most advocates prepare two lists or outlines: a short version, in which they list only those points that they must make, and a long version, in which they list the points they would like to make if they have time. If the court is hot and asks a number of questions, they argue from the short list or outline; if the court is cold, they use the long one.

§ 19.3.3 Practicing the Argument

The next step is to practice, both by yourself and with colleagues. Working alone, practice your opening, your closing, your statements of the law, and the arguments themselves. Think carefully about the language you will use and about how you will move from one issue to the next and, within an issue, from argument to argument. Also list every question that a judge could be reasonably expected to ask, and decide (1) how you will respond and (2) how you can move from the answer to another point in your argument.

Then, with colleagues, practice delivering the argument. Ask your colleagues to play the role of the judge(s), sometimes asking almost no questions and at other times asking many. As you deliver the argument, concentrate on "reading" the court, adjusting your argument to meet its concerns; on responding to questions; and on the transitions between issues and arguments. Before a major argument, you will want to go through your argument five to ten times, practicing in front of as many different people as you can.

§ 19.3.4 Reviewing the Facts and the Law

You will also want to review the facts of the case, the law, and both your brief and your opponent's brief. When you walk into the courtroom, you should know everything there is to know about your case.

In practice, months or years may pass between the writing of the brief and the oral argument. When this is the case, it is essential that you update your research, and, when appropriate, file a supplemental brief with the court.

§ 19.3.5 Organizing Your Materials

Part of the preparation is getting your materials organized. You do not want to be flipping through your notes or searching the record during oral argument.

a. Notes or Outline

To avoid the "flipping pages syndrome," limit yourself to two pages of notes: a one-page short list or outline and a one-page long list or outline. These pages can then be laid side by side in front of you on the podium. (So that they don't blow off, many advocates staple the pages to the inside of a manila folder.) Colored markers can be used to highlight the key portions of the argument.

b. The Briefs

You will want to take a copy of your brief and your opponent's brief with you to the podium, placing them on the inside shelf. Make sure that you know both what is in the briefs and where that information is located.

c. The Record

In arguing an appeal, you will usually want to have the relevant portions of the record in the courtroom, either on the podium shelf or on counsel table. You should also be fully familiar with the record, as with the briefs, knowing both what is in the record and where particular information can be found. To assist in quickly locating information, many attorneys tab the record or prepare a quick index.

d. The Law

Although you do not need to have copies of all of the statutes and cases with you, you should be familiar with both the statutes and cases you cited in your brief and those on which your opponent's case is based. If you do bring cases with you, have them indexed and highlighted for quick reference.

§ 19.4 Courtroom Procedures and Etiquette

Like much of law, oral argument has its own set of conventions and procedures.

§ 19.4.1 Seating

In most jurisdictions, the moving party sits on the left (when facing the court) and the responding party sits on the right.

§ 19.4.2 Before the Case Is Called

If court is not in session, sit at counsel table, reviewing your notes or quietly conversing with co-counsel. If court is in session, sit in the audience until the prior case is completed. When your case is called, rise and move to counsel table.

§ 19.4.3 Courtroom Etiquette

Stand each time you are instructed to do so by the bailiff. For example, stand when the bailiff calls court into session and announces the judge or judges, and stand when court is recessed or adjourned. In the first instance, remain standing until the judges are seated, and in the latter instance, remain standing until the judges have left the courtroom.

Also stand each time you address the court, whether it be to tell the court that you are ready to proceed, to make your argument, or to respond to a question.

In addressing the court, you will want to use the phrases "Your Honor," "Your Honors," "this Court," "the Court," or, occasionally, the judge's name: "Judge Brown" or "Justice Smith." Never use a judge's or justice's first name.

Finally, never speak directly to opposing counsel. While court is in session, all your comments must be addressed to the court. Also remember that you are always "on." While opposing counsel is arguing, sit attentively at counsel table, listening and, if appropriate, taking notes.

§ 19.4.4 Appropriate Dress

As a sign of respect, both for the court and the client, most attorneys dress well for oral argument. Men wear conservative suits and ties, and women wear conservative dresses or suits. The key is to look professional but not severe. During oral argument, the judge's attention should be focused on your argument, not on your attire.

§ 19.5 Making the Argument

Like the brief, the oral argument has a prescribed format. See Chart 19.1.

§ 19.5.1 Introductions

Begin your oral argument by introducing yourself and your client. At the trial court level, the language is relatively informal. Most attorneys say "Good morning, Your Honor," and then introduce themselves and the client. At the appellate level, the language is more formal. By convention, most attorneys begin by saying, "May it please the Court, my name is _____, and I represent the [appellant] [respondent], _____."

Chart 19.1   **Outline of Oral Argument**

Outline of Oral Argument

A. *Moving party* (party bringing the motion or, on appeal, the appellant)
   1. Introductions
   2. Opening
   3. Statement of the issue(s)
   4. Brief summary of the significant facts (when appropriate)
   5. Argument
   6. Conclusion and request for relief
B. *Responding party* (party opposing the motion or, on appeal, the respondent or appellee)
   1. Introductions
   2. Opening
   3. Statement of position
   4. Brief summary of significant facts (when appropriate)
   5. Argument
   6. Conclusion and request for relief
C. *Moving party's rebuttal*
D. *Sur-rebuttal* (when allowed)

In many courts, the introduction is also used to reserve rebuttal time. The attorney for the moving party reserves rebuttal either before introducing himself or herself or immediately afterwards. "Your Honor, at this time, I would like to reserve _____ minutes for rebuttal."

§ 19.5.2 Opening

The first minute of your argument should be memorable. The opening sentences should catch the judge's attention, making the case's importance clear, establishing the theme, and creating the appropriate context for the argument that follows.

§ 19.5.3 Statement of the Issues

a. The Moving Party

If you are the moving party, you need to set out the issues. Sometimes this is best done as part of the opening. From the issue statement alone, the case's importance is clear: "In this case, the appellant asks the Court to overrule *Roe v. Wade.*" At other times, such a strategy is not effective. For example, few trial judges would find the following opening memorable: "In this case, the defendant asks the court to suppress identification testimony." In such cases, the opening and the statement of the issues should not be combined.

As a general rule, the statement of the issues should precede the summary of the facts. Before hearing the facts, the court needs a context. There are times, however, when it is more effective to set out the issues after the summary of the facts.

Wherever they are presented, the issue statements must be tailored to oral argument. What is effective in writing may not be effective when spoken. For example, although the under-does-when format works well in a brief, it does not work well orally. In oral argument, the issue needs to be presented more simply. "In this case, the court is asked to decide whether..." or "This case presents two issues: first, whether...and second, whether...."

Even though they are streamlined, the issues should be presented in the light most favorable to the client. The questions should be framed as they were in the brief, and the significant and emotionally favorable facts should be included. See sections 17.6.1 and 18.12.3.

b. The Responding Party

As a general rule, the responding party does not restate the issue or issues. Instead, it states its position, either as part of its opening or as a lead-in to its arguments: "The cocaine and Rolex watch should not be suppressed. At the time he told the defendant to stop, Officer Hanson had an articulable suspicion...."

§ 19.5.4 Summary of Facts

a. The Moving Party

When arguing to a cold court, you will want to include a summary of the facts, in one to three minutes telling the court what the case is about. You may also want to include a summary of the facts when arguing to a hot court. If the facts are particularly important, you will want to summarize them, refresh the court's memory, and present the facts in the light most favorable to the client. There will, however, be times when a separate summary of the facts is not the best use of limited time. In these cases, instead of presenting the facts in a separate summary at the beginning, integrate them into the argument.

b. The Responding Party

As the responding party, you do not want to use your time repeating what opposing counsel just said. Consequently, for you a summary of the facts is optional even if the court is cold. If opposing counsel has set out the facts accurately, the summary can be omitted. Just integrate the significant facts into the argument. You will, however, want to include a summary if opposing counsel has misstated key facts or has omitted facts that are important to your argument or if you need to present the facts from your client's point of view.

c. References to the Record

In presenting the facts, you will not, as a matter of course, include references to the record. You must, however, be able to provide such references if asked to do so by the court or if you are correcting a misstatement made by opposing counsel.

§ 19.5.5 The Argument

Unless the issues and arguments build on each other, start with your strongest issue and, in discussing that issue, your strongest argument. This allows you to take advantage of the positions of emphasis and ensures that you will have the opportunity to make your best, or most crucial, arguments. In addition, it usually results in better continuity. Because the moving party's strongest issue is usually the responding party's weakest, the moving party's final issue will be the responding party's first, providing the responding party with an easy opening for his or her argument.

Moving Party	*Responding Party*
Issue 1 → Issue 2	Issue 2 → Issue 1

In presenting the arguments, do what you did in your brief but in abbreviated form. When the law is not in dispute, begin by presenting the rule of law, presenting that law in the light most favorable to your client (see sections 17.9.3 and 18.15.3). Then argue that law, explaining why the court should reach the result that you advocate. When it is the law itself that is in dispute, argue your interpretation.

In both instances, you must support your position and present arguments based on the plain language of the statute or rule, legislative intent, policy, the facts of the case, or analogous cases. When appropriate, cite to the relevant portions of a statute or to a common law rule and, in using analogous cases, be specific: explain the rule that the court applied, the significant facts, and the court's reasoning. Although you should have the full case citations available, you do not need to include them in your argument.

Although you want to cite to the relevant authorities, you do not, as a general rule, want to quote them or your brief. Reading more than a line is seldom effective. If it is important that the court have specific language before it, refer the judge or judges to the appropriate page in the brief or, better yet, prepare a visual aid.

There are several other things that you need to keep in mind in making your argument. First, it is usually more difficult to follow an oral argument than a written one. As a result, it is important to include sufficient roadmaps, signposts, and transitions. Make both the structure of your argument and the connections between ideas explicit.

Second, you need to manage your time. Do not spend so much time on one issue or argument that you do not have time for the other issue or issues or other arguments. Because it is difficult to predict how many questions the court will ask, practice both a short version and a long version of each argument.

§ 19.5.6 Answering Questions

You should welcome the court's questions. They tell you what the court is thinking about your case, what the judges understand, and what they still question. If you're not getting questions, it is usually a bad sign. The judges have either already made up their minds or are not listening.

Questions from the bench fall into several categories. Some are mere requests for information. The judge wants to clarify a fact or your position on an issue or wants to know more about the rule or how you think it should be applied.

Other questions are designed to elicit a particular response from you: Judge A agrees with your position and wants you to pursue a particular line of argument for the benefit of Judge B, who is not yet persuaded. Still other questions are designed to test the merits of your argument. These questions may have as their focus your case or, at the appellate level, future cases. If the court applies rule A, what does that mean for cases X, Y, and Z?

Whatever the type of question, when the judge begins to speak, you must stop. Although judges can interrupt you, you should not interrupt them. As the judge speaks, listen — not only to the question that is being asked but also for clues about how the judge is perceiving the case.

The hardest part comes next. Before answering the judge, think through your answer. Although the second or two of silence may make you uncomfortable, the penalty for answering too quickly can be severe. Although few cases are won at oral argument, some are lost, usually because in answering a question the attorney conceded or asserted too much. The second or two of silence is by far better than an unfavorable ruling.

When you know what you want to say, answer. In most instances, you will want to begin by giving the judge a one-, two-, or three-word answer. "Yes." "No." "Yes, but . . . ." "No, but . . . ." "In some cases, ..." Then explain or support your answer, integrating the points that you want to make into your answer when possible. Instead of thinking of questions as interruptions, think of them as another vehicle for making your argument.

There are a number of things that you should not do in responding to a question. First, do not tell the judge that you will answer the question later. It is you, not the judge, who must be flexible.

Second, do not argue with the judge. Answer all questions calmly and thoughtfully. Do not raise your voice, and even if you are frustrated, don't let it show. If one line of argument isn't working and the point is essential to your case, try another, and if that line doesn't work, try still another. When the point is not important or you have given all the answers you have, answer, and then, without pausing, move as smoothly as you can into the next part of your argument.

Third, after answering the question, don't stop and wait for the judge's approval or permission to continue. Answer the question, and then, unless asked another question, move to the next part of your argument. Finally, don't answer by asking the judge a question. In oral argument, it is inappropriate to question a judge.

§ 19.5.7 The Closing

The closing is as important as the opening. Because it is a position of emphasis, you want to end on a favorable point.

One way of doing this is to end with a summary of your arguments, reminding the court of your strongest points and requesting the appropriate relief. Although this is often effective, it can also be ineffective. Many judges stop listening when they hear the phrase "In conclusion" or "In summary." Consequently, when using a summary, avoid stock openers. Catch the court's attention by repeating a key phrase, weaving the pieces together, or returning to the points made in your opening.

Another way is to end on a strong point. If you are running out of time, it may be better to stop at the end of an argument or after answering a question than to rush through a prepared closing. Like a good comedian, a good advocate knows when to sit down.

§ 19.5.8 Rebuttal

Perhaps the hardest part of the oral argument is rebuttal. In one or two minutes you must identify the crucial issues and make your strongest argument or response.

As a general rule, do not try to make more than one or two points during rebuttal. The points should be selected because of their importance to your case: do not merely repeat what you said in the main portion of your argument or respond to trivial points made by opposing counsel. Instead, make your rebuttal a true rebuttal by responding to significant points made by opposing counsel or questions or concerns raised by the court during opposing counsel's argument.

Because time is so limited, most advocates begin their rebuttal by telling the court how many points they plan to make: "I would like to make two points." This introduction tells the court what to expect. The advocate then makes his or her first point and supports it and, unless interrupted by a question, moves to the second point. Most advocates close by quickly repeating their request for relief.

§ 19.6 Delivering the Argument

Every advocate has his or her own style. While some are soft-spoken, others are dynamic; while some are plain-speaking, others strive for eloquence. As an advocate, you will need to develop your own style, building on your strengths and minimizing your weaknesses. Whatever your style, there are certain "rules" that you should follow.

§ 19.6.1 Do Not Read Your Argument

The first, and perhaps most important, rule is not to read your argument. Similarly, do not try to deliver a memorized speech. Know what you want to say and then talk to the court. You are a teacher, sharing information and answering the court's questions.

§ 19.6.2 Maintain Eye Contact

If you don't read, you will be able to maintain eye contact with the judge. This is important for several reasons. First, it helps you keep the judge's attention. It is very difficult not to listen to a person who is looking you in the eye. Second, it helps you "read" the court. By studying the judges, you can often determine (1) whether they already agree with you on a point and you can move to the next part of your argument; (2) whether they are confused; or (3) whether you have not yet persuaded them. Finally, eye contact is important because of what it says about you and your argument. An advocate who looks the judge in the eye is perceived as being more confident and more competent than one who doesn't.

When you are arguing to an appellate court, maintain eye contact with all of the judges. Even when answering a specific judge's question, maintain eye contact with all of the judges.

§ 19.6.3 Do Not Slouch, Rock, or Put Your Hands in Your Pockets

In delivering an oral argument to the court, stand erect, but not stiffly, behind the podium. Do not rock from foot to foot, and do not put your hands in your pockets.

Although it may be appropriate to move around the courtroom when arguing to a jury, you should not do so when arguing to the court.

§ 19.6.4 Limit Your Gestures and Avoid Distracting Mannerisms

Gestures are appropriate in an oral argument. They should, however, be natural and relatively constrained. If you talk with your hands, mentally put yourself inside a small telephone booth.

You also want to avoid distracting mannerisms. Do not play with a pen, the edge of your notes, or the keys in your pocket. In addition, do not repeatedly push hair out of your eyes or your glasses back up on your nose.

§ 19.6.5 Speak So That You Can Be Easily Understood

In delivering your oral argument, speak loudly and clearly enough that you can be easily heard by the judges.

Also try to modulate your voice, varying both the pace and how loudly you speak. If you want to emphasize a point, speak more slowly and either more softly or more loudly.

§ 19.7 Making Your Argument Persuasive

In delivering your oral argument, you will want to use many of the same techniques that you used in writing your brief. In stating the issue, frame the question so that it suggests the answer favorable to your client and, in presenting the facts, emphasize the favorable facts by placing them in positions of emphasis and by using detail and sentence structure to your advantage. See sections 17.5.3 and 18.12.5. Also present the law in the light most favorable to your client. State favorable rules broadly, use cases to your advantage, and emphasize the policies that support your client's position. See sections 17.9.3 and 18.15.3.

You should also pick your words carefully. Select words both for their denotation and their connotation and avoid words and phrases that undermine the persuasiveness of your argument. If you represent the defendant, don't say, "It is the defendant's position that the line-up was suggestive." Instead, say "The line-up was suggestive." Similarly, don't say, "We feel that the prosecutor acted improperly when she referred to the defendant's post-arrest silence." Say instead, "The prosecutor acted improperly when she referred to the defendant's post-arrest silence."

§ 19.8 Handling the Problems

Because an oral argument isn't scripted, you need to prepare for the unexpected and decide in advance how you will handle the problems that might arise.

§ 19.8.1 Counsel Has Misstated Facts or Law

If opposing counsel misstates an important fact or the governing law, you will usually want to bring the error to the attention of the court. This should, however, be done carefully.

First, make sure you are right. If there is time, double-check the record, the statute, or the case. Second, make sure you are correcting a misstatement of fact or law, not the opposing party's interpretation of a fact, statute, or case. Third, correct the mistake, not opposing counsel. Instead of criticizing or attacking opposing counsel, simply provide the court with the correct information and, if possible, the citation to the record or the language of the statute or case.

EXAMPLE

Correcting a Statement Made by Opposing Counsel

"Ms. Martinez did not see the assailant three times. She testified that she saw him twice: once when he drove by slowly and then when he pulled in front of her."

Finally, correct only those errors that are significant.

§ 19.8.2 You Make a Mistake

If you make a significant mistake, correct it as soon as you can.

§ 19.8.3 You Don't Have Enough Time

Despite the best planning, you will sometimes run out of time. You may have gotten more questions than you expected, leaving you little or no remaining time for your last issue or your final points. When this happens, you have two options. You may either quickly summarize the points that you would have made, or you may tell the court that, because you are out of time, you will rely on your brief for the issues and arguments that you didn't cover.

What you don't want to do is exceed the time that you have been allotted. Unless the court gives you permission to continue, you must stop when your time is up.

§ 19.8.4 You Have Too Much Time

This is not a problem. You do not need to use all of your allotted time. When you have said what you need to say, thank the court and sit down.

§ 19.8.5 You Don't Know the Answer to a Question

Occasionally you will be asked a question that you can't answer. If it is a question about the facts of your case or about the law, don't try to bluff. Instead, do one of the following: (1) if you can do so in a few seconds, look up the answer; (2) tell the judge that at this point you can't answer the question but that you will be glad to provide the information after oral argument; or (3) give the best answer you can.

Statements That You Can Make When You Do Not Know the Answer   EXAMPLE

"So that I may answer correctly, let me quickly check the record."

"I'm not sure what the actual words were. I will check and provide you with that information after oral argument."

"As I recall, the police officer testified that he asked the question twice."

If the question raises an issue you hadn't considered, the options are slightly different. You can either trust yourself and, on the spot, give your best answer or tell the court that you need to give the question some thought.

§ 19.8.6 You Don't Understand the Question

If you don't understand a question, tell the judge and either ask him or her to repeat the question or repeat the question in your own words, asking the judge whether you understood correctly. "I'm sorry, I'm not sure that I understand your question. Could you please rephrase it?" "If I am correct, you are asking whether . . . ."

§ 19.8.7 You Become Flustered or Draw a Blank

It happens, at some time or another, to almost everyone. You become flustered or draw a blank. When this happens, "buy" a few seconds by either taking a drink of water or taking a deep breath and looking down at your notes. If you still can't continue with the point you were making, move to another one.

§ 19.8.8 You're Asked to Concede a Point

Concessions can work both to your advantage and to your disadvantage. You will win points by conceding points that you can't win or that are not important to your argument. You can, however, lose your case if you concede too much. You must, therefore, know your case, and concede when appropriate and otherwise politely but firmly stand your ground.

§ 19.9 A Final Note

No matter how much they dread it, initially most individuals end up enjoying oral argument for what it is, a stimulating dialogue among intelligent people.

§ 19.9.1 Checklist for the Oral Argument

I. Preparation

- The advocate knows the law and the facts of the case.
- The advocate has anticipated and prepared rebuttals for the arguments the other side is likely to make.

- The advocate has anticipated and prepared responses to the questions the court is likely to ask.
- The advocate has determined what arguments he or she needs to make to win.
- The advocate has prepared two outlines: a long outline, which can be used if the court asks only a few questions, and a short outline, which can be used in case the court asks more questions.

II. Content and Organization

A. *Introduction*
- The advocate identifies himself or herself and the client.
- When appropriate, the advocate requests rebuttal time.

B. *Opening and Statement of Issues or Position*
- The advocate begins the argument with a sentence or phrase that catches the attention of the court and establishes the client's theory of the case.
- The advocate then presents the question or states his or her position.
- The question or statement of position is framed so that it supports the advocate's theory of the case and suggests an answer favorable to the client.
- The question or statement of position is presented using language that is easily understood.

C. *Summary of Facts*
- When appropriate, the advocate includes a short summary of the facts in which he or she explains the case and establishes an appropriate context. When a separate summary of the facts is not appropriate, the advocate weaves the facts into the argument.
- The facts are presented accurately but in the light most favorable to the client. The positions of emphasis and detail are used effectively, and words have been selected for both their denotation and their connotation.

D. *Argument*
- The advocate discusses the issues and makes the arguments needed to win.
- The argument is structured in such a way that it is easy to follow: (1) issues and arguments are discussed in a logical order and (2) sufficient roadmaps, signposts, and transitions are used.
- The arguments are supported. The advocate uses the law, analogous cases, policy, and the facts to support each of his or her assertions.
- The law, analogous cases, policies, and facts are presented accurately.

- The law, analogous cases, policies, and facts are presented in the light most favorable to the client.

E. Questions from the Bench
- When a judge asks a question, the advocate immediately stops talking and listens to the question.
- The advocate thinks before answering.
- As a general rule, the advocate begins his or her answer with a short response ("Yes," "No," "In this case") and then supports that answer.
- After answering the question, the advocate moves back into his or her argument without pausing or waiting for the judge to give permission to continue.
- The advocate sees questions not as an interruption but as another opportunity to get his or her argument before the court.
- As he or she listens to the questions, the advocate adjusts the argument to match the concerns and interests of the court.

F. Closing
- The advocate ends the argument by summarizing the main points or on a strong point.
- When appropriate, the advocate includes a request for relief.

G. Rebuttal
- The advocate uses rebuttal to respond to the one or two most important points raised by opposing counsel or the court.

III.　Delivery

- The advocate treats the argument as a dialogue; he or she does not read or recite the argument.
- The advocate maintains eye contact with all of the judges.
- The advocate has good posture, uses gestures effectively, and speaks so that he or she can be easily understood.
- The advocate does not use phrases like "I think," "We maintain," or "It is our position that."
- The advocate is composed and treats the court and opposing counsel with respect.

A Guide to Effective and Correct Writing

Introduction

When people watch law-related television programs and movies or read novels about lawyers, they may get the impression that attorneys divide their time between exciting courtroom scenes and even more exciting personal relationships with their clients and coworkers. Sophisticated viewers know that the writers for the big and small screen use a fair amount of artistic license in portraying those personal relationships; after all, there are rules of professional responsibility that prohibit much of this behavior. These same viewers, however, may assume that the dramatic courtroom scenes are how most attorneys spend much of their time.

While it is true that many attorneys spend a fair amount of time in court, what the TV programs, movies, and lawyer novels fail to show is all the preparation that goes on before trial. What's more, they fail to show all the everyday work of a lawyer advising clients and handling cases that do not go to trial.

Earlier in this textbook you may have been surprised to find out how much of a lawyer's life is spent being a legal researcher. Somehow the screenwriters and novelists fail to show their lawyer heroes toiling away in the library or online with LexisNexis and Westlaw. You may be even more surprised to find out how much of a lawyer's life is spent being a writer. Yes, a writer. Virtually every type of legal practice entails a considerable amount of writing. Whether it is an office memo to a senior partner, a contract drafted for a business deal, a letter advising a client, or even a brief to the United States Supreme Court, the typical lawyer is the author of many *many* pieces of "legal writing." In fact, it is not an exaggeration to say that the ability to write well is an absolute must for lawyers. More often than the dramatic courtroom scene, the well-crafted piece of writing is how the typical lawyer demonstrates his or her legal skill.

Book 4 is designed to be your writing reference book — you will find anything and everything you need to know about writing for law. Part 1 focuses on techniques that make writing effective; Part 2 focuses on the grammar and punctuation rules of correct writing. Together the two parts cover what the movies, novels, and TV shows failed to dramatize — how to pick just the right word, craft the memorable sentence, polish a paragraph, organize ideas into an effective framework, check the document for errors — and be able to do it all with style. It might not make great TV, a blockbuster movie, or a bestselling novel, but writing well as a lawyer will be satisfying and a key to your success.

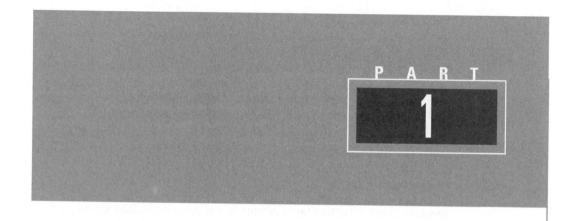

A Guide to Effective Writing

Introduction

This part of the book gives legal writers general recommendations about what makes legal writing effective. We believe what follows is good advice, but we also want to alert readers to three caveats about the notion of "effective legal writing."

First, effectiveness in legal writing is a relative thing. The same level of effectiveness is not needed in every situation. The trick, of course, is to make the writing effective enough so that it accomplishes its goal without laboring over the writing to the point that it consumes all of the working day and night. In short, some balance is appropriate.

Second, effectiveness in legal writing—and in all writing for that matter—always depends on the context. What will please and even delight one reader may irritate or anger another. An organizational scheme that is effective in one instance may be dead wrong in another. Even precision and conciseness, those most sought-after characteristics of effective legal writing, can be ineffective in instances in which vagueness and verbosity accomplish the desired objective. In other words, writing that most readers would consider competent, stylistically pleasing, and even eloquent in the abstract but that does not work in a given context is, in that context, ineffective.

Finally, effectiveness is a fairly subjective notion. Again, we can give you the standard advice and some insights of our own about what is and is not effective legal writing, but then you must filter all that through your own sense of whether you think something works. If, as you are writing a given piece, your instincts tell you it is working (or it is not working) and all the theory and advice tell you the opposite, we suggest that you look at it again. If your instincts and common sense still insist that the conventional wisdom about effective legal writing is not working in that situation, then trust your instincts.

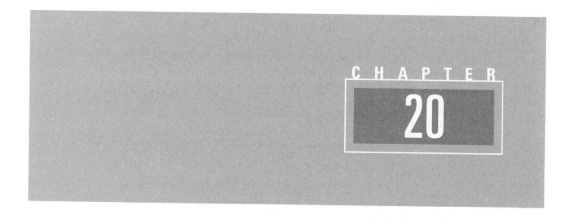

Effective Writing — The Whole Paper

§ 20.1 The Psychology of Writing

Writing is not for the faint-hearted. It takes courage, perseverance, creativity, and flexibility, not to mention intelligence and a solid foundation of writing skills. A fair number of lawyers and judges profess to like writing and even say that they find the process satisfying. If you are in this fortunate group, this chapter is not addressed to you.

If you are among the less fortunate — those who have felt overwhelmed by the prospect of writing, who have struggled with writer's block, who have found writing to be a difficult, perhaps even painful process — there is hope. Writing, like most other skills, becomes more pleasurable with each successful experience. It also helps to know where the usual stumbling blocks are in the process and how to get past them.

Few legal writers have trouble getting started on the research phase of a writing project. Many encounter their first stumbling block when it is time to move from research to writing. A typical avoidance mechanism is to keep researching long past the point of need. Writers who have developed this pattern of approaching writing tasks usually postpone putting pen to paper or fingers to keyboard until the last possible moment. Then they write, almost out of desperation, and end up turning in as a final product something that is really a rough draft. By delaying the writing process, they make it virtually impossible to do any high-quality drafting, revising, editing, and proofreading. The result is yet another unsatisfying writing experience.

If this describes your typical writing process, you may be able to break out of this habit by developing a schedule for the completion of the entire document. In this schedule, allot a reasonable amount of time to complete the research, but be firm about when you will begin writing. Give yourself mini-deadlines for completing an outline, producing a first draft, revising, editing, and proofreading. Allow breathing room in this timetable for problems such as a printer malfunction or a flat tire. If at all possible, plan as though your deadline is sooner than the real deadline. To do this, you may find it easier to write the schedule backwards, starting with the final deadline and allowing time for proofreading, then editing, all the way back to researching.

Sample Schedule for a Two-Week Writing Project

Week 1		Research and organize research into template
Week 2	Day 1	brainstorm, create plan, outline
	Day 2	drafting
	Day 3	drafting
	Day 4	revising
	Day 5	editing, last-minute citation checks
	Day 6	proofreading
	Day 7	final product (ready a day early!)

For shorter time frames and quick turnarounds, a schedule is even more critical. In such cases, you will probably be working with half-day, quarter-day, or even hourly units, but the principles are still the same. Figure out how much of the total time should be spent researching and how much should be spent writing. Create mini-deadlines for yourself. Start with your final deadline and work backwards as you plan.

Sample Schedule for a Two-Day Writing Project

Day 1	Research and organize research into template
Day 2	by 10:00 a.m. brainstorm, create plan, outline
	by 2:00 p.m. drafting
	by 3:00 p.m. revising
	by 4:00 p.m. editing
	by 4:30 p.m. proofreading
	by 5:00 p.m. final product completed (and in the partner's hands!)

With practice, you may find that you do not need as much time for research and that you can allow a larger percentage of your time for writing.

Schedules are invaluable, but many writers need more than a schedule to get them started writing. One key to success is to organize your research in a way that will facilitate the writing process. For example, instead of organizing your research around cases, organize it around the law or the points you want to make. Under each point, list the statutes, cases, or authorities on which you will rely and a quick summary of how they support that point.

If you record your research on a template like the ones set out in Chapters 5 and 8, you will find that you are halfway toward an organizational scheme by the time you begin drafting. The template can be easily transformed into an outline for the discussion section. Under your heading for the introductory section, you have the text of the general rules, under your heading for the elements, you have the text of the specific rules and briefs of the possible analogous cases. With luck, you also have a list of the arguments that each side may make.

Another method is to copy the applicable statutes and cases and color code them. Color coding helps during the drafting phase because it gives you a quick way to gather up all the information you have collected on a given point (grab all the red) and then physically order those sheets. The same sheets may have other colors on them, but while you are writing about the "red point," you can stay focused on the parts of the notes and photocopied cases that concern that point. When it comes time to do the "blue point," the same sheets get picked up and sequenced into the information about that point.

If color coding does not appeal to you, you may find that having separate file folders or a tabbed notebook does. The key is to develop files or sections of the notebook for the points you want to make in the whole document, not separate files or notebook sections for each analogous case. This means you may need two or more photocopies of the same page of a case so that it may be filed under each of the appropriate points.

§ 20.2 Outlines, Writing Plans, and Ordered Lists

Unfortunately, student writers are taught to write outlines long before they ever need one. Sometime in junior high most of us were first exposed to outlines, but the outlines were for relatively short, uncomplicated papers whose organization we could keep in our heads. The task wasn't large enough or complex enough to warrant an outline. As a result, many student writers believe outlines or written plans are useless because they were useless for papers in the seventh grade.

For professional writers (and lawyers *are* professional writers) who must organize extensive and complex material, spending time creating an outline or writing plan or even just an ordered list almost always saves time in the end. Filling in the standard templates achieves the same goal. Done properly, an outline, plan, or template will keep you from backtracking, repeating yourself, missing a key point, or finally discovering what it is you want to say after you have written the whole thing the wrong way.

But creating order in extensive and complex material is not easy; it takes the writer's complete attention. Consequently, it deserves a distinct block of time for just that task. Don't fall into the trap of trying to create order at the same time you are drafting sentences and paragraphs. That approach is needlessly stressful because it forces you to keep track of several big tasks all at once.

Writing a good outline, template, or plan may also mean that you have to change some of your preconceived ideas about outlines. First of all, the outline, template, or plan is for you, the writer, not for a teacher. Roman numerals and capital A's and B's are not important. Use them if they help; discard them if they hinder. Even if you discard the roman numerals, letters, and numbers, keep the indentations. They will help you distinguish among main points, subpoints, sub-subpoints, and supporting details.

There are as many ways to go about creating an outline or writing plan as there are writers. Below are some time-tested techniques you may find helpful.

§ 20.2.1 Read It All; Mull It Over

Before beginning to write, read through all of your research. Let your mind mull it over while you do some mindless task such as mowing the lawn or taking a bath. While you are engaged in the mindless task, your mind will almost certainly begin organizing the ideas.

§ 20.2.2 Don't Overlook the Obvious Ways to Organize

One obvious way of beginning to organize is to determine how the court will approach the problem. Are there any threshold questions the court will consider first? If so, place them first in your outline. What will the court look at and decide second, third, and so on? Your organizational scheme should mirror the process the court will follow.

Furthermore, in creating an organization for your document, do not assume that you always have to create a brand-new, never-seen-before organizational scheme. Most documents fit comfortably in one of the common organizational plans. Borrow freely from the bank of common knowledge about how to organize an elements analysis, a balancing test, or a discussion of the development of a trend, to name but a few. Many discussion sections follow an IRAC (issue, rule, analysis, conclusion) plan or use mini-IRACs in some of the sections.

§ 20.2.3 Find Order Using a Three-Column Chart

The three-column chart can be an effective way to find order in a document, particularly when the document does not immediately appear to fall into any of the typical organizational patterns. In the first column, make one giant list of everything you think the final document should include. Be as comprehensive as possible. Dump everything you have in your brain about the problem into this list. Do not worry about the order of the items.

Below is an example of a brain dump used to find organization for a legal problem concerning whether some carpeting made for a customer fell within the UCC exception to specially manufactured goods.

Column One: The Brain Dump

- Requirements for exception
    1. goods specially manufactured for buyer
    2. unsuitable for sale to others in ordinary course of seller's business
    3. manufacture commenced
- no written contract
- oral contracts should be the rule
- "specially manufactured" not defined
- "specially manufactured" refers to nature of goods
- manufacturer had to specially set looms
- *Flowers*: buyer's name/artwork on wrapping material
- wrapping material & carpet are personalized
- a family flower is not a name
- *Colorado Carpet*: carpeting available at outlets
- policy: goods themselves are evidence of contract
- seller of custom-made goods not exempt from Statute of Frauds
- if all goods custom, no written contract necessary
- seller of custom goods as likely to fabricate contract as seller of ready-made goods
- quote from *Wackenhut* court
- undue hardship for seller
- wholesaler easily sold rugs to a third party

Once the first column is complete, the writer then uses the second column to begin doing some preliminary ordering of the list in Column One. Column One will probably already contain some natural groupings of ideas. If so, the writer places them together in Column Two at roughly the point in the document where she guesses they will go.

For example, the writer of the specially manufactured goods memo knew that the rule section should come early in the memo, so she moved the requirements for the exception close to the top of Column Two. She then considered whether anything should precede or immediately follow the requirements. A quick glance down Column One yielded at least one other point about rules: there is no written contract. She added this point before a discussion of the exception and its requirements.

After the list of requirements, it seemed natural to move right to the first requirement and to *Flowers*, the case that helps explain what constitutes "specially manufactured for the buyer." Because the writer knew she wanted to make an argument for Boliver Custom Carpets based on *Flowers*, that argument was placed next on the list.

The writer proceeded down the list from Column One and found roughly where each item fit in Column Two. By the end, she had some stray items: "Goods themselves are evidence of the contract" and "undue hardship for seller." Stray items can be worked into the organization now or saved for Column Three.

Column Two: Preliminary Ordering of Ideas

- no written contract
- specially manufactured goods exception
- requirements for exception
  1. goods specially manufactured for buyer
  2. unsuitable for sale to others in ordinary course of seller's business
  3. manufacture commenced under circumstances... & prior to receipt of notice of repudiation
- First requirement: goods specially manufactured for buyer
- *Flowers*: buyer's name & artwork on wrapping paper
- wrapping paper is personalized
- BCC's argument: like wrapping paper, rugs are personalized
- Therefore, rugs specially manufactured for buyer
- ....

Column Three is used to further refine the order of the list. This is the time to test out various places where the stray items may fit. In this case, because two of the items seemed to be policy reasons for the specially manufactured goods exception, they could fit right before or after the list of requirements. The other two items — "'specially manufactured' not defined" and "'specially manufactured' refers to nature of goods" — belong in the rule section of the first requirement.

While preparing Column Three, also check to see if anything has been forgotten. Look for all the standard features of legal analysis (burden of proof, plain language arguments, policy arguments, and so on) and all the standard "moves" a lawyer makes (argument, counterargument, rebuttal, countervailing policy argument, and so on).

In the specially manufactured goods case, who has the burden of proof? Does the other side have an argument based on the first requirement? Based on *Flowers*? Based on policy? Where will these counterarguments and rebuttals fit? Given the rough plan from Column Two, it is relatively easy to add in those pieces as needed. The added pieces are in bold-face type in the following chart.

Column Three: Refined Order/Check for Standard Features and "Moves"

- no written contract
- specially manufactured goods exception
- requirements for exception
- **party seeking exception has burden of proof**
  1. goods specially manufactured for buyer
  2. unsuitable for sale to others in ordinary course of seller's business
  3. manufacture commenced under circumstances... & prior to receipt of notice of repudiation
- **policy underlying exception**

1. goods themselves are evidence of contract
2. undue hardship for seller

- First requirement — goods specially manufactured for buyer
- "specially manufactured" not defined
- "specially manufactured" refers to nature of goods
- *Flowers*: buyer's name & artwork on wrapping material
- wrapping paper is personalized
- contrast with *Colorado Carpet*: carpeting available at outlets, so not specially manufactured
- BCC's plain language argument
- BCC's argument: like wrapping material, rugs are personalized
- distinguish rugs from carpet in *Colorado Carpet*
- Therefore, rugs specially manufactured for buyer

Working in this way, you will find that the secret to the three-column chart is that you focus on one main task with each column, and as you move through the columns, you get more and more control over the material. For example, when the writer of the specially manufactured goods memo moved from her Column Two to Column Three, she began to see that the material did fit into one of the standard organizational plans after all. By the time she had reached Column Three, she had an outline.

§ 20.2.4 Organize with Index Cards or Post-It Notes

Another way of creating organization that is similar to the three-column chart is to organize with index cards or post-it notes. Simply write down each point on one card or note and then lay them all out on a large surface — the kitchen table or your bedroom floor will work. Start grouping the cards as you see points that are related to each other. Once you have a few groups, make some basic decisions about what goes before what. Because each point is on a card, it is easy to manipulate the points and try out different organizational schemes. Once you have them in order, voila! You have your outline.

§ 20.2.5 Try a Tree-Branching Diagram

If you are struggling to figure out how to organize the pieces of a complex law, use a sheet of paper (it is hard to do one of these on a computer) and construct a tree-branching diagram. Tree-branching diagrams can help you get a clear picture of how the pieces and steps work together.

Below is a chart for a Family and Medical Leave issue. See Chart 20.1.

Once you have a map in your mind of the legal terrain, you will need to convert the tree-branching diagram into an organizational plan for writing. The key to doing this is to use headings, roadmaps, signposts, transitions, and a mini-conclusion to help readers follow where they are in the analysis.

Chart 20.1   Tree-Branching Diagram

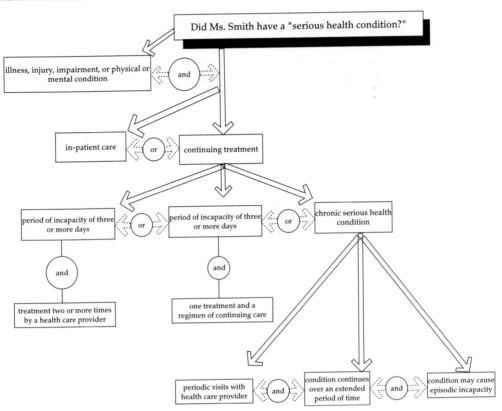

Start by creating a coherent numbering and lettering system for the headings so that they signal how the pieces fit together. Then use a roadmap sentence to introduce each "branch" in the diagram and signposts to make it clear when several "twigs" are all under one branch. Add transitions such as "in addition to proving [insert element or sub-element] for conjunctive elements or "in the alternative" to signal disjunctive elements to remind readers how the parts work together. Finally, include mini-conclusions to wrap up a section or subsection and keep readers (and yourself) clear about how the pieces were adding up.

The outline below contains only the headings, roadmaps, signposts, and transitions for the FMLA issue in the tree-branching diagram; the ellipsis indicates where the analysis would be developed. Citations have been omitted for the example.

I. Did Ms. Smith have a serious health condition?

To establish that she had a serious health condition, Ms. Smith must prove the following: (1) that she had an illness, injury, impairment, or physical or mental condition that prevented her from working for three weeks and (2) either that she received (A) inpatient care or (B) continuing treatment.

. . . .

1. Did Ms. Smith have an illness, injury, impairment, or physical or mental condition that prevented her from working for three weeks?

    . . . .

2. Did Ms. Smith receive either inpatient care or continuing treatment?

In addition to proving that she had an illness, injury, impairment, or physical or mental condition that prevented her from working for three weeks, Ms. Smith must also prove that she received either (A) inpatient care or (B) continuing treatment.

A. Did Ms. Smith receive inpatient care?

    . . . .

B. Did Ms. Smith receive continuing treatment?

Even if Ms. Smith cannot prove that she received inpatient care, she can try to prove that she received continuing treatment. To do this, she will have to prove (a) that she was incapacitated for three or more days and received treatment two or more times by a health care provider; or (b) that she was incapacitated for three or more days and received treatment by a health care provider on at least one occasion, which resulted in a regimen of continuing treatment; or (c) that she suffered from a chronic health condition.

(a)   Was Ms. Smith incapacitated for three or more days and did she receive two or more treatments?

Although conceding that Ms. Smith was incapacitated for three or more days, we will argue that she did not meet the additional treatment requirement.

(b)   Was Ms. Smith incapacitated for three or more days and did she receive one treatment that resulted in a regimen of continuing treatment?

In the alternative, Ms. Smith can try to prove that in addition to being incapacitated for three or more days, she received treatment by a health care provider on at least one occasion that resulted in a regimen of continuing treatment

    . . . .

(c)   Did Ms. Smith have a chronic serious health condition?

Assuming Ms. Smith will be unable to prove the first option, that she received two or more treatments, or the second option, that she received one treatment resulting in a regimen of continuing treatment, she is left with a third and last option for proving she received continuing treatment: showing that she has a chronic serious health condition. . . .

§ 20.2.6 Talk to a Colleague

Whenever you are having trouble getting a large amount of material organized in your mind, try talking it over with a colleague. Use the approach that you are going to explain the issue(s) to your listener. As you are talking, notice how you naturally organize the material. Jot down key words and phrases that come to mind as you are speaking. Don't be afraid to talk through the parts with which you are having the most difficulty. It may free you to address these areas if you begin by saying something like "this is the part I'm having trouble with" or "this is the part that is still rough in my mind." Let your listener question you and provide his or her own insights.

If talking out the issue(s) seemed helpful, sit down immediately afterwards and write out the organization you discovered as you were speaking. If talking-before-writing becomes a valuable organizing technique for you, you may even want to tape-record the talking-before-writing sessions.

§ 20.2.7 Try a New Analogy or Format

If you have a phobia about outlines, rename what it is you are doing when you develop the organization for a document. Some writers are more comfortable developing a "writing plan." Others like to think in terms of an "ordered list." You may need an entirely new analogy for what you are doing. Think instead of an architect creating a blueprint for a building or an engineer designing an aircraft.

Some people prefer horizontal flowcharts to vertical outlines. There is nothing magical about organizing ideas from top to bottom in an outline. If working from left to right in a flowchart feels more comfortable to you, do it.

Others can find and better visualize an organizational scheme by using a technique called clustering. To use clustering, simply begin by putting one main idea in a circle and then attach related subpoints. Chart 20.2 is an example of a cluster diagram.

Chart 20.2   **Cluster Diagram**

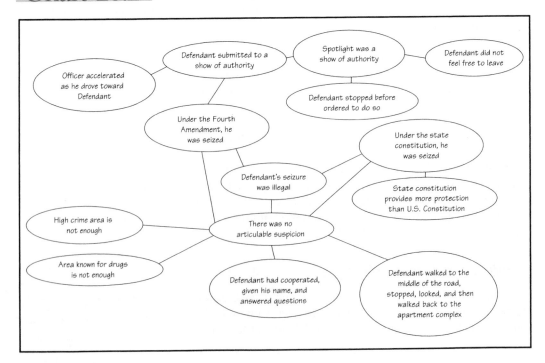

Once you have a basic cluster, begin a new circle for each main idea, each time attaching related subpoints. By continuing to expand the cluster diagram, you will end up with a map of how you are thinking about a legal problem.

Now look for clusters of ideas. These will usually become sections in the final document. You may even find that after doing the clustering diagram you can see that the material fits into one of the standard organizational plans. The final step is to translate the clustering diagram into a traditional outline.

§ 20.2.8 Consider Your Reader, Your Purpose, and How You View the Case

After spending hours doing research — in the trenches, so to speak — it is a good idea to review the basics before composing a battle plan. For either a memo or a brief, ask yourself, for whom am I writing this document? What are that reader's purposes? What are my purposes? For briefs, ask yourself, what is my overall theme? Is this a case about mistaken identity, inappropriate police procedures, self-defense, or freedom to assemble? The theme, or what some lawyers call "the theory of the case" in persuasive writing (see sections 17.3 and 18.6.2), should be evident in every section of the outline, from the statement of facts or statement of the case to the rule, discussion, or argument sections.

One final note before leaving the subject of outlines: like the blueprint for a building or the design for an aircraft, outlines should be aids for the writer, not straitjackets. Don't be afraid to change an outline when it isn't working or when you get a better idea.

§ 20.3 Drafting the Document

If creating an outline is the first stumbling block for most writers, the second comes when it is time to start drafting. Some people develop "writer's block." Faced with what seems to be an overwhelming task, the writer freezes. Nothing seems like the perfect beginning, so nothing gets written. If you tend to freeze when you must start writing, try some of the following techniques.

§ 20.3.1 Give Yourself Optimum Writing Conditions

Make writing as pleasant as possible. Start drafting at the time of day and in the place where you do your best thinking and writing. If you are a morning person, don't start drafting at 5 p.m. unless you absolutely must. If you prefer a legal pad to a computer, by all means use a legal pad. Treat yourself to a fancy new pen if that will make you feel better about writing.

§ 20.3.2 Trick Yourself into Getting Started

If you have written an outline, worked with a template, or kept research notes in your own words, you have already started drafting. By expanding outline labels into phrases, then clauses, then sentences, you can gradually slip into creating the first draft. By fleshing out your research notes, you begin developing the language that will appear in your draft. For some writers, this gradual "drift" into drafting helps them avoid writer's block.

§ 20.3.3 Write First What You Know Best

For some reason, many writers seem to think that they must write a document in order — the first sentence first, then the second sentence, the first paragraph before the second paragraph, and so on. This notion about writing is not a problem as long as the writer knows how to begin.

However, when you are not quite sure how to begin, it's often a good idea to start writing a draft at the point in the material where you are the most confident. This might be something as simple as raising and dismissing the undisputed elements. Get the writing rolling and let your subconscious work through how to begin the document.

The same is true when you are hopelessly stuck in the middle of a document. Try skipping over the problem area for a time and write another section. With a bit of luck, you may figure out what to do about the problem area without letting it bring the project to a halt.

One caution, though: if you start in the middle of a document or if you skip over a problem area for the time being, you will have to come back and make sure the sections are logically and stylistically connected.

§ 20.3.4 Get the Juices Flowing

Athletes who are preparing to perform do warm-up and stretching exercises. Some writers find that freewriting, or simply sitting down and starting to write without stopping, has similar benefits when done before drafting. The idea is to get some flow and momentum going. Other writers find that they can "get the writing juices flowing" by reading similar documents or rereading other documents they have written.

§ 20.3.5 Take It One Step at a Time

Many writers are overwhelmed by the prospect of drafting twenty pages or more. Writing a page or even just a paragraph, however, seems relatively easy. The trick then is to give yourself small parts of the whole document to do at a time.

Your goal for the next hour, for example, may be to write the rule section. Before lunch you may want to complete a paragraph about the plaintiff's policy argument on the last element. By breaking the large task into several smaller tasks, you allow yourself to focus on one part at a time and direct all your energy toward writing that part well.

§ 20.3.6 Reward Yourself

As you complete small parts of the larger writing task and as you see yourself meeting deadlines in your personal timetable, reward yourself. A reward can be something as small as a coffee break or as large as an evening off at a movie. What matters is that writing becomes a pleasurable task at which you feel successful.

§ 20.3.7 Defeat Procrastination

When it comes to writing, most of us procrastinate to some extent. We need to start drafting that motion for summary judgment, and suddenly we get an urge to check email, clean out a filing cabinet, or invite a colleague out for coffee — anything to postpone putting pen to paper or fingers to keyboard.

All the ideas presented up to now go a long way toward defeating procrastination before it starts. Tried and true time management techniques (the "to do" list, a daily schedule, rewards along the way) may do the trick. Simple things like finding the right place to work, breaking a big project into small tasks, and tricking oneself into getting started right away can also help break the negative reinforcement cycle of procrastination. Even with this bag of tricks, though, some writers find that the procrastination habit is a hard one to defeat. One reason is that we may have an overly simplistic idea about procrastination and how it affects us as writers.

Fortunately, psychologists who have studied procrastination extensively have a few insights that apply to legal writing. Some experts have described two fundamentally different types of procrastinators: the relaxed type and the tense-afraid type.[1] Relaxed procrastinators often have negative feelings about their work and blow it off by having fun, socializing, or engaging in some distracting activity. Ellis and Knaus[2] call these individuals the "easily-frustrated, self-indulgent procrastinators." They tend to describe the work as boring or stupid, and procrastinate by finding something fun to do and then rationalize that behavior.

In contrast, tense-afraid procrastinators[3] are often overwhelmed and unrealistic about how much time things take, indecisive about how to proceed, and angry or resentful about the demands being made on them. Tense-afraid procrastinators often lack confidence in their ability and fear falling short or failing.

While most experts agree that there are distinctly different types of procrastinators, they disagree on how to categorize them. L. J. S. Walker,[4] for example, divides procrastinators into four types: the Perfectionist, the Postponer, the Politician, and the Punisher. Sapadin[5] categorizes them into six types: the Perfectionist; the Dreamer, who has big ideas but can't work out the details; the Worrier; the Defier, who resists what others expect or want; the Crisis-Maker; and the Over-Doer, who is chronically over-extended.

These descriptive labels vividly capture one important truth about procrastination: there are often dramatically different reasons why people

---

1. Laura J. Solomon & Esther D. Rothblum, *Academic Procrastination: Frequency and Cognitive-Behavioral Correlates*, 31 J. Counseling Psychol. 503 (1984).

2. Albert Ellis & William Knaus, *Overcoming Procrastination* (New American Library 1977).

3. *http://mentalhelp.net/psyhelp/chap4/chap4r.htm.*

4. Lilly J. Schubert Walker, *Procrastination: Fantasies and Fears*, 25 Manitoba J. Counseling 23 (1988).

5. Linda Sapadin, *It's About Time! The Six Styles of Procrastination and How to Overcome Them* (Penguin 1997).

procrastinate. For example, some procrastinators' delaying behavior comes from an overdeveloped sense of optimism ("Why start? I have plenty of time"), while other procrastinators' habit stems from an overdeveloped sense of pessimism ("Why start? Whatever I do won't be good enough").

What does all of this mean for the legal writer who is struggling with a procrastination habit? Simply put, the advice or strategy that might be helpful for one type of procrastinator may be counterproductive for another. The key is to match the advice and strategy to the type of procrastinator and the reasons for procrastination.

For example, if you are a relaxed procrastinator, you may respond well to writing schedules with multiple mini-deadlines for each step along the way. (See § 20.1.) Because relaxed procrastinators seem to need to feel deadline pressure in order to get started, having a self-imposed deadline for completing the research, for developing an outline or organizational plan, or even for small steps such as getting the rules section drafted may help. Reporting in to someone about whether each of these mini-deadlines was met may also be helpful.

If you are a tense-afraid procrastinator, what may be most important is to recognize what not to do. Exhorting yourself to "try harder" or "get organized" may be counterproductive.[6] If you are this kind of procrastinator, better strategies are those that increase the pleasantness or reduce the unpleasantness (or the perception of unpleasantness) of the task. (See §§ 20.3.1, 20.3.6.)

One simple approach some tense-afraid procrastinators find helpful is to recall the last time they had a successful writing experience. What did they write? How did they go about completing this writing task? If they still have that successful piece of writing, they may find it helpful to reread it before starting the new writing task. The key to this approach is to build on past successes.

The fear of failure in some tense-afraid procrastinators tends to be a deep-seated psychological phenomenon far beyond the scope of this book, but the literature about procrastination provides some strategies that you may find helpful if you are a tense-afraid procrastinator. Chief among them are some simple changes in self-talk[7] from procrastinating ways of thinking to productive ways of thinking:

Procrastinating	*Productive*
I must/have to _____ or (something awful will happen).	I'd like to/choose to . . . .
I've got to finish	When can I get started on . . . ?
Oh, God, this assignment is enormous.	Where is the best place to start?
I can't succeed.	I have a better chance of succeeding if I . . . .

If you are a "perfectionist" procrastinator, you may need help setting realistic goals and developing judgment about how much time to spend on any given part of the writing task. Gently reminding yourself about

---

6. *http://mentalhelp.net/psyhelp/chap4/chap4r.htm*; Neil Fiore, *The Now Habit* 49 (Jeremy P. Tarcher, Inc., 1989).

7. Marjory Roberts, *Eight Ways to Rethink Your Work Style*, 23 Psychol. Today, no. 2 (Mar. 1989): 42; *http://mentalhelp.net/psyhelp/chap4/chap4r.htm*.

the law of diminishing returns and how it relates to efficiency versus perfectionism may help you focus on the goal — to be an effective writer, not a perfect writer — and remember that "effective" often means knowing when something is good enough to get the job done.

Perfectionists can also get bogged down when any given paragraph, sentence, or even word choice is not going well. To avoid grinding to a halt in such situations, try skipping over the problem area, at least for the moment, and continuing to work on another section while the subconscious mind works on a solution for the problem. See § 20.3.3.

If you are a "postponer" procrastinator, you may tend to have a short attention span and difficulty staying on task for long periods. Good strategies for you include (1) adjusting your writing schedule so that the writing sessions are shorter and have more variety, (2) having others structure and direct your writing activities, and (3) creating a writing schedule and sending in progress reports to someone whom you do not want to disappoint.

"Politicians" are the high-profile members of any group. They involve themselves in numerous activities and often have difficulty saying no when asked to organize an event or participate in a project. Social butterflies by nature, they want to please others. Consequently, they may have a hard time making their writing a priority. As a rule, politicians have two root causes to their procrastination: (1) they are overextended, and (2) they resist focusing on any task like writing that is more solitary than social.

If you are a "politician" procrastinator, you will probably have to cut one or more activities. Once you have carved out enough time to do your writing, consider using the strategies that make writing a more social activity. Working to develop a clear sense of who the reader is may help you see writing more as lively dialogue than lonely monologue. You may work best at writing tasks that allow you to collaborate with another writer.

Finally, no discussion of procrastination would be complete without mentioning the importance of controlling distractions. For some writers that means turning off the cell phone, cleaning the clutter from one's desk, or shutting the office door. For the majority who write on their computers, it means turning off email and the Internet and using laptops in locations that encourage rather than discourage staying focused.

§ 20.4 Revising

"Revision," or "re-vision," means "to see again." When you revise, you step back from the project and try to see it with fresh eyes. This is not an easy thing to do. Many writers have difficulty adopting a revisionist perspective. Most avoid rethinking the whole document and prefer the safety of tinkering with smaller editing issues such as sentence structure or word choice. To help make the shift from drafter to reviser, you may find one of the following techniques helpful.

§ 20.4.1 Develop a Revision Checklist

A revision checklist should focus on the large issues in writing. Below is a sample revision checklist that can be used for most documents.

Revision Checklist

- Will this document meet the reader's needs?
- Is the tone right for this document and this reader?
- Is the document well organized?
- Are the ideas well developed?
- Is the analysis conclusory or superficial? What would make it more sophisticated?
- What else should be included?
    - A plain language argument?
    - An argument based on an analogous case?
    - A policy argument?
    - A countervailing policy argument?
    - A rebuttal to an argument?
- What can be omitted?
- Is the theme, or theory of the case, evident in all sections of the document?

In the earlier chapters on writing office memoranda and briefs, we included sample revision checklists. On your own revision checklist, add any other habitual writing problems that have been pointed out to you by your legal writing professor, classmates, colleagues, or other readers.

§ 20.4.2 Write an After-the-Fact Outline

Of all the areas to rethink when you are revising, the most challenging is often the organization. One simple way to check the paper's organization is to create an after-the-fact outline, which is an outline of what you have actually written, not a plan that precedes the writing.

To create an after-the-fact outline, read each of your paragraphs and try to sum up the point in that paragraph in a phrase, clause, or, at most, a sentence. (If you can't do this summarizing, that alone suggests that the paragraph needs revision.) Record the summarizing phrase, clause, or sentence on the outline, using indentations to show the main points, subpoints, and sub-subpoints. Keep the outline on one side of a page or pages so that you can lay out the whole outline and see it all at once.

Use after-the-fact outlines the way you would an aerial photograph of ground you just covered on a hike. Seen from this perspective, is the way you traveled through the material the most efficient one? Did you do any needless backtracking? Repetition? Did you miss anything along the way? If so, where can you easily add it?

Now that you have the "big picture" in mind, are there ways you can prepare your reader for the twists and turns your path will take? For example, are there insights you should add to your roadmap paragraph that will help your reader? What kinds of signposts will help the reader stay on track? See section 21.2.

§ 20.4.3 Do a Self-Critique

Leave the role of the writer and become a critical reader. Play the devil's advocate. Where can you punch holes in this thing? Where are its weaknesses? Where are its strengths? Using what you find, you can return to the role of the writer and improve the draft.

§ 20.4.4 Check for Unity and Coherence

For a draft to be well written, the entire document, as well as each paragraph and section, must have unity and coherence. Unity at the document level means that every part of the document contributes to the overall thesis. In a legal memorandum, the thesis is essentially the same as your conclusion.

Many writers, though, do not have a clear idea of what their thesis is until they have completed a draft. While drafting, however, they discover what it is they are trying to say. This way of arriving at a thesis, or controlling idea, is perfectly fine. What it means, though, is that now that the writer has discovered the thesis he or she must go back through the draft with that thesis in mind and make sure that all parts are working toward that goal.

The same process may be true at the paragraph level. The writer may begin drafting the paragraph without a clear idea of what point he or she is trying to make. After drafting the paragraph, however, the writer discovers what the point is and how it contributes to the larger whole. At this point, then, the writer should first add or revise the topic sentence and then go back through the paragraph to make sure all the parts contribute to the paragraph's point. (See section 22.2.1 for more about unity.)

Like unity, coherence is also important at both the document and the paragraph level. Consequently, a good revision strategy is to check at both the document and the paragraph levels to see if you are using the common devices for creating coherence.

- logical organization
  - chronological, spatial, topical
  - general to specific, specific to general
  - IRAC: issues, rules, application, conclusion
- roadmap paragraphs
- topic sentences
- signposts, dovetailing, and transitions
- repetition of key terms
- parallelism
- pronouns

See section 22.3.2 for more about how these devices create coherence.

Two final points about revising: first, drafting and revising are not always distinct stages in the writing process; some revising occurs even as the first draft is being written. Second, if possible, do some revising on a hard copy. Seeing your writing just on a computer screen can be misleading. Because you can see only a small portion of the whole document at a time, you may overlook problems with some of the larger issues in writing.

§ 20.5 Editing

Editing is an examination of the smaller issues in writing. As with revising, you must once again step out of the role of the drafter and look at the writing with a critical eye, but this time the critical eye is focused on smaller issues such as sentence structure and word choice.

When editing sentence structure, writers should pay particular attention to the subjects and verbs of their sentences. If the subject-verb combination is effective, many other writing problems will clear up automatically. See Section 8.2.1 and Chapter 24.

Legal writers should also make an extra effort to edit for precision and conciseness. See sections 25.1 and 25.2. Sloppy word choice and added verbiage may be overlooked in other types of writing, but they are unforgivable in legal writing. In addition to editing for sentence structure and word choice, each writer should edit for his or her habitual problem areas.

If this seems like a lot to think about all at once, you are right. For this reason, many writers find it easier to edit for just one or two writing problems at a time. If, for example, your habitual problem is wordiness, do one reading with the single goal of editing out all unnecessary words.

Editing Tips

1. Don't let yourself fall in love with a particular phrase or sentence. No matter how well crafted it might be, if it doesn't work with the whole paragraph, indeed the whole document, it is not an effective phrase or sentence.

2. Be selective about whom you ask for editing advice. Although you can sometimes get excellent editing advice from others, there are far too many examples of the blind leading the mildly nearsighted. What often works better is to notice the parts of the paper that your reader/editor pointed out as problems and figure out with that reader what threw him or her off track. This procedure is much less risky than the unquestioning use of an inexperienced editor's rewrites.

3. Read your writing aloud or, better yet, have a colleague read it aloud to you while you follow along on another copy. Mark any part that the reader misreads or stumbles over or anything that just doesn't sound right. This technique will not tell you how to fix something, but it will give you a good idea of what needs to be fixed.

4. Spend the majority of your editing time on the section(s) of the document that you found hardest to write. No need to keep massaging the opening sentence long after you know it reads smoothly. Force yourself to focus your editing energy on the rockiest parts of the paper.

5. As with revising, if at all possible, do some of your editing on hard copy. The same language looks slightly different on a page than it does on a computer screen. For some reason, that small change from screen to page allows you to see the writing with different, fresh eyes.

§ 20.6 Proofreading

Whether you or your secretary types your writing, you will be the one who is responsible for the final product. Any missed words, format problems, and typos are ultimately your missed words, format problems, or typos. Consequently, every lawyer, no matter how competent his or her support staff, needs to know a few simple proofreading strategies.

First of all, proofreading is a distinct skill. It is not the same as normal reading or revising or editing. It is reading for errors. Consequently, to proofread properly, you need to remember a few important things.

Slow down. Speed-reading and proofreading are mutually exclusive terms. Proofreading should be done at your slowest reading rate. One technique for slowing yourself down is to cover up all but the line you are proofreading with another sheet of paper. This technique also helps you to focus on the individual words on the page, so you will see transposed letters in the middle of words and notice missing words rather than read them in where they should be.

Consider proofreading the last third of your document first. Chances are there are more errors in the last sections simply because you or your typist were probably more tired and rushed when they were done. If that's true, then it makes sense to use the time when you are freshest on the part of the document that needs your energy the most.

If at all possible, do your proofreading at a completely separate time — ideally, a day or more after you have completed your drafting and revising. Even a small break in time allows you to see the document anew and to bring fresh eyes to the pages.

Proofread all parts of the document, including headings, charts, appendices, captions, and page numbers.

Double check all dates and monetary figures and the spelling of every name.

Finally, do not be lulled into complacency by spell-check. Even the best computer software does not know a "trail" from a "trial."

§ 20.7　Myths About Writing

No one seems to know exactly where they come from, but over the years a number of myths have developed about writing. Many of these myths have been repeated and even taught to several generations of students so that they now have an air of legitimacy. They seem to be part of the common knowledge about writing, although one never sees them repeated in reputable composition textbooks.

The most unfortunate consequence of these myths is the unnecessary constraints they place on sophisticated writers. A good writer, for example, may labor mightily to avoid splitting an infinitive only to find that all the other options are awkward or imprecise. Still, the myth hovers over the writer's head, creating uneasiness about using split infinitives.

What to do? Because at least some of the myths are treated as gospel by some readers, it is probably unwise to make split infinitives or any of the other myths a trademark of your writing style. When another equally good construction is available, use it instead. But when the best thing to do is to split the infinitive or start the sentence with "but" (as this sentence does) or to violate any of these other non-rules, do so — and do so without guilt.

Myth: Never Split an Infinitive

Grammar historians tell us that we acquired this non-rule at the time grammarians attempted to force the English language into the Latin grammar system. In Latin, infinitives are one word; hence, Latin infinitives are never split. Without regard to either the obvious fact that infinitives are two words in English (to see, to argue, to determine) or the obvious fact that speakers of English regularly split infinitives with a modifier, the non-rule was created so that English grammar would conform to Latin grammar.

This all seems terribly silly until you remember that at the time English was considered an inferior, upstart, unruly language and Latin was considered a superior, well-designed, systematic language. Moreover, devising a grammar that actually described the way English was used was unheard of at the time. The purpose of grammar, it was thought, was to bring order to a language raging out of control.

What should a legal writer do then about split infinitives? Because the split infinitive myth is entrenched in many educated readers' minds, it is not worth the possible negative reaction to a given split infinitive if there are reasonably good ways to change it. In fact, many split infinitives are redundant ("to completely comprehend," "to finally finish") and need the modifier removed.

However, when the split infinitive is the best, indeed the most precise, way to express a point, stand your ground and use it. Note, however, that infinitives should not be split by the word "not." The correct way to write the negative form of an infinitive is to place the "not" before the infinitive.

EXAMPLE   **Incorrect**

The defendant explained that to not attend the meeting would have drawn undue attention to him.

EXAMPLE   **Revised**

The defendant explained that not to attend the meeting would have drawn undue attention to him.
or

The defendant explained that not attending the meeting would have drawn undue attention to him.

Myth: Never Start a Sentence with "And," "But," or "Or"

Although there is no real rule that you may not start a sentence with "and," "but," or "or," it is often a good idea to choose a more specific transition. If using one of these three words is a hasty or lazy choice, it is probably the wrong choice.

Occasionally, however, one of these three words is the perfect transition, especially because each is a one-syllable word that gets the next sentence started quickly. For this reason, it is usually not a good idea to start a sentence with "and," "but," or "or" and then follow the conjunction with a comma. When you do, you start the sentence up quickly only to immediately slow it down.

One final caveat about using "and," "but," or "or" at the beginnings of sentences: as transitions, these three words tend to sound informal.

Myth: Never Start a Sentence with "Because" or "However"

Legal writers often need to describe cause/effect relationships. In such cases, the best sentence structure is often "Because [fill in the cause], [fill in the effect]." This is an exceedingly useful sentence structure, and no rule prohibits its use.

Similarly, no rule prohibits beginning a sentence with "however." Stylistically, however, it is often a better idea to move the transition "however" further into the sentence so that it immediately precedes the point of contrast, as is the case in this sentence.

Myth: Never End a Sentence with a Preposition

Winston Churchill did more than anyone else to debunk this writing myth. Churchill pointed out the idiocy of this non-rule when he wrote the following marginal comment on a state document: "This is the sort of English up with which I will not put."

Notwithstanding Churchill's remark, many readers claim to be offended by sentences that end with prepositions. For this reason, it is not a good practice to end sentences with prepositions when they can be easily revised.

Draft

EXAMPLE

Winfield may be able to get title to the entire triangle, not just the part that the bathhouse is built on.

Revised

Winfield may be able to get title to the entire triangle, not just the part on which the bathhouse is built.

Notice that some sentences ending with a preposition are not easily revised using the technique above because the preposition works with the verb to create a meaning that is different from the meaning of the verb alone. For example, "to put up with" has a meaning far different from the meaning of "to put." Consequently, the best way to revise such verb + preposition combinations is to use a synonym ("to put up with" = "to tolerate").

Myth: Never Write a One-Sentence Paragraph

One-sentence paragraphs are not wrong per se, although they are often a sign of lack of development of the ideas in the writing. Numerous one-sentence paragraphs have the added drawback of making the writing seem unsophisticated.

For these reasons, use one-sentence paragraphs infrequently. Save them for occasions when the paragraph serves as a transition between two large sections of a document or when a shorter paragraph will give the reader a breather between two extremely long paragraphs. Notice too that a well-written one-sentence paragraph is usually made up of a fairly long sentence, although on rare occasions a one-sentence paragraph composed of a short sentence can be quite dramatic. See section 22.4 for more about paragraph length.

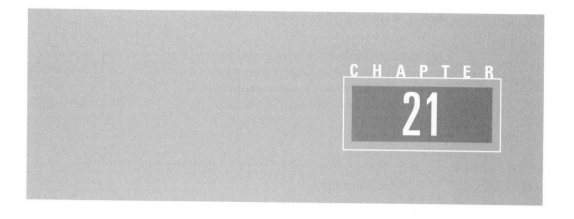

CHAPTER

21

Connections Between Paragraphs

§ 21.1 Headings

Headings serve two purposes for the reader: they signal the overall organization, and they help the reader locate where he or she is in a document. As indicators of organization, headings work a bit like a table of contents. They give the reader the framework within which to fit the ideas.

As locating devices, headings are invaluable to readers. A reader who does not have the time to read the whole document can use the headings to find the exact section he or she must read. For readers who have read the whole document and later need to refer to a point, headings are a quick way to locate that point.

Like all other headings, argumentative headings in briefs must be both indicators of overall organization and locating devices. In addition, they must persuade. See section 17.9 for more on writing argumentative headings.

Even though headings in objective memos are somewhat less important to the overall document than argumentative headings are in a brief, they still must be well written. The best headings in memos are fairly short — not more than one typed line and usually less than half a line — and they capture the content in a nutshell.

For headings to be helpful organizational indicators, they must be written in parallel form (see section 27.7) and in a consistent format. If the document has headings and subheadings, the reader will be able to identify the different levels of headings if they use compatible but different formats. For example, the main headings may use roman numerals and boldface and the subheadings may use capital letters and underlining. See section 29.2.2 for capitalization in headings.

EXAMPLE   **Format for Headings**

I. Main Heading

A. <u>Subheading</u>
B. <u>Subheading</u>

II. Main Heading

A. <u>Subheading</u>
B. <u>Subheading</u>

When creating headings, remember the time-honored advice that "You can't have a 1 without a 2, and you can't have an A without a B." In other words, do not create a heading or a subheading unless there is at least one more heading or subheading at that same level.

Developing a good format for headings is simple. The bigger challenge is composing their content. To be useful finding devices, headings must capture the essence of the section that the heading introduces with enough specificity to be meaningful and enough generality to encompass the entire section.

Often the law itself will suggest the content of various sections of the document and hence the headings. An elements analysis or a list of factors, for example, lends itself to a document with the elements or factors as the headings.

But do not automatically assume that each element or factor deserves its own heading. Because undisputed elements will probably require minimal discussion, the document will appear chopped up if the writer uses a separate heading for each one. More important, the reader is not likely to need a heading for each undisputed element.

To compose good headings, find the key words and phrases that sum up the section. Sometimes the easiest way to write a heading is to reread the section and ask yourself, "In a nutshell, what is this section about?" The answer should be close to what would make a good heading. For example, if the answer is "the court's lack of jurisdiction in this matter," then omit what can be easily inferred and the heading becomes "Lack of Jurisdiction."

But suppose you are writing an office memo for a case and your answer to the question "what is this section about?" is something like "whether or not the court will admit the eyewitnesses' line-up identifications." Although this clause may accurately sum up the section, consider how it will look as a heading:

Weak Heading

A. Whether or Not the Court Will Admit the Eyewitnesses' Line-Up Identifications

The example heading exceeds the one-line limit and includes some information that the reader can easily infer. Now consider these four substitute headings for the same section:

Substitute Headings

1. The Line-up

2. Line-Up Identifications

3. Admissibility of Line-Up Identifications

4. Admissibility of Eyewitnesses' Line-Up Identifications

Option 1 is probably too general. It is unlikely the following section will include everything about the line-up. Option 2 is better. Even so, if the focus of the following section is on the admissibility of the identifications, that key word in the heading will be helpful to the reader. Option 4 is also acceptable, but the word "eyewitnesses" can probably be inferred. Option 3 is the best. It sums up the section; it includes the key words and phrases; and it is short enough to be read at a glance.

One last thought about headings: headings are for the reader, not the writer. The most common mistake legal writers make regarding headings is to use them as crutches for the writer. Headings should not be used as artificial bridges between two sections of the document. The connection between the sections should be made without the heading. If the headings in a document are removed, the sections should still flow naturally from one to the next.

§ 21.2 Roadmaps and Signposts

§ 21.2.1 Roadmaps

Roadmaps are introductory paragraphs that give readers an overview of the entire document. They give readers the "big picture" perspective so that the readers will be able to understand how numerous discrete bits of information fit together in the larger whole.

Like real roadmaps, roadmap paragraphs orient readers in several ways: they establish the overall structure of the discussion; they suggest what will be important and hence what deserves the readers' particular attention; and they create expectations for how the discussion will unfold and conclude.

Although not every objective memo needs a roadmap paragraph, those with several steps in the analysis are easier to read if the writer uses a roadmap to set the stage for what follows. For example, the attorney writing a memo on whether electromagnetic fields are a nuisance used the following roadmap to show the two steps in the court's analysis.

EXAMPLE   **Sample Roadmap Paragraph**

In deciding whether New Mexico will allow a cause of action in nuisance, the New Mexico courts are likely to look first at whether EMFs constitute a public nuisance and then at whether they constitute a private nuisance.

A roadmap paragraph like the one that follows provides a helpful overview of how the court will analyze a particular issue.

EXAMPLE   **Sample Roadmap Paragraph**

The McKibbins claim that because there was no written contract, the oral contract is unenforceable under this state's version of the UCC Statute of Frauds. The first thing the court will have to determine, then, is whether the UCC applies at all. If the court finds that the UCC does govern the contract, the court will then have to decide whether the Statute of Frauds bars BCC's claim. Because BCC did not comply with the formal requirements of the Statute of Frauds, the court will find that the contract is unenforceable unless one of the exceptions included in the Statute applies. The only exception likely to apply is the specially manufactured goods exception.

A good roadmap paragraph also tells readers where to focus their attention. For example, if the applicable law includes several elements or factors, the reader will find it helpful to be told in the roadmap paragraph which elements or factors are critical to a case.

EXAMPLE   **Sample Roadmap Paragraph**

To claim a prescriptive easement, the Oregon Wilderness Watchers will have to satisfy four elements by clear and convincing evidence: (1) that its use was open and notorious; (2) that its use was continuous and uninterrupted; (3) that its use was adverse to the right of the owner; and (4) that its use of the property met each of the other requirements for over ten years. *See Martin v. G.B. Enters., LLC*, 98 P.3d 1168, 1170 (Or. Ct. App. 2004). Although OWW should have no difficulty satisfying the first and fourth elements, the second element and especially the third element will be difficult to satisfy.

Roadmap paragraphs that use the "first, we will look at _____;
then we will look at _____; and finally we will look
at _____" approach tend to sound unsophisticated. Substituting
"I" or "this memorandum" is no better. A better approach is to use the court as
the actor. "First, the court must determine _____; if the court
finds _____, it must then consider _____."

Compare the following roadmap paragraphs. Notice how much more sophisticated Examples 2 and 3 sound. Example 2 uses the two parties as actors to get away from the "you and me, dear reader" approach and to set up a logical progression of subissues. Notice that "we" in Example 2 refers to the client and attorney, not to the writer and reader. Example 3 uses the court as the actor, so it is now clear to the reader that the memorandum is tracking the court's decisionmaking process.

Unsophisticated Roadmap   EXAMPLE 1

In this memorandum, we will examine three issues. First, we will look at whether the statute applies. If we find that it does not, then we will look at whether the Oregon Wilderness Watchers had an easement. If we find that an easement was created, then we will examine the scope of the easement.

Better Roadmap   EXAMPLE 2

Our client would like to prevent or limit the use of a path across his property by the Oregon Wilderness Watchers (OWW). An Oregon statute exists that provides for public recreational use while protecting the owner's interest in his land, and we will argue that it applies to this case. OWW will contend that the statute does not apply and that a prescriptive easement exists. If a prescriptive easement does exist, our client wants to limit the scope of its use.

Better Roadmap   EXAMPLE 3

In deciding this case, the court will consider three issues. First, the court will determine whether the statute applies. If it does not, the court will then determine whether the Oregon Wilderness Watchers had an easement. If the court determines that an easement had been created, the court will then decide the scope of the easement.

§ 21.2.2 Signposts

Signposts are those words and phrases that keep readers oriented as they progress through a piece of writing. They can be used as a connecting thread throughout a whole document or throughout a smaller section.

To be the most effective, a series of signposts need to be signaled in advance. For example, a writer may signal a series of signposts when he or she opens a section by saying, "There are four exceptions to the Statute of Frauds." In the subsequent discussion, the writer can then use the words "first," "second," "third," "fourth" (or "final" or "last"), and "exception" to signal shifts to each new exception.

The following example is an excerpt from a memo about whether a contract is enforceable under the UCC Statute of Frauds. The setup for the signpost series and the signposts are in boldface type.

EXAMPLE   ## Signposts

There are four exceptions to the Statute of Frauds, but three of them are not applicable. The first of these inapplicable exceptions, Col. Rev. Stat. § 4-2-201(2)(2005), applies only to transactions "between merchants." In an earlier section, § 4-2-104(1), a merchant is defined as "a person who deals in goods of the kind or otherwise holds himself out as having knowledge or skill peculiar to the practices or goods involved in the transaction or to whom such knowledge or skill may be attributed by his employment of an agent or broker or other intermediary who by his occupation holds himself out as having such knowledge or skill." Because the McKibbins presumably had little or no experience in the carpeting business and because they hired no intermediary to negotiate the transaction for them, the court will probably not find that they are merchants. This exception, then, does not apply.

The second inapplicable exception, § 4-2-201(3)(b), provides that a contract that does not satisfy the requirements of subsection (1) is still enforceable if the party against whom enforcement is sought admits in his pleading, testimony, or otherwise in court that a contract for sale was made. Because we are not at the litigation stage of this case yet, this exception does not apply.

The third inapplicable exception, § 4-2-201(3)(c), provides that a contract is enforceable with respect to goods for which payment has been made and accepted or which have been received and accepted. The McKibbins made no payment for the rugs, and they never received the rugs, so this exception also does not apply.

The exception that may be applicable is the exception for specially manufactured goods. . . .

Notice that most signpost series use the ordinal numbers (first, second, third, and so on) before a noun such as "element," "exception," "factor," "issue," "part," "prong," "reason," "requirement," "question," or "section."

EXAMPLE   ## Signposts

Three Issues

the first issue, the second issue, the third issue

A Two-Part Test

the first part of the test, the second part of the test

Three Questions to Consider

the first question, the second question, the final question

Once a signpost series is set up, do not change terminology. If there were "three questions" in the introduction to the series, it may confuse readers if the second question is suddenly relabeled "the second issue." See section 25.1.4.

Do not worry that legal readers will find such consistency boring. Legal readers are reading for information, not entertainment. Consistent terminology in signposts adds to the document's clarity.

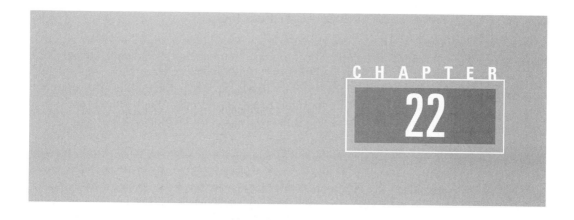

Effective Paragraphs

§ 22.1 The Function of a Paragraph

Paragraphs exist for many reasons. First, they help writers organize what they are writing. Second, they help readers see and understand that organization. Third, they give readers a psychological, as well as a logical, break.

Writers need paragraphs to help them stay in control of what they are writing. Paragraphs are like tidy boxes in which to sort information. They make writing a manageable task.

Readers need paragraphs so that they can absorb information in manageable bits. If the typical legal reader must comprehend twenty hours' worth of research in the roughly twenty minutes it takes to study an eight-page memo, he or she will need some way to see significant groupings of ideas. That way is the paragraph.

But paragraphing is more than a matter of logic and organization. It is also a matter of reader comfort and aesthetics. After all, those "boxes" into which the writer is fitting ideas can be huge containers that are too heavy to lift or small cartons with barely enough room for half an idea.

When paragraphs are too long, readers tend to become bewildered, even lost, or worse, lulled into inattention. Paragraphs that are too short, on the other hand, make the writing and the thinking seem skimpy and inconsequential. Readers need paragraphs that are the right size to comfortably follow what the writer is saying.

Paragraphs also change the look of a page. They create more white space, which can be a welcome relief. Anyone who has opened a book to see a solid mass of type on page one knows how intimidating overly long paragraphs can be. In contrast, the visual break at the beginning of a paragraph signals a brief mental breather.

As the first significant grouping of sentences, a paragraph becomes a kind of mini-composition all its own. It has a beginning, a middle, and an end.

The following paragraph, which is taken from the middle of an argument section of a brief in opposition to a motion to disclose the identity of a state informant, illustrates how a paragraph is a mini-composition.

EXAMPLE

Beginning   The fact that the informant is present at the alleged drug transaction is not determinative of whether the testimony of that informant is relevant or necessary. *Lewandowski v. State*, 389 N.E.2d 706, 710 (Ind. 1979). In *Lewandowski*, the Indiana Supreme Court held that "[m]ere presence of the informer when marijuana was sold to a police officer has been held to be insufficient to overcome the privilege of nondisclosure." *Id.* The court reached the same conclusion **Middle**   on nearly identical facts in *Craig v. State*, 404 N.E.2d 580 (Ind. 1980) (informant introduced officer to defendant and was present during purchase of illegal drugs). In the present **Ending**   case, the State's informant served mainly as a line of introduction and as such her testimony does not automatically become relevant or necessary to the defendant's case simply because she was present at the scene.

---

§ 22.2 Paragraph Patterns

Every paragraph needs a focus, a topic, a point to make. In addition, every paragraph needs a shape, a way of moving through sentences to make that point. The example paragraph in section 22.1 about the relevance of the informant's testimony has one of the most common shapes or patterns: that of a fat hourglass.

An hourglass paragraph begins with a general statement about the topic. This statement may take up one or more sentences. The paragraph then narrows to the specific support or elaboration or explanation the writer has

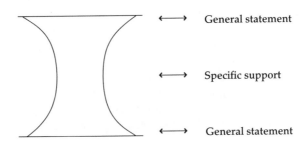

⟷ General statement

⟷ Specific support

⟷ General statement

for that general statement. The paragraph concludes with a more general sentence or two about the topic.

More common in legal writing is a variation of this pattern: the V-shaped paragraph. Like the hourglass paragraph, the V-shaped paragraph begins with a general discussion of the topic and then narrows to the specific support. The V-shaped paragraph ends with the specific support; it does not return to a general statement.

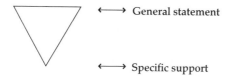

General statement

Specific support

Both the hourglass and the V-shaped paragraph patterns work well in legal writing. Both use the opening sentence or sentences as an overview of what is to come and then proceed to support that generalization with specifics.

V-Shaped Paragraph

Kraft Savings, one of three savings and loans repre-   **General statement**
sented on Kraft Island, does a significant amount of the
banking business on Kraft Island. As of 2000, Kraft Savings
had 2.2 million dollars in deposits, 9.6 million dollars in
outstanding loans, and a large volume of business with the   **Specific support**
Kraft City Council. In 2000, Kraft Savings handled 40 million
dollars in transactions for almost 1,900 customers in about
2,400 accounts.

---

§ 22.3   Unity and Coherence in Paragraphs

§ 22.3.1   Paragraph Unity

To be a mini-composition, a paragraph must have its own topic — that is, its own point to make, and all elements in the paragraph must work together to make that point. When they do, the paragraph has unity. Look again at the paragraph about the state informant.

Unified Paragraph

The fact that the informant is present at the alleged drug transaction is not determinative of whether the testimony of that informant is relevant or necessary. *Lewandowski v. State*, 389 N.E.2d 706, 710 (Ind. 1979). In *Lewandowski*, the Indiana

Supreme Court held that "[m]ere presence of the informer when marijuana was sold to a police officer has been held to be insufficient to overcome the privilege of nondisclosure." *Id.* The court reached the same conclusion on nearly identical facts in *Craig v. State*, 404 N.E.2d 580 (Ind. 1980) (informant introduced officer to defendant and was present during purchase of illegal drugs). In the present case, the State's informant served mainly as a line of introduction and as such her testimony does not automatically become relevant or necessary to the defendant's case simply because she was present at the scene.

All of the information is about one topic: the informant's testimony is not necessarily relevant or necessary simply because the informant was present at the drug transaction. This topic is introduced at the beginning of the paragraph by a topic sentence, developed and supported by two sentences in the middle of the paragraph, and then concluded by the last sentence.

What the paragraph does not do is stray from this topic. Even though the writer will need to refer to both *Lewandowski* and *Craig* later in the memo to support other points, he or she did not get sidetracked and try to do it here. The paragraph stays on course and makes its point. It has a clear focus; it has unity.

§ 22.3.2 Paragraph Coherence

When a paragraph is coherent, the various elements of the paragraph are connected in such a way that the reader can easily follow the writer's development of ideas. Coherence can be achieved in a number of ways: by using familiar organizational patterns, particularly those that are established patterns for legal writing; by establishing and then using key terms; and by using sentence structure and other coherence devices to reinforce the connections between ideas.

a. Using Familiar Organizational Patterns

All readers expect certain patterns — cause/effect, problem/solution, chronological order — and when writers meet those expectations, the ideas are easy to follow. Legal readers have some additional patterns they expect in legal writing. For example, once a rule, standard, or definition has been laid out, legal readers expect it to be applied. They expect a court's holding to be followed by its rationale. In office memos, arguments are almost always followed by counterarguments. In both office memos and briefs, the IRAC pattern (issue, rule, analysis/application, and conclusion) and all its variations are commonplace and expected.

Writers can also achieve coherence in paragraphs by creating reader expectations and then fulfilling them. For example, when a writer sets up a list of factors, elements, reasons, or issues, the reader expects the writing to follow up on that list. In the following paragraph, the writer uses this technique to create a coherent discussion of how the statutory term "ways of this state" will be construed in a case in which an intoxicated driver was on the shoulder of the road.

Coherent Paragraph

A narrow construction of the term "ways" is unlikely. In fact, there are two strong indications that Montana will favor a broad construction: (1) an extension stated in the statutory definition of "highway"; and (2) an interpretation of "ways" given in a Montana Supreme Court decision. By statutory definition, "[h]ighway means the entire width between the boundary lines of every publicly maintained way when any part thereof is open to the use of the public for purposes of vehicular travel, *except that for the purpose of chapter 8 the term also includes ways which have been or shall be dedicated to public use*" (emphasis added). Mont. Code Ann. § 61-1-201 (2003). Chapter 8 includes offenses committed while under the influence of alcohol. Because the legislature expanded the statutory definition for alcohol-related offenses, it follows that the legislature intended to broaden, not narrow, the term. Following the legislature's lead, the Montana Supreme Court stipulated that "ways" encompasses state and county right-of-ways, including borrow pits, which road maintenance crews use as sources of dirt and gravel. *State v. Taylor*, 661 P.2d 33, 35 (Mont. 1983). It is highly unlikely that the court would include borrow pits but exempt shoulders from the term "ways." Therefore, the court will probably conclude that Mr. Renko's truck was on the ways of the state open to the public.

b. Using Key Terms

Of the various methods writers have for creating coherence, repetition of key terms is the easiest and one of the most important. In the following example paragraph about the state informant, we have used different typefaces for each of the key terms — informant, **present** or **presence**, testimony, and RELEVANT OR NECESSARY — so you can see how the repetition of key terms gives the paragraph coherence. Together the key TERMS are part of a network of connecting threads that create a coherent theme for the paragraph.

With Key Terms Highlighted

The fact that the informant is **present** at the alleged drug transaction is not determinative of whether the testimony of that informant is RELEVANT OR NECESSARY. *Lewandowski v. State*, 389 N.E.2d 706, 710 (Ind. 1979). In *Lewandowski*, the Indiana Supreme Court held that "[m]ere **presence** of the informer when marijuana was sold to a police officer has been held to be insufficient to overcome the privilege of nondisclosure." *Id.* The court reached the same conclusion on nearly identical facts in *Craig v. State*, 404 N.E.2d 580 (Ind. 1980) (informant introduced officer to defendant and was **present** during purchase of illegal drugs). In the present case, the state's informant served mainly as a line of introduction and as such her testimony does not automatically become RELEVANT OR NECESSARY to the defendant's case simply because she was **present** at the scene.

The following paragraph from the memo concerning the intoxicated driver on the shoulder of the road also demonstrates the repetition of key terms. Notice how the writer makes logical connections between the key terms to show that **ways of the state open to the public** may not be construed to include SHOULDERS of the road.

EXAMPLE

With Key Terms Highlighted

Although the primary issue of the case focuses upon resolving questions pertaining to actual physical control, the issue of whether Mr. Renko's truck was on the **ways of the state open to the public** deserves brief analysis. The traffic code states that " '**ways of the state open to the public**' means any highway, road, alley, lane, parking area, or other public or private place <u>adapted and fitted for public travel</u> that is in common use by the public." Mont. Code Ann. § 61-8-101(1) (2003). The language specifically states "<u>adapted and fitted for public travel</u>." Because Mr. Renko's truck was found on the SHOULDER, the court would have to determine whether the SHOULDER of a highway is <u>adapted and fitted for public travel</u>. In defining other statutory language, the Montana Supreme Court resorted to dictionary definitions. Webster defines "SHOULDER" as "either edge of a roadway; specifically: the part of the roadway *outside the <u>traveled</u> way*" (emphasis added). It is possible, then, that the court could interpret the statutory language narrowly and conclude that the term **"ways"** does not encompass SHOULDERS.

c. Using Sentence Structure and Other Coherence Devices

Writers can also create coherence through sentence structure and through a number of other common coherence devices. Dovetails (beginning a sentence with a reference to the preceding sentence) and other transitions create connections by establishing links between sentences. See section 23.3. Parallelism within a sentence or between sentences shows the reader which ideas should be considered together and which should be compared and contrasted. See section 27.7. Even pronouns in their own small way provide subtle links within the writing because they are a connection to the noun they replace.

For the following paragraph, notice how the parallel phrases "on the defendant's ability to operate the vehicle" and "on the vehicle's condition" in the opening topic sentence set up the organizational pattern. The writer then signals the beginning of each half of the discussion by using the parallel sentence openers "in focusing on the defendant's condition" and "in focusing on the vehicle's condition." Note too the dovetailing between sentences 2 and 3 ("he would have been able to operate the vehicle" → "not only is it possible that he could have operated the truck") and between sentences 4 and 5 ("defined" → "by that definition"). Pronouns also subtly provide coherence ("defendant," → "he," "truck," → "it," "court," → "it").

EXAMPLE

Creating Coherence

If some form of operability is required, then the court must decide whether to focus on the defendant's ability to operate the vehicle or on the vehicle's condition. *See State v. Smelter*, 36 Wn. App. 439, 444, 674 P.2d 690 (1983). In focusing on the defendant's condition, the court could find that because the defendant had the key and was in the cab of the truck, he would have been able to operate the vehicle had he been awakened. Not only is it possible that he could have operated the truck, it is evident that he did drive the truck from the tavern to the freeway before parking it on the shoulder. In focusing on the vehicle's condition, the Washington court used the trial court's "reasonably operable" standard and defined that term as any malfunction short of a cracked block or a similar problem that would render the vehicle totally inoperable. *Id.* at 693. By that definition, Mr. Renko's truck was reasonably operable regardless of whether it would start. Therefore, if the Montana court considers operability an issue, it would probably find that Mr. Renko was capable of operating the vehicle and that the vehicle was in reasonably operable condition.

To sum up, then, if a paragraph has unity, it has all the right pieces. If a paragraph is both unified and coherent, then all the right pieces are arranged and connected in such a way that the reader can easily follow them.

§ 22.4 Paragraph Length

First, the truth. Not all paragraphs are three to five sentences long. Most are, but not all. In fact, quite a few well-written paragraphs are as short as two sentences; and, yes, some well-written paragraphs contain only one sentence. One-sentence paragraphs are neither a goal to strive for nor a taboo to be feared. Writers simply need to know when they have finished what they set out to do in the paragraph.

Similarly, good paragraphs may run many sentences longer than five. It is not outrageous for a paragraph in legal writing to include seven or even eight sentences, as long as the writer needed that many to make the point. However, writers should keep in mind the reader's comfort and avoid seven- and eight-sentence paragraphs about complicated discussions of law. Remember too that an eight-sentence paragraph is likely to create a solid page of type, which has a negative psychological impact on readers.

The following five-paragraph example is from a section in an appellate brief. Notice the number of sentences in and the length of each paragraph. Citation sentences are not counted as substantive sentences.

Variety in Paragraph Length

EXAMPLE

I. The Trial Court Erred in Holding That the Plaintiff Is a Public Figure as a Matter of Law

The states have a legitimate interest in compensating plaintiffs for damage to reputation inflicted through defamatory publications. *Gertz v. Robert Welch, Inc.,* 418 U.S. 323, 341 (1974). While recognizing that "[s]ome tension necessarily exists between the need for a vigorous and uninhibited press and the legitimate interest in redressing wrongful injury," the United States Supreme Court has stressed that the plaintiff's right to the protection of his reputation must not be sacrificed when the court balances these two competing interests. *Id.*

Two-sentence paragraph

In an attempt to balance the interests of the media against the interests of plaintiffs injured by defamatory statements, the Court developed three classes of plaintiffs: public officials, public figures, and private figures. *Gertz,* 418 U.S. at 343; *Curtis Publishing Co. v. Butts,* 388 U.S. 130 (1966); *New York Times, Co. v. Sullivan,* 376 U.S. 254, 279 (1964). Because public figure plaintiffs are held to a higher standard of proof in defamation suits, the Court has made it clear that the public figure standard is to be construed narrowly. *Gertz,* 418 U.S. at 341, 352. The Court will not lightly find a plaintiff to be a public figure. *Id.*

Three-sentence paragraph

Three-sentence paragraph   The first class of public figure defined by the Court in *Gertz* is the limited purpose public figure. To become a limited purpose public figure, a plaintiff must voluntarily inject himself or herself into a particular public controversy and attempt to influence its outcome. *Id.* at 351, 352. By doing so, the plaintiff invites public attention and comment on a limited range of issues relating to his involvement in the controversy. *Id.* at 351.

One-sentence paragraph   The Court described the second class of public figure, the all-purpose public figure, as having "assumed roles of especial prominence in the affairs of society," or as occupying "positions of such persuasive power and influence," or as "achieving such pervasive fame or notoriety that he becomes a public figure for all purposes and in all contexts." *Id.* at 345, 351.

Six-sentence paragraph   Under these narrow definitions laid down by the United States Supreme Court, Vashon Savings and Loan is neither a limited purpose public figure nor an all-purpose public figure. Therefore, the trial court erred in granting defendants' motion for partial summary judgment on the public figure issue. Furthermore, this error was prejudicial because it resulted in the plaintiffs being held to a higher standard of proof at trial. But because the standard of review is *de novo* when a partial summary judgment order is appealed, this court is not bound by the erroneous trial court decision below. *Herron v. Tribune Publishing Co.,* 108 Wn.2d 162, 169, 736 P.2d 249, 255 (1987); *Noel v. King County,* 48 Wn. App. 227, 231, 738 P.2d 692, 695 (1987). Rather, the court should apply the *Gertz* public figure standard to the facts of this case and reach its own independent determination. Correct application of the standard will result in a holding that Vashon Savings and Loan is a private figure for purposes of this defamation suit.

First, a few comments about the preceding example. Notice that the length of each paragraph is primarily determined by content. The writer wrote as few or as many sentences as she needed to make each point. The length of each paragraph is further determined by reader comfort and interest. Some variety in paragraph length helps keep the writing interesting. Short, one- or two-sentence paragraphs tend to work in places where the reader needs a bit of a break before or after an unusually long paragraph. Too many short paragraphs, though, and the writing begins to seem choppy and undeveloped.

An occasional long paragraph allows the writer to go into depth on a point. Too many long paragraphs, though, and the writing slows down to a plod and seems heavy and ponderous.

Short paragraphs can also be effective when the writer is making a major shift, change, or connection between ideas. Consequently, short paragraphs frequently serve as transitions between major sections and as introductions or conclusions to major sections.

See Exercises 22A and 22B in the *Practice Book*.

§ 22.5 Topic and Concluding Sentences

Again, the truth. Not all paragraphs have topic and concluding sentences. In fact, many well-written paragraphs have neither.

However, and this is a big "however," most well-written paragraphs do have topic sentences, and those that don't have an implied topic sentence that governs the paragraph as firmly as any written topic sentence. The truth about concluding sentences is that sometimes they are useful to the reader and sometimes they are not. You have to use your common sense about when to include a concluding sentence and when to leave one out. Readers are most likely to find concluding sentences helpful after longer, more complicated points. If, on the other hand, you are confident that the information in the concluding sentence would be painfully obvious, then leave it out.

The point then is to know what topic and concluding sentences do for a paragraph. Once you know how they work, you can decide whether a stated or an implied topic or concluding sentence works in a given situation.

§ 22.5.1 Stated Topic Sentences

The following examples demonstrate how the standard topic sentence works. Notice that the topic sentence has two functions: it introduces or names the topic and it asserts something about the topic.

Standard Topic Sentence   EXAMPLE 1

In determining whether service was proper under Fed. R. Civ. P. 4(d)(1), courts have considered several other factors. First, the courts recognize that "each decision proceeds on its own facts." *Karlsson*, 318 F.2d at 668. Second, the courts consider whether the defendant will return to the place where service was left. *Id*. Third, the courts look at whether service was reasonably calculated to provide actual notice to the defendant. *Elkins v. Broome*, 213 F.R.D. 273, 275 (M.D.N.C. 2003).

Standard Topic Sentence   EXAMPLE 2

Defendants have successfully used the following articulated reasons to rebut a plaintiff's *prima facie* case. In *Kelly*, the defendant testified that the plaintiff was terminated because he was the least effective salesman. *Kelly*, 640 F.2d at 977. Similarly, in *Sakellar*, the defendant alleged that the plaintiff lacked the skills and experience for the position. *Sakellar*, 765 F.2d at 1456. And in *Sutton*, the defendant discharged the plaintiff for "intemperate and impolitic actions." *Sutton*, 646 F.2d at 410.

One common weakness of some novice legal writers is to write topic sentences that merely name the topic. These "topic sentences" fall under the category of "The next thing I'm going to talk about is. . . ."

Compare the following two topic sentences. Which will a reader find more helpful?

EXAMPLE 1	**Poor Topic Sentence**

Another case that discussed actual malice is *Journal-Gazette Co., Inc. v. Bandido's Inc.*, 712 N.E.2d 446 (Ind. 1999).

EXAMPLE 2	**Improved Topic Sentence**

The court extended these protections in *Journal-Gazette Co.*, holding that plaintiffs in a defamation action would have to prove actual malice if the published statements were of public or general interest. *Journal-Gazette Co., Inc. v. Bandido's Inc.*, 712 N.E.2d 446 (Ind. 1999).

The topic sentence in Example 1 does little more than name a case. The topic sentence in Example 2 is far superior. It introduces the point the paragraph will make — that plaintiffs in a defamation action would have to prove actual malice if the statements published were of public or general interest.

In addition, the topic sentence in Example 2 demonstrates an excellent method for writing topic sentences that introduce a new case: it begins with a transition that relates the point from the new case to the previous discussion and then follows with a paraphrase of the holding. The following example shows how the writer completed the paragraph.

EXAMPLE 3	**Complete Paragraph**

The court extended these protections in *Journal-Gazette Co.*, holding that plaintiffs in a defamation action would have to prove actual malice if the published statements were of public or general interest. *Journal-Gazette Co., Inc. v. Bandido's Inc.*, 712 N.E.2d 446 (Ind. 1999). The court wrote, "If a matter is a subject of public or general interest, it cannot suddenly become less so merely because a private individual is involved, or because in some sense the individual did not 'voluntarily' choose to become involved." *Id.* at 452 (quoting *Rosenbloom v. Metromedia*, 403 U.S. 29, 43 (1971)).

The next two examples also show how to use a court's holding for the topic sentence. In Example 1, the writer develops the topic sentence by setting out the facts in the analogous case and then distinguishes the facts from the client's case.

EXAMPLE 1	**Holding for Topic Sentence**

In *Messenger*, the court held that the trespassory slashing of trees was a permanent form of property damage. *Messenger v. Frye*, 28 P.2d 1023 (Wash. 1934). However, the tree slashing in that case was extensive. It was the extent of the injury, not the type of injury, which made the damage irreparable and therefore permanent. Unlike the slashed trees, the damage to the rosebushes in our case should not be considered extensive because only four out of twenty rosebushes were destroyed. The rosebushes can probably be replaced, thus restoring the Archers' property to its original condition. Therefore, the damage to the rosebushes and buds is temporary, and the Archers will recover only for the restoration cost of the rosebuds and bushes, as well as the diminished use value of their property.

In Example 2, the writer develops the topic sentence by setting out the facts of the case and then returns to the holding.

Holding for Topic Sentence

EXAMPLE 2

In an analogous Arizona case, _State v. Thomas_, the court held that the trial court committed an error of constitutional magnitude when it allowed the prosecution to do exactly as the prosecution did in the present case. _Thomas_, 636 P.2d at 1219. In _Thomas_, the only pertinent evidence was the testimony of the defendant, who stood accused of rape, and the testimony of the prosecuting witness. During the trial, the prosecution questioned the witness about her religious beliefs and church-related activities, eliciting from her that she was a religious person. _Id._ at 1217. In closing argument, the prosecution told the jury that the ultimate issue was the credibility of the witnesses, and that before the jury could believe the defendant, it had to believe that the prosecuting witness, an "uprighteous, religious, moralistic type," was a liar. _Id._ The appellate court held that admission of the religious references was an error of constitutional magnitude. _Id._ at 1219.

Writing strong topic sentences is critical to your analysis. Often the topic sentence is the spot where the writer synthesizes a group of analogous cases. Notice in the following examples from the sample memo in Chapter 5 how the topic sentences sum up the key features the writer has uncovered in a group of cases with the same holding.

Topic Sentence Synthesizes Cases

In the cases in which the courts have found that there was sufficient evidence to support a finding of constructive possession, the defendant had been staying on the premises for more than a few days and had no other residence; had personal property on the premises; and had done some act that indicated that he had dominion and control over the property. _See, e.g., State v. Weiss_, 73 Wn.2d 372, 438 P.2d 610 (1968); _State v. Collins_, 76 Wn. App. 496, 886 P.2d 243 (1995). In _Collins_, the defendant admitted staying on the premises fifteen to twenty times during the prior month and having no other residence; boxes filled with the defendant's personal property were found in a hallway; and, while the police were in the house, the defendant received several phone calls. _Id._ at 499. Similarly, in _Weiss_, the evidence indicated that the defendant had been staying on the premises for more than a month and had helped pay the rent; a bed belonging to the defendant was found in the house; and the defendant had invited others to spend the night. _Id._ at 374. In both cases, the courts held that the facts were sufficient to support the jury's verdict that the defendant had dominion and control over both the premises and the drugs.

The writer uses the same strategy for writing a topic sentence by synthesizing the cases with the opposite holding.

Topic Sentence Synthesizes Cases

In contrast, in the cases in which the courts have found that there was not sufficient evidence to support a finding of constructive possession, the defendant was only a temporary visitor and had another residence. *See, e.g., State v. Callahan,* 77 Wn.2d 27, 459 P.2d 400 (1969); *State v. Davis,* 16 Wn. App. 657, 558 P.2d 263 (1977). In *Callahan,* the defendant, Hutchinson, had been on the houseboat for only a few days, had only a limited number of personal possessions on the premises, and was not paying rent. In addition, another individual admitted that the drugs belonged to him. Based on these facts, the court held that the defendant did not have constructive possession of either the premises or the drugs, which were found on a table next to the defendant. *Id.* at 32. Likewise, in *Davis,* the court held that the defendant did not have dominion and control over either the premises or the drugs when the defendant was staying at the apartment for only the weekend while his mother entertained guests at home. Even though the defendant's clothing and sleeping bag were found in the apartment, the court held that the presence of these items was not enough to establish constructive possession. *Id.* at 658-59.

As we have seen, the first sentence of a paragraph is usually the topic sentence. Topic sentences may, however, appear later in a paragraph, particularly if the opening sentence or sentences are used to provide a transition to or background for the topic.

The following example is taken from the beginning of the second argument in a memorandum in opposition to the defendants' motion for partial summary judgment. Notice how sentence 1 serves as a transition between the two arguments and sentence 2 provides background for sentence 3, the topic sentence.

EXAMPLE   **Transition to and Background for Topic**

Transition	*Sullivan* and *Gertz* dealt with individual citizens who had been libeled and who had sought redress in the courts. The
Background	case before the court today is different; the plaintiff is a state chartered savings and loan, a business entity. The significance of the different status of a business entity and its reputation,
Topic sentence	as compared to a private individual, has been recognized in several federal courts. In *Martin Marietta v. Evening Star Newspaper,* 417 F. Supp. 947, 955 (D.D.C. 1976), the court stated that "[t]he law of libel has long reflected the distinction between corporate and human plaintiffs" and that "a corporate libel action is not a basic [sic] of our constitutional system, and need not force the first amendment to yield as far as it would be in a private libel action." *Martin Marietta,* 417 F. Supp. at 955 (citations omitted). The *Marietta* court continued, "Corporations, which do not possess private lives to begin with, must similarly [to public figures] be denied full protection from libel." *Id.*

See Exercise 22C in the *Practice Book.*

§ 22.5.2 Implied Topic Sentences

Many paragraphs with implied topic sentences occur in statements of fact. Although some statements of fact have paragraphs that are thematically organized and use traditional topic sentences, most have a chronological organization with implied topic sentences. Many use a mix of the two.

Practically all paragraphs in statements of fact depend on their narrative, or storytelling, quality to keep the writing organized. The organizing principle, or topic, of such paragraphs may be what happened in a given time period, what happened to a given person, or what facts make up a given part of the situation.

The following paragraph appeared in the statement of facts from a case about whether service of process was valid when it was left at a spouse's home. The preceding paragraph explained that the defendant, Ms. Clay-Poole, has a job and residence in New York and that her husband has a job and residence in California. In this paragraph, no topic sentence is stated, but one is certainly implied.

No Stated Topic Sentence

Ms. Clay-Poole and Mr. Poole usually see each other about once a month for three or four days. They split the traveling about equally, although Ms. Clay-Poole travels to San Diego somewhat more frequently than Mr. Poole travels to Albany. They are happy with this arrangement; consequently, they do not intend to move in together permanently.

The implied topic sentence of this paragraph is that Ms. Clay-Poole and Mr. Poole have a commuter marriage. The writer could have stated the topic sentence, but in this case it was sufficiently obvious to leave it implied.

§ 22.5.3 Concluding Sentences

To be worthwhile, concluding sentences need to do more than just restate the topic sentence. If they don't, then the paragraph will not have advanced the line of reasoning in the memo or brief. Look again at the paragraph about whether a drug informant's testimony is relevant. Notice how the topic and concluding sentences are not simply artful clones of each other.

The concluding sentence advances the line of reasoning by taking that topic, or that point, and applying it to the present case. It rather neatly argues that the rationale in *Craig v. State* is applicable in the present case because in both cases the informant "served mainly as a line of introduction." This concluding sentence is not just extra baggage — the obligatory "Now I'm going to tell you again what I told you before." It is a working sentence, a significant sentence, perhaps the most significant sentence in the paragraph.

Earlier we saw how a paraphrase of the holding often makes an excellent topic sentence. Paraphrasing the holding can also be an effective way to conclude a paragraph about an analogous case.

Concluding Sentence Paraphrases Holding

The Georgia appellate court addressed the issue of consent in relation to the disposal of a stillborn child. *See McCoy v. Georgia Baptist Hospital,* 306 S.E.2d 746 (Ga.

Ct. App. 1983). In that case, the mother delivered a stillborn child in the defendant hospital. Both parents had signed a consent form authorizing the hospital to dispose of the body "in any manner they deem advisable." *Id.* at 747. Thereafter, the mother discovered that the body had been placed in a freezer and left there for approximately one month. The court held that the parents released their quasi-property interests in the child's body to the defendant hospital when they signed the consent form. *Id.*

Another effective technique for writing concluding sentences is to use a particularly apt quotation.

EXAMPLE   ### Quotation for Concluding Sentence

The California Court of Appeals has decided that an individual is entitled to full property rights in his organs and other bodily tissue. In *Moore v. Regents of UCLA*, 249 Cal. Rptr. 494 (Cal. Ct. App. 1988), the appellant's diseased spleen was removed by the appellee research hospital. Appellee subsequently discovered that Moore's spleen and other bodily tissue had unique characteristics that could be used to develop substances with potential commercial value. Moore was never told of appellee's discovery and continued to allow appellee to extract bodily tissue from him under the guise of continuing treatment. The appellate court held that Moore had certain rights in his bodily tissue that should be recognized and protected. The court went on to say that "[t]he rights of dominion over one's own body, and the interests one has therein . . . are so akin to property interests that it would be a subterfuge to call them something else." *Id.* at 505.

One word of caution, though: many legal writers overuse quotations. For the technique of concluding with a quotation to be effective, it should be used only occasionally and only when the quotation is unusually well stated.

Remember, too, that every paragraph does not have to have a stated concluding sentence. Like implied topic sentences, implied concluding sentences are permissible as long as the reader can easily surmise what the paragraph's conclusion is.

See Exercise 22D in the *Practice Book*.

§ 22.6 Paragraph Blocks

One reason why many paragraphs may not have topic sentences or concluding sentences yet function well in a piece of writing is that the paragraphs are part of a larger organizational element: a paragraph block. Like paragraphs, paragraph blocks are mini-compositions, only this time the beginning is likely to be a paragraph or two, the middle is usually several paragraphs, and the ending is also a paragraph or more.

The beginning paragraph or paragraphs work like a topic sentence. They are general statements that introduce the topic of the paragraph block and assert something about that topic.

The middle paragraphs contain the subpoints — the specifics that support the topic paragraph. Ideally, each of the middle paragraphs is organized like a mini-composition with its own topic sentence, supporting sentences, and concluding sentences.

The concluding paragraph or paragraphs work in the block the same way a concluding sentence works in a paragraph. They bring the discussion back to the broad general topic but in a way that advances the line of reasoning.

The following example demonstrates how a typical paragraph block works.

Paragraph Block

There is only one case in which a court has found a financial institution to be an all-purpose public figure. That case, *Coronado Credit Union v. KOAT Television, Inc.,* 656 P.2d 896 (N.M. Ct. App. 1982), was decided incorrectly. In holding that a credit union was an all-purpose public figure, the New Mexico Court of Appeals extended and broadened the *Gertz* standard in a way the Supreme Court never intended. By ignoring the Court's mandate to construe the all-purpose public figure standard narrowly, the *Coronado* court extended this standard to include all financial institutions. The court considered the following factors to reach this per se rule: (1) Financial institutions as corporations are chartered by the state; (2) Financial institutions are regulated by the state through statutes; and (3) Financial institutions deal in areas of general public concern. *Id.* at 904.

Topic paragraph

The fatal flaw in the court's analysis is best illustrated by applying these three factors to the fact pattern in *Gertz*. In *Gertz*, the Supreme Court held that the plaintiff attorney was not an all-purpose public figure. 418 U.S. at 352. But if the *Coronado* analysis is used, the opposite result would have been reached: (1) Attorneys must be licensed by the state to practice law and must meet certain state requirements to obtain that license; (2) Attorneys are subject to regulation by the state through Professional Codes of Conduct; and (3) Attorneys deal in areas of general public concern and interest. In fact, lawyers are officers of the court and, as such, must seek the public good in the administration of justice.

Supporting paragraph

Thus, under the *Coronado* analysis, Mr. Gertz and indeed all attorneys would be classified as all-purpose public figures. Such a result is in direct opposition to the Court's holding in *Gertz*. Consequently, the rule applied in *Coronado* is far too broad and could not withstand constitutional scrutiny.

Concluding paragraph

The following excerpt from a memo shows how two paragraph blocks work together to complete a section under the heading of "negligence." An element of the law analysis lends itself nicely to paragraph block writing. In the example, notice how the paragraph that concludes one paragraph block also serves as the topic paragraph for the second block.

EXAMPLE

Negligence

Topic paragraph   If Dennis's negligence created the emergency, then he may not use the emergency doctrine. "Negligence" is defined as failing to act like a reasonable person. This general principle is best explained by way of illustration, and the courts provide numerous examples. *Martini ex rel. Dussault v. State,* 89 P.3d 250, 256 (Wash. App. 2004).

Topic sentence   Speed excessive to conditions can be negligent. For example, when a defendant's logging truck rounded a curve and was unable to stop within 375 feet, his speed was found to be negligent. *Sandberg v. Spoelstra,* 285 P.2d 564 (Wash. 1955). **Supporting paragraph** When early morning visibility was restricted to 75 feet by a heavy rainfall, the court held that a speed of fifty miles per hour could be negligent. *Pidduck v. Henson,* 467 P.2d 322 (Wash. App. 1970). Finally, when daylight visibility exceeding 100 feet was restricted to about three car lengths at night because of the glare of a street light, the court held that a speed under the twenty-five miles per hour posted limit could be negligent. *Sonnenberg v. Remsing,* 398 P.2d 728 (Wash. 1965).

Topic sentence   Failure to heed road hazard warnings can also be negligent. Thus, when a driver confronted a multiple-car accident on the freeway, where patrol cars were present with flashing lights and other cars were parked along the shoulder and median, the driver was negligent for not slowing down. **Supporting paragraph** *Schlect v. Sorenson,* 533 P.2d 1404 (Wash. App. 1975). Likewise, when a driver is warned of a fog hazard, drives into a deteriorating fog bank, and collides with a stopped vehicle, the driver is negligent. *Hinkel v. Weyerhaeuser Co.,* 494 P.2d 1008 (Wash. App. 1972).

Topic sentence   Finally, violations of the rules of the road can be negligent *per se.* When the driver of a semitrailer observed a car stalled in the road ahead of it, slowed, switched lanes, and passed to the rear of the automobile where it struck one of the occupants on the highway, the driver was negligent. The **Supporting paragraph** driver was negligent as a matter of law for failing to obey several rules of the road: (1) reducing speed when confronted with hazards, (2) sounding horn to warn pedestrians of danger, (3) changing lanes only when safe to do so, and (4) signaling a lane change for 100 feet before turning. *Nesmith v. Bowden,* 563 P.2d 1322 (Wash. App. 1977).

Concluding paragraph/topic paragraph   Plaintiff is likely to employ all the above arguments. She will argue that Dennis was negligent because his speed was excessive, because he failed to heed road hazards, and because he violated the rules of the road.

Dennis's speed was not excessive for the conditions he faced. Although plaintiff may cite *Sandberg, Pidduck,* and *Sonnenberg,* Dennis can distinguish the conditions in *Pidduck* and *Sonnenberg* from the conditions that Dennis faced. In both cases, visibility was restricted by unusual circumstances. Dennis faced no unusual circumstances. He was rounding a gradual curve under the speed limit, and there is no indication that the curve was so sharp that it required a reduced speed limit. Nor is there any indication that there was a lower speed limit for night driving as opposed to day driving. In *Sandberg,* the driver had 375 feet in which to stop, and there was no obstruction in his lane when the driver collided with a vehicle in the other lane. Although the exact distance is unknown in Dennis's case, apparently Dennis had much less space in which to stop. Also, he faced an obstruction in his own lane.

Topic sentence

Supporting paragraph

Dennis's situation is analogous to the situation in *Ryan v. Westgard,* 530 P.2d 687 (Wash. App. 1975), where the driver was found to be not negligent. There, the driver was following approximately 100 feet behind another car. This car swerved into another lane, and the following driver confronted yet another car going extremely slowly. He attempted to stop, but collided with the slower vehicle. The court reasoned that the plaintiff was following the car in front of him at a proper speed until the moment that vehicle swerved out into the adjoining lane. *Id.* at 501. Like the driver in *Ryan,* Dennis too was traveling at a proper speed until the moment his vehicle encountered the stalled bus. Therefore, Dennis's speed was not excessive.

Topic sentence

Supporting paragraph

Concluding sentence

Plaintiff will also argue that Dennis was negligent for failing to slow when confronted with a road hazard. Again, Dennis can distinguish the warning that he had from the warnings given in *Schlect* and *Hinkel.* Dennis was not warned several miles in advance of the obstruction, as was the driver in *Hinkel.* Nor did he confront a multiple-car accident with flashing patrol car lights and cars parked along the highway as did the driver in *Schlect.*

Pair of topic sentences

Supporting paragraph

Dennis rounded a curve and confronted a bus with flashers on that was stopped in the left lane of the freeway at 11:30 p.m. His situation is more analogous to the cases in which drivers faced sudden and unexpected obstacles after little warning. *Haynes v. Moore,* 545 P.2d 28 (Wash. App. 1975); *Leach v. Weiss,* 467 P.2d 894 (Wash. App. 1970). In *Haynes,* the driver confronted a car, which he first saw when he was fifty feet away, stopped on a bridge. He braked but collided with the car. He was found to be not negligent. Likewise, in *Leach,* the driver confronted a car stopped on a bridge, braked, crossed the center line, and collided with another vehicle. The driver was not negligent. Neither is Dennis negligent.

Topic sentence

Supporting paragraph

Concluding sentence

Finally, plaintiff will argue that our client was negligent for violating the rules of the road. Dennis was driving in the left-hand lane and was not passing or turning. This conduct

Topic sentence

Supporting paragraph — violates Wash. Rev. Code § 46.61.100 (2004), which requires that a driver stay in the right-most lane except when passing or turning. Under *Nesmith*, 563 P.2d at 1326, this violation creates a *prima facie* case of negligence. However, Dennis can argue that this conduct was not negligence because it did not endanger the class of persons that this rule was designed to protect. The purpose of Wash. Rev. Code § 46.61.100 (2004) is to protect vehicles traveling in the same direction by promoting safe passing. *Sadler v. Wagner*, 486 P.2d 330 (Wash. App. 1971). Edith was not passing Dennis, and Dennis was not **Concluding sentence** — passing Edith. Thus, Edith does not fall within the class of persons this rule was designed to protect, and Dennis was not negligent.

Concluding paragraph — Dennis was not negligent because of excessive speed, he was not negligent for failing to heed road hazard warnings, and he was not negligent for failing to obey the rules of the road. His conduct did not create the emergency. He can submit substantial evidence in support of this second element, even though he can expect opposing counsel to make this a difficult issue.

See Exercises 22E, 22F, and 22G in the *Practice Book*.

Connections Between Sentences

Transitions are the primary connectors between sentences. Used properly, transitions express the relationship between the ideas in the sentences they connect and signal how the ideas are moving in a line of reasoning.

Three types of transitions connect sentences:

1. generic transitions,
2. orienting transitions, and
3. substantive transitions.

Still other transitions, headings and signposts, are used to make connections between paragraphs and over a longer piece of writing. See Chapter 21.

§ 23.1 Generic Transitions

Generic transitions include those words and phrases that are used in every kind of writing. Chart 23.1 lists the most common generic transitions grouped by function.

§ 23.1.1 Using Generic Transitions

The first question writers have about generic transitions is when to use them. In theory, that seems simple. Because generic transitions signal those shifts or changes inherent in human thought, it would seem that all writers should have to do is insert an appropriate transition to signal each time they make such a shift in their writing.

Chart 23.1   Generic Transitions

For Contrast

however	nevertheless*	but
on the other hand	conversely	still
by (in) contrast	notwithstanding	yet
on the contrary	nonetheless*	instead
contrary to_____	alternatively	though
unlike_____	even so*	although
despite_____	rather	even though

For Comparison

similarly	analogously	in like manner
likewise	in the same way	
	for the same reason	

For Cause and Effect

therefore*	accordingly	hence
consequently*	thus*	since
as a result	because	so
		for

For Addition

also	moreover	besides
further	too	and
in addition	additionally	
furthermore		

For Examples

for example	to illustrate	specifically
for instance	namely	that is*

For Emphasis

in fact	certainly	still*
above all	indeed	clearly

For Evaluation

more important	surprisingly	unquestionably
unfortunately	allegedly	
fortunately	arguably	

*Generic transition that falls under more than one category.

For Restatement

in other words	more simply	to put it differently
that is*	simply put	

For Concession

granted	of course	to be sure

For Resumption After a Concession

still*	nonetheless*	all the same
nevertheless*	even so*	

For Time

subsequently	later	earlier
recently	eventually	afterwards
meanwhile	shortly thereafter	until now
initially	simultaneously	since
formerly	at the time	by the time

For Place

adjacent to	here	nearby
next to	beyond	opposite to

For Sequence

first, second, third	next	then
former, latter	final	later
in the first place	finally*	primary, secondary

For Conclusion

in summary	in brief	thus*
in sum	in short	therefore*
to sum up	to conclude	consequently*
finally*	in conclusion	to (in) review

*Generic transition that falls under more than one category.

In practice, it is not so simple. For one thing, there are no hard and fast rules for when a transition is needed. In fact, experienced writers do not always agree about when a transition is appropriate and when it is cumbersome. For beginning law students and new associates in a firm, such differences in opinion can be confusing: one reader wants more transitions added, the next reader edits them out.

The truth is that, to some extent, the number and placement of generic transitions is a matter of personal style and preference. That being said, there is still a general consensus about when to use generic transitions. You can find that consensus and develop your own sense about when to use generic transitions in one or more of the following ways.

First, observe how other writers, particularly professional writers, use generic transitions. For example, notice how they rarely omit transitions that signal contrast and those that show movement up or down the ladder of abstraction. Observe the ways skilled legal writers use generic transitions to keep their readers on track.

Second, read your own writing aloud. Let your ear tell you when a new sentence starts with a jolt rather than with a smooth connection.

Third, listen to someone else read your writing aloud. Stop that reader at several points along the way (particularly when there is no transition) and ask if he or she can guess what the next sentence will discuss. If the connections between the ideas are so obvious that the reader can anticipate where the writing is headed, probably no transition is needed. Conversely, if your reader needs more guidance through your points, add the appropriate generic transitions as needed.

Fourth, and most important, when writing, constantly ask yourself what will help your reader. Keeping the reader's perspective and needs in mind will help you decide when a generic transition is a helpful guide and when it is extra baggage.

§ 23.1.2 Problems with Generic Transitions

Some legal writers have a tendency to write as though others can read their minds. These writers omit transitions because the connections between the ideas are obvious to the writers themselves. They forget to consider whether these connections are obvious to the reader. For example, notice in the first pair of sentences that follow how jarring the second sentence seems without the transition for contrast, and then notice how in the revised second sentence the reader easily adjusts once the generic transition for contrast is added.

EXAMPLE   **First Draft**

Mr. Wry, the owner of the Fitness Club, may claim that although Hillary's restaurant has lost several customers, the majority of the customers will return. Mr. Hillary may argue that the loss of several customers is significant to his business.

Revised

Mr. Wry, the owner of the Fitness Club, may claim that although Hillary's restaurant has lost several customers, the majority of the customers will return. Mr. Hillary, on the other hand, may argue that the loss of several customers is significant to his business.

Other writers omit transitions in hopes of being more concise. They forget that being concise, although important, is a relative luxury compared to being clear.

Legal writers should also take great care to select the precise transition that best describes the relationship between the two ideas or sentences. In the following example, the writer mistakenly selected a transition for comparison rather than a transition for addition.

Wrong Transition

EXAMPLE

Because some overt physical activity and noise are normally generated by fitness and aerobics classes, the Fitness Club's classes are not unreasonably noisy or offensive. Similarly, bathing suits are not unusual or unanticipated sights in a waterfront area.

Revised

Furthermore, bathing suits are not unusual or unanticipated sights in a waterfront area.

The need for precision in transitions also means that it is not enough simply to select the right category of generic transition. Generic transitions within the same category often have distinct meanings and connotations. For example, two transitions for conclusion — "to sum up" and "finally" — have entirely different meanings. "To sum up" should signal a brief overview or general statement about the entire piece of writing; "finally" should signal that the last point is about to be made.

In some instances, generic transitions are similar in meaning but quite different in tone. For example, two transitions for cause and effect — "therefore" and "hence" — mean almost the same thing, but "therefore" creates a matter-of-fact tone while "hence" carries with it a feeling of heavy solemnity and old wisdom.

A word of warning then: use the list of generic transitions in Chart 23.1 with care. Do not automatically assume that transitions grouped in the same category are synonymous.

Of course, you will find that some generic transitions in the same category are virtually synonymous. In such instances, you may find that the list offers some variety that may free you from using the same generic transition ad nauseam.

Some final advice about transitional expressions: first, because transitions show the connection between two ideas, it is best to place the transition right at the point of connection. In the following example, the transition showing the cause/effect relationship comes too late to help the reader very much.

Late Transition

EXAMPLE

Hillary was made insecure in the use of his property when patrons threatened not to return. The Fitness Club and its activities constitute a nuisance as a result.

Revised

As a result, the Fitness Club and its activities constitute a nuisance.

The break between paragraphs also serves as a kind of transition. The white space is a strong signal that the writing is moving to a new point.

See Exercise **23A** in the *Practice Book*.

§ 23.2 Orienting Transitions

Orienting transitions provide a context for the information that follows. They serve to locate — physically, logically, or chronologically — the ideas or points in the rest of the sentence.

Two of the most common orienting transitions in legal writing are those that include times and dates and those that refer to cases.

EXAMPLES   **Reference to Time, Dates, Cases**

At 2:00 a.m. on January 1, 2006, David Wilson was arrested and charged with reckless driving and driving while intoxicated.

In *Bugger*, the court found that the position of the driver was insignificant.

In the case at hand, there is no indication that the defendant intended to deceive the plaintiff about her rights under the contract.

Other orienting transitions create a context by directing the reader to adopt a certain point of view, by supplying the source of the information that follows, or by locating the information historically or chronologically.

EXAMPLES   **Transitions That Create Context**

From the bank's perspective, granting a second loan would be ill-advised and risky.

According to Dallas Police Department Officer James Richardson's report, Officers Richardson and Loe entered the warehouse at 12:30 a.m.

Over the last twenty years, courts have realized that some exceptions to the general principle were necessary.

Orienting transitions frequently occur at the beginning of a section. In such positions, orienting transitions are not so much connections between points within the writing as they are connections between the writing and the mind of a reader first coming to the material.

Orienting transitions also occur at the beginning of paragraphs. From this position, they help readers adjust or "shift gears" as they mentally move along a line of reasoning within a larger idea. Of course, orienting transitions may occur within a paragraph, and when they do, they work like all other transitions to bridge the gap between sentences and between ideas.

Here are several more examples of orienting transitions. Note the variety of ways orienting transitions provide a context for what follows.

To Give an Historical Perspective

EXAMPLES

In the 1990s, the court narrowed the scope of the "discretionary" category by emphasizing that the State must show that "a policy decision, consciously balancing the risks and advantages, took place . . . ."

In a recent decision, the court upheld a conviction when the driver was asleep or passed out and remained in a position to regulate the vehicle's movement.

To Suggest a Case's Importance

EXAMPLE

In an often cited case, the court overturned a conviction for "actual physical control" when the motorist's vehicle was parked on the shoulder of the highway.

To Give a Chronology

EXAMPLE

In March of 1999, the Wilsons were advised that their fence encroached approximately thirty feet on the Anders' property. In response, the Wilsons claimed previous and current exclusive right, as well as title and interest to the disputed property.

To Announce a Shift in Topic

EXAMPLES

As for damages, the court will probably enjoin those activities that constitute a private nuisance.

In regard to the prosecution's allegation that Mr. Hayes's original attorney thwarted the discovery process, Mr. Hayes will point out that he was unaware that his original attorney shredded the requested documents.

Some legal writers avoid the orienting transitions beginning with "as for," "as to," "in regard to," and "regarding" in sentences like the preceding examples on the grounds that these transitions are an abrupt, an ineffective, or a lazy way to make a significant shift in topic. These writers prefer that significant shifts in topics be introduced by full sentences.

Revised

EXAMPLES

The question of damages will be more difficult to predict. The court will probably enjoin those activities that constitute a private nuisance, but awarding damages for Hillary's lost profits is less likely.

Revised

The prosecution's second allegation, that Mr. Hayes's original attorney thwarted the discovery process, should be directed at Mr. Hayes's original attorney, not at Mr. Hayes. Mr. Hayes was unaware that his original attorney shredded the requested document. He cannot be held responsible for the unsanctioned actions of his lawyer.

As with generic transitions, the biggest problem writers have with orienting transitions is the question of when to use them. The answer is the same for all types of transitions: use them when the reader needs them.

§ 23.3 Substantive Transitions

Thus far, we have looked at generic transitions, which are like glue between sentences, and at orienting transitions, which are backdrops for information or sometimes windows through which information can be seen.

The third type of transition, substantive transitions, can best be compared to the interlocking links of a chain. Like the links of a chain, substantive transitions serve two functions: they make a connection and they provide content. In short, they live up to their name — they are both substantive and transitional.

EXAMPLE   **Substantive Transition**

Bugger and *Zavala* are the only cases in which a conviction was overturned when the motorist's vehicle was totally off the road. While these holdings could be helpful to Mr. Renko, the Montana court will still probably interpret the statute to include the shoulder of the highway.

In the preceding example, the substantive transition is "while these holdings could be helpful to Mr. Renko." It serves as a transition connecting the two sentences for two reasons: first, it is placed at or near the beginning of the following sentence, where it can help bridge the gap between the ideas; and, second, it uses the phrase "these holdings" to refer back to the information in the previous sentence. In short, the transition looks both forward and back.

But, as we said before, a substantive transition does not serve merely as a transition; it also provides new content. It points out that "these holdings" "could be helpful to Mr. Renko" before going on to the main point of the sentence, that the court still is likely to interpret the statute as including the shoulder of the highway.

§ 23.3.1 The Structure of Substantive Transitions

Substantive transitions often employ a technique called "dovetailing" as the basis for their structure. A carpenter who wants a strong joint to connect two pieces of wood is likely to use a dovetail joint, a special joint characterized by the tight fit of the interlocking pieces of wood. Similarly, a writer who wants a strong joint between two sentences uses a dovetail of words to connect the ideas. Through the dovetail, the writer interlocks ideas by creating an overlap of language, which may be as simple as the repetition of terms from one sentence to the next or use of pronouns to refer back to an earlier noun.

Repetition of Terms Dovetail

In *Esser*, four people agreed to share costs and build a road. After the road was built, each person used the road under a claim of right.

Sentence 1	Sentence 2
. . . four people . . . build a road.	After the road was built, each person used the road . . . .

Note that words may be repeated in their exact form or in a similar or related form.

A slightly more complicated dovetail requires the writer to find a word or phrase to use in the second sentence that sums up the idea of the previous sentence.

Summarizing Phrase Dovetail

Searches and seizures are governed by the Fourth Amendment to the United States Constitution and Article I, section 7, the Washington Constitution. Both of these provisions have been interpreted as requiring that search warrants be valid and that searches and seizures be reasonable.

Sentence 1	Sentence 2
Fourth Amendment . . . and Article 1. . . .	Both of these provisions . . .

Note that in both cases the words in the dovetail tend to be toward the end of the first sentence and toward the beginning of the second.

Often the summarizing noun or phrase will be preceded by a hook word such as "this," "that," "these," "those," or "such."

Hook + Summarizing Phrase

Realizing that she would not be able to stop in time to avoid hitting the bus, Mrs. Long swerved her vehicle around the bus and into the parallel lane of traffic. This evasive action resulted in her sideswiping another vehicle in the oncoming lane.

Connecting idea	Connecting idea
swerved . . . into . . . traffic	This evasive action (*hook* (*summarizing word*) *noun phrase*)

To form an effective dovetail, then, a legal writer may use one or more of the following techniques:

1. move the connecting idea to the end of the first sentence and to the beginning of the second sentence;
2. repeat key words from the first sentence in the second sentence;
3. use pronouns in the second sentence to refer back to nouns in the first sentence;
4. state the connecting idea in a specific form in the first sentence and then restate it in a summarizing noun or phrase in the second sentence;
5. use hook words such as "this," "that," "these," "those," and "such" before a repeated key word or summarizing noun or phrase.

Another way to think about dovetailing is to remember that most sentences are made up of two parts: old information and new information. The old information is what has already been named or discussed. It usually appears near the beginning of a sentence. The new information is the point the writer wants to add. It usually appears near the end of a sentence.

Sentence	
old information	new information

A dovetail takes the new information from the end of one sentence and restates it as the now old information at the beginning of the subsequent sentence.

Sentence 1		*Sentence 2*	
A	B	B	C
old information	new information	old information	new information

Obviously, though, it is unrealistic to assume that all sentences should follow a strict A + B, B + C, C + D pattern. In reality and in good legal writing, the pattern is not followed rigidly. Quite often, for example, Sentence 3 will start with old information B.

Sentence 1		*Sentence 2*		*Sentence 3*	
A	B	B	C	B	D
old	new	old	new	old	new

EXAMPLE   **Dovetailing**

In 1983, the Montana legislature adopted new and stricter laws to deal with drunk drivers. This legislation extended law enforcement jurisdiction and generally provided for faster and stiffer penalties. Brendon J. Rohan, *Montana's Legislative Attempt to Deal with the Drinking Driver: The 1983 DUI Statutes*, 46 Mont. L. Rev. 309, 310 (1985).

This legislation also demonstrates a definite trend in Montana toward greater liability for the individual and a preference toward upholding drunk driving convictions regardless of mitigating circumstances.

Another useful variation of the pattern is to begin a sentence with a combination of two earlier pieces of old information.

Sentence 1		Sentence 2		Sentence 3	
A	B	B	C	B + C	D
old	new	old	new	old+old	new

Dovetailing

EXAMPLE

When the defendant entered his hotel room, he was surprised to find two men rummaging through his suitcase. One of the men turned toward him, drew his gun, and aimed it at the defendant. Under these circumstances, the defendant had every reason to believe that he was being robbed and that his life was in danger.

This pattern works well when the writer wants to point out the similarity in two or more cases just cited.

Dovetailing

EXAMPLE

Courts in both Arizona and Utah did not uphold convictions when the vehicle's motor was off. *State v. Zavalo*, 666 P.2d 456 (Ariz. 1983); *State v. Bugger*, 483 P.2d 442 (Utah 1971). These cases are significant because in both instances the engine was off and the vehicle was completely off the highway.

Some writers unconsciously reverse the old → new pattern. They begin a sentence with new information and tack on the old, connecting information at the end. The result is a halting, disjointed style.

First Draft

EXAMPLE

The defendant need not ensure the plaintiff's safety; he need exercise only reasonable care. *Potter v. Madison Tavern*, 446 P.2d at 322. He has breached his duty to the plaintiff if he has not exercised reasonable care.

Revised

If he has not exercised reasonable care, he has breached his duty to the plaintiff.

Occasionally, however, it is awkward, if not impossible, to move the old information to the very beginning of a sentence and the new information to the very end. In such cases, remember that the old → new pattern is a general principle, not an absolute rule.

A final bit of advice about dovetailing: avoid using hook words without repeating a key term or using a summarizing noun or phrase. See section 27.5.2 on broad pronoun reference.

EXAMPLE   **First Draft**

At common law, a duty is established when the defendant stands in a special relationship to the plaintiff. This can exist between a specific plaintiff and a specific defendant.

Revised

This special relationship can exist....

See Exercises **23B, 23C, 23D,** and **23E** in the *Practice Book.*

§ 23.3.2 The Content of Substantive Transitions

The content in substantive transitions can be compared to half steps in a line of reasoning. Sometimes these half steps are articulated inferences that one can reasonably draw from the previous sentence or idea.

EXAMPLE   **Substantive Transition**

The owners of the factory could agree to release the fumes only after certain hours at night or only under certain weather conditions. While these steps may ameliorate the situation, the question remains whether any emission of toxic fumes is reasonable.

In the preceding example, a thoughtful reader would surely be able to infer the content of the substantive transition — "while these steps may ameliorate the situation" — after reading the first sentence. Consequently, some may argue that it would be better to replace the substantive transition with a more concise generic transition like "even so" or "still." Obviously, writers must exercise judgment and weigh the relative merit of completeness versus conciseness.

In the following two examples, notice how the generic transition, although more concise, is less persuasive for the Bells than the substantive transition.

EXAMPLE   **Generic Transition**

The Bells' doctor, Peter Williams, advised them that future pregnancies had a 75 percent chance of ending in a stillbirth. Consequently, the Bells decided that Mr. Bell would have a vasectomy.

Substantive Transition

The Bells' doctor, Peter Williams, advised them that future pregnancies had a 75 percent chance of ending in a stillbirth. Relying on Dr. Williams's advice, the Bells decided that Mr. Bell would have a vasectomy.

Notice how the generic transition "consequently" seems fairly neutral. It suggests that the Bells' decision to have Mr. Bell undergo a vasectomy was the expected consequence of an unfavorable statistical probability. The substantive transition "relying on Dr. Williams's advice," on the other hand, stresses the Bells' dependence on their doctor's professional opinion. Mentioning the doctor again by name not only reminds the reader that the doctor was the source of the information but also emphasizes the role he played in the Bells' final decision.

Although it would be impossible to enumerate the many ways substantive transitions are used in legal writing, there are a few common situations in which they are particularly effective.

a. Bridging the Gap Between Law and Application

Perhaps the most common use of substantive transitions in legal writing occurs at junctures between law and application. Compare the following two examples and note how the substantive transition "under the rule announced in *Parnell*" draws the rule and its application together better than a generic transition can.

Generic Transition

When a juror could have been excused for cause, reversible error occurs when the accused is forced to exercise all his peremptory challenges before the jury is finally selected. *State v. Parnell*, 463 P.2d 134 (Wash. 1969); *see also State v. Gilchrist*, 590 P.2d 809 (Wash. 1979). In the present case, Chapman accepted the jury with one peremptory challenge unexercised. Thus, he was not forced to use all his peremptory challenges before the final selection of the jury. **Therefore,** the Court of Appeals' decision in finding harmless error is sustainable.

Substantive Transition

When a juror could have been excused for cause, reversible error occurs when the accused is forced to exercise all his peremptory challenges before the jury is finally selected. *State v. Parnell*, 463 P.2d 134 (Wash. 1969); *see also State v. Gilchrist*, 590 P.2d 809 (Wash. 1979). In the present case, Chapman accepted the jury with one peremptory challenge unexercised. Thus, he was not forced to use all his peremptory challenges before the final selection of the jury. **Under the rule announced in *Parnell*,** the Court of Appeals' decision in finding harmless error is sustainable.

b. Applying Another Court's Rationale

Similarly, substantive transitions are often used when the reasoning of one court has been laid out in detail and this reasoning will now be applied to the present case. Note how the author of the following example has used the substantive transition "Applying the *McAlindin* rationale to the present case" to bridge from the analogous case to the present case.

EXAMPLE

Substantive Transition

One test used to analyze whether an individual is substantially limited in a major life activity under the Americans with Disabilities Act (ADA) was developed by the court in *McAlindin v. County of San Diego*, 192 F.3d 1226 (9th Cir. 1999), *amended by* 201 F.3d 1211 (9th Cir. 2000). Under the *McAlindin* test, an individual is "substantially limited" in interacting with others if his or her relations with others are "characterized on a regular basis by severe problems, for example, consistently high levels of hostility, social withdrawal, or failure to communicate when necessary." *Id.* at 1235.

In *McAlindin*, the plaintiff claimed that his diagnosed anxiety, panic, and somatoform disorders substantially limited his ability to interact with others. *Id.* at 1230. The court reversed the entry of summary judgment in favor of the defendant, holding that McAlindin established an issue of material fact as to whether he was substantially limited in his ability to interact with others. *Id.* at 1235. The court reasoned that McAlindin had become increasingly withdrawn, spending most of his time around the house, and feeling that he had to constrict his outside activities and stay away from crowds and shopping centers. *Id.*

Applying the *McAlindin* rationale to the present case, the court will likely find that Mr. Porter suffers from consistently high levels of social withdrawal and is similarly socially isolated. Like McAlindin, Mr. Porter avoids crowded places, shops late at night, and eats at restaurants during off hours to avoid contact with people. In fact, the court will likely find that Mr. Porter is even more socially limited than McAlindin was. In *McAlindin*, the plaintiff was married and confined his social activities to his family. *Id.* In contrast, Mr. Porter has no close relationships with anyone. He lives alone, as his relationships with roommates never worked out, and he gave up trying to date long ago. Mr. Porter has not seen his family in years, and he has no friends.

Therefore, the court will likely find there is an issue of material fact as to whether Mr. Porter is substantially limited in his ability to interact with others, and, thus, Mr. Porter's case will, at the very least, survive a motion for summary judgment.

---

c. Gathering Together Several Facts

Another juncture where substantive transitions can be used effectively occurs between a list of numerous individual facts and a statement about their collective significance. In the following example, the substantive transition, "based on these admissions," is essential. It is the one place where the point is made that three facts taken together were the basis for the court's action.

Substantive Transition

In his deposition, Singh acknowledged that the railroad tie had appeared wet and slippery before he stepped on it. He also stated that he had regularly delivered mail to the Bates's residence for two years and that he was familiar with the premises, including the railroad tie. Finally, Singh acknowledged that he attended weekly postal safety meetings and knew about the hazards posed by wet surfaces. Based on these admissions, the trial court granted summary judgment in favor of Bates and dismissed Singh's negligence action.

d. Bridging the Gap Between Sections of a Document

Substantive transitions are more effective than generic transitions at junctures between large sections of a paper. Even when headings are used for larger sections, substantive transitions are still needed to show the similarities or differences between the sections.

In the following example, the writer has just completed a section on the Supreme Court's comments on an actual termination, which is always effected through an official company act. The following sentence begins a new section under the heading Constructive Discharge. The substantive transition — "unlike an actual termination" — shows the connection between the sections.

Substantive Transition After Heading

Constructive Discharge
Unlike an actual termination, a constructive discharge may or may not involve official action. *Pennsylvania State Police v. Suders*, 542 U.S. 129, 133 (2004).

To sum up then, substantive transitions are those special points in writing where the writer pulls two or more thoughts together and, in doing so, creates a powerful bond between ideas. By overlapping the language and merging the ideas, the writer does more than just connect the points; he or she weaves them together.

Some final thoughts about transitions: although the artificial division of transitions into separate categories makes it easier to understand their separate functions, it also masks the ways in which generic, orienting, and substantive transitions are similar. One can argue, for example, that all transitions, including generic transitions, provide some content or that all transitions orient the reader. Consequently, how you categorize a particular transition is not really important; what is important is that you be able to use all three categories of transitions to create connections in your own writing.

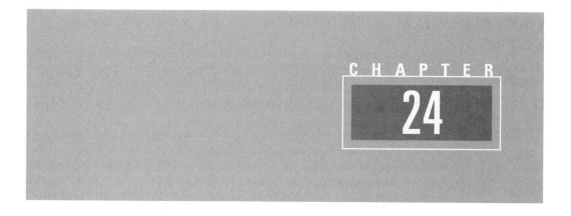

Effective Sentences

E ffective sentence writing begins with the subject-verb unit. Those two key sentence positions should contain the crux of the sentence's message. If these two parts of the sentence are written well, then many of the other parts of the sentence will fall into place.

Consequently, our discussion of effective sentence writing begins with four points about the subject-verb unit: the use of active and passive voice, the use of concrete subjects, the use of action verbs, and the distance between subjects and verbs. The remainder of the chapter addresses points that concern the whole sentence: sentence length, emphasis, and sentence structures that highlight similarities or differences.

§ 24.1 Active and Passive Voice

The term "voice," when it is applied to the subject-verb unit, refers to the relationship of the subject to the action expressed in the verb. This rather vague concept is easier to understand in terms of the difference between active and passive voice.

§ 24.1.1 Identifying Active and Passive Voice

In the active voice, the subject of the sentence is doing the action described by the verb.

The judge overruled the objection.
(subject)   *(verb)*   *(direct object)*

In the sentence above, the subject "judge" is doing the verb "overruled." Another way to look at it is to remember that in the active voice the subject is "active," or acting. In contrast, in the passive voice, the subject of the sentence is having the action of the verb done to it.

The objection was overruled by the judge.
   (subject) *(verb)*

In this last sentence, the subject "objection" is not doing the overruling; rather, the verb "was overruled" is being done to the subject. Another way to look at it is to remember that in the passive voice the subject is "passive." It is not acting; it is acted upon.

Note that in the passive voice the person or thing doing the verb is either mentioned in a prepositional phrase ("by the judge," as in the previous example) or omitted, as in the example below.

The objection was overruled.
   (subject) *(verb)*

Also note that passive voice is different from past tense. Even though both concern the verb, past tense refers to the time of an action, and passive voice refers to the relationship of an action to the subject of the sentence.

See Exercise 24A in the *Practice Book.*

§ 24.1.2 Effective Use of Active Voice

Generally, the active voice is preferred over the passive voice for several reasons:

1. It is more concise.

EXAMPLES   **Active Voice Is Concise**

The marshal left the summons.

(active voice — 5 words)

The summons was left by the marshal.

(passive voice — 7 words)

---

2. It uses a crisp, vigorous verb.

EXAMPLES   **Verbs in Active Voice**

The plaintiffs filed a complaint in the Superior Court of Chavez County, New Mexico.

(active voice — verb "filed" is crisp and vigorous)

A complaint was filed by the plaintiffs in the Superior Court of Chavez County, New Mexico.

(passive voice — verb "was filed" loses much of its vigor; the auxiliary verb "was" and the preposition "by" dilute the energy of "filed")

3. It allows information to be processed more readily.

Active Voice

EXAMPLE

The defendant's attorney must offer the deposition into evidence.

This active voice sentence is easy to process mentally. The reader can visualize the subject "defendant's attorney" doing the verb "must offer" to the object "deposition" as quickly as the words are read. The sentence suggests a mini-drama that readers can visualize in their minds.

Passive Voice

EXAMPLE

The deposition must be offered into evidence by the defendant's attorney.

Although the information in this passive voice sentence is not difficult to process, readers must read the entire sentence before they will be able to visualize the sentence in their minds. By the midpoint in the sentence, "The deposition must be introduced into evidence," the action has begun, but it is being done by unseen hands. The "actor" in the mini-drama does not come in until the end of the sentence.

In both objective and persuasive legal writing, active voice is usually preferred when you want to make a point that someone or something performed a particular action. Active voice emphasizes who or what is responsible for committing an act.

See Exercise 24B in the *Practice Book*.

Voice Affects Emphasis

EXAMPLES

The defendant embezzled over $1,000,000.

(active voice — emphasizes that the defendant is responsible for the act)

Over $1,000,000 was embezzled by the defendant.

(passive voice — it is still clear that the defendant performed the act, but now the emphasis is on the amount of money)

Over $1,000,000 was embezzled.

(passive voice — doer of the action is either unknown or left unsaid; emphasis is on the amount of money)

§ 24.1.3 Effective Use of Passive Voice

Although it is true that active voice is generally preferable to passive voice, there are several situations in which passive voice is more effective.

1. Use passive voice when the person or thing performing the action is unknown or relatively unimportant.

EXAMPLES   **Active Unknown or Unimportant**

A portion of the tape was erased.

The safe's hinges must be examined before the manufacturer's liability can be determined.

---

2. Use passive voice when you do not want to disclose the identity of the person or thing performing the action.

EXAMPLES   **Actor Not Identified**

The plaintiff's retirement benefits were discontinued.

Toxic fumes were ventilated out of the plant between 2:00 and 3:00 a.m.

---

3. Use passive voice when the deed, rather than the doer, should be emphasized.

EXAMPLE   **Emphasis on the Deed**

All four defendants were convicted of first degree murder.

---

4. Use passive voice when it allows the writer to keep the focus of the writing where it belongs, as in the following example from a paragraph about a mistake in a contract.

EXAMPLE   **Control Focus**

A mistake can also be attributed to Lakeland Elementary School for believing the price of the playground equipment included installation.

---

5. Use passive voice when it provides a stronger link between preceding and subsequent sentences or clauses. See section 23.3 on dovetailing. This link is enhanced by moving the connecting ideas to the end of the first sentence (or clause) and then picking up on that point at the beginning of the second sentence (or clause).

Sentence 1	*Sentence 2*
connecting idea	connecting idea

EXAMPLE

Dovetailing

Under the Revised Code of Washington, Title 62A, contracts for the sale of goods are regulated by the Uniform Commercial Code. The UCC outlines the requirements for a valid contract for the sale of goods and the various steps necessary to the contract's performance.

The first sentence uses passive voice so that "Uniform Commercial Code" will be at the end of the sentence. The second sentence begins with "The UCC" to provide a strong link between the sentences. The second sentence is in active voice.

Sentence 1	*Sentence 2*
. . . by the Uniform Commercial Code.	The UCC . . . .

In persuasive writing, you will find that the passive voice allows you to downplay who performed certain actions. For example, counsel for the defense may want to use the passive voice when admitting wrongdoing by the defendant.

EXAMPLE

Downplays Actor

A purse was taken from the plaintiff by the defendant.
(passive voice used to downplay defendant's action)

Counsel for the plaintiff will use active voice to emphasize that it was the defendant who took the purse.

EXAMPLE

Emphasizes Actor

The defendant took the plaintiff's purse.

See Exercise 24C in the *Practice Book*.

§ 24.2 Concrete Subjects

Effective subjects of sentences are concrete rather than abstract. They are real people and real things that readers can mentally visualize.

Unfortunately, in legal writing we are often forced to use abstractions as subjects of our sentences. The law and its application often require that we focus on ideas and concepts; consequently, we often end up placing these ideas and concepts in the subject position. Even so, legal readers appreciate having as many concrete subjects as possible to help bring the writing back down to earth.

To find the most effective concrete subject of a sentence, ask yourself, "Who (or what) is doing something in this sentence?" Then place that real person (or thing) in the subject position of the sentence.

EXAMPLE

Draft: A <u>decision</u> <u>was</u> <u>made</u> by the district manager to
                 (subject)   *(verb)*
              eliminate all level-four positions.

Revised: The <u>district manager</u> <u>decided</u> to eliminate all level-
                      (subject)   *(verb)*
               four positions.

Note that the preceding example illustrates a common problem in legal writing known as nominalization. Nominalization is the process of converting verbs into nouns (for example, "decide" → "decision"). The effect in the sentence is twofold: (1) the real action of the sentence is buried in a noun, making the sentence more ponderous and turgid; and (2) the verb becomes either a passive voice substitute or a "to be" verb substitute, making the sentence less energetic.

In many sentences, the real person or thing acting in the sentence has been buried in an abstraction or omitted altogether.

EXAMPLE

Draft: The <u>awarding</u> of damages <u>will be left</u> to judicial
                 (subject)   *(verb)*
              discretion.

Revised: The <u>judge</u> <u>will decide</u> whether to award damages.
                  (subject) *(verb)*

Often the subject position in the sentence is taken up by an almost meaningless abstraction such as "nature of," "kind of," "type of," "aspect of," "factor of," or "area of." Notice how the sentence improves when these meaningless abstractions are omitted and real people and real things are placed in the subject position.

Draft: The <u>nature</u> of the defendant's argument <u>was</u> that he
    (subject)   *(verb)*
    was "temporarily insane."

Revised: The <u>defendant</u> <u>argued</u> that he was "temporarily
     (subject) *(verb)*
    insane."

Both the subject position and the verb position are often taken up by the many weak subject-verb combinations that use the "it is _____ that" pattern.

It is important to note that
It is likely (unlikely) that
It is obvious (clear) that
It is essential that

To revise sentences with this weakness, look after the "that" for the real subject and verb.

See Exercise 24D in the *Practice Book.*

Draft: <u>It</u> <u>is</u> obvious that the defendant was not read his
   (subject/verb)
   rights.

Revised: The <u>defendant</u> <u>was</u> not <u>read</u> his rights.
    (subject)   *(verb)*

---

§ 24.3 Action Verbs

Effective verbs show real action rather than vague action or state of being. To find the most effective verb for a sentence, ask yourself, "What is someone (or something) actually doing in the sentence?" Then place that action in the verb position.

Common Pitfalls to Avoid When Selecting a Verb

1. Avoid overusing a form of the verb "to be" ("am," "are," "is," "was," "were") as a main verb. Use a form of the verb "to be" as the main verb only when the point of the sentence is that something exists.

Draft: The <u>owner</u> of the land <u>is</u> East Coast Properties, Inc.
               (subject)   *(verb)*

Revised: <u>East Coast Properties, Inc.</u> <u>owns</u> the land.
                    (subject)   *(verb)*

Draft: There <u>are</u> four <u>elements</u> that must be proved to
                    (verb)   *(subject)*
               recover damages under the family car or purpose
               doctrine.

Revised: Four <u>elements</u> <u>must be proved</u> to recover damages
                    (subject)   *(verb)*
               under the family car or purpose doctrine.

Revised to Active Voice

To recover damages under the family car or purpose doctrine, the plaintiff must prove four elements.

Notice that the sentence openers "There is" or "There are" or "There was" or "There were" are weak unless the point of the sentence is that something exists. With these four sentence openers, the subject comes after the verb.

2.   Avoid using vague verbs. Verbs such as "concerns," "involves," "deals (with)," and "reveals" tell the reader little about the real action in the sentence.

Draft: *Swanson* <u>dealt</u> with a sales contract that contained
               (subject) (verb)
               an open item and that was signed by a homebuilder
               and a couple who were prospective buyers of a
               home.

Revised: In *Swanson*, a <u>homebuilder</u> and a <u>couple</u> who were
                              (subject)   *(subject)*
               prospective buyers of a home <u>signed</u> a contract that
                                            (verb)
               contained an open item.

3. Avoid nominalization, that is, burying the real action in a noun, and avoid burying the action in an adjective.

   See Exercise 24E in the *Practice Book.*

Draft: The <u>corporate officers</u> <u>had</u> an informal meeting at an
                    (subject)   *(verb)*
               undisclosed location.

Revised: The <u>corporate officers</u> <u>met</u> informally at an
                    (subject)   *(verb)*
               undisclosed location.

Draft: The <u>policy</u> underlying the doctrine of adverse
                    (subject)
               possession <u>is</u> favorable to the Morgans.
                          (verb)

Revised: The <u>policy</u> underlying the doctrine of adverse
                    (subject)
               possession <u>favors</u> the Morgans.
                          (verb)

---

§ 24.4 Distance Between Subjects and Verbs

An effective sentence has its subject and verb close together. When they are close together, the reader can identify the subject-verb unit quickly and comprehend the entire sentence more easily. When they are far apart and separated by many intervening words, the reader will find it much more difficult to understand the sentence.

Draft: <u>Information</u> about Mutual Trust Bank's standard
               (subject)
               operating procedures and about how the contractor
               drew up his loan application <u>will be required</u> by the
                                            (verb)
               court.

Revised: The <u>court</u> <u>will require</u> information about Mutual Trust
                    (subject) *(verb)*
               Bank's standard operating procedures and about how the contractor
               drew up his loan application.

In some cases, the writer will have to rewrite one sentence as two sentences to keep the subjects and verbs close together.

Draft: A <u>case</u> in which a section 11-902 charge was
            (subject)
            dropped because the driver was found lying on the
            highway near his truck <u>shows</u> that a driver's presence
                                    (verb)
            in the vehicle is a prerequisite for finding him guilty.

Revised: In one case, the <u>court</u> <u>dismissed</u> a section 11-902
                            (subject)   *(verb)*
            charge because the driver was found lying on the
            highway near his truck. The <u>court</u> <u>reasoned</u> that a
                                        (subject) (verb)
            driver's presence in a vehicle is a prerequisite to
            finding the defendant guilty.

Another reason for keeping subjects and verbs close together is to reduce the chance that they will not agree in number. See section 27.4. In the following example, the writer has mistakenly made the verb agree with the singular noun "script" when the plural subject "quality and mutilation" requires the plural verb "are."

Incorrect — Subject and Verb Do Not Agree

Inferior <u>quality and mutilation</u> of the musical play *Not Enough*
            (subject)
Lovin' as a result of Skylark Productions' revisions of the script <u>is</u>
                                                                    (verb)
hard to establish.

Occasionally a writer must separate the subject and verb with quite a bit of information. In such cases, if the intervening information can be set off by punctuation, the reader will still be able to identify the subject-verb unit fairly easily.

Set Off Intervening Information

The <u>Lanham Trademark Act</u>, a law primarily designed to prevent
            (subject)
deceptive packaging of goods in interstate commerce, <u>has been</u>
                                                            (verb)

<u>interpreted</u> to include false attribution and distortion of literary
    (verb)
and artistic works.

Remember too that keeping subjects and verbs close together is desirable but not absolutely required. There will be times in legal writing when it is all but impossible to keep subjects and verbs close together.

See Exercises **24F** and **24G** in the *Practice Book*.

§ 24.5 Sentence Length

Whenever a legal writer asks "how long should my sentences be?" the only possible answer is "it depends." Obviously sentence length is primarily governed by what you are trying to say. In addition, decisions about sentence length should be based on two other factors: the reader and the context.

§ 24.5.1 The Reader

Effective sentence length is that which the reader can handle comfortably. Educated readers — judges, attorneys, some clients — can comfortably read somewhat longer sentences than the general public. Consequently, legal writers can usually write sentences for their readers that average about twenty-two words per sentence, with only a rare sentence exceeding a thirty-five word limit. For readers with less education, shorter sentences are usually more effective.

Notice how the overly long sentence in the following example can create a feeling in the reader of mental overload. Several overly long sentences written one after another only compound this feeling.

Overly Long Sentence   EXAMPLE

The post-trial motion was supported by an affidavit from a juror that stated that a fellow juror discussed the case with a professional truck driver who was familiar with the accident scene and who told the juror that the accident could not have occurred as the plaintiff stated. (48 words)

There are several ways to revise overly long sentences such as the one in the example above so that they become more readable. One way is to break up an overly long sentence into two or more separate sentences.

Revised   EXAMPLE

The post-trial motion was supported by an affidavit by a juror. In his affidavit, the juror stated that a fellow juror discussed the case with a professional truck driver who was familiar with the accident scene. The truck driver told the juror that the accident could not have occurred as the plaintiff stated.

Another way to revise an overly long sentence is to create manageable units of meaning within the sentence. A writer can do this by identifying structural components within the sentence, especially phrases and clauses, and setting them off with appropriate punctuation.

Notice how much more readable the following example becomes when, in Revision 1, the "if" clause is moved to the front of the sentence where it can be set off from the rest of the sentence by a comma.

EXAMPLE   **Draft**

The Reynoldses will be responsible for both the attacks on the Halversons' chickens and Mr. Halverson's medical bills resulting from the dog bite if the plaintiff can show that the Reynoldses should have known of their dog's viciousness. (38 words)

Revision 1

If the plaintiff can show that the Reynoldses should have known of their dog's viciousness, (15 words) then they will be responsible for both the attacks on the Halversons' chickens and Mr. Halverson's medical bills resulting from the dog bite. (23 words)

Other punctuation marks, such as the colon, can sometimes be added to create a break within a sentence.

EXAMPLE   **Revision 2**

If the plaintiff can show that the Reynoldses should have known of their dog's viciousness, (15 words) then they will be responsible for the following: (8 words) the attacks on the Halversons' chickens and Mr. Halverson's medical bills resulting from the dog bite. (16 words)

This technique of arranging phrases and clauses so they can be set off by punctuation is particularly helpful when writing issue statements or questions presented. In the following example, the reader is expected to absorb the information in fifty-six words straight without a punctuation break.

EXAMPLE   **Draft**

Under New Hampshire law did the trial court commit prejudicial error by refusing plaintiffs' motion for a new trial because of jury misconduct when the motion was supported by a juror affidavit stating that another juror discussed the case with an alleged expert outside the trial context and then related the information to the entire jury?

In Revision 1, the writer has broken up this same information into more readable units by using a comma to set off the introductory phrase and a conjunction between the two main clauses. See section 28.1, Rules 1 and 2.

Revision 1

EXAMPLE

Under New Hampshire law, did the trial court commit prejudicial error by refusing plaintiffs' motion for a new trial because of jury misconduct when the motion was supported by a juror affidavit, (32 words) and that affidavit stated that another juror discussed the case with an alleged expert outside the trial context and then related the information to the entire jury? (27 words)

In Revision 2, the writer has used commas between a series of parallel clauses (here, "when" clauses) to help break up the information into manageable units. See section 27.7. Even though the revised sentence is longer than the original, it is more readable because the reader gets the information in smaller, more manageable units.

Revision 2

EXAMPLE

Under New Hampshire law, did the trial court commit prejudicial error when it refused plaintiffs' motion for a new trial because of jury misconduct, (24 words) when the motion was supported by a juror affidavit, (9 words) and when that affidavit stated that another juror discussed the case with an alleged expert outside the trial context and then related the information to the entire jury? (27 words)

The third way to solve sentence length problems is to eliminate wordiness. See section 25.2.

See Exercises **24H** and **24I** in the *Practice Book*.

§ 24.5.2 The Context

Earlier we said that decisions about sentence length should be based on both the reader and the context. Readers rarely see a sentence in isolation. Most sentences are preceded by other sentences and followed by other sentences. Consequently, how readers respond to the length of any given sentence depends, in part, on the sentences that surround it.

For example, a forty-word sentence that is unwieldy in one context may work in another. A short, snappy sentence that drives a point home in one paragraph may seem trite and unsophisticated in another. Even a steady diet of medium-length sentences is unappetizing. Such writing tends to be monotonous and bland. Thus, when it comes to sentence length, consistency is not a virtue. Effective sentences vary in length.

The following example from a statement of facts shows how lack of variety in sentence length makes the writing less interesting to read. In the eleven sentences that follow, the range in sentence length is only from nine words in the shortest sentence to nineteen words in the longest sentence.

Draft

On December 15, 2006, Officers Jack Morrison and Wayne Fiscis of the Phoenix Police Department searched Victor Ehrlich's apartment. (17 words) They had in their possession a valid search warrant for marijuana. (11 words) Marijuana was found in both the living room and the kitchen. (11 words) While searching the bedroom, Officer Morrison found a large manila envelope in one of the dresser drawers. (17 words) Photographs were protruding from the top of the envelope. (9 words) Morrison looked inside and found photographs of Ehrlich with three young girls sitting on his lap. (16 words) Ehrlich was wearing only boxer shorts, and the girls were nude from the waist up. (15 words) Considering the photographs to be perverted, Morrison showed them to Fiscis, who agreed that they looked suspicious. (17 words) They seized the photographs as well as the marijuana. (9 words) The defendant, Victor Ehrlich, has now contested this seizure. (9 words) He has made a motion to suppress the photographic evidence as the result of an unconstitutional seizure. (17 words)

The following revised version is more interesting to read because sentence length now ranges from six words in the shortest sentence to twenty-nine words in the longest.

Revised

On December 15, 2006, Officers Jack Morrison and Wayne Fiscis of the Phoenix Police Department searched Victor Ehrlich's apartment. (17 words) They had in their possession a valid search warrant for marijuana. (11 words) After finding marijuana in both the living room and the kitchen, they searched the bedroom, where Officer Morrison found a large manila envelope in one of the dresser drawers. (29 words) Seeing photographs protruding from the top of the envelope, Morrison looked inside and found photographs of Ehrlich with three young girls sitting on his lap. (25 words) Ehrlich was wearing only boxer shorts. (6 words) The girls were nude from the waist up. (8 words) Considering the photographs to be perverted, Morrison showed them to Fiscis, who agreed that they looked suspicious. (17 words) They seized the photographs as well as the marijuana. (9 words) The defendant, Victor Ehrlich, has now contested this seizure and has made a motion to suppress the photographic evidence as the result of an unconstitutional seizure. (26 words)

Part of what makes the revised version effective is its use of short sentences. The four short sentences were all used to highlight particularly significant facts.

§ 24.5.3 The Power of the Short Sentence

Used sparingly, short sentences can energize writing. Not only can they provide relief to readers who have just labored through several long sentences, they also tend to highlight the information they contain.

Note how in the following example the short sentence serves both as a welcome break after two fairly long sentences and as a way to emphasize the significant point that individuals in both cases were possibly motivated by a reward.

Short Sentence for Emphasis

EXAMPLE

In two older decisions, *United States v. Snowadzki,* 723 F.2d 1427 (9th Cir. 1984), and *United States v. Black,* 767 F.2d 1334 (9th Cir. 1985), individuals conducting unlawful searches were considered to have acted as private parties, not as government agents. In both cases, the individuals obtained the documents unlawfully and then turned them over to the government, which later submitted them as evidence at trial. In each instance, a reward had been offered.

See Exercises 24J and 24K in the *Practice Book.*

§ 24.6 Emphasis

Emphasis is a natural part of all writing. In objective writing, the writer uses emphasis to let the reader know where to focus his or her attention. In persuasive writing, emphasis allows the advocate to spotlight those points that favor the client and downplay those that hurt the client. It also allows the advocate to hammer home his or her theory of the case. In the previous section, we saw how short sentences can be used to emphasize key points. Notice again how the revision of the following sentence demonstrates the startling effect a short sentence can have.

Original

EXAMPLES

The defendant lied when she testified that she was in St. Paul, Minnesota, at the time of the robbery.

Revised

The defendant testified that she was in St. Paul, Minnesota, at the time of the robbery. She lied.

Besides short sentences, emphasis can be achieved in several other ways:

A.   telling the reader what is important
B.   underlining (or italics or boldface)

C.   using positions of emphasis
D.   using punctuation to highlight a point
E.   using single-word emphasizers
F.   changing the normal order of a sentence
G.   repeating key words
H.   setting up a pattern (and sometimes breaking it)

Of all these strategies, the most common and least sophisticated are the first two: (A) simply telling the reader what is important and (B) underlining. Some writers consider these first two strategies too obvious and overused to be effective. Others feel that they can be effective if used selectively.

§ 24.6.1 Telling the Reader What Is Important

Sentence openers such as "it is important to note that," "it is noteworthy that," "most important," or "above all" alert the reader to the importance of the point that follows. Used rarely, these sentence openers can help the reader identify which points deserve heightened emphasis. Used frequently, these same sentence openers bog down the writing and make it wordy.

EXAMPLES   **Sentence Openers for Emphasis**

Above all, the court should consider the defendant's past record as a good husband, model father, and leader in the community.

It is important to note that the check was postdated.

Notice that the last example may be even more emphatic when revised into a short sentence: The check was postdated.

Expressions such as "especially," "particularly," and "most important" also signal importance when they are inserted right before the point to be emphasized.

EXAMPLE   **Signaling Emphasis**

The court should consider the defendant's past record as a good husband, a model father, and, most important, a leader in the community.

---

§ 24.6.2 Underlining

Underlining is undoubtedly the simplest and least sophisticated strategy to create emphasis. It requires no restructuring of the sentence and little, if any, planning. If you do decide to use underlining for emphasis, be extremely selective.

EXAMPLE   **Underlining for Emphasis**

The contract <u>permits</u> but does not <u>require</u> the tenant to add landscaping and similar outdoor improvements.

It is sometimes tempting to assume that readers will not detect subtle emphasis and must be told which words are crucial. Many writers would consider the underlining in the previous example unnecessary and possibly even condescending. The remaining strategies for emphasis are significantly more subtle and therefore more suitable for sophisticated readers.

§ 24.6.3 Using Positions of Emphasis

When it comes to emphasis, not all parts of the sentence are created equal. That is, the beginning, middle, and end of a sentence are not equally emphatic.

In most sentences, writers place new information at the end of a sentence. Also, the end of the sentence is the point of climax. Everything in the sentence builds toward the words at the end. Consequently, in most sentences, the most emphatic position is at the end.

The next most emphatic position is usually at the beginning. Here the writer typically sets the stage for the rest of the sentence. The reader expects the beginning of the sentence to demonstrate how the new information in this sentence is connected with what has already been discussed.

The middle of the sentence is usually the least emphatic. Skillful advocates know that in this part of the sentence they can place unfavorable information and points they do not wish to highlight.

The following grid illustrates the positions in a sentence and their degree of emphasis.

SENTENCE

beginning	middle	end
somewhat emphatic	least emphatic	most emphatic

Examine the following two examples, either of which could appear in an objective memo. Example 1 places "are not attractive nuisances" in the end position, so this version should occur in a memo that emphasizes the point that natural streams are usually not attractive nuisances.

Changing Emphasis

EXAMPLE 1

Unless they are concealing some dangerous condition, natural streams that flow through the hatchery are not attractive nuisances.

Example 2 places "unless they are concealing some dangerous condition" in the end position, so this version is likely to occur in a memo that emphasizes that a concealed dangerous condition made a natural stream an attractive nuisance.

EXAMPLE 2 | **Changing Emphasis**

Natural streams that flow through the hatchery are not attractive nuisances, unless they are concealing some dangerous condition.

In the following example from a persuasive brief, note how placing the clause in the end position emphasizes that the error was harmless.

EXAMPLE | **Changing Emphasis**

Even if the trial court mischaracterized the property, the entire division was fair; thus, the error was harmless.

To emphasize that the entire division of property was fair, the same sentence can be revised.

EXAMPLE | **Changing Emphasis**

Even if the trial court mischaracterized the property, the error was harmless because the entire division was fair.

As ethical members of the legal profession, legal writers must often include information that is unfavorable to their client. Rather than concede a point in a short sentence, which will highlight the unfavorable point, it is often better to include it with the favorable point and arrange the material so the reader ends with the point favorable to your client.

EXAMPLE | **Controlling Emphasis**

Although Mr. Brown admits that he raised his voice during the altercation with Mrs. Smith, he never threatened Mrs. Smith, as Mrs. Smith claims, but rather reminded her of his rights as a property owner.

Combining the End Position with Other Strategies for Emphasis

By using the emphatic end position in combination with another strategy for emphasis, legal writers can achieve even more emphasis.

Here the end position, combined with punctuation, is used for dramatic effect.

EXAMPLE | **Emphasis in End Position**

The court suppressed all of the evidence except for one piece: the suicide note.

In the next example, the end position, combined with the use of a phrase telling the reader what is important, is used to suggest a climax.

Emphasis in End Position　　　　　　　　　　　　　EXAMPLE

Before awarding custody, the court must consider the mental and physical health of all individuals involved, the child's adjustment to home and school, the relationship of the child with his parents and siblings, the wishes of the parents, and, most important, the wishes of the child.

In the next example, the end position, combined with the technique of setting up a pattern and breaking it, is used to startle the reader.

Breaking a Pattern　　　　　　　　　　　　　　　EXAMPLE

Daniel Klein was loyal to his parents, loyal to his wife, loyal to his friends, and disloyal to the company that had employed him for thirty years.

Two final points before leaving the topic of positions of emphasis: first, the positions of emphasis can also be applied at the paragraph and document levels; second, the characterization of most emphatic, somewhat emphatic, and least emphatic for the end, beginning, and middle of sentences is a general, not an absolute, principle. In the following subsections we will see how punctuation, single-word emphasizers, and the changing of normal word order can make the beginning and even the middle of sentences strong points of emphasis.

§ 24.6.4　Using Punctuation for Emphasis

Commas, colons, and dashes can all be used to set up a point in an appositive at the end of a sentence. An appositive is a restatement of an earlier word or group of words. It is often a more detailed substitute for the earlier word or group of words. In the following examples "expert witness" is an appositive for "one term," "bribe" is an appositive for "exchange of money," and "greed and more greed" is an appositive for "two things."

Punctuating for Emphasis　　　　　　　　　　　　EXAMPLES

All of the prosecution's arguments depend on the definition of one term, "expert witness."

Throughout the United States, such an exchange of money is known by one name: bribe.

The defendant was motivated by only two things — greed and more greed.

Notice in the three following examples how all three marks of punctuation cast a slightly different light on the words that follow them. The comma, as a rather commonplace punctuation mark, suggests in the first of these examples that there is nothing too surprising about the silent partner being his brother.

EXAMPLE 1   **Punctuation and Emphasis**

The construction contract included a silent partner, his brother.

The colon requires a longer pause; consequently the phrase "his brother" receives more emphasis in the example that follows. Colons also have an aura of formality that somehow suggests the seriousness of what follows them.

EXAMPLE 2   **Punctuation and Emphasis**

The construction contract included a silent partner: his brother.

The longer pause created by the dash gives even more emphasis to "his brother." Also, the dash suggests that it is rather surprising that the brother is the silent partner.

EXAMPLE 3   **Punctuation and Emphasis**

The construction contract included a silent partner — his brother.

One thing legal writers should consider before using dashes, however, is that some readers feel dashes also convey a sense of informality. Consequently, many legal writers avoid the dash in legal prose.

Pairs of commas or pairs of dashes can also be used to set off appositives and parenthetical expressions in the middle of sentences. Because pairs of commas are the standard punctuation in such cases, they give the enclosed information less emphasis than a pair of dashes.

See Exercise 24L in the *Practice Book*.

EXAMPLES   **Punctuation and Emphasis**

Defense counsel's final argument, that the accident was unavoidable, will fail because the defendant's earlier statement shows that she considered the possibility of an injury during a high wind storm.

Defense counsel's final argument — that the accident was unavoidable — will fail because the defendant's earlier statement shows that she considered the possibility of an injury during a high wind storm.

§ 24.6.5 Using Single-Word Emphasizers

Certain words ("no," "not," "never," "only," "any," "still," "all," "every," "none") convey natural emphasis because they either dramatically change or intensify the meaning of the words they modify.

Draft

EXAMPLES

A change made to the contract must be approved by both parties.

Revision 1

Any change made to the contract must be approved by both parties.

Revision 2

A change may be made to the contract only if approved by both parties.

Note that the most effective way to use "not" for emphasis is to place a comma before it and use it as a contrasting element.

"Not" for Emphasis

EXAMPLES

It is the taxpayer, not the tax preparer, who is responsible for the accuracy of all information on the form.

Mrs. Field's express wish was for the jewelry to go to her niece, not to her daughter.

Three other single-word emphasizers ("clearly," "obviously," and "very") are so overused by legal writers and, in the case of "very," by the general public, that they have lost much of their ability to emphasize. Ironically, then, sentences that contain "clearly," "obviously," and "very" often seem to have more impact when these words are omitted.

Weak

EXAMPLE

Clearly, the defendant knew she was committing a crime.

Revised

The defendant knew she was committing a crime.

Notice that in the example, "clearly" would be stressed. In the revision, "knew" gets the natural stress.

EXAMPLE

Weak

Many residents complained about the very loud noise coming from the factory.

Revised

Many residents complained about the loud noise coming from the factory.

"Very" is often an unnecessary prop for a word. Usually, a word such as "loud" conveys the right level of meaning by itself. If, however, "loud" is too weak a term for your purpose, it is better to choose a stronger term rather than to rely on "very" to bolster its meaning.

See Exercise 24M in the *Practice Book.*

EXAMPLE

Revised

Many residents complained about the ear-splitting noise coming from the factory.

§ 24.6.6 Changing the Normal Word Order

Readers expect the traditional subject-verb-object order in sentences. When a writer changes this expected order, the change draws attention to itself and emphasizes whatever words are out of the traditional order.

The most common change is from active voice to passive voice (see sections 24.1.1 to 24.1.3).

EXAMPLE

Changing Word Order

Over $1,000,000 was embezzled by the defendant.

Another fairly common change is to insert the words to be emphasized between either the subject and the verb or between the verb and its object.

EXAMPLES

Martin Fuller, blinded by grief, lost his grip on reality and opened fire in the parking lot.
(subject and verb separated by "blinded by grief")

He shot—apparently at close range—both of Tim O'Connell's parents.
(verb and object separated by "apparently at close range")

Another, less frequent change is to delay the subject and verb and open the sentence with a part of the sentence that would normally come at the end.

Draft   EXAMPLE

Mrs. Taylor rewrote her will only one week before she died.

Revised

Only one week before she died, Mrs. Taylor rewrote her will.

Notice that some of the preceding examples seem to contradict the earlier advice about keeping subjects and verbs close together and using the end position in sentences to achieve emphasis. None of the strategies for emphasis works as an absolute rule. The writer should use his or her judgment in selecting which strategy is effective in each instance.

See **Exercise 24N** in the *Practice Book*.

§ 24.6.7 Repeating Key Words

Many writers mistakenly assume that repetition is a weakness. This assumption leads them to search desperately for synonyms of words that recur frequently in a given office memo or brief.

While it is true that needless repetition is ineffective, it is also true that deliberate repetition can be a powerful strategy for emphasis. Key terms and key points should reverberate throughout a piece of legal writing. Like the dominant color in a beautiful tapestry, key words and phrases should be woven throughout to create an overall impression that this is what the case is about.

Consider the following excerpt from the respondent's brief in a case where the appellant, a church, wants to operate a grade school without the special use permit required by the city's zoning ordinance for all schools in residential areas. Throughout the excerpt, three different words — "code," "use," and "school" — are deliberately repeated for emphasis. We have bold-faced these three words so you can see how frequently they appear.

EXAMPLE

Argument

I. THE TRIAL COURT PROPERLY CONSTRUED AND APPLIED BOTH THE ZONING AND BUILDING **CODES** BECAUSE THE CHURCH HAS CHANGED THE **USE** OF ITS BUILDING BY OPERATING A FULLTIME GRADE **SCHOOL**.

The church must comply with the requirements of the zoning and building **codes** before it may legally operate its **school**. Each of these **codes** makes accommodation for **uses** that legally existed before enactment of the **code**. However, the church never operated a **school** before the **codes'** enactment, so full compliance with the **codes** is required for the new **use** involved in operating a **school**.

---

§ 24.6.8 Setting Up a Pattern

The earlier strategy of repeating key words is closely tied to another strategy for emphasis: setting up a pattern. In such cases a pattern is set up and key words are repeated within that pattern. This kind of deliberate repetition can be used effectively within one sentence or in a sequence of sentences.

EXAMPLES   **Deliberate Repetition**

Lieutenant Harris has been described by his superiors as an "exemplary officer" — exemplary in his demeanor and professionalism, exemplary in his management of subordinates, exemplary in his performance of duty, and exemplary in his loyalty to the service.

Both women were abducted in the same locale. Both women were abducted at night. Both women were abducted while alone. Both women were abducted by the same man: Edward Smith.

Note that to achieve a climactic effect, the writer usually used parallel structure (see section 27.7) to create the pattern and then arranged the material in an order of increasing importance. Thus, emphasis was achieved by the pattern, the repetition of key words, and the end position. Notice too that this strategy for emphasis is best suited for persuasive writing.

§ 24.6.9 Variation: Deliberately Breaking a Pattern

A rather dramatic variation of the pattern strategy is to set up the pattern and then deliberately break it. This variation depends on the pattern and repetition of key words to create a certain expectation in the reader. The reader's surprise when the pattern is broken creates heightened emphasis.

See Exercise 24O in the *Practice Book*.

EXAMPLE   **Breaking a Pattern**

The defendant acted under a common scheme, for a common motive, but with uncommon results.

See Exercises 24P and 24Q in the *Practice Book*.

§ 24.7 Sentence Structures That Highlight Similarities or Differences[1]

Legal writers often need to compare and contrast facts. In arguing that a case is analogous to or distinguishable from the present case, writers must spell out exactly how the two sets of facts are similar or different. All too often, though,

---

1. The material and examples in the following section first appeared in a column written by Anne Enquist: *Teaching Students to Make Explicit Factual Comparisons*, 12 Perspectives 147 (Spring 2004).

novice legal writers are tentative and vague when they set up these comparisons. Instead of making explicit factual comparisons, the novice writer is likely to start a comparison sentence with something like "Like *Smith*, the defendant in our case...."

This approach has at least two problems. First, the sentence has a basic precision problem. It is comparing a whole case, *Smith*, to a person, the defendant. See section 11.2. Second, it is very likely sending the reader scurrying back a page or two to where *Smith* was discussed. "Like *Smith*, the defendant in our case..." makes it the reader's responsibility to figure out what the factual similarity is between *Smith* and the present case. What exactly is it in *Smith* that is analogous to the present case?

The first problem can be easily solved by simply making sure that the comparison (or contrast) is apples to apples and oranges to oranges: "Like the <u>defendant</u> in *Smith*, the <u>defendant</u> in our case..." or "Unlike the <u>driver</u> in *Lee*, the <u>driver</u> in our case...." That lining up of at least one fact (defendant to defendant or driver to driver) gives the reader a start at understanding the argument, but it is still just a start. The second problem can be solved by stating enough of the salient facts about the defendants or the drivers for the reader to see the similarities or differences.

Step one, then, might be to make a parallel chart of the similarities or differences before beginning to write sentences.

<u>analogous case</u>	<u>the present case</u>
defendants in *Smith*	defendants in our case (the Joneses)
allowed daughter's boyfriend	allowed family friend
to use the family car	to use the family car
to drive to a dance	to drive to work
boyfriend used car for a prank	friend used car for work-related errand
and got into an accident	and got into an accident

holding	*argument*
family car doctrine does not apply because	family car doctrine should not apply because
defendants' permission limited to driving to and from dance, not prank	defendants' permission limited to driving to and from work, not work-related errands
driver acted beyond the scope of permission	driver acted beyond the scope of permission
defendants not liable	defendants should not be liable

Step two is to translate the chart into sentences. The reader will readily see the comparison if the writer matches the sentence structure in the first and second parts of the sentence so that the information about the analogous case parallels the information about the present case. In the following example, the parallel parts are labeled A and A^1, B and B^1, and so on.

<u>"Like the defendant in *Smith* who allowed his daughter's boyfriend to use the family car</u>
      A   B

<u>to drive to a dance, the defendants in our case allowed their family friend to use the</u>
   C   A^1 B^1

family car to drive to work. The *Smith* court held that the defendants were not liable
 C¹   D
because the driver acted beyond the scope of their permission. (cite) Their permission
                                      E
was limited to driving to and from the dance; it did not extend to using the
                                                                 F
car for a prank. (cite) Similarly, the Joneses should not be held liable because
 G   D¹
the driver acted beyond the scope of their permission. Their permission was limited to
                                   E¹
driving to and from work; it did not extend to work-related errands.
       F¹   G¹

Of course, writers do not have to rigidly and mindlessly repeat the exact sentence structure in the second part that they used in the first part, but notice that *some* repetition makes the comparison easier for the reader to follow.

Below are a few more examples of comparing or contrasting charts followed by "like" or "unlike" sentences. An "equals sign" (=) in the chart indicates similarities; an equals sign with a line through it (≠) indicates differences.

EXAMPLE   **Comparing and Contrasting Cases**

defendant in *Sheldon*	=	Ms. Olsen (the defendant in this case)
used parents' house	≠	used halfway house
for many activities	≠	for only a few activities
indicates	≠	does not indicate
center of domestic activity		center of domestic activity

"Unlike the defendant in *Sheldon*, who used her parents' home for many activities indicative of a center of domestic activity, Ms. Olsen used the halfway house for only a few activities indicative of a center of domestic activity."

EXAMPLE   **Comparing and Contrasting Cases**

driver in *Cook*, Whitner,	=	Ms. Foster (the driver in this case)
paid room and board	=	paid room and board
family's adult daughter	≠	family friend
lived with parents	≠	lived with Nguyens
since death of husband	≠	while attending university

"Like the driver in *Cook* who paid for room and board, Ms. Foster also paid for room and board; however, unlike Whitner, who was the family's adult daughter who had lived with her parents since the death of her husband, Ms. Foster was only a family friend who was living with the Nguyens while she attended the university."

When the facts in both the analogous and the present case are virtually identical on one or more points, writers often use a sentence structure like the one below.

Sentence Structure When Facts Are Identical   `EXAMPLE`

"As in *Cook*, the driver in our case paid for room and board; however, unlike Whitner, who was the family's adult daughter who had lived with her parents since the death of her husband, Ms. Foster was only a family friend who was living with the Nguyens while she attended the university."

Note, however, that the "As in case name," sentence opening should be used with some care. Consider a situation in which the writer has found the following similarity between two cases:

Chea employee's stress   = Officer Wu's stress (the employee in this case)

resulted from a series of incidents   = resulted from three different incidents

The incorrect sentence in the example below is imprecise because it says the employee's stress in *Chea* also came from these same three incidents that caused Officer Wu's stress.

Precision when Comparing/Contrasting Cases   `EXAMPLE`

Incorrect

"As in *Chea*, Officer Wu's stress resulted from three different incidents: the Aurora Bridge accident, the City's failure to notify him about his exposure to HIV, and the WTO riots."

Correct

"Like *Chea*, in which the employee's stress resulted from a series of incidents, in this case, Officer Wu's stress resulted from three different incidents: the Aurora Bridge accident, the City's failure to notify him about his exposure to HIV, and the WTO riots."

In some situations, writers need to list many facts in order to compare or contrast cases, and doing so in one long sentence would affect readability. For those situations, companion sentences in which all of sentence 1 mirrors all of sentence 2 are often preferable.

Examples of Companion Sentences   `EXAMPLES`

In *Cook,* because Ms. Whitner ate most meals with the family, had her own room in the family home, was assigned several family-related chores, and was included in the family holiday photo, the court held that she was "treated as a member of the family." (cite) Similarly, because Ms. Foster ate three to four times a week with the

Nguyens, shared a room with their daughter, and vacationed in Oregon with them, the court should decide that she was treated as a member of the family.

In *Cook*, the court noted numerous examples of how Ms. Whitner was treated as a member of the family: she ate most meals with the family, had her own room in the family home, was assigned several family-related chores, and was included in the family holiday photo.

Similarly, in our case Ms. Foster can also point to numerous examples of how she was treated as a member of the family: she ate three to four times a week with the Nguyens, shared a room with their daughter, and vacationed in Oregon with them.

Interestingly, however, distinguishing facts often works best through a series of sentences with juxtaposed parts.

EXAMPLE   ## Sentences with Juxtaposed Parts

Cook is easily distinguishable from our case. Ms. Whitner ate most meals with the family; Ms. Foster ate only three to four times a week with the Nguyens. Whitner had her own room in the family home; Foster shared a room with the Nguyens' daughter, but after October spent most nights at her boyfriend's apartment. Whitner was assigned several family-related chores, including cooking once a week and taking out the trash; Foster was never asked to perform any chores and was instead treated more like a guest. Whitner was included in the family holiday photo and wrote her own paragraph in the family Christmas letter; Foster was included in the Nguyens' Oregon vacation, but she paid for her own room, meals, and souvenirs. Therefore, although Ms. Foster was still living with the Nguyens at the time of the accident, the court is unlikely to find that Ms. Foster was treated as a member of the family.

The examples above are but a few of the many sentence structures for making factual comparisons. The key is to think through how the facts are similar or different and then consciously construct a sentence that highlights those similarities and differences.

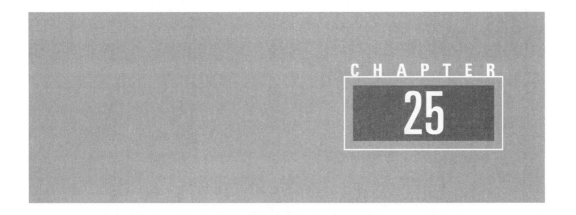

Effective Words

A powerful agent is the right word. Whenever we come upon one of those intensely right words in a book or a newspaper the resulting effect is physical as well as spiritual, and electrically prompt.

— Mark Twain,
Essay on William Dean Howells

§ 25.1 Diction and Precision

Such a seemingly simple thing. Use the right word, Twain tells us, and the effect is physical, spiritual, electric, prompt. But right is a relative thing, isn't it? Some words are more right than others. Some words approach the desired meaning; others capture it, embody it, nail it to the wall in a way that leaves both the writer and reader satisfied, almost breathless.

Take the word "right," for example. Twain chose "right" to describe the kind of word he meant, even though the thesaurus suggests that he might have chosen any number of so-called synonyms. How about the "noble" word, the "proper" word, the "suitable" word, the "exact" word, the "accurate" word, the "correct" word, or even the "precise" word?

What is it about "right" that makes it the right choice?

First of all, denotation — that is, the word's definition. "Noble" is the wrong choice because it has the wrong denotation. Webster tells us that "noble" means "possessing outstanding qualities." The definition of "noble" also includes a tie to some kind of superiority. Something is "noble" because it has a "superiority of mind or character or ideals or morals." The kind of words Twain talks about do something different from possessing outstanding qualities or superiority.

"Proper" seems to have the right denotation. "Proper" is defined as "marked by suitability, rightness, or appropriateness." Later in the definition we find "strictly accurate" and "correct." These meanings seem closer to Twain's intention. But wait a minute. Further still in the definition we see "respectable," "strictly decorous," and "genteel." But do we have to include all of the possible definitions of a word when we use it? Obviously not, but in the case of "proper," these later definitions are clues about the connotations, or associations, that the word carries.

The word "proper" has close ties with the word "propriety," which means "the quality or state of being proper." "Propriety" also means "the standard of what is socially acceptable." If "the proper thing to do" has overtones of decorum and civility, then "the proper word" might also suggest a bit of politeness in its selection. It's doubtful that Twain meant that a "polite word" is a powerful agent.

"Suitable" has similar denotation and connotation problems. Part of the definition of "suitable" is "adapted to the use or purpose." If "suitable words" are those that are adapted to a certain use or purpose, then it is unlikely anything with such a chameleon-like quality can ever be physical, spiritual, electric, or prompt.

"Exact" has the virtue of meaning in "strict, particular, and complete accordance with fact" and the minor flaw of connoting a kind of mathematical or scientific measurement. Still, it is a far better choice than "noble," "proper," or "suitable."

In fact, "exact," "accurate," "correct," "precise," and "right" all have what dictionaries call "the shared meaning element." They all mean "conforming to fact, truth, or a standard."

What is it then about the word "right" that makes it preferable to the other four words, that makes it just right? It has the right denotation and the right connotation, and it has the right sound.

Go back to the quotation at the beginning of the chapter. Try reading the first sentence aloud as it is. Now, one at a time, substitute the words "exact," "accurate," "correct," and "precise" for "right." Read each of these versions aloud. Notice how much harder it is to get the desired emphasis with the three-syllable "accurate." Even the two-syllable words dilute, albeit just a bit, the punch that we hear in the one-syllable "right." Furthermore, "right" has a kind of honesty and simplicity that captures the spirit of Twain's insight.

Now what does all of this mean for a writer of legal briefs and memos? The same thing it means for any good writer. Finding the right word to express one's meaning is critical to clear communication. With anything other than the right word, you have sacrificed precision; you have sacrificed exact meaning.

In cases like Twain's in which several words can express the intended meaning, the writer can then go beyond precision to eloquence to find the word with just the right sound. See Chapter 26: Eloquence. For now, though, we will focus just on diction and precision and the word choice problems that frequently occur in legal writing. (Three categories of word choice problems — legalese, gender-neutral language, and bias-free language — deserve special attention. They are discussed in sections 25.3, 25.4, and 25.5 respectively.)

§ 25.1.1 Colloquial Language

Because legal writing is done for serious reasons and in a professional context, legal writers should select words that reflect seriousness and professionalism. Slang, colloquialisms, or informal expressions that are acceptable in everyday spoken language are usually out of place in legal writing.

EXAMPLE

Poor

The prosecutor noted that Mr. Webb is hung up about how clean his car is, what gas is used in it, and how it is driven.

Revised

The prosecutor noted that Mr. Webb feels strongly about how clean his car is, what gas is used in it, and how it is driven.

There is only one exception to the general ban on using slang, colloquialisms, and informal language in legal writing — when the writer is quoting. While a writer of a trial brief would be ill-advised to call the defendant "a bad dude," he or she may effectively use that expression if it appeared in the record.

§ 25.1.2 The Reader's Expectations and Idioms

A writer's choice among synonyms should also be affected by the reader's expectations. Legal readers, for example, expect to hear about "analogous" cases or "similar" cases, not "comparable" cases or "matching" cases.

Read the following example and see if any word is jarring to legal readers.

EXAMPLE

Draft

Boliver Custom Carpets will probably argue that there are significant parallelisms between its case and *Flowers*.

Revised

Boliver Custom Carpets will probably argue that there are significant similarities between its case and *Flowers*.

Similarly, some synonyms have the correct denotation and connotation, but their use is jarring because the reader expects certain idiomatic combinations.

Consider the following example. Which word doesn't seem quite right?

EXAMPLE

Draft

Corporations can elude liability by dissolution.

Although the thesaurus may list "elude" as a synonym for "avoid" and "escape," legal readers expect either the idiom "avoid liability" or the idiom "escape liability."

EXAMPLE   **Revised**

Corporations can avoid liability by dissolution.

Numerous verbs have certain prepositions with which they commonly combine. In common usage, for example, one always "infers from" something. A client may "agree to" sign a contract, but she may not "agree with" the way you are handling her case. Although one can fear for one's life, one can live in fear of a lawsuit.

When in doubt about which idiom or preposition is appropriate, consult one of the better dictionaries or a usage guidebook. Another strategy is to read the sentence aloud. Native speakers of English can usually "hear" which preposition is correct.

EXAMPLE   **Draft**

Publishers must be able to publish matters of public concern without fear for a lawsuit.

Revised

Publishers must be able to publish matters of public concern without fear of a lawsuit.

---

§ 25.1.3 Not-Really-Synonymous Synonyms

Of the many types of imprecision, the most common is the simple substitution of a not-really-synonymous "synonym." In the following example, the writer knew that there were several things he had to prove under the doctrine of adverse possession, but he forgot what to call those "things."

EXAMPLE   **Draft**

The adverse possessor must prove the condition of hostility.

"Condition" is not completely wrong; the reader can probably figure out what the writer intended. But "condition" is not precise. By using the precise term "element," the writer conveys the exact intended meaning, and he makes it clear that he is doing an elements analysis of the problem.

EXAMPLE   **Revised**

The adverse possessor must prove the element of hostility.

Notice that in the above example the term "element" is used when there are indeed "elements" that must be proved. Some legal writers mistakenly use the terms "element" and "factor" as if they were synonyms. The term "element" refers to a requirement — something that must be proved or met. "Factor," on the other hand, refers to what a court must consider. For example, courts must examine several factors to determine which parent gets custody of a child.

Another group of problematic terms that some legal writers and even some courts use imprecisely includes the words "part," "prong," and "step." If there is a two-part test, then both parts must be satisfied. If there are two prongs to a test, then the test can be satisfied in either of the two ways. If there is a two-step test, both steps must be satisfied in sequence.

Unfortunately, however, you may occasionally find that courts themselves sometimes use the terms "factor," "element," "part," "prong," and "step" imprecisely when describing a test. In such instances, you will probably want to adopt the court's word choice if you are writing to that same court. In writing for others, however, you will probably want to adopt the precise term.

Yet another precision problem occurs when writers try to dress up a simple idea in a fancy vocabulary word and end up instead with a word choice that misses the mark.

EXAMPLE

Draft

The McKibbins may argue that rugs are totally diverse from closed circuit television camera security systems because few consumers have a need for such elaborate security systems.

Revised

The McKibbins may argue that rugs differ from closed circuit television camera security systems because few consumers have a need for such elaborate security systems.

The most serious type of "not-really-synonymous synonym" problem occurs when writers attempt to use words they have not completely mastered. Needless to say, it can be embarrassing to find that you have used a word that only sounds like the word you intended. Undoubtedly, the writer of the following example intended the point to be "salient," not salty.

See Exercise 25A in the *Practice Book*.

EXAMPLE

Misused Word

Mrs. Harris's most saline point is that Mr. Harris intends to move the children over 250 miles away.

---

§ 25.1.4 The Same Term for the Same Idea

Another common precision problem in legal writing is the misuse of elegant variation. In other words, legal writers sometimes try to use synonyms for key terms in their writing in the mistaken belief that using the same term over and over again bores their readers.

What they have forgotten, though, is that their legal readers have been carefully trained to read statutes and, according to the rules of statutory construction, a different term signals a different idea. Many legal readers carry this rule over into their memo and brief reading. A change in a key term starts them wondering: "Does the writer mean the same thing as before, or is this really something new?"

Read the following example, and note how the writer uses the phrase "best interests of the child" and its variations consistently but imprecisely floats back and forth among the terms "factor," "principle," and "element."

EXAMPLE   **Inconsistent Terms**

In a custody proceeding, the court's "paramount consideration" is the best interests of the child. *Waters v. Magee*, 877 A.2d 658, 664 (R.I. 2005). In assessing the child's best interests, the court may consider several **factors**, including the wishes of the child's parents, the reasonable preference of the child, and the quality of the relationship between the child and his or her parents. *Id.* Additional **elements** that the court may consider include the mental and physical health of the individuals involved, as well as the moral fitness of the parents. *Id.* at 664-65. Furthermore, the stability of the child's home life is another **principle** that the Rhode Island courts have considered in deciding custody disputes. *Id.* This list is non-exclusive, and no one **element** is determinative; rather, the court should consider a combination of and interaction among all the relevant **factors**. *Id.* at 665.

In a case like the example above, the reader does not know whether to accuse the writer of sloppy writing or to try to make some fine distinction between "factor," "principle," and "element." In many cases, there is a legal distinction between "factor" and "element" or between "factor" and "principle." In those cases, substituting the terms for each other would be more than confusing; it would be legally inaccurate.

In short, then, legal readers appreciate appropriate variety, but they do not appreciate variety at the expense of clarity.

See Exercise 25B in the *Practice Book*.

§ 25.1.5 Precise Comparisons

In the preceding sections, we saw how disconcerting it can be for readers when writers are not careful about what they call something. Equally disconcerting for readers are situations in which writers are sloppy about the comparisons they make.

EXAMPLE   **Draft**

The facts in *Turner* are similar to the present case.

Because a case includes more than just the facts, it is incongruous to compare just the facts of one case to another entire case.

Revised   EXAMPLE

The facts in *Turner* are similar to the facts in the present case.

In the following examples, the writer has forgotten that the italic type signals the case, not the defendant.

Draft   EXAMPLE

Unlike *Callahan,* Richardson was not just a temporary visitor.

Revised

Unlike Callahan, Richardson was not just a temporary visitor.

Draft   EXAMPLE

Like *Collins,* Richardson had personal possessions on the premises.

Revised

Like the defendant in *Collins,* Richardson had personal possessions on the premises. As in *Collins,* in the present case Richardson had personal possessions on the premises.

See Exercise 25C in the *Practice Book.*

§ 25.1.6 Subject-Verb-Object Mismatch

Not all problems of precision are a matter of just one poorly chosen word. All too frequently, the problem is a poorly chosen combination of words. Read the following example from a case about a custody dispute and see if the subject, verb, and object go together.

Draft   EXAMPLE

Dr. Davis's <u>occupation</u> as an obstetrician <u>has shown</u> a <u>diminished ability</u> to provide
       (subject)   *(verb)*   *(object)*
consistent care and guidance for her children.

Can an occupation show a diminished ability to do anything? Obviously not. What has happened to this writer is that she has gotten tangled in her own verbiage and has written something nonsensical. What she wants to say is that Dr. Davis is an obstetrician and that people who are obstetricians often have demanding, irregular schedules and therefore have less time and energy to give consistent care and guidance to their own children.

Consider the following possible revision.

EXAMPLE   **Possible Revision**

As an obstetrician, Dr. Davis may have a diminished ability to provide consistent care and guidance for her children.

Of course, the revision's meaning is somewhat different from the meaning in the original sentence. Dr. Davis, rather than the profession of being an obstetrician, has become the subject.

Consider the following compromise revisions.

EXAMPLE   **Possible Revision**

Dr. Davis's occupation, obstetrician, may impair her ability to provide consistent care and guidance for her children.

To determine whether this or any other subject-verb-object combination is mismatched, lift those three parts out of the sentence and see if they make sense as a unit.

occupation	may impair	ability
(subject)	*(verb)*	*(object)*

Does "occupation may impair ability" make sense? Most readers would say that it does; some, however, would argue against the personification of "occupation" and suggest that occupations cannot "impair" anything. Precision, as we said earlier, is a relative thing.

One common personification used in law that many readers consider imprecise is the use of a case in the subject position when the writer actually means the court that decided that case.

EXAMPLE   **Draft**

The case *Randall v. State*, 806 So. 2d 185 (Miss. 2001), reversed the trial court's decision because the trial court did not give an additional limiting instruction to the jury.

Using the "lift-out" strategy, we get the following combination:

case	reversed	decision
(subject)	*(verb)*	*(object)*

To be more precise, place the real actor, the supreme court, in the subject position.

Revised   EXAMPLE

In *Randall v. State*, 806 So. 2d 185 (Miss. 2001), the Mississippi Supreme Court reversed the trial court's decision because the trial court did not give an additional limiting instruction to the jury.

Mississippi Supreme Court	reversed	trial court's decision
(subject)	*(verb)*	*(object)*

Occasionally, legal writers mistakenly end up with a combination that essentially means "X equals X"; that is, the subject or beginning of the sentence and object or end of the sentence are the same.

Draft   EXAMPLE

The purpose of the legislation is compensatory intent.

purpose	is	intent
(subject)	*(verb)*	*(predicate nominative)[1]*

There is virtually no difference between "the purpose of the legislation" and "the intent of the legislation." More than likely, the writer intended to say that the purpose of the legislation was to compensate someone.

Revised   EXAMPLE

The purpose of the legislation is to compensate victims of such crimes.

Part of matching the right subject with the right verb is understanding how the legal system works. Knowing exactly what courts, juries, parties to litigation, legislatures, and agencies do and don't do makes it easier to select appropriate verbs. Chart 25.1 lists some typical subject-verb-object combinations.

For example, "the court finds" is the right combination for describing the action a court takes in making a finding of fact. "The court held" is the right combination when describing the court's holding in a case. "The court ruled" is the right combination for describing the actions a court takes on a motion or an objection in a particular case. Courts can also "deny motions" or "grant injunctions"; they can "take something under advisement."

---

1. The term "predicate nominative" is used instead of "object" with linking verbs. See section 27.1.

Chart 25.1   Typical Subject-Verb-Object Combinations

the court found (findings of fact)
the court ruled (ruling on an objection or a motion)
the court held (law applied to facts of a specific case)
the court determined (or must determine)
the court granted an injunction
the court granted the motion
the court denied the motion
the court applied the law (the test, the rule, the standard)
the court adopted the test
the court ordered (psychological testing, discovery)

the court relied on
the court followed
the court concluded
the court examined
the court reasoned

the appellate court affirmed the trial court's decision
the appellate court modified the trial court's decision
the appellate court reversed the trial court's decision
the appellate court upheld the trial court's decision
the appellate court remanded the case

In *Smith*, the court criticized the court's holding in *Jones*.
In *Smith*, the court explained the court's holding in *Jones*.
In *Smith*, the court followed the court's holding in *Jones*.
In *Smith*, the court limited the court's holding in *Jones*.
In *Smith*, the court questioned the court's holding in *Jones*.
In *Smith*, the court expanded upon the court's holding in *Jones*.
In *Smith*, the court overruled *Jones*.

the jury found the defendant (guility or not guility)
the jury determined that the defendant was (was not) liable
the jury awarded damages

the defendant (or plaintiff) argued, stated, maintained, asked, claimed, alleged,
asserted, responded, rebutted, countered, moved

the legislature passed, enacted, amended
the legislature intended to (promote, encourage, prevent, protect)
the legislature wanted to (promote, encourage, prevent, protect)

the agency determined, decided
the agency ruled
the agency promulgated, investigated, proposed, mediated

Courts can "apply the law," they can "apply a standard," and they can "apply a test"; they never "apply the facts." In other words, courts apply law to fact, not fact to law.

Incorrect

Applying the facts of this case to the law, the court held that the defendant was negligent.

Correct

Applying the law to the facts of this case, the court held that the defendant was negligent.

In cases in which the court is both the decider of law and the trier of fact, courts perform an additional set of duties. When no jury is present, the court will "find" the criminal defendant guilty or not guilty, and the court will "award" civil damages.

As both the decider of law and the trier of fact, the court may "make determinations" or simply "determine" something about the law or the facts. Even so, "determine" is more commonly used for findings of fact.

For cases up on appeal, appellate courts have a variety of actions they can perform. They can "affirm," "modify," "reverse," or "remand" a case; they can also "criticize," "distinguish," "explain," "follow," "limit," "overrule," or "question" the decisions in another case.

The court never takes on the role of one of the parties to litigation. Consequently, as a general rule, the court does not "claim," "allege," "assert," or "argue." The court is in a position to "say," not to "claim."

Even though it is technically incorrect to say "the court claimed," "the court asserted," or "the court argued," there are a few times when these combinations may be strategic word choices. In instances in which the writer is disagreeing with another court, for example, a writer may deliberately use "the court claimed" as a pejorative attack on another court's reasoning. The effect, of course, is the subtle undermining of the court's authority.

Another instance in which it is appropriate to use a combination like "the court argued" occurs when members of the same court differ. Consequently, a law professor or the author of a law review article may say "Justice X argued" to describe a position that Justice X took when trying to persuade the other members of the same court.

Juries, on the other hand, are charged with tasks that are different from judges. They "find" that a defendant is guilty or not guilty, they "determine liability," and they "award damages," but they do not "rule" on the law. Consequently, "a jury found," "a jury determined," and "a jury awarded" are appropriate combinations. In a jury trial, the jury, not the judge, "renders a verdict," and the judge, not the jury, "enters a judgment" based on that verdict. In a bench trial, the judge "renders a verdict."

Defendants and plaintiffs perform certain acts as well. They "argue," "state," "ask," "claim," "contend," "allege," "assert," "respond," "rebut," and "counter," but they do not "apply" the law. That is for the court to do.

Incorrect

Applying the majority rule, the defendant will argue that the benefit of having a healthy baby outweighs the burden.

Correct

The defendant will argue that the court should apply the majority rule and hold that having a healthy baby outweighs the burden.

Either party to litigation may make a preliminary motion. Although you often hear, for example, that "the plaintiff made a motion for summary judgment," it is more concise to say "the plaintiff moved for summary judgment."

Legislatures, of course, perform entirely different functions from judges, juries, and litigants. The legislature may "enact a statute," it may "amend a statute," and it may "pass a law." It does not "hold" or "find." When it comes to policy, it is appropriate to say that the legislature "intended," "wanted to promote," "wanted to encourage," "wanted to prevent," or "wanted to protect."

Like judges, agencies "make determinations" (or just "determine"), and they "decide" things. Rarely does an agency "hold"; save "hold" for the few times when an agency issues an opinion. Even then, it is more likely to "rule." And, of course, agencies perform many other functions, such as "promulgate," "investigate," "propose," and "decide."

Perhaps the most glaring errors in word choice made by novice legal writers are those that stem from confusion over criminal and civil cases. Use "accused," "prosecuted," and "charged" for criminal cases. The defendant in a civil suit may be "sued" or "an action may be filed" against him or her; a civil suit defendant is not "accused," "prosecuted," or "charged."

Similarly, defendants in civil suits are not "found guilty or not guilty"; they are "found liable" or "not liable."

The outcome of a trial is a "judgment," not a "settlement." Use "settlement" for those agreements reached by parties through negotiation, not litigation. Parties may "settle out of court."

See **Exercise 25D** in the *Practice Book*.

Criminal Cases	Civil Cases
accused	sued
charged	action filed against
guilty	liable
not guilty	not liable

§ 25.1.7 Grammatical Ambiguities

Before leaving the topic of precision, we must consider those times when writing becomes ambiguous and imprecise because the writer has not paid close attention to the grammar of the sentence. Modifiers in particular can create unintended meanings because modifiers seem to be free-floating spirits that can find a home in many different spots in a sentence. See section 27.6 for more on modifiers.

§ 25.2 Conciseness

Imagine for a moment that you are at a great steak house. It's a special occasion, so you order the best steak on the menu. When your meal arrives, however, you find that the steak is surrounded by an inch of fat. Appealing? Hardly. The meat itself may be tender and juicy, but you find it hard to appreciate its flavor with all that fat staring up at you from the plate. Why, you wonder, didn't the chef trim off the fat before your meal was served to you?

Wordy writing is like a steak surrounded by fat. The writing may have great analysis and brilliant arguments, but if you haven't trimmed the fat, the reader is still likely to find the writing unappealing.

The question for most legal writers is how to transform fatty writing into writing that is lean and appealing. What follows are numerous strategies for trimming excess verbiage.

§ 25.2.1 Don't State the Obvious

Judges, lawyers, and most clients are busy people. They don't want to spend time reading the legal equivalent of "the sky is blue" or "people breathe air," unless, of course, you have something new to say about what is obvious.

Wasting time with sentences like "Now I am going to discuss the cases that are relevant to this issue" or "The appellate court will not reconsider factual issues" annoys legal readers. It is a given that an office memo will discuss cases that are relevant to the issue; it is old news that appellate courts don't retry a case on its facts.

Novice legal writers often state the obvious because it reminds them of the steps they must go through in legal analysis. For example, a writer who begins the discussion section of a memo with "To determine the answer to this question, we must first look at the rule that . . . " has not recognized that a legal reader would be shocked to find something other than the rule at this point in the memo.

Consider the following excerpt from a draft of a memo.

Stating the Obvious   EXAMPLE

Thompson bears the burden of establishing that the action meets the federal removal requirements. Some of these requirements are more important than others, but all are required before removal may occur. To understand these requirements, it is easiest to break down 28 U.S.C. § 1441(a) (1988) into its component parts and discuss each part separately.

Besides the wordiness that comes from the redundancy in the first two sentences — requirements are required — the last sentence is no more than an announcement that one should do the obvious: analyze the requirements.

Novice and experienced legal writers often fall into the "stating the obvious" trap when they are trying to compose topic and transitional sentences within a discussion or argument section.

Suppose, for example, that a writer has just completed a paragraph about the holding, rationale, and facts of an analogous case. The writer now wants to compare the facts of the analogous case with those of the present case. At first the writer may be tempted to begin with something like *"Moore* and the present case are factually similar." This announcement should be quickly obvious, however, and unworthy of mention. What the writer needs to discuss in this topic sentence is the nature of these similarities or why those similarities suggest a certain outcome.

§ 25.2.2 Don't Start Too Far Back

Some novice legal writers fall prey to a cousin of the "stating the obvious" problem — starting too far back. They forget that there is common knowledge among legal readers. Consequently, the writing problem is determining where to begin and what not to say.

Consider the following example of starting too far back from a draft of a memo about a case in which criminal charges had been filed against the client who had photocopied a dollar bill and, after a friendly bet, had tried it in a change-making machine.

EXAMPLE   **Unnecessary Background**

Counterfeiting has been classified as an offense affecting the administration of governmental functions because the power to coin money was expressly granted to Congress and denied to the states by the terms of the Constitution. Hence, counterfeiting is a federal crime, and the penalty for passing counterfeit money is found in the *United States Code*. Congress has enacted statutes making counterfeiting a federal offense; the various counterfeiting crimes are defined by these statutes, and these statutes determine the essential elements of the respective crimes.

The background information in the preceding example is unnecessary. The writer of this excerpt seems to have forgotten who the reader is and what that reader is likely to know.

Writers who have a tendency to start too far back often fill their writing with background information that they needed in order to focus their ideas or to clarify a point. Even if they needed the information to analyze the problem, that does not automatically mean that their reader will need it too.

For example, because of a lack of experience, the writer may have had to do a fair amount of spade work to fill in a skimpy background in a given area of law. Unless the writer believes the reader needs the same kind of review or preliminary discussion, it should be omitted from the reader's version.

Furthermore, writers are obliged to save their readers from at least some of the blind alleys they explored. Legal writers who were successful writers as undergraduates often have a difficult time realizing this. In law there is no extra credit for arguments that don't work.

Thus far, we have primarily discussed legal writing that starts too far back analytically. Occasionally legal writers start too far back historically. They give long, careful explanations of how a particular area of law has evolved when all the reader wants is a discussion of how the end result of that evolutionary process applies to the facts of the case at hand.

This is not to say that tracing the history of a statute or a judicial trend is never appropriate. The point is to consider your specific reader and that reader's purposes, and then ask yourself if it is appropriate in the document you are writing. Put another way, don't write a law review article when the senior partner has assigned you to write an office memo.

§ 25.2.3 Don't Overuse Quotations

When to quote and how much to quote — these are two tough questions for all legal writers. Like many other issues in legal writing, there is a range of opinion about when quoting is appropriate, even required, and when the writer should merely paraphrase and cite to authority.

Most legal readers agree that relevant portions of statutes should be quoted. The trick, of course, is to pare the quotation down to that which is relevant.

In the following example, the writer has mistakenly quoted more of the statute than her reader needs. The case she is working on does not have anything to do with obstruction of a highway or the closing of a channel, but rather with whether a noisy aerobics club with patrons in skimpy attire is a private nuisance.

Overquoting a Statute   EXAMPLE

In determining whether there is a cause of action for private nuisance, the court is guided by Washington Revised Code § 7.48.010 (2006), which provides the following:

> The obstruction of any highway or closing the channel of any stream used for boating or rafting logs, lumber or timber, or whatever is injurious to health or indecent or offensive to the senses, or an obstruction to the free use of property, so as to essentially interfere with the comfortable enjoyment of the life and property, is a nuisance and the subject of an action for damages and other and further relief.

First, edit out all of the statute that is extraneous to the case:

> [t]he obstruction of any highway or closing the channel of any stream used for boating or rafting logs, lumber or timber, or whatever is injurious to health or indecent or offensive to the senses, or an obstruction to the free use of property, so as to essentially interfere with the comfortable enjoyment of the life and property, is a nuisance and the subject of an action for damages and other and further relief.

Appropriately pared down then, the quotation looks like this:

> [W]hatever is . . . indecent or offensive to the senses, or an obstruction to the free use of property, so as to essentially interfere with the comfortable enjoyment of the life and property, is a nuisance . . . .

Note the use of ellipses to indicate words omitted in the middle and at the end of the quotation. The brackets, which are used to show that the "w" was not capitalized in the original, also show that the original did not begin at the word "whatever." See section 28.5 for more on the use of ellipses and brackets in quotations.

Although there is a great deal of agreement about quoting relevant portions of statutes, there is some disagreement about whether common law should be set out verbatim. One general rule is that if a specific phrase reappears in the cases, then that phrase has become the standard or familiar "rule" and should therefore be quoted.

Generally, it is best to paraphrase the holding and rationale and cite to authority. Occasionally, however, the particular language of the holding or court's reasoning is so apt or well stated that a quotation is effective. This tactic works best when used rarely.

Never quote facts of a case, although you may want to quote the exact words of a person in a fact statement when those words suggest the person's attitude, motive, or intention.

When deciding how much to quote, consider what your purpose is. In persuasive writing, you will probably use fairly extensive quoting from the record to make points about errors and conflicting testimony. You might also use a few more quotations from analogous cases because they allow you to create emphasis and effective repetition. A well-written lead-in to a quotation that makes your point, followed by a carefully selected quotation that makes your point, allows you to make that point twice without being tedious. The same tactic used in objective writing, however, would be tedious.

The cardinal rule of quotations can be summed up as follows: quote only when the language itself is worth attention. The language of statutes is always worth our attention; the specific language of common law is sometimes worth our attention; and, occasionally, the language of a court stating its holding or expressing its rationale is so memorable that it should not escape our attention. In all three instances, quote; otherwise, don't.

§ 25.2.4 Create a Strong Subject-Verb Unit

The quickest way to achieve an energetic yet lean style is to make sure that the subject-verb unit carries the core of meaning in the sentence. In other words, put the real action in the verb; put the doer of that action in the subject.

All too frequently in ineffective legal writing the real action of the sentence is buried in a noun. This practice of changing verbs to nouns, known as nominalization, tends to make sentences wordy (see section 24.3). Because the real action in the sentence is somewhere other than the verb, the writer must find a substitute to fill the verb slot in the sentence, usually either a form of the verb "to be" or some other filler verb that expresses no real action.

EXAMPLE   **Draft**

The present case <u>is</u> an illustration of this point.
        (verb)

Revised

The present case <u>illustrates</u> this point.
        (verb)

The following examples are but a few of the many ways legal writers can make their writing more concise by finding the real action in the sentence. The trick is to ask yourself "what are the people really doing?" Are they "reaching" or are they "agreeing"? Is the court "making" something or "stating" something?

reached an agreement	→	agreed
made a statement	→	stated
perform a review	→	review
made a recommendation	→	recommended
supports an inference	→	infers
made the assumption	→	assumed

If the real doer of the action is somewhere other than in the subject, then the subject of the sentence is also inevitably wordy because the writer has had to manufacture some language to fill that slot in the sentence.

Sometimes writers fill the subject slot with wordy expletives like "there is," "there are," "there was," "there were," "it is," or "it was." Avoid these expletive constructions unless the point of the sentence is that something exists.

Draft   EXAMPLE

It was his intention to return to Maryland.

Revised

He intended to return to Maryland.

When writers inadvertently slip into the passive voice (see section 24.1), they inevitably create a wordy sentence with a weak subject.

Draft   EXAMPLE

Authorization for the contract was given by the district manager.

Revised

The district manager authorized the contract.

---

§ 25.2.5 Avoid Throat-Clearing Expressions

Frequently legal writers create wordy sentences because they fill both the subject and verb slots with throat-clearing expressions that add little, if any, meaning to the sentence. These expressions seem to have more to do with getting the writer warmed up to the task of articulating his or her point than with content.

EXAMPLE   **Draft**

It must be remembered that the statute requires that service be made at the dwelling house or usual place of abode.

Revised

The statute requires that service be made at the dwelling house or usual place of abode.

Most but not all of these throat-clearing expressions fall into the pattern "It is _____ that":

It is expected that
It is generally recognized that
It is significant that
It is a known fact that
It is obvious that
It is essential that
It is crucial that
It is conceivable that

Notice how the following throat-clearing expressions may be reduced to one word or completely edited out.

It seems more likely than not that   →   probably
It can be presumed that   →   presumably
It may be argued that   →   arguably or say who may argue

A fair number of the throat-clearing expressions spend time saying that someone should take note of something.

It should also be noted that
It is interesting to note that
It is worth noting that
It is crucial to note that
It is important to note that

If the writer can presume that the reader is already taking special note of all that is written, then such expressions are superfluous. For an extended discussion on writing strong subject-verb units, see sections 24.2 and 24.3.

Two commonsense reminders: (1) do not edit out every conceivable bit of wordiness from your writing. If you do, your writing will become sparse and lifeless. (2) Do not focus on wordiness in the early stages of drafting: being concerned about wordiness in the early stages is premature. First efforts and early drafts are, by nature, wordy and overwritten. In fact, at the beginning of the writing process, it may even be healthy for a writer to have an excess of words to work with. Thus, all the suggested strategies for conciseness in this section should be applied late in the writing process.

See Exercise 25E in the *Practice Book*.

§ 25.2.6 Don't Use Pompous Language

A traveling geological formation acquires little vegetative growth. Translation: A rolling stone gathers no moss.

If only that were true. All too often, legal writers who are really "rolling" through an analysis begin gathering all kinds of moss in the form of stuffy, overly formal words. Instead of valuing their ideas for their clarity and simplicity, legal writers sometimes feel they have to "dress up" the words so that they look lawyerly and sound erudite. They may have forgotten that their readers want to understand what they are saying, not be impressed by their vocabulary.

The following are but a few of the many words and expressions that legal writers use to dress up an otherwise simple point. Resist the temptation. Keep it simple. Your readers will love you for it.

allocate	→	give, divide
ascertain	→	make sure
cease	→	stop
commenced	→	began
constitute	→	make up
emulate	→	copy
endeavor	→	try
finalize	→	complete, finish, end
implement	→	carry out or put into effect
initiated	→	began
objective	→	goal, aim
originate	→	start
preclude	→	shut out, prevent
prior to	→	before
promulgate	→	issue, publish
pursuant	→	under
render	→	make, give
secure	→	get, take, obtain
subsequent	→	after
terminated	→	ended, finished
utilize	→	use
verification	→	proof

§ 25.2.7 Don't Repeat Yourself Needlessly

Language seems to be inherently redundant. Start trying to string a few words together and fairly soon some of those words will start making the same point. No matter how hard we try, words just keep coming out at a faster rate than the ideas, so naturally some words double up and say the same thing.

Some of this doubling up seems to come from a lack of faith in the words themselves. For example, why does anyone ever say or write "close proximity"? Isn't proximity always close? What logic is there in the expression "sworn affidavit"? If an affidavit is a "sworn statement in writing," then is a "sworn affidavit" a "sworn sworn statement in writing"?

The following is a sampling of many common redundancies adapted from a list called "Dog Puppies" compiled by writer and editor Yvonne Lewis Day.[2] A few extra redundant phrases have been added by the authors. The word or words in parentheses should be omitted.

3 a.m. (in the morning)
11 p.m. (at night)
red (in color)
(a distance of) twenty feet
(a period of) six months
(absolute) guarantee
(absolutely) clear
(actual) experience
(advance) planning
at (the) present (time)
(basic) fundamentals
belief (system)
(but) however
(but) nevertheless
(close) scrutiny
combine (together)
(complete) monopoly
(completely) destroyed
consensus (of opinion)
crisis (situation)
(current) trend
daily (basis)
depreciate (in value)
descend (down)
(different) kinds
(direct) confrontation
during (the course of)
during (the year of) 2005
each (and every)
each (separate) incident
(many) (different) ways
(mass) media
merged (together)
my (own) opinion
my (personal) opinion
never (at any time)
never (before)
off (of)
(over) exaggerate
(past) experience
(past) history
(past) records

(advance) warning
alongside (of)
(and) moreover
appreciate (in value)
(as) for example
ascend (up)
ask (a question)
(as to) whether
(at a) later (date)
emergency (situation)
(empty) space
(end) result
eradicate (completely)
(essential) element
(established) pattern
estimated (roughly) at
(false) pretenses
few (in number)
(foreign) imports
free (of charge)
(future) plans
(general) public
healing (process)
(important) essentials
indicted (on a charge)
(integral) part
is (now) pending
join (together)
(local) residents
(major) breakthrough
recur (again)
refer (back)
reflect (back)
reiterate (again)
repeat (again)
reported (to the effect) that
revert (back)
risk (factor)
scrutinize (carefully)
(separate) entities
shooting (incident)
(specific) example

---

2. Adapted from "The Economics of Writing" by Yvonne Lewis Day, reprinted with permission from the August 1982 issue of *The Toastmaster*.

permeate (throughout)	(State's) prosecutor
(personal) friendship	(subtle) nuance
(plan) ahead	(sudden) outburst
postponed (until later)	(suddenly) exploded
(pre-) planned	(temporary) reprieve
probed (into)	(thorough) investigation
protest (against)	(underlying) (basic) assumption
(rate of) speed	(unexpected) surprise
	(usual) custom

Many redundancies and wordy expressions have an "of" in them. Some legal writers find that they can spot many wordy constructions simply by searching for "of"'s and editing out about half of them.

The preceding list of redundancies includes those expressions that are common to writers in all disciplines. The language of law is much worse; it has made redundancy an art.

One source of these redundancies, according to David Mellinkoff,[3] has been the law's tendency to draw on more than one language at a time to describe a single idea. Consequently, we get tautologies such as "null and void" when either "null" or "void" alone would be sufficient.

buy (Old English) or purchase (French)
own (Old English) or possess (French)
minor (Latin) or child (Old English) or infant (French)
will (Old English) or testament (Latin)
property or chattels (French) or goods (Old English)
pardon (French) or forgive (Old English)
constable (French) or sheriff (Old English)
larceny (French) or theft or stealing (Old English)
attorney (French) or lawyer (Old English)

Mellinkoff adds that other redundancies such as "aid and abet," "part and parcel," and "safe and sound" come from law's early oral tradition when the rhythm and sound of the words made them not only more memorable but also more powerful in the minds of the people.[4]

The question for modern legal writers, then, is whether doubling phrases serve any purpose for their readers. Is there some important distinction between "perform" and "discharge"? Is "cease and desist" more memorable or more emphatic than just "cease" or "desist"?

If the answer to these questions is no, then what the writer has done by using doubling phrases is to double the words the reader must read. No new content, just more words — not exactly the way to win over a busy reader.

(Admittedly, some repetition in legal writing is done for effect. Used properly, repetition can be persuasive and even eloquent. Obviously, the discussion in this section refers to mindless, not deliberate, repetition.)

---

3. David Mellinkoff, *The Language of the Law* 58 (1963).
4. David Mellinkoff, *supra*, 42-44.

§ 25.2.8 Clean Out the Clutter

Some legal writers are word pack rats. They love words and collect them for their own sake. And like most pack rats, they are not particularly discriminating. They have extra words, often meaningless words, stashed in every nook and cranny of their writing.

Real pack rats have a right to the clutter they collect. After all, they are the only ones who live in it. Unfortunately, legal writers who are word pack rats force their readers to live in their clutter as well. Most readers would rather not.

Clutter in writing takes several forms. One of the most common is the extraneous prepositional phrase. Notice how easily prepositional phrases can begin to grow and multiply.

EXAMPLES

Avoiding the Clutter Habit

Rubenstein is filing a motion for summary judgment.

Clutter

Rubenstein is in the process of filing a motion for summary judgment.

More Clutter

At this point in time, Rubenstein is in the process of filing a motion for summary judgment.

Still More Clutter

At this point in time, Rubenstein is in the process of filing a motion for summary judgment with the court.

Eight words have quickly grown to twenty, with no real gain in content.

Again, as we saw in the earlier list of redundancies, the "of" preposition tends to be a frequent offender. Although we cannot write without any "of" phrases, in most people's writing about half of them can be eliminated or tidied up.

EXAMPLE

Draft

In the absence of any evidence of drugs on the premises, the police officers' actions can be given the interpretation of an invasion of privacy.

Revised

Without evidence of drugs on the premises, the police officers' actions invaded the defendant's privacy.

Notice that the "of the" can be eliminated from some phrases and made into possessives in others.

all of the defendants	→	all defendants
none of the witnesses	→	no witness
the family of the victim	→	the victim's family
the reasoning of the court	→	the court's reasoning

Before leaving the topic of extraneous "of" phrases, we should discuss their frequent companion: empty nouns. Nouns like "area," "aspect," "basis," "character," "circumstances," "field," "kind," "manner," "matter," "nature," "situation," and "type" rarely add any real content to writing. Most should be edited out.

the basis of the testimony	→	the testimony
the field of chemical engineering	→	chemical engineering
the nature of the defendant's argument	→	the defendant's argument

Other modifiers besides prepositional phrases like to clutter up sentences. Adverbs in particular like to creep into legal writing sentences, often in the disguise of precision. You can usually (there's one!) spot adverbs by their -ly ending, but look out for "quite," "rather," "somewhat," and "very," too.

Adverb Clutter

EXAMPLE

Basically, the witness seemed quite relaxed as she carefully outlined the rather long list of extremely technical calculations she had made.

Revised

The witness seemed relaxed as she outlined the long list of technical calculations she had made.

Frequently, adverbs do add a shade of meaning that the writer intends. "The witness spoke softly" is not the same as "the witness spoke." The question for the careful legal writer, then, is (1) whether the adverb adds important content, and, (2) if so, whether the adverb is the best way to express that content. "Spoke softly" may be more precisely and more concisely written as "whispered," "murmured," or "mumbled."

One adverb that deserves special mention is "clearly." It is so overused in legal writing that one has to wonder if it has any meaning left. Clearly, it is time to think of a more sophisticated way to begin sentences.

See Exercise 25G in the *Practice Book*.

§ 25.2.9 Focus and Combine

A clear focus will help you decide which sentences can be combined and, when combining, which parts to keep as the main subject and verb and which parts to subordinate. For example, two sentences can often be combined into one by changing one of the sentences into a relative clause beginning with "which," "who," "whom," "whose," or "that."[5]

| EXAMPLE | **Draft** |

The State's main witness was Arthur Hedges. Arthur Hedges agreed to testify after reaching a favorable plea bargain.

Combined

The State's main witness was Arthur Hedges, who agreed to testify after reaching a favorable plea bargain.

In some cases, these same relative clauses can be reduced to phrases by deleting unnecessary "who's," "which's," and "that's."

| EXAMPLE | **Draft** |

The defendant lived in a room that was over the garage.

Revised

The defendant lived in a room over the garage.

Frequently, two sentences can be combined when one of them defines or identifies part of the other.

| EXAMPLE | **Draft** |

Upon entering the house, the police smelled phenyl-2-propanone. Phenyl-2-propanone is an organic chemical that is a necessary precursor ingredient of amphetamine.

Combined

Upon entering the house, the police smelled phenyl-2-propanone, an organic chemical that is a necessary precursor ingredient of amphetamine.

A colon can sometimes be used to combine two sentences when the first sentence introduces a list or an explanation that will be given in full in the second sentence.

---

5. Use "who" for persons and the nominative case; use "whom" for the objective case; use "whose" when you need the possessive. Use "that" and "which" for things. Use "that" for restrictive clauses and "which" for nonrestrictive clauses.

Draft

To assert the emergency doctrine, the defendant must be able to satisfy four elements. The four elements are (1) that he was suddenly confronted by an emergency; (2) that he did not cause the emergency by any negligence on his part; (3) that he was compelled to decide a course of action instantly; and (4) that he made such a choice as a reasonably careful person placed in such a position might have made.

Combined

To assert the emergency doctrine, the defendant must satisfy the following four elements: (1) he was suddenly confronted by an emergency; (2) he did not cause the emergency by any negligence on his part; (3) he was compelled to decide a course of action instantly; and (4) he made such a choice as a reasonably careful person placed in such a position might have made.

Occasionally, two or more sentences that have the same subject can be combined by using compound verbs or by changing one set of verbs into participles.

Draft

The police officers discovered the laboratory used to make the amphetamine. The officers found a propane burner.

Combined (compound verbs)

The police officers discovered the laboratory used to make the amphetamine and found a propane burner.

Draft

Deascon asks this court to review the lower court's decision. He argues that the reasons given by the trial court for imposing an exceptional sentence are not supported by the record.

Combined (participle)

Deascon asks this court to review the lower court's decision, arguing that the reasons given by the trial court for imposing an exceptional sentence are not supported by the record.

To reduce phrases to words, be on the lookout for wordy constructions like "the fact that," most phrases built around "regard," "of" prepositional phrases, and phrases that end in "that."

because of the fact that	→	because
despite the fact that	→	although, even though
due to the fact that	→	because
except for the fact that	→	except for
in spite of the fact that	→	although, even though
in view of the fact that	→	because, considering that
owing to the fact that	→	because
the fact that he asked	→	his question
in regard(s) to	→	about, concerning
with regard to	→	about, concerning
by means of	→	by
by virtue of	→	by, under
for the purpose of	→	to
has the option of	→	may
in compliance with your request of	→	as requested, as you requested
in favor of	→	for
in the absence of	→	without
in the neighborhood of	→	about, approximately
on the basis of	→	from
over the signature of	→	signed by
in the event that	→	if
for the reason that	→	because

Legal writers are divided over whether (or not) to omit the "or not" in the expression "whether or not." Notice, for example, that the "or not" can be deleted from the preceding sentence with no loss in meaning. In such cases, it is better to delete it. Sometimes, however, the sentence becomes nonsensical if the "or not" is omitted. Usually, the "or not" can be omitted when the word "if" can substitute for "whether." Retain "or not" if the substitution of "if" for "whether" changes the meaning.

Some phrases are deadwood and can be omitted or replaced with one word.

See Exercises 25H, 25I, and 25J in the *Practice Book*.

at this point in time	→	omit or use "now"
at that point in time	→	omit or use "then"
in this day and age	→	omit or use "now," "nowadays"
in the case of	→	omit or use "in"
in reality	→	omit
in terms of	→	omit
in a very real sense	→	omit

§ 25.2.10 Avoid Excessive Conciseness

The question, of course, with the reducing and combining advocated in this section is how much is too much? When does editing for conciseness improve the writing, and at what point does it hinder the readability of sentences?

Properly done, reducing and combining can make writing more focused and concise. Overdone, it can ruin writing by packing it too tightly and by creating overly long and overly complicated sentences.

One result of overdone combining is compound noun phrases, also known as noun strings. Like those Russian dolls that have a seemingly endless progression of smaller and smaller dolls inside each doll, compound noun phrases have modifier modifying modifier modifying modifier to the point that the reader forgets where the whole thing began. Such overpacking in a sentence strains even the most cooperative reader.

Draft

Alabama's silent prayer statute's failure to satisfy "the purpose" prong of the *Lemon* test renders it unconstitutional.

Revised

Alabama's silent prayer statute fails to satisfy "the purpose" prong of the *Lemon* test; therefore, the statute is unconstitutional. OR

Alabama's statute on silent prayer fails . . .

Notice that in the preceding example a nominalization, "failure," became the verb and the revision eliminated one of the possessives, "statute's." Because multiple possessives are always awkward, avoid them whenever possible.

Also remember that some nominalizations can be unpacked and improved by changing the noun into the participle, or adjective form, as is done with "exclusion" in the following example.

Draft

a broad prior conviction evidence exclusion rule

Revised

a broad rule excluding evidence of prior convictions

Like all tricks of the trade, then, editing for conciseness must be used with discretion and with an eye toward what the reader will find easier to read and understand.

§ 25.3 Plain English Versus Legalese

Early in law school there seems to be an almost irresistible urge to clothe everything in the diction and style of the most incomprehensible insurance policy.

— Norman Brand and John O. White[6]

---

6. *Legal Writing: The Strategy of Persuasion* 107 (1988).

> To communicate upon matters of technicality and complexity ... is impossible with (and for) the nontechnical and simple person; and to use the language of simplicity in addressing a learned profession is to insult that profession.
>
> — Ray J. Aiken[7]

Above are but samplings of the heated, ongoing debate over legalese. Proponents of the traditional style of legal writing argue that legalese is part of the specialized discourse of lawyers and that it serves worthwhile purposes for lawyers and their readers. Proponents of "plain English," on the other hand, argue that legalese is responsible for many of the ills that plague legal writing, not the least of which is that lay readers cannot readily comprehend what their attorneys are writing.

If you read the law journals, you may get the impression that the advocates for simplified, plain English are winning the debate. Article after article decries the use of such mainstays of legal writing as Latin phrases and legal argot. Perhaps a more significant indication that legalese is on the way out is that several state legislatures have passed legislation requiring "simple," "clear," "understandable" language that uses "words with common and everyday meanings" in consumer contracts and insurance policies.[8]

If you read the writing of most practicing attorneys, however, you might get the impression that the advocates for the traditional style of legal writing have won the day. Corporate lawyers rely heavily on boilerplate, and most practitioners seem to have absorbed the language of their law school casebooks. They may have heard that legalese is dead, but they don't write like they believe it.

And so the debate rages on, and although the plain English versus legalese issue has been before the collective "court" of legal professionals and their clients for some time now, we have yet to reach a verdict. The trend seems to be toward plain English, but the resistance is strong. In short, in the matter of Plain English v. Legalese, the jury is still out.

So what is a legal writer to do? While the profession continues to wrestle with this issue, we would like to offer a simple test for determining whether any given bit of legalese should be used or should be relegated to the dustbin.

The Test

Given the document's reader, writer, purpose, and surrounding circumstances, does the legalese increase or decrease communication between writer and reader?

With the test as a backdrop, let's examine legalese and its characteristics.

First of all, there is no agreed-upon definition of "legalese." One law review author has defined a legalism as "a word or phrase that a lawyer might use in drafting a contract or a pleading but would not use in conversation with his wife."[9]

---

7. *Let's Not Oversimplify Legal Language*, 32 Rocky Mtn. L. Rev. 364 (1960).

8. *See, e.g.,* Minn. Stat. § 325G. 30.3, N.Y. Gen. Oblig. Law § 5-702, N.J. Rev. Stat. § 56:12-1, Conn. Gen. Stat. §§ 38-68s-x.

9. George R. Smith, *A Primer of Opinion Writing, for Four New Judges*, 21 Ark. L. Rev. 197 (1967).

With a bit of editing, we can modify the definition to omit the sexism and to describe legalese: legalese is language a lawyer might use in drafting a contract or a pleading but would not use in ordinary conversation. In short, legalese is distinct from human talk; it is law talk.

What then are the characteristics that distinguish law talk from ordinary human talk?

Group 1

- long sentences, especially those with excessive modification and qualification
- abstractions as subjects — the real "doers" or actors are often omitted or relegated to a prepositional phrase
- weak verbs — both passive voice and nominalizations sap the sentences of their natural energy

Group 2

- archaic word choice
- foreign phrases
- terms of art and argot
- use of "said" and "such" as articles
- omission of articles, especially "the"
- avoidance of the first and second person (I, we, you)
- doubling phrases

The first group of characteristics primarily involves sentence structure. They are discussed in the following sections: long sentences, section 24.5; abstractions as subjects, section 24.2; and weak verbs, sections 24.1 and 24.3.

The second group of characteristics occurs at the word level. It is more about vocabulary: Is it better to use a formal word, an unfamiliar word, a foreign word, or a simple word? When is a word or phrase an unnecessary legalism, and when is it a term of art? When is one word enough, and when should it be bolstered by one or more synonyms to cover every possible contingency?

These characteristics of legalese are the focus of this section.

§ 25.3.1 Archaic Word Choice

Consider a story told by an attorney who was an advocate of plain English. Her client wanted her to draft a will. She drafted two versions: a plain English version and a traditional version. Although the attorney recommended the plain English version, the client selected the traditional version because it "sounded like a will." For this document and its purpose, the formality of "I hereby give, devise, and bequeath" was appropriate. It created the tone, the solemnity, and the timeless quality that the client wanted.

But what about client letters, office memoranda, and briefs to the court? Although these documents are formal in nature, do they require archaic language? Most authorities on legal language agree that they don't. In fact, research shows that appellate judges, who are the readers of the most formal of these documents, appellate briefs, strongly prefer plain English.[10]

---

10. Robert W. Benson & Joan B. Kessler, *Legalese v. Plain English: An Empirical Study of Persuasion and Credibility in Apppellate Brief Writing*, 20 Loy. L.A. L. Rev. 301-319 (1987).

The standard argument that "if I don't sound like a lawyer, I won't be believable" was strongly refuted in this research. In fact, the research showed that the judges were more likely to categorize writing in legalese as "poorly worded, unconvincing, vague, not concise, unpersuasive, uncreative, unscholarly, from a non-prestigious firm or an ineffective appellate advocate, unpowerful, incomprehensible and ambiguous."[11]

The legalese-ridden documents that the judges read included Old and Middle English words like "thereby" and "herein." Below is a fairly comprehensive list of other Old and Middle English words and phrases that should be avoided in client letters, office memoranda, and briefs. In some cases, a more appropriate substitute word or phrase follows in italics.

Compound words that begin with *here-*, *there-*, and *where-*

hereafter	thereabout	whereas[12]
herebefore	thereafter	whereat
hereby	therefrom	whereby
herein	therein	wherefore
hereinabove → above	thereof	wheresoever
hereinafter	thereon	wherein → there
hereinunder → below	thereto	whereof
hereof	thereunto	whereon
heretofore → before, up to this time	therewith	whereupon
hereunder		
herewith (enclosed herewith → *enclosed*)		

aforementioned (omit or substitute *previously mentioned*)
aforesaid (omit or substitute *above*)
behoove → *to be necessary, to be proper*
comes now the plaintiff
foregoing (for the foregoing reasons) → *for these reasons*
forthwith → *immediately*
henceforth[13]
hitherto → *until this time, up to now*
pursuant to → *under or according to*[14]
thence → *from there, from that place, time, or source, for that reason*
thenceforth → *from that time on, after that*
thereafter → *from that time on*
to wit → *namely, that is to say*
whence → *from where*
whensoever → *whenever*

---

11. *Id.* at 315.

12. "Whereas" can often be eliminated or replaced with "because," "considering that," "while on the contrary," or "inasmuch as." At other times, it can be used but with care. Frequently, writers use it without seeming to know what it means. At times, "whereas" is the best choice; for example, using "whereas" is certainly better than the wordy "in view of the fact that."

13. Many would not object strenuously to "henceforth," but find it a bit dated. "From now on" is a satisfactory plain English substitute.

14. Sometimes "pursuant to" is a useful legalism that lawers and judges find acceptable, but you should avoid the term with nonlawyers.

§ 25.3.2 Foreign Phrases

Many of the Latin phrases that appear in legal writing create a barrier between writer and reader. Only a student on the way home from Latin class (or possibly a lawyer specializing in property) will be comfortable with a phrase like *Cujus est solum ejus est usque ad coelum et usque ad inferos.* The rest of us would do one of two things: use the context to try to figure out what the writer meant or reach for the *Unabridged Black's Law Dictionary.* In either case, the Latin has not aided communication. Even the conscientious consulter of the dictionary will understand the writer's meaning only by looking up the explanation the writer should have given the reader in the first place.

More often, the Latin is not so much confusing as it is unnecessary. Why say "supra" when "above" works just as well? Unnecessary Latin phrases make the writing appear stuffy and pretentious. When a simple English equivalent can be used without loss of meaning, use it.

Latin Words or Phrases to Avoid

arguendo → for the sake of argument
et al. → and others
infra → below
inter alia → among other things
per curiam → by the court
seriatim → in turn, serially, one after another
sui generis → unique
supra → above
viz. (abbreviation for "videlicet") → namely or that is to say

Not all Latin should be replaced, however. Some Latin phrases ("gratis," "per diem," "persona non grata") are sufficiently familiar to educated readers that their use does not impair communication. In fact, these phrases are often accepted as English.

Other Latin phrases ("amicus curiae," "per se") are equally familiar to lawyers and judges and can be used for these readers without a second thought. They are the "shop talk" of law. The same phrases, though, may need substitutes or explanation for client readers.

A final group of Latin phrases are so useful that few are willing to discard them. "Respondeat superior," for example, sums up a whole doctrine in tort law; "res judicata" is a fundamental rule of civil procedure. While these phrases will probably need clarification for readers who are not lawyers, the average legal reader would find them not only familiar but indispensable.

Latin Words or Phrases to Keep for Readers Who Are Lawyers

ad hoc	mens rea
ad litem	modus operandi
amicus curiae	nexus

bona fide	nolo contendere
caveat emptor	non sequitur
certiorari	penumbra
consortium	per diem
corpus delicti	per se
de facto, de jure	post mortem
de novo	prima facie
dicta, dictum	pro bono
ex parte	quorum
ex post facto	quid pro quo
gratis	res ipsa loquitur
habeas corpus	res judicata
id. (abbreviation for *idem*)	respondeat superior
in limine	scintilla
in personam	stare decisis
ipso facto	sua sponte
mandamus	supersedeas

Of course, Latin is not the only foreign language that appears frequently in legal writing. Thanks to the Norman Conquest and its subsequent effect on the language of England, French plays an important role in the language of law.

The vast majority of the words derived from French are common terms that are already fully incorporated into English and as such pose few if any problems for readers ("assault," "defendant," "heir," "larceny," "mortgage," "plaintiff," "pleadings," "tort," "reprieve," and "verdict," to name just a few).

More likely troublemakers are those words and phrases that are Old French. For the following French terms, use the suggested plain English substitutes.

alien or *aliene* (used as a verb) → to convey or to transfer
cestui que trust → beneficiary
cy-pres → as near as possible
en ventre sa mere → in its mother's womb
en vie → alive
feme covert → married woman
feme sole → single woman
save → except
seisin → possession or ownership

As we saw with Latin, though, there are French words and phrases that are terms of art for which we have no satisfactory plain English substitute. Although they will almost certainly require explanations for readers who are not lawyers, they are indispensable vocabulary for a lawyer.

French Words and Phrases to Keep

estoppel   laches   voir dire

§ 25.3.3 Use of Terms of Art and Argot

Terms of art, by definition, do not have satisfactory substitutes. Even though one might be able to give a short explanation of a term of art's meaning, complete understanding would take an extensive explanation.

A "term of art," according to David Mellinkoff, is "a technical word with a specific meaning."[15] In *The Dictionary of Modern Legal Usage*, "terms of art" are defined as "words having specific, precise significations in a given specialty."[16]

Given these requirements, it should not be surprising that there are relatively few terms of art in law. "Certiorari" is an excellent example of a true term of art. Perhaps a satisfactory short explanation is that it refers to the order written by a higher court to a lower court requiring the lower court to produce a certified record of a certain case.

For a full understanding of "certiorari," however, one would have to lay out a much larger context: how discretionary review and the appellate process work in general and specifically how the Supreme Court of the United States chooses cases it wishes to hear.

Argot, by contrast, is legal jargon, or lawyers' shop talk. It is the shorthand of law, the quick-and-easy term or phrase that lawyers use among themselves. For this reason, argot is inappropriate when communicating with nonlawyers. Used with discretion, it can be effective communication among lawyers.

"Case on all fours" is a classic example of argot. Other common examples include "adhesion contract," "attractive nuisance," "Blackacre," "case at bar," "case-in-chief," "clean hands," "cloud on the title," "court below," "four corners of the document," "horse case," "instant case," "off the record," "pierce the corporate veil," "reasonable man," "res ipsa loquitur," "sidebar," and "Whiteacre."

In writing, avoid argot that has degenerated into slang. "Cert denied" or "resipsey case" sounds cute rather than professional.

§ 25.3.4 Use of "Said" and "Such" as Adjectives

If you were a stand-up comic trying to make fun of the way lawyers write, all you would have to do is put "said" or "such" before almost every noun.

Ineffective "Said" and "Such"   EXAMPLE

It was snowing and icy on January 9, 2006, when Mr. Smith, the plaintiff, was driving home from work along a deserted highway in his 2002 Honda Accord with chains on said vehicle's tires. Suddenly said plaintiff felt said vehicle jerk violently, and then said plaintiff heard a loud clanging of metal. Such clanging continued until such time as said plaintiff was able to pull said vehicle over to the shoulder of said highway. Upon inspection of said vehicle, said plaintiff realized that such clanging was caused

---

15. David Mellinkoff, *The Language of the Law* 16 (1963) (quoting *Webster's New International Dictionary* (2d ed. 1934).

16. Bryan A. Garner, *The Dictionary of Modern Legal Usage* 872 (2d ed. 1995).

when said chains had broken and then wrapped around the axle of said plaintiff's said vehicle. "Oh, *!?*/!" said said plaintiff.

In client letters, office memos, and briefs, rigorously avoid all use of "said" as an adjective. Replace with "the," "that," "this," or an appropriate, unambiguous pronoun.

"Such" can be used as an adjective with categories of persons, things, or concepts. For example, "such instances of neglect," "such witnesses as these," and "such an example of compassion" is not legalese. These phrases are good writing.

Do not, however, use "such" with singular nouns that are not categories of persons, things, or concepts but rather are specific references to the same previously mentioned singular noun. For example, "such payment" should be revised to "this payment"; "such stock certificate" should be changed to "the stock certificate."

§ 25.3.5 Omission of the Article "The"

Occasionally, one sees legal writing that has the sound of a police report.

EXAMPLE   **Draft**

Defendant denies that she hit plaintiff.

This rather terse style is achieved by omitting the article "the." The reason for omitting "unnecessary" articles in police reports may be that information needs to be recorded on forms. Happily, lawyers do not have such requirements, so they do not have to sacrifice a fluid writing style.

EXAMPLE   **Revised**

The defendant denies that she hit the plaintiff.

---

§ 25.3.6 Avoidance of First-Person and Second-Person Pronouns

By convention, legal writers use the pronouns "I," "me," "we," "us," "you," and "your" rarely. Occasionally, in a client letter, a lawyer might write "I recommend" or, more commonly, "in my opinion." Much less frequent would be the phrase "I think" or (horrors!) "I feel" (the common explanation for the horrified reaction being that lawyers are paid to think, not to feel) in an office memorandum. Pity the naive attorney, though, who writes in a brief "you should rule" or "you must determine."

To get around the I's and you's in legal writing, because after all it is I, the writer, who is recommending and thinking, and it is you, the judge and reader, who is ruling and determining, legal writers resort to all sorts of linguistic gymnastics. Before discussing which of these gymnastic moves work and which lead to new problems, let's examine why the first- and second-person pronouns are *persona non grata* in legal writing.

First of all, remember the long-standing tradition of avoiding first and second person in any formal writing. While the recommendations about this issue have relaxed considerably for undergraduate research papers and the like, the original rationale applies to most legal writing. The facts and the application of law to those facts are the focus of attention for both writer and reader. As such, they should occupy center stage.

Second, the use of "I" and "you" often creates an inappropriately informal tone. While a bit of informality and familiarity may be appropriate in some client letters and an occasional office memo, generally these documents should be formal and professional in tone. (Remember, though, formal does not mean stilted.)

Third, indiscreet use of "you" in client letters and especially in briefs may make the writer appear arrogant, pushy, and disrespectful. Readers rarely like to be ordered around. Not surprisingly, "you must" or "you should" language often backfires. Rather than encouraging the reader to act as the writer wants, such language sets the stage for resistance to the writer's recommendations and arguments.

In the following example, the inclusion of "my," "I," and "you" is both distracting and inappropriate. The first-person references incorrectly place the emphasis on the writer, and the second-person references may even anger the judge.

Draft

EXAMPLE

In my research, I found that you must apply Washington Rule of Evidence 609(a) to determine the admissibility of evidence of a criminal defendant's prior convictions.

Revised

In Washington, the admissibility of evidence of a criminal defendant's prior convictions is governed by Washington Rule of Evidence 609(a). OR

Washington Rule of Evidence 609(a) governs the admissibility of evidence of a criminal defendant's prior convictions.

The first revision of the example illustrates one of the common gymnastic moves that legal writers use to avoid the first- and second-person pronouns: use of the passive voice. While the passive voice is a good choice in some instances (see section 24.1.3), it can easily lead to dull, lifeless writing. Use with care.

Some legal writers use the pronoun "one" to get around using "you." This tactic works reasonably well as long as the writer does not use "one" several times and then shift — incorrectly — from "one" to the third-person pronoun "he," "she," "him," "her," "it," "they," or "them."

EXAMPLE

Incorrect

One should avoid first-person pronouns in his or her legal writing.

Revised

One should avoid first-person pronouns in one's legal writing.

Better

One should avoid first-person pronouns in legal writing.

In office memos, some writers slip into a we-they style as they describe the various arguments the two sides can make. While this practice is accepted in some firms, it can easily be avoided by simply naming the parties. Thus, instead of "they will argue...and we will rebut this argument by showing...," legal writers can easily say "Smith will argue...and Jones will rebut this argument."

Frequently, a writer of an office memo is tempted to use "we" in the following situation. The writer has just explained the law or just described an analogous case to the reader. Now the writer wants the reader to follow along as he or she applies that law or case.

The writer might begin by saying "If we apply the plain meaning of statute X to the facts in the present case, we can see that the photocopy is a similitude" or "If we compare the actions of the defendant in *Smith v. Jones* to the actions of Brown, we can see that unlike Jones, Brown knew he was lying to the F.B.I." This is not a serious writing sin, of course, but it is one that can be easily avoided.

Unfortunately, some writers try to write around the "we" in such instances and end up with a dangling modifier. See section 27.6.2.

EXAMPLE

Incorrect

Applying the plain meaning of statute X to the facts in the present case, the photocopy is a similitude.

Comparing the actions of the defendant in *Jones* to the actions of Brown, Brown, unlike Jones, knew he was lying to the F.B.I.

There is a better way. The writer does want the reader to follow along as he or she makes the next logical connection, but the writer also wants to suggest that the court must see the same logical connection. Therefore, it makes good sense, both in terms of writing style and strategy, to say "If the court applies the plain meaning of statute X to the facts in the present case, it will find..." or "Applying the plain meaning of statute X to the facts in the present case, the court will find...."

One final note about first- and second-person pronouns: because these pronouns have gained acceptance in some other types of formal writing, they are likely to gain increasing acceptance in all but the most formal documents in legal writing. Watch the trend, and you will be able to adjust accordingly.

See Exercise **25.K** in the *Practice Book*.

§ 25.4 Gender-Neutral Language

The language of law, while a bit slower to change than the language of other fields, is moving in the direction of gender-neutral word choices. Numerous states now require gender-neutral language in their legislation. Increasingly, legislators, practitioners, and jurists are realizing that some language they previously considered to be inclusive has just the opposite effect: it excludes.

For legal writers, there are at least four good reasons for making the effort to use gender-neutral language: fairness, clarity, precision, and reader reaction. These reasons more than justify the effort it takes to master the five problem areas legal writers face when trying to use gender-neutral language.

§ 25.4.1 Generic Use of "Man"

Avoid using the term "man" to mean all people or all of humanity. Similarly, avoid using expressions and other derivatives built on this broad use of the term man.

Sexist Terms	*Gender-Neutral Substitutes*
man (noun) or mankind	people, humanity, human race, human beings, human population, humankind
man (verb) as in "man the office"	staff, operate, run, work
a man who...	an individual who..., a person who..., one who..., someone who...
the common man, the average man, the man in the street	the common individual, the average citizen, the person on the street, ordinary people
man hours	worker hours, work days
man-made	hand-crafted, handmade, manufactured, machine-made, fabricated, synthetic, created, constructed
manpower	human energy, human resources, work force, personnel, staff, workers, employees, labor, labor supply/force

§ 25.4.2 Generic Use of "He"

It used to be standard practice for grammar and writing texts to advise writers to use masculine pronouns when the gender of the antecedent noun or pronoun could be either male or female. Now most grammar and writing texts advise writers to avoid the generic use of "he." Unfortunately, though, we have been unable to agree on a gender-neutral singular pronoun as a substitute. Until we do, we will need to use one or more of several approaches for avoiding the generic use of the masculine pronouns.

a. Revise the Sentence So That the Antecedent and Its Pronoun Are Plural

EXAMPLE

Draft

The holding suggests that a defendant waives his constitutional rights only through an affirmative or overt act.

Revision

The holding suggests that defendants waive their constitutional rights only through affirmative or overt acts.

b. Revise the Sentence So That a Pronoun Is Not Needed

EXAMPLE

Draft

As a general rule, an employer is not liable for the work performed by his independent contractors.

Revision

As a general rule, an employer is not liable for the work performed by independent contractors.

c. Replace the Masculine Noun and Pronoun with "One," "Your," or "He" or "She," as Appropriate

EXAMPLE

Draft

Every man has a right to defend his home.

Revisions

One has a right to defend one's home.

You have a right to defend your home.

Everyone has a right to defend his or her home.

d. Repeat the Noun Rather than Use an Inappropriate Masculine Pronoun

Draft

Joinder of counts should not be used to embarrass or prejudice a defendant or to deny him a substantial right.

Revised

Joinder of counts should not be used to embarrass or prejudice a defendant or to deny a defendant a substantial right.

One approach that is occasionally recommended for avoiding the generic "he" is to use the plural pronouns "they" and "their" for singular nouns and indefinite pronouns, such as "everyone" or "anybody." While using this approach may arguably solve the sexism problem, it still may leave the writer with an error in pronoun agreement (see section 27.4.2) as well as with more than a few logical inconsistencies; for example, "Everyone is entitled to their opinion." Rather than trade one problem for another, use one of the other five strategies outlined above for avoiding the generic "he."

§ 25.4.3 Gender-Neutral Job Titles

Avoid job titles that suggest it is nonstandard for women to hold the position.

Sexist Terms	Gender-Neutral Substitutes
businessman	business executive, manager, business person
chairman	coordinator, presiding officer, head, chair, chairperson, director
Congressman	Representative, member of Congress, congressional representative, Senator
councilman	council member
deliveryman	delivery clerk, courier
draftsman	drafter
doorman	doorkeeper
fireman	firefighter
forefather	founder, ancestor
foreman (as the head of a group of workers)	supervisor, head worker, section chief
insuranceman	insurance agent
juryman	juror
landlord	owner, manager, lessor
layman	layperson
mailman, postman	postal carrier, postal worker, mail carrier

Sexist Terms	*Gender-Neutral Substitutes*
middleman	negotiator, liaison, intermediary
newspaperman	reporter, editor
paperboy	newspaper carrier
policeman	police officer
salesman	sales associate, sales representative
spokesman	representative, spokesperson
steward, stewardess	flight attendant
watchman	guard

§ 25.4.4 Sexist Modifiers

Unconsciously, writers sometimes assign needless sexist modifiers to words. Avoid modifiers that suggest that it is unusual for either a woman or a man to occupy a certain position.

Sexist Modifier	*Revised*
female judge	judge
lady lawyer	lawyer
male nurse	nurse
woman attorney	attorney

§ 25.4.5 Other Sexist Language

Avoid feminizing a word with a suffix; for example, "actress," "executrix," "testatrix." Such endings suggest that it is nonstandard for women to fill certain roles.

Avoid terms with connotations of youth (girl), decorum (lady), or informality (gal) unless the comparable term for males (boy, gentleman, guy) is also appropriate.

When using titles (Miss, Mrs., Ms.) before women's names, follow the particular woman's preference, if known, or, if unknown, use no title. In professional contexts, professional titles take precedence over social titles for both women and men; for example, Justice Sandra Day O'Connor, not Mrs. O'Connor. In salutations in letters, avoid using the outdated "Dear Sir" or "Gentlemen" when the gender of the receiver is unknown. Acceptable substitutes include "Dear Sir or Madam," "Ladies and Gentlemen," or the title of the receiver(s), as in "Dear Members of the Board." Some writers omit the salutation and use a reference line such as "To the Director of Operations" or "Re: Credit Department."

Sexist Term	*Gender-Neutral Substitutes*
coed	student
divorcee	divorced person
forefathers	ancestors, forerunners, forebears
girl or girls (when applied to adult females)	woman or women

Sexist Terms	*Gender-Neutral Substitutes*
lady or ladies	woman or women (unless the equivalent "gentleman" or "gentlemen" is also used for men)
househusband, housewife	homemaker
man and wife	man and woman, husband and wife
old wives' tale	superstitious belief or idea

See Exercises 25L, 25M, and 25N in the *Practice Book*.

§ 25.5 Bias-Free Language

In addition to the concern that legal writers use gender-neutral language in their documents, there are related concerns that the language of law and legal argument be free of bias against other groups, such as racial, religious, and ethnic minorities; the gay, lesbian, bisexual, transgender/transsexual (GLTB) community; persons who are elderly or poor; and persons with disabilities.

Making bias-free language choices is not always easy, though, particularly when one realizes that the preferred terms are constantly changing and not all members of any given group have the same preferences. These challenges tempt some to ignore or just give up on the issue of bias-free language of law. The argument seems to go something like this: "Why should I bother when they can't even decide what they want to be called?"

The temptation to avoid the issue is easier to resist, however, when one considers the power of language and its ability to shape perception. This concern is more than just being "politically correct"; how we label something affects how we see it. Thus, language can serve to perpetuate stereotypes, or it can bring new insight and perspective. Choices in language can suggest that members of a group are inherently inferior or that they are valued members of society. In short, what we call ourselves or someone else matters. Naming, or labeling, is both an enormous power and an enormous responsibility, and, like all legal writing, it should be done with a lot of thought and care.

The following general recommendations outline some advice for legal writers concerning the issue of bias-free language. Many of the specific recommendations and examples for commonly encountered terms are taken from McGraw-Hill's "Guidelines for Bias-Free Publishing," the National Lesbian and Gay Journalists Association (NGLJA) Stylebook Supplement, from the President's Committee on Employment of People with Disabilities, or the Guidelines for Reporting and Writing About People with Disabilities. The recommendations also rely on the *Guidelines for Bias-Free Writing* and numerous usage notes in *The American Heritage Dictionary of the English Language*.[17]

---

17. Marilyn Schwartz & the Task Force on Bias-Free Language of the Association of American University Presses, *Guidelines for Bias-Free Writing* (Indiana U. Press 1995); *The American Heritage Dictionary of the English Language* (4th ed. Houghton Mifflin 2000).

§ 25.5.1 Avoid Irrelevant Minority References

Perhaps the most subtle and possibly the most insidious forms of prejudice in some legal writing are unnecessary references to race, ethnic origin, or other minority categories. In a case in which the description of an individual is necessary to the analysis (such as a case in which the police apprehended an individual based on the individual matching a victim's description), including the race of the individual is obviously appropriate. Unless a crime was racially motivated, however, it is probably inappropriate to include the race of the victim.

Similarly, before using an adjective to indicate that a person's sexual orientation is public knowledge, such as in the phrase "openly gay councilmember," consider whether the public nature of that person's sexual orientation is relevant. (Note too that if it is relevant, the term "openly" is preferred over "avowed," "admitted," "confessed," or "practicing.")

§ 25.5.2 Stay Abreast of the Preferred Terminology

All language changes over time. Some parts of language tend to change more rapidly, however, because of rapid changes in sensibilities and society's collective thinking about certain issues.

Notice, for example, the changes in terminology for these groups of people.

Colored People → Negro → Black → Black American OR African American[18]

Indian → American Indian → Native American

Oriental[19] → Asian OR Asian American

Homosexual → Gay, Lesbian, Bisexual, Transgender (GLBT)

Handicapped → Disabled → Physically Challenged OR Persons of Differing Abilities OR Persons with Exceptionalities OR Exceptional Persons → Persons with disabilities

Elderly → Senior Citizens

Notice too that some of these progressions end with two or more choices, indicating a lack of consensus among the members of the group about the currently preferred term. For example, younger members of the black community may prefer to be called African Americans, while their parents or grandparents may prefer to be called blacks.

How then does a legal writer decide what term to use? In addition to doing research to stay abreast of the preferred terminology, legal writers may

---

18. While early forms of many terms that combined races or nationalities often had hyphens ("African-American'" "Mexican-American"), the current trend is toward omitting the hyphen. The argument for omitting the hyphen is that it conveys something less than full membership in both groups.

19. Although the word "Oriental" is still considered appropriate in some phrases such as "an Oriental rug," it is now widely considered to be offensive when it is used to refer to people native to Asia or descended from an Asian people.

use the following general guidelines when deciding which words or labels will work best in any given situation:

    a. Prefer self-chosen labels (and avoid terms that may offend members of that group);

    b. Choose precise, accurate terms;

    c. Whenever possible, prefer the specific term over the general term;

    d. Prefer terms that describe what people are rather than what they are not;

    e. Notice that a term's connotations may change as the part of speech changes (e.g., the same word that is offensive as a noun may be acceptable as an adjective);

    f. In selecting terms, emphasize the person over the difference; and

    g. Avoid terms that are patronizing or overly euphemistic or that paint people as victims.

a. Prefer Self-Chosen Labels

While it may be difficult to determine what a whole group of individuals prefers to be called, it is often simple to determine what a given person wants to be called. One can just ask. If a client prefers to be labeled as "black" rather than "African American," for example, that preference should be honored. If the applicable law uses a specific label for a group that differs from the individual's preferred term, the sensible solution is for the lawyer writer to explain to the client why it *might* be preferable to use the term used in the law but then leave the final decision about word choice up to the client.

Of course there are situations in which a group has a developing consensus about preferred terminology. In the gay, lesbian, bisexual, transgender (GLBT) community, for example, "gay" is now the preferred adjective for men who are sexually attracted to other men. The rule of thumb tends to be to use "homosexual" only if "heterosexual" would be used in a comparable situation. "Lesbian," on the other hand, is generally preferred for females as both a noun and an adjective, although some women prefer to be called "gay." When referring to both men and women, "gay men and lesbians" is preferred, but "gays" is sometimes used as a shorter replacement. The preferred term for an individual in a committed GLBT relationship is "partner." "Sexual orientation" is strongly preferred over "sexual preference" or "lifestyle." "Cross-dresser" is strongly preferred over "transvestite," and "transgender" is the preferred umbrella term for individuals whose biological and gender identity are not the same (cross-dressers, transsexuals,[20] male or female impersonators, etc.). In choosing names and pronouns to refer to transgendered persons, the preference is for the name, sex, and corresponding pronouns of the individual at the time of the action.

Equally important to preferring self-chosen labels is to avoid offensive labels. Perhaps the best example of a term that members of a group find offensive is the label "Oriental" when used to refer to persons. The objections

---

20. A "transsexual" is an individual who has acquired the physical characteristics of the opposite sex.

to the term are twofold. First, the word "Oriental," which means "eastern," identifies people from Asian countries in relationship to being east of Europe; hence the term smacks of a Eurocentric perspective. Second, and probably more important, the word "Oriental" has connotations of Asian countries as being "exotic" and the people as being "inscrutable." As a result, many Asian Americans consider it nothing short of an ethnic slur to be called "Orientals." Using the word "Oriental" as an adjective such as in terms like "Oriental rug," "Oriental cuisine," or "Oriental medicine," however, is generally considered acceptable.

Similarly, the terms "handicap" and "handicapped" are not considered offensive when they refer to laws or situations, but they are offensive when used to describe people. Replace language such as "the handicapped" or "handicapped person" with "people with disabilities" or with the terminology for the specific disability, such as "person who walks with crutches."

Some whites, most notably the Irish, find it offensive to be labeled "Anglos." The alternative term "Caucasian" is still used in many police departments, but "Caucasian" is not generally a recommended term because it is based on an outmoded notion of a Caucasian race that is no longer accepted in the scientific community. The preferred term, "white," is also not without problems, not the least of which is that its parameters are ambiguous. The term obviously refers to skin color, and its generally accepted meaning is any white or light-skinned person of non-Latin extraction. In some cases, however, "white" includes Latinos and Latinas.

Some words that have historically been slurs and epithets have begun to be reclaimed by members of a given community. For example, some members of the GLBT community have reclaimed the word "queer" and now use it in a variety of contexts, such as "queer studies." As a general rule, however, reclaimed words may be used only by "insiders" in any given community, and their use by "outsiders" is still considered offensive.

Examples of Self-Chosen Terminology for Persons with Disabilities

Avoid These Terms	*Self-Chosen/More Accurate Terms*
hyperactive	person with ADHD (attention deficit hyperactivity disorder)
brain damaged	person with a brain injury
harelip	person with a cleft lip or cleft palate
Mongol/Mongoloid	person with Down's syndrome
retarded/slow learner	person with a learning disability

b. Choose Precise, Accurate Terms

Precision and accuracy are highly valued in all word choices in legal writing, and even more so when selecting words that describe race, ethnicity, national origin, religion, and disabilities. For this reason it is important not to assume that terms are interchangeable. "Mexican American," for example, should be used only to refer to a person who is a United States citizen or permanent resident of Mexican ancestry. "Spanish" refers to persons whose ancestors were from Spain. "Latino" and "Latina" are accurate terms only for persons who have Latin American ancestry.[21]

Similarly, the terms "Arab," "Middle Easterner," and "Muslim" are not synonyms; they refer to language, geography, and religion respectively. The term "Arab," for example, refers to persons who speak the Arabic language. The term "Middle Easterners," which focuses on geography, is obviously accurate for only those individuals from the Middle East, not people from Algeria, Tunisia, Morocco, and Libya. Remember too that there are non-Arab countries — Iran, Turkey, and Israel — in the Middle East.

People who come from republics that were part of the former Soviet Union often resent being incorrectly labeled as "Russians." Use instead the appropriate precise term, such as "Armenians" or "Kazahks."

The term "Muslim" refers to a person who believes in the Islamic religion. Thus, not all Muslims are Arabs, nor are all Arabs Muslims. Likewise, not all Israelis are Jewish, nor are all Jewish people Israelis.

In writing about people with disabilities, note the difference between specific terms such as "blind" versus "visually impaired" and "deaf" versus "hearing loss." A person who is blind has "a loss of vision for ordinary life purposes"[22] while the term "visually impaired" is a generic umbrella term for all degrees of vision loss. Similarly, "deaf" refers to profound hearing loss, while "hearing loss" is the generic umbrella term for any degree of hearing loss. Like "hearing loss," the term "hearing impaired" is a generic term for any degree of hearing loss, but some people with a hearing disability dislike the term. The self-chosen terms tend to be "person who is deaf" or "person who is hard of hearing."

c. Whenever Possible, Prefer the Specific Term over the General Term

Unnecessarily lumping groups of people with varying histories, cultures, and languages under a generic term can be interpreted as not making the effort to understand or respect the differences captured by the specific terms. Thus, while there are differences within the group over whether to use "Indian" or "Native American" or even the newest term, "First American,"

---

21. In addition to concerns about accuracy, some terms are self-chosen and others are rejected because of their varying emphasis on geographic, historical, and cultural roots or political identity. For example, although "Hispanic" is an accurate term for people in the United States who trace their ancestry back to one or more Spanish-speaking countries, some Spanish-speaking persons resent the term, not only because it homogenizes so many diverse peoples but also because it came into common use by way of the government (particularly through the census), the media, and the public at large. Other people resent the term "Hispanic" because they associate it with Spanish colonialism and feel it overemphasizes Spanish ancestry and ignores the African and indigenous roots of Latino culture. "Latino," on the other hand, is preferred by many because it has both a Spanish sound and connotations of ethnic pride. Whether a given individual prefers to be called "Hispanic," "Latino," or "Chicano" may also depend on where the person resides in the United States or on the person's politics. "Hispanic" is the more popular choice in Florida and Texas; "Latino" is more commonly used in California; "Chicano" has connotations of political activism.

22. *Guidelines for Reporting and Writing About People with Disabilities, www.lsi.ku.edu/lsi/internal/guidelines.html* (last visited Aug. 24, 2005).

what is consistently preferred is to use a more specific term such as "Mohawk" or "Navajo" whenever possible rather than a generic term. This principle also applies to the term "Asian American." Although "Asian American" is appropriate when a generic term is needed, it is better to use a more specific term such as "Japanese American" whenever possible.

d. Prefer Terms That Describe What People Are Rather than What They Are Not

Three terms that designate a person as a member of a group other than the majority white population — "non-white," "minority," and "person of color" — demonstrate the interplay of several principles related to bias in language. "Non-white" is often considered offensive because it classifies people by what they are not rather than by what they are. The term "minority" does not seem to create the same level of resentment as "non-white," although some members of minority communities that are not African American complain that the term "minority" is often treated as synonymous with the black community. All three terms have the disadvantage of grouping widely disparate peoples together and, at least in some instances, should be replaced by a specific reference. In some situations, long lists of specific references are impractical. In such cases, the generic term "person of color" is the preferred option.

e. Notice That a Term's Connotations May Change as the Part of Speech Changes

Earlier we saw that while the term "Oriental" is considered offensive when used as a noun to label a person, it is acceptable as an adjective in such phrases as "Oriental rug" or "Oriental food." This same principle comes into play in the preferred terminology for disability and aging.

Members of the disability community tend to prefer the adjective form of "disabled," as in "disabled persons," over the noun form, "the disabled," but the generally preferred term is "persons with disabilities." The adjective form of "elderly" as in "an elderly man" is less offensive than the noun form "the elderly." Members of this community tend to prefer the term "senior citizen."

f. In Selecting Terms, Emphasize the Person over the Difference

The disability community has endorsed what is known as the "person first" principle, which is selecting terms that put the person before the disability whenever possible. The idea is that the individual should be emphasized over the difference and that the difference should not be treated as the person's total identity. Consequently, although as we read in the last section, members of the disability community prefer the adjective form of "disabled," as in "disabled persons," over the noun form, "the disabled," others further recommend "persons with disabilities" over "disabled persons" because it puts the person before the disability. Similarly, "person with epilepsy" is preferred over the term "epileptic," "person with an amputated leg" over "amputee," "person with diabetes" over "diabetic," and "person with paraplegia" (or quadriplegia) over "paraplegic" (or "quadriplegic").

g. Avoid Terms That Are Patronizing or Overly Euphemistic or That Paint People as Victims

While there is a temptation to move toward more euphemistic terms for persons who have physical and mental disabilities, that temptation should be tempered not only by the importance of communicating clearly but also by the realization that sugar coated euphemisms can be patronizing. Some options also seem to be too long to be practical. Consider the following progression:

Handicapped → Disabled → Physically Challenged OR → Persons
     with Disabilities
Persons of Differing Abilities OR
     Differently Abled Persons OR
     Persons with Exceptionalities OR
     Exceptional Persons

Well-meaning persons have tried to introduce terms such as "persons of differing abilities," "differently abled persons," "persons with exceptionalities," "exceptional persons," and "physically challenged" to try to put a positive gloss on having a disability. Such euphemisms tend to fail because they are both imprecise and patronizing. The term "persons with disabilities" is the preferred term because it is factual, not condescending, and it uses the "person first" principle.

Within the disability community, there is also a controversy over terms that paint persons with disabilities as being weak and helpless victims. Note the difference, for example, between "burn victim" and the preferred term "burn survivor" and "stroke victim" and the preferred term "stroke survivor." Some also argue that writers should omit or replace the clichéd verbs in phrases such as "person *confined* to a wheelchair" (replace with "person in a wheelchair" or "person who uses a wheelchair"); "person *stricken* with multiple sclerosis" (replace with "person with multiple sclerosis"); "person *suffering* from arthritis" (replace with "person who has arthritis"); and "person *afflicted* with AIDS" (replace with "person with AIDS"). Verbs such as "stricken," "suffering," "afflicted," and the like sensationalize the disability.

In some instances, a lawyer may feel that the "language of victimization" works towards the client's advantage. The question, of course, is whether to use this kind of short-term "advantage" when it contributes to a particular cultural bias and stereotyping. As with so many decisions such as this, it may be appropriate to consult the described individual to determine his or her preference.

For an in-depth discussion of bias in legal language and argument, see Lorraine K. Bannai & Anne Enquist, *(Un)Examined Assumptions and (Un)Intended Messages: Teaching Students to Recognize Bias in Legal Analysis and Language*, 27 Seattle U. L. Rev. 1 (2003).

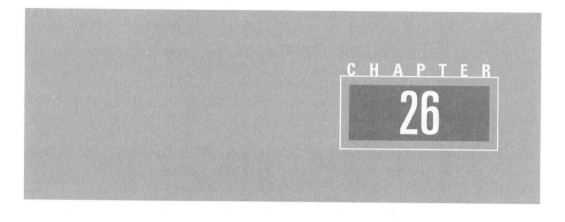

Eloquence

I s it unrealistic to think that legal writing can be eloquent? After all, lawyers write under enormous time pressure. Who has the time to massage language to the point at which someone would call it "eloquent"?

Further, is it appropriate for legal writing to be eloquent? Should an office memo sound like it was written by Shakespeare? What client is willing to pay for a client letter that waxes poetic? Are judges more impressed by arguments or by the language they are wrapped in?

All these good questions really boil down to one question: should a lawyer strive to write eloquently?

Yes, at least sometimes.

While it would not hurt if every office memo and client letter were written eloquently, the one area in which eloquence undoubtedly pays off is briefs. An eloquent brief is a more persuasive brief. Of course the arguments must be sound and persuasive in and of themselves, but one cannot divorce the content of the argument from the form in which it is written. What one says and the way one says it are inextricably linked.

One striking bit of evidence that eloquent briefs are persuasive is the frequency with which well-articulated arguments from briefs reappear in judicial opinions. If imitation is the highest form of flattery, there can be nothing more flattering to a brief writer than to have a judge "lift" a phrase or more from the brief and incorporate it into the opinion.

But as we suggested before, eloquence is not something legal writers can add as a kind of finishing touch. Eloquence is not a tuxedo or an evening gown. A writer cannot "put on" eloquence any more than an artist can put on originality.

Eloquence in legal writing and originality in art are there throughout the creative process, often at the point of conception, again through the drafting and revising, and yet again in the final polishing.

§ 26.1 Purple Prose

Like artists who try to force themselves to be original, legal writers who try to force themselves to be eloquent will probably end up creating something that is either absurd or monstrous.

The following excerpt is from the Statement of Facts in a case about whether racial slurs create a cause of action for the tort of outrage.

> Our client, Mr. Silvino Gomez, is a twenty-year-old of Mexican American descent. Gomez's prowess as a basketball player brought him to the delighted attention of enthusiastic recruiters from several private colleges. He ultimately accepted an athletic scholarship from the University of Newton, where he matriculated and began playing his chosen sport in September 2006. His maiden voyage into the waters of college life was off to a promising start: barely out of the starting gate, he showed himself to be as talented in the classroom as on the court, and his grades reflected his academic acumen. His interests that fall also included the very beautiful Elizabeth Jaynes, former girlfriend of the team's star guard, Michael Wilson. Gomez's freshman year was not to be without troubles, however. Storm clouds gathered on the horizon as the season got underway. Gomez, playing well, sensed that Wilson considered him a threat, and tension between the two stirred the air as Wilson harassed Gomez on the court. Although there was no "name-calling" during October, the dust flew in November when Wilson thundered at Gomez, "You fucking spic!" At first, the insults were made only when the coaches were absent, but in late November Wilson hurled them like lightning bolts during several practices in the presence of the coaches. In December, even the fans at several games were listening as Wilson's insults fell like hailstones on Gomez.

Some call writing like the excerpt above "purple prose." Like the color purple, it can be a bit much. Instead of focusing the reader's attention on the point being made, it calls attention to itself. What's worse, the effort shows.

How to prevent the "purple prose" syndrome? The best safeguard is the axiom "when in doubt, don't." If you think the writing may be "too much," it probably is. Err on the side of subtlety.

Or if you are fortunate enough to have a candid colleague, get a second opinion. If you fear that something you have written may be overdone, ask that colleague to read the writing and let you know if you have stepped over the invisible line and into the realm of purple prose.

You might also try watching out for some of the common features of purple prose, many of which appear in the example above.

- excessive use of adjectives and adverbs: *delighted* attention, *enthusiastic* recruiters, *the very beautiful* Elizabeth Jaynes
- cliche-ridden phrases and images: *the dust flew, hurled them like lightning bolts*
- mixed metaphors: *maiden voyage* mixed with *out of the starting gate*
- overdeveloped metaphors: the weather metaphor in the second paragraph
- pretentious vocabulary: academic *acumen*

Other common features of purple prose not demonstrated in the previous example include the following:

- too much of any one of the poetic devices (for example, excessive alliteration, or the Peter Piper effect)
- heavy-handed use of stylistic devices
- excessive use of underlining and italics for emphasis

§ 26.2 Common Features of Eloquent Writing

Before writing can be considered eloquent, it must be clear, competent, and readable. Eloquent writing, however, goes a step beyond competence. The language is more than clear and energetic: it is memorable, striking, even poetic, because the writer has paid attention to the sound, rhythm, and imagery of language.

Features of language that one may not have thought about since that last class in poetry — alliteration, assonance, cadence, stressed and unstressed syllables, onomatopoeia, simile, and metaphor — may be used, but they do not overwhelm eloquent legal writing. Rhetorical features that one may have noticed in aphorisms — parallelism, balance, antithesis — may also be used, particularly at key points.

Other features, such as electric verbs (see section 24.3), occasional short sentences (see section 24.5), variety in sentence length and sentence openers, and subtle devices for creating emphasis (see section 24.6), are fairly common.

Best of all, all this occurs naturally, apparently effortlessly, even though we know better. Like a pair of dancers who move as one body or a well-executed double play, eloquent writing is the perfect, harmonious matching of form and content. The reader feels satisfied, perhaps even uplifted, by the writing.

§ 26.2.1 Alliteration and Assonance

Eloquent writing begs to be read aloud. One wants to savor the language. Every word and phrase seems to be just the right choice. Quite simply, the writing sings.

Of the numerous features that affect the sound of a piece of writing, alliteration and assonance are probably the easiest to identify. Alliteration, or the repetition of consonant sounds, must be subtle or the writing will begin to sound like "Peter Piper picked a peck of pickled peppers." One way accomplished writers work in alliteration without overpowering the prose is to use it in the middle of words as well as at the beginning.

The following example demonstrates a subtle use of alliteration. The example is taken from the amicus brief for the United States in the landmark Supreme Court case *Wallace v. Jaffree*, which concerned the constitutionality of a state statute authorizing public school teachers to allow a moment of silence at the beginning of the school day for "prayer or meditation."

EXAMPLE

Moment of silence statutes are libertarian in the precise spirit of the Bill of Rights: they accommodate those who believe that prayer should be an integral part of life's activities (including school), and do so in the most neutral and noncoercive spirit possible. The student may pray, but is equally free to meditate or daydream or doze. No one can even know what the other chooses to do: silence is precious because it creates the possibility of privacy within public occasions. To hold that the moment of silence is unconstitutional is to insist that any opportunity for religious practice, even in the unspoken thoughts of schoolchildren, be extirpated from the public sphere. It is to be censorial where the Religion Clauses are libertarian; it would make the very concept of religious accommodation constitutionally suspect.

The alliteration in this example is unobtrusive. In fact, most of us can read this passage and never consciously notice that it includes alliteration. Look again at these phrases:

> the most neutral and noncoercive spirit possible
> daydream or doze

The brief writer could have said "the most impartial and noncoercive spirit possible" or "the most objective and noncoercive spirit possible" or even "the most equitable and noncoercive spirit possible," but didn't. "Neutral," when coupled with "noncoercive," has both the right meaning and the right sound.

The same is true of "daydream or doze." Rather than select "doze," the writer could easily have said "nap," "rest," "sleep," or "snooze." All have similar meanings, but try substituting any one of the four in the original sentence to see what is gained by the alliterative "doze."

The brief writer saves the most subtle and arguably the most powerful alliteration for the clause "silence is precious because it creates the possibility of privacy within public occasions." This clause has two layers of alliteration. The more obvious is the repetition of the p sounds: "silence is precious because it creates the possibility of privacy within public occasions." The second layer is the repetition of s sounds, which is done by both the letters s and c: "silence is precious because it creates the possibility of privacy within public occasions."

The soft "s" and "sh" sounds work perfectly in this context. They underscore the writer's meaning by gently, almost imperceptibly, reminding the reader of the kind of quiet the writer wants the schoolchildren to have.

Assonance, or the repetition of vowel sounds, is similar to alliteration. In the following example, the brief writer repeated the a sound.

EXAMPLE   ### Repeating Vowel Sounds

The absurdity of this implicit assumption is apparent when applied to the motivations of those responsible for the First Amendment itself.

Is the assonance overdone in the example above? Read it aloud to determine if it works.

§ 26.2.2 Cadence

Cadence is the rhythmic flow of the writing, what musicians might call "the beat." Unlike music, though, writing has no apparent time signature and few overt signals for where to place the emphasis. Even so, good writers control the pace and emphasis in their sentences by artful use of sentence structure, sentence length, punctuation, and stressed and unstressed syllables. Like good musicians, they "hear" what they are creating.

Read aloud the following selection from Supreme Court Justice Louis Brandeis.

> In a government of laws, existence of the government will be imperiled if it fails to observe the law scrupulously. Our Government is the potent, the omnipresent teacher. For good or for ill, it teaches the whole people by its example. Crime is contagious. If the Government becomes a lawbreaker, it breeds contempt for law; it invites every man to become a law unto himself; it invites anarchy. To declare that in the administration of the criminal law the end justifies the means — to declare that the Government may commit crimes in order to secure the conviction of a private criminal — would bring terrible retribution. Against that pernicious doctrine this Court should resolutely set its face.

This excerpt is rich with the features of eloquent prose, but for now let's look just at the rhythm in the language. Consider, for example, the phrase "the potent, the omnipresent teacher." The more common way to write two adjectives before a noun is "the potent, omnipresent teacher," without the extra "the." Why the extra "the" in the Brandeis version? Try scanning the phrase as you would a piece of poetry.

⌣ / ⌣ / ⌣ / ⌣ / ⌣
the po-tent, om-ni-pres-ent teach-er

The unvarying unstressed, stressed, unstressed, stressed syllable pattern is flat and lifeless, particularly when it comes in two-syllable, sing-song units. It does not give "omnipresent" enough emphasis. Add the extra "the," however, and the rhythm is more interesting and, more important, more compatible with the desired emphasis.

Now look at the last sentence of this selection.

. . . this Court should resolutely set its face.

This clause is easy to read aloud. It is a grand, solemn conclusion. Why? Scan the last four words.

/ ⌣ / ⌣ / ⌣ /
res-o-lute-ly set its face

The three one-syllable words "set its face" break up any sing-song effect. Further, notice where the stress falls — on "set" and "face." Thus, by ending the selection on a stressed syllable, a strong note, Justice Brandeis creates the sound of finality and conviction. Had Brandeis arranged the last clause so that it ended on "resolutely" (as he had the earlier one, "to observe the law scrupulously"), the unstressed syllable at the end of "resolutely" would have fought against the decisive closure he wanted.

$$/ \smile / \quad / \smile / \smile$$

set its face res-o-lute-ly

Does this mean Justice Brandeis scanned his prose for stressed and unstressed syllables as he was writing it? That's highly unlikely. What is likely is that he heard the sound he was creating and, perhaps through trial and error, manipulated the words until he achieved the aural effect he wanted.

The preceding examples show that adding an extra syllable here or there or changing a stressed to an unstressed syllable or vice versa can make a difference in how writing sounds. Adding or deleting an extra word or syllable also makes a difference in the pace of the writing. Such a change in pace is particularly obvious when the word added or omitted is a conjunction in a series.

A typical series reads like "red, white, and blue." Asyndeton, or the deliberate omissions of conjunctions in a series, quickens the pace. The same series without the conjunction — "red, white, blue" — sounds slightly rushed.

Polysyndeton, or the deliberate use of many conjunctions in a series, slows the pace and drags out the prose. Now the series takes more time: "red and white and blue."

Compare the following examples from a child custody case in which the court looks at which of the parties was the child's primary caregiver. In an objective, neutral discussion of the father's care of the child, the following series may appear.

EXAMPLE   **Neutral Version**

Mr. Lundquist had certain responsibilities regarding his daughter Anna's care: he drove her to school, checked her homework, and took her to medical appointments.

The attorney for Lundquist's former wife may use asyndeton to create the impression that Mr. Lundquist's care of his daughter was minimal.

EXAMPLE   **Mother's Version**

Mr. Lundquist had few responsibilities regarding his daughter Anna's care: he drove her to school, checked her homework, took her to medical appointments.

Mr. Lundquist, on the other hand, will probably want to create the impression that he was an involved parent who spent a great deal of time with his daughter. Notice how the use of polysyndeton, in combination with other persuasive devices, such as characterizing the facts and adding detail, creates the desired effect.

Father's Version

Mr. Lundquist had several significant responsibilities regarding his daughter Anna's care: he drove her to school each day and checked her homework every evening and took her to all regularly scheduled and emergency medical appointments.

§ 26.2.3 Variety in Sentence Length

In section 24.5, we said that legal readers can comfortably read sentences that average around twenty-two words in length. We also suggested that long sentences, thirty-five words or more, are difficult to read unless they are broken into manageable units of meaning. Finally, we briefly touched on the power of the short sentence. All of these points apply to eloquent writing.

Let's look again at the earlier excerpt from Justice Brandeis.

> In a government of laws, existence of the government will be imperiled if it fails to observe the law scrupulously. Our Government is the potent, the omnipresent teacher. For good or for ill, it teaches the whole people by its example. Crime is contagious. If the Government becomes a lawbreaker, it breeds contempt for law; it invites every man to become a law unto himself; it invites anarchy. To declare that in the administration of the criminal law the end justifies the means — to declare that the Government may commit crimes in order to secure the conviction of a private criminal — would bring terrible retribution. Against that pernicious doctrine this Court should resolutely set its face.

A reader's sense of how long a sentence is depends partly on the number of words but also on the number of syllables in the sentence. Here's how the sentences in the Brandeis excerpt break down, in both the number of words and the number of syllables they contain.

sentence 1	20 words	32 syllables
sentence 2	8 words	15 syllables
sentence 3	13 words	17 syllables
sentence 4	3 words	5 syllables
sentence 5	24 words	38 syllables
sentence 6	37 words	62 syllables
sentence 7	11 words	18 syllables

The variety in sentence length in this selection is remarkable — from 3 words to 37 words, from 5 syllables to 62 syllables. Having variety, though, is not an end in itself. Notice how Justice Brandeis uses sentence length. The one extremely short sentence, "Crime is contagious," is startling in its brevity. It hits the reader like a slap in the face. Its terseness creates the emphasis this point deserves.

The longest sentence in the selection has to be longer just to get across its points, but it also needs more words to create the effect of building to a climax. This sentence needs time to gather momentum. And even though it is fairly long — 37 words or 62 syllables — this sentence is easy to read because it comes in manageable units of meaning: 15 words, 18 words, and 4 words.

Such variety in sentence length helps create an interesting and varied pace. Deliberately breaking the "rules" can be another effective way to create reader interest. In the following excerpt from *Edwards v. Aguillard*, 482 U.S. 578, 107 S. Ct. 2573, 96 L. Ed.2d 510, Justice Scalia uses a marathon sentence to help make a point.

> But the difficulty of knowing what vitiating purpose one is looking for is as nothing compared with the difficulty of knowing how or where to find it. For while it is possible to discern the objective "purpose" of a statute (i.e., the public good at which its provisions appear to be directed), or even the formal motivation for a statute where that is explicitly set forth (as it was, to no avail, here), discerning the subjective motivation of those enacting the statute is, to be honest, almost always an impossible task. The number of possible motivations, to begin with, is not binary, or indeed even finite. In the present case, for example, a particular legislator need not have voted for the Act either because he wanted to foster religion or because he wanted to improve education. He may have thought the bill would provide jobs for his district, or may have wanted to make amends with a faction of his party he had alienated on another vote, or he may have been a close friend of the bill's sponsor, or he may have been repaying a favor he owed the Majority Leader, or he may have hoped the Governor would appreciate his vote and make a fundraising appearance for him, or he may have been pressured to vote for a bill he disliked by a wealthy contributor or by a flood of constituent mail, or he may have been seeking favorable publicity, or he may have been reluctant to hurt the feelings of a loyal staff member who worked on the bill, or he may have been settling an old score with a legislator who opposed the bill, or he may have been mad at his wife who opposed the bill, or he may have been intoxicated and utterly unmotivated when the vote was called, or he may have accidentally voted "yes" instead of "no," or, of course, he may have had (and very likely did have) a combination of some of the above and many other motivations. To look for the sole purpose of even a single legislator is probably to look for something that does not exist.

Sentence 5 is a linguistic tour de force. At 202 words, it must set some kind of record for sentence length, yet the sentence is quite readable because it is broken up into manageable units that vary between 8 and 24 words.

But no one thinks Justice Scalia wrote this sentence to demonstrate that he can write a long sentence that is readable. Rather, in this rare instance, an extremely long sentence dramatically made his point that there is an extremely long list of reasons why any single legislator may vote for a bill.

The selection also demonstrates our earlier point about variety in sentence length. Here the range is from 15 words to 202 words.

sentence 1	27 words
sentence 2	64 words
sentence 3	15 words
sentence 4	30 words
sentence 5	202 words
sentence 6	21 words

Notice what points Justice Scalia makes in his two shortest sentences.

§ 26.2.4 Variety in Sentence Openers

It is risky to suggest that legal writers should occasionally vary the openings of their sentences. In the hands of the wrong writer, this advice can lead to some clumsy prose.

For the most part, writers should follow the more traditional advice and begin the majority of their sentences with the subject. Writers who use all sorts of sentence openers other than the subject tend to write prose that sounds jumpy and disjointed, but writers who oversubscribe to the idea of starting sentences with the subject write incredibly boring prose.

The question then is when should a writer use something other than the subject to begin a sentence? Even in garden-variety prose, subjects are frequently preceded by phrases or clauses that establish a context or pick up on a previously established theme. (See sections 23.2 and 23.3 on orienting transitions and dovetailing.)

What is far more unusual and, when done well, more striking, is the inverted word order of some sentences. Such an inversion, known in classical rhetoric as anastrophe, focuses particular attention on whatever words are out of their normal or expected order. The Brandeis excerpt ended with an example of inverted word order.

Inverted Order　　　　　　　　　　　　　　　　　　`EXAMPLE`

Against that pernicious doctrine this Court should resolutely set its face.

As always, to understand the drama and power this arrangement creates, all one has to do is read the sentence in the normal, expected word order.

Normal Word Order　　　　　　　　　　　　　　　　　`EXAMPLE`

This Court should resolutely set its face against that pernicious doctrine.

Here are some more excerpts from the briefs in *Wallace v. Jaffree*. From the brief of the appellees:

Inverted Word Order　　　　　　　　　　　　　　　　`EXAMPLE`

With great difficulty the state attempts to argue that this case creates tension between the Establishment and Free Exercise clauses.

From the amicus brief from the American Jewish Congress:

Inverted Word Order　　　　　　　　　　　　　　　　`EXAMPLE`

The public schools serve as vehicles for "inculcating fundamental values," including "social, moral, or political" ones. *Bd. of Educ. v. Pico*, 102 S. Ct. 2799, 2806 (1982). Pointedly absent from this list are religious values. Education in those values is not, under the Constitution, the responsibility of the public schools; it is that of family and church.

The expected word order of the second sentence in the second example is "Religious values are pointedly absent from this list." Notice that by inverting the order, the brief writer not only places emphasis on what is out of order, "pointedly absent," but also strengthens the emphasis on "religious values" by moving it to the end of the sentence.

§ 26.2.5 Parallelism

Parallelism, or the use of similar grammatical structures in a pair or series of related words, phrases, or clauses, is required in some contexts. See section 27.7. Accomplished writers, however, treat parallelism not just as a grammatical requirement but as a stylistic opportunity. They use parallelism and its related forms to create special effects, emphasis, and euphony.

Here again is an excerpt from the appellants' brief in *Wallace v. Jaffree:*

EXAMPLE   **Parallel Phrases**

This development is a tribute not only to the good sense of the American people, but also to the genius of the Framers of the body of the Constitution.

| not only | to the good sense of the American people, |
| but also | to the genius of the Framers of the body of the Constitution |

Look again at the Scalia excerpt. Justice Scalia uses a specialized version of parallelism called isocolon when he matches both the structure and the length of the parallel elements in the following sentence.

EXAMPLE   **Isocolon**

In the present case, for example, a particular legislator need not have voted for the Act either because he wanted to foster religion or because he wanted to improve education.

| either | because he wanted to foster religion |
| or | because he wanted to improve education |

Some examples of isocolon go beyond matching the number of words and even match the number of syllables. The same excerpt from Justice Scalia includes examples of another specialized form of parallelism: balance. In the sentence below, notice how the first half of the sentence is balanced against the second half.

EXAMPLE   **Balance**

To look for the sole purpose of even a single legislator is probably to look for something that does not exist.

> To look for   is   to look for
> the sole purpose   probably   something that
> of even a   does not exist.
> single legislator

The amicus brief of the United States in *Wallace v. Jaffree* also includes an excellent example of balance.

Balance   EXAMPLE

To hold that the moment of silence is unconstitutional is to insist that any opportunity for religious practice, even in the unspoken thoughts of school children, be extirpated from the public sphere.

> To hold that ...   is   to insist that ....

Balance can also be created in a number of other ways. Here's an excerpt from Justice Cardozo's opinion in *Hynes v. New York*:

Balance   EXAMPLE

The approximate and relative become the definite and absolute.

> approximate   become   definite
> and   and
> relative   absolute

From the brief of the appellees in *Wallace*:

Balance   EXAMPLE

The First Amendment is as simple in its language as it is majestic in its purpose.

> as simple   as (it is) majestic
> in its language   in its purpose

Also fairly common in eloquent legal writing is a related form of parallelism known as antithesis. Like balance, antithesis repeats similar parallel structures on both sides of the equation, but, unlike balance, the ideas are in contrast. In other words, balance says X equals X, and antithesis says X does not equal X.

The structure of antithesis is usually quite simple and falls into one of two patterns:

> not _____ but _____

> _____, not _____

Examples from the amicus brief of the United States in *Wallace*:

EXAMPLE   ## Antithesis

The touchstone is not secularism, but pluralism.

We believe that provision for a moment of silence in the public schools is not an establishment of religion, but rather a legitimate way for the government to provide an opportunity for both religious and nonreligious introspection in a setting where, experience has shown, many desire it. It is an instrument of toleration and pluralism, not of coercion or indoctrination.

---

not *secularism* but *pluralism*
of *toleration and pluralism*, not of *coercion or indoctrination*

Yet another variation of parallelism is the use of parallel openers, which can start sentences, clauses, or phrases. They often have the effect of building to a climax or suggesting that a point is well established. From the Brandeis excerpt:

EXAMPLE   ## Parallel Openers

If the Government becomes a lawbreaker, it breeds contempt for law; **it invites** every man to become a law unto himself; **it invites** anarchy. **To declare that** in the administration of the criminal law the end justifies the means — **to declare that** the Government may commit crimes in order to secure the conviction of a private criminal — would bring terrible retribution.

And from the Scalia excerpt:

EXAMPLE   ## Parallel Openers

He may have thought the bill would provide jobs for his district, or **may have** wanted to make amends with a faction of his party he had alienated on another vote, or **he may have** been a close friend of the bill's sponsor, or **he may have** been repaying a favor he owed the Majority Leader, or **he may have** hoped the Governor would appreciate his vote and make a fundraising appearance for him, or **he may have** been pressured to vote for a bill he disliked by a wealthy contributor or by a flood of constituent mail, or **he may have** been seeking favorable publicity, or **he may have** been reluctant to hurt the feelings of a loyal staff member who worked on the bill, or **he may have** been settling an old score with a legislator who opposed the bill, or **he may have** been mad at his wife who opposed the bill, or **he may have** been intoxicated and utterly unmotivated when the vote was called, or **he may have** accidentally voted "yes" instead of "no," or, of course, **he may have** had (and very likely did have) a combination of some of the above and many other motivations.

In the following excerpt from the EEOC brief in *Hishon v. King & Spaulding*, the brief writer combined parallel openers with antithesis.

Parallel Openers and Antithesis

EXAMPLE

But the two Senators did not obliquely approach, let alone confront, even the "employment" of lawyers at law firms. They did not mention lawyers; they spoke of doctors instead. They did not discuss law partnerships; they spoke of hospitals instead.

§ 26.2.6 Onomatopoeia

"Snap," "crackle," and "pop" — these words are examples of onomatopoeia; that is, they sound like what they mean. So do "sizzle," "plop," "hiss," "click," "twang," "crinkle," and a host of others. These words sound like the natural sounds they represent.

Other words have an onomatopoeic quality even though the words do not represent a sound. Consider the word "weird." Not only does it sound weird, it is even spelled weird. The word "bizarre" works the same way: it looks and sounds bizarre. The list goes on. There is something grotesque in the look and sound of "grotesque," and it is hard to imagine a word that looks and sounds more unattractive than "ugly."

Consider the sound of words like "sensual," "lascivious," and "licentious." Notice how the rolling "s" and "l" sounds combine in various ways to give the words a lazy, even erotic, sound. "Sultry" works the same way.

The "slippery slope" one hears so much about in law puts the "s" and "l" together as a consonant blend and achieves a slippery effect. The words seem to *slide* off the tongue with slow ease. Like a judicial system that has started down that slippery slope, there are no natural brakes to stop these words once they are formed on the lips. Notice too that "slick," "slime," "slink," "slither," "slush," and "sludge" all somehow share this same slippery, even oily, quality.

Should legal writers use onomatopoeia in their writing? Consider the following versions of essentially the same point.

Draft

EXAMPLES

Harris suddenly took the keys and ran out the door.

Revised

Harris snatched the keys and ran out the door.

"Snatched" says in one word — even one syllable — what the first of the examples takes two words and four syllables to say. The word's quickness mirrors the quickness in the action. "Snatched" sounds like a quick grab at those keys.

§ 26.2.7 Simile and Metaphor

Similes are indirect comparisons.

Simile

EXAMPLE

Lowell's mental irresponsibility defense is like the toy gun he used in the robbery — spurious.

Metaphors are direct comparisons.

EXAMPLE   **Metaphor**

Our Government is the potent, the omnipresent teacher.

To be effective, similes and metaphors need to be fresh and insightful. Unfortunately, all too many metaphors used in legal writing are cliche-ridden. How often must we hear that something or other is "woven into the fabric of our society"? When was the last time you actually thought about wolves and sheep when something or someone was described as a "wolf in sheep's clothing"?

Timeworn similes and metaphors suggest that the writer's thought processes are on autopilot, and no more than that will be expected of the reader. We can all mentally coast.

A fresh simile or metaphor makes demands on the reader. It asks the reader to bring to the new subject matter all the associations it has with the other half of the metaphor.

So powerful is metaphor that metaphors have become issues themselves. Consider again *Wallace v. Jaffree*, which involved the Alabama "silent meditation or prayer in public schools" statute. Throughout that case's history, both sides argued whether there was "an absolute wall of separation" between federal government and religion.

§ 26.2.8 Personification

Like so many of the suggestions in this chapter, personification, or giving human traits or abilities to abstractions or inanimate objects, must be used with a light hand if it is to be used at all in legal writing.

In the brief of the appellees in *Wallace v. Jaffree*, the writer used personification to make a point about the intent of the Alabama legislature.

EXAMPLE   **Personification in a Brief**

In 1982, in order to breathe religious life into its silent meditation statute, the Alabama legislature amended 16-1-20 to expressly include "prayer" as the preferred activity in which the students and teachers may engage during the reverent moment of silence.

In his dissenting opinion in *Hoffa v. United States*, Chief Justice Warren uses personification to make a point about the government's actions and its witness.

EXAMPLE   **Personification in an Opinion**

Here the Government reaches into the jailhouse to employ a man who was himself facing indictments far more serious (and later including one for perjury) than the one confronting the man against whom he offered to inform.

Eloquent language does one of two things. It creates a satisfying sound or, as in the Warren excerpt above, it creates a memorable image. The best of the best does both. Such writing is memorable, even unforgettable. It grabs the reader's attention long enough to make the reader see something new or see something old in a new way.

A Guide to Correct Writing

Introduction

This section of the *Handbook* was written as a review of grammar, punctuation, and mechanics. While many legal writers have a good command of these aspects of writing, some students complain that they never really understood how to use a semicolon or that they have heard about dangling modifiers but what in the world are they, anyway?

This section is designed to be a quick refresher and explanation for those students who have forgotten some of the basic rules or who, for some reason, never learned some of them. Even students who have strong backgrounds in grammar, punctuation, and mechanics may find it helpful to review some of the chapters in this section simply because legal writing puts more demands on the writer than do most other types of writing. Consequently, it may make your writing more efficient and more effective if you have all the rules, and hence all the options, at your fingertips.

Finally, although this section is titled "A Guide to Correct Writing," the term "correct" is a slightly troubling one because it may suggest that the choices outlined in these chapters are the absolutely "right" ones in all circumstances. This is not true. In informal language, for example, certain other usage choices are not only acceptable but preferred. In legal writing, however, standard English is the norm and therefore the "correct" choice.

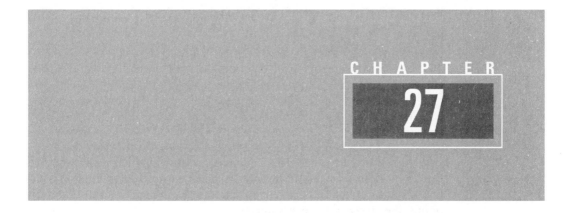

Grammar

§ 27.1 Basic Sentence Grammar

Grammar, like law, is a system. Once you understand the basic workings of the system, you can begin to use the system effectively and efficiently.

Much of Part 1, A Guide to Effective Writing, and Part 2, A Guide to Correct Writing, depends on understanding the grammar of an English sentence. This section is a quick review of basic sentence structure and the various components of most English sentences.[1]

§ 27.1.1 Sentence Patterns

In legal writing, as in most other writing, most sentences are statements. These statements name someone or something (the subject) and then describe an action that someone or something is performing (the predicate).

Smith   hit Jones.
(subject)   *(predicate)*

Smith's car   smashed into the railing.
(subject)   *(predicate)*

---

1. Although modern grammarians have persuasively argued that structural and transformational grammars more accurately describe the English sentence, the authors have elected to use traditional grammar, partly because it is more familiar to most readers and partly because it is sufficient for our purposes.

Occasionally, the predicate describes the state in which the subject exists or the subject's state of being.

Smith's car	is a total loss.
(subject)	*(predicate)*

At the heart of every subject is a noun or a pronoun. Nouns name persons (Supreme Court Justice David Souter), places (Austin, Texas), things (savings bond), and concepts (negligence). Because pronouns are substitutes for nouns, they too can serve as subjects.

At the heart of every predicate is a verb. Some verbs express an action ("sue," "plead," "argue," "allege"); others show a state of being (such as forms of the verb to be). Frequently, the main verb is preceded by other verbs known as auxiliary, or helping, verbs ("might have been" assaulted), which express time relationships and shades of meaning. See section 30.1.2.

Pattern 1: Subject + Verb

To write a sentence, you need at least one noun or pronoun for a subject and at least one verb for a predicate. This is the simplest sentence pattern.

subject	predicate
Lawyers	argue.
(noun)	*(verb)*

Pattern 2: Subject + Verb + Direct Object

Many verbs, however, cannot stand alone. They require a noun that will receive the action of the verb. We cannot, for example, simply say "lawyers make" and call that a sentence. "Make" what? To make sense, the verb needs a direct object. Notice that the direct object is part of the predicate.

subject	predicate	
Lawyers	make	arguments.
(noun)	*(verb)*	*(noun)*
		(direct object)

Direct objects "receive" the action of the verb.

Lawyers	make arguments.
Judges	deny motions.
	(direct object)

Another way of thinking about this point is to say that the subject performs the action of the verb, and the verb "is done to" the direct object.

You can often find the direct object in a sentence by simply asking the question "what?" after the verb. Make what? Make "arguments." Deny what? Deny "motions."

Pattern 3: Subject + Linking Verb + Subject Complement

Similarly, state of being, or linking verbs, need nouns (or sometimes adjectives) to complete the idea. Because these words do not directly receive the action of the verb in the same way as a direct object, they are not called direct objects. Instead, they are called subject complements because they complement the subject by renaming or describing it.

subject	predicate	
Lawyers	are	advocates.
(noun)	*(linking verb)*	*(noun)*
		(subject complement)

subject	predicate	
Lawyers	are	aggressive.
(noun)	*(linking verb)*	*(adjective)*
		(subject complement)

Note that some of the same words ("am," "is," "are," "was," "were") function as linking verbs in some sentences and as auxiliary, or helping, verbs in other sentences. You can always tell whether one of these words is a linking verb or a helping verb by checking to see whether it is the only main verb in the sentence (then it is a linking verb) or whether it is followed by another main verb (then it is an auxiliary, or helping, verb).

Linking Verb "Is"

EXAMPLE

The judge is the trier of fact.

In the preceding example, "is" is the only main verb; therefore, it is a linking verb.

Helping Verb "Is"

EXAMPLE

The judge is speaking to the jury.

In the preceding example, "is" is followed by another main verb, "speaking"; therefore, "is" is an auxiliary, or helping, verb in this example. Notice that the combination "is speaking" is an action verb.

Pattern 4: Subject + Verb + Indirect Object + Direct Object

In another common pattern, the verb is followed by two nouns. The second noun after the verb, the direct object, receives the action of the verb. The first noun after the verb, the indirect object, identifies to whom or for whom (or what) the action is performed.

subject	predicate		
Lawyers	tell	clients	their options.
	(verb)	*(noun)*	*(noun)*
		(indirect object)	*(direct object)*

Pattern 5: Subject + Verb + Direct Object + Object Complement

In this last pattern, we also have two nouns following the verb, but in this pattern, the first noun is the direct object and the second noun is an object complement. An object complement renames or describes the direct object.

subject	predicate		
Smith	called	Jones	a liar.
	(verb)	*(noun)*	*(noun)*
		(direct object)	*(objective complement)*

Using these basic sentence patterns, we can now begin adding all those extras that make sentences interesting and complex.

§27.1.2 Single-Word Modifiers

Modifiers change, limit, describe, or add detail. Words that modify nouns or pronouns are, by definition, adjectives (*illogical* argument, *nervous* witness, *bearded* suspect).

Words that modify verbs, adjectives, or adverbs are adverbs (*quickly* responded, finished *soon*, *extremely* angry, *very recently*). Notice that adverbs often end in "-ly."

Any of our basic sentences can be expanded by using adjectives and adverbs as modifiers.

EXAMPLES   **Basic Sentences Expanded by Modifiers**

Thoughtful lawyers make very persuasive arguments.
adjective   adverb adjective

Too many lawyers are overly aggressive.
adv. adj.   adverb adjective

---

§27.1.3 Phrases

When expanding the basic sentence patterns, we are not limited to single-word modifiers. Groups of related words, or phrases, may also serve as modifiers. A phrase is easily distinguished from other groups of related words because a phrase always lacks a subject or a verb or both.

Probably the most common type of modifying phrase is the prepositional phrase. Prepositional phrases are made up of a preposition (words that show relationships between other words, such as "about," "at," "by," "for," "in," "of," "on," "to"), its object, and any modifiers.

Preposition	Modifiers	Object
at	the same	time
by	an	affidavit
for	a new	trial
in	the	verdict
under	this	section

Prepositional phrases can modify nouns, verbs, adjectives, or adverbs.

Prepositional Phrases

EXAMPLE

At 10:00 p.m. on April 5, 2006, a two-truck collision occurred <u>in Delaware</u> <u>between a truck</u> driven <u>by Constance Ruiz</u> and a truck driven <u>by Fred Miller</u>.

Basic sentence patterns can also be expanded with verbals. Verbals are made from verbs, but they cannot serve as the main verb of a sentence. Instead, verbals are ways of using verb forms in other roles in a sentence. The three types of verbals — gerunds, infinitives, and participles — are described below. Notice that each can be expanded into a phrase.

a. Gerunds

Gerunds always act as nouns, so they are found in slots in the sentence that require nouns (subject, objects). They are formed by adding "-ing" to the base form of a verb.

Gerunds in Sentences

EXAMPLES

<u>Impeaching</u> his testimony will be difficult.
(gerund)

Forgery includes <u>writing</u> a bad check.
        (gerund)

---

b. Participles

Participles act as adjectives. Present participles are formed by adding "-ing" to the base form of the verb; past participles usually add "-d" or "-ed." Irregular verbs have a special past participle form (for example, "brought," "drunk," "stolen").

Participles in Sentences

EXAMPLES

A computer <u>wrapped</u> in a blanket was found in Johnson's trunk.
      (participle)

<u>Applying</u> this rule, the New York Supreme Court held that the
(participle)
appellant's constitutional rights were not violated.

<u>Given</u> that forgery is not a crime of dishonesty, the court found that
(participle)
evidence of the prior conviction is inadmissible.

Notice that the only way to distinguish between a gerund and a present participle is to determine the roles they perform in a sentence.

c. Infinitives

Infinitives can act as nouns, adjectives, or adverbs. The infinitive form is always "to" plus the base form of the verb.

EXAMPLE   **Infinitives in Sentences**

<u>To extend</u> the all-purpose public figure standard <u>to include</u> all financial institutions ignores the Supreme Court's mandate <u>to construe</u> the standard narrowly.

---

d. Absolutes

One additional type of phrase, the absolute phrase, can also be used to expand the basic sentence patterns. Absolute phrases do not modify any one word or phrase in a sentence; instead, they are whole sentence modifiers. Absolute phrases are made up of a noun (or pronoun), a participle, and their modifiers.

attention		diverted
noun	**+**	*participle*

EXAMPLE   **Absolute in Sentences**

<u>His attention diverted by the fire,</u> the witness was unlikely to have viewed the fleeing arsonist for more than a second.

---

§27.1.4 Clauses

A clause is a group of related words that has both a subject and a verb. There are two types of clauses: main (or independent) clauses and subordinate (or dependent) clauses. A main clause can stand alone as a sentence. A subordinate clause cannot stand alone as a sentence because by definition it is introduced by a subordinating conjunction or relative pronoun.

Common Subordinating Conjunctions

after	if	though
although	if only	till
as	in order that	unless
as if	now that	until
as long as	once	when

as though	rather than	whenever
because	since	where
before	so that	whereas
even if	than	wherever
even though	that	while

Relative Pronouns

that	which	whom
what	who	whomever
whatever	whoever	whose

Notice that in subordinate clauses introduced by a relative pronoun, the subject of the clause is often the relative pronoun (Defendants *who do not take the stand* risk having jurors infer that they are guilty.).

Main Clauses

EXAMPLES

Martin retained full possession of the stock.

The trial court abused its discretion.

It failed to consider the statutory factors.

Subordinate Clauses

EXAMPLE

although Martin retained full possession of the stock

that the trial court abused its discretion

when it failed to consider the statutory factors

Subordinate Clauses Attached to Main Clauses

EXAMPLE

Although Martin retained full possession of the stock, the trial court awarded the stock to Judith.

The appellate court found that the trial court abused its discretion when it failed to consider the statutory factors.

§ 27.1.5 Appositives

Appositives are words or groups of words that follow a noun and rename it. They may also further describe or identify the noun.

Appositives

EXAMPLES

The sexual assault charges against Los Angeles Lakers' basketball player <u>Kobe Bryant</u>
(appositive)
were dismissed when his accuser told prosecutors she would not testify.

Jim Bakker, <u>television evangelist</u>, was convicted of twenty-four
(appositive)
counts of fraud and conspiracy.

In *Texas v. Johnson,* <u>a case about a state criminal statute forbidding "the desecration of a venerated object,"</u> the Supreme Court ruled that burning the American flag as an expression of political discontent is protected by the First Amendment.

Appositives are frequently introduced by phrases (that is, such as, for example).

EXAMPLE   **Phrases Introducing Appositives**

Evidence of some crimes, <u>such as fraud, embezzlement, and false pretense,</u> may be probative of a defendant's credibility as a witness.

---

§27.1.6 Connecting Words

The five basic sentence patterns can also be expanded by using connecting words that allow us to combine words or word groups of equal rank. For example, we can add one or more nouns to a subject to create a compound subject (Smith and Wilson hit Jones), or we can add one or more verbs to the predicate to create a compound predicate (Smith hit and kicked Jones).

a. Coordinating Conjunctions

The most common connecting words are the seven coordinating conjunctions.

and	nor	yet
but	for	so
or		

"And," "but," "or," and "nor" can connect any two (or more) of the same kind of word or word group. "For" and "so" connect main clauses.

EXAMPLE   **Connecting Two Nouns**

Crimes of dishonesty involve **fraud <u>or</u> deceit**.

EXAMPLE   **Connecting Two Verbs**

The complaint stated that the defendants **had published <u>but</u> not retracted** a defamatory article about Kraft Savings and Loan.

EXAMPLE   **Connecting Three Phrases**

Copies of the article were distributed **to subscribers, to newsstands, <u>and</u> to at least three civic groups**.

EXAMPLE   **Connecting Two Subordinate Clauses**

Because there are only two witnesses <u>and</u> because each witness has a different version of the facts, the jury will have to choose which one to believe.

Connecting Two Main Clauses

Kraft Savings and Loan has not assumed a role of especial prominence in the affairs of society, nor **does it occupy a position of pervasive power or influence.**

b. Correlative Conjunctions

Correlative conjunctions come in pairs.

both . . . and	either . . . or	whether . . . or
not . . . but	neither . . . nor	as . . . as
not only . . . but also		

Correlative Conjunctions

Plaintiff's contact with the community is <u>both</u> **conservative** <u>and</u> **low-key.**

The jury <u>either</u> **will not hear the defendant's testimony** <u>or</u> **will completely disregard it** if his prior convictions are admitted.

c. Conjunctive Adverbs

Even though conjunctive adverbs do not connect parts of the sentence grammatically, they are useful because they show the relationship between two or more ideas.

The Most Common Conjunctive Adverbs

accordingly	further	likewise	similarly
also	furthermore	meanwhile	still
anyway	hence	moreover	then
besides	however	nevertheless	thereafter
certainly	incidentally	next	therefore
consequently	indeed	nonetheless	thus
finally	instead	otherwise	undoubtedly

Conjunctive Adverbs in Sentences

Mrs. Davis admits that her physician told her that she has a drinking problem. She refuses, <u>nevertheless</u>, to attend Alcoholics Anonymous. <u>Instead</u>, she claims that she drinks only an occasional glass of wine.

Mrs. Davis will have $33,872 a year to spend as she sees fit; <u>therefore</u>, she has no need for the dividend income from the stock.

Mr. Davis has no means from his present income to repurchase the stock; <u>con-sequently</u>, the option to repurchase is worthless.

Notice too that because they do not connect parts of the sentence grammatically, conjunctive adverbs can often move in the sentence.

EXAMPLES ## Moving Conjunctive Adverbs

Tom Davis owned his own business; <u>however</u>, his son did not participate in the business because the two did not get along.

Tom Davis owned his own business; his son did not participate in the business, <u>however</u>, because the two did not get along.

§ 27.2 Fragments

Although there are a few exceptions, fragments are generally taboo in legal writing. In fact, of the kinds of errors a writer can make, fragments are considered one of the most egregious.

Simply defined, a sentence fragment is an incomplete sentence. Theoretically, it may be missing its subject,[2] but more than likely it is missing a main verb, or it is a subordinate clause trying to pose as a sentence.

§ 27.2.1 Main Verb Missing

All verbals — gerunds, participles, and infinitives — are formed from verbs, but they cannot fill verb slots in a sentence. Consequently, they cannot serve as the main verb of a sentence. Some legal writers who are prone to writing fragments mistake verbals for main verbs. See section 27.1.3 for definitions and explanations of verbals.

EXAMPLE ## Fragment

The attorney objecting to the line of questioning.

In the example above, "objecting" is not a verb; it is a participle modifying "attorney." Because the example has no main verb, it is a fragment, not a sentence. To make it a sentence, either add a main verb or change "objecting" from a participle to a main verb.

EXAMPLE ## Possible Revisions

The attorney objecting to the line of questioning <u>rose</u> to her feet.

The attorney <u>objects</u> to the line of questioning.

The attorney <u>was objecting</u> to the line of questioning.

Notice that the same word, "objecting," can be a participle or, with an auxiliary verb added, a main verb.

---

2. Imperative, or command, sentences such as "Sit down" or "Hang your coat in the cloakroom" may appear to have a missing subject, but the subject is always understood to be "you." Therefore, imperative sentences are not fragments even if they contain only one word, like "Run!"

§ 27.2.2 Subordinate Clauses Trying to Pose as Sentences

Take any main, or independent, clause and add a word like "although," "because," "if," "until," or "when" in front of it and it automatically becomes a subordinate, or dependent, clause.

until + main clause = subordinate clause

As a main clause, it is a sentence; as a subordinate clause standing alone, it is a fragment.

Main Clause   EXAMPLE

The attorney objects to the line of questioning.

Subordinate Clause   EXAMPLES

Until the attorney objects to the line of questioning.

Subordinate clauses must be attached to a main, or independent, clause.

Subordinate Clause Attached to Main Clause   EXAMPLE

Until the attorney objects to the line of questioning, the judge will
        (subordinate clause)   *(main clause)*
not rule.
(main clause cont'd)

"Although," "because," "if," "until," and "when" are not the only words, or subordinating conjunctions, that can change a main clause into a subordinate clause. Below is a fairly complete list of the most common subordinating conjunctions used in legal writing. Remember: if one of these words or phrases introduces a clause, that clause will be subordinate. It cannot stand alone.

Subordinating Conjunctions

after	before	now that	till
although	even if	once	unless
as	even though	provided	until
as if	if	rather than	when
as long as	if only	since	whenever
as soon as	in order that	so that	where
as though	in that	than	whereas
because	no matter how	that	wherever
		though	while

Notice, too, that subordinate clauses may follow a main clause. Take care, however, to attach the subordinate clause to its main clause. Some writers mistakenly treat the subordinate clause as a separate sentence, which creates a fragment.

EXAMPLE

Fragment

Kaiser's statement acknowledging our client's ownership of the land may have no effect on the hostility of his claim. Because Kaiser never acted in subordination to the true owner.

EXAMPLES

Correct

Kaiser's statement acknowledging our client's ownership of the land may have no effect on the hostility of his claim because Kaiser never acted in subordination to the true owner.

The relative pronouns — "who," "whoever," "whom," "whomever," "whose," "what," "whatever," "which," and "that" — also lure some writers into writing fragments.

EXAMPLE

Fragment

The admission of a defendant's prior convictions may affect that defendant's decision to take the stand. Which would interfere with his right to testify freely on his own behalf.

EXAMPLES

Correct

The admission of a defendant's prior convictions may affect that defendant's decision to take the stand. Therefore, admission of his prior convictions would interfere with his right to testify freely on his own behalf.

"Who," "which," and "what" are also interrogative pronouns that introduce questions. Questions introduced by "who," "which," and "what" are not fragments.

EXAMPLE

"Which" to Introduce a Question

Which witness will corroborate the defendant's alibi?

In short, to determine if you have written a sentence rather than a fragment, (1) make sure you have a verb, (2) make sure you have a subject, and (3) make sure your subject and verb are not preceded by a subordinating conjunction or a relative pronoun.

See Exercises 27A and 27B in the *Practice Book.*

§27.2.3 Permissible Uses of Incomplete Sentences

There are a handful of permissible uses for incomplete sentences in legal writing.

a. in issue statements beginning with "whether"
b. as answers to questions
c. in exclamations or exact quotations

d. for stylistic effect
e. as transitions

a. In Issue Statements Beginning with "Whether"

Many issue statements, or questions presented, begin with the word "whether."

"Whether" Issue Statement

Whether, under Washington tort law on wrongful death or conversion, the Hoffelmeirs may collect punitive damages for the destruction of their pet cat when the cat was impounded and when, after Mr. Janske of the Humane Society tried unsuccessfully to contact the Hoffelmeirs, the animal was destroyed before the time required by the Sequim City Ordinance.

Although a grammarian would not consider the above example to be a complete sentence, most attorneys and judges find this format acceptable in legal writing. It is as though legal readers read in an elliptical "The issue is" before "whether."

b. As Answers to Questions

Many office memos contain a brief answer section. Typically, a brief answer will begin with an incomplete sentence that is a short response to the legal question. This is an acceptable use of a fragment. The following example is the brief answer to the question presented in the preceding example.

Acceptable Fragment in Brief Answer

Probably not. In Washington, there is a strong policy against the award of punitive damages and, unless there is a statutory provision allowing for punitive damages, the courts will not award them. In this instance, there is no statutory provision allowing for punitive damages.

---

c. In Exclamations or Exact Quotations

Exclamations rarely occur in legal writing because they make the tone of the writing appear inflammatory, effusive, or sarcastic. The one place exclamations do appear in legal writing is in quoted dialogue. On such occasions, quote exactly what the speaker said and how he or she said it, including fragments.

d. For Stylistic Effect

Sophisticated writers who are well schooled in the rules of grammar can occasionally use an intentional fragment for stylistic effect. Most writers, however, should avoid writing any fragments.

Fragment for Stylistic Effect

It may have been unavoidable, but it still took courage. More courage than most of us would have had.

e. As Transitions

Like fragments used for stylistic effect, intentional fragments used as transitions are a risk. Use them only if you are secure about and in complete control of your writing.

If you have already read sections 22.4 and 22.5 of this book, you may have noticed that the authors used two incomplete sentences as transitions to begin those sections.

Fragments as Transitions

First, the truth.

Again, the truth.

See Exercise 27C in the *Practice Book*.

§ 27.3 Verb Tense and Mood

§ 27.3.1 Tense

Verb tense does not pose problems for most legal writers who are native speakers of English. Native speakers tend to "hear" when the verb is right or wrong. Consequently, verb tense is one of those areas of writing that is best left alone, unless a writer is having problems.

For those native and non-native speakers of English who are having problems with verb tense in legal writing, the following is a quick review of the basic verb tense structure. See Chapter 30 for more on verbs and verb tense, particularly how auxiliary verbs create shades of meaning.

Throughout this review of verb tense, we will use a capital "X" to indicate the present on all time lines.

The term "tense" refers to the time in which the verb's action occurs in relation to the time when the writer is writing. For example, present tense is used for actions that occur in the present — that is, at the time the writer is writing.

Present Tense

The defendant <u>pleads</u> not guilty.

Time line: _____ X _____
the present
(the action is occurring
at the same time
the writer is writing)

Notice, however, that the "X" on the time line that represents "the present" may be as short as a fraction of a second or as long as several centuries, depending on what time frame the writer sets up.

Past tense refers to actions that occurred before the writer is writing.

Past Tense

Two years ago, this same prosecutor <u>charged</u> the defendant with aggravated assault.

> Time line: _____ X _____
> ← the past →

Legal writers usually use the past tense when describing analogous cases.

In *Colorado Carpet,* the court <u>rejected</u> the argument for the specially manufactured goods exception because the carpet <u>was</u> not cut to a room size.

Future tense refers to actions that will occur after the writer is writing.

Future Tense

The plaintiff <u>will call</u> an expert witness.

> Time line: _____ X _____
> ← the future →

The simple tenses — present, past, and future — are just that: simple and easy to use. Only the present tense offers a few noteworthy wrinkles.

In addition to its common use for actions that occur in the present, present tense is also used to express general truths and to show habitual actions.

Present Tense for General Truths/Habits

Appellate courts <u>do</u> not <u>retry</u> a case on its facts.

The defendant <u>drinks</u> a six-pack of beer every Friday night.

Present tense can also be used to indicate the future when the sentence contains other words and phrases to signal a future time.

Present Tense with other "Future" Signals

The court <u>hears</u> oral arguments later this afternoon.

The perfect tenses are a bit more complicated. Perfect tenses are designed to show that an action is completed before a certain time. For example, the present perfect tense usually shows that an action is completed at the time of the statement. It is formed by using "have" or "has" before the past participle. In the sentence below, the present perfect "have tried" occurred before the present.

EXAMPLE   **Present Perfect Tense**

The plaintiffs <u>have tried</u> this strategy before, but it is not working this time.

Time line: _____ X _____
           ───────────────▶
           (action begun in the
           past and completed
           before the present)

The present perfect tense is also used when the action was begun in the past and it continues on into the present.

EXAMPLE   **Present Perfect Tense**

The United States Supreme Court <u>has held</u> that states can be sued under federal disability law for failing to provide persons with disabilities access to the courthouse. *Tennessee v. Lane*, 514 U.S. 509 (2004).

Time line: _____ X _____
           ───────────────▶
           (action begun in the
           past and continues
           on into the present)

The past perfect tense is used when one past action was completed before another past action. For example, a legal writer may find it useful to use the past perfect to distinguish the time sequence of the facts of the case from the time sequence of a court's actions, both of which occurred in the past.

Note that the past perfect tense is formed by adding "had" before the past participle.

EXAMPLE   **Past Perfect Tense**

The court <u>noted</u> that the defendant <u>had known</u> about the defective brakes for three months.

Time line: _____ X _____ X _____ X _____
                  had   noted
                  known   (past)   (present)
                  (past
                  perfect)

The past perfect tense is also useful when discussing court proceedings at different levels. For example, a writer may use the simple past tense to describe the decisions of an appellate court and the past perfect to describe the decisions of the trial court.

Past and Past Perfect

EXAMPLE

The Court of Appeals <u>affirmed</u> the trial court, which <u>had ruled</u> that the statute did
     (simple past)   *(past perfect)*
not apply.

The future perfect tense is used when an action that started in the past ends at a certain time in the future. It is formed by adding "will have" before the past participle.

Future Perfect Tense

EXAMPLE

By the time you finish dinner tonight, drunk drivers <u>will have claimed</u> five more victims on United States highways.

Time line: _____ X _____X _____

             →
         will have
         claimed

Every verb can also be progressive; that is, it can show continuing action by adding "-ing."

Present progressive: is claiming
Past progressive: was claiming
Future progressive: will be claiming
Present perfect progressive: has been claiming
Past perfect progressive: had been claiming
Future perfect progressive: will have been claiming

One last word about verb tenses: one common myth is that writers have to maintain a consistent verb tense. Although writers should avoid needless shifts in verb tense, shifts are required when there is a shift in time, which may occur even within the same sentence.

See Exercises 27D and 27E in the *Practice Book*.

Acceptable Shifts in Verb Tense

EXAMPLES

Her landlord <u>knows</u> that she <u>will be</u> unable to pay her rent.
  (present)   *(future)*

Although Mr. Henderson <u>built</u> the shed on the northwest corner of the property in
       (past)

1990, he <u>admits</u> that Ms. Kyte <u>has owned</u> that corner since 1995.
   (present)   *(present perfect)*

Smith <u>will argue</u> that he <u>did</u> not knowingly or willingly <u>consent</u> to a search of his wallet.
  (future)   *(past)*   *(past)*

§27.3.2 Mood

In grammar, the term "mood" refers to the approach the writer gives the verb. English has three moods: indicative, imperative, and subjunctive. The indicative mood is used for statements of facts or questions.

EXAMPLE | **Indicative Mood**

The defendant <u>pleaded</u> not guilty.

The imperative mood is used for sentences that are orders or commands. The subject of a sentence in the imperative mood is understood to be "you," the reader or listener.

EXAMPLE | **Imperative Mood**

<u>Plead</u> not guilty.

The subjunctive mood is the only mood that is a bit tricky. Although grammarians are constantly discussing its demise, the subjunctive mood is still used in a variety of situations.

1. The subjunctive is used to express ideas contrary to fact.

EXAMPLE | **Subjunctive Mood**

If I <u>were</u> the defendant, I would plead not guilty.

2. The subjunctive is used to express a requirement.

EXAMPLE | **Subjunctive for a Requirement**

The law requires that contracts <u>be signed</u> willingly, not under duress.

3. The subjunctive is used to express a suggestion or recommendation.

EXAMPLE | **Subjunctive for a Recommendation**

His attorney recommended that he <u>be allowed</u> to give his own closing argument.

4. The subjunctive is used to express a wish.

EXAMPLE | **Subjunctive for a Request**

The clerk asked that the check <u>be post-dated</u>.

Note that the contrary-to-fact clauses begin with "if" and the requirement, suggestion, recommendation, or wish clauses all begin with an expressed or elliptical "that."

In addition, there are a few idioms such as "far be it from me" and "suffice it to say" that use the subjunctive mood.

The subjunctive mood is formed slightly differently depending on how it is used. For present conditions that are contrary to fact, it is formed from the past tense of the verb. For the verb "to be," it uses "were."

Forming the Subjunctive   EXAMPLES

If the inspection team <u>took</u> a reading on the toxic particles being emitted right now, it would show that the factory has completely disregarded EPA guidelines.

If she <u>were</u> to testify, the defendant's sister would corroborate his story.

For past conditions that are contrary to fact, the subjunctive mood is formed from the past perfect.

Forming the Subjunctive   EXAMPLE

<u>Had</u> the contract been signed, there would be no question that it is valid.

For requirements, recommendations, and suggestions, the subjunctive mood is formed from the infinitive form of the verb without the "to."

Forming the Subjunctive   EXAMPLE

The law requires that the adverse possessor <u>prove</u> that the possession was open and notorious.

---

§ 27.4 Agreement

Simply put, agreement is matching the form of one word to another. In legal writing, agreement can be a problem in two areas: (1) the agreement in number between a subject and verb and (2) the agreement in number between a pronoun and its antecedent.

§ 27.4.1 Subject-Verb Agreement

Singular subjects take singular verbs, and plural subjects take plural verbs. For most native speakers of English, this kind of subject-verb agreement comes almost as naturally as breathing, as long as the sentence is short and simple.

Subject-Verb Agreement   EXAMPLES

The law requires that all drivers wear seat belts.

    singular subject = law
    singular verb = requires

The immigration laws require that all workers provide proof of citizenship before starting a job.

    plural subject = laws
    plural verb = require

In English, we often think that adding "s" makes the plural form of words. This is true for nouns but not for verbs. We add an "s" to the singular form of present tense verbs (except the verb "to be") when they are matched with a singular noun or the pronouns "he," "she," or "it." For example, we say "a client maintain<u>s</u>," "he reject<u>s</u>," "she allege<u>s</u>," or "it confirm<u>s</u>."

In simple sentences, a writer can usually make subjects and verbs agree by listening to the way the sentences sound. The writer's ear tells him or her what matches and what does not. In longer, more complicated sentences, like those that often occur in legal writing, the ear is more likely to be fooled. The following rules cover those situations.

RULE 1   **A subject and its verb must agree even when they are separated by other words**

When other words, particularly nouns, come between a subject and its verb, the writer may inadvertently match the verb to a word other than the subject. The following example demonstrates this error in agreement.

EXAMPLE   **Incorrect**

Custom-made <u>towels</u> imprinted with the hotel's logo <u>satisfies</u> the
             (subject)   *(verb)*
requirement that the goods be specially manufactured.

The writer has mistakenly chosen the singular verb "satisfies" to match with the intervening noun "logo" when the verb should be the plural form "satisfy" to agree with the plural subject "towels." One way writers can check for this kind of agreement error is to read their subjects and verbs together without the intervening words. "Towels satisfy" will sound right to native speakers.

The number of the subject is not changed by adding intervening words that begin with expressions such as "accompanied by," "as well as," "in addition to," "with," "together with," or "along with." These expressions are considered prepositions and not coordinating conjunctions (see section 27.1), so they modify the subject; they do not change its number.

In the following example, the verb "suggests" correctly agrees with the subject "statement."

EXAMPLE   **Correct**

The defendant's <u>statement</u> to the police, as well as her testimony at trial, <u>suggests</u> that her actions were premeditated.

RULE 2   **Two or more subjects joined by "and" usually take a plural verb**

Subjects joined by "and" are plural. This rule does not change even if one or all of the subjects are singular.

Correct

EXAMPLE

North Star Cinema and Highland Heights Theater question the validity of the admissions tax.

Unfortunately, writers sometimes hear only the second half of the subject with the verb and mistakenly select a singular verb ("Highland Heights Theater question<u>s</u>"). To correct this agreement error, you may find it easier to mentally substitute the word "they" for plural subjects when trying to use your ear to find the correct form of the verb ("they question").

Exception A

Occasionally two or more parts of the subject make up one idea or refer to one person or thing. In such cases, use a singular verb.

Correct

EXAMPLE

His wife and beneficiary was the only person mentioned in the will.

Exception B

Occasionally the words "each" or "every" precede one or more of the parts of a plural subject. In such cases, use a singular verb.

Correct

EXAMPLE

Every juror and spectator in the courtroom expects the defendant to testify.

Subjects joined by "or" or "nor" take verbs that agree with the part of the subject closest to the verb

RULE 3

To check subject-verb agreement in sentences with subjects joined by "or" or "nor," simply read only the second half of the subject with the verb and let your ear help you select the correct verb form. In the following examples, read "Lazar Television is" and "her older sisters have."

Correct

EXAMPLES

Neither Horizon Telecommunications nor Lazar Television is the type of enterprise that the bulk sales statutes seek to regulate.

The child's mother or her older sisters have been caring for her after school.

In a verb phrase like "have been caring" in the preceding example, the helping, or auxiliary, verbs are the ones that change.

singular:	has been caring
plural:	have been caring

RULE 4	**Most indefinite pronouns take singular verbs**

Indefinite pronouns are pronouns that do not refer to any definite person or thing, or they do not specify definite limits. The following is a list of the most common indefinite pronouns:

all	each	everything	none
any	either	neither	somebody
anyone	everyone	nobody	someone
anybody	everybody	no one	something

Usually these pronouns refer to a single, indefinite person or thing, so they take singular verbs.

EXAMPLE	**Correct**

Everyone who ate in the restaurant is suffering the same symptoms.

A few indefinite pronouns — "none," "all," "most," "some," "any," and "half" — may take either a singular or a plural verb depending on the noun to which they refer.

EXAMPLES	**Correct**

All of the jewelry was recovered.

All of the rings were recovered.

RULE 5	**Collective nouns take singular verbs when the group acts as one unit; collective nouns take plural verbs when the members of the group act separately**

"None" tends to be the most troublesome word in the group. Traditionally in formal usage, "none" was considered singular because it derives from the Old English word for "no one." Consequently, writers can feel confident about using a singular verb in most instances. In general usage, however, "none" is singular or plural depending on the situation and the effect the writer wants to achieve. All three of the following examples are correct.

EXAMPLES	**Correct**

None of the courts in this jurisdiction have ruled on this issue.

None of the courts in this jurisdiction has ruled on this issue. OR

Not one of the courts in this jurisdiction has ruled on this issue.

The following is a list of the most common collective nouns in legal writing:

jury	committee	board
audience	team	majority
family	crowd	number
Supreme Court	appellate court	fractions (when used
names of companies/		as nouns)
corporations		

The following examples all use collective nouns that are acting as one unit, so the verbs are singular.

Correct

EXAMPLES

The jury has reached its verdict.

The appellate court has affirmed the conviction.

Boeing is concerned about its liability.

An easy way to tell if the collective noun "number" is singular or plural is to check whether "number" is preceded by "a" or "the." "A number" requires a plural verb; "the number" requires a singular verb.

Correct

EXAMPLES

A number of witnesses are willing to testify that they saw the defendant drive out of the parking lot.

The number of union members who are seeking early retirement is growing.

Nouns ending in "s" that are singular in meaning take singular verbs

RULE 6

Despite their "s" ending, words such as "aesthetics," "athletics," "economics," "mathematics," "news," "physics," "politics," and "statistics" are usually considered singular because they describe a whole concept or body of knowledge.

Correct

EXAMPLE

Politics is inappropriate in a court of law.

When "statistics" refers to individual facts, it takes a plural verb.

Correct

EXAMPLE

The enrollment statistics show that the university has consistently discriminated against Asian students.

RULE 7	**Linking verbs agree with their subjects, not their subject complements**

In the following example, the linking verb "was" agrees with "testimony," not the subject complement "contradictory and intentionally misleading."

EXAMPLE	**Correct**

The defendant's testimony was contradictory and intentionally misleading.

In the next example, the linking verb "is" agrees with "reason," not "evaluations."

EXAMPLE	**Correct**

The reason for firing Jones was his low evaluations.

See section 27.1 for more on subject complements.

RULE 8	**Verbs agree with their subjects even when the subjects come after the verb**

Subjects follow verbs after expletive constructions such as "there is" and "there are."

EXAMPLES	**Correct**

There is a possibility that the defendant will plead "temporary insanity."

There are several options for ensuring that the loan is repaid.

Subjects may also follow verbs when normal word order is changed for emphasis.

EXAMPLE	**Correct**

At no time was Brown aware that his conversations were being tape recorded.

At no time were Brown and Smith aware that their conversations were being tape recorded.

RULE 9	**The title of a work or a word used as a word takes a singular verb**

EXAMPLE	**Correct**

Tactics in Legal Reasoning is an excellent resource for both law students and practitioners.

When a word is used as a word, it is often enclosed in quotation marks or preceded by "the word"; a word used as a word takes a singular verb.

Correct

"Premises" has at least three different meanings: (1) the introductory propositions to a syllogism, (2) the area of land surrounding a building, or (3) a building or part of a building.

The word "premises" has three different meanings.

Compare the previous examples, both of which used the singular verb "has," with the following example, which requires the plural verb form "have."

Correct

The premises have been searched by the police.

See Exercise 27F in the *Practice Book*.

§ 27.4.2 Pronoun-Antecedent Agreement

Pronouns are substitutes for nouns. They have no independent meanings. Consequently, they must refer to a noun and be consistent with that noun in gender, person, and number.

An antecedent is the noun to which the pronoun refers. A pronoun must agree with its antecedent.

Legal writers usually do not have problems making their pronouns and antecedents agree in gender or person. Agreement in number, however, can be a bit more difficult.

Singular antecedents require singular pronouns; plural antecedents require plural pronouns

Pronoun Agreement

William MacDonald may claim that <u>his</u> constitutional rights were violated.
 (antecedent)   *(pronoun)*

William MacDonald and Grace Yessler may claim that <u>their</u> constitutional rights were
 (antecedent)   *(antecedent)*   *(pronoun)*
violated.

This rule, although simple on the surface, becomes a little trickier when the pronoun substitutes for a generic noun that is singular. Because English does not have a singular generic pronoun to fit these situations, writers are left with less than ideal choices.

For example, in informal writing and oral language, you may frequently see or hear a plural pronoun used as a substitute for a singular generic noun, as in the ungrammatical example below. In formal writing, such as legal writing, this practice is unacceptable.

EXAMPLE   ## Ungrammatical

The <u>defendant</u> may claim that <u>their</u> constitutional rights were violated.
   (antecedent)   *(pronoun)*

Some writers try to solve the problem by resorting to the traditional masculine pronoun for all generic nouns. This practice is unacceptable to the many modern writers who believe that language should be gender-neutral. See section 25.4.

EXAMPLE   ## Masculine Pronoun

A <u>defendant</u> may claim that <u>his</u> constitutional rights were violated.
  (antecedent)   *(pronoun)*

Occasionally, the problem can be solved by making the generic noun plural. Unfortunately, not all sentences will allow this quick fix.

EXAMPLE   ## Plural Noun

<u>Defendants</u> may claim that <u>their</u> constitutional rights were violated.
(antecedent)   *(pronoun)*

Even fewer sentences will allow a writer to remove the pronoun altogether without substantial revision or loss in meaning.

EXAMPLE   ## Removed Pronoun

A defendant may claim that the constitutional rights were violated.

The example above avoids the grammatical problem but with a significant loss in meaning: the belief that one actually possesses constitutional rights is no longer included in the sentence's meaning. What is left, then, is the option of using the slightly awkward "he or she," "his or her," "himself or herself."

EXAMPLE   ## "His or Her"

A <u>defendant</u> may claim that <u>his or her</u> constitutional rights were violated.
  (antecedent)   *(pronouns)*

While not perfect, this option seems to be the best choice, provided the writer does not put more than one "he or she," "his or her," or "himself or herself" in a sentence.

Exception to Rule 1:

Occasionally the word "each" or "every" precedes one or more of the parts of a plural antecedent. In such cases, use a singular pronoun.

Correct   EXAMPLE

Every girl and woman in the community feared for her safety.

When a pronoun refers to two or more antecedents joined by "or" or "nor,"   RULE 2
the pronoun agrees with the nearer antecedent

Pronoun Agreement   EXAMPLE

Either <u>David Wilson</u> or <u>Donald Wilson</u> left <u>his</u> keys in the car.
      (antecedent)   (antecedent)   (pronoun)

Notice that this rule for pronoun agreement is similar to Rule 3 for subject-verb agreement.

When a singular and a plural antecedent are joined by "or" or "nor," place the plural antecedent last so that the pronoun can be plural.

Correct: EXAMPLE

Neither the <u>defendant</u> nor his <u>brothers</u> admit knowing where <u>their</u> neighbors keep items of value.

When an indefinite pronoun is the antecedent, use the singular pronoun   RULE 3

Indefinite pronouns are those that do not refer to any specific person or thing, or they do not specify definite limits. The most common indefinite pronouns are "all," "any," "anyone," "anybody," "each," "either," "everyone," "everybody," "everything," "neither," "nobody," "no one," "none," "somebody," "someone," and "something."

EXAMPLE

Correct

Anyone would have noticed that his or her license plate was removed.

Notice that this rule for pronoun agreement is similar to Rule 4 for subject-verb agreement. (See section 27.4.1.)

As with Rule 1, writers must take care not to use the informal and ungrammatical plural pronoun or the traditional generic "he" as a pronoun substitute for an indefinite pronoun.

EXAMPLES

Ungrammatical

Somebody must have used their phone to call the police.

EXAMPLE

Masculine pronoun

Somebody must have used his phone to call the police.

EXAMPLE

Corrected

Somebody must have used his or her phone to call the police.

OR

Somebody must have used the phone to call the police.

RULE 4

When a collective noun is the antecedent, use a singular pronoun if you are referring to the group as one unit and a plural pronoun if you are referring to the individual members of the group

Some common collective nouns are "jury," "committee," "appellate court," "Supreme Court," "majority," "board," "team," "family," "audience," "crowd," "number," "State," "defense," "prosecution," and the names of companies and corporations.

See Exercise 27G in the *Practice Book*.

EXAMPLES

Singular Collective Nouns

The jury must not be misled about Jason Richardson's credibility when it is considering his testimony.

Shopping Haven discriminated against John Adams when it failed to issue him a new credit card for an existing account.

§ 27.5 Pronoun Reference

Pronouns are substitutes for nouns. Consequently, pronouns usually[3] refer back to a noun, and that noun is known as the antecedent.

Pronoun and its Antecedent   EXAMPLE

<u>Marino</u> moved for reconsideration, but <u>her</u> motion was denied.
(antecedent)   *(pronoun)*

Legal writers tend to have two kinds of problems with pronouns and their antecedents: (1) they use plural pronouns to refer back to singular antecedents; and (2) they use pronouns that have unclear or ambiguous antecedents. The first problem is one of grammatical agreement, discussed in the second half of section 27.4. The second problem is the focus of this section.

---

§ 27.5.1 Each Pronoun Should Clearly Refer Back to Its Antecedent

Consider the following sentence:

Ambiguous Pronoun   EXAMPLE

Officer Robert O'Malley, who arrested Howard Davis, said that he was drunk at the time.

As it stands, the sentence has two possible readings because the pronoun "he" has two possible antecedents: Officer Robert O'Malley and Howard Davis. To clear up the ambiguity, do one of two things:

1. repeat the noun rather than use a pronoun, or
2. revise the sentence so that the pronoun is no longer ambiguous.

Possible Revisions   EXAMPLE

Officer Robert O'Malley, who arrested Howard Davis, said that Davis was drunk at the time.

Howard Davis was drunk when he was arrested by Officer O'Malley.

Officer O'Malley was drunk when he arrested Howard Davis.

According to the arresting officer, Robert O'Malley, Howard Davis was drunk at the time of the arrest.

---

3. Indefinite pronouns such as "someone," "anybody," "everything," and "neither" do not refer back to nouns. Also, some pronouns that are parts of idioms ("it is likely that . . . ," "it is clear that . . . ," "it is raining") do not have antecedents.

Officer Robert O'Malley, who arrested Howard Davis, admitted being drunk at the time of the arrest.

See Exercise 27H in the *Practice Book*.

§ 27.5.2 Avoid the Use of "It," "This," "That," "Such," and "Which" to Refer Broadly to a General Idea in a Preceding Sentence

Consider the following sentences:

EXAMPLE   **Pronoun Error**

Even if Mr. Smith's testimony about possible embarrassment caused by Acme is adequate to justify a damage award, emotional harm is difficult to quantify. This makes it unlikely that Mr. Smith will receive any substantial recovery.

To what does "this" in the second sentence refer? Because it does not seem to refer back to any specific noun in the preceding sentence, the reader is left to guess exactly how much or how little of the preceding discussion "this" is supposed to encompass.

The solution to many broad pronoun reference problems is often a rather simple one: add a summarizing noun after the pronoun to show the limits of the reference.

EXAMPLE   **Correct**

This difficulty makes it unlikely that Mr. Smith will receive any substantial recovery.

The same technique often works well with "that" and "such."

EXAMPLE   **Draft**

Mrs. Marquette has testified that Mr. Marquette has beaten her and their children on at least three occasions, that he has locked them out of their home twice, and that he has threatened to "cut their throats" if they told anyone. According to Mr. Marquette, that is a lie.

EXAMPLE   **Correct**

Mrs. Marquette has testified that Mr. Marquette has beaten her and their children on at least three occasions, that he has locked them out of their home twice, and that he has threatened to "cut their throats" if they told anyone. According to Mr. Marquette, that testimony is a lie.

The use of the pronoun "which" to refer broadly to a preceding idea is a trickier problem to correct. Look at the following example and see if you can determine what the "which" stands for. Keep in mind the basic rule that a pronoun is a substitute for a noun.

Pronoun Error

In *Boone v. Mullendore,* Dr. Mullendore failed to remove Mrs. Boone's fallopian tube, which resulted in the birth of a baby.

The nouns that "which" could possibly refer to are the case name, Dr. Mullendore, and the fallopian tube. Obviously none of these resulted in the birth of a baby. Instead, the writer seems to suggest that "which" is a substitute for the following idea: Dr. Mullendore's failure to remove Mrs. Boone's fallopian tube. Notice that in expressing what the "which" referred to, we had to use the noun "failure" rather than the verb "failed." To correct the error, then, we must add the noun "failure" to the sentence.

Correct

In *Boone v. Mullendore,* Dr. Mullendore's failure to remove Mrs. Boone's fallopian tube resulted in the birth of a baby.

Be sure to distinguish between the incorrect use of "which" to refer broadly to a previously stated idea and the correct use of "which" to introduce nonrestrictive clauses.

§ 27.5.3 Pronouns Should Refer Back to Nouns, Not to Adjectives

Occasionally a word that appears to be a noun is actually an adjective because it modifies a noun.

Adjective That Looks Like a Noun

the <u>Rheams</u> <u>building</u>
  (adjective) (noun)

Often the possessive form of a noun is used as an adjective in a sentence.

Adjective That Looks Like a Noun

the <u>defendant's</u> <u>alibi</u>
  (adjective) (noun)

But because a pronoun must always refer to a noun, adjectives that are noun look-alikes cannot serve as antecedents for pronouns.

EXAMPLE	**Incorrect**

The Rheams building has undergone as many facelifts as he has.

EXAMPLE	**Correct**

The Rheams building has undergone as many facelifts as Rheams himself has.

EXAMPLE	**Incorrect**

After hearing the defendant's alibi, the jurors seemed to change their opinion of him.

EXAMPLE	**Correct**

The jurors seemed to change their opinion of the defendant after they heard his alibi.

Admittedly, this rule is a grammatical technicality. Infractions rarely create ambiguity. Even so, because correctness and precision are required in legal writing, it is best to heed the rule.

See Exercises 27J and 27K in the *Practice Book*.

§ 27.6 Modifiers

Using modifiers correctly is simple. All one has to do is (1) remember to keep modifiers close to the word or words they modify and (2) make sure the words they modify are in the same sentence as the modifiers.

§ 27.6.1 Misplaced Modifiers

Forgetting to keep modifiers close to the word or words they modify leads to misplaced modifiers. Some words — "almost," "also," "even," "ever," "exactly," "hardly," "just," "merely," "nearly," "not," "only," "scarcely," "simply" — are particularly prone to being misplaced. These words should adjoin the words they modify and ideally should be placed right before the word or words they modify.

Notice, for example, how the placement of "only" changes the meaning in the following sentences.

EXAMPLE	**Placement of "Only" Changes Meaning**

<u>Only</u> the defendant thought that the car was rented.
No one but the defendant thought that.

The defendant <u>only</u> thought that the car was rented.
He did not know for sure.

The defendant thought <u>only</u> that the car was rented.
He thought one thing, nothing else.

The defendant thought that the <u>only</u> car was rented.
Only one car was available, and it was rented.

The defendant thought that the car was <u>only</u> rented.
He did not think it was leased or sold.

In speech, such single-word modifiers are often put before the verb even when the speaker does not intend them to modify the verb. Some authorities accept placing "only" immediately before the verb if it modifies the whole sentence.

Speech: He only drove ten miles.
Writing: He drove only ten miles.

There is a growing trend toward placing "only" earlier in a sentence if it fits there more naturally, but "strict grammarians still insist that the rule for placement of only should always be followed."[4]

Phrases, particularly prepositional phrases, can also be easily misplaced in sentences. The result can be imprecise writing, an awkward construction, and unintentional humor.

The writer of the following example was surprised to find out that because of a misplaced modifier he had inaccurately placed the brother instead of the cabin in New Hampshire.

Misplaced Modifier   EXAMPLE

The defendant owned a cabin with his brother in New Hampshire.

Revised

The defendant and his brother owned a cabin in New Hampshire.

The misplaced modifier in the following example gave the writer a meaning she never intended.

Misplaced Modifier   EXAMPLE

The witness to the events may be unavailable after the accident.

Although there are contexts in which this sentence is correctly written, the writer intended to say, "The witness to the events after the accident may be unavailable." Her version made it sound like an intentional "accident" was being planned for the specific purpose of making the witness "unavailable"!

Take care to place clauses that begin with "who," "which," and "that" immediately after the noun they modify.

Misplaced Modifier   EXAMPLE

The victim described her attacker as having a tattoo on his right buttock, which was shaped like a peace sign.

---

4. *The American Heritage Dictionary of the English Language* 1230 (4th ed., Houghton Mifflin Co. 2000).

This sentence suggests that the attacker's right buttock, not his tattoo, was shaped like a peace sign.

EXAMPLE   **Revised**

The victim described her attacker as having a tattoo that was shaped like a peace sign on his right buttock.

See Exercises **27L, 27M,** and **27N** in the *Practice Book*.

§ 27.6.2 Dangling Modifiers

Dangling modifiers are those modifiers that do not have a noun in the sentence to modify; hence, they are "dangling," or unattached to an appropriate noun. Legal writers tend to write dangling modifiers for one of two reasons: (1) the noun or pronoun the modifier is intended to modify is in the mind of the writer but inadvertently omitted from the sentence; or (2) the writer wanted to avoid the first person pronouns "I" or "we"[5] and, in doing so, left a modifier dangling.

EXAMPLE   **Dangling Modifier**

By calling attention to the defendant's post-arrest silence, the jury was allowed to make prejudicial and false inferences.

In the example above, the modifier "by calling attention to the defendant's post-arrest silence" should modify the noun "the prosecutor," which does not appear in the sentence. Unfortunately, it seems to be modifying the noun closest to it: "the jury."

EXAMPLE   **Revised**

By calling attention to the defendant's post-arrest silence, the prosecutor encouraged the jury to make prejudicial and false inferences.

Notice how in the following example the dangling modifier can be corrected by including the pronoun it modifies, "we," or by revising the sentence so that the dangling modifier is no longer a modifier.

EXAMPLE   **Dangling Modifier**

In deciding whether to attempt to quash service, more than the technical merits of the case have to be considered.

---

5. Many authorities in legal writing still advise legal writers to avoid using first-person references.

Revised

In deciding whether to attempt to quash service, we must consider more than the technical merits of the case. *OR*

A decision about whether to attempt to quash service must be based on more than the technical merits of the case.

You can see that the majority of dangling modifiers occur at the beginnings of sentences. One way to avoid writing this type of dangling modifier is to remember to place the noun the modifier modifies right after the comma separating the modifier from the main clause.

$$\underline{\text{Modifier,} \quad \text{Main Clause}}$$
$$(noun)$$

$$\underline{\text{By calling attention} \ldots \text{silence, the prosecutor} \ldots.}$$

If you are having difficulty deciding what noun the modifier should modify, ask yourself who or what is doing the action described in that modifier. Then place the answer to that question right after the comma separating the modifier from the main clause.

$$\underline{\text{In deciding} \ldots \text{service, we must consider} \ldots.}$$

Notice too that when the real actor in a sentence is in the subject position, the problem of dangling modifiers is usually solved. See section 24.2 for more on using effective subjects in sentences.

Many kinds of grammatical structures can be dangling. The most common are participles (words with "-ing," "-ed," or past endings), infinitives (to + verb; for example "to show"), and prepositional phrases.

Some dangling modifiers can also be corrected by adding a subject to the modifier.

Dangling Modifier

While petitioning for a permit, zoning regulations in the area were changed.

Revised

While the hospital was petitioning for a permit, zoning regulations in the area were changed.

Subordinate clauses, like the one in the revision above, are not dangling modifiers.

Dangling modifiers may also occur at the ends of sentences. Again, the problem is that the noun the modifier modifies does not appear in the sentence.

EXAMPLE   **Dangling Modifier**

This motion was denied in the interest of judicial economy, reasoning that there was evidence that raised a question regarding Anderson's knowledge of the relationship.

Who or what is doing the reasoning that there is evidence? Most certainly the court, but the noun "court" does not appear in the sentence.

EXAMPLE   **Revised**

Reasoning that there was evidence that raised a question regarding Anderson's knowledge of the relationship, the court denied this motion in the interest of judicial economy.

It is also permissible to leave the modifier at the end of the sentence as long as it modifies the subject of the sentence.

EXAMPLE   **Revised**

The court denied this motion in the interest of judicial economy, reasoning that there was evidence that raised a question regarding Anderson's knowledge of the relationship.

This example could also be correctly revised by changing the modifier to a subordinate clause.

See Exercise 27O in the *Practice Book*.

EXAMPLE   **Revised**

The court denied this motion in the interest of judicial economy because there was evidence that raised a question regarding Anderson's knowledge of the relationship.

---

§27.6.3 Squinting Modifiers

Squinting modifiers are labeled as such because they appear to be looking both backward and forward in a sentence; that is, they appear to be modifying both the word that precedes them and the word that follows them.

EXAMPLE   **Ambiguous Modifier**

The bridge inspection that was done frequently suggested that the drawbridge electrical system was beginning to fail.

This sentence has two possible interpretations: are the inspections themselves done frequently, or are there frequent suggestions throughout the inspection report?

Revised

The bridge inspection that was frequently done suggested that the drawbridge electrical system was beginning to fail. *OR*

The bridge inspection that was done suggested frequently that the drawbridge electrical system was beginning to fail.

§ 27.7 Parallelism

Consider the following pairs of sentences. What is it about version B of each pair that makes it easier to read?

Correcting Lack of Parallelism

1A. The defendant claims that on the day of the murder he was at home alone washing his car, he mowed his lawn, and his dog needed a bath so he gave him one.
1B. The defendant claims that on the day of the murder he was at home alone washing his car, mowing his lawn, and bathing his dog.

2A. Dr. Stewart is a competent surgeon with over twenty years of experience and who is respected in the local medical community.
2B. Dr. Stewart is a competent surgeon who has over twenty years of experience and who is respected in the local medical community.

3A. The defendant claimed the evidence was prejudicial and that it lacked relevance.
3B. The defendant claimed the evidence was prejudicial and irrelevant.

In all the preceding pairs, the version A sentences lack parallelism and, as a result, are grammatically incorrect, as well as clumsy and unsophisticated. The version B sentences do not change the content significantly; they simply use the structure of the sentence to make that content more apparent and more accessible. Specifically, they use parallelism.

In grammar, "parallelism" is defined as "the use of similar grammatical form for coordinated elements." This definition may seem overly abstract or vague until it is broken into its components.

"Coordinated elements" are parts of a sentence joined by conjunctions, such as "and," "but," "or," "nor," and "yet." Sometimes they are pairs, but often they are a series or a list.

"Similar grammatical form" simply means that a noun is matched with other nouns, verbs are matched with other verbs, prepositional phrases are matched with other prepositional phrases, and so on. For example, look at the poorly coordinated elements in sentence 1A above.

washing his car,
he mowed his lawn, and
his dog needed a bath so he gave him one

Even without analyzing exactly what kind of phrase or clause each one of these elements is, we can see that they do not have similar grammatical form. Now look at the coordinated elements of sentence 1B. Note how the "-ing" endings make the items parallel.

washing his car
mowing his lawn, and
bathing his dog

Matching endings of the first key word in each of the elements is one way to make elements parallel.

Now compare the coordinated elements in 2A and 2B.

2A. with over twenty years of experience and
      who is respected in the local medical community

2B. who has over twenty years of experience and
      who is respected in the local medical community

Again, without doing an analysis of the grammar of each element, we can see, or perhaps hear, that 2B has parallel structure, but this time the parallelism is signaled by using the same word, "who," to introduce each element.

In some cases, however, you will not be able to rely on matching endings to key words or matching introductory words; you will have to find the same grammatical form in order to make the elements parallel.

In 3A, for example, the writer has tried to match an adjective, "prejudicial," with a relative clause, "that it lacked relevance." The writer could have used the second tip — matching introductory words — and created the following parallel elements:

that the evidence was prejudicial and
that it lacked relevance

The more concise and better choice is to find the appropriate adjective to match "prejudicial."

prejudicial and
irrelevant

Because many sentences in legal writing are long and complicated, parallelism is critical for keeping the content and its presentation manageable. In the following sentence, for example, the defendant's two concessions are easier for the reader to see because they are set out using parallel constructions.

EXAMPLE

Parallelism in Long Sentences

Counsel for the defendant conceded that she did assault Coachman and that a trial would determine only the degree of the assault.

$$\text{conceded} \begin{cases} \underline{\text{that she did assault Coachman}} \\ \underline{\text{that a trial would determine only the degree}} \\ \text{of the assault} \end{cases}$$

Notice too in both the preceding and subsequent examples that by repeating the introductory word "that," the writer has made the parallelism more obvious, which, in turn, makes the sentence easier to read.

Repeating Introductory "That"

EXAMPLE

When questioned at the parole hearing, Robinson claimed that it was wrong to tell only one side of the story, that he had not received permission but felt he had a right to write what he wanted, and that people had a right to hear the other side of the story.

$$\text{claimed} \begin{cases} \underline{\text{that it was wrong to tell only one side of the story,}} \\ \underline{\text{that he had not received permission but felt he had a right}} \\ \underline{\text{to write what he wanted, and}} \\ \underline{\text{that people had a right to hear the other side of the story.}} \end{cases}$$

Writing parallel elements is required for grammatical sentences; repeating an introductory word to heighten the parallelism is not required but is recommended for making the parallelism more obvious to the reader.

Issue statements can also become much more manageable when the legally significant facts are laid out using parallel construction. The following example uses "when" as the introductory word to each element. Notice how the legally significant facts are not only written using parallel construction but also grouped according to those that favor the defendant and those that favor the plaintiff. The conjunction "but" helps the reader see the two groupings.

Parallelism in Issue Statements

EXAMPLE

Under Federal Rule of Civil Procedure 4(d)(1), is service of process valid when process was left with defendant's husband at his home in California, when defendant and her husband maintain separate residences, when defendant intends to maintain a separate residence from her husband, but when defendant regularly visits her husband in California, when defendant keeps some personal belongings in the California house, when defendant receives some mail in California, and when defendant received actual notice when her husband mailed the summons and complaint to her?

when process was left with defendant's husband at his home in California
when defendant and her husband maintain separate residences
when defendant intends to maintain separate residence from her husband, BUT

when defendant regularly visits her husband in California
when defendant keeps some personal belongings in the California house
when defendant receives some mail in California
when defendant received actual notice when her husband mailed the
    summons and complaint to her

Parallelism is also critical, indeed it is required, when setting out lists.

EXAMPLE

Parallelism in Lists

Wilson challenges the admission of three photographs, which he claims are grue-
some: (1) the photograph of Melissa Reed as she appeared when discovered at the
crime scene; (2) the photograph of Melinda Reed as she appeared when discovered at
the crime scene; and (3) a photograph of Wilson wearing dental retractors to hold his
lips back while exposing his teeth.

Lists require parallelism when they are incorporated into the writer's text,
as in the example above, and when they are indented and tabulated, as in the
example below.

EXAMPLE

Parallelism in Lists

The school district will probably be liable for the following:

  1. the cost of restoring the Archers' rose bushes, as well as the lost use value of
      their property during restoration;
  2. the cost of replacing Mr. Baker's windows and the market value of his vase;
      and
  3. compensation to the Carlisles for the annoyance and inconvenience they
      have experienced.

To create parallelism, match the key words in each element; the parallelism is not destroyed if all the modifying words and phrases do not match
exactly.
In the following examples, the key words "received" and "released"
match, and the key words "for … harm" and "for … expenses" match.

EXAMPLES

Matching Key Words

In *Pepper,* the injured plaintiff <u>received</u> medical treatment and <u>released</u> the defendant
from liability.

The Bells are seeking damages <u>for severe emotional and financial harm</u> and <u>for
substantial medical expenses related to the pregnancy.</u>

To summarize, then, writers can correct problems in parallelism in one of three ways:

1. match the endings of key words,
2. match introductory words, or
3. use the same grammatical form.

See Exercise 27P in the *Practice Book*.

Earlier we said that parallelism is required for coordinated elements joined by "and," "but," "or," "nor," and "yet." Parallelism is also required for elements joined by correlative conjunctions, which are conjunctions that come in pairs. The most common correlative conjunctions are "either ... or," "neither ... nor," "not only ... but also," "both ... and," "whether ... or," and "as ... as."

To make the elements joined by one of these pairs parallel, simply match what follows the first half with what follows the second half.

either _____   either <u>similar</u>

or _____   or <u>identical</u>

Either/Or   EXAMPLE

Campbell's prior convictions are either similar or identical.

neither _____   neither <u>the photographs</u>

nor _____   nor <u>the testimony</u>

Neither/Nor   EXAMPLES

Neither the photographs nor the testimony can prove who actually committed the alleged assault.

not only _____   not only <u>verbally</u>

but also _____   but also <u>physically</u>

Not Only/But Also   EXAMPLE

The defendant admits that she not only verbally but also physically abused her children.

Take care when using these pairs. All too frequently legal writers lose the parallelism in their sentences by misplacing one of the words in these pairs.

Lack of Parallelism

The purpose of the rule is to ensure that actual notice is provided either by personal or constructive service.

either _____	either <u>by personal</u>
or _____	or <u>constructive</u>

Note that "by personal" is not parallel with "constructive."

Revised:

The purpose of the rule is to ensure that actual notice is provided either by personal or by constructive service. *OR*

The purpose of the rule is to ensure that actual notice is provided by either personal or constructive service.

Parallelism is also required when elements are compared or contrasted. Many of the comparing and contrasting expressions use "than." Notice in each of the following pairs where the blanks are for the parallel elements.

more _____ than _____

less _____ than _____

_____ rather than _____

Parallelism to Compare/Contrast

Wilson's attention was centered more <u>on the assailant's gun</u> than <u>on his face.</u>

The court applied <u>the "clearly erroneous" standard</u> rather than <u>the arbitrary and capricious standard</u>.

See Exercise 27Q in the *Practice Book*.

CHAPTER 28

Punctuation

§ 28.1 The Comma

Commas are everywhere. They are the most frequently used punctuation mark and, unfortunately, the most frequently misused punctuation mark. They give most legal writers fits. Few writers seem to be able to control the little buzzards, and most seem to be more than a bit controlled by them. Many fairly good legal writers admit that they punctuate by feel, especially when it comes to commas. They rely on the "rule" that one should use a comma whenever the reader should pause — advice that works only about 70 percent of the time.

It is no wonder that few legal writers know and apply all the rules for commas. There are too many of them. In this section, we discuss no fewer than twenty rules, all designed to govern one little punctuation mark. Even so, these twenty rules do not cover every conceivable use of the comma, just the high spots.

The good news, however, is that not all these rules are equally important. Some are critical; misapplication of these rules will either miscue the reader or change the meaning of a sentence as significantly as a misplaced decimal point can change the meaning of a number. The critical rules are listed under the heading "Critical Commas: Those That Affect Meaning and Clarity."

Section 28.1.2, "Basic Commas: Those That Educated Readers Expect," includes all the commonly known comma rules. Using these rules incorrectly probably will not affect meaning, but it may distract the reader and even cause him or her to wonder about the writer's professionalism.

There are other comma rules, though, that the average reader will not know, and he or she will not notice whether they are applied correctly. Still, these rules are helpful to writers who not only care about writing correctly but also recognize that knowing the more esoteric comma rules allows them to add to their repertoire those sentence structures that require using these rules.

Finally, the last group of comma rules includes those situations in which commas are inserted unnecessarily. Please notice, too, that some of the last rules are marked with an asterisk (*). The asterisk indicates those few comma rules about which some authorities disagree. See Chart 28.1.

Chart 28.1   Overview of the Comma Rules

OVERVIEW OF THE COMMA RULES

CRITICAL COMMAS: Those That Affect Meaning and Clarity

Rule 1: **Use a comma before a coordinating conjunction joining two main clauses.**

The prosecutor spoke about the defendant's motive, and the jury listened carefully.

Rule 2: **Use a comma to set off long introductory phrases or clauses from the main clause.**

Using their overhead lights and sirens, the police followed the defendant out of the area.

Rule 3: **Use a comma to prevent a possible misreading.**

At the time, the prosecution informed Jones that it would recommend a sentence of eighteen months.

Rule 4: **Use a comma to set off nonrestrictive phrases or clauses.**

Officer Bates, acting as a decoy, remained outside on the sidewalk.

BASIC COMMAS: Those That Educated Readers Expect

Rule 5: **Set off nonrestrictive appositives with commas.**

A corrections officer called Diane Cummins, the defendant's girlfriend.

Rule 6: **Set off nonrestrictive participial phrases with a comma or commas.**

The trial court denied the motion, finding that the seizure fell under the plain view doctrine.

Rule 7: **Use a comma or commas to set off transitional or interrupting words and phrases.**

The trial court, however, imposed an exceptional sentence of thirty months.

Chart 28.1   Overview of the Comma Rules *(cont'd)*

Rule 8:   Use commas according to convention with quotation marks.

Corbin said, "I never saw the other car."

Rule 9:   Use a comma or commas to set off phrases of contrast.

Adams initially indicated that he, not Wilson, was involved in the robbery.

Rule 10:   Use commas between items in a series.

Wong had no money, identification, or jewelry.

Rule 11:   Use a comma between coordinate adjectives not joined by a conjunction.

The contract was written in concise, precise language.

Rule 12:   Use commas according to convention with dates, addresses, and names of geographical locations.

The land in Roswell, New Mexico, was surveyed on October 4, 1991, and purchased less than a month later.

ESOTERIC COMMAS: Those That Are Required in Sophisticated Sentence Structures

Rule 13:   Use commas to set off absolutes.

His career destroyed, Williams lapsed into a state of depression.

Rule 14:   Use a comma to indicate an omission of a word or words that can be understood from the context.

The first witness said the attacker was "hairy"; the second, bald.

Rule 15:   Use commas to set off expressions that introduce examples or explanations.

Collins testified that Adams had participated in the robbery and had fenced some of the items, namely, a camera, stereo, and silver.

UNNECESSARY COMMAS: Those That Should Be Omitted

Rule 16:   Do not use a comma to set off restrictive adverbial clauses that follow the main clause.

Complicity may be found if a defendant participates in the early stages of an activity that results in the attack on the victim.

Chart 28.1   Overview of the Comma Rules *(cont'd)*

Rule 17:   Do not use a comma to separate a subject from its verb or a verb from its object.

The idea that an individual can obtain another person's property through adverse possession is difficult for many people to accept.

Rule 18:   Do not use a comma to separate correlative pairs unless the correlatives introduce main clauses.

Neither the United States Supreme Court nor this court has ever ruled that a defendant has a due process right to an instruction on lesser included offenses.

*Rule 19:   Do not use a comma between a conjunction and introductory modifiers or clauses.

The fire had completely destroyed the trailer, and according to the fire chief, there was some concern that the overhead structure of the barn would collapse.

*Rule 20:   Do not use a comma between "that" and introductory modifiers or clauses.

He testified that when they returned to his hotel room, Wells demanded a $150 fee

*Some authorities disagree on these comma rules.

§ 28.1.1 Critical Commas: Those That Affect Meaning and Clarity

Commas are like the signs along the highway. They signal, usually subtly, how the sentence structure will unfold. The correct use of commas, like the correct use of highway signs, prepares the reader for what's to come, whether it be another main clause, an explanatory appositive, or a shift from an introductory element to the main clause. Seasoned readers absorb the information they get from commas in much the same way seasoned drivers absorb the information they get from highway signs. Sometimes it grabs their attention; more often than not, it works almost subconsciously. The comma rules that follow are the ones that affect meaning and clarity. If they are used incorrectly, they will miscue the reader in much the same way that an incorrect highway sign would miscue a driver.

Use a comma before a coordinating conjunction joining two main, or independent, clauses

Reminder

There are seven coordinating conjunctions: "and," "but," "or," "for," "nor," "yet," and "so."[1]

Reminder

A main, or independent, clause has its own subject and verb, and it can stand alone as a sentence.

$$\underline{\qquad\qquad\qquad\qquad}_{,}\overset{\substack{\text{coordinating}\\\text{conjunction}}}{\underline{\qquad\qquad\qquad\qquad\qquad\qquad}}.$$

         [*main clause*]   [*main clause*]

Brackets mark the main clauses in the following examples.

Before Conjunctions Joining Main Clauses

[The prosecutor spoke about the defendant's motive], and [the jury listened carefully.]

[The corrections officer contacted several other persons], but [none knew of Wilson's disappearance.]

When applying Rule 1, be sure that you are not mistakenly assuming that a comma must precede every coordinating conjunction. It precedes those coordinating conjunctions that join two main clauses.

In the next example, "but" is preceded by a comma because it joins two main clauses. "And," on the other hand, joins two noun phrases ("the motion to sever" and "the motion for a new trial"), not two main clauses, so it is not preceded by a comma.

[The trial court did not err in denying the motion to sever and the motion for a new trial], but [it did err in giving the accomplice liability instruction.]

In addition, be sure to distinguish between sentences with two main clauses (subject-verb, and subject-verb), which require a comma before the conjunction, and sentences with compound verbs (subject-verb and verb), which should not have a comma before the conjunction.

---

1. Some writers prefer to use a semicolon before "yet" and "so." The semicolon signals a longer pause.

Two Main Clauses

The defendant's girlfriend denied that she knew where he was, and she refused to answer any more questions.

Compound Verbs

The defendant's girlfriend denied that she knew where he was and refused to answer any more questions.

Writers who omit the comma before a coordinating conjunction joining two main clauses miscue their readers. No comma before a coordinating conjunction signals the second half of a pair of structures other than main clauses. This error is often labeled a fused sentence or run-on sentence. When the main clauses are short and closely related, however, the comma before the coordinating conjunction may be omitted.

Short Main Clauses

The prosecutor spoke and the jury listened.

Exception to Rule 1

When the main clauses are long or when they have internal punctuation, use a semicolon before the coordinating conjunction.

Long Main Clauses with Internal Punctuation

After analyzing the defendant's claim under ER 401, the court rejected it, explaining that the evidence at issue was relevant to the question of falsity; and because falsity was an element to be proved by the plaintiff, the evidence met the ER 401 requirements of probative value and materiality.

See Exercise 28A in the *Practice Book*.

Use a comma to set off long introductory clauses or phrases from the main, or independent, clause

If a main, or independent, clause is preceded by introductory material, the reader will need a comma to signal where the introductory material ends and where the main clause begins.

_____,_____.

[*long introductory*   [*main clause*]
clause or phrase]

Long introductory clauses that must be set off with a comma are easy to spot. Because they are clauses, they will have a subject and a verb. Because they are subordinate, not main, clauses, they will also begin with a subordinating conjunction such as "after," "although," "as," "because," "before," "if," "unless," "until," "when," or "where." See section 27.1 for more on subordinate clauses and subordinating conjunctions.

Long Introductory Clauses   EXAMPLES

If the accident were unavoidable, Smith's intoxication was not "a cause . . . without which the death would not have occurred."

When Abbott failed to return to the work release facility, a corrections officer called his mother's home.

Of the many kinds of introductory phrases used in legal writing, the most common are prepositional phrases, infinitive phrases, and participial phrases. (Section 27.1 defines and explains prepositions, infinitives, and participles. It is not critical, however, to be able to identify the types of introductory phrases to punctuate them correctly.)

Introductory Prepositional Phrase   EXAMPLE

In the present case, the record shows that Thompson initially assaulted Blevins.

Introductory Infinitive Phrase   EXAMPLE

To support an argument that the trial court abused its discretion, a defendant must point to specific prejudice.

Introductory Participial Phrase   EXAMPLE

Using their overhead lights and sirens, the police followed the defendant out of the area.

Notice that long introductory phrases are often made up of several prepositional phrases or a combination of prepositional, infinitive, and participial phrases.

Two Introductory Prepositional Phrases   EXAMPLE

[On the evening] [of August 13, 2006], Larry Utter was robbed at gunpoint while making a deposit at a local bank.

Introductory Prepositional and Infinitive Phrases   EXAMPLE

[At the hearing] [on McDonald's motion] [to dismiss], the parties stipulated to the admission of an incident report prepared by McDonald's probation officer.

Furthermore, there is no specific rule for what constitutes a "long" phrase or clause. An introductory phrase or clause of four or more words is usually set off with a comma, but writers have some discretion, particularly with introductory phrases.

Short prepositional phrases, for example, are often set off by a comma, especially when the writer wants to emphasize the information in the phrase, such as dates or case names.

EXAMPLES   ## Short Introductory Phrases

In 1997, the Oltmans removed the fence separating their property from the farm.

In Harris, the defendant was charged with first degree robbery.

Short, introductory transitional expressions, such as "consequently," "for example," "however," "nevertheless," "therefore," and "on the other hand," are almost always set off by a comma.

EXAMPLE   ## Introductory Transitions

Consequently, unlawful restraint is invariably an element of the greater offense of attempted kidnapping.

See Exercise **28B** in the *Practice Book*.

RULE 3   ### Use a comma to prevent a possible misreading

A reader should be able to understand your sentences correctly on the first reading. If a comma can prevent a possible misreading, it should be included.

EXAMPLES   ## Confusing

People who can usually hire their own lawyer.

Revised

People who can, usually hire their own lawyer.

Although under Rule 2 you have the discretion to omit a comma after short introductory material, you must use the comma if a reader might at first mistakenly assume that part of the main clause is part of the introductory material.

Confusing

At the time the prosecution informed Singh that it would recommend a sentence of eighteen months.

Revised

At the time, the prosecution informed Singh that it would recommend a sentence of eighteen months.

See Exercise 28C in the *Practice Book*.

Use a comma to set off nonrestrictive phrases or clauses

Nonrestrictive phrases or clauses do not restrict or limit the words they modify. They give additional information.

Restrictive phrases or clauses restrict or limit the words they modify. They add essential information.

Nonrestrictive Phrase

Officer Bates, <u>acting as a decoy</u>, remained outside on the sidewalk.

Nonrestrictive Clause

Officer Bates, <u>who acted as a decoy</u>, remained outside on the sidewalk.

In both of the examples above, "Officer Bates" is completely identified by her name. "Acting as a decoy" or "who acted as a decoy" does not give restricting or limiting information, so both are set off by commas.

If the name of the officer were unknown, the writer may need to use the phrase or clause as a way to identify the officer. The phrase or clause would then be restrictive because it would limit the meaning of "officer." When used as a restrictive phrase or clause, the same words are not set off by commas.

Restrictive Phrase

An officer acting as a decoy remained outside on the sidewalk.

Restrictive Clause

An officer who acted as a decoy remained outside on the sidewalk.

A few more examples may be helpful in learning to distinguish which phrases and clauses are nonrestrictive and therefore set off by commas.

Nonrestrictive Clause

The child's father, who is six months behind in his child support payments, has fled the state.

"The child's father" clearly identifies the individual in question; "who is six months behind in his child support payments" does not restrict or limit the meaning of "the child's father," even though it is important information for understanding the sentence.

Restrictive Clause

The uncle who lives in Oklahoma has agreed to care for the child until an appropriate foster home is found.

This sentence suggests that the child has more than one uncle. "Who lives in Oklahoma" restricts or limits the meaning of "the uncle." It is the uncle in Oklahoma, not the one in Arkansas, who has agreed to care for the child.

Notice that whether a phrase or clause is punctuated as restrictive or nonrestrictive can significantly change the meaning of a sentence.

Without Commas

Attorneys who intentionally prolong litigation for personal gain misuse the legal system.

The preceding sentence says that there is a restricted or limited group of attorneys — those who intentionally prolong litigation for personal gain — who misuse the legal system.

With Commas

Attorneys, who intentionally prolong litigation for personal gain, misuse the legal system.

The preceding sentence does not refer to a restricted or limited group of attorneys. It says that all attorneys misuse the legal system and that all attorneys intentionally prolong litigation for personal gain.

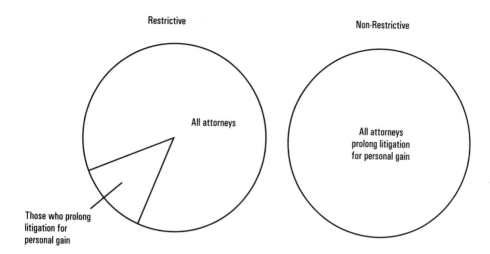

Restrictive and nonrestrictive clauses that modify people begin with "who" or "whom." See the Glossary of Usage for more on "who" and "whom." Careful writers still observe the usage rule that restrictive clauses that modify things or objects use "that" and nonrestrictive clauses that modify things or objects use "which." See the Glossary of Usage for more on the distinction between "that" and "which."

Incorrect Usage

EXAMPLE

The instruction which is unchallenged is an accomplice instruction that includes the "ready to assist" language.

Revised

EXAMPLE

The instruction that is unchallenged is an accomplice instruction that includes the "ready to assist" language. *OR*
Instruction 21, which is unchallenged, is an accomplice instruction that includes the "ready to assist" language.

The following chart sums up the key points in Rule 4.

Restrictive	restricts the word it modifies	no commas	who/whom that
Nonrestrictive	does not restrict the word it modifies	commas	who/whom which

See Exercises **28D** and **28E** in the *Practice Book*.

§28.1.2 Basic Commas: Those That Educated Readers Expect

RULE 5	**Set off nonrestrictive appositives with commas**

Reminder

Appositives are nouns or noun substitutes that follow another noun to identify it or further describe it.

EXAMPLE	**Comma with Appositive**

A corrections officer called <u>Diane Cummins</u>, <u>the defendant's girlfriend.</u>
                  (noun)   *(appositive)*

Because most appositives are nonrestrictive, they need to be set off with commas. However, restrictive appositives, like the restrictive phrases and clauses in Rule 4, add information that restricts or limits the preceding noun; therefore, restrictive appositives are not set off with commas.

EXAMPLE	**Nonrestrictive Appositive**

The court sentenced the defendant, a juvenile, to a term outside the standard range.

There is only one defendant; "a juvenile" adds information, but it does not restrict or limit the meaning of "defendant."

EXAMPLE	**Restrictive Appositive**

The defendant's brother Joseph contradicted the story another brother Daniel told to the police.

The defendant has more than one brother, so the noun phrases "defendant's brother" and "another brother" must be restricted or limited by the brothers' names.

Some appositives are introduced by the word "or." Be sure to distinguish between the appositional "or," which is a restatement of or explanation for the preceding noun, and the disjunctive "or," which introduces an alternative to the preceding noun.

EXAMPLE	**Appositional "or":**

You may designate an attorney-in-fact, or agent, to make your health care decisions in the event you are unable to do so. ("Attorney-in-fact" and "agent" are the same thing.)

Disjunctive "or":

EXAMPLE

The girl's father or uncle always accompanied her on dates. ("Father" and "uncle" are alternatives.)

Set off nonrestrictive participial phrases with a comma or commas

RULE 6

Reminder

Participles, which are formed from verbs, can serve as adjectives. Present participles have an "-ing" ending; past participles have a variety of endings, depending on whether the verb is regular or irregular. Common past participle endings include "-d," "-ed," "-t," "-n," and "-en."

verb	present participle	past participle
reason	reasoning	reasoned
find	finding	found

Many sentences in legal writing use a beginning or an ending participial phrase to describe the rationale for the action expressed in the main verb. Such participial phrases are not dangling or misplaced (see section 27.6.2) if, as in the following examples, they modify the subject of the sentence.

Nonrestrictive Participial Phrases

EXAMPLES

Reasoning that the sentence imposed was disproportionate to the gravity of the offense, the State Supreme Court reversed and remanded for resentencing.

The State Supreme Court reversed and remanded for resentencing, reasoning that the sentence imposed was disproportionate to the gravity of the offense.

Finding that the seizure fell under the plain view doctrine, the trial court denied the motion.

The trial court denied the motion, finding that the seizure fell under the plain view doctrine.

Restrictive participial phrases should not be set off with commas. In the following example, "washing his hands" restricts or limits the meaning of "the man."

See Exercise 28 F in the *Practice Book*.

Restrictive Participial Phrase

EXAMPLE

The attendant noticed blood on the shirt of the man washing his hands.

RULE 7	**Use a comma or commas to set off transitional or interrupting words and phrases**

Legal writers frequently break the flow of a sentence intentionally by inserting a word or phrase in the middle of a main clause. Readers have no trouble understanding what the main clause is and what the transitional or interrupting word or phrase is as long as those transitions or interrupters are set off with commas.

$$\underline{\hspace{3cm}}, \text{interrupter}, \underline{\hspace{3cm}}.$$

(main)   *(clause)*

EXAMPLES	**Commas With Interrupters**

The trial court, however, imposed an exceptional sentence of thirty months.

The Court of Appeals held that Wells, through her own fault and connivance, caused the delay between the time the State filed the information and the time of Wells's arraignment.

Note, however, that many of the same transitional words and phrases (for example, "however," "therefore," "on the other hand," "for example") that interrupt a main clause can also be used between two main clauses. Be sure to distinguish between the two and punctuate accordingly.

EXAMPLES	**Interrupter**

His vision, therefore, was blurred.

EXAMPLE	**Transition Between Two Main Clauses**

The driver lost his contact lenses; therefore, his vision was blurred.

RULE 8	**Use commas according to convention with quotation marks**

Commas are frequently used to separate short or informal quotations from words in the same sentence that introduce, interrupt, or follow the quotation.

EXAMPLES	**Commas With Quotation Marks**

Corbin said, "I never saw the other car."

"I never saw the other car," Corbin said, "until it was right on top of me."

"I never saw the other car," said Corbin.

Commas are placed inside closing quotation marks[2] but outside closing parentheses or brackets.

Inside Closing Quotation Marks   `EXAMPLE`

A twenty four-month sentence does not appear to be "clearly excessive," especially when the presumptive range of twelve-fourteen months could have been increased by twelve months under Wash Rev. Code § 9.94A 310 (2006)

Outside Closing Parentheses   `EXAMPLE`

Both of the defendants are young (19 and 20), and both of them are first-time offenders.

Quotations that are immediately preceded by "that" do not have a comma between the quotation and "that."

Quotation Preceded by "That"   `EXAMPLE`

In *Herron v. King*, the court stated that "actual malice can be inferred from circumstantial evidence including . . . the reporter's knowledge that his sources are hostile to the plaintiff. . . ." *Id.* at 524.

See Exercise 28G in the *Practice Book*.

Use a comma or commas to set off phrases of contrast   `RULE 9`

Phrases of contrast usually begin with "not," "but," or "yet."

Commas for Contrast   `EXAMPLES`

Adams initially indicated that he, not Wilson, was involved in the robbery.

The court of appeals affirmed the trial court, but on different grounds.

Some writers occasionally omit commas with phrases of contrast that begin with "but." These writers would omit the comma before the "but" in the preceding example. Either way is correct. In addition, commas are usually omitted between elements joined by the paired conjunctions "not only . . . but also. . . ." See Comma Rule 18.

No Comma with Paired Conjunctions   `EXAMPLE`

The trial court not only overruled defense counsel's repeated objections but also accused the defendant's attorney of intentionally delaying the proceedings.

---

2. In Great Britain a comma is placed inside closing quotation marks only if it is part of the quotation.

RULE 10	**Use commas between items in a series**

Reminder

A series is three or more items that are grouped together and that are in the same grammatical form. Each item may be as short as one word or as long as a clause.

EXAMPLE	**Series of Single Words**

Wong had no money, identification, or jewelry.

EXAMPLE	**Series of Verb Phrases**

Mason moved at least twice during the period of his escape, changed his name and his appearance, and held four or five jobs.

EXAMPLE	**Series of Clauses**

MacNeill could not remember who he was, where he lived, what he did for a living, or what he had done during the last two weeks.

Even a series composed of short main clauses may use commas to separate the items.

EXAMPLE	**Series of Main Clauses**

Matthews pulled a knife on O'Hara, she screamed, and he turned and ran away.

Although the comma before the final "and" in a series is sometimes described as "optional," legal writers should make a habit of including it because some sentences become ambiguous when that comma is omitted.

EXAMPLE	**Ambiguous Without Serial Comma**

Mrs. Corsini wants her property divided equally among the following relatives: Michael Corsini, Glenda Corsini, Ralph Meyers, Joanna Mitchem, Louis Mitchem, Donna Mitchem and Donald Mitchem.

Should the property be divided six or seven ways? Assume Donna Mitchem and Donald Mitchem are married. Did Grandmother Corsini intend for the couple to get one-sixth of her property, or did she intend for each of them to receive one-seventh?

Adding a comma before the final "and" tells the reader that the property should be divided seven ways. Adding another "and" before "Donna Mitchem" says that it should be divided six ways and that Donna and Donald should, as a couple, receive a one-sixth share.

Ordinarily, commas are not used to separate pairs of words, phrases, or clauses that are joined by coordinating conjunctions.

Pair of Words   EXAMPLE

Lundquist was <u>arrested</u> and <u>charged</u> with negligent homicide.

Pair of Phrases   EXAMPLE

The Supreme Court is remarkably free <u>to emphasize certain issues of the case over others</u> or <u>to stress completely new issues</u>.

Pair of Clauses   EXAMPLE

The trial court asked the defendant <u>whether he understood his right to a jury trial</u> and <u>whether he received any promises of better treatment if he waived that right</u>.

Commas are not used between items in a series when all the items are joined by coordinating conjunctions. As a stylistic technique, joining all the items in a series with conjunctions has the effect of slowing down the series, which may be desirable on rare occasions when the writer wants the reader to focus special attention on each of the individual items in the series. See Exercise 28.H in the *Practice Book*.

All Items Joined by Conjunctions   EXAMPLE

There is no indication that the delay was negligent or deliberate or unusual.

Use a comma between coordinate adjectives not joined by a conjunction   RULE 11

Coordinate adjectives are two or more adjectives that independently modify the same noun.

concise,   precise   language
(*adjective*)   (*adjective*)   (*noun*)

The test for whether adjectives are coordinate is simple: (1) reverse the order of the adjectives; or (2) add an "and" between the adjectives. If the adjectives are modifying the noun independently, then changing their order or adding an "and" will not change the meaning.

1. precise, concise language
2. concise, precise language
3. precise and concise language

The following example does not contain coordinate adjectives. Instead, "black" modifies "leather" and "leather" modifies "briefcase." Notice that you can tell that the adjectives are not coordinate by applying either part of the test. Both create awkward constructions.

Not Coordinate Adjectives

black leather briefcase

Reverse Order

leather, black briefcase

Add "and"

black and leather briefcase

Use commas according to convention with dates, addresses, and names of geographical locations

When a full date is written out in the month-day-year order, use a comma after the day so that a reader can easily see the correct groupings of the digits.

July 4, 1776

Dates in this order also require a comma (or other punctuation) after the year when the sentence continues after the date.

Comma After Year

The land was surveyed on October 4, 1996, and purchased less than a month later.

If the day is omitted or if the full date has the month and date reversed, omit commas because there are no adjacent groupings of digits.

July 1776   4 July 1776

No Comma When Month/Date Reversed

Martin and Hughes were arrested on 21 December 1998 and charged with first-degree assault.

Use commas to set off individual elements in addresses and geographical names. Note that the state and zip code are considered one element and therefore are not separated by a comma. When addresses or geographical names are followed by the remainder of a sentence, they should be followed by a comma.

Chicago, Illinois   Ontario, Canada

Commas with Address/Geographical Names

Send the bill to Mr. and Mrs. Arthur Meiering, 3000 La Jolla Lane, Roswell, New Mexico 88201, before Tuesday.

The string of robberies began in San Diego, California, and ended in Oakland, California, after the police arrested the defendant.

When possible, rephrase a date or geographical name used as a modifier when the date or geographical name will have to be followed by a comma.

Awkward

the June 21, 2005, meeting

Revised

the meeting on June 21, 2005

Awkward

the Atlanta, Georgia, public health official

Revised

the public health official from Atlanta, Georgia

See Exercise 28I in the *Practice Book.*

§ 28.1.3 Esoteric Commas: Those That Are Required in Sophisticated Sentence Structures

Use commas to set off absolutes

Reminder

Absolutes are made up of either a noun or pronoun followed by a participle. They modify an entire sentence or main clause and can appear at the beginning, at the end, or within a sentence.

his <u>career</u> <u>destroyed</u> *(noun) (participle)*	their <u>lights</u> <u>flashing</u> *(noun) (participle)*
his <u>gun</u> <u>drawn and loaded</u> *(noun) (participles)*	the <u>last</u> <u>being</u> a year ago *(noun)(participle)*

EXAMPLES   ## Commas With Absolutes

His career destroyed, Williams lapsed into a state of depression.

The police followed the defendant for less than one mile, their lights flashing.

The defendant reentered the tavern, his gun drawn and loaded, and proceeded to order the tavern's patrons to line up against the wall.

She testified that on four or five occasions, the last being a year ago, he demanded that she rewrite her will.

RULE 14   **Use a comma to indicate an omission of a word or words that can be understood from the context**

EXAMPLES   ## Comma to Show Omission

The first witness said the attacker was "hairy"; the second, bald.

In Texas there are five elements to the crime; in Delaware, four.

RULE 15   **Use commas to set off expressions that introduce examples or explanations**

"For example," "for instance," "that is," "namely," "i.e.," "e.g.," and "viz." are usually followed by a comma. A comma can also be used before these expressions if the break in the flow of the sentence is slight. Dashes or semi-colons are used before these expressions if the break is substantial.

EXAMPLES   ## Punctuation With Examples

Collins testified that Adams had participated in the robbery and had fenced some of the items, namely, a camera, stereo, and silver.

The State must prove that the defendant acted by color or aid of deception — that is, that he operated to bring about the acquisition of the property or services by either creating or confirming another's false impression, which he knew to be false, or by failing to correct another's impression, which he had previously created.

Crestwood Elementary accepted all standard forms of identification, *e.g.*, birth certificate, driver's license, or military identification.

Some authorities suggest that writers avoid the abbreviations "*i.e.*," "*e.g.*," and "*viz.*" in the text of their writing and use their English equivalents instead ("that is," "for example," and "namely" respectively). The rationale for this suggestion is that many readers misunderstand the abbreviations. If you decide to use the abbreviations, remember to italicize or underline them.

See Exercise 28 J in the *Practice Book*.

§ 28.1.4 Unnecessary Commas: Those That Should Be Omitted

Do not use a comma to set off restrictive adverbial clauses that follow the main clause	RULE 16

Reminder

Adverbial clauses have their own subject and verb, and they are introduced by an adverb such as "although," "because," "before," "when," and "while."

A restrictive adverbial clause restricts or limits the action of the verb to a time, manner, or circumstance. Nonrestrictive adverbial clauses give additional information.

Clauses introduced by the adverb "if" are always restrictive, so they are not set off by commas.

### No Comma with "If" Clause	EXAMPLE

Complicity may be found if a defendant participates in the early stages of an activity that results in the attack on the victim.

Clauses introduced by the adverbs "because" and "unless" are usually restrictive, although they can be nonrestrictive.

### No Comma with "Because"/"Unless" Clauses	EXAMPLES

Summary judgment was granted because the plaintiff failed to establish the *prima facie* elements.

Special damages may not be presumed without proof unless actual malice is proved.

When clauses beginning with "after," "as," "before," "since," "when," and "while" restrict the time of the main verb, they should not be set off with commas.

### Restrict Time of Verb	EXAMPLES

The tractor trailer entered the parking lot as the game was ending and the crowd was beginning to leave the stadium.

Morton was drinking beer while he was driving the boat.

When adverbial clauses beginning with "as," "since," or "while" do not restrict the time of the verb but rather express cause or condition, they are nonrestrictive and should be set off by commas.

EXAMPLES   ## Express Cause or Condition

Southworth returned to the scene of the assault, as he feared that he had lost his neck chain in the scuffle.

Clauses introduced by the adverbs "although" and "though" are always nonrestrictive, so they must be set off with commas.

EXAMPLES   ## Commas with "Although" and "Though"

Del Barker admits that he received his 2005 tax statement, although he claims that the only notice he received of the filing requirements was from general news articles in the newspaper.

Each physician received compensation and paid expenses in direct proportion to his or her production of the gross income of the partnership, even though the partnership was an equal partnership.

See Exercise 28K in the *Practice Book*.

RULE 17   ## Do not use a comma to separate a subject from its verb or a verb from its object

Legal writers are often inclined to write long subjects. When they do, it is tempting to insert a comma after the subject and before the verb because the reader will need a pause. The comma is the wrong solution; instead, the writer should revise the sentence.

In the following example, the subject is enclosed in brackets.

EXAMPLE   ## Incorrect

[The idea that an individual can obtain another person's property through adverse possession], is difficult for many people to accept.

EXAMPLE   ## Revised

Many people find it difficult to accept the idea that an individual can obtain another person's property through adverse possession.

In the following example, the verb "received" is incorrectly separated from its object, "the note," by a comma.

Incorrect

EXAMPLE

Bloomquist had received from a fellow employee at Landover Mills, a note describing where the "crack house" was located.

Revised

EXAMPLE

A fellow employee at Landover Mills sent Bloomquist a note describing where the "crack house" was located.

Exception

EXAMPLE

Nonrestrictive modifiers and interrupters that separate a subject from its verb should be preceded and followed by commas, even though the commas separate the subject from its verb. See Rules 4, 5, and 7 in this section.

Do not use a comma to separate correlative pairs unless the correlatives introduce main clauses

RULE 18

Reminder

Correlative pairs include "either . . . or," "neither . . . nor," "both . . . and," and "not only . . . but also."

Incorrect

EXAMPLE

Neither the United States Supreme Court, nor this court has ever ruled that a defendant has a due process right to an instruction on lesser included offenses.

Revised

EXAMPLE

Neither the United States Supreme Court nor this court has ever ruled that a defendant has a due process right to an instruction on lesser included offenses.

Main Clauses

EXAMPLE

Either the manager will have to describe the damage done to the apartment, or he will have to return the deposit.

The correlative pair "not only . . . but also" connects two elements, so a separating comma is inappropriate. Some authorities, however, do recommend a comma to separate the "not . . . but" pair because it is used to contrast elements.

RULE 19	**Do not use a comma between a conjunction and introductory modifiers or clauses**

When a coordinating conjunction joins two main clauses, the second main clause frequently begins with introductory modifiers or its own subordinate clause. Although some writers add a comma after the conjunction and before the introductory modifier or clause, this extra comma is needless; it merely slows the sentence down.

_____,and _____.
  [*main clause*]   [*introductory modifiers/clause*]   [*main clause*]

EXAMPLE	**Incorrect**

The fire had completely destroyed the trailer, and, according to the fire chief, there was some concern that the overhead structure of the barn would collapse.

EXAMPLE	**Revised**

The fire had completely destroyed the trailer, and according to the fire chief, there was some concern that the overhead structure of the barn would collapse.

EXAMPLE	**Incorrect**

The woman demanded that Thomas hand over his wallet, but, when Thomas replied that he did not have his wallet, the woman shot him in the chest.

EXAMPLE	**Revised**

The woman demanded that Thomas hand over his wallet, but when Thomas replied that he did not have his wallet, the woman shot him in the chest.

RULE 20	**Do not use a comma between "that" and introductory modifiers or clauses**

EXAMPLE	**Incorrect**

He testified that, when they returned to his hotel room, Wells demanded a $150 fee.

EXAMPLE	**Revised**

He testified that when they returned to his hotel room, Wells demanded a $150 fee.

See Exercises 28L, 28M, and 28N in the *Practice Book*.

§28.2 The Semicolon

The semicolon is one of the easiest punctuation marks to learn how to use. Unfortunately, some legal writers avoid using semicolons because they believe semicolons are quite complicated and will require learning numerous rules. Exactly the opposite is true. There are only two general rules for using semicolons; all other uses are variations or exceptions to these two rules.

_____ main clause   ;   main clause.   _____ .

Use a semicolon to separate main, or independent, clauses not joined by a coordinating conjunction   RULE 1

Reminder

Main clauses contain a subject and verb. They can stand alone as a sentence. There are only seven coordinating conjunctions: "and," "but," "or," "for," "nor," "yet," and "so."

Correct Use of Semicolon   EXAMPLES

Officer Thompson administered the breathalyzer test; the results showed that the defendant's blood alcohol level was over the maximum allowed by the state.

The plaintiff is a Nevada resident; the defendant is a California resident.

If you use a comma or no punctuation between main clauses, you will produce a comma splice or run-on sentence. See section 28.6.

Main clauses joined by a semicolon should be closely related in meaning. Often the semicolon suggests that the ideas in the connected main clauses work together as a larger idea. (See the first example above.) The semicolon can also be used to balance one idea against another. (See the second example above.) In all cases, the semicolon signals to the reader to pause slightly longer than for a comma but shorter than for a period. This length of pause helps the reader to see the ideas in the main clauses as more closely related to each other than the ideas would be in two separate sentences.

Variation on Rule 1

To show the relationship between the main clauses, a conjunctive adverb frequently follows the semicolon separating main clauses. The conjunctive adverb is usually followed by a comma. The most commonly used conjunctive adverbs are "accordingly," "also," "besides," "consequently," "furthermore," "hence," "however," "indeed," "instead," "likewise," "meanwhile," "moreover," "nevertheless," "still," "then," "therefore," and "thus." See section 26.1.

_____ main clause   ; *therefore,*   main clause _____ .
               [*conjunctive*
                 adverb]

Conjunctive Adverbs

The summons was not delivered to his usual place of abode; therefore, service was not effected in the manner prescribed by law.

The elements of the test have not been completely defined; however, the court has clarified the policies underlying the rule.

Conjunctive adverbs may also occur in the middle of main clauses. In such cases, they are usually preceded and followed by a comma.

main, *therefore*, clause
_____.

In the Middle of a Main Clause

The motor was not running, however, because of a problem with the distributor cap.

Compare the preceding example with the following example.

Between Two Main Clauses

The motor was not running because of a problem with the distributor cap; however, the inoperability of the vehicle was irrelevant.

See Exercises 28O and 28P in the *Practice Book*.

Use semicolons to separate items in a series if the items are long or if one or more of the items has internal commas

Reminder

A series is three or more items of equal importance. If the items in a series are relatively short or if they do not have internal commas, then the items can be separated by commas.

item 1, item 2, and item 3
_____
typical series with items
separated by commas

item 1 ; item 2 ; and item 3
_____
long items separated by semicolons

item 1 ; , item 2 , ; and item 3
_____
internal commas in one or more
items separated by semicolons

Long Items

The Montana court has applied these definitions to cases with the following fact patterns: the driver was asleep and intoxicated; the driver was positioned behind the steering wheel; the vehicle's motor was running; and the vehicle was parked.

Long Items   EXAMPLE

The court must determine the following issues to resolve your claim:

1. whether your ex-landlord sent you a written statement within thirty days of termination;
2. whether your ex-landlord withheld your deposit in bad faith; and
3. whether the court wishes to include attorneys' fees as part of a possible damage award.

Internal Commas   EXAMPLE

The prosecutor called the following witnesses: Linda Hastings, an advertising executive; Samuel Hedges, an accountant; and Timothy Lessor, president of the company.

Internal Commas   EXAMPLE

The defendant claims to reside in Maryland, even though (1) his car is registered in California; (2) he is registered to vote in California; and (3) all of his financial assets, including stocks, bonds, and a savings and checking account, are in a California bank.

See Exercise 28Q in the *Practice Book*.

§ 28.2.1 Use of the Semicolon with "Yet" or "So"

Some writers prefer to use a semicolon rather than a comma before the coordinating conjunctions "yet" and "so" when they join two main clauses. Either the comma or the semicolon is correct in the following examples, but note that the longer pause suggested by the semicolon adds a bit more emphasis to the conjunction and to the words that immediately follow the semicolon.

Comma or Semicolon with "So"   EXAMPLES

Our client was legally intoxicated at the time of the arrest, so being asleep or unconscious is not a defense.

Our client was legally intoxicated at the time of the arrest; so being asleep or unconscious is not a defense.

---

§ 28.2.2 Use of the Semicolon with Coordinating Conjunctions

Usually main clauses joined by a coordinating conjunction require only a comma before the conjunction. See section 28.1, Rule 1. However, when the main clauses are long and grammatically complicated or when they have internal commas, it is helpful for the reader if a semicolon rather than a comma precedes the coordinating conjunction. The semicolon makes it easier to spot the break between the main clauses.

> _____ ;but , , ____.
>
> *main clause*   *main clause*

EXAMPLE   **Semicolon with Coordinating Conjunction**

Your landlord can withhold a reasonable amount to cover the cost of repairing the window; but if he failed to send you a check for the remainder of the deposit, or if he failed to state why he withheld the deposit, or if he failed to do both within thirty days of termination of the lease, then he forfeited his right to withhold any part of the deposit.

---

§ 28.2.3 Use of the Semicolon with Citations

Because citations are either sentences or clauses, they should be treated as main clauses. Consequently, multiple citations are separated with semicolons.

See Exercises **28R** and **28S** in the *Practice Book*.

EXAMPLE   **Semicolons Between Citations**

Connecticut courts have consistently held that a party waives its constitutional claims if it does not raise those claims in the trial court and it affirmatively acquiesces in the trial court's order. *State v. Barley*, 839 A.2d 1281, 1284 (2004); *Falls Church Group, Ltd. v. Tyler, Cooper and Alcorn, LLP*, 874 A.2d 266, 271 (Conn. App. Ct. 2005); *State v. Tyson*, 862 A.2d 363, 366 (Conn. App. Ct. 2004).

---

§ 28.3 The Colon

Colons are useful to legal writers for a number of reasons. They are regularly used to introduce quotations or lists, and they are often the best way to set up explanations or elaborations.

EXAMPLES   **Quotation**

In support of this result, the court noted that the limitation on the use of the *corpus delicti* rule is based on the "suspect nature" of out-of-court confessions: "Corroboration of the confession is required as a safeguard against the conviction of the innocent persons through the use of a false confession of guilt." *Id.* at 419.

List:

There are three ways to measure a plaintiff's recovery for personal property damage: (1) if the destroyed personal property has a market value, the measure is that market value; (2) if the destroyed property has no market value but can be replaced, then the measure is the replacement cost; or (3) if the destroyed property has no market value and cannot be replaced, then the measure is the property's intrinsic value.

Explanation/Elaboration:

The periodic polygraph examinations are arguably connected logically to the ultimate goal of Nyles's rehabilitation: to deter him from molesting children.

The main function of a colon is to introduce what will follow. For this reason, a colon requires a lead-in main clause that is grammatically complete.

<u>grammatically complete lead-in main clause:</u> _____.

In the example that follows, "the subsections that do not apply are" is not grammatically complete; therefore, the colon is used incorrectly.

Incorrect　　　　　　　　　　　　　　　　　　　　　　EXAMPLE

The subsections that do not apply are: 201-1, 201-1(3)(b), and 201-1(3)(c).

One way to correct the example is to omit the colon.

Revised　　　　　　　　　　　　　　　　　　　　　　　EXAMPLE

The subsections that do not apply are 201-1, 201-1(3)(b), and 201-1(3)(c).

Another option is to add filler expressions, such as "the following" or "as follows," to make the lead-in main clause grammatically complete.

Revised　　　　　　　　　　　　　　　　　　　　　　　EXAMPLE

The subsections that do not apply are the following: 201-1, 201-1(3)(b), and 201-1(3)(c).

What follows the colon may or may not be a main clause. If what follows the colon is not a main clause, do not capitalize the first word after the colon; if more than one main clause follows the colon, capitalize the first word of the main clauses.

Phrase Follows Colon　　　　　　　　　　　　　　　　EXAMPLES

Mr. Baker has sustained personal property damage: broken picture windows and a smashed vase.

More Than One Main Clause Follows Colon

Mr. Baker has sustained personal property damage: His picture windows and vase were smashed. The shrubs outside the window were destroyed.

Quotations that are integrated into the writer's own sentences are not introduced by a colon.

Integrated Quotations

The first letter the Bakers received stated that "permits are issued subject to existing water rights."

The court in *HLP* presumed that Congress intended § 2339B to have a broad reach, regardless of a violator's intent, because "giving support intended to aid an organization's peaceful activities frees up resources that can be used for terrorist acts." *See id.*

Because colons set up the endings of sentences, they can be used effectively and stylistically to create emphasis. See section 24.6.4. Notice how the writers of the following sentences use colons to highlight a point.

Colons That Create Emphasis

Orlando's trial was originally scheduled for May 16, 2005: ninety-three days after his arraignment.

The legislature has already determined the standard range for Norris's offense: fourteen to eighteen months.

Gibson claimed that his intent was to do a lawful act: administer parental discipline.

Traditionally typists were taught to include two spaces after a colon. In recent practice, however, more and more writers and publishers are using only one space after a colon. A similar debate has developed over whether one or two spaces should follow a period ending a sentence. The 15th edition of *The Chicago Manual of Style* recommends one space after colons and after periods ending sentences.

See Exercise 28T in the *Practice Book.*

§ 28.4 The Apostrophe

Apostrophes determine possession — who owns what. If you and your clients care about who owns what and about whether ownership is clearly stated, then apostrophes are worth the few minutes it takes to learn how to use them correctly.

All the apostrophe rules are important, but take special note of Rules 5 and 6. Misusing these two rules can create either ambiguity or the appearance of incompetence.

Use " 's" to form the possessive of singular or plural nouns or indefinite pronouns not ending in "-s"

defendant's alibi	expert's testimony
family's income	children's guardian
a day's wages	a year's revenue
anybody's guess	everyone's concern

Use "'s" to form the possessive of singular nouns ending in "-s"[3] as long as the resulting word is not difficult to pronounce

> James's contract   Congress's authority
> business's license   witness's testimony

Three or more "s" sounds together are difficult to pronounce. When necessary, avoid three "s" sounds together by dropping the "s" after the apostrophe.

In the examples above, the double "s" ending in "business" or "witness" makes only one "s" sound, so when the "s" is added, as in "business's" and "witness's," only two "s" sounds are required. However, when these same words are followed by words that begin with "s," then the "s" after the apostrophe is dropped for ease in pronunciation.

> business' sales   witness' signature

For the same reason, many idioms that include the word "sake" drop the "s" after the apostrophe.

> for goodness' sake   for righteousness' sake
> for appearance' sake   for conscience' sake

Although almost all singular proper names follow the standard rule and form their possessive by adding "s," those few proper names with internal and ending "s" sounds also drop the "s" after the apostrophe for ease in pronunciation. Note that the "s" sound may be made by a "z" or an "x" as well as an "s."

> Velasquez' hearing   Alexis' prior conviction
> Kansas' case law

> **But** Arkansas's case law (because the final "s" in
> Arkansas is silent)

Use only an apostrophe to form the possessive of plural nouns ending in "-s"

> framers' intent   workers' rights
> four cities' plan   two agencies' concern
> ten dollars' worth   thirty days' notice

Plural proper nouns follow the same rule.

> the Smiths' attorney   the Thomases' dog

It is easier to form plural possessives correctly if you form the plural first and then apply the rules for possessives.

---

3. A few recognized authorities, including *The Associated Press Stylebook and Libel Manual*, recommend using only an apostrophe with singular proper names.

Singular	*Plural*	*Plural Possessive*
day $\longrightarrow$	days $\longrightarrow$	two days' labor
family $\longrightarrow$	families $\longrightarrow$	families' petition
Jones $\longrightarrow$	Joneses $\longrightarrow$	Joneses' pre-nuptial agreement

Occasionally a singular idea is expressed in words that are technically plural — for example, "United States," "General Motors," or "Olson Brothers." In such cases, apply the rule for forming plural possessives and add just an apostrophe.

United States' commitment   General Motors' lobbyists

RULE 4   **Use "'s" after the last word to form the possessive of a compound word or word group**

mother-in-law's statement   district manager's idea
attorney general's office   somebody else's problem
the Governor of Florida's
recommendation

RULE 5   **To show joint possession, use "'s" only after the last noun in a group of two or more nouns; to show individual possession, use "'s" after each of the nouns in a group of two or more nouns**

John and Mary's stocks $\longrightarrow$ stocks are jointly owned

John's and Mary's stocks $\longrightarrow$ some stocks are owned by John; some are owned by Mary

the governor and legislature's report $\longrightarrow$ one report from both

the governor and legislature's reports $\longrightarrow$ more than one report but still from both

the governor's and legislature's reports $\longrightarrow$ one or more reports from the governor; one or more reports from the legislature

---

RULE 6   **To form the possessive of personal pronouns, do not use the apostrophe**

hers   its   ours   theirs   whose   yours

Many writers confuse the contractions "it's," "they're," and "who's" with the possessive of the personal pronouns "its," "their," and "whose."

it's = it is	its = possessive of "it"
they're = they are	their = possessive of "they"
who's = who is	whose = possessive of "who"

Besides showing possession, the apostrophe has a few other uses, including the formation of contractions and some plurals.

To form contractions, use the apostrophe to substitute for one or more omitted letters or numbers   RULE 7

it's = it is	ma'am = madam
they're = they are	class of '68 = class of 1968

Note that contractions are used rarely in formal writing, including most legal writing.

To form the plural of numbers, letters, or words referred to as words, add "'s"   RULE 8

seven 0's	cross all the t's and dot all the i's
1950's	replace all the and's with or's
two Boeing 767's	

Some authorities recommend adding just "s" to make numbers plural: 1990s, two Boeing 767s.

See Exercises 28U, 28V, and **28W** in the *Practice Book.*

§ 28.5 Other Marks of Punctuation

§ 28.5.1 Quotation Marks

a. Identification of Another's Written or Spoken Words

There is nothing mysterious about quotation marks; they do just what their name suggests: they mark where something is quoted.

Although many legal writers have a problem with excessive quoting (see section 25.2.3), there are still several occasions, most notably statutes and memorable phrasing, where quoting is necessary or appropriate. For these occasions, use quotation marks around those words that are not your own and that you have taken from the cited source.

EXAMPLE 1

Quoting Written Words

The relationship between Southwestern Insurers and each of its agents is governed by an agreement that includes the following statement: "The location of the agent's office cannot unduly interfere with the business established by another agent."

EXAMPLE 2

Quoting an Opinion

In the *Ryan* case, the Court of Appeals ruled that the plaintiff's choice in not swerving was "prudent under the circumstances." *Id.* at 508.

EXAMPLE 3

Quoting Spoken Words

The bartender testified that he overheard the defendant say he would "get even" with Meyers.

Take care to quote the source's words exactly; use the ellipsis (see section 28.5.2) to indicate any omissions you have made to the wording and brackets (see section 28.5.3) to indicate changes in capitalization and additions for clarity and readability.

EXAMPLE 4

Quoting With Changes and Omissions

In his *Roviaro* dissent, Justice Clark observed that "[e]xperience teaches that once this policy [of confidentiality] is relaxed . . . its effectiveness is destroyed. Once an informant is known, the drug traffickers are quick to retaliate." *Id.* at 67.

Notice that in Examples 2, 3, and 4 the quotation is integrated into the writer's own sentence. When you integrate a quotation into one of your own sentences, be sure that the parts fit. The grammar of your sentence must be compatible with the grammar of the quotation.

EXAMPLE

Incorrect

An actionable nuisance is "an obstruction to the free use of property, so as to essentially interfere with the comfortable enjoyment of life and property, is a nuisance and the subject of an action for damages and other further relief." RCW 7.48.010.

EXAMPLE

Revised

An actionable nuisance is "an obstruction to the free use of property, so as to essentially interfere with the comfortable enjoyment of life and property. . . ." RCW § 7.48.010.

b. Block Quotations

Do not use quotation marks around quotations of fifty words or more. A quotation of this length should be set off as a block quotation; that is, it should be single-spaced, indented on the left and right margins, and without quotation marks. Block quotations should be separated from the text above and below the quotation with extra space.

Unfortunately, some court rules require quotation marks for block quotations. As a writer, then, determine which method your reader prefers and apply it. Know too that the trend seems to be toward using block quotations for long quotations that are not quite fifty words. The rationale seems to be that it is easier for the reader to see where the quotation begins and ends.

Block Quotation   EXAMPLE 5

Davis argues that the trial court erred in giving instruction 19, which reads as follows:

> Evidence has been introduced in this case regarding the fact that stop signs were installed in the neighborhood of Ohio and Texas Streets approximately one and one-half years after the accident of December 24, 1999. You are not to consider this evidence as proof of negligence nor as an admission of negligence on the part of the City.

Block Quotation   EXAMPLE 6

The *Sholund* court held that no contract arose between the insured and the insurance company:

> [W]here the agent represents two or more companies, no one of them can be bound until the agent allocates the risk, or some portion thereof, to it by some word or act. Until that is done, there is no contract, because of failure of parties.... In the present case, the record is totally devoid of any act or word on the part of the agent to designate the appellant as the company to take the risk until after the property was destroyed by fire. He merely thought the appellant would take it. Thoughts can become binding as contracts only when transformed into acts or words.

Id. at 113-15.

Block quotations also tend to highlight the quoted material; consequently, some writers use them for persuasive reasons even when the quotation is fairly short.

c. Effective Lead-ins for Quotations

In Examples 1, 5, and 6, the quotations are not integrated into the writer's own sentences; instead, they are formally introduced and set up as separate statements.

Notice how the lead-ins to these formally introduced quotations are written. The language in the lead-ins prepares the reader for the quotation, sometimes by summarizing or paraphrasing the quotation, sometimes by explaining in advance why the quotation is significant.

Compare the lead-ins in the following examples. Notice how the ineffective lead-ins do little more than indicate that a quotation will follow. In contrast, the effective lead-ins guide the reader into the quotation and suggest what the reader should look for in the quotation.

EXAMPLE

Ineffective Lead-in

The court found the following:

> The juvenile has an extensive record of adjudications and diversions for a variety of criminal offenses.... The court concludes that a sentence within the standard range would constitute a manifest injustice.... [C]ommitment...for a period of fifty-two (52) weeks is a more appropriate and reasonable sentence, taking into consideration the age of the defendant, his level of criminal sophistication and lack of success in rehabilitation....

EXAMPLE

Effective Lead-in

The court found a "manifest injustice" and increased Boyd's sentence because of his criminal history:

> The juvenile has an extensive record of adjudications and diversions for a variety of criminal offenses. ... The court concludes that a sentence within the standard range would constitute a manifest injustice.... [C]ommitment...for a period of fifty-two (52) weeks is a more appropriate and reasonable sentence, taking into consideration the age of the defendant, his level of criminal sophistication and lack of success in rehabilitation....

EXAMPLE

Ineffective Lead-in

In *Curtis v. Blacklaw*, the court said the following:

EXAMPLE

Effective Lead-in

In *Curtis v. Blacklaw*, the court explained the relationship between the standard of ordinary care and the emergency doctrine:

> [T]he existence of a legally defined emergency does not alter or diminish the standards of care imposed by law upon the actors.... With or without an emergency instruction, the jury must determine what choice a reasonably prudent and careful person would have made in the same situation.

Id. at 363.

Notice too that when a quotation is formally introduced and preceded by a colon, the portion of the sentence before the colon — the lead-in — must be grammatically complete. See section 28.3.

d. Quotations Within Quotations

Occasionally, something you want to quote will already have quotation marks in it, either because the source quoted someone else or because the source used a term in a special way. For a quotation within a quotation, use single quotation marks (an apostrophe on most keyboards).

Quotation Within a Quotation   EXAMPLE

"Police must discover incriminating evidence 'inadvertently,' which is to say, they may not 'know in advance the location of [certain] evidence and intend to seize it,' relying on the plain view doctrine as a pretext." *Texas v. Brown*, 460 U.S. 730, 743 (1983) (quoting *Coolidge*, 403 U.S. at 370).

---

e. Quotation Marks with Other Marks of Punctuation

Periods and commas go inside closing quotation marks; semicolons and colons go outside closing quotation marks. Dashes, question marks, and exclamation points go inside closing quotation marks when they are part of the quotation and outside closing quotation marks when they are part of the larger sentence.

Correct   EXAMPLES

Davis's employer described him as a "street-smart youngster who knew what not to get involved with."

The jury could have arguably considered Wilson's insulting remarks to Harris as "unlawful," thereby depriving Harris of her self-defense claim.

Parole is a "variation on imprisonment"; therefore, parole and its possible revocation are a continuing form of custody relating back to the criminal act.

---

f. Other Uses for Quotation Marks

Quotation marks may also indicate that a word is being used in some special way.

Words Used in a Special Way   EXAMPLES

Mrs. Hartley claims that her husband played "mind games" with her to get her to sign the agreement.

The court of appeals held that the attorney's phrasing was calculated to imply that Morris was a "hired gun" for insurance carriers.

Special terms are often introduced by phrases like "the word" or "the term." Put the words that follow these phrases in quotation marks, but do not use quotation marks around words that follow "so-called."

EXAMPLE   ## Special Terms

The words "beyond a reasonable doubt" in the constitutional error test created confusion in the Arizona courts for some time.

As a general rule, use quotation marks around a word or phrase that is a special term the first time it is used. Thereafter, the quotation marks should be omitted.

Quotation marks should also be used around words that follow the terms "signed," "endorsed," or "entitled."

EXAMPLE   ## Correct

The contract was signed "Miss Cathryn Smith," not "Ms. Kathryn Smith."

Do not use quotation marks around the single words yes and no.
Do not use quotation marks around a paraphrase.

EXAMPLE   ## Paraphrase

When the officer asked her if she needed a ride home, she said yes.

---

§ 28.5.2 Ellipses

Use the ellipsis — three spaced dots — to indicate an omission in a quotation. (The dots are the same as periods on the keyboard.) The ellipsis allows you to trim quotations down and focus the reader's attention on the parts of the quotation that are relevant to your case.

EXAMPLE   ## Ellipsis to Show Omission

Helen signed a quitclaim deed to Richard, disclaiming "an interest in the . . . property."

You should allow a space before the first dot and after the last dot in an ellipsis. When the omission occurs in the middle of a quoted sentence, retain any necessary punctuation. Notice, for example, that the comma after "union" is retained in the following quotation because it is necessary punctuation for the sentence as it is quoted.

Retain Necessary Punctuation

"We the people of the United States, in order to form a more perfect union, ... do ordain and establish this Constitution for the United States of America."

When the omission occurs at the end of a quoted sentence, use the ellipsis dots to indicate that omission and then space and add a fourth period for the punctuation to end the sentence.[4]

Fourth Period to End Sentence

"We the people of the United States, in order to form a more perfect union, ... do ordain and establish this Constitution ...."

When the omission occurs after the end of a quoted sentence, punctuate the quoted sentence and then insert the ellipsis. In such a case, the sentence period is closed up to the last word in the sentence. This is demonstrated in the next two examples, both of which are quotations from the following original material.

Original Material

The hostility/claim of right element of adverse possession requires only that the claimant treat the land as his own as against the world throughout the statutory period. The nature of his possession will be determined solely on the basis of the manner in which he treats the property. His subjective belief regarding his true interest in the land and his intent to dispossess or not dispossess another is irrelevant to this determination.

Id. at 860-61.

Quotation from the Preceding Material

The hostility/claim of right element of adverse possession requires only that the claimant treat the land as his own as against the world throughout the statutory period.... His subjective belief regarding his true interest in the land and his intent to dispossess or not dispossess another is irrelevant to this determination.

Id. at 860-61.

---

4. *The Chicago Manual of Style*, 15th ed., recommends a closing period followed by the ellipsis rather than the ellipsis followed by a space and period. The result would be "We the people of the United States, in order to form a more perfect union, ... do ordain and establish this Constitution ...."

EXAMPLE   ## Another Quotation from the Same Original

"The hostility/claim of right element of adverse possession requires only that the claimant treat the land as his own as against the world throughout the statutory period. . . . [H]is intent to dispossess or not dispossess another is irrelevant to this determination." *Id.* at 860-61.

When the omission occurs at the beginning of the quotation, do not use an ellipsis. The reader will be able to tell that the original quotation did not begin at that point because the quotation begins with a lower case letter.

EXAMPLE   ## Incorrect

In 2001, King granted to the State a ". . . permanent easement assignable in whole or in part" over King's property. CP 106.

EXAMPLE   ## Correct

In 2001, King granted to the State a "permanent easement assignable in whole or in part" over King's property. CP 106.

When the quoted material is just a phrase or clause, no ellipsis is needed before or after the quoted material.

EXAMPLE   ## No Ellipsis for a Phrase

An omission, to be actionable, must constitute "tacit authorization" or "deliberate indifference." *Gray-Hopkins v. Prince George's County, Md.,* 163 F. Supp. 2d 571, 581 (D. Md. 2001).

When a paragraph or more is omitted, indent and use the usual three ellipsis dots plus the fourth period for the end punctuation.[5]

EXAMPLE   ## Omitted Paragraph

The Safe Drivers' Insurance policy contains the following relevant provisions:

Definitions

. . . .

A car is a 4-wheel motor vehicle licensed for use on public roads. It includes any motor home that is not used for business purposes and any utility trailer.

---

5. The *ALWD Citation Manual* recommends centering an ellipsis indicating the omission of one or more paragraphs and placing five to seven spaces between each ellipsis dot.

. . . .

A motor vehicle is a land motor vehicle designed for use on public roads. It includes cars and trailers. It also includes any other land motor vehicle while used on public roads.

Like all good things, ellipsis marks can be misused. Never use the ellipsis to change the original intent in the quotation. Also, take care not to overuse the ellipsis in any one quotation. Too many omissions make the quotation difficult to read.

§ 28.5.3 Brackets

Brackets are used to show changes in quotations. The most common are additions of clarifying material and changes in capitalization and verb tense.

Addition of Clarifying Material

"The privilege [of nondisclosure] recognizes the obligation of citizens to communicate their knowledge of the commission of crimes to law enforcement officials and, by preserving their anonymity, encourages them to perform that obligation." *Lewandowski v. State*, 389 N.E.2d 706, 708 (Ind. 1979) (quoting *Roviaro v. United States*, 353 U.S. 53, 62 (1957)).

Capitalization Change

"[A] municipality may be held liable under 1983 for the intentional conduct of its governing body, . . . [b]ut we have held city police chiefs *not* to be such officials, . . . as they are almost uniformly subordinate to the city's governing body." *Languirand*, 717 F.2d at 227 (emphasis in original).

Change in Verb Tense

The Council authorized the construction of a twelve-story tower, finding that reducing the tower to this height "substantially mitigate[s] adverse impacts on the land use pattern in the vicinity."

Use empty brackets [ ] to indicate where a single letter is omitted.

In some cases, a pronoun in a quotation may be ambiguous in the new context, so for clarity the writer should substitute the appropriate noun in brackets. In such cases, the omission of the pronoun does not need to be indicated.

To Replace an Ambiguous Pronoun

At the time of her medical release, Wainwright made the following admission: "I did continue to have some pain and discomfort in my back, neck, and arms, but [Dr. Rodgers] felt this was normal pain and discomfort and that it would go away."

Occasionally, something that you want to quote has a significant error in it. In such cases, use a bracketed *sic* immediately after the error to indicate that the error was in the original and not inadvertently added. Note that *sic* is italicized.

EXAMPLE   **To Indicate an Error in a Quote**

On the day after the union vote was held, the shop supervisor issued a memo to all machinists stating that how they voted "would not effect [*sic*] their performance reviews."

---

§ 28.5.4 Parentheses

In everyday writing, parentheses are used to add additional information to sentences. They are one way to signal that that information is of lesser importance.

EXAMPLE   **Additional Information**

Newcombe removed one-eighth ounce of marijuana (worth $40) from Tyson's pocket.

Because conciseness is a cardinal virtue in legal writing, legal writers usually edit out any information that is of lesser importance. As a natural consequence, you will rarely encounter parenthetical inserts in legal writing. This does not mean that parentheses themselves do not appear anywhere in legal documents. They are frequently used in the following ways.

a. To Enclose Short Explanations of Cases Within Citations

EXAMPLE   **Explanation Within Citation**

Washington courts have consistently held that releases executed in connection with voluntary, high-risk adult sport activities do not violate public policy. *Vodopest v. MacGregor*, 128 Wn.2d 840, 848, 913 P.2d 779 (1996) (mountain climbing release did not violate public policy). *See also Chauvlier v. Booth Creek Ski Holdings, Inc.*, 109 Wn. App. 334, 345, 35 P.3d 383 (2001) (snow skiing release did not violate public policy).

---

b. To Refer Readers to Attached or Appended Documents

EXAMPLE   **Separate Parenthetical Sentence**

Before signing the agreement, Jones crossed out the language "at time of closing" in paragraph 12 and inserted the language "pro ratio as received by sellers" in paragraph 24. (See appendix 1.)

When a parenthetical reference is set up as a separate sentence, as in the example above, the period goes inside the closing parentheses. When the parenthetical reference is inserted in the middle of a sentence, place any punctuation required for the sentence outside the closing parenthesis.

Inserted Within Sentence

EXAMPLE

Before signing the agreement, Jones crossed out the language "at time of closing" (paragraph 12, appendix 1), and Smith inserted the language "pro ratio as received by sellers" (paragraph 24, appendix 2).

c. To Confirm Numbers

Numbers

EXAMPLE

In 1999, Patrick and Rose Milton borrowed five thousand dollars ($5,000) from Southern Security Company.

d. To Enclose Numerals That Introduce the Individual Items in a List

Enclose Numerals

EXAMPLE

The company's regulations list seven circumstances under which an employee may be separated from his or her job: (1) resignation, (2) release, (3) death, (4) retirement, (5) failure to return from a leave of absence, (6) failure to return from a layoff, and (7) discharge or suspension for cause.

e. To Announce Changes to a Quotation That Cannot Be Shown by Ellipses or Brackets

Changes to Quotation

EXAMPLES

"[I]solated incidents are normally insufficient to establish supervisory inaction upon which to predicate § 1983 liability." *Wellington*, 717 F.2d at 936 (footnote omitted).

The court held that "[a]n instruction, *when requested*, defining intent is required when intent is an element of the crime charged." *Id.* (emphasis added).

f. To Introduce Abbreviations after a Full Name Is Given

EXAMPLE   **Abbreviations**

Boliver Custom Carpets (BCC) has been in business for one year.

See Exercise 28X in the *Practice Book*.

§ 28.5.5 The Hyphen

Hyphens combine words to form compound modifiers or compound nouns. The trick is knowing when a pair or grouping of modifiers or nouns should be joined by hyphens to show that they are acting as one unit.

For modifiers, the first step is a simple one: if the modifiers do not precede the noun they modify, then they are not hyphenated. (The very few exceptions are modifying words that are always hyphenated. When you look them up in a dictionary, they are spelled with a hyphen. Ex. "short-lived" "tax-exempt")

EXAMPLES   **Correct**

Owens's argument ignores other rules of statutory construction that are <u>well established</u>.

Owens's argument ignores other <u>well-established</u> rules of statutory construction.

This case has set precedents that are <u>far reaching</u>.

The case has set <u>far-reaching</u> precedents.

Notice that legal writers use many compound modifiers that begin with "well." As long as these modifiers precede the noun they modify, they are hyphenated.

a well-reasoned opinion	a well-defined test
a well-known fact	a well-founded argument

Obviously, though, not all compound modifiers begin with "well," and unfortunately, often the only way to know whether to hyphenate is to consult a good dictionary with a recent publication date. The recent publication date is important because our language changes: what was once two or more separate words may later be hyphenated and eventually combined into one word.

on line ⟶ on-line ⟶ online

Still Separate

trier of fact
leave of absence   *prima facie* case

Hyphenated

price-fixing contract	take-home pay
out-of-pocket expenses	stop-limit order
sudden-emergency doctrine	court-martial
cross-examination	hit-and-run accident

Combined

wraparound mortgage	quitclaim deed
counterclaim	

Our changing language also gives us new hyphenated nouns.

frame-up   split-off   squeeze-out

Many words are in transition. For example, you may notice that "line-up" is spelled with a hyphen in some cases and as the combined word "lineup" in others. The same is true for "pre-trial" and "pretrial" and "email" and "e-mail." In such instances, consult your most recent authority and try to be consistent within the document you are writing. Note too that the trend seems to be to spell words without the hyphen as soon as they have a level of acceptance as a permanent compound.

In addition to using the dictionary as a guide to hyphen use, there are a few general rules about when to use hyphens.

1. Always hyphenate modifiers and nouns that begin with the prefixes "all," "ex," and "self."

all-American	all-purpose
ex-partner	ex-judge
self-defense	self-incrimination

2. Other prefixes, including "anti," "co," "de," "inter," "intra," "multi," "non," "para," "pro," "re," "semi," and "super," generally should not use a hyphen.

antitrust	nonpayment
codefendant	paralegal
degenerate	prorate
interagency	reallocate
intrastate	semiannual
multinational	supersede

Unfortunately, however, there are enough exceptions to this general rule that you may often have to look up the word you need. For example, "co-worker" and "pro-life" are exceptions. The following exceptions apply to larger categories of words:

     a. Use a hyphen when it is needed for clarity ("re-create," not "recreate");

   b. Use a hyphen when it is needed to prevent a doubled vowel ("re-enact," "de-emphasize," "co-opt") or a tripled consonant;
   c. Use the hyphen when it is needed because the second element is capitalized ("post-World War II," "un-American," "anti-Semitic").

3. "Elect" is the one suffix that usually requires a hyphen. The one exception occurs when the office consists of two or more words.

>   governor-elect   president-elect   secretary-treasurer elect

4. Hyphens are used to form compound numbers from twenty-one to ninety-nine. Hyphens are also used with fractions functioning as adjectives, but not with fractions functioning as nouns.

>   the twenty-fourth objection
>   one-half acre *but*
>   one half of the employees
>   two-thirds majority *but*
>   two thirds of the board

5. Hyphens are often used to join a number and a noun to make a compound modifier.

>   twenty-year-old appellant   ten-year lease
>   three-mile limit   ten-acre tract
>   nine-year-old conviction   first-year student

6. Do not use a hyphen in the following instances:

   a. when the first word in a two-word modifier is an adverb ending in "-ly" ("previously taxed income," "jointly acquired property");
   b. when the compound modifier contains a foreign phrase ("*bona fide* purchaser," "*per se* violation");
   c. when a civil or military title denotes one office ("justice of the peace").

Sometimes two or more compound modifiers share the same second element. In such cases, use a hyphen after each first element; do not use the second element twice.

high- and low-test gasoline

nine- and ten-acre parcels

Hyphens are also frequently used to combine two parties into one modifier. Note, however, that the en dash, which is slightly longer than a hyphen, is preferred when joining two equal parties. The en dash is created by inserting it as a symbol.

>   attorney-client privilege   husband-wife tort actions (hyphens)
>   attorney–client privilege   husband–wife tort actions (en dashes)

See Exercises 28Y and 28Z in the *Practice Book*.

§ 28.5.6 The Dash

The em dash, or what is sometimes called the "long dash," is used infrequently in legal writing. The consensus seems to be that em dashes are somewhat informal for the serious work of law. Still, there are a few occasions when the em dash is useful. For example, in sentences in which a list is an appositive, a pair of em dashes can be used to signal the beginning and end of the list.

Em Dashes with Internal Lists

EXAMPLES

By 1999, the defendant had opened up bank accounts in several foreign countries — Switzerland, Brazil, South Africa, and Spain — all under different names.

The conservative bloc — Rehnquist, O'Connor, Scalia, and Kennedy — controlled the major cases of the 1988-1989 term.

Similarly, an em dash is needed to set off an introductory list containing commas.

Em Dashes with Introductory List

EXAMPLE

Name-calling, threats, and repeated beatings — these were the ways Wilson gave attention to his son.

When used with discretion, em dashes can also be an effective way to create emphasis (see section 24.6.4). Notice how in the following pairs of sentences, the em dashes do more than the commas to highlight what they enclose.

To Create Emphasis

EXAMPLES

Commas:

The prosecution's questions, over repeated objections, about Ms. Patten's religious beliefs cannot be deemed inadvertent.

Em Dashes:

The prosecution's questions — over repeated objections — about Ms. Patten's religious beliefs cannot be deemed inadvertent.

Commas:

The victim's age, eighteen months, made him particularly vulnerable.

Em Dashes:

The victim's age — eighteen months — made him particularly vulnerable.

Em dashes can also be used to show abrupt shifts or to cue the reader that the words that follow are shocking or surprising.

To Indicate Surprise

Several witnesses — including the defendant's mother — testified that they believed Willie was capable of committing such a heinous crime.

On a keyboard, the em dash is created by hitting the hyphen key twice or by inserting it as a symbol. There is no space before or after the em dash.

The en dash, which was traditionally created by simply typing a hyphen, can now be added to text by inserting it as a symbol. An en dash is shorter than an em dash but longer than a hyphen. The primary uses of the en dash are to show spans in dates and page numbers (2003–2006, pages 39–44) or the joining of two things that are equal (attorney–client privilege, secretary–treasurer).

§ 28.6 Comma Splices and Fused Sentences

§ 28.6.1 Comma Splices

Perhaps the most common punctuation error in all writing, not just legal writing, is the comma splice. Simply put, a comma splice is the joining of two main, or independent, clauses with just a comma. This is the pattern for a comma splice:

main clause   ,   main clause.

Reminder

A main clause has both a subject and verb and can stand alone as a sentence.

Comma Splices — Incorrect

The prosecutor spoke about the defendant's motive, the jury listened carefully.

The corrections officer contacted several other persons, none knew of Wilson's disappearance.

Mr. Baker sustained personal property damage, his picture windows and vase were smashed.

When correcting a comma splice, use one of the five simple methods that best suits the context.

1. Make each main clause a separate sentence.

Correct   EXAMPLE

The prosecutor spoke about the defendant's motive. The jury listened carefully.

---

2. Add a coordinating conjunction ("and," "but," "or," "for," "nor," "yet," "so") after the comma separating the two main clauses. See Rule 1 in section 28.1.

Correct   EXAMPLE

The corrections officer contacted several other persons, but none knew of Wilson's disappearance.

---

3. Change the comma separating the two main clauses to a semicolon. See section 28.2.

Correct   EXAMPLE

The corrections officer contacted several other persons; none knew of Wilson's disappearance.

---

4. Change one of the main clauses to a subordinate clause.

Correct   EXAMPLES

While the prosecutor spoke about the defendant's motive, the jury listened carefully.

Although the corrections officer contacted several other persons, none knew of Wilson's disappearance.

---

5. If the second main clause is an explanation or illustration of the first main clause, use a colon to separate the two main clauses. See section 28.3.

Correct   EXAMPLE

Mr. Baker sustained personal property damage: his picture windows and vase were smashed.

Comma splices often occur in sentences that have two main clauses and a conjunctive adverb introducing the second main clause. This is incorrect:

<u>main clause, therefore,   main clause.</u>

Reminder

The most commonly used conjunctive adverbs are "accordingly," "also," "besides," "consequently," "furthermore," "hence," "however," "indeed," "instead," "likewise," "meanwhile," "moreover," "nevertheless," "still," "then," "therefore," and "thus."

EXAMPLE   **Incorrect**

The summons was not delivered to his usual place of abode, therefore, service was not effected in the manner prescribed by law.

Such comma splices are usually best corrected by using the third method, changing the comma to a semicolon.

EXAMPLE   **Correct**

The summons was not delivered to his usual place of abode; therefore, service was not effected in the manner prescribed by law.

They can also be corrected by changing the comma to a period.

EXAMPLE   **Correct**

The summons was not delivered to his usual place of abode. Therefore, service was not effected in the manner prescribed by law.

---

§ 28.6.2 Fused Sentences

Fused sentences, also known as run-on sentences, are a less frequent but even more serious writing error than comma splices. A fused sentence has no punctuation or coordinating conjunction between two main clauses. This is the pattern for a fused sentence:

<u>main clause</u>   <u>main clause.</u>

EXAMPLE   **Fused Sentence**

The prosecutor spoke about the defendant's motive the jury listened carefully.

Fused sentences can be corrected using the same methods for correcting comma splices.

Occasionally, one hears an overly long, rambling sentence described as a "run-on sentence." This is an incorrect use of the term. A run-on sentence is the same thing as a fused sentence: either the punctuation or the coordinating conjunction is omitted between two main clauses.

See Exercises 28AA and 28BB in the *Practice Book*.

C H A P T E R

29

Mechanics

§ 29.1 Spelling

With the advent of spellcheck on everyone's computer, it might seem as though misspelled words are no longer an issue in legal writing. Spellcheckers have been a godsend, but they have not solved all the problems related to spelling in legal writing.

First, spellcheckers still do not have many commonly used legal words in their dictionaries. For example, "articulable," as in the phrase "articulable suspicion" will show up as a misspelling. The way to solve this problem is to add the correct spelling to your computer's dictionary. You may also find it useful to add other common abbreviations like those that appear in many citations to your computer's dictionary.

Second, spellcheckers accept secondary spellings that many legal readers dislike. For example, most legal readers consider "judgment" without the "e" a misspelling, but the computer dictionary will accept "judgement" without comment.

Third, computer spelling programs check spelling by making a blind match between the words you have typed and the words in the dictionary. The program does not consider context. Consequently, it will read "torte" as spelled correctly without knowing whether the writer intended a wrongful act or a cake with rich frosting.

Finally, spelling programs do not include most proper names. This means that writers have to be particularly careful proofreading names and not just click "ignore" or "ignore all" too quickly. Make a point of checking whether it is Stephen with a "ph" or Steven with a "v," Schmitt with a "t" or Schmidt with a "d." There is no quicker way to alienate someone than to misspell his or her name.

§ 29.2 Capitalization

§ 29.2.1 General Rules

In English, there are two general rules for capitalization: (1) to mark the beginning of a sentence, and (2) to signal a proper name or adjective. Unfortunately, however, there is occasional disagreement about what is a proper name or adjective.

Two additional principles may serve as useful guides: first, be consistent. Once you have decided that a word or type of word is capitalized or lowercase, apply that decision consistently throughout the document you are writing. Second, note that the tendency in English now is toward what is called the "down" style,[1] which is a lowercase rather than an uppercase style.

a. Beginning of a Sentence

The first word of a sentence is always capitalized. Even sentence fragments such as those that begin brief answers in legal memoranda have their first word capitalized.

A complete sentence enclosed in parentheses starts with a capital letter unless the parenthetical sentence occurs within another sentence.

EXAMPLE   **Capitalization with Parentheses**

The Wilsons extended their garden beyond the property line and onto the disputed strip. (See Attachment A.) *but*

The Wilsons extended their garden beyond the property line (see Attachment A) and onto the disputed strip.

---

1. Quotations

Capitalize the first word of a direct quotation when the quotation is formally introduced and set up as a separate sentence.

EXAMPLE   **Formally Introduced Quotations**

The Supreme Court unanimously struck down a policy banning women of child-bearing age from hazardous but top-paying jobs: "Decisions about the welfare of future children must be left to the parents who conceive, bear, support, and raise them rather than to the employers who hire those parents."

Do not capitalize the first word of a direct quotation when the quotation is integrated into the writer's sentence. See section 28.5.3 for discussion of the use of brackets when making a change to a quotation.

---

1. See *The Chicago Manual of Style* 311 (15th ed. U. of Chicago Press 2003).

Integrated Quotation

The Supreme Court unanimously struck down a policy banning women of child-bearing age from hazardous but top-paying jobs, stating that "[d]ecisions about the welfare of future children must be left to the parents who conceive, bear, support, and raise them rather than to the employers who hire those parents."

Do not capitalize the beginning of the second segment of a split direct quotation.

Split Quotation

"Concern for a woman's existing or potential offspring," wrote Justice Blackmun for the majority, "historically has been the excuse for denying women equal employment opportunities."

2. Sentences Following a Colon

When a colon introduces two or more full sentences, capitalize the first word of each of those sentences. When a colon introduces a single full sentence, that sentence does not begin with a capital letter.

A Colon Introduces Two or More Full Sentences

The company has evidence that Mrs. McKibbin accepted the written proposal: She made a telephone call to place the order for the rugs. She sent an email that included the rugs' measurements.

A Colon Introduces a Single Sentence

The company has evidence that Mrs. McKibbin accepted the written proposal: she made a telephone call to place the order for the rugs.

Do not capitalize the first word after the colon if what follows the colon is less than a complete sentence.

Phrase Follows Colon

In *Traweek*, the court found that the appearance of the defendants differed from the witness's description in just one detail: the color of the shirts worn by the defendants.

If the items in a series following a colon are not complete sentences, do not capitalize the first word in each item.

Incomplete Sentences Follow Colon

The parties will dispute whether three of the four elements of the sudden emergency doctrine are met: (1) whether Mr. Odoki was confronted by a sudden and unexpected emergency, (2) whether his own negligence created or contributed to that emergency, and (3) whether he made a choice such as a reasonable person placed in the same situation might make.

---

b. Proper Nouns and Adjectives

As a general rule, capitalize a word used to name someone or something specific; use a lowercase letter when the same word is used as a general reference.

the President of Shell Oil
a president of a company

Stanford Law School
a law school

Environmental Protection Agency
an agency of the federal government

Traditionally, the short forms of proper nouns were also capitalized. If, for example, the defendant in a lawsuit was the "Green River Community College," after the first reference the writer then used the short form "the College," and "College" was capitalized. Rule 8 in the 18th edition of the *Bluebook* seems to suggest a similar approach. *The Chicago Manual of Style* 15th edition, however, now says that the short forms may be lowercased but that writers should use their judgment and discretion when making the decision.[2]

Unfortunately, there is also disagreement about whether to capitalize the words "defendant" and "plaintiff" (and similar terms such as "appellant," "appellee," "respondent," and "petitioner"). Some authorities capitalize these words only when they refer to the parties in the matter that is the subject of the document.[3] Others simply say not to capitalize the terms at all[4] or not to capitalize them when they appear before a name,[5] as in the example "defendant Smith." All agree that these words should be capitalized on cover sheets for briefs. Once you have started capitalizing (or not capitalizing) a particular term, be consistent throughout that document.

Particularly difficult for legal writers is determining when to capitalize certain words that commonly occur in legal writing ("act," "amendment," "bill," "circuit," "code," "congressional," "constitution," "court," "federal," "national," "statute," and "the"). Use the following list as a quick reference.

"Act"

Capitalize the word "act" when it is part of a full title.

---

2. See *The Chicago Manual of Style* 311-12 (15th ed. 2003).
3. See *The Bluebook* B10.6.2 (18th ed. 2005).
4. See *Texas Law Review Manual on Usage, Style & Editing* 38 (9th ed. 2002).
5. See *The Chicago Manual of Style* (15th ed. 2003).

the Clean Air Act
the Controlled Substance Act of 1970, *but*
an act passed by the legislature

"Act" is also capitalized when it is used as the short form of a proper name.

the Clean Air Act → the Act

"Amendment"

Most authorities, including the 18th edition of *The Bluebook* capitalize "amendment" when referring to amendments of the United States Constitution.

Fifth Amendment

A general reference to an amendment should not be capitalized.

an amendment to the tax laws

Notice that when referring to one of the amendments to the Constitution, most writers spell out ordinals through the Ninth Amendment and use figures for the 10th amendment and above.

Fifth Amendment   14th Amendment

When two or more amendments are mentioned together, use figures if either is for the 10th Amendment or above.

the 5th Amendment and the 14th Amendment

"Bill"

With the exception of the Bill of Rights, "bill" should be written in lowercase. This practice does seem to be an exception to the general rule of capitalizing words that are part of a full title.

Senate bill 47   House bill 11

"Circuit"

Capitalize "circuit" when it is used as part of a full title or with a circuit number. Use lowercase when "circuit" is part of a general reference.

United States Court of Appeals for the Second Circuit, *but* circuit courts

"Code"

Capitalize "code" when it is part of a full title or when it refers to a specific code. Use lowercase for all general references.

The United States Internal Revenue Code
United States Code, but
the tax code
state codes
unofficial code

"Congress"

Capitalize "Congress" when it is part of the full title of the United States Congress or the short form "the Congress." The adjective "congressional," on the other hand, is usually lowercase unless it is part of a full title such as the *Congressional Record.*

"Constitution"

Capitalize "constitution" when used as part of the full title of any constitution or when used as a short form reference to the United States Constitution.

the United States Constitution
the Constitution (short for United States Constitution), *but*
a new state constitution

"Court"

Probably the most common capitalization question in legal writing is when should "court" be capitalized.

1. The official and full names of all international and higher courts are capitalized.

International Court of Justice
United States Court of Appeals for the Third Circuit
Texas Court of Appeals
Arizona Supreme Court

2. Always capitalize "court" when referring to the United States Supreme Court. Note that even the short forms for referring to the United States Supreme Court are capitalized.

the Supreme Court of the United States
the United States Supreme Court
the Supreme Court
the Court (short form for Supreme Court)

3. Do not capitalize "court" if it is part of the name of a city or county court.

Phoenix night court
Hampton municipal court
juvenile court

Despite the agreement among the authorities about not capitalizing "court" if it is part of the name of a city or county court, most practitioners seem to ignore the rule and capitalize "court" in such instances.

4. Capitalize "court" in a document when referring to the very court that will receive that document.

5. Capitalize "court" when the term specifically refers to the judge or presiding officer.

> It is the opinion of this Court. . . .

Other personifications such as "Your Honor" and "the Bench" are also capitalized.

"Federal"

The word "federal" is capitalized only when it is part of a specific name or when the word it modifies is capitalized.

> Federal Bureau of Investigation
> Federal Deposit Insurance Corporation
> Federal Energy Regulatory Commission, *but*
> federal government
> federal agents
> federal court

"National"

The word "national" is capitalized only when it is part of a specific name or when the word it modifies is capitalized.

> National Security Council, *but*
> national security interests

Another test for whether to capitalize "federal" or "national" is whether the word following those terms is capitalized. If it is, then capitalize "federal" or "national" because it is part of a specific name.

"State"

Capitalize when "state" is part of the full title for a state or when referring to the governmental actor or party to a suit.

> State of Washington
> The State will argue that the evidence should be admitted.

"Statute"

Use lowercase for "statute," unless it is part of a title.

> federal statutes
> state statutes
> statute of limitations, *but*
> Statute of Frauds

"The"

In names and titles, capitalize "the" only if it is part of an official name.

The Hague
The Bluebook but
the United States Supreme Court
the American Bar Association

§ 29.2.2 Headings

The most important thing to remember about capitalization in headings is consistency. If local rules or convention dictates that certain types of headings require all capital letters, be consistent with that rule or convention. If there are no rules governing capitalization in the type of headings you are writing, develop a system that can be used consistently throughout the document.

Elaine C. Maier, in her book *How to Prepare a Legal Citation*, outlines the following suggested scheme "in descending order of subordination":

1. All letters of all words in the heading are capitalized.
2. All initial letters of all words in the heading are capitalized.
3. All initial letters of all words in the heading except articles, conjunctions, and prepositions of four letters or fewer are capitalized.
4. The sentence style of capitalization is used; that is, only the first letter of the first word and proper nouns are capitalized.[6]

Use the same capitalization level to indicate comparable levels in your text. (Boldface, underlining, and other typefaces may also be used to create levels in text.)

In situations in which you are developing your own scheme of capitalization in headings, remember that having more than five words typed in all capitals slows your reader down. For this reason, it may be best to use all capitals at a level where you have only relatively short headings.

§ 29.2.3 Miscellaneous Rules for Capitalization

Academic Degrees

Academic degrees are capitalized, but some have lowercase internal letters.

J.D.   LL.M.   M.D.   Ph.D.

Acronyms

Most acronyms are written in all capitals (CEO, OPEC, NASA, CERCLA). Abbreviations of government agencies, corporations, and military organizations are also all capital letters (EEOC, FCC, IBM, USMC).

---

6. Elaine C. Maier, *How to Prepare a Legal Citation* 158 (Barron's Educational Series, Inc. 1986).

Compass Points, Geographical Names, and Topographical Names

Compass points are capitalized when they refer to a geographical region; adjectives derived from compass points are also capitalized. The compass points themselves are lowercased if they just name a direction.

the Middle West
the Northeast
Southern hospitality
Southwestern cuisine, *but*
the car was heading west
the fence runs along the northern boundary

Topographical Names

Capitalize topographical names when they are part of a proper name.

Lake Superior	*but*	a lake
the Mississippi River		the river
the Rocky Mountains		those mountains

In legal documents, words such as "state," "county," or "city" are capitalized when they are part of a specific name.

Washington State
Chaves County
the City of Spokane
the State of Florida
Commonwealth of Virginia

Similarly, capitalize words such as "bridge," "square," "building," "park," and "hotel" when they are part of a place name.

Brooklyn Bridge	Central Park
Transamerica Building	Tiananmen Square

Judges' Names

The Supreme Court has a tradition of spelling judges' names in all capitals when the names are referred to in opinions.

Rules of Law

Despite efforts at uniformity, several rules of law are known by several versions of their name, all with differing capitalization. The common issue is whether a certain phrase is part of the title of the rule. The general guideline is to capitalize the words that are essential to the rule's name. Another reasonable guideline is to use the most common form of the rule's name.

Is it, for example, "the rule in Shelley's case," "the Rule in Shelley's case," "the Rule in Shelley's Case," or "The Rule in Shelley's Case"? Using the guideline of capitalizing those words that are essential to the rule's name, "rule" and "case" should be capitalized because they are commonly treated as part of the name. "The," on the other hand, should probably be lowercase to avoid making the phrase look like a book title

Is it the "rule against perpetuities," the "Rule against Perpetuities," or the "Rule Against Perpetuities"? Professor Dukeminier asked this question in his article *Perpetuities: Contagious Capitalization*,[7] and determined that "Rule against Perpetuities" and "rule against perpetuities" were both commonly used and therefore acceptable. "Rule against Perpetuities" is preferable, according to Dukeminier, for historical reasons.

What should a legal writer do, then, when faced with a similar question? One easy suggestion is to go online and do a quick search to see what the courts do. If that does not solve the problem, consider the following factors:

1. What words are essential to the rule's name?
2. What capitalization is most common?
3. Is there a historical reason for preferring one version over another?

The most important consideration of all, though, is consistency. Once you have determined which version you will use, use it consistently throughout the document.

Titles

Capitalize titles of court documents. Use all capitals for titles on the documents themselves.

Titles are capitalized when they precede a personal name and are treated as part of that name. Titles are also capitalized when they immediately follow a name as an appositive. The same titles are then normally lowercased when they follow a personal name or when they are used as a short form for the name.

Dean Kellye Testy
Kellye Testy, Dean of Seattle University School of Law
the dean

Governor George E. Pataki
George E. Pataki, Governor of the State of New York,
the governor

Trademarks

Use all capitals to distinguish a trademark from the name of a company or corporation.

XEROX (trademark)   Xerox (corporation)

---

7. Jesse Dukeminier, *Perpetuities: Contagious Capitalization*, 20 J. Legal Educ. 341 (1968).

Vessels

Although one occasionally sees all capitals used for the name of a vessel, capitalizing only the first letter is preferred.

Titanic   *Valdez*

§ 29.3 Abbreviations and Symbols

§ 29.3.1 General Rules for Abbreviations

Abbreviations, or shortened forms, should be used primarily for the convenience of the reader. Properly used, an abbreviation saves the *reader* time and energy. It gets across the same message in less space.

The temptation for writers, of course, is to use abbreviations that are convenient for them. A writer who fails to adopt the reader's perspective may use an abbreviation to save the writer time and energy only to find that the reader is unsure, confused, or even frustrated by the abbreviation.

One source of abbreviation confusion is the sheer number of specialized abbreviations used in some legal documents.[8] The result of such overuse is obvious: the harried reader has to keep turning back in the document to keep the abbreviations straight. The solution to the problem is equally obvious: avoid using numerous specialized abbreviations in the same document.

All of the abbreviation rules that follow apply to abbreviations in textual sentences, not in citations.

Rule 1.   Abbreviate only when the abbreviation will be clear to the reader.

Rule 2.   If an abbreviation will be initially unfamiliar to the reader, use the full form first and then follow with the abbreviation in parentheses.

Full Form Followed by Abbreviation

EXAMPLES

Mrs. Kearney telephoned Boliver Custom Carpets (BCC) and asked if it manufactured custom-made carpets. BCC's representative took down a description of the carpets she wanted made.

Mr. Chung wants to know whether the Oregon Wilderness Watchers (OWW) can create a prescriptive easement across his land. OWW has been using a path across Chung's property to reach its property.

Abbreviations created for a specific document, such as BCC and OWW in the examples above, are usually written in all capitals. Notice that common abbreviations that are acronyms (ERIC, SARA, ERISTA) are also written

---

8. Writing about a case in which no fewer than seven different groups of initials were used, Justice Rehnquist complained that "the 'alphabet soup' of the New Deal era was, by comparison, a clear broth." *Chrysler Corp. v. Brown*, 441 U.S. 281, 284, 286-87 (1979).

in all capitals, unless they have been fully incorporated into the language ("radar," "sonar," "scuba," and "zip code").

§ 29.3.2 Miscellaneous Rules for Abbreviation

Geographical Names

United States Postal Service abbreviations are acceptable when used on envelopes and in other situations when an address is written in block form. Note that state abbreviations are all capitalized without end periods. (This rule does not apply to states in case citations.)

Professor Sven Bloomquist
8990 Union St.
Brooklyn, NY 11215

The same words (avenue, street, northeast, New York) should be spelled out when they appear in text. All compass points (northeast, southwest) are also lowercase, unless they are used as the name of a region (the Pacific Northwest, the South).

"Saint" may be abbreviated when it is part of the name of a city (St. Louis); follow the bearer's preference when it is part of a person's name (David Saint-Johns, Ruth St. Denis).

Foreign Phrases

Some Latin words commonly used in legal texts and citations are abbreviations, so they should be followed by periods (*id.*, *i.e.*, *e.g.*). Others are complete words (the *ex* in *ex parte* or *re*), so a period should not be used.

Names of Laws

The first time a law is mentioned in text, its title should be typed out in full; thereafter, abbreviations may be used. (See *The Bluebook* or *ALWD Citation Manual* for how to write the names of laws in citations.)

first mention: Article II, Section 3
later references: Art. II, Sec. 3

Academic Degrees

Academic degrees are abbreviated. Note that capitalization should be checked in a dictionary.

Ph.D.	LL.D.	M.B.A.	C.P.A.
J.D.	LL.B.	LL.M.	M.D.

Time

The abbreviations for *ante meridiem* and *post meridiem* are most commonly written as unspaced, lowercase letters with periods.

9:00 a.m.

Measures and Weights

When the numeral is written out,[9] the unit must also be written out. When the figure is used, the unit may be abbreviated.

one hundred square miles   *or* 100 sq. mi.
one hundred eighty pounds *or* 180 lbs.

Double Punctuation

Occasionally, an abbreviation will be the last word in a sentence. In such cases, do not add an additional period after the period for the abbreviation.

The officer had checked in at 8:00 p.m.
Clark claimed she had a Ph.D.

A period for an abbreviation is used with a question mark or an exclamation point.

Did the officer check in at 8:00 p.m.?

§ 29.3.3 Inappropriate Abbreviations

Informal abbreviations

Avoid informal abbreviations such as "ad," "cite," "exam," "memo," "quote" (as a noun), and "&" in formal legal writing. Use the more formal, full name: "advertisement," "citation," "examination," "memorandum," "quotation," and "and."

Dates

Do not abbreviate dates. Write them out in full.

Monday, February 13, 2006, *not*
Mon. Feb. 13, '06

Abbreviations Between Lines or Pages

Do not separate parts of an abbreviation. The full abbreviation should be on one line on one page.

Beginnings of Sentences

Avoid beginning a sentence with an abbreviation unless the abbreviation is a courtesy title (Mr., Mrs., Ms., Dr., Messrs.).

---

9. According to *The Bluebook* Rule 6.2(a), numbers from zero to ninety-nine are written out and larger numbers use numerals, unless the number begins a sentence. Numbers used at the beginning of a sentence must be written out.

Titles

Most titles other than Mr., Mrs., Ms., Dr., and Messrs. are not abbreviated.

Professor John Q. LaFond
General Tommy Franks

When "Honorable" and "Reverend" are preceded by "The," then "Honorable" and "Reverend" are spelled out; when used without "The," they can be abbreviated.

The Reverend James P. Coyne　*but*　Rev. James P. Coyne
The Honorable Walter Jackson　*but*　Hon. Walter Jackson

§ 29.3.4 General Rules for Symbols

Rule 1.　Do not begin a sentence with a symbol. "Section" and "paragraph" are always spelled out at the beginning of a sentence.

Section 289 was amended in 1989, *not*
§ 289 was amended in 1989.

The symbol for "section," §, or §§ for "sections," must be used in footnotes or citations as long as the symbol does not begin a sentence. Be sure to separate the symbol from the number following it with a space.

Rule 2.　Use the symbol for dollar ($) and percent (%) with numerals. Spell out the words if the numbers are spelled out.

fifteen dollars　　*or*　　$15.00
sixty percent　　*or*　　60%

There is no space between $ or % and their accompanying numerals.

§ 29.4　Italics

In legal writing, italics are most commonly used for case names, titles of publications, foreign phrases, introductory signals, and, occasionally, emphasis. Underlining is an acceptable substitute, and some firms and indeed some courts prefer underlining for case names.

Rule 1.　All case names, including the v.,[10] should be in italics.

Smith v. Jones
United States v. Foster

If underlining is used, underline the blank spaces between the words.

Smith v. Jones
United States v. Foster

---

10. Some attorneys do not italicize the *v.*, presumably because the Supreme Court of the United States does not. *The Bluebook* and *ALWD Citation Manual* rules, however, require that the *v.* be italicized.

Rule 2. Italicize all introductory signals, phrases introducing related authority, and explanatory phrases in citations. (See *The Bluebook* or the *ALWD Citation Manual* for a complete list.)

Accord	*See also*	*Cf.*	*E.g.,*
aff'd	*cert. denied*	*rev'd*	*withdrawn*
cited with		*construed in*	
approval in			

"See" is not italicized when it is used in text, rather than as part of the citation, to introduce an authority.

Rule 3. Italicize all titles of publications when they appear in text. (See *The Bluebook* or the *ALWD Citation Manual* for titles in citations.) Titles of books, reports, periodicals, newspapers, and plays are all italicized when they appear in textual sentences. Even titles of nonprint media, such as television and radio programs, musical works, and works of visual art are italicized.

Handbook of Federal Indian Law
Index to Legal Periodicals
Yale Law Review
New York Times
Presumed Innocent
Law and Order

The Bible, however, is not italicized.

Rule 4. Italicize names of aircraft, ships, and trains.

        Hindenburg   *Nimitz*   *Orient Express*

Rule 5. Italicize foreign words that are not incorporated into the English language.

carpe diem
qua
infra
supra

Rule 6. Italics may be used to indicate that a word is being used as a word.

Article 6 is silent about what constitutes *service* as opposed to *merchandise*.

Rule 7. If used sparingly, italics may be used for emphasis.

Italics for Emphasis

EXAMPLE

Fremont's coach insists that he asked *all* of his players to participate in the drug-testing program.

Use of italics or underlining for emphasis occurs most commonly in long quotations. In such cases, the writer must indicate whether the emphasis was added or whether it was part of the original quotation.

EXAMPLE

Italics for Emphasis Added

The relevant portion of § 2339B reads as follows:

§ 2339B. Providing material support or resources to designated foreign terrorist organizations

    (a) Prohibited activities.

        (1) Unlawful conduct. Whoever knowingly provides material support or resources to a foreign terrorist organization, or attempts or conspires to do so, shall be fined under this title or imprisoned not more than 15 years, or both, and, if the death of any person results, shall be imprisoned for any term of years or for life. *To violate this paragraph, a person must have knowledge that the organization is a designated terrorist organization..., that the organization has engaged or engages in terrorist activity..., or that the organization has engaged or engages in terrorism....*

    . . . .

    (g) Definitions. As used in this section — ...

    . . . .

        (4) the term "material support or resources" has the same meaning given that term in section 2339A (including the definitions of "training" and "expert advice or assistance" in that section); ...

    . . . .

    (i) Rule of construction. *Nothing in this section shall be construed or applied so as to abridge the exercise of rights guaranteed under the First Amendment to the Constitution of the United States.*

18 U.S.C.A. § 2339B (West, Westlaw through P.L. No. 109-3) (emphasis added).

---

§ 29.5 Conventions of Formal Writing

The conventions of formal writing apply to legal writing, particularly briefs and memoranda. Consequently, some practices that are acceptable in informal writing or oral language are generally considered inappropriate in formal legal documents.

§ 29.5.1 Use of First-Person Pronouns

Although in recent years there has been a bit more acceptance of first-person pronouns (I, me, my, we, our, us) in legal writing, most legal writers still use only third person in legal memoranda and briefs.

"Our" is fairly well accepted when used in office memos to refer to the client's case ("in our case"), although purists still prefer that the client's name be used ("in Brown's case"). "My" is well accepted in client letters ("in my opinion"), and many attorneys use other first-person pronouns throughout client letters ("I received your letter"; "please call me if you have any questions").

§ 29.5.2 Use of Contractions

Contractions are closely associated with the informality of most oral language. For this reason, there has been strong resistance to the use of contractions in legal writing. Occasionally, you will see a contraction used in a client letter, but these instances are not the norm. As a general rule, avoid contractions in all legal writing.

§ 29.5.3 Use of Numbers

The Bluebook sets the standard for what is the acceptable way to write numbers in legal writing. In a nutshell, the rule is to spell out numbers from zero to ninety-nine in text and from zero to nine in the content of a footnote. For larger numbers, use numerals unless the number begins a sentence or the number is a round number (hundred, thousand).

If a series of numbers includes one or more numbers that should be written with numerals, then numerals should be used for the entire series.

Numerals for Entire Series   EXAMPLE

The dispatch operator received 104 calls on Friday, 72 calls on Saturday, and 11 calls on Sunday.

Numerals should be used with numbers that contain a decimal point, with numbers used for sections or subdivisions, and in contexts in which numbers are used frequently to refer to percentages and dollar amounts.

§ 29.5.4 Use of Questions and Exclamations

As a general rule, avoid questions in legal writing. With the exception of the question presented, or issue statement, sentences in legal writing are almost always statements, not questions or exclamations.

When you want to use a question, revise the question into a statement that says, in effect, this question exists.

Question   EXAMPLE

Will the court apply the center of activity test or the nerve center test?

Revised

The question is whether the court will apply the center of activity test or the nerve center test.z

---

When you are tempted to use a rhetorical question, revise that point into a positive assertion or statement.

Question

How can the police do their job if they are not allowed to stop suspects who match an eyewitness's description?

Revised

The police will be unable to do their job if they are not allowed to stop suspects who match an eyewitness's description.

Exclamatory statements may appear to be forceful and therefore persuasive, but they often achieve the opposite effect. Instead of strengthening a position, exclamatory statements may weaken it because they make the writer appear unsophisticated, immature, or inflammatory. As a general rule, then, unless you are quoting another person, do not use exclamatory sentences.

Legal Writing for English-as-a-Second-Language Students

Introduction

Legal writing courses are challenging for native speakers of English who have spent their lives immersed in a culture heavily influenced by the United States legal system. Even for these law students, some of the terminology of legal prose is new, and many of the conventions are unfamiliar.

If you are an English-as-a-second-language (ESL) law student, you have two additional language-related challenges. First, there are numerous grammatical rules that native speakers have internalized but that non-native speakers must still learn. The first half of this chapter focuses on three grammatical areas that many ESL law students find difficult: articles, verbs, and prepositions.

Second, if you are an ESL law student who was raised in a different culture, you will have naturally internalized your native culture's approach to writing. Consequently, as an ESL law student, you will face a second challenge: learning how native speakers of English, particularly those in the United States legal culture, approach writing. These different approaches to writing, or what we will call "rhetorical preferences," tend to affect the whole piece of writing and include such things as what is assumed about the writer-reader relationship, how direct and explicit writers are when they explain and support their arguments, and what writing patterns are commonplace and expected. The second half of this chapter addresses how the rhetorical preferences in the United States and particularly in the legal culture may differ from the rhetorical preferences of other cultures.

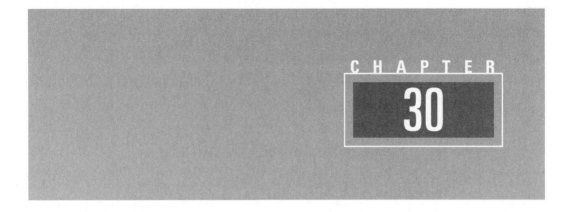

Grammar and Rhetoric for ESL Law Students

§ 30.1 Grammar Rules for Non-Native Speakers of English

This section will address the most common grammatical problems for ESL law students: (1) how articles are used; (2) how auxiliary, or helping, verbs change meaning; (3) which form of the verb to match with certain auxiliary verbs; (4) which verb tense to use in certain sentence structures; (5) which verbs commonly used in law are followed by objects, gerunds, or infinitives; and (6) which prepositions follow certain verbs, adjectives, and nouns commonly used in law.

§ 30.1.1 Articles

Errors in the use of articles ("a," "an," and "the") are distracting to many readers. Too many missing or incorrect articles draw attention away from content and toward the errors. Consequently, most ESL law students find that if they want their writing to be considered professional, they must devote time and energy to mastering the use of articles in English.

One of the simplest and most effective strategies for learning the correct use of articles is to note how they are used in judicial opinions and other writing about law. Many ESL law students simply memorize phrases and law terminology, including how articles are used in these phrases and with these terms, from the writing of capable native speakers.

A second strategy is to learn the rules governing the use of articles in English. Unfortunately for most ESL law students, many of their native languages do not use articles, and others use articles in ways that are different from English. As a result, most ESL law students cannot rely on their native languages to help them with the rules of English articles. Instead they must learn the general rules and then be aware that there are still many exceptions.

Chart 30.1 is a decision tree that summarizes the following discussion about how to use articles with common nouns in English.

a. "A" and "An"

Rule 1.   Use the indefinite articles "a" and "an"[1] with count nouns when the noun is singular and when the reader does not know the specific identity of the noun.

"Count nouns"[2] refer to persons, places, or things that can be counted. Count nouns have both a singular and plural form.

EXAMPLES

Singular Form of Count Nouns

a contract   an easement   a trial court   an appellate court
one juror

Plural Form of Count Nouns

contracts   easements   trial courts   appellate courts
twelve jurors

Non-Count Nouns

anger   equipment   harassment   insurance
pollution science   testimony   wealth

See Exercise 30A in the *Practice Book*.

Remember that "a" and "an" are only used (1) with the singular form of a count noun (2) when the reader does not know the specific identity of that noun. The second part of the rule usually applies when a particular noun is mentioned for the first time in the writing because at that point the reader does not know the specific identity of the noun.

---

1. "A" is used before consonant sounds; "an" is used brfore vowel sounds. Examples: "a jury," "a contract," "an assault," "an incident," "an unusual request," "an alleged victim," "an hour," "an honest man" ("h" is silent in "hour" and "honest"), "a unique opportunity," "a university," "a unit" "a unanimous jury" ("u" has the consonant "y" sound in "unique," "university," "unit," and "unanimous"), and "a one-hour delay" ("o" has "w" sound in "one"). See Glossary of Usage on **a/an**.

2. Many nouns like "paper" can be used as count or non-count nouns, depending on the particular sense in which they are used. Most ESL dictionaries indicate wheather a noun is a count or non-count noun and, for nouns that can be both, under which meanings the noun is a count or non-count noun.

Chart 30.1 — Decision Tree and General Definitions for Articles in English

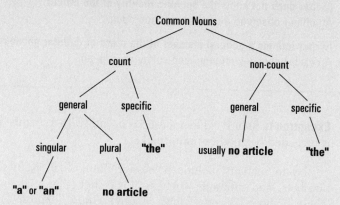

Step 1:   Decide if the noun is a count or non-count noun.

Step 2:   If the noun is a count noun, decide if the use of the noun is general or specific. If the use is specific, usually "the" is the correct article. Rule 3.

Step 3:   If the use of a count noun is general, decide if the noun is singular or plural. If the noun is singular, usually "a" or "an" is the correct article. Rule 1. If the noun is plural, usually no article is needed. Rule 4.

Step 4:   If the noun is a non-count noun, decide if its use is general or specific. If the use is general, usually no article is needed. Rule 2. If the use is specific, use "the." Rule 3.

Count nouns refer to persons, places, or things that can be counted. Count nouns have both a singular and plural form.

a contract	contracts	an appellate	appellate courts
an easement	easements	court	
a trial court	trial courts	one juror	twelve jurors

Non-count nouns refer to entities or abstractions that cannot be counted.

negligence   evidence   violence   arson   discretion

General use of a noun usually occurs the first time a noun is used in a given context. General use of a noun also occurs when the writer intends any one of a group or class.

Specific use of a noun usually occurs for any one of the following reasons:

1. The noun has already been used once in a given context;
2. The noun is followed by a phrase or clause that restricts its identity;
3. The noun is preceded by a superlative or a ranking adjective;
4. The writer and the reader have shared knowledge about the identity of the noun.

Specific nouns will have a specific answer to the question "which one (or ones)?"

"A" with Singular Count Noun

EXAMPLE

(assume "truck" is being mentioned for the first time)
A truck slowly approached.

Rule 1 also applies when the specific identity of the noun is unknown to the writer or when the writer intends to name a general member of a class or group.

Use of "A"/"An"

(writer does not know the specific identity of the officer)
<u>An</u> officer observed a truck slowly approach.

(writer intends a general member of the class of cellular phones)
<u>A</u> cellular phone is often a good safety precaution.

Exception to Rule 1:   Do not use "a" or "an" with a singular count noun that is preceded by another noun marker.

Noun markers include possessive nouns like "Kelly's" or "Florida's," numbers, and pronouns such as "his," "her," "its," "their," "this," "that," "these," "those," "every," "few," "many," "more," "most," "much," "either," "neither," "each," "any," "all," "no," "several," and "some."

Incorrect

A this officer observed a truck slowly approach.
("this" is a noun marker, so "a" should be omitted)

An one officer observed a truck slowly approach.
("one" is a noun marker, so "an" should be omitted)

Correct

This officer observed a truck slowly approach.
One officer observed a truck slowly approach.

Other common exceptions to Rule 1 include many prepositional phrases that are idiomatic expressions.

on vacation	by plane	by car	at home	in school
to bed	to college	in class	at night	at school
in bed				

No Article with Idioms

The defendant testified that he was <u>at home</u> by 8 p.m. and <u>in bed</u> by 8:30 p.m.

Rule 2.   Do not use "a" or "an" with non-count nouns.
"Non-count" nouns refer to abstractions that cannot be counted. Non-count nouns do not have a plural form.

Non-Count Nouns

negligence   evidence   violence   arson   discretion

However, if an amount of a non-count noun is expressed by adding a quantifier, then an article is used before the quantifier.

a piece of evidence   an act of violence

In most instances, the following words are non-count nouns.

Nouns naming drinks and food

water, milk, coffee, tea, wine, juice
fruit, fish, beef, chicken, meat

Nouns naming generalized objects

ammunition, clothing, equipment, freight, furniture, jewelry, luggage, lumber, machinery, mail, money, propaganda, scenery, stationery, traffic, vegetation

Nouns naming substances, matter, or material

(asterisks indicate the substance, not an object)
air, coal, dirt, electricity, gasoline, gold, grass, hair, ice, iron*, oil, oxygen, paper*, plastic, steel, wood

Nouns related to weather

fog, ice, rain, snow

Nouns naming subject matter

architecture, art, chemistry, civics, economics, engineering, geology, grammar, history, literature, mathematics, music, philosophy, physics, science, and all names of languages (Arabic, Chinese, English, French, German, Italian, Japanese, etc.) when they are used as nouns

Nouns related to games, sports, and recreation

(asterisks indicate the game, not an object)
baseball*, basketball*, bowling, bridge, camping, chess, dancing, football*, golf, hiking, hockey, hunting, opera, sailing, singing, soccer, swimming, tennis, television*, volleyball*

Abstract nouns

advice, anger, beauty, capitalism, communism, confidence, democracy, education, employment, energy, fun, happiness, health, help, homework, honesty, ignorance, information, intelligence, justice, kindness, knowledge, laughter, liberty, life, love, merchandise, nature, news, pollution, poverty, recreation, research, satisfaction, society (in the sense of people in general), strength, technology, transportation, trouble, truth, violence, virtue, wealth, wisdom, work

Law-related nouns

abandonment, abatement, access, acquiescence, adultery, alimony, arson, authentication, capital (in the sense of money or property), commerce, conduct, depreciation, discretion, duress, evidence, extortion, insurance, harassment, housing, insolvency, insurance, intent, land, malice, negligence, privacy, real estate

---

EXAMPLES   ## No Article with Non-Count Nouns

The detective found a weapon and ammunition in the defendant's trunk.
(no article before non-count noun "ammunition")

Magistrates must exercise discretion when determining whether to authorize hidden recording devices.
(no article before non-count noun "discretion")

Gerunds[3] and gerund phrases are non-count nouns and therefore do not require "a" or "an."

EXAMPLES   ## Gerunds as Non-Count Nouns

Drowning was the cause of death.
(gerund)

Most attorneys enjoy making arguments.
        (gerund phrase)

See Exercises 30B and 30C in the *Practice Book*.

b. "The"

Rule 3.   Use the definite article "the" with count[4] and non-count nouns when the specific identity of the noun is clear to the reader.
    The specific identity of a noun can be clear to the reader for a number of reasons.

Reason #1: Readers know the specific identity of a noun after it has already been used once in a given context.

EXAMPLE   ## Switch from "A" to "The"

A truck slowly approached. An officer noticed the truck contained several garbage cans.

---

3. Gerunds are verbals that end in "-ing" and that function as nouns. Gerunds with modifying phrases fall under Rule 3 and are preceded by "the." Example: "The drowning of her second child raised the prosecutor's suspicions."
    4. Notice that this rule applies to both singular and plural count nouns.

(Use "a" before "truck" when it is first mentioned; use "the" before "truck" for subsequent references.)

Reason #2: Readers know the specific identity of a noun when it is followed by a phrase or clause that restricts or limits its identity.

Phrase Restricts Meaning

EXAMPLE

The driver of the truck appeared nervous.
(Use "the" before "driver" because "of the truck" is a phrase that restricts or limits the meaning of "driver.")

Many but not all modifying phrases and clauses that follow a noun restrict or limit the noun's identity, thereby making it specific. You can determine which "of" prepositional phrases restrict or limit the identity of a noun by testing to see if they can be changed to the possessive form. If they can be changed to the possessive form, they are restricting or limiting the noun, so "the" should precede the noun.

Restricting Phrases Can Be Possessive

EXAMPLES

the driver of the truck → the truck's driver
the cost of a trial → a trial's cost
the length of the skidmarks → the skidmarks' length

Other "of" phrases, however, do not restrict or limit the identity of a noun; they show that only a part or a measured amount of the noun is intended. These "of" phrases cannot be changed to the possessive form. Use "a" or "an" before these nouns.

Phrases That Show a Part

EXAMPLES

a pound of marijuana   a third of her salary
a slice of bread   a gallon of gasoline

Similarly, when a noun is followed by a phrase or clause that defines rather than restricts or limits, use "a" or "an" before the noun.

Phrase That Defines

EXAMPLE

A contract that has all of its terms in writing is a formal contract.
("a" is used before "contract" because "that has all of its terms in writing" defines it)

Reason #3: Readers know the specific identity of a noun when it is preceded by a superlative[5] or ranking adjective.[6]

Superlative or Ranking Adjectives

<u>The</u> best example of a public figure is a film star.
(Use "The" because "example" is preceded by the superlative "best.")

The defendant was <u>the</u> tallest man in the line-up.
(Use "the" because "man" is preceded by the superlative "tallest.")

The plaintiff will be unable to satisfy <u>the</u> third element.
(Use "the" before the ranking adjective "third.")

Reason #4: Readers know the specific identity of a noun when both the writer and the reader have shared knowledge about the identity of the noun. Shared knowledge can be universal, like knowledge of the sun, and it can be local, like knowledge of a local landmark.

Shared Knowledge About a Noun

The moon provided enough light for the officers to see the defendant open his trunk.
(Use "the" before "moon" because the writer and the reader have shared knowledge about its identity.)

Numerous gang-related activities have occurred at the shopping mall.
(Use "the" before "shopping mall" if the writer and reader have shared knowledge about its identity as a local landmark.)

One way to determine whether a noun is specific is to ask "which one (or ones)?" For specific nouns, you will have a specific answer. When you have a specific answer, use "the." For example, if the test is applied to some of the earlier example sentences, the questions and answers are as follows:

Question: Which driver?	Answer: The driver of the truck
Question: Which example?	Answer: The best example
Question: Which element?	Answer: The third element
Question: Which moon?	Answer: The moon we all know about
Question: Which shopping mall?	Answer: The shopping mall that is a local landmark

---

5. Superlatives compare the thing modified with two or more things. Superlatives include "best," "worst," words ending in -est ("biggest," "smallest," "tallest," "shortest," "wisest," "fastest," "slowest," "luckiest," "loudest"), and comparisons that use "most" or "least" ("the most beautiful," "the most egregious," "the least responsible," "the least humiliating"). Be sure not to use comparative or superlative forms with things that cannot be compared ("perfect," "unique," "pregnant," "dead," "impossible," and "infinite").

6. Ranking adjectives include sequential adjectives like "first," "second," "third," and "next," as well as adjectives that show the noun is one of a kind ("unique").

If the answer to the "which one (or ones)?" question is "any one" or "all" or "I don't know which one" or "one that has not been mentioned before," then the noun is general.

Rule 4. Do not use "the" before plural nouns meaning all in a class, all of a group, or "in general."

Omit "The" Before General Plural Nouns

Defendants have the right to an attorney.
(No "the" before "defendants" because it is plural and all defendants are intended, but "an" before "attorney" because it is singular and no specific attorney is intended.)

Appellate courts do not re-try the facts of a case.
(No "the" before "appellate courts" because it is plural and the intended meaning is appellate courts "in general"; "the" before "facts" because the restricting phrase "of a case" makes it specific, and "a" before "case" because it is singular and no specific case is intended.)

Rule 5. Do not use "the" before most singular proper nouns, including names of persons, streets, parks, cities, states, continents, and most countries.

Omit "The" Before Singular Proper Nouns

Smith was last seen in Yellowstone National Park.

Jones offered trips to New York City, Florida, Germany, and Uganda as sales incentives.

The possessive form of a singular name is also not preceded by "the."

Omit "The" Before Possessive

Mr. Hempstead learned of the affair by reading Carol's diary.
(No "the" before possessive "Carol's")

Notice, however, that the plural form of proper nouns that are family names is preceded by "the." See Rule 7.

"The" Before Plural Family Names

The Smiths were last seen in Yellowstone National Park.

Rule 6. Use "the" with proper nouns containing the word "of," a political word like "kingdom," "union," or "republic," or organizational words like "institute," "foundation," or "corporation."

EXAMPLES   **"The" Before Political/Organization Words**

the city[7] of Los Angeles   the Republic of Korea
the University of Notre Dame   the Ford Foundation
the Boeing Corporation   the Commonwealth of Virginia

Notice that many things have two proper noun names and that "the" is only used with the form containing "of" or the political or organizational word.

the city of Los Angeles   *but*   Los Angeles
the Republic of Korea   *but*   Korea
the University of Notre Dame   *but*   Notre Dame
the Ford Foundation   *but*   Ford
the Boeing Corporation   *but*   Boeing
the Commonwealth of Virginia   *but*   Virginia

Do not use "the" with names of universities, colleges, or schools unless the name is written with an "of."

EXAMPLES   **When to Use "The" with Schools**

Harvard University Law School   the School of Law
Smith College   the College of Engineering

Rule 7. Use "the" before most plural proper nouns, including the plural form of a family name.

EXAMPLES   **"The" with Proper Names**

the United States   the United Nations   the Bahamas
the Rockies   the Philippines   the Cayman Islands
the Smiths   the Joneses

Rule 8. Use "the" before the names of most bodies of water and the names of specific geographic regions.

---

7. Words like "city" are usually, but not always, written in lowercase when they precede the noun and when they appear in text. In citations, however, capitalize geographic terms like "city." See Rule 10.2.1(f) in *The Bluebook*.

"The" with Geographic Terms

the Atlantic Ocean   the Mississippi River   the Persian Gulf
the Southwest   the Midwest   the Middle East

See Exercise 30D in the *Practice Book*.

c. No Article

Rule 9.   Do not use "a," "an," or "the" before non-count nouns used in a general sense or plural common nouns used in a general sense.

No Article

Information can lead to justice.
(No article before non-count nouns "information" and "justice.")

Expert witnesses have become common in courtrooms.
(No article before plural nouns "expert witnesses" or "courtrooms.")

See Exercise 30E in the *Practice Book*.

§ 30.1.2 Verbs

Verbs present many challenges to both native and non-native speakers of English. Some of these challenges are addressed in other chapters. (Sections 27.3.1 and 27.3.2 discuss verb tense and mood, section 27.4.1 discusses subject-verb agreement, section 24.1 discusses active and passive voice, and sections 24.3 and 24.4 discuss action verbs and the distance between subjects and verbs.)

As an English-as-a-second-language law student, you also need to pay special attention to verb phrases that contain auxiliary, or helping, verbs and verb tense in conditional and speculative sentences. In addition, you will need to learn which verbs commonly used in legal writing are followed by gerunds, infinitives, and objects.

a. Verbs with Auxiliary, or Helping, Verbs

Unlike article errors, errors in verbs often change the meaning and are therefore much more serious. Fortunately, few ESL law students have difficulty with the main verbs in English verb phrases. The challenge is to learn the subtle yet often significant differences in meanings that auxiliary, or helping, verbs add to the main part of the verb phrase.

For example, "can" (or "cannot") before a verb shows ability or knowledge.

"Can" Shows Ability

Despite his back injury, the plaintiff can still drive a semi-truck.
("Can" indicates the ability to drive.)

"Can" is also used to suggest that the action is a possibility or an option.

"Can" Shows Possibility

The defendant can argue that *Smith* applies.
("Can" indicates the possibility of the defendant arguing that Smith *applies.)*

Chart 30.2 lists the most common meanings for many auxiliary, or helping, verbs.

In addition to learning how meanings change based on auxiliary, or helping, verbs, ESL law students have to master which form of the verb to use with various helping verbs.

Auxiliary, or helping, verbs that are followed by the base form

Use the base form of a verb after the following auxiliary, or helping, verbs: "can," "could," "do," "does," "did," "may," "might," "must," "shall," "should," "will," and "would."

Helping Verbs + Base Form

| can argue | could deny | did object | may plead |
| might consider | must rely | should admit | will determine |

Auxiliary, or helping, verbs that are followed by objects and then the base form

A few verbs ("make," "let," and "have") must be followed by a noun or pronoun object and then by the base form of a verb.

Verbs + Objects + Base Form

The children's father lets <u>them</u> <u>leave</u> for school without eating breakfast.
(pronoun) (base form)

The mother makes the <u>children</u> <u>do</u> their homework.
(noun) (base form)

The verb "help" can be followed by a noun or pronoun and then a base form or the infinitive form of a verb.

"Help" + Object + Base Form

Both parents helped the children <u>learn</u> different sports.
(base form)
Both parents helped the children <u>to learn</u> different sports.
(infinitive)

Chart 30.2   Common Meanings for Auxiliary, or Helping, Verbs

Auxiliary Verb	Meanings	Example Sentences
can	shows ability or knowledge	Despite his back injury, the plaintiff can still drive a semi-truck.
	suggests possibility	The defendant can argue that *Smith* applies.
	gives an option	The prosecutor can charge the defendant with first- or second-degree murder.
could	shows past ability	Before his back injury, the plaintiff could drive a semi-truck.
	shows possibility	The defendant could argue that *Smith* applies.
could have	suggests past opportunity that was missed	The plaintiff could have learned to drive a semi-truck, but he cannot now because of his back injury.
may	asks or gives permission	Students may leave the campus during the lunch hour.
	shows possibility	The court may grant a motion to dismiss.
might	shows possibility	The court might grant a motion to dismiss.
should	shows advisability or expectation	The court should grant a motion to continue when the State amends a change the day before trial.
	shows obligation	The court should instruct the jury to disregard that remark.
	shows expectation	You should receive the signed agreement in tomorrow's mail.
should have	shows obligation that was not met	The court should have instructed the jury to disregard that remark, but it failed to do so.
	shows expectation that was not met	You should have already received the signed agreement in the mail; I do not know why it is late.
	shows advisability after the fact	The officer should have handcuffed the suspect, but he did not.
ought to	shows advisability or expectation	The court ought to grant a motion to continue when the State amends a change the day before trial.
	shows obligation	The court ought to instruct the jury to disregard that remark.
	shows expectation	You ought to receive the signed agreement in tomorrow's mail.
ought to have	shows obligation that was not met	The court ought to have instructed the jury to disregard that remark, but it failed to do so.
	shows expectation that was not met	You ought to have received the signed agreement in yesterday's mail; I do not know why it is late.
	shows advisability after the fact	The officer ought to have handcuffed the suspect, but he did not.

CHART 30.2	*(continued)*	
Auxillary Verb	*Meanings*	*Example Sentences*
must	shows requirement	The court must ask the defendant how she pleads.
	shows probability	The defendant must be considering a plea bargain.
must not	shows prohibition	The prosecution must not suggest that the defendant's post-arrest silence implies guilt.
will	shows future	The verdict will be announced after the parties return to the courtroom.
	shows a promise or willingness	Acme will clean up the toxic waste site.
would	indicates a repeated past action	The arsonist would often warn his victims.
	indicates a future act in a past tense sentence	The arsonist warned his victims that he would set fire to the building.

<u>Auxiliary, or helping, verbs that are followed by the past participle of the verb</u>

Use the past participle of a verb with "have," "has," or "had."

EXAMPLES   **"Have," "Has," "Had" + Past Participle**

have determined   has begun   had stolen   has written

<u>Auxiliary, or helping, verbs that are followed by the present participle of the verb</u>

Use the present participle of a verb after forms of "be," including "am," "are," "is," "was," "were," "have been," and "had been."

EXAMPLES   **Helping Verbs + Present Participle**

are relying   is considering   was driving

See Exercises 30F and 30G in the *Practice Book.*

b. Verb Tense in Conditional Sentences

Lawyers frequently use conditional sentences to express possibilities or to suggest what might happen in the future. "If" and "unless" clauses are commonly used either before or after the main clause. Use present tense in the "if" or "unless" clause and future tense in the main clause.

Conditional Sentences

If the court <u>applies</u> the *Reed* test, it <u>will find</u> that the element is met.
       (present tense)   *(future tense)*

The prosecutor <u>will charge</u> the defendant with arson unless she <u>has</u> an alibi.
     (future tense)   *(present tense)*

---

c. Verb Tense in Speculative Sentences

To show that an outcome is possible but unlikely, use past tense in an "if" clause and "would" "could," or "might" as the auxiliary, or helping, verb in the main clause.

Speculative Sentences

If the witness <u>saw</u> the defendant's car at the accident scene, he would have also seen
        (past tense)
the defendant.

The jury might ignore its instructions if it <u>believed</u> the police fabricated the evidence.
                                        (past tense)

To speculate about something that did not happen, use the past perfect tense in an "if" clause and "would have," "could have," or "might have" as auxiliary, or helping, verbs with the past participle. Remember that "had" is the helping verb that creates the past perfect tense.

Speculative Sentences

If the defendant had spoken to Mr. Torres, he would have apologized to him, not threatened him.

The tenants could have complained to the building superintendent if he had been accessible.

To express conditions that are contrary to fact, use "were" in an "if" clause and "would," "could," or "might" in the main clause.

Contrary to Fact

If I were you, I might try apologizing to the plaintiff.

If Mrs. Henderson were alive, she would not want the jury to find the defendant guilty of manslaughter.

d. Verbs Plus Gerunds, Infinitives, or Objects

Some verbs should be followed by gerunds (a verb form ending in "-ing" and used as a noun); other verbs should be followed by infinitives (a verb form made up of "to" plus the base form of the verb); others require objects (nouns or pronouns); and some verbs can be followed by either a gerund or an infinitive.[8] Some ESL law students may find that the most effective strategy for determining whether to use an infinitive or a gerund after a certain verb is to apply the "Bolinger principle," which is to use infinitives to express something "hypothetical, future, unfulfilled" and to use gerunds to express something "real, vivid, fulfilled." (Bolinger, 1968)

EXAMPLES   **Bolinger Principle**

The defendant wants <u>to enter</u> a plea of not guilty.
(The sentence expresses an as yet unfulfilled action so the infinitive is used.)

The defendant admits <u>hitting</u> the pedestrian.
(The sentence expresses a past action so the gerund is used.)

The neighbors hope <u>to obtain</u> an easement.
(The sentence expresses a future action so the infinitive is used.)

His responsibilities include <u>hiring</u> employees.
(The sentence expresses a real, not a hypothetical action.)

Exceptions

Unfortunately, the Bolinger principle does not apply to approximately one-fourth of the verbs in question, including the following verbs:

<u>Verbs that are exceptions to the Bolinger principle and use gerunds:</u>

anticipate, consider, delay, envision, imagine, keep, mind, postpone, recommend, risk, suggest, understand

<u>Verbs that are exceptions to the Bolinger principle and use infinitives:</u>

claim, continue, fail, get, have, hire, manage, teach, tell

EXAMPLES   **Exceptions to the Bolinger Principle**

Her attorney will recommend <u>accepting</u> the offer.
(gerund)
(Sentence expresses a future action but still uses a gerund after the verb.)

The officer managed <u>to distract</u> the gunman.
(infinitive)
(Sentence expresses a past action but still uses an infinitive after the verb.)

---

8. Most verbs can also be followed by "that" clauses.

Consequently, many ESL law students may prefer using lists that group verbs according to what must follow them. Below are lists of verbs commonly used in law grouped by what follows them. The patterns for each combination are in boldface type.

Verbs that are usually followed by a gerund rather than an infinitive.[9]

(**verb** + _____**-ing**)

acknowledge	justify
admit	keep
advocate	resent
anticipate	keep on
appreciate	mention
approve	mind
avoid	miss
begrudge	necessitate
cannot help	postpone
complete	practice
condemn	put off
consider	quit
contemplate	recall
defend	recollect
defer	recommend
delay	resent
deny	relinquish
detest	relish
disclaim	renounce
discuss	report
dislike	resist
enjoy	resume
entail	risk
escape	sanction
evade	shirk
facilitate	suggest
finish	tolerate
get through	understand
give up	visualize
imagine	withhold
involve	witness

Verb + Gerund   EXAMPLE

The defendant admits <u>knowing</u> the victim, but he denies <u>killing</u> him.
             (gerund)   *(gerund)*

---

9. Although gerunds rather than infinitives often follow these verbs, using a gerund is not required. Many of these verbs are followed by "that" clauses.

Some verbs can be immediately followed by an infinitive; others are followed by an object and then an infinitive; still other verbs can be followed by either an object or an infinitive. When an object is between the verb and the infinitive, the object performs the action of the infinitive.

Verbs that can be followed by either an infinitive or a "that" clause with little or no change in meaning are indicated by an asterisk.

Verbs that are usually followed by an infinitive rather than a gerund.

(**verb** + to _____)

agree*	know how
appear	learn
arrange	manage
ask	need
attempt	offer
bother	plan
care	prepare
claim	pretend*
condescend	promise*
consent	refuse
decide*	say
demand	seem
deserve	struggle
desire	swear
endeavor	tend
expect	threaten
fail	venture
happen	volunteer
have	want
hesitate	wait
hope*	wish

EXAMPLES   **Verb + Infinitive**

The workers expect _to reconcile_ their differences with management.
        (infinitive)

Management plans <u>to offer</u> them a contract with a 5% salary increase.
        (infinitive)

The mediator hoped <u>to extend</u> the negotiation deadline.
(verb followed by infinitive "to extend")

The mediator hoped that the negotiation deadline would be extended.
(verb followed by "that" clause)

Verbs that can be followed by either a gerund or an infinitive:

A few verbs can be followed by either a gerund or infinitive with little change in meaning.

(<u>verb</u> + _____ -ing OR verb + to_____)

abhor	disdain
afford	dread
attempt	endure
bear	go
begin	hate
cannot bear	intend
cannot stand	like
cease	love
choose	neglect
commence	propose
continue	scorn
decline	start

Verb + Infinitive or Gerund

EXAMPLES

Landowners continue <u>to assert</u> their rights.
            (infinitive)

Landowners continue <u>asserting</u> their rights.
            (gerund)

A few verbs can be followed by a gerund or infinitive but with a significant change in meaning. One common pattern, which is supported by the Bolinger principle (infinitive expresses fulfilled action, gerund expresses unfulfilled action), is that when the verb is followed by a gerund, past time is indicated; when the verb is followed by an infinitive, future time is indicated.

forget   prefer   regret   remember   sense   stop   try

Meaning Changes

EXAMPLES

Mrs. Warren remembered <u>locking</u> the safe.
            (gerund)
(She has a past memory of locking the safe.)

Mrs. Warren remembered <u>to lock</u> the safe.
            (infinitive)
(She did not forget to lock the safe.)

Mrs. Warren must remember <u>to lock</u> the safe.
            (infinitive)
(She must remember this for the future.)

Verbs usually followed by objects, then infinitives (except in the passive[10] voice):

(**verb** + (**object**) + **to** _____)

advise	oblige
allow	order
appoint	permit
authorize	persuade
cause	remind
challenge	request
command	require
convince	select
encourage	teach
forbid	tell
force	tempt
get	train
hire	trust
instruct	urge
invite	warn

EXAMPLES   **Verb + Object + Infinitive**

Opposing counsel will advise her client to settle.
              (verb)   (object) (infinitive)

The judge permitted the prosecutor to ask questions about prior convictions.
              (verb)   (object)   (infinitive)

Acme encouraged its employees to participate in the political campaign.
        (verb)   (object)   (infinitive)

Acme instructed them to use their lunch hour stuffing envelopes.
        (verb) (object)(infinitive)

Employees were permitted to attend the rally.
              (passive verb) (infinitive)

(No noun or pronoun before infinitive because verb is in passive voice.)

Verbs that can be followed by either an object or an infinitive

(**verb** + (**object**)) OR (**verb** + **to** _____)

ask	need
beg	prefer
choose	prepare
dare	promise
expect	want

10. In passive voice the action of the verb is done to the subject. Example: The motion was denied. In the example, "was denied" is done to "the motion." In active voice, the subject performs the action in the verb. Example: The judge denied the motion. In this example, the judge is doing the denying. See section 24.1 for an extensive discussion of passive and active vioce.

help   wish
intend   would like
like

Verb + Object or Infinitive

The landlord expected the tenants to check the batteries in the smoke detectors.
(Object "the tenants" follows "expected.")

The landlord expected to hear tenants complain about the rent increase.
(Infinitive "to hear" follows "expected.")

Verbs followed by "too," "enough," and "how" expressions and an infinitive

Use infinitives when expressions with "too," "enough," or "how" follow a verb.

"Too," "Enough," "How" + Infinitive

The police arrived too late to apprehend the burglar.
("too" expression followed by infinitve "to apprehend")

The defendant is not strong enough to kick that door down.
("enough" expression followed by infinitive "to kick")

A 20-year-old woman knows how to protect herself.
("how" expression followed by infinitive "to protect")

See Exercise 30H in the *Practice Book.*

e. Two- or Three-Word Verbs

Learning which prepositions[11] to use in two- or three-word verbs, or phrasal verbs, is crucial because the prepositions in these verbs often completely change the meaning of the verb.

Phrasal Verbs

One-Word Verb	*Meaning of One-Word Verb*
"catch"	find and stop
Two-Word Verb	*Meaning of Two-Word Verb*
"catch up"	to improve and reach the same standard
Three-Word Verb	*Meaning of Three-Word Verb*
"catch up with"	to come from behind and reach OR to find someone doing something illegal and punish that person

---

11. The prepositions in phrasal verbs are often called particles.

Because there are so many two- or three-word verbs in English and because several of them (like "catch up with") have different meanings for different contexts, the best strategy for learning them is to note how they are used in native speakers' oral and written language. In addition, note that most of these verbs have more formal synonyms that are preferred in legal writing.

Phrasal Verbs

The brief must be *turned in* by 5:00. → The brief must be *submitted* by 5:00.

The protester *handed out* leaflets. → The protester *distributed* leaflets.

The attorney *put off* the meeting. → The attorney *postponed* the meeting.

Firefighters *put out* the blaze. → Firefighters *extinguished* the blaze.

§ 30.1.3 Prepositions

The preceding section discussed two- or three-word verbs in which the addition of one or more prepositions made a significant change to the base verb's meaning. Other English verbs, adjectives, and nouns must also be followed by specific prepositions. Unfortunately, prepositional use is idiomatic and not based on rules. Consequently, we have resorted to alphabetical lists of verbs, adjectives, and nouns commonly used in legal writing and their correct prepositions. When more than one preposition can be used with a given verb, adjective, or noun, the different preposition choices are separated by slash (/) marks. Parentheses show the types of words that may follow a given preposition. Brackets indicate meaning. Some verbs are in their present tense form; others are in their past tense form.

a. Prepositions That Follow Verbs Commonly Used in Law

absolved from (wrongdoing)
absolved of (financial liability)
accompanied by
accused of
acquainted with
acquiesced in/to
adhered to
affected by
agree on (a contract, a date)
agree to [means "to acquiesce"]
agree with [means "to be in accord with" or "have the same opinion"]
allude to
amenable to

apply for (a position)
apply to
approve of [means to find something good or suitable]
attribute to
based on/upon
blamed for
caused by
charge at/toward/into
charge with (murder)
comment on
commit to
communicate to [means to express thoughts or feelings]

communicate with [used when two people understand thoughts or feelings]

compare to [used with similarities]

compare with [used with similarities and differences]

compensate for

compete for/against

compete with

complain about

composed of

confined to

consent to

contrast with [used with differences]

convicted of (crimes)

convicted on (counts)

cooperate with

covered with

decide for/against (the plaintiff)

decide in favor of (the plaintiff)

decide on (a date)

derived from

discriminate against

distinguish between/from

divided into

divorced from

experiment with (drugs)

fill in (a hole or crack)

filled out (an application)

filled up (a tank)

filled with (sound, light, emotion)

finished with

founded by (a person)

founded in (a date)

founded on [means the main idea that something else develops from]

free from/to

gain access to

impressed by/with

informed about [means to give information]

informed on [used when information is given to police or an enemy]

interfere with

object to

participate in

prevent from

prohibit from

protect against/from

questioned about/concerning

reach (a conclusion) about

reach for (a gun)

recover from

refer to

rely on/upon

rescue from

resigned from

respond to

save for [means to keep money to use for a specific purpose]

save from (harm or danger)

suffer from

suspected of

worry about

b. Prepositions That Follow Adjectives Commonly Used in Law

accustomed to

afraid of

amazed at

angry about/at/over/with

anxious about

appreciative of

appropriate for

ashamed of

averse to

aware of

bad at

bored with

capable of

careful about/with

certain about/of

clever at

comparable to/with

concerned about/with

confident about

confused about

conscious of

consistent with

c. Prepositions That Follow Nouns Commonly Used in Law

access to
amendment to
approval of
attempt at
authority on [area of expertise]
belief in
choice between/of
commitment to
complaint about/against
concern about/for/over
confidence in
confusion about/as to/over
dedication of/to
difference among (three or more)
difference between (two)
division between/of
doubt about/as to
effect of/on
experience in/of/with
explanation for/of
fear for/of
idea about/for/of
knowledge about/of

liability for
means of
need for
in need of
objection to
opposition to
participation in
possibility for/of
preference for
prevention of
process of
protection against/from
reason for
reference to
reliance on
respect for/of
response to
responsibility for
satisfaction from/in/of
search for
skill at/in
success as/in

d. Prepositions in Idioms

during the course of (his employment)
in circumstances like (our case)
in contrast
in favor of
in light of
on the contrary

§ 30.2 Rhetorical Preferences in Writing[12]

Discourse patterns vary from language to language and from culture to culture. The way an expert writer makes a point in one culture is often quite different from how an expert writer in another culture would make the same point. Indeed, what one culture may consider a good point in a given context, another culture might consider irrelevant in the same context.

What is particularly fascinating about this phenomenon, though, is that it often goes unnoticed. In fact, most writers have internalized their own

---

12. This section concerns expository and argumentative writing, not literary prose.

culture's rhetorical preferences to the point that these preferences are sub-conscious choices. Most people seem to assume that their culture's world view and how it is expressed in writing is the way all human beings "naturally" think and write.

Because these cultural differences in discourse are so deeply embedded in language and in our subconscious, they are rarely taught to students. Most ESL law students report that their foreign language classes concentrated only on vocabulary and sentence grammar; they stopped short of addressing the larger cultural issues that affect the overall approach to writing. If this was true of your language classes, you may be unconsciously assuming that what was appropriate and conventional when writing in your native language is also appropriate and conventional when writing in English.

This section examines the rhetorical preferences in expository and argu-mentative writing in United States culture, with particular emphasis on how those preferences are manifested in legal writing. The section also compares and contrasts these preferences with some of the more common rhetorical preferences from other cultures in hopes of giving ESL law students insights about writing in English. Chart 30.5 starting on page 853 summarizes the differences between rhetorical preferences in English and those in other languages and cultures.

Remember, however, that this is a discussion of what is generally true about writing in the discourse community of United States lawyers and judges, and that in certain instances, the generalizations will not apply. For example, while it is generally true that writing that is direct is preferred in the United States legal culture, there are occasions when vagueness or indirection better serves the writer's purposes. The discussion makes similar generalizations about writing preferences in other cultures based on the research done by contrastive rhetoricians.[13] Again, like all generalizations, they may not be true in every instance, and unfortunately, the research avail-able on rhetorical preferences in other cultures is somewhat incomplete. Even more important to remember is that language, including rhetorical preferences, does not stand still. The information that follows will need con-stant updating as the rhetorical preferences of various cultures evolve.

§ 30.2.1 Cultural Assumptions About Readers and the Purposes for Writing

All cultures treat writing as an act of communication, but they differ widely in their assumptions about that communication. Some operate under the assumption that the reader bears the heavier responsibility; it is the reader who must strive to understand the writer. Other cultures operate under the assumption that the writer has the heavier responsibility; it is the writer who must strive to be understood by the reader.[14] In

---

13. The sources for the information in the following section are in two bibliographies: one for ESL law students at the end of this chapter and one for legal writing professors at the end of the Teaching Notes for Chapter 30 in the Teacher's Manual. Students who are interested in reading the source material that applies to their specific native language and culture should consult the bibliography at the end of this chapter.

14. John Hines, *Reader versus Writer Responsibility: A New Typology* in WRITING ACROSS LANGUAGES: ANALYSIS OF 2L TEXT (Ulla Connor & Robert B. Kaplan eds., 1987).

Chart 30.3   Writer-Responsible vs. Reader-Responsible

English ⇓ Writer-Responsible	Most East Asian and Middle Eastern Languages ⇓ Reader-Responsible
▪ Primary responsibility for successful communication lies with the writer. ▪ If the reader has trouble understanding, it is the writer's fault. ▪ Writers are expected to work at being clear.	▪ Primary responsibility for successful communication lies with the reader. ▪ If the reader has trouble understanding, it is his or her own fault. ▪ Writers may intentionally obscure meaning; good writing often has an element of mystery to it.
▪ Writers are expected to present their ideas in ways that can be easily understood. ▪ Writing clear sentences that can be understood the first time they are read is expected.	▪ Readers are expected to work at understanding what is written. ▪ Readers do not expect sentences that can be automatically understood the first time they are read.
▪ Being able to make a complicated topic easy for a reader to understand is admired.	▪ Not fully grasping a writer's intended meaning does not frustrate these readers.

reader-responsible cultures, writers may intentionally obscure meaning. Good writing often has an element of mystery to it. Readers are expected to work at understanding what is written. If they fail to understand, it is their fault.

In writer-responsible cultures, writers are expected to work at being clear. Good writing is not mysterious. Writers are expected to present their ideas in ways that can be easily understood. If the reader has trouble understanding, it is the writer's fault.

a. Assumptions and Expectations in the United States and in the United States Legal Culture

Because English is a writer-responsible language, the primary responsibility for successful communication lies with the writer. Writing clear sentences that can be understood the first time they are read is expected.[15] Being able to make a complicated topic easy for a reader to understand is admired.

The Reader's Time Is Valuable

An underlying assumption of the United States legal culture is that the reader's time is more valuable than the writer's time. Legal readers — including judges and partners in law firms — tend to have positions of power over the writers of legal prose: lawyers writing briefs for the court, interns and associates writing memoranda for supervising attorneys. Consequently, writers are expected to expend their time and energy writing clearly so that readers do not have to spend extra time and energy understanding.

---

15. Clarity has not always been a top priority in legal writing. In the past, consumer contracts and statutes were often written in long, complex sentences that were difficult to understand because they were filled with abstractions and other legalese. See section 25.3.

In addition, United States readers tend to be far less patient than readers from other cultures. Consequently, beginnings in writing in the United States tend to get to the point quickly. They answer the question, "What is this about?"

United States legal readers tend to expect a quick overview at the beginning of a piece of writing that sets out its content and structure. Many prefer statements of facts with an overview paragraph that introduces the parties, the legal problem, and the source of the facts. Discussion sections in legal memoranda are almost always begun by giving an overview of the law and a roadmap to its application. Even when writers must describe how the law developed over a period of time, such historical discussions tend to be brief, hitting only the high points and moving rapidly toward the current state of the law. Giving some background and context for understanding the policy underlying the law is also common, but these discussions tend to be short and to the point. In general, United States legal readers want only enough background and context for the law to deal with the case before them.

As a rule, judges are even more impatient than other United States legal readers. They are eager for brief writers to get to the application of the law to the facts. Long-winded introductions or treatises on the applicable law are likely to irritate judges who are already knowledgeable about the law and who are reading the brief with the primary purpose of thinking through how that law applies to the case before them.

Introductory paragraphs in letters to clients also tend to have some features of an overview. They may include a short, polite beginning that helps establish or reinforce the relationship between the writer and reader, but then they usually move rather quickly to stating the purpose of the letter. In many cases that means stating the legal question the client brought to the attorney and, particularly when the answer to that question is one the client will like, introducing or setting out the answer the attorney found after researching the problem.

The Reader Wants to Know What You Are Thinking; Be Direct and Explicit

To ensure that their meaning is clearly conveyed to their readers throughout a document, attorneys use two common features of the prose style in the United States: directness and explicitness. In office memos, writers are expected to be direct and candid with their readers. Writers should lay out the facts, the rules, the relevant cases, and the arguments that each side is likely to make. Writers should tell their readers when, in the writer's opinion, the court will probably find an argument weak or persuasive. Some firms also want office memoranda to include some candid strategic advice, such as whether the firm should take the case or whether settling out of court might be the client's best option.

Unfavorable facts, rules, analogous cases, and weaknesses in the client's case are dealt with openly. In most (but not all) instances, office memoranda are in-house documents that are read only by members of the firm, who want a frank and honest assessment of the situation.

Directness manifests itself in briefs when the writer tells the court exactly what he or she wants from the court (for example, denial of summary judgment, admission of some evidence). Directness may lead a brief writer to concede a point, but it does not mean that a brief writer should be neutral or lay out the opponent's arguments in a favorable light.

It is possible, of course, to be too direct with a court. Some judges and justices admit that they do not like being told by an attorney that they "must" do something even when that something is required by law. Using "should" rather than "must" in sentences like "The court should grant the motion to suppress..." or "This court should find that the trial court abused its discretion..." allows the writer to be direct without seeming to be ordering the court around. Passive voice is another way to avoid sounding like the writer is bossing the court around. Revising "The court must grant the motion..." to "The motion should be granted..." is less likely to elicit a negative reaction from a judge. Yet another way of being direct without seeming to boss the court is to make the law the subject of the sentence — "Section 409 requires that...."

In letters to clients, directness tends to be most obvious when an attorney writer is telling the client about his or her options. Attorneys writing to clients also find that it is effective to be direct about any instructions or deadlines they must convey to the client, even though these instructions and deadlines may be softened a bit with a word like "please" (for example, "Please sign and return the enclosed documents to my office by Monday, December 18, 2006."). Attorney writers are also invariably direct in pointing out that their predictions are their professional opinions, not guarantees of a certain outcome. On the other hand, attorneys writing to clients tend to be slightly less direct about conveying bad or disappointing news. While the writer may save unhappy news for the end of a letter or soften the blow with an empathetic word like "unfortunately," the attorney writer will still be clear about what the bad news is.

Despite the preference for directness, most attorneys avoid first and second person references ("I" and "you") in both legal memoranda and briefs. Rather than write "I think the court will find the first element is met" in an office memorandum, most attorneys write "the court will probably find that the first element is met." Rather than write "you should consider" when addressing the court, virtually all attorneys write "the court should consider." Use of "I" and "you" is more common in letters to clients, but even there many attorneys prefer "in my opinion" to "I think" or "I believe." Even though the use of "you" is commonplace in letters to clients, indiscriminate use of "you" can make a letter seem bossy or too informal. Many attorneys prefer using "we" in letters to clients to mean both the client and the attorney. "We" conveys the impression that the two are or will be working together as a team.

Explicitness is most evident when legal memo and brief writers construct their arguments. Facts are analogized and distinguished explicitly. Little is left to the imagination as the writer makes explicit connections between points and draws explicit conclusions from the points he or she has made. Summaries that synthesize and repeat earlier points are admired. Indeed, explicitly drawn conclusions are hallmarks of United States legal writing.

The Writing Has to Get the Job Done

Another assumption of the United States legal culture is that writing is primarily functional; it has a job to do — explain, persuade, or both — and its value is judged almost exclusively by whether it accomplishes its purpose. Legal writers would not create prose that is aesthetically pleasing for its own sake. Eloquence is admired only when it serves the underlying purposes of explaining or persuading. Further, excessive elaboration is not considered eloquent writing; rather, it is treated as fluff or padding.

Writers Should State and Support a Position

Writing is assumed to be the writer's own view or opinion. Readers in the United States expect writers to state a position and then defend it. Other people's writing is considered "fair game"; that is, it is completely acceptable to challenge, disagree with, or criticize the writing of another, including an expert in the field or even a court, as long as the challenge, disagreement, or criticism is well supported and directed at the ideas and arguments, not at the individual. Attacking the arguments of one's opponents is expected, but once again the criticism should address the weaknesses in the arguments and not become personal.

Support for one's ideas can take a number of forms. In United States writing in general, facts, statistics, and other "hard data" are favorite forms of support. Readers expect concrete support for most of a writer's points. The use of detail as evidence supporting one's position is considered persuasive. Simple assertions that are not backed up by supporting evidence are widely criticized as unpersuasive.

In the United States legal culture, support for one's ideas or arguments generally falls into three categories: plain language arguments, analogous case arguments, and policy arguments. (See pages 158-160.) United States legal readers expect that most of a legal writer's points will be supported by cited authority. A plain language argument relies on the authority of the law and a common sense reading of it. An analogous case argument relies on the authority of another court and how it ruled in a similar case. Policy arguments often cite legislative history as the authority for statements about the policy underlying a rule. Citing to the record and using detailed facts from the case to support one's arguments are all considered effective advocacy. Conversely, assertions without support are considered poor advocacy.

When an attorney uses facts and cases to support an argument, the expectation is that attorneys will be meticulously accurate. If an attorney is caught misrepresenting a fact or a case, he or she loses credibility. Legal readers would become suspicious of that attorney's other representations of fact and law. What is also expected in the United States legal culture, however, is that attorneys writing as advocates will "characterize" the facts and case law in a light that is favorable to their clients. Attorneys disagree about where the line is drawn between characterizing and misstating facts. Most agree that characterization includes emphasis. For example, favorable facts are highlighted and discussed in detail; unfavorable facts are downplayed and only mentioned briefly. (See pages 391-392.) Most agree that omitting key facts or cases that are unfavorable is not only dishonest and ineffective advocacy, but also a probable violation of the rules. Virtually all agree that misstating key facts or cases is totally unacceptable and possibly even malpractice.

One way to determine whether a given way of expressing a fact or discussing a case is just a favorable characterization or an outright misstatement is to ask what the opponent would say in response. If an opponent would be inclined to say something like "I wouldn't put it that way," then the attorney can assume he or she has stayed within the legitimate boundaries of characterization. If an opponent would say "that's not true," then the attorney can assume he or she has stepped over the line into misstatement.

Assuming, then, that misstatement is not an option, what is still confusing is whether it is better to err on the side of understatement or on the side of overstatement. Many lawyers would argue that understatement is safer and better for building one's reputation with other attorneys and judges. Even so, a quick survey of writing in the profession would probably show that, if an attorney is erring on one side or the other, most err on the side of overstatement.

Writing Is Like Personal Property; Avoid Plagiarism

An added complication to the United States culture's views about writing and support for ideas is its notion of plagiarism. Because people in the United States place a high value on originality, an original idea or an original expression in words is considered a valuable possession. Consequently, people in the United States culture tend to think that a writer's ideas, and especially the words a writer uses to express those ideas, are that writer's personal property. Using someone's ideas or words *without attribution* is treated like stealing that person's ideas or words. Using someone's ideas or words *with attribution*,[16] however, is a commonplace and respectable form of supporting one's own points. In fact, use of attributed quotations from experts and other authorities is considered effective support as long as the writer is selective about what he or she quotes. Overquoting, while not nearly as serious a mistake as plagiarism, is frowned upon because it suggests the writer has borrowed too heavily from other sources and has not contributed any original thinking.

Concerns about plagiarism also appear in legal writing, but they are somewhat overshadowed by the heavy emphasis on having authority for one's arguments. Citing cases, statutes, books, law review articles, and other secondary sources is considered of paramount importance. These citations show that the writer has the support of the law, other courts, and other legal minds behind his or her arguments. There is universal agreement about not only the need for citations to authority but also the use of quotation marks[17] to show that a writer has set out the exact language of a rule.[18]

There is a difference of opinion, however, in the United States legal culture about whether legal writers need to use quotation marks as well as the citation when they are using the exact language of a court. Some legal writers and readers seem to feel that court opinions are almost like public property. Others continue to be careful to use quotation marks around exact

---

16. In some instances, writers also need the original author's express permission.

17. Long quotations of fifty words or more are written as block quotations. No quotation marks are used with block quotations even though the wording is exactly the same as the original. See section 27.5b in this book Rule 5.1 in *The Bluebook*, and Rule 48.5 in the *ALWD Citation Manual*.

18. Using ellipses to omit parts of the rule that are not applicable to the matter at hand is completely acceptable.

Chart 30.4 Plagiarism

- People in the United States culture tend to think that a writer's ideas, and especially the words a writer uses to express those ideas, are that writer's personal property.
- Using someone's ideas or words without attribution is treated like stealing that person's ideas or words.
- When using someone else's ideas, include citations to the source; when using someone else's words, include citations to the source and use quotation marks around that person's words.

language from another court. The safe choice is to apply the same standards in legal writing as in other writing in the United States and use quotation marks around another's words.

An additional important point concerns plagiarism in law school settings: in all United States law schools, plagiarizing is considered a serious ethical offense. Despite the recent shift to encouraging some limited collaboration in legal writing classes, virtually every United States law school has a student code of conduct that strictly forbids copying another student's work and representing it as one's own. Plagiarizing the words, ideas, or even the key organizational features of another student's writing has serious consequences, often including expulsion from law school. Similarly, law students writing seminar papers and law review articles must be conscientious about citing their sources and using quotation marks when they are using the language of an authority. The penalties for plagiarizing the work of a published author are usually identical to the penalties for plagiarizing the work of another student.

In United States law firms, however, very different standards apply. Attorneys who are members of the same firm often share sample forms, in-house memoranda, and even rule sections from briefs. Using the writing of another member of the firm as a model is common. Some firms even have memo and brief "banks," which are copies of office memoranda and briefs written by firm members that other firm members can use when they are writing about similar legal problems. This sharing within a firm is not considered plagiarism; rather, it is considered a practical way to save time and resources.

b. Assumptions and Expectations in Other Cultures

Most East Asian and Middle Eastern languages are reader-responsible languages. Consequently, not fully grasping a writer's intended meaning does not frustrate these readers. They do not expect sentences that can be automatically understood the first time they are read. Japanese readers, for example, assume that the writer may have deliberately hidden some of the meaning. Even though a Japanese writer may continually return to the theme of an article, the theme may not be stated explicitly. Similarly, Hebrew and Arabic readers expect to "read between the lines" and draw the appropriate conclusions on their own.

The tradition in Russian academic writing is for writers to show their intelligence and the importance of their ideas by being intentionally complex. Long sentences, long paragraphs, and even long paragraphs that are made up of one long sentence are admired. Writers achieve some of the complexity by using subordination, parallelism, and parenthetical comments. Using technical terms, sometimes without even defining them, adds to the complexity.

A few cultures and their written languages seem to be in a transition period from reader-responsible to writer-responsible communication. Experts in contrastive rhetoric believe, for example, that modern Chinese (Mandarin) is shifting from a reader-responsible to a writer-responsible approach.

In some cultures, the best way to begin a piece of expository writing is with an appropriate proverb, parable, or anecdote. This sets a tone for the discussion that follows and also underscores the "truth" of what will be said. Thai writing, for example, tends to begin with an anecdote, followed by specific detail, and then ended by an overall statement of the main point in the very last sentence. In Haitian Creole, or Kreyòl, essays begin with flowery and philosophical introductions and then may go on to include numerous proverbs. In Japanese prose, *ki*, which is comparable to the introduction, does not include the thesis. German writers are also taught not to state a thesis before they have set out the evidence that supports it. Other cultures favor a personal approach to beginnings. Relating how the topic is connected to the writer is a common way to introduce a topic. Still others rely heavily on beginnings that develop a historical context. Arabic speakers tend to set the stage for their topics by broad statements about the general state of affairs.

The length of the introduction or how much of the total piece of writing should be taken up by the introduction also varies greatly from culture to culture. Lengthy introductions are a noteworthy feature of Spanish writing. An introduction that takes up to a third of the total pages would not be uncommon.

Rather than introducing the main point quickly, Chinese writers use a "brush clearing" or "clearing the terrain" approach. In this approach, the writer begins by discussing all the ideas related to his or her main idea. Once this is done (the brush is cleared), the main idea is ready to be explored.

As a general rule, writers in East Asian languages prefer indirectness to directness and inferring meaning rather than writing explicitly. Stating one's point baldly is equated with a lack of sophistication. Chinese writers, for example, may give concrete examples but the cultural preference is to stop after listing the examples and allow the reader to make the connections and draw the inevitable conclusion. Explicit conclusions are considered repetitious and possibly even insulting to educated readers.

Japanese writers may, as a general rule, be even more indirect than Chinese writers. Good Japanese writing implies or alludes to rather than explicitly states its points. Making a point indirectly or hinting at meaning is regarded as a sign of intelligence and sensitivity. Directness is equated with brashness. Korean writers rarely use direct persuasion and explicit description. Arguing directly or explicitly is apt to have a negative effect on readers. The more common approach is to hide criticisms in metaphors. The preference to be indirect is not limited, however, to writers of Asian languages. Finnish writers also tend to leave things unsaid that seem obvious.

In many cultures, writing is treated as received wisdom. Writers strive to pass along the insights of the past; consequently, readers do not assume that a writer is expressing his or her own opinion. Instead, students are encouraged first to memorize and later to repeat in their own writing the words of the respected authorities from the past. It is not considered plagiarism to use the words of another without citation. The purpose of writing in these cultures is to create harmony between writer and reader, not to debate or explicate a point of view. In China, for example, being a writer is equated with being a scholar and therefore one who knows and writes the truth.

Other cultures, by contrast, have developed a long history of skepticism about their governments and so-called expert opinion that may be based on officially sanctioned "truth." As a result, writers in these cultures tend not to support their arguments by quoting other authorities, citing statistics that come from governmental agencies, or offering concrete proof. Polish writers, for example, tend not to refer to the work of others; instead, the dominant rhetorical techniques in their tradition are comparing and contrasting and defining and redefining.

In Japanese writing, there is a tendency to use a mix of arguments for and against a position. Japanese writers also may end an argument taking a different position from their beginning position. Even in argumentative essays, Japanese writers tend to be somewhat tentative and use more hedges and qualifiers than do writers from other cultures. Korean writers may use a formulaic expression like "some people say" as a way to introduce their own point of view, particularly when the position they are taking is a controversial one. The formula expression allows the writer to avoid being too direct and to suggest that there is other support for the position the writer states.

Other cultures treat writing more as an art than as a functional skill. Japanese writers, for example, tend to be very concerned about the aesthetics of their writing. Writers of Romance languages like Spanish or French pride themselves in using the language beautifully. Writers in Arabic also tend to place a stronger emphasis on the form of language. They prefer richness in language, particularly in the form of metaphors and other figurative language, over conciseness.

The best support for one's points varies from culture to culture. Some cultures support points through analogies, appeals to intuition, beautiful language, or references to sages from the past. Chinese writers prefer elaborate metaphors and literary references. They also use numerous references to historical events. Rather than using different pieces of evidence as support, some cultures prefer to argue the same point in many different ways. Different cultures also disagree about what is understatement and overstatement. Middle Eastern law students, particularly those who were educated in Classical Arabic, may consider a supporting statement as neutral that a typical person from the United States would consider an exaggeration. What native speakers would consider neutral, they would tend to view as examples of understatement.

§ 30.2.2 Culturally Determined Patterns in Writing

a. Preferences in the United States

As a general rule, students in the United States receive more direct instruction in rhetorical patterns in writing than do students in most other school systems. Composition textbooks stress paragraphs that use a general topic sentence, specific supporting sentences, and a general concluding sentence. The five-paragraph essay taught in junior high and high school expands this same general → specific → general structure over a slightly longer piece of prose. The typical term paper or research paper with its thesis statement expands the structure over a still longer piece of writing.

In other words, United States students internalize a hierarchical approach with numerous levels of subordination as the appropriate way to present ideas. In fact, the degree to which a writer uses a hierarchical approach to writing is often the basis for judging whether that writer's work is mature. Conversely, frequent use of coordination (this point "and" this point "and" this point "and" this point) is considered a sign of an immature prose style. One-sentence paragraphs are also generally frowned upon and thought to be the mark of undeveloped ideas.

Writing in the United States legal culture emulates this same hierarchical approach. An effective prose style in law typically uses an overview → analysis → synthesis organizational strategy. In fact, successful attorney writers deliberately use topic sentences, roadmaps, signposts, and enumeration to reveal the hierarchical organization of their line of reasoning.

Writing that is deemed "coherent" prose in the United States usually has very explicit language links to guide readers across the levels of generality and specificity. Indeed, lexical ties are the primary ways native speakers of English create coherence in their prose. Favorite metatextual elements include signposts such as "first," "second," and "third," and transitions that signal how the line of thought is shifting, such as "in contrast," "on the other hand," "consequently," and "in conclusion." These sentence-to-sentence connections result in a linear prose style. Narratives in English also tend to be linear because speakers of English perceive time as linear. Temporal-causal sequencing is typical.

English sentences tend to be written in an old information → new information pattern. Topics tend to be in the first half of sentences.

b. Preferences in Other Cultures

The traditional American formula for writing (introduction, body, conclusion) with roadmaps and signposts along the way is considered mechanical, unsophisticated, and even childish in many other cultures. French writing, for example, uses more of a meandering approach. The writer might touch on the topic initially and then circle back to it later in the writing. Topic sentences are not part of the French writing tradition, primarily because they are deemed too obvious and condescending to readers. Contrary to the English tradition of conclusions simply summarizing what has already been said, French writers often conclude an essay by introducing a new but related topic.

The Japanese formula for prose, *ki-shoo-ten-ketsu*, is as predictable as the traditional American structure of introduction, body, and conclusion, but the Japanese version has distinct differences. *Ki*, which is roughly comparable to the introduction, will not typically include the thesis; *shoo* will develop the argument; *ten* will abruptly shift and introduce a new sub-theme, which is often an examination of the thesis from a new angle; and *ketsu*, which is the conclusion, may state the thesis, but rather than just summarize the earlier ideas, *ketsu* may introduce some new ideas. *Ketsu* need not have the closure expected from an American conclusion. It may end with a question or otherwise express some lingering doubt.

Korean expository essays also tend to be organized from specific to general. Like the Japanese *ketsu*, Korean conclusions may contain the thesis but only in an indirect form.

The Slavic countries like Poland use yet another form of organization known as "circumvoluted discourse."[19] In this approach, the writer tackles a point from numerous perspectives and works toward a thesis, which is finally revealed near the end. Like the Japanese *ten*, the circumvoluted approach may seem to English readers to take the writing off course when in fact the technique is more about tackling a topic from many points of view.

Several cultures, particularly Arabic-speaking cultures, do not particularly value hierarchy and subordination in ideas. As a rule, Arabic writers are inclined to restate their positions, often with warnings, rather than support them with examples. In fact, most Arabic languages have relatively few markers for subordination. Instead, parallelism is a key ingredient in Arabic for conveying a rich array of parallel ideas. Coordination and balance are other hallmarks of sophisticated Arabic prose. Unlike in English, where excessive coordination is treated as "unsophisticated," mature Arabic writers tend to join many of their ideas together with "wa," the Arabic word for "and." Writers in many other languages, including Chinese, also favor additive conjunctions to connect ideas.

Unlike United States writers, who tend to move from the general to the specific, Japanese writers prefer to move from the specific to the general. This tradition is reinforced in Japanese journalistic writing, which begins with details and saves the lead until much later in the story. Chinese writers also tend to use an inductive approach.

Many other cultures prefer to hide the underlying organization of a piece of writing. Numbering one's points or reasons is not favored. In general, writers in most other cultures use fewer language links than do their United States counterparts. In a few languages, most notably in Puerto Rican Spanish, one- or two-sentence paragraphs are common.

Native speakers of Chinese tend to use centrifugal rather than linear organizational patterns, and native speakers of Spanish tend to use linear

---

19. Leslie Kosel Eckstein et al., *Understanding Your International Students: An Educational, Cultural, and Linguistic Guide* (Jeffra Flaitz ed., 2003).

organizational patterns but with tangential breaks. Spanish writers do not tend to use signposts or transitional words and phrases to guide readers through the text.

Because both Chinese and Japanese are languages that rely heavily on the concept of topic, the typical sentence structure in these languages is a topic-comment structure. Consequently, ESL law students who have Chinese or Japanese as their first language may be inclined to replicate this sentence structure preference in English and produce what native speakers of English would consider too many sentences that begin with "as for," "in regards to," "there is," or "there are."

§ 30.2.3 Conciseness Versus Repetition

a. Preferences in the United States

In all types of expository prose in the United States, conciseness is heralded as a writing virtue. Saying a great deal in a few words is considered a sign of the writer's intelligence and respect for his or her readers. In the United States legal culture, conciseness is even more highly prized as lawyers fight to keep their heads above the paper blizzard created by complex litigation. Courts require lawyers to write within page limits. Judges admonish attorneys to "be brief." Supervising attorneys chastise young lawyers to "get to the point."

In the United States legal culture, writers are expected to be concise in two different ways: they are expected to edit their sentences of all excess verbiage (see section 25.2), and they are expected to stay on track and focus on points that are central to developing a line of reasoning. Straying, even slightly, from the point puzzles and irritates legal readers in the United States, who are likely to view writing with digressions as disorganized, unfocused, and a waste of their time. In fact, one of the strongest condemnations of any part of a piece of legal writing is to label it "irrelevant."

Only in law review articles is exploration of a related side issue encouraged, and even in law review articles, this type of digression must be done in footnotes, not in the main body of the text. A few writers have borrowed the law review footnote system as a means for exploring tangential points in memoranda and briefs, but this practice is the exception, not the norm. Many more memorandum and brief writers use appendices when they believe that some but not all of their readers might appreciate extensive supporting, background, or related information. In any case, the virtually unanimous view is that anything in the body of the text of any memorandum or brief must be directly "on point."

Although writing textbooks, including legal writing textbooks, often advise writers to be concise and denounce "needless" repetition, at least two kinds of repetition are favored in legal prose style. First, legal writers tend to repeat their conclusions. In legal memoranda, the overall conclusion may appear in both the brief answer and in the separate conclusion section. In addition, legal writers often state mini-conclusions after an extended discussion of a significant point and then draw these mini-conclusions together into an overall conclusion.

Second, when writing as advocates, lawyers tend to repeat points, albeit subtly, that are favorable to their case. In fact, many effective advocates expend a great deal of effort finding slightly different ways to emphasize essentially the same point. Brief writers who write an argumentative point heading and then open the next section with a positive assertion are often making exactly the same point but choosing a different sentence structure and slightly different words. The net effect of deliberate but subtle repetition is to create an overall theme, or theory of the case, that the writer hopes the reader will adopt. Lawyers in the United States who use subtle repetition as a form of advocacy generally know that they must use this technique selectively and carefully because they are aware that they risk annoying legal readers, particularly judges, if the repetition becomes too obvious.

b. Preferences in Other Cultures

In many other cultures, elaborate and extended prose is greatly admired. In most Romance languages, for example, sophisticated writers use frills and flourishes to embellish their points. The very kinds of digressions that United States legal readers find irritating and irrelevant are admired in many other cultures. Spanish readers, for example, consider the exploration of side points a sign that the writer is highly intelligent and well versed in the topic. French and Chinese writers also have much more freedom to digress and introduce related material. Earlier we saw how Japanese writers use an organizational framework called *ki-shoo-ten-ketsu*. They shift the topic and look at it from a new angle when they are in the *ten* element.

Many cultures prefer to argue the same point in many different ways. Paragraph after paragraph says essentially the same thing with only modest additions or changes. Arabic writers, for example, pride themselves in making the same point in many different ways. Polish writers have a tradition of restating the same idea. Chinese writers return several times to a main idea before moving on. Their readers expect repetition; indeed, they expect Chinese writers to use and re-use stock phrases. Naturally, the repetition in all these rhetorical traditions lengthens a typical piece of writing.

§ 30.2.4 Some Final Thoughts

The work of contrastive rhetoricians is far from complete. As a result, readers of this chapter may be somewhat disappointed that their country or culture is not represented in the examples or that the examples do not cover every point that they would like to see made. Admittedly, more work must be done before we have a complete picture of the rhetorical preferences of various cultures.

In the meantime, our hope is that by being more explicit about some of the preferences of the United States legal culture and comparing those preferences with those of some non-United States and non-legal cultures, ESL writers can more easily assimilate into writing for the United States legal culture. After all, being explicit is one of the valued characteristics of legal writing in the United States!

Chart 30.5   Contrasting Rhetorical Preferences

U.S. Legal Writing	Chinese	Japanese	Korean	French	Spanish	Arabic	Russian
Introductions							
▪ U.S. legal writers tend to give a quick overview at the beginning of a piece of writing that sets out its content and structure. Beginnings in writing tend to get to the point quickly, answering the question, "What is this about?"	▪ Chinese writers often use a "clearing the terrain" approach, discussing all of the ideas related to the main idea before exploring the main idea.	▪ Japanese writers using the organizational framework called *ki-shoo-ten-ketsu* do not typically include the thesis in *ki*, which is roughly comparable to the introduction.			▪ Spanish writers tend to compose lengthy introductions that may take up to a third of the total pages.	▪ Arabic writers tend to set the stage for topics by broad statements about the general state of affairs.	

Chart 30.5 Contrasting Rhetorical Preferences *(cont'd)*

U.S. Legal Writing	Chinese	Japanese	Korean	French	Spanish	Arabic	Russian
Conciseness							
▪ Conciseness—saying a great deal in a few words—is considered a sign of the writer's intelligence and respect for his or her readers. ▪ Writers are expected to be concise by (1) editing their sentences of all excess verbiage and (2) staying on track and focusing on points	▪ Chinese writers return several times to the main idea before moving on. ▪ Chinese readers expect repetition. ▪ Chinese readers expect writers to use and re-use stock phrases.					▪ Arabic writers prefer richness in language, particularly in the form of metaphors and other figurative language, over conciseness. ▪ Arabic writers pride themselves in making the same point in many different ways.	

Chart 30.5 Contrasting Rhetorical Preferences *(cont'd)*

U.S. Legal Writing	Chinese	Japanese	Korean	French	Spanish	Arabic	Russian
that are central to developing a line of reasoning.							

Directness

U.S. Legal Writing	Chinese	Japanese	Korean	French	Spanish	Arabic	Russian
▪ Writers are generally expected to be direct and candid with their readers. Writers should lay out the facts, the rules, the relevant cases, and the arguments each side is likely to make. Unfavorable facts, rules, analogous	▪ Chinese writers may give concrete examples but the cultural preference is to stop after listing the examples and allow the reader to make the connection and draw the inevitable conclusion.	▪ Japanese writers may continually return to the theme of an article, although the theme may not be stated explicitly. ▪ Making a point indirectly or hinting at meaning is regarded as a sign of intelligence and sensitivity. Good writ...	▪ Korean writers rarely use direct persuasion and explicit description. Arguing directly or explicitly is apt to have a negative effect on Korean readers. ▪ It is common to hide criticisms in metaphors.			▪ Arabic writers expect readers to "read between the lines" and draw appropriate conclusions on their own.	▪ Russian writers tend to show their intelligence and the importance of their ideas by being intentionally complex.

Chart 30.5   Contrasting Rhetorical Preferences *(cont'd)*

U.S. Legal Writing	Chinese	Japanese	Korean	French	Spanish	Arabic	Russian
in the client's case are dealt with openly. ▪ Although brief writers should be direct by telling a court exactly what they want, writers do not want to sound like they are ordering the court around. ▪ Despite the preference for directness, most attorneys avoid first		or alludes to rather than explicitly states its points. ▪ Directness is equated with brashness.					

Chart 30.5   Contrasting Rhetorical Preferences *(cont'd)*

U.S. Legal Writing	Chinese	Japanese	Korean	French	Spanish	Arabic	Russian
and second person references ("I" and "you") in both legal memoranda and briefs.							

Digressions

U.S. Legal Writing	Chinese	Japanese	Korean	French	Spanish	Arabic	Russian
▪ U.S. legal readers are likely to view writing with digressions as disorganized, unfocused, and a waste of their time. ▪ Only in law review articles is exploration of a related	▪ Chinese writers have much more freedom to digress and introduce related material.	▪ Japanese writers, using the organizational framework called *ki-shoo-ten-ketsu,* shift the topic and look at it from a new angle when they are in the *ten* element.		▪ French writers have much more freedom to digress and introduce related material.	▪ Spanish readers consider the exploration of side points a sign that the writer is highly intelligent and well versed in the topic.		

Chart 30.5 Contrasting Rhetorical Preferences *(cont'd)*

U.S. Legal Writing	Chinese	Japanese	Korean	French	Spanish	Arabic	Russian
side issue encouraged, and even in law review articles, this type of digression must be done in footnotes, not in the main body of the text.							

Writer's Opinion

U.S. Legal Writing	Chinese	Japanese	Korean	French	Spanish	Arabic	Russian
▪ Writers are assumed to be expressing their own view or opinion. Readers in the U.S. expect writers to state a position	▪ Writers are equated with scholars and therefore people who know and write the truth.	▪ Japanese writers tend to be more tentative and use more qualifiers than writers from other cultures.	▪ Korean writers may use a formulaic expression like "some people say" as a way to introduce their view, particularly when they				

Chart 30.5 Contrasting Rhetorical Preferences (cont'd)

U.S. Legal Writing	Chinese	Japanese	Korean	French	Spanish	Arabic	Russian
and stick to it. It is acceptable to challenge, disagree with, or criticize the writing of another, including an expert in the field or even a court, as long as the challenge, disagreement, or criticism is well supported and directed at the ideas and arguments and not at the individual.			are taking a controversial position.				

Chart 30.5   Contrasting Rhetorical Preferences *(cont'd)*

U.S. Legal Writing	Chinese	Japanese	Korean	French	Spanish	Arabic	Russian
Support							
■ Writers use facts, statistics, and other "hard data" as forms of support. Legal writers are expected to be meticulously accurate when using facts and cases to support an argument. ■ In the U.S. legal culture, it is also expected that attorneys, writing as	■ Chinese writers prefer to support their points through elaborate metaphors and literary references. ■ Chinese writers also use numerous references to historical events.	■ Japanese writers tend to use a mix of arguments for and against a position. ■ Japanese writers may also end an argument by taking a different position from their beginning position.				■ Arabic writers are inclined to restate their positions, often with warnings, rather than support them with examples.	

Chart 30.5 Contrasting Rhetorical Preferences *(cont'd)*

U.S. Legal Writing	Chinese	Japanese	Korean	French	Spanish	Arabic	Russian
advocates, will "characterize" the facts and case law in a light that is favorable to their client. Citing cases, statutes, books, law review articles, and other secondary sources is important to show that the writer has the support of the law, other courts, and other legal minds behind his or her argu-							

Chart 30.5   Contrasting Rhetorical Preferences *(cont'd)*

U.S. Legal Writing	Chinese	Japanese	Korean	French	Spanish	Arabic	Russian
Rhetorical Patterns/ Organizational Strategies							
▪ U.S. writers use a linear prose style that moves from the general to the specific. Writers generally use a hierarchical approach with numerous levels of subordination to express their ideas. Frequent use of coordination is considered	▪ Chinese writers tend to use an inductive approach, moving from the specific to the general. Native Chinese speakers tend to use centrifugal rather than linear organizational patterns. ▪ Chinese writers	▪ Japanese writers move from the specific to the general. ▪ The Japanese formula for prose, *ki-shoo-ten-ketsu*, is as predictable as the traditional American structure of introduction, body, and conclusion, but	▪ Korean expository essays tend to be organized from specific to general.	▪ French writing uses more of a meandering approach; the writer might touch on the topic initially and then circle back to it later in the writing. Topic sentences are not used because they are deemed too obvious and	▪ Spanish writers tend to use linear organizational patterns but with tangential breaks. Spanish writers do not tend to use signposts or transitional words and phrases to guide readers through the text. One- or	▪ Arabic writers do not particularly value hierarchy and subordination in ideas. Parallelism is a key ingredient for conveying a rich array of parallel ideas. ▪ Coordination and balance are signs of sophisticated	▪ Writers are intentionally complex, using subordination, parallelism, parenthetical comments, and technical terms, sometimes without defining them. ▪ Long sentences, long paragraphs, and even

Chart 30.5   Contrasting Rhetorical Preferences *(cont'd)*

U.S. Legal Writing	Chinese	Japanese	Korean	French	Spanish	Arabic	Russian
a sign of an immature prose style. One-sentence paragraphs are generally disfavored. An effective prose style in law typically uses an overview → analysis → synthesis organizational strategy. Successful writers use topic sentences, signposts, and enumeration to reveal the hierarchical	favor additive conjunctions to connect ideas. The typical sentence structure in Chinese is a topic-comment structure.	the Japanese version has distinct differences. The typical sentence structure in Japanese is a topic-comment structure. Japanese writers tend to be very concerned about the aesthetics of their writing.		condescending to readers. Writers of Romance languages, like French, pride themselves in using the language beautifully.	two-sentence paragraphs are common. Writers of Romance languages, like Spanish, pride themselves in using the language beautifully.	Arabic pros. Arabic writers tend to join many of their ideas together with "wa," the Arabic word for "and." Arabic writers tend to place a strong emphasis on the form of language.	long paragraphs that are made up of one long sentence are admired.

Chart 30.5 Contrasting Rhetorical Preferences *(cont'd)*

U.S. Legal Writing	Chinese	Japanese	Korean	French	Spanish	Arabic	Russian
organization of their line of reasoning.							
Conclusions							
■ Summaries that synthesize and repeat earlier points are admired. Explicitly drawn conclusions are hallmarks of U.S. legal writing. ■ Legal writers tend to repeat their conclusions. The overall conclusion may appear in more than one place, such	■ Explicit conclusions are considered repetitious and possibly even insulting to educated readers.	■ *Ketsu,* which is roughly comparable to the conclusion, may state the thesis, but rather than just summarize the earlier ideas, *ketsu* may introduce some new ideas. ■ *Ketsu* need not have the closure expected from an American	■ Korean conclusions may contain the thesis but only in an indirect form.	■ French writers often conclude an essay by introducing a new but related topic.			

Chart 30.5 Contrasting Rhetorical Preferences *(cont'd)*

U.S. Legal Writing	Chinese	Japanese	Korean	French	Spanish	Arabic	Russian
as in office memoranda, where the overall conclusion may appear in both the brief answer and in the separate conclusion section.		English conclusion. ▪ It may end with a question or otherwise express some lingering doubt.					

The many empty boxes in the chart highlight the point that the work of contrastive rhetoricians is far from complete. We still have much to learn about the rhetorical preferences of many cultures.

BIBLIOGRAPHY FOR ESL LAW STUDENTS

For more information for international lawyers on rhetorical preferences, linguistic specializations, and current conventions for writing in the United States legal system:

Jill J. Ramsfield, CULTURE TO CULTURE: A GUIDE TO U.S. LEGAL WRITING (2005).

For more information on reader-responsible and writer-responsible languages:

John Hinds, *Reader Versus Writer Responsibility: A New Typology* in WRITING ACROSS LANGUAGES: ANALYSIS OF L2 TEXT (Ulla Connor & Robert B. Kaplan eds., 1987).

For an excellent discussion of the differences between the rhetorical preferences in the United States and many other cultures:

Leslie Kosel Eckstein et al., UNDERSTANDING YOUR INTERNATIONAL STUDENTS: AN EDUCATIONAL, CULTURAL, AND LINGUISTIC GUIDE (Jeffra Flaitz ed., 2003).

William Grabe & Robert Kaplan, "Writing Across Cultures," THEORY AND PRACTICE OF WRITING (Christopher Candlin ed., 1996).

John Hinds, "Inductive, Deductive, Quasi-Inductive: Expository Writing in Japanese, Korean, Chinese, and Thai," *Coherence in Writing: Research and Pedagogical Perspectives* (Ulla Connor & Ann M. Johns eds., 1990).

Ilona Leki, UNDERSTANDING ESL WRITERS: A GUIDE FOR TEACHERS (1992).

For other common problem areas that appear in ESL students' writing:

Diane Hacker, *ESL Trouble Spots*, in A WRITER'S REFERENCE (2d ed. 1992).

Raymond C. Clark, Patrick R. Moran, Arthur A. Burrows, THE ESL MISCELLANY: A TREASURY OF CULTURAL & LINGUISTIC INFORMATION (2d ed. 1981).

The remaining sources are grouped by country or language.

Arabic:

Shirley E. Ostler, *English in Parallels: A Comparison of English & Arabic Prose* in WRITING ACROSS LANGUAGES: AN ANALYSIS OF L2 TEXT (Ulla Connor & Robert B. Kaplan eds., 1987). (Note that Ostler's research has subsequently been criticized by John Swales because Ostler compared student essays written in Arabic with published texts in English. Swales believes that contrastive rhetoricians must compare writing in the same genre.)

Terry Prothro, *Arab-American Differences in the Judgment of Written Messages*, 42 J. Soc. Psychol. 3-11 (1955).

English for Specific Purposes in the Arab World, (John Swales & Hassan Mustafa eds., 1984).

Richard Yorkey, *Practical EFL Techniques for Teaching Arabic-Speaking Students* in THE HUMAN FACTORS IN ESL (J. Alatis & R. Crymes eds., 1977).

Japan:

John Hinds, *Japanese Expository Prose,* 13 Papers in Linguistics: Int'l J. of Human Comm. 158 (1980).

John Hinds, *Linguistics & Written Discourse in Particular Languages: Contrastive Studies: English & Japanese,* in ANN. REV. APPLIED LINGUISTICS, (Robert B. Kaplan et al. eds., 1979).

H. Kobayashi, *Rhetorical Patterns in English and Japanese,* Dissertation Abstracts Int'l 45(8):2425A.

Hebrew:

Michael Zellermayer, *An Analysis of Oral & Literate Texts: Two Types of Reader-Writer Relationships in Hebrew & English* in THE SOCIAL CONSTRUCTION OF WRITTEN COMMUNICATION (Bennett A. Rafoth & Donald L. Rubin eds., 1988).

China:

Carolyn Matalene, *Contrastive Rhetoric: An American Writing Teacher in China,* 47 Coll. Eng. 789 (1985).

Robert T. Oliver, COMMUNICATION & CULTURE IN ANCIENT INDIA & CHINA (1971).

B. A. Mohan & A. Y. Lo, *Academic Writing & Chinese Students: Transfer & Developmental Factors,* TESOL Q. 19:515-534.

Shelley D. Wong, *Contrastive Rhetoric: An Exploration of Proverbial References in Chinese Student L1 & L2 Writing,* 6 J. Intensive Eng. Stud. 71 (1992).

India:

Robert T. Oliver, COMMUNICATION & CULTURE IN ANCIENT INDIA & CHINA (1971).

Korea:

Chunok Lee & Robin Scarcella, "Building upon Korean Writing Practices: Genres, Values, and Beliefs," in *Cross Cultural Literacy: Global Perspectives on Reading and Writing* (Fraida Dubin & Natalie A. Kuhlman eds., 1992).

Harold Chu, "Linguistic Perspective on the Education of Korean-American Students," in *Asian-American Education: Prospects and Challenges* (Clara C. Park & Marilyn Mei-Ying Chi eds., 1999).

William G. Eggington, *Written Academic Discourse in Korean: Implications for Effective Communication* in WRITING ACROSS LANGUAGES: ANALYSIS OF L2 TEXT (Ulla Connor & Robert B. Kaplan eds., 1987).

Thailand:

Indrasuta Chantanee, *Narrative Styles in the Writing of Thai & American Students*, in WRITING ACROSS LANGUAGES & CULTURES: ISSUES IN CONTRASTIVE RHETORIC 206 (Alan C. Purves ed., 1988).

In addition to this bibliography, which was designed for students who may wish to read the source material relevant to a particular language or culture, *The Teacher's Manual for The Legal Writing Handbook*, (4th ed.) contains a bibliography for legal writing professors at the end of the teaching notes for Chapter 30 that list other source material.

Glossary of Usage

In grammar, "usage" simply means what word or phrase a native speaker of the language would use in certain situations. In legal writing, appropriate usage will typically be that of the educated professional. Choices will usually reflect a conservative, more traditional view of language.

Even in law, though, usage is not static. The language of law may be traditional and formal, but it is still living and changing. As a consequence, "correct" usage varies from time to time. What was once unacceptable may, in a decade, become the appropriate choice. For this reason, astute legal writers should consider the date of publication for any authority they consult about usage and, as always, they should consider the reader and purposes of the document they are producing.

In addition, all usage errors are not created equal. Some are egregious errors; others, more forgiveable. While it is certainly best to master all the usage questions in the following glossary, those marked with an asterisk (*) are important to learn first either because they appear frequently in legal writing or because they represent an error that would distract most readers.

*A/An.** Use "a" before words that begin with a consonant sound, and use "an" before words that begin with a vowel sound. Notice that some words begin with a vowel but still use "a" because the initial sound in the word is a consonant sound. This situation occurs when the word begins with a long "u" or "eu" and before the word "one" (a university, a one-hour delay). A few words (usually silent "h" words) begin with a consonant but still use "an" because the initial sound in the word is a vowel sound (an honor, an heir).

*A lot.** "A lot" as in the expression "a lot of time" is always spelled as two words. "Alot" as one word is never correct. Notice, however, that "a lot" tends to sound rather informal and may also be imprecise. For these reasons, "a lot" is often not the best choice in legal writing ("a lot of time" → "a great deal of time"; "a lot of prior convictions" → "numerous prior convictions"; "a lot of experience" → "considerable experience").

*Adverse/Averse.** "Adverse" means "unfavorable," "opposed," or "hostile." One can get an "adverse verdict" or "adverse criticism." "Averse" means "disinclined" or "reluctant." Use "averse" to show a distaste for something or a tendency to avoid something. One may be averse to representing certain types of clients.

*Advice/Advise. "Advice" is the noun; "advise" is the verb. One can advise a client, or one can give advice to a client.

*Affect/Effect. Generally, "affect" is used as a verb meaning "to influence, impress, or sway": "The jury did not seem to be affected by the defendant's emotional appeal for mercy." "Affect" may also be used as a verb meaning "to pretend or feign": "The witness affected surprise when she was told that the signature was forged." Less common is "affect" used as a noun in psychology meaning "emotion."

The most common use of "effect" is as a noun meaning "the result, consequence, or outcome." "Effect" is also used to mean "goods," as in "one's personal effects," and "impression" as in "done for effect."

"Effect" is used as a verb meaning "to bring about or accomplish": "The mediator successfully effected an agreement between labor and management." Had the preceding example been "the mediator affected an agreement between labor and management" the meaning would have been significantly different. "Effected an agreement" means the agreement was reached; "affected an agreement" means the mediator had some influence on the agreement.

Study Aid

Part of what seems to confuse writers about "affect" and "effect" is that "affect" as a verb means "to have an effect on." For this reason, it may be helpful to analyze the grammar of a sentence in which "affect" or "effect" would appear. If the sentence needs a verb and you cannot substitute "to bring about," then use "affect." If the choice requires a noun, use "effect."

*Among/Between. Use "among" when discussing three or more objects or people; use "between" when discussing two objects or people: "The members of the Board of Directors could not agree among themselves." "Attorney-client privilege refers to those confidential communications that occur between a client and her attorney."

Amount/Number. Use "amount" with nouns that cannot be counted and "number" with nouns that can be counted: "The amount of grief this mother has suffered cannot be measured by the number of dollars a jury awards her."

And/or. Although this usage is gaining in popularity, many authorities consider it cumbersome; others point out that it can be ambiguous, unless you use "and/or" to show that three possibilities exist (for example, husband and/or wife can mean (1) husband, (2) wife, or (3) both). Consequently, because the reader has to stop and sort through the three possibilities, it is easier on the reader to present each of the three possibilities separately (for example, "husband or wife or both").

Anxious/Eager. "Anxious" comes from the root word "anxiety." Consequently, if one is "anxious," one is "concerned or worried": "I feel anxious about the interview." "Eager," on the other hand, means "looking forward to": "When asked what happened, the defendant was eager to talk to the police."

Opposition to the use of "anxious to" to mean "eager to" is abating, but careful writers still observe the distinction.

Study Aid

Use "anxious about," but "eager to." A defendant may be "anxious about" (worried about) testifying or "eager to" (looking forward to) testify.

As/Like. "Like" can be used as a preposition, not just as a conjunction. Consequently, if a full clause follows, use "as" or "as if": "The defendant looked as if she were lying."

A While/Awhile. "A while" is an article plus a noun; "awhile" is an adverb. Use "awhile" only when it modifies a verb, not as an object of a preposition: "The shopkeeper waited awhile before answering the officer's question; then he paused for a while before showing the officer the safe."

But however/But yet. These phrases are redundant; avoid them. Use just "but" or just "however" or just "yet" alone.

Compare to/Compare with/Contrast. Use "compare to" when pointing out only similarities; use "compare with" when pointing out similarities and differences; use "contrast" when pointing out only differences.

Complement/Compliment. A complement completes something: "Ajax, Inc. considered Smith to be the perfect complement to its sales department." A compliment is a flattering remark.

Comprise/Compose/Include. "Comprise" means "to contain": "The panel comprises three judges." Notice that "is composed of" can substitute for "comprise." For precision's sake, do not substitute "include" for "comprise." "Comprise" denotes a complete listing; "include" may mean a partial listing or complete listing.

Study Aid

The whole comprises all the parts. The whole is composed of all the parts. The whole includes some or all of the parts.

Continual/Continuous. "Continual" means "frequently repeated"; "continuous" means "unceasing": "His clients' continual complaint was that he never returned telephone calls." "Continuous water flow cools the reactor."

Criteria/Criterion. "Criteria" is the plural form; "criterion" is the singular form. "Acme published the following criteria for the new position: a four-year college degree, experience in sales, and willingness to travel. It waived the first criterion for applicants who had completed Acme's own in-house training program."

Different from/Different than. Use "different from" when comparing two things; use "different than" when the usage is followed by a clause. "The new contract is different from the old one." "The court's reasoning in this case is different than it was ten years ago."

Disinterested/Uninterested. "Disinterested" means "neutral, unbiased"; "uninterested" means "bored": "We want judges to be disinterested, not uninterested, in the cases before them."

e.g./i.e. In textual sentences, the English equivalents for "e.g." (for example) and "i.e." (that is, or namely) are generally preferable to the Latin abbreviations, although "i.e." and "e.g." are appropriate in footnotes and parenthetical matter. When the Latin abbreviations are used, they should be italicized and followed by a comma. Some writers mistakenly use "i.e." to mean "for example." In citations, use the signal "e.g." according to Rule 1.2(a) in *The Bluebook* or 45.3 in the ALWD *Citation Manual*.

Eminent/Imminent. "Eminent" means "distinguished," "prominent," or "high ranking." An expert witness may be an "eminent scholar." "Imminent" means "about to happen" or "impending." "Imminent" is often used with danger or misfortune as in the phrases "imminent attack," "imminent disaster," or "imminent harm."

Etc. Avoid using "etc." in legal writing. Whenever possible, replace "etc." with specifics, or use the appropriate English equivalent ("and so forth" or "and others") instead. Never use "and etc." This phrase is redundant; it means "and and so forth."

Farther/Further. Use "farther" for geographical distances and "further" for showing other additions: "The placement of the fence suggested that the property line was farther north." "We can discuss this matter further after we have more facts."

Fewer/Less. Use "fewer" for objects that can be counted; use "less" for generalized quantities or sums that cannot be counted: "Elaine used fewer sick days than any other employee. She also had less work." "Less than" can be used with plural nouns of time, amount, or distance. "Less than four weeks."

*Good/Well. Use "good" as an adjective and "well" as an adverb, except when referring to health: "The prosecutor is a good lawyer who prepares well for trial." "Will the witness be well enough to testify in court?"

Hanged/Hung. Use "hung" as the past tense for "hang" in all situations except executions: "The counterfeit bill was framed and hung in the lobby." "The whistleblower was hanged by the members as a warning to others."

*Have/Of. "Have," not "of," should be used after the auxiliary verbs "could," "should," and "would": "The plaintiff could have offered a compromise before initiating the lawsuit."

*Imply/Infer. "To imply" means "to indicate, suggest, or express indirectly": "At the show-up, the police officer implied that the defendant was the assailant when he said, 'Don't you think that's him?'" "To infer" means "to deduce, conclude, or gather": "The jury may infer that the defendant is guilty if it hears about her prior convictions."

Study Aid

Use "infer" when the actors in the sentence are drawing inferences from something.

Is when/Is where. Do not use these constructions in sentences that are definitions. A well-crafted definition should have a noun following "is": "An endowment is the transfer of money or property to an institution." Not: "An endowment is when someone transfers money or property to an institution."

*__Its/It's.__ "Its" is the possessive form of "it." Like many other pronouns, "it" forms the possessive by simply adding "s," not "'s" (hers, yours, ours). "It's" is a contraction for "it is" or sometimes "it has." Because contractions are generally avoided in legal writing, "its" or spelling out the words "it is" will be the correct choice in most legal writing.

Lay/Lie. "Lay" is a transitive verb, which means it must have an object. "Lay" means to "put, place, or set down": "Just lay the file on my desk." "Lie" is an intransitive verb, which means it does not have an object. "To lie" means "to recline or remain": "The file will lie unopened on my desk until the bill is paid."

Study Aid

The confusion over "lay/lie" stems from the conjugation of these verbs. "Lay" is a regular verb (lay, laid, laid), but "lie" is an irregular verb (lie, lay, lain) with a past tense that matches the present tense of "lay." The simplest way to determine which word to use is to (1) decide which verb you need ("lay" or "lie") and then (2) decide which tense is required.

Literally. "Literally" is not an all-purpose intensifier. It has a specific meaning: "exactly what the words say." The sentence "The defendant was literally on pins and needles waiting to hear the verdict" means that somehow the defendant was positioned atop pins and needles.

*__Loose/Lose.__ "Lose" is the opposite of "win": "I am afraid you will lose in court." It can also mean "to mislay." "Loose" is the opposite of "tight": "The victim described his attacker as wearing loose clothing."

*__Principal/Principle.__ "Principle" is a noun meaning a "rule, truth, or doctrine": "The principle of negligence per se may make the plaintiff's evidentiary burden easier." "Principal" can be a noun meaning "the head person or official." In finance, "principal" also means "the capital sum," as distinguished from interest: "The principal of Lincoln High School authorized an investment that earned less than one percent on the principal." In criminal law, a principal is the chief actor or perpetrator or aider and abettor present at the commission of the crime. In real estate, a principal is a person who empowers another to act as his or her representative: "The broker owes his principal, the seller, loyalty and good faith."

"Principal" as an adjective means "main" or "chief": "The principal question before the jury is whether the eyewitness is credible."

Supposed to/Used to. Be sure to include the final "d" in both expressions.
Sure and/Sure to. Always use "be sure to."

*Than/Then. Use "than" for comparisons, such as "taller than," "greater than," "more than," and "rather than." Use "then" to denote a time.

That. (When it cannot be omitted). Do not omit the subordinate conjunction "that" when it will prevent a possible misreading. This problem occurs when a noun clause is used as the direct object. In such cases, the subject of the noun clause alone can be misread as the direct object. Incorrect: "Florida courts found a woman who had attempted three suicides and had been committed to a state mental hospital was an unfit and improper person." Corrected: "Florida courts found that a woman who had attempted three suicides and had been committed to a state mental hospital was an unfit and improper person."

That/Which/Who. Use "that" and "which" for things; use "who" for people. Use "that" for restrictive clauses and "which" for nonrestrictive clauses: "The defendant's truck, which does not have oversized tires, was identified by the victim as the vehicle that hit him." The clause "which does not have oversized tires" is nonrestrictive because it does not restrict or limit the meaning of "defendant's truck." Unless the defendant has more than one truck and the reader needs the clause to determine which truck is meant, the phrase "defendant's truck" is already clearly identified. The clause "that hit him," on the other hand, restricts or limits the meaning of the noun "vehicle."

Exception: "Which" is used in restrictive clauses that use the constructions "that which," "of which," or "in which."

*Their/There/They're. "Their" is the possessive form of "they." "There" denotes a place ("stay there"), or it can be used as an expletive ("There is one last point I want to make"). "They're" is a contraction for "they are."

Through/Thru. Always use "through."

Thus/Thusly. Always use "thus."

*To/Too/Two. "To" is a preposition with a great number of functional and idiomatic uses: "The defendant drove back to the city. To his surprise, the police had set up a roadblock. Ultimately, he was sentenced to death." "Too" is an adverb meaning "also," "very," or "excessively": "His story was too implausible." "Two" is the number.

Toward/Towards. Both are acceptable; "toward" is preferred in the United States because it is shorter.

Try and/Try to. Always use "try to."

When/Where. "When" denotes a time; "where" denotes a place. When indicating a particular situation, choose "when" or "in which," not "where." Avoid the expression "a case where...." A case is not a place. Replace with "a case in which...." Common practice, however, seems to be to use "where" in parentheticals after citations.

Which/Who. "Which" should not be used to refer to people.

Who/Whom. Use "who" in most subject positions and "whom" in most object positions. (See below for the exception.)

This general rule means, however, that you will have to analyze a sentence before you can determine whether "who" or "whom" is correct. One easy way to analyze question sentences is to answer the question. If in the answer you use the subjective form ("I," "we," "he," "she," or "they"), then use "who" in the question. If in the answer you use the objective form ("me," "us," "him," "her," or "them"), then use "whom" in the question.

> Who is calling? (He is calling.)
> *(subject)*

> To whom does the clerk report? (The clerk reports to her.)
> *(object)*

For some questions, you may find it easier to determine whether to use "who" or "whom" if you recast the sentence in normal subject/verb/object order.

> Whom should I pay?
> *(object)*

> I should pay whom? (I should pay them.)

The greatest confusion concerning "who/whom" occurs in sentences in which the same pronoun appears to be the object of one part of the sentence and the subject of another part of the sentence.

> The police questioned a woman who they thought matched the victim's description.

The sentence above is correct. Although "who" may appear to be the object of "they thought," it is actually the subject of "matched the victim's description." A simple way to determine which form of the pronoun is correct in such situations is to mentally delete the subject/verb immediately after the "who" or "whom." If the sentence still makes sense, use "who"; if not, use "whom."

> The police questioned a woman who ~~they thought~~ matched the victim's description.

Use the same method to determine that "whom" is the correct choice in the following example.

> The man whom the police questioned matched the victim's description of her assailant.

> The man whom ~~the police questioned~~ matched the victim's description of her assailant.

When the subject and verb following the "who/whom" slot are deleted, the sentence no longer makes sense. Notice too that you can isolate the clause "whom the police questioned," put it in normal order, "the police questioned whom," and answer the question ("the police questioned him") to determine that "whom" is the correct form.

Exception: The one exception to the rule is that "whom" is used for subjects of infinitives.

Whom does our client want to represent him?

Our client wants whom to represent him? (normal word order)

Our client wants her to represent him. (Answer the question or substitute another pronoun.)

Your/You're. "Your" is the possessive form of "you." "You're" is the contraction for "you are."

Glossary of Terms

Active voice. Active voice is the quality of a transitive verb in which the action of the verb is performed by the subject: "Judges decide cases." (Compare with Passive Voice.)

Advance sheets. Advance sheets are paperback pamphlets that contain copies of recent published decisions. They are usually filed at the end of a set of reporters and are used to keep the reporter up-to-date.

Alliteration. Alliteration is the repetition of consonant sounds as in "Peter Piper picked a peck of pickled peppers."

ALWD Citation Manual. The *ALWD Citation Manual*, which is published by Aspen Publishers, is a manual that sets out rules for citing to constitutions, statutes, cases, secondary sources, and other materials in legal memos and briefs. Because the *ALWD Citation Manual* is easier to use than *The Bluebook*, an increasing number of law schools, law reviews, and courts are adopting the *ALWD Citation Manual*.

American Jurisprudence, Second Series (Am. Jur. 2d). *American Jurisprudence* (Am. Jur.) is a comprehensive multivolume legal encyclopedia that is available both in book form and on LexisNexis and Westlaw. Am. Jur. 2d has over 440 articles, covering a wide range of legal topics. The topics are set out in alphabetical order and include references to selected cases and to A.L.R. annotations. Am. Jur. is not jurisdiction specific. Instead of the setting out federal law or a particular state's law, it talks about the law in general terms. Most attorneys use Am. Jur. 2d to obtain an overview of an area of law and as a finding tool.

American Law Reports (A.L.R.). *American Law Reports* collect and summarize cases that relate to a particular topic or issue. For example, A.L.R. Fed collects and summarizes cases that discuss federal issues, and A.L.R.1st, A.L.R.2d, A.L.R.3d, A.L.R.4th, and A.L.R.5th collect and summarize state law issues. A.L.R. is available both in book form and on LexisNexis and Westlaw.

Analogous case. An analogous case is a case that is similar to the client's case. An analogous case argument is an argument in which the attorney compares and contrasts the facts in an analogous case to the facts in the client's case and explains why those similarities or differences are legally significant.

Analysis. When you analyze something, you examine it closely, identifying each part and determining how the parts are related. In law, there are two types of analysis: statutory analysis, which involves the close examination of a statute, and case analysis, which involves the close examination of a case.

Annotated codes. An annotated code is a code that contains not only the text of the statutes but also historical notes, cross-references to other sources published by the same publisher, and notes of decision. Thus, an annotated code is a primary authority because it sets out the law itself and a finding tool because you can use it to find other primary authorities (cases that have interpreted and applied the statute) and secondary authorities (for example, practice books and treatises that discuss the statute.)

Assonance. Assonance is the repetition of vowel sounds.

Atlantic Reporter (A., A.2d). The *Atlantic Reporter* sets out the published decisions of the highest court and intermediate courts of appeals in the following states: Connecticut, Delaware, District of Columbia, Maine, Maryland, New Hampshire, New Jersey, Pennsylvania, Rhode Island, and Vermont. The decisions are organized by date and not by jurisdiction.

Attorney general opinions. The United States Attorney General is the attorney for the federal government's executive branch, and a state attorney general is the attorney for a state's executive branch. Some of the opinion letters that attorney generals write answering their clients' questions are made available to the public in the form of attorney general opinions. The opinions that are made available to the public are persuasive authority and are usually available in both book and electronic formats.

Bias-free language. Bias-free language is language that suggests that persons from minority racial, religious, and ethnic groups are valued members of society. The term is also used to refer to language that is sensitive to perceptions about people who are poor, people who are elderly, people who are disabled, or people who are homosexuals.

Black's Legal Dictionary. *Black's Legal Dictionary* is a popular legal dictionary that is available in hardbound form, paperback form, and on Westlaw.

The Bluebook: A Uniform System of Citation. Because *The Bluebook* was originally written as a guide to citing authorities in law review footnotes, most of the text and examples describe how to cite material in footnotes. There is, however, a section that describes how to modify the rules and examples for citations in memos and briefs. Although *The Bluebook* can be difficult to use, many courts base their citation systems on it.

Boolean searching. Boolean searches are named after George Boole, the British mathematician who developed the set of "connectors" that carry his name and that describe the logical relationships among search terms. When you do Boolean or "terms and connectors" searching, you search for documents using "search terms" and "connectors" that describe the relationship between terms. Some of the more common connectors are "and," which retrieves only those documents that contain both search terms; "or," which retrieves documents that contain at least one of the search terms; "but not," which retrieves documents that contain the first search term but not the second search term; "/s," which retrieves documents that contain the documents that contain both search terms in the same sentence; and "/50," which retrieves documents in which the search terms are within 50 words of each other ("noise" words may not be counted.) Because the connectors may vary from service to service, check the services' documentation to see what connectors are available and what they mean.

Briefs. A brief is a document submitted to the court by a party or interested individual in which the party or individual argues that the court should or should not take a particular action. Some briefs are now available online. For example, both LexisNexis and Westlaw have databases containing the briefs.

Case briefing. Case briefing is a technique used to analyze a court's written opinion. A case brief usually contains a summary of the facts, a statement of the issue(s), the court's holding, and the court's rationale.

Case law. Case law includes both those cases that set out the common law and those cases that interpret and apply enacted law.

Citation. A typical legal citation identifies an authority and gives readers the information that they need to locate that authority. In addition, many citations give readers information that they can use in determining how much weight to give to the authority. The two most frequently used citation manuals are the *ALWD Citation Manual* and *The Bluebook: A Uniform System of Citation*. In addition, many states and courts have their own citation manuals or rules.

Citators. Citators serve two purposes. First, they are used to determine whether a particular authority, for example a case, is still good law. Second, they are used to find other authorities that have cited to a particular case, statute, regulation, law review article, or other authority. Today, the two most commonly used citators are KeyCite,® which is on Westlaw, and *Shepard's*,® which is available on LexisNexis and in book form.

Cite checking. Cite checking is the process used to determine the current status of an authority and to locate sources that have cited that authority. The two most common systems for cite checking an authority are *Shepard's*, which is available both in book form and on LexisNexis, and KeyCite, an online service available on Westlaw.

Code. A code sets out statutes and regulations not in the order in which they were enacted but by topic. Thus, in a code, all of the statutes or regulations relating to a particular topic are placed under a single title. For instance, in the *United States Code*, all of the federal statutes relating to interstate highways are placed under one title, all of the statutes relating to endangered species are placed under a different title, and all of the statutes relating to Social Security benefits are placed under yet a different title.

Code of Federal Regulations (**C.F.R.**). The *Code of Federal Regulations* contains federal regulations currently in effect. These regulations are set out not in the order in which they were promulgated but by topic. For example, all of the federal regulations relating to income tax are set out under one title and all of the federal regulations relating to the Americans with Disabilities Act are set out under another title. The *Code of Federal Regulations* is published in book form and is available on both free Internet sites and on fee-based Internet sites like LexisNexis, Loislaw, VersusLaw, and Westlaw.

Common law. The common law is a system of law that is derived from judges' decisions rather than statutes or constitutions.

Compiled legislative histories. A compiled legislative history is a legislative history that has been compiled by an individual, an organization, or a service. Some of the best sources for compiled legislative histories are *United States Code Congressional and Administrative News* (U.S.C.C.A.N.) (in book form and on Westlaw); Nancy Johnson, *Sources of Compiled Legislative Histories* (2000, Fred B. Rothman & Co. now William S. Hein & Co)(book); *Union List of Legislative Histories, 7th Edition* (2000) (see *http://www.llsdc.org/sourcebook/about-union-histories.htm*); and the LexisNexis and Westlaw legislative histories databases.

Concluding sentence. A concluding sentence in a paragraph is the sentence that sums up the main point of the paragraph. Although not every paragraph will have a concluding sentence, in those that do, the concluding sentence is invariably the last sentence in the paragraph.

Congressional Information Service (CIS). The *Congressional Information Service* is a fee-based service that collects and provides access to Congressional materials. The bound volumes have a wide range of indexes and abstracts summarizing bills, committee reports, and hearings. The full text of bills, committee reports, and hearings are available on microfiche and on LexisNexis.

Congressional Record. The *Congressional Record* is the official record of the proceedings and debates of the United States Congress and is available both in book form and online. In book form, the daily version is published at the end of each day that Congress is in session, and the multivolume version is published at the end of each Congressional session. One of the best online sources is GPOAccess.gov. Its databases are updated daily, and, at the back of each daily issue, is the "Daily Digest," which summarizes the day's floor and committee activities.

Connotation. The connotation of a word is all the associations the word carries with it. For example, the word "lawyer" may have positive connotations for individuals who respect lawyers or who aspire to be lawyers, but it may have negative connotations for people who have had bad experiences with lawyers. (Compare with Denotation.)

Corpus Juris Secundum (C.J.S.). *Corpus Juris Secundum* (C.J.S.) is a multivolume legal encyclopedia that is available both in book form and on LexisNexis and Westlaw. Like Am. Jur. 2d, C.J.S. has over 400 articles, covering a wide range of legal topics set out in alphabetical order. C.J.S. is not jurisdiction specific. Instead of the setting out federal law or a particular state's law, it talks about the law in general terms. Most attorneys use C.J.S. to obtain an overview of an area of law or as a finding tool. C.J.S. uses West's Key Number system.

Denotation. The denotation of a word is its dictionary definition. (Compare with Connotation.)

Dicta. Comments made by a court that are not directly related to the issue before it or that are not necessary to its holding are dicta. Such comments are often preceded by the word "if": "If the evidence had established. . . ." Although in some cases dicta are easily identifiable, in other cases they may not be. When the issue is broadly defined, the statement may be part of the court's holding; when the issue is narrowly defined, the statement is dicta. (Compare with Holding.)

Digests. Digests are a finding tool that is used to find cases. Each digest contains a number of topics, for example, criminal law, evidence, and real estate. Under each of these topics are a series of subtopics and under these subtopics are annotations describing cases that have discussed those subtopics. Most states have state digests, which list cases from that state, and Thomson West publishes a series of regional digests and federal digests. Most digests also have descriptive word indexes and other finding aids. Although historically digests were available in only book form, some digest information is now available online. For example, Westlaw has the Thomson-West digests.

Dovetailing. Dovetailing is the overlap of language between two sentences that creates a bridge between those two sentences. Dovetails are often created by moving the connecting idea to the end of the first sentence and the beginning of the second sentence, repeating key words, using pronouns to refer back to nouns in an earlier sentence, and using "hook words" (this, that, these, such) and a summarizing noun.

Elements analysis. When you do an elements analysis, you systematically analyze a set of requirements set out either in a statute or as part of a common law doctrine by determining whether, given a particular set of facts, each requirement is met.

Emotionally significant fact. An emotionally significant fact is one that, while not legally significant, may affect the way the judge or jury decides the case.

Enacted law. Enacted law is a system of law created by the legislative and executive branches. For example, statutes and regulations are enacted law.

ESL. The acronym "ESL" stands for "English as a second language."

***Federal Civil Rules Handbook*.** The *Federal Civil Rules Handbook* sets out the text of each Federal Rule of Civil Procedure; the authors' commentary, which includes a description of the rule; and citations to key cases.

Federal legislative histories. Federal legislative histories contain some or all of the documents that were created during the process of enacting or amending a federal statute. For example, a federal legislative history might contain the text of the bill as it was originally submitted, transcripts from committee hearings, committee reports, and transcripts from any floor debates. While some judges use legislative histories as a tool for determining what Congress intended when it enacted or amended a particular statute, other judges give such histories little weight. As a legal researcher, look first for a compiled legislative history.

Federal Practice and Procedure (**Second Edition**). *Federal Practice and Procedure* is a multivolume treatise that sets out and discusses the Federal Rules of Civil Procedure, the Federal Rules of Criminal Procedure, the Federal Rules of Evidence, and other federal rules in detail.

***Federal Register*.** The *Federal Register* publishes copies of proposed federal regulation, copies of proposed changes to existing federal regulations, and the final version of the regulations that are ultimately promulgated. In addition, the *Federal Register* also publishes notices of hearings, responses to public comments on proposed regulations, and helpful tables and indexes. It is published almost every weekday, with continuous pagination throughout the year. Because the *Register* uses continuous pagination, page numbers in the thousands are common. An online version of the *Federal Register* is available on GPOAccess.gov and on LexisNexis and Westlaw.

Federal Reporter; Federal Reporter, Second Series; Federal Reporter, Third Series. The decisions of the United States Court of Appeals are published in the *Federal Reporter* (F.), *Federal Reporter, Second Series* (F.2d), or *Federal Reporter, Third Series* (F.3d) The *Federal Reporter* has decisions issued between 1889 and 1924; the *Federal Reporter, Second Series*, has decisions issued between 1924 and 1993; and *Federal Reporter, Third Series*, has decisions issued since 1993. Decisions are set out not by topic or by circuit but in chronological order.

Federal Rules of Evidence Manual (Eighth Edition). The *Federal Rules of Evidence Manual* is a multivolume treatise that sets out the text of each federal rule of evidence along with commentary and an annotated list of cases.

Federal Supplement, Federal Supplement, Second Series. While most United States District Court decisions are not published, some are published in the *Federal Supplement, Federal Supplement, Second Series*, or in another specialized reporter, for example *Federal Rules Decisions* or *Bankruptcy Reporter. Federal Supplement* has decisions issued between 1932 and 1998 and *Federal Supplement, Second Series*, has decisions issued after 1998.

Finding. A finding is a decision on a question of fact. For example, a trial court judge may find a defendant incompetent to stand trial, or a jury may find that a police officer acted in good faith. (Compare with Holding.)

Finding tools. Finding tools are what the name suggests: they are tools that help you locate primary and secondary authority. Some examples of finding tools are digests, annotated codes, and search engines. While digests serve only as finding tools, annotated codes contain both the primary authority (the statutes) and finding tools (notes of decision, which are one-paragraph summaries of a point of law set out in a case, and cross-references to other primary and secondary authorities.)

FindLaw.com. FindLaw.com is a website sponsored by Thomson West that either sets out or has links to the electronic version of federal and state statutes and regulations, selected cases, court rules, and other legal materials.

Gender-neutral language. Gender-neutral language is language that treats males and females as having equal value. It does not assume being male is the norm or that certain jobs or positions are primarily filled by males or females.

Generic transition. Generic transitions are those transitions that are commonly used in writing to describe standard mental moves, such as "consequently" to show cause/effect or "however" to show contrast.

Google.com. Google is one of a number of search engines that can be used to locate websites on the Internet. Some other commonly used search engines are Yahoo, MSN, and A9. By using Google's Advanced Search option, you can find websites that set out specific types of information.

Headnotes. A headnote is a one-sentence summary of a rule of law found at the beginning of a court's opinion. Because headnotes are written by an attorney employed by the company publishing the reporter in which the opinion appears and not the court, they cannot be cited as authority.

Holding. A holding is the court's decision in a particular case. "When the court applied the rule to the facts of the case, it held that. . . ." Thus, a holding has two components: a reference to the applicable rule of law and a reference to the specific facts to which that rule was applied. Because the holding is the answer to the legal question, it can be formulated by turning the issue (a question) into a statement. (Compare with Dicta).

Hornbooks. Hornbooks are books written for law students that summarize an area of law and provide citations to key constitutional provisions, statutes, cases, and regulations. Legal researchers use a hornbook to obtain an overview of a particular area of law or issue.

Hypertext. Hypertext allows a user to move from one part of a text to another part of the text or to an entirely separate text. Moving is done by clicking on links. Links are created by the designer and/or publisher of the text (often a Webpage).

Integrated format. The phrase "integrated format" refers to a method of organizing the discussion section of an objective memorandum. Instead of using the script format, in which the discussion section is organized around the arguments that each side makes, the writer organizes the discussion around legal principles or points. (Compare with Script format.)

Internet. The Internet is an international network that allows a computer user to access information.

Jump cite. A jump, or pinpoint cite, tells you the specific page on which a particular quote, rule, or statement appears.

KeyCite®. KeyCite is Westlaw's cite checking system. You can use it to determine if a case, statute, or regulation is still good law and to find other authorities that have cited to that case, statute, or regulation.

Key Number. Key Numbers are part of West's Key Number system. West has divided the law into more than four hundred topics. Under these topics, each point of law is assigned a Key Number. Once you identify the topic and Key Number for a particular point of law, you can use that topic and Key Number to locate information related to that point of law in almost all of West's publications. For example, you can use the topic and Key Number to locate information in C.J.S.; in West's state, regional, and general digests; in secondary sources published by West; and on Westlaw.

Law Reviews and Journals. Law reviews and journals are periodicals that contain articles written by law school professors, law students, judges, and attorneys. Law reviews and journals published by law schools are edited by students: second- and third-year law students select and edit the articles that are published in these journals. Law reviews and journals published by other groups are usually edited by members of that group. For instance, the *Journal of Legal Writing* is edited by law school professors who teach legal writing.

Legalese. Legalese is a broad term used to describe several common features of legal writing such as the use of archaic language, Latin terms, boilerplate language, and long and convoluted sentences. "Legalese" is usually a pejorative term.

Legally significant fact. A legally significant fact is a fact that a court would consider significant either in deciding that a statute or rule is applicable or in applying that statute or rule.

Legislative history. Legislative histories are a tool that attorneys and courts use to determine what Congress or a state legislature intended when it enacted a particular statute. In general, a legislative history consists of the original and amended texts of the bills, transcripts of committee hearings, committee reports, and transcripts of floor debates.

LexisNexis. LexisNexis is a fee-based computer-assisted research service.

List of CFR Sections Affected (LSA). As a legal researcher, you will use the *List of CFR Sections Affected* (LSA) to determine whether there have been any actions that have affected a particular C.F.R. section. If there has been an action that affected a particular regulation, the LSA lists the page number or numbers where that action is noted. If there has not been an action, the C.F.R. section will not be listed. Because LSA is published monthly, you will also need to do final updating to check for changes since the most recent version of LSA

Loislaw. Loislaw is a fee-based computer-assisted research service.

Looseleaf services. Historically, looseleaf services were what their name suggests: a service that provided information in "looseleaf" notebooks, which were updated by taking out a page and replacing it with a new page. Today, most looseleaf services are available both in book form and on fee-based services like LexisNexis, Loislaw, VersusLaw, or Westlaw. Although each looseleaf service is different, most deal with specialized areas of law. For example, there are looseleaf services that deal with federal tax issues, with federal benefits issues (for example, Social Security), and with many federal issues (for example, environmental issues). Most looseleaf services provide a wide range of up-to-date information about these specialized areas. For example, many of them set out the text of the applicable statutes and regulations, the text of proposed legislation and regulations, and summaries of relevant court and administrative decisions.

Mandatory authority. Mandatory authority is law that is binding on the court deciding the case. The court *must* apply that law. In contrast, persuasive authority is law that is not binding. Although the court may look to that law for guidance, it need not apply it. Determining whether a particular statute or case is mandatory or persuasive authority is a two-step process. You must first determine which jurisdiction's law applies (that is, whether federal or state law applies and, if state law applies, which state's law); you must then determine which of that jurisdiction's statutes and cases are binding on the court that will be deciding the case.

Metaphor. A metaphor is a direct comparison. For example, a journey is often a metaphor for life.

Moore's Federal Practice (Third Edition). *Moore's Federal Practice* is a multi-volume treatise that sets out and discusses in detail the Rules of Civil Procedure, the Rules of Criminal Procedure, and the United States Court of Appeals and Supreme Court rules.

Municipal Research & Service Center (MRSC). The Municipal Research & Service Center (MRSC) is a non-profit, independent organization that provides services to city and county governments in Washington. Its database is searchable. See *www.mrsc.org.*

Natural language searching. Unlike Boolean or terms and connectors searching, which allows you to determine the logical relationships between your search terms, natural language searching uses an algorithm that weighs each search term based on its "rareness" and on its proximity to other search terms. In addition, unlike Boolean searching, which lists your results by date, natural language searches list your results based on their "relevance" scores.

New York Supplement **(N.Y.S.2d).** The *New York Supplement* sets out the published decisions of the New York Court of Appeals. The decisions are set out in date order.

Nominalization. Nominalization is the process of converting verbs into nouns (determine → determination).

Northeastern Reporter **(N.E., N.E.2d).** The *Northeastern Reporter* sets out the published decisions of the highest court and intermediate courts of appeals in the following states: Illinois, Indiana, Massachusetts, and Ohio, The decisions are organized by date and not by jurisdiction.

Northwestern Reporter **(N.W., N.W.2d).** The *Northwestern Reporter* sets out the published decisions of the highest court and intermediate courts of appeals in the following states: Iowa, Michigan, Minnesota, Nebraska, South Dakota, and Wisconsin. The decisions are organized by date and not by jurisdiction.

Notes of decision. A note of decision is a one-sentence summary of a point of law set out in a case. Because notes of decision are written by attorneys who work for a legal publishing company, you cannot cite them as authority. Instead, you must read and cite the cases from which they were drawn.

Nutshells. *Nutshells* are one-volume books written for students summarizing an area of law. The books are written by an expert in the area of law and are published by Thomson West.

Onomatopoeia. Onomatopoeia is the quality some words have when they sound like what they mean. For example, both "plop" and "slap" tend to sound like what they mean.

Orienting transitions. Orienting transitions are transitions that provide a context for the information that follows. They locate the reader physically, logically, or chronologically.

Overruled. A case is overruled when, in a different case, a court determines that, in an earlier decision, the court applied the wrong rule of law. In contrast, a decision is reversed when, in the same case, a higher court reverses the decision of a lower court.

Pacific Reporter **(P., P.2d, P.3d).** The *Pacific Reporter* sets out the published decisions of the highest court and intermediate courts of appeals in the following states: Alaska, Arizona, California, Hawaii, Idaho, Kansas, Nevada, New Mexico, Oklahoma, Oregon, Utah, Washington, and Wyoming. The decisions are organized by date and not by jurisdiction.

Paragraph block. A paragraph block is a group of two or more paragraphs that together develop a point within a larger document.

Paragraph coherence. A paragraph has coherence when the various points raised in the paragraph are connected to each other. Common connecting devices include repetition of key words, transitional phrases, parallelism, and pronouns.

Paragraph unity. A paragraph has unity when all the points raised in the paragraph are related to one larger point, the paragraph's topic.

Parallel citation. If a case is published in more than one reporter, the citation to that case may include references to more than one reporter. The first reference will be to the official reporter. Any other references are called parallel citations. For example, the United States Supreme Court's decision in *Terry v. Ohio* is published in three reporters: *United States Reports*, *Supreme Court Reporter*, and *United States Supreme Court Reports, Lawyer's Edition, Second*. The first reference is to the official reporter, and the second and third references are parallel cites to unofficial reporters.

Passive voice. Passive voice is the quality of a transitive verb in which the subject receives rather than performs the action of the verb: "Cases are decided by judges." (Compare with Active Voice.)

Personification. Personification is the attribution of human qualities or characteristics to abstractions or inanimate objects.

Persuasive authority. Persuasive authorities are cases, statutes, regulations, and secondary authorities that a court may consider, but is not required to follow, in deciding a case.

Pinpoint cite. A pinpoint, or jump, cite tells you the specific page on which a particular quote, rule, or statement appears.

Plain English. Plain English is the term used to describe a movement to encourage the use of simple, straightforward language (in professions such as law) that is readily understandable by lay people. In other countries, the same movement is referred to as the "Plain Language Movement."

Policy argument. A policy argument is one in which the attorney argues that a particular interpretation of a statute, regulation, or common law rule is (or is not) consistent with current public policy, that is, the objective underlying a particular law. For example, child custody laws usually seek to provide stability for children; environmental laws usually try to balance the interests of developers and preservationists.

Primary authority. Primary authority is the law. For example, the constitution, statutes, regulations, and cases are primary authorities. Some primary authorities are mandatory authority, and some are only persuasive authority. For example, while a decision of the California Supreme Court is always primary authority, the only courts that are bound by that decision are California state courts. Thus, California Supreme Court decisions are mandatory authority in California but only persuasive authority in other states.

Purple prose. Purple prose is the overuse of flowery language that draws attention to itself.

Raise and dismiss. You can raise and dismiss issues, elements, and arguments. In each case, both sides will agree on the point; therefore, extensive analysis is not necessary. However, a writer goes through the raise-and-dismiss process to assure the reader that the point was considered.

Regulation. Regulations are promulgated by the executive branch under authority granted to it by the legislative branch. Regulations are similar in form and substance to statutes and are usually compiled into codes. For example, regulations promulgated by federal agencies are compiled and published in the *Code of Federal Regulations*.

Reporters. Reporters are sets of books that set out the published decisions of one or more courts in the order in which the decisions were issued. For example, *United States Reports* has the decisions of the United States Supreme Court set out in date order, the *Pacific Reporter* has decisions from the state courts in the Pacific region set out in date order, and *Nebraska Reports* has decisions of the Nebraska Supreme Court set out in date order.

Reversed. A decision is reversed when, in the same case, a higher court reverses the decision of a lower court. In contrast, a case is overruled when, in a different case, a court determines that in an earlier decision the court applied the wrong rule of law.

Roadmap. Roadmaps are introductory paragraphs that give readers an overview of an entire document or a section of a document.

Rule. The rule is the legal standard that the court applies in deciding the issue before it. In some cases, the rule will be enacted law (a constitutional provision, statute, or regulation); in other cases, it will be a court rule (one of the Federal Rules of Civil Procedure); and in still other cases, it will be a common law rule or doctrine. Although in the latter case the rule may be announced in the context of a particular case, rules are not case-specific. They are the general standards that are applied in all cases. (Compare with Test.)

Script format. When you use the script format to organize the arguments in an objective memo, you set out all of the plaintiff's or moving party's arguments, all of the defendant's or responding party's arguments, the plaintiff's or moving party's rebuttal, and then a mini-conclusion in which you predict how the court will decide that element or issue. Thus, while the integrated format used a form of deductive reasoning (conclusion and then reasons supporting that conclusion), the script format uses a form of inductive reasoning (arguments and then conclusion).

Search engine. Search engines allow you to search for and retrieve websites.

Secondary authority. A secondary authority is an authority that explains or comments on the law. For example, practice books, treatises, and law reviews are secondary authority. A court is never bound by a secondary authority.

Session laws. Session laws are the laws enacted during a particular legislative session arranged in date order. The federal session laws are set out in a set called *Statutes at Large*.

***Shepardize*™.** When you *Shepardize* a case, you cite check the case to determine whether it is still good law and to identify other authorities that have cited that case.

***Shepard's*®.** *Shepard's* is a system that you can use to cite check cases, statutes, and regulations. Although it is still available in book form, most attorneys now use the version that is on LexisNexis. You can use *Shepard's* to determine whether a case, statute, or regulation is still good law and to find other authorities that have cited to that case, statute, or regulation.

Signposts. Signposts are words and phrases that keep readers oriented as they move through a document. Transitional phrases, particularly ones like "first," "second," and "third," are the most common signposts. Topic sentences can also be considered a type of signpost.

Simile. Similes are indirect comparisons that use "like" or "as," such as "his mind is like a steel trap."

Slip opinion. The phrase "slip opinion" refers to the court's opinion in the form that it is initially released by the court. Slip opinions do not have volume numbers, page numbers, or editorial features, for example, headnotes.

***South Eastern Reporter* (S.E., S.E.2d).** The *South Eastern Reporter* sets out the published decisions of the highest court and intermediate courts of appeals in the following states: Georgia, North Carolina, South Carolina, Virginia, and West Virginia. The decisions are organized by date and not by jurisdiction.

***Southern Reporter* (So., So. 2d).** The *Southern Reporter* sets out the published decisions of the highest court and intermediate courts of appeals in the following states: Alabama, Florida, Louisiana, Mississippi, The decisions are organized by date and not by jurisdiction.

***South Western* (S.W., S.W.2d).** The *South Western Reporter* sets out the published decisions of the highest court and intermediate courts of appeals in the following states: Arkansas, Kentucky, Missouri, Tennessee, and Texas. The decisions are organized by date and not by jurisdiction.

Standard of review. "Standard of review" refers to the level of scrutiny an appellate court will use to review a trial court's decision. For example, in *de novo* review the appellate court does not give any deference to the decision of the trial court; it decides the issue independently. In contrast, when the standard of review is abuse of discretion, the appellate court defers to the trial court, reversing its decision only when there is no evidence to support it.

Statute. A statute is a law enacted by the legislative branch of federal and state governments (municipal and county enactments are called ordinances). Statutes can be contrasted with common law (or case law), which is made by the judicial branch.

***Statutes at Large*.** *Statutes at Large* contains the session laws enacted by Congress during a particular Congressional session. You may use the *Statutes at Large* when doing a legislative history for a federal statute.

Substantive transitions. Substantive transitions are connecting words and phrases that also add content. Unlike generic transitions, which signal standard mental moves, substantive transitions tend to be document-specific. (Compare with Dovetailing.)

Synthesis. When you synthesize, you bring the pieces together into a coherent whole. For example, when you synthesize a series of cases, you identify the unifying principle or principles.

Term of art. Although sometimes used to describe any word or phrase that has a "legal ring" to it, "term of art" means a technical word or phrase with a specific meaning. "Certiorari" is a true term of art; "reasonable person" is not.

Test. Although the words "rule" and "test" are sometimes used interchangeably, they are not the same. A test is used to determine whether a rule is met. (Compare with Rule.)

Topic sentence. A topic sentence is the sentence in a paragraph that introduces the key point in the paragraph or that states the topic of the paragraph. Topic sentences are often the first sentence in a paragraph.

Unannotated codes. An unannotated code has the text of statutes currently in effect. It does not, however, have cross-references to other sources or notes of decision describing cases that have discussed a particular statutory section.

United States Code (U.S.C.). The *United States Code* is the official source for United States statutes. Although the *United States Code* sets out the text of all of the federal statutes currently in effect and historical notes, it does not have cross-references to other sources or notes of decision.

United States Code Annotated (U.S.C.A.). The *United States Code Annotated* (U.S.C.A.) is an unofficial version of the *United States Code* published by Thomson West. In addition to setting out the current version of the federal statutes, the U.S.C.A. has historical notes, which summarize amendments; cross-references to other materials published by West; and notes of decisions, which describe cases that have interpreted and applied the statute. The U.S.C.A. is available in book form and on Westlaw.

United States Code Congressional and Administrative News (U.S.C.C.A.N.). The *United States Code Congressional and Administrative News* (U.S.C.C.A.N.) contains copies of legislative history materials for selected pieces of legislations.

United States Code Service (U.S.C.S.). The *United Code Service* is an unofficial version of the *United States Code* published by LexisNexis. In addition to setting out the current version of the federal statutes, the U.S.C.S. has historical notes, which summarize amendments; cross-references to other materials published by LexisNexis; and notes of decisions, which describe cases that have interpreted and applied the statute. The U.S.C.S. is available in book form and on LexisNexis.

United States Constitution. The easiest place to find a copy of the United States Constitution is the Internet. There are copies on the Cornell website, (*http://www.law.cornell.edu/constitution/constitution.overview.html*) and on FindLaw.com (*http://www.findlaw.com/casecode/constitution/*). Use the search function on the FindLaw site to search for particular words or phrases. You can also find the text of the United States Constitution in the first volume of the *United States Code*, the *United States Code Annotated*, and the *United States Code Service*, and in most state codes.

URL (Uniform Resource Locator). The URL is the "address" for a particular webpage. Through it, a computer user can access the information on the page.

VersusLaw. VersusLaw is a fee-based computer-assisted research service.

Voice. Voice is the active or passive quality of a transitive verb.

Washington Practice. *Washington Practice* is a multivolume set that provides attorneys with an overview of Washington law and citations to Washington statutes, regulations, rules, and cases. For example, one of the volumes summarizes Washington law on adverse possession and provide citations to key Washington statutes and cases. *Washington Practice* is available in book form and on Westlaw.

Website. A website is place on the World Wide Web where information is posted (published).

West's Key Number System. West's Key Number System is a system developed by Thomson West. The system works as follows. Through the years, West has created a series of topics and within those topics, Key Numbers for each point of law. This set of topics and Key Numbers is West's Key Number System. When a court publishes an opinion, it sends a copy of its opinion to West, which assigns the case to an editor. The editor identifies each point of law set out in the court opinion, writes a single sentence summarizing that point of law, and then assigns that summary a topic and Key Number. These summaries are used in two ways. First, West uses these summaries as headnotes for the case. In West publications, these headnotes are placed at the beginning of the case, after the name of the case but before the court's opinion. Second, these summaries are placed in the appropriate digests under their assigned topic and Key Number.

Westlaw. Westlaw is a fee-based computer-assisted research service.

World Wide Web (Web). The World Wide Web is a component of the Internet that allows a computer user to move from site to site by way of hypertext links. The World Wide Web also allows for graphical representations (for example, graphs or photographs) unlike other Internet systems.

Index